Mergers and Acquisitions

Images Series

Books in the series interrogate conventional categories in today's fast-changing business world. By applying new perspectives, they redefine established territories and extend our view of important business phenomena. Select international contributions to each volume are integrated by the Editor to provide a richer insight into the business landscape and open up new conceptual horizons.

Published

Images of Strategy	Stephen Cummings and David Wilson
Mergers and Acquisitions	Duncan Angwin

Forthcoming

The Multinational	Simon Collinson and Glenn Morgan

Mergers and Acquisitions

Duncan Angwin

Blackwell
Publishing

© 2007 by Blackwell Publishing Ltd
except for editorial material and organization © 2007 by Duncan Angwin

BLACKWELL PUBLISHING
350 Main Street, Malden, MA 02148-5020, USA
9600 Garsington Road, Oxford OX4 2DQ, UK
550 Swanston Street, Carlton, Victoria 3053, Australia

The right of Duncan Angwin to be identified as the Author of the Editorial
Material in this Work has been asserted in accordance with the UK Copyright,
Designs, and Patents Act 1988.

First published 2007 by Blackwell Publishing Ltd

1   2007

Library of Congress Cataloging-in-Publication Data

Mergers and acquisitions / Duncan Angwin.
    p. cm.—(Images of strategy)
  Includes bibliographical references and index.
  ISBN 978-1-4051-2239-9 (hardcover : alk. paper) – ISBN 978-1-4051-2248-1
(pbk. : alk. paper)   1. Consolidation and merger of corporations.   I. Angwin, Duncan.

  HD2746.5.M453 2007
  658.1′62—dc22

                                                          2006037935

A catalogue record for this title is available from the British Library.

Set in 10.5/13pt Minion
by Graphicraft Limited, Hong Kong

For further information on
Blackwell Publishing, visit our website:
www.blackwellpublishing.com

Contents

Notes on Contributors

Duncan Angwin

Dr Duncan Angwin is associate professor in strategic management at Warwick Business School, University of Warwick. After graduating from Cambridge University, Duncan spent 8 years in the City of London where he held a number of senior corporate finance positions in merchant and investment banks. He then returned to academia and obtained a PhD from the University of Warwick. He now holds senior visiting appointments at a number of universities in the US, Europe and Australia, including Saïd Business School, Oxford, Georgetown University, US, École Nationale des Ponts et Chaussées, Paris, and Ecole Hassania, Casablanca, Morocco.

Duncan is the author of many articles in leading US and European academic journals, including *Academy of Management Executive*, *European Management Journal*, *Journal of World Business*, *Long Range Planning* and *Organization Studies*. He has also been published in many practitioner journals and national newspapers. He has authored a book on post-acquisition management with the *Financial Times*, entitled *Implementing Successful Post-Acquisition Integration* (2000), and, with co-authors Stephen Cummings and Chris Smith, has recently published a book on strategic management with Blackwell Publishing, Oxford, entitled *The Strategy Pathfinder* (2007).

Duncan's primary area of research is strategy-as-practice as an approach to mergers and acquisitions. He is currently program chair for the practice of strategy at the Strategic Management Society. His close links with industry, with firms such as AVIVA, Ernst & Young, HSBC, JLL, Prudential, TNT and Vodafone, both as researcher and consultant, allow the in-depth, real-time exposure necessary for this sort of research. Duncan is currently working with several European universities on EU funded research into M&A in the food industry.

Ken Bates

Ken Bates, BA, FCA, an associate professor, has been at Warwick Business School, University of Warwick, since 1990, lecturing in financial accounting, financial analysis and management accounting on undergraduate and postgraduate courses. Ken has also been involved in the design and delivery of the accounting and finance content of numerous tailored executive courses for WBS blue chip clients and has been academic director of the WBS/Severn Trent Water Executive Development Programme. Ken is the study note author for the Distance Learning MBA Management Accounting module and has also contributed to the Financial Accounting study notes. He is currently the distance learning MBA academic director.

Ken was formerly with Thomson McLintock & Co. (now KPMG) and Arthur Andersen & Co., where he gained audit and investigation experience with both private and public corporations, including audit commission value for money studies at a local authority. Ken also has experience in industry as a company secretary and finance director within the Caparo Group where he was involved in M&A activity. Ken's research interests include: financial analysis and valuation; strategic management accounting; performance measurement and cost management systems in both manufacturing and service industries; customer profitability analysis; and accounting education.

Matthew Checkley

Dr Matthew Checkley specializes in venture capital strategy at Warwick Business School, where he also lectures in corporate strategy. He has published work on how brokers' equity analysts in the City of London compete, and is currently publishing on venture capital strategy. He also advises technology entrepreneurs on business planning and raising equity finance. He runs workshops and offers business coaching.

Matthew's research interests include dynamic social networks, risk, entrepreneurialism and venture capital, as well as mergers and acquisitions. His professional background is in technology industry analysis. Having worked for 8 years with major investment banks in equity research, and with specialist research firms, Matthew has experience of valuing both quoted and private companies, and tracking their development over time. He is well attuned to the market's changing views of M&A. He also has the mixed blessing of having lived through six mergers!

Simon Collinson

Dr Simon Collinson is reader in international business at Warwick Business School, University of Warwick, and Lead Ghoshal Fellow at the Advanced Institute of Management (AIM). His research interests include: global innovation strategies, knowledge management and adaptability in multinational firms, and business practices, FDI and innovation in Japan and China.

Simon has published widely, such as in *Organization Studies*, *International Journal of Technology Management*, *R&D Management* and *Organizational Dynamics*, and has received funding awards from the ESRC, EPSRC, DTI, Royal Society and CEC. With Professor Alan Rugman, Simon is also co-author of the *FT Pearson International Business* (4th edn, 2006) textbook. He has research, consulting and executive teaching experience with firms such as British Aerospace, Corus Steel, Diageo, HSBC, ICI, GKN, Jones Lang LaSalle, Kodak (Japan), Lloyd's Register, Nippon Steel, Philips, Prudential and Sony.

Stephen Cummings

Stephen Cummings obtained his doctorate from Warwick Business School and is now professor of strategic management at Victoria Management School (VMS) and visiting professor at École Nationale des Ponts et Chaussées, Paris, and Ecole Hassania, Casablanca, Morocco. He is VMS's director of executive programmes and has developed programmes for a number of corporations, including HSBC, GKN Westland, Philips, *Financial Times*, Corus and Prudential.

Stephen is the author of *Recreating Strategy* (London: Sage, 2002), editor (with David Wilson) of *Images of Strategy* (Oxford: Blackwell, 2003), and co-author (with Duncan Angwin and Chris Smith) of *The Strategy Pathfinder* (Oxford: Blackwell Publishing, 2007). He has published on strategy and its links to ethics, history and change in journals such as *Academy of Management Executive*, *Organization Studies*, *Deusto Harvard Business Review*, *Long Range Planning*, *Journal of Organizational Change Management* and *Business Horizons*.

Scott Dacko

Dr Scott G. Dacko is associate professor of marketing and strategic management at Warwick Business School, The University of Warwick. He holds a PhD in business administration from the University of Illinois at Urbana-Champaign, and MBA and BME degrees from the University of Minnesota.

Scott has 10 years' new product development, management and marketing experience in large and small companies in the US. His research interests include the role of timing in marketing strategy development and success for services and products (e.g. market entry and new product/service introduction timing), marketing management, and consumer behaviour as well as skill development in business and marketing education. He has published articles in journals including *Marketing Intelligence & Planning*, *Benchmarking: An International Journal*, *International Journal of Advertising*, *International Journal of New Product Development and Innovation Management*, *Journal of Marketing Management* and *Journal of Marketing Education*.

Laura Empson

Dr Laura Empson, BSc (Economics), MBA, PhD, is director of the Clifford Chance Centre for the Management of Professional Service Firms and reader in the management of professional service firms.

Laura's research focuses on law, accounting and consulting firms. She is interested in the management of change in professional services firms and, under this broad theme, has explored a wide range of issues, such as managing the post-merger integration process, overcoming impediments to knowledge-sharing among professionals, and changing organizational and professional identities. Her current research project, funded by the Economic and Social Research Council, is concerned with changing forms of governance in professional service firms. This study explores various themes associated with the partnership form of governance, including the way the partnership 'ethos' is expressed through organizational structures, systems and cultures. It examines the implications of moving towards more 'corporate' styles of managing.

In 1999, she established the Professional Service Firm Management Conference at Oxford, which brings together leading academics from around the world every year to discuss their research on professional service firms. Laura is on the editorial board of *Organization Studies* and *Journal of Management Inquiry*. She is a member of the Research Awards Committee of the Organization and Management Theory Division of the Academy of Management.

Prior to becoming an academic, Laura worked for several years as an investment banker and subsequently as a strategy consultant. She has acted as a consultant to a number of leading professional service firms in the consulting, accounting, law and investment banking sectors.

Laura is currently editing a book, *Managing the Modern Law Firm*, to be published by Oxford University Press.

Stephen Gates

Dr Stephen Gates, CFA, is professor of strategy at Audencia Nantes École de Management (sgates@audencia.com). He has published a series of articles concerning strategic performance measurement systems, including performance measurement during M&A integration, performance measurement in European executive compensation, and human capital performance measurement. His publications have appeared in *MIT Sloan Management Review*, *Long Range Planning*, *World at Work*, *Journal of Applied Corporate Finance*, and *Journal of International Business Studies*. Dr Gates is also currently project director for two European councils of The Conference Board: Corporate Strategy and Investor Relations.

Glenn Morgan

Glenn Morgan is professor of organizational behaviour at Warwick Business School, University of Warwick, UK. He is joint editor of the journal *Organization*, 'the critical journal of organization, theory and society', and he has published widely in organization and management journals. In recent years, he has been researching multinational firms, global financial markets and transnational regulation, and the impact of these on change in national business systems such as Japan, Germany and the UK.

His current research focuses on three main themes: firstly, theories of comparative capitalisms and the impact of globalization and regionalization on the establishment, reproduction and change of institutions; secondly, the internationalization of law firms and how this interacts with changing forms of regulation and economic organization at the national, regional and global levels (research being conducted jointly with Dr Sigrid Quack at the Wissenschaftszentrum, Berlin); thirdly, the development of a sociological theory of multinational firms relating their structures of control and coordination to the dynamics of power within and across local social contexts (research being conducted with Professor Peer Hull Kristensen at Copenhagen Business School).

Derek O'Byrne

Derek O'Byrne is head of strategic planning at Waterford Institute of Technology. A graduate of Dublin Institute of Technology, Trinity College Dublin and Dublin City University, he commenced his career in the commercial sector working in a number of different industries before joining academia in 1995. Since then he has lectured widely on strategy and change management and has presented a number of modules on merger integration to executive MBA groups. His current research interests include action research-based approaches to understanding change, particularly in the area of mergers and acquisitions.

Sally Riad

Sally Riad is a senior lecturer in management at Victoria University of Wellington, New Zealand, and director of post-graduate programmes in management at Victoria Management School. Her research interests broadly focus on organizational change and culture. Specifically, Sally has extensively researched mergers, both public and private; she has published papers on various aspects of the integration process and has received international awards for work on the topic. Earlier in her career, Sally was a management practitioner, an experience that lends pragmatic emphasis to her research and writing.

David M. Schweiger

Dr Schweiger is the Buck Mickel/Fluor Daniel professor of international business at the University of South Carolina and adjunct professor of strategic management at EM Lyon in France. He is also is actively involved in executive development programmes for Emory University, London School of Economics and Duke University Corporate Education. He is managing director of Schweiger, Lippert and Associates, a strategic management consulting firm. He holds a DBA in Management from the University of Maryland, and a MS and BS from the Polytechnic Institute of New York.

Prior to his academic career, he was an engineer with the Sperry Rand Corporation. He has worked with numerous US and international organizations, including Texaco, Ameritech, Home Depot, Verizon, Basic Element (Russia), BBA Nonwovens (England), 3M, Ingersoll Rand, Robert Bosch (Germany), Cox Communications, Hitachi, Westinghouse Nuclear Fuels, Sonoco Products, General Motors, Alcatel (France), Bank of America, Societe Generale (France).

Dr Schweiger's research has been widely published in scientific and professional journals, including *Strategic Management Journal*, *Academy of Management Journal*, *Organizational Dynamics*, *Personnel Administrator*, *Academy of Management Executive*, and *Human Resource Management*. He has also published the book *M&A Integration:*

A Framework For Executives and Managers (McGraw-Hill, 2002). He is currently working on a new book, *The Heart of Senior Leadership*, and is international strategic management editor for *Journal of World Business*.

Chris Smith

Chris began his working life as a clinical psychologist based in an acute psychiatric unit. In this setting, delusion and illusion were rampant and powerful in driving the behaviour of staff and patients. A career move to general management (via the human resources function) brought him into contact with a narrower, but no less powerful, set of delusions, focused mainly on money (see chapter 3) and power. His most recent shift was into academia – firstly to Warwick Business School, where he gained his PhD, and then to his current position at the Adelaide Graduate School of Business in South Australia. This has enabled him to partake in the more educated and articulate delusions of understanding and prediction. In the service (some might say grip) of such delusions, he writes, researches and teaches strategic management around the world. He is co-author, with Duncan Angwin and Stephen Cummings, of *The Strategy Pathfinder* (2007) published by Blackwell Publishing, Oxford.

Janne Tienari

Janne Tienari is professor of management and organizations at Lappeenranta University of Technology, Finland, and ajunct professor (Docent) at the Helsinki School of Economics. His research interests include cross-cultural studies for organizing, management and gender, mergers and acquisitions, media discourse and the diffusion of management ideas and practices.

Eero Vaara

Eero Vaara is professor of management and organization at the Swedish School of Economics and Business Administration in Helsinki, Finland, and visiting professor at École de Management de Lyon, France.

   His research interests focus on organizational change, industrial restructuring, and globalization. In particular, he has studied mergers and acquisitions from various theoretical and methodological perspectives. He has lately worked especially on narrative and discursive perspectives and philosophical questions in organization management research.

Philippe Very

Philippe Very is professor of strategic management at EDHEC Business School, France, and the author of many publications (books, academic journals, business press). His last book entitled *Des fusions et des Hommes* (Organisation, 2002), a best-seller in France, received the prestigious Manpower Award for the 'best 2002 book dealing with HR management'. The book has been translated into English: *The Management of Mergers and Acquisitions* (Wiley, 2004).

Philippe is involved in research projects dealing with the themes of mergers and acquisitions, international management, and corporate governance. He is also currently occupying the position of associate dean in charge of faculty development at EDHEC Business School.

Mark Whittington

Mark Whittington, BSc, MBA, ACMA, recently joined Aberdeen University after working as a lecturer in accounting and finance at Warwick Business school for 13 years. While at Warwick, Mark lectured financial accounting, financial analysis and management accounting to MBA students and strategic management accounting to final-year undergraduates. Mark is the study note author for the Distance Learning MBA Financial Accounting module and has also contributed to the Management Accounting study notes. Mark has worked with numerous companies and organizations delivering financial training and offering advice.

Prior to joining WBS, Mark worked as an accountant in the steel industry before becoming a management trainer specializing in designing and delivering accounting and commercial courses. Mark's research interests include financial analysis and valuation, customer profitability analysis, strategic management accounting, international accounting, pension accounting and accounting education.

Preface

We may again be experiencing record levels of M&A activity. $75bn (£38.8bn) of deals have just been announced in only a 24 hour period, the largest private equity deal ever has just been recorded and the peaks of 2000 are looking to be surpassed. M&A is again in full flow as a major force for reshaping corporate landscapes.

Complementing the flurry of interest in M&A is a tidal wave of M&A book titles. Searching Amazon.com reveals over 2,214 business books on acquisitions, and ten times this number on mergers. It is therefore pertinent to ask, why another book on M&A?

The vast majority of M&A books fall into categories: 1) text books (generally with a strong orientation towards one discipline); 2) practical manuals with step by step guides through the intricacies of financial and legal processes; 3) consultancy style books; 4) academic books either as collected papers or research based. Despite this 'wealth' of material, it is apparent that there are real concentrations of focus and scholarship as well as unexplored territories. It is also evident that there is little interrogation between different approaches to M&A, so that overlaps and tensions are not investigated and mutual areas of interest rarely developed.

This book is distinctive in exposing and addressing both of these weaknesses. It reveals M&A to be a much broader, richer and more intensely interwoven tapestry than is generally acknowledged and captured in the literature. It also suggests that a more complete understanding of obscured and unrecognised aspects of M&A and interactions between different approaches may help solve problems in the field, such as why so many M&A appear to fail.

Specifically, the book has two main aims: 1) to broaden M&A horizons through plural perspectives; and 2) to provide integrating mechanisms for interpreting multiple views of M&A. The presentation of different perspectives on M&A at once shows how bounded current M&A treatment has become, as well as revealing new aspects and nuances of these complex phenomena.

Each of the chapters of the book can be viewed as a work of scholarship in its own right. The book also synthesizes these contributions by using different integrating mechanisms. These mechanisms are used to illustrate how comparison between elements of different perspectives may reveal important dynamics in M&A which may help in deciphering its complexity. These approaches are intended as a beginning, rather than an end, in a process of revealing new horizons to M&A.

Part I Overview

Chapter 1 M&A as Horizons

Duncan Angwin

'At last the horizon appears free to us, even granted it is not bright; at last our ships may venture out; . . . the sea, **our sea,** *lies open again; perhaps there has never been such an 'open sea'.*

Nietzsche

The aim of this book is to rebalance efforts in understanding mergers and acquisitions (M&A). Predominant approaches towards M&A miss a great deal. They have been shown to be inadequate, in some instances are highly questionable, and yet continue to enjoy academic hegemony. To achieve a fuller understanding of M&A, there is an urgent need to reconceptualize from an academic perspective. New approaches and sensitivities are required for researchers to engage with the rich variety and complexity inherent in M&A. This richness appeals to the virtues of a pluralist approach, where many points of view, methods and theories are legitimate or plausible. This approach enables the phenomena of M&A to be explored so that conventional boundaries of M&A research may be extended and new horizons revealed.

To regain the 'open sea' we must first be aware that dominant currents in M&A research exert a powerful hold over our understandings and perceptions. We are pulled inexorably towards familiar horizons and dragged away from other potential streams and eddies that might reveal new seascapes. This book aims to resist the pull of these undertows by attempting to reveal new richness in M&A. Its objective is to extend, broaden and reveal currents that may allow us to voyage to new horizons and appreciate a more open sea. This will help rebalance a literature overly oriented towards the financial and economic and which tends to obscure contextual, temporal, and social issues. It will also challenge the neat prescriptive theories arising from traditional perspectives that dominate M&A studies. More complex, less predictable and more dynamic processes, with less coherent outcomes, will be offered which are more in keeping with what 'actually happens' in M&A. This more pluralistic approach may help to reveal new horizons and suggest ways in which variety itself may be theorized. But first we must ask if this M&A 'sea' is worth exploring?

M&A activity has a number of characteristics that make it worthy of the attention of researchers. M&A have been around for a long time – indeed may be as old as business itself. Large waves of activity may be more recent in occurrence but still date back over 100 years, with a major wave recorded in the US at the end of the nineteenth century. The scale of M&A activity makes it hard to ignore and it dominates the world economic scene. Global M&A deals over the past ten years (1996–2005) have totalled in excess of a staggering $23.4 trillion. This dollar amount has immediate implications for the transfer of ownership of large volumes of business and the movement of vast amounts of payment, as well as having widespread impacts on a large group of stakeholders. In the aggregate, changes in ownership through M&A can affect national and regional economies, industry structures, firms and their commercial linkages, owners, creditors, advisers, management, employees and other stakeholders. The rise of mega-deals, deals in excess of $1bn, is resulting in growing interaction with regulators at national and pan-national levels and with governments who wonder whether M&A activity is in the national economic and social interest. The geographic distribution of M&A is also changing, with rapidly rising levels of cross-border deals. Many countries, such as China, recognize M&A as having a transformative power. Cross-border M&A in many countries is now encouraged as a way to stimulate and restructure aspects of their economies.

At the level of the firm, M&A are frequently major strategic events, demonstrating tangible evidence of firm strategy and vision. Whether actively sought or unbidden, they can substantially affect a firm's future through revitalizing, reorienting and in some instances completely transforming the business. M&A may also mark the dissolution of the firm and in some instances its complete demise. The speed with which M&A can be executed and their 'transformational' power makes them an attractive way for firms to grow rapidly and improve their competitive position. For this reason, it is currently a popular dynamic strategy. However, M&A activity also represents a powerful threat to firms in terms of loss of independence and identity. For some the threat of M&A is a mechanism for keeping top managers of potential target firms 'on their toes'.

It is apparent that M&A activity affects a very broad range of constituents across a wide range of industries and geographies. Its importance on many levels has led to very large quantities of research over a long, sustained period of time. The earliest scholarly studies have been identified as those by economists in the United States concerned with concentration in manufacturing leading to exploitative practices (see Bower, 2004). The influence of their reasoning was to prompt Congress into passing a series of acts, such as the Sherman Anti-trust Act of 1898, the Clayton Act and the setting up the Federal Trade Commission. By the 1960s new strands of research were adding breadth to the traditional focus on the effects of M&A on competition. Strategists began to investigate the implications of M&A at the firm level (Andrews, 1971; Rumelt, 1974; Salter and Weinhold, 1979), rather than at the level of industry and some studies investigated how firms might integrate post-acquisition (Kitching, 1967; Searby, 1969; Howell, 1970; Ansoff et al., 1971). In the 1970s finance academics began investigating the effects of M&A on performance (Weston and Mansinghka, 1971; Weston, Smith and Shrieves, 1972; Lev and Mandelker, 1972). In this renaissance of interest in M&A, observers began to recognize that many M&A failed, giving rise to interest in the negative outcomes for employees and managers (Levinson, 1970; Meeks, 1977; Hayes, 1979; Magnet, 1984; Hunt et al., 1986; Marks and Mirvis, 1986). From these beginnings, major research streams have developed so that today there are very significant concentrations of scholarship with sources in economics/strategy, finance and organizational behaviour. Each seeks to answer questions that are coherent with the intellectual foundations of these disciplines and which they deem to be the most important aspects of M&A.

For the **economics/strategy school**, key questions include: 'how does M&A activity affect competition in different market structures?'; 'which strategic motives are most successful for creating value?'; 'which integration approaches are best for capturing or creating value?' A central concern of this school is the nature of synergy in M&A. For the **finance school**, core questions are: 'do M&A create value?'; 'who benefits from M&A?'; 'how much are acquisitions worth?' A central issue for the finance school is how M&A should be paid for. The **organizational behavioural school** asks 'what impact do M&A have on employees?' and 'how can organizational fit be managed post-acquisition to minimize human costs?' For organizational behaviouralists, the notion of culture clash has assumed centrality in many of these studies. A more detailed examination of these schools is contained in the M&A Primer following chapter 14.

These questions have gained intellectual dominance in the research domain of M&A and tended to obscure features that are evident to practitioners. Whilst not denying the contribution of current streams of research to our understanding of M&A, the richness and complexity of the phenomena are not fully captured. Many paradoxical findings litter the dominant streams of enquiry, such as: 'why do so many M&A still take place when most are deemed to fail?'; 'why do M&A persist when they cause so much human suffering?'; 'with all the vast amount of research that has taken place on M&A, why do the success rates recorded seem to be falling rather than rising?' (Angwin, 2000). Indeed despite the wealth of learned articles on M&A, it is doubtful whether many are of profound use to a practitioner faced with managing an M&A deal for the first time. For instance, how does the knowledge that half of all M&A fail help a practitioner? Other academic observers are also aware of the shortcomings of traditional avenues of enquiry in not providing satisfactory answers to the questions raised above and being limited in their guidance to the practitioner. For this reason, academics have recently been exhorted to draw on multiple bodies of theory and to mix methods for better insights (Bower, 2004).

This book suggests a different approach, which is to recognize that the 'richness' of M&A is underappreciated. Rather than just finding alternative theories to apply, or new methods to use for their own sake, we should be more sensitive to what the M&A process actually is, and allow it to speak for itself. We should not 'gag' M&A activity and its practitioners with our dominant theories in use. For this reason, we should reappraise our view on the expanse of M&A and enquire whether we really have fully appreciated the extent of their horizons.

The task of this book is to rebalance efforts to understand M&A, to expose new horizons for research and to regain 'the open sea'. It is about expanding the horizons of M&A awareness by breaking out of a certain set of artificial intellectual constraints that currently dominate. Drawing on my own 20 years of combined practical and academic endeavour in M&A, I perceive a richness in the phenomena that is rarely brought together within the covers of one book. In many discussions with current practitioners, questions arise that are not addressed in extant literature and which are of central importance to crafting a deal. These questions may lie outside those dominant paradigms. Questions may also arise from new industries and new situations that are too recent to have attracted researcher attention. They may result from the continual need for new advisory products and approaches, and from companies wanting advice on the saliency of these new initiatives. There is also a category of questions that practitioners face and which represents a major challenge for which the literature does not offer the solutions it might. Practitioners have to engage with *all aspects* of M&A and rarely have the luxury of being able to separate and isolate aspects in a hermetic way to make it more manageable. Practitioners need a broad appreciation of *all* elements that may influence M&A, be aware of how all items of an M&A deal interact and understand how to manage a series of dialectical and tangential tensions. These issues are rarely if ever discussed in the prevailing literature as major currents of intellectual enquiry rarely interrogate each other.

Each dominant current is guilty of ignoring important factors and connections in M&A if they do not sit comfortably within their core disciplines. For example, organizational behaviour studies generally ignore the way deals are financed, the strategic intent that drives them and the legal conditions that surround them. Strategic perspectives are often woefully ignorant of the importance of the influence of legal systems and regulations on M&A and also ignore the critical role that key negotiators play in crafting a deal. Financial studies generally ignore the problems organizations face in post-acquisition management and the roles managers play.

Within the phenomena of M&A there are pools of activity and expertise that remain untapped. Within academia there are also large bodies of knowledge that have yet to connect with M&A despite their importance in many deals. For instance, while many surveys show that expanding market share is a major driver – some say *the* major driver – of M&A activity, how many articles are there in top journals that delve beneath gross measures of market share to examine exactly how marketing advantages are actually realized? Similarly, further along the supply chain, integrating the operations of firms is often a key way to achieve synergy benefits, but articles in top journals on integrating operational processes are hard to find. Central to the completion or failure of a deal is the way in which negotiations are handled, the content, the trade-offs and bargaining. Again, despite its critical position in the M&A process, articles on M&A negotiation are largely absent.

To rise to the challenge of illustrating the richness of M&A and to evaluate critically many of the core assumptions that pervade current understandings, a new approach is required. One way is to place the practitioners at the heart of the enquiry. This orientation helps give credence to their concerns and questions, rather than questions driven from purely theoretical foundations. It allows us to focus on their problems and to examine their activities and actions. This allows us to get closer to the 'action' of doing M&A. We can gain insight into the languages and metaphors they employ, how different types of practitioners actually work together and how they handle paradoxes and tensions inherent in M&A. In other words, by focusing on the practitioners, their concerns, language, activities and actions, we can perceive directly where the complexities and interconnections in the M&A process lie and how they attempt to manage them. In moving away from a discipline-based approach to M&A we are no longer constrained to see M&A through those lenses, but rather to perceive the process through all the practitioners involved. This approach inevitably results in overlaps with traditional research to a greater or lesser extent, but it also allow us to see around the edges of those currents.

To put this approach into action I created a list of images, assumptions and metaphors that pervade the practice of M&A. These included M&A as . . . 'success', 'illusion', 'warfare', 'power', 'risk', 'project', 'boundaries', 'knowledge', 'stereotypes', 'imperialism', 'linkages', 'practice', and 'time'. While many will be instantly recognizable to those in the field, few have been addressed explicitly or critically in the literature. For instance, the language employed, actions taken and activities inherent in M&A are infused with connotations of *warfare* – M&A as hostile takeover, dawn raid, poison pill – and yet this image has rarely been analysed or critiqued. Similarly, the notion of M&A as a form of commercial, social and even political *imperialism* is prevalent across many levels of analysis in many cross-border M&A – such as the hostile takeover of Mannesman by Vodafone or the acquisition of Rowntree by Nestlé – and yet the concept is rarely analysed. Of course, it has not been possible to be comprehensive in selecting images for consideration and there are strong images, such as M&A as fear, terraforming (remodelling the business landscape through M&A) or creativity, which have escaped this book. Nevertheless the images we do have, capture elements of the phenomena which will be familiar to all those engaged in M&A and deserve closer inspection. For those unfamiliar with M&A, a Primer is included after chapter 14. This details the main elements of the phenomena; key terms; processes; main research streams; practical issues for researchers.

I approached a number of leading contributors in the field of M&A to address these images and explicitly avoided framing the requests in disciplinary or theoretical terms to allow them the freedom to choose their own frames of reference. The resulting chapters tap into a wide set of issues relating to M&A and serve to illustrate the richness and pluralism of the phenomena. The chapters stem from a wide range of theoretical positions, adopt varying levels and units of analysis, and draw on quite different sets of data as a consequence. Some chapters adopt what might be described as a traditional approach, examining the firms involved from a detached external 'objective' point of view. Deal characteristics are compared with outcomes – an ex post closed world-view, where analysis focuses on correlating variables with financial performance and risk assessment. This approach provides strong prescriptions for what works and what does not: success and failure. Others also take an external objective view of M&A but are sensitive to different contexts. Under these conditions, institutional variation is viewed as critical in setting the stage for M&A to be played out in various ways. A number of chapters look inside the firms for their unit of analysis. Some adopt a senior manager perspective, focusing on their pre-acquisition intents and expectations. This is treated in different ways depending on the extent to which the top manager is viewed as self-contained or influenced by unique histories and path dependencies, institutional pressures and social interactions. The general recognition that many M&A do not work out is cause for some to focus on the post-acquisition phase, where the integration process itself is worked out and where value is gained or lost. Attention here focuses on how capabilities may transfer, such as knowledge, the process of socialization, how boundaries may form and dissolve and how the whole phase, or project, may be monitored over time. While these foci reveals new insights for parts of M&A, some authors argue for greater connectivity between key aspects. Different integrative frameworks are put forward to enable more insightful appreciation of M&A performance and practice. The final chapter observes that a key variable that underlies all the chapters but which is rarely addressed explicitly is the use and handling of time. A more sensitive appreciation of time may well help understanding of why there are so many apparent contradictions and paradoxes in the field.

In reading the chapters, the reader will become aware of a wide variety of approaches to M&A as well as considerable 'in chapter' complexity in treating an image of M&A. Some take cross-sectional views of M&A whereas others are longitudinal and dynamic, giving explicit treatment of time. Many chapters pursue a particular level of analysis and draw on different types of data to illustrate their arguments. Others examine interactions between such levels and some look at interaction between different types of analysis. Some prefer to examine how a particular stream of literature gives insights into an image, and then suggest how that stream may evolve and expand into new waters. This pluralism is welcome and a major objective of this book. In part it illustrates the complexity of M&A activity as a phenomenon and is an expression of legitimate messiness. However, while pluralism is an end in itself, it is useful to attempt to organize the chapters in such a way that the reader can perceive how they may link in relation to one another. Contrasting and comparing the chapters enriches the reader's perception of the 'ocean' that is M&A.

A natural order that emerges from the chapters, and is adopted as the structure of this book, is the M&A process itself. This structure is likely to strike a chord with practitioners and has the advantage of ease of navigation through M&A as a process. Taken as a linear sequence, the chapters can be grouped in terms of: **pre-acquisition**, where the attention is on the events and pressures leading up to the signing and completion of the deal; **post-acquisition**, where attention is directed to events, actions and activities that take place in the enlarged firm post deal; **integration**, where chapters aim at being more holistic and integrative of the whole process.

This sequential approach has its advantages in that it is broadly a narrative through the M&A process and lends itself to an ordered flow through the chapters with which practitioners would feel comfortable. It also has the advantage of offering the reader juxtaposed approaches to similar phases of the M&A process and illustrates how a different 'take' on similar moments results in quite different interpretations. Its drawbacks are that it appears to compartmentalize the M&A process and prevents key parts of M&A being connected. This has been identified as a limitation in the study of M&A itself (Angwin and Vaara, 2005) and justifies the closing 'integration' section, where there are three quite different approaches to handling this important issue. Later in this chapter, alternative courses are plotted through the book for readers wishing to pursue alternative directions.

To handle the images offered to them, some authors make recourse to the main bodies of M&A research, whereas others clearly depart from such safe havens, either moving into less usual spaces or locating themselves between different perspectives. Perhaps unsurprisingly, the authors were quick to realize that the 'dominant' images in M&A can be perceived as part of dialectical tensions. In some instances the authors have chosen to address explicitly the balance within a tension, such as whether M&A is 'War *and* Peace' rather than 'War *or* Peace'. Others have decided to concentrate on the 'anti-image' in order to expose our blind-sidedness, such as M&A as 'Illusion' rather than 'Certainty', and some have decided to attack the image head-on as self-serving explanation, such as M&A as 'Stereotypes'. These treatments add a depth and dynamic quality to the images supplied. These images as dialectical tensions are illustrated in figure 1.1.

The following reviews in more detail the contents of the book and how authors have handled their image of M&A.

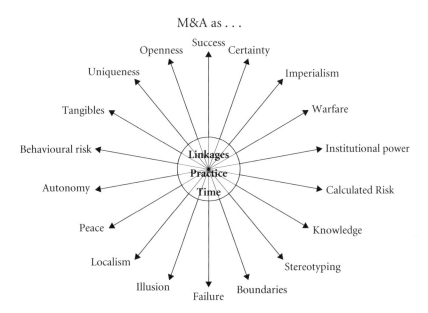

Figure 1.1   Dialectical tensions between images of M&A

Part I: Pre-Acquisition

The question that has concerned M&A scholars more than any other is whether M&A are successful and so it is apposite that we begin the book with this long-standing question. In chapter 2, 'M&A as Success', Ken Bates and Mark Whittington take a classical perspective and draw on a substantial finance and accounting literature. They ask: 1) does M&A activity add value, and for whom, and 2) how can the right price for the target company be determined? In terms of M&A adding value, Ken and Mark examine benefits to acquiring and acquired shareholders as well as the economy as a whole while bearing in mind that there are significant variations between countries, firm characteristics and types of deal. The amount paid for an acquisition is viewed as critical for a successful outcome and to determine the 'right' price they consider valuation techniques such as: 1) 'multiples'; 2) dividend discount models; 3) asset-based models; 4) cash flow methods (including a detailed worked example); 5) accounting-based approaches; and 6) real option approaches. Where acquirers are deemed to have overpaid, the 'winner's curse', 'hubris', or human weakness is blamed. Ken and Mark emphasize there is no one perfect approach to valuation and argue that contextual awareness is a vital skill to avoid the 'myopia' of spurious accuracy. They also argue that valuation approaches need greater dynamism and should be more closely linked to managerial activity in the M&A process.

Mark and Ken's handling of the question of M&A 'success' may be regarded as the 'classical' approach to M&A. It is regarded as central to the study of M&A and dominates all texts that are designed to be 'comprehensive' on the subject. This serves as a rich backdrop against which the other images in this book can be contrasted. Many of the hints in M&A as success are picked up and amplified in several of the subsequent chapters, whereas others can be seen to work from quite different sets of first principles. It is against the 'classical view' espoused in this chapter that the plurality of subsequent images and the diversity and richness of M&A can be observed.

Mark and Ken's chapter on success offers certainty about M&A outcome. In a deterministic sense, provided managers follow certain 'laws', a successful outcome is inevitable. Success therefore denies human agency, which is only inferred when failure occurs – or the irrationality of acting outside of classical prescriptions. This sense of 'certainty' was offered to Chris Smith – a seasoned senior executive and M&A practitioner turned academic. Chris has negotiated many M&A transactions as buyer and seller and has considerable professional experience to bring to bear on this question. His take on 'certainty' was to attack this image by depicting 'M&A as Illusion' in chapter 3. For Chris, M&A activity is a process of social interaction revolving around uncertainties inherent in the phenomena. This general manager perspective will resonate with practitioners of M&A in terms of what managers actually do, think and perceive when entering into a bidding contest.

As a previous general manager of a large multinational company, Chris was charged with selling off a business to a friendly purchaser. He was surprised to encounter irrational behaviour from the well-known counterparty in the face of incontrovertible evidence. To explain this surprising behaviour, Chris suggests that illusions and delusions are endemic in M&A. False perceptions and false beliefs over key aspects of the target firm, its value and the qualities of the acquirer and its management, can seriously affect the final agreed price. These illusions can infect the entire management team, and related external groups, such as financial advisers. All of these parties may have vested interests in promoting such illusions and particular social/ economic/legal contexts may also help encourage and legitimate such distortions. As Chris notes in his opening quotation *whole communities may be seized with fits of insanity*. Using the image of M&A as illusion, Chris then analyses how a major bidding competition between two large Australian supermarket chains evolved and resulted in probable overpayment. M&A as illusion looks directly at the practitioners involved in the pre-acquisition process and how they interact, to understand why they may overpay for M&A.

While Chris has offered a picture of top manager psychology during the lead up to a transaction, the 'atmosphere' of M&A is captured in chapter 4, 'M&A as Warfare', by Stephen Cummings and Sally Riad. They observe that the language of war, for which they coin the term 'warspeak', pervades M&A practice, dominating other possible languages. They observe that 'warspeak' offers dynamic, colourful, heroic images and 'legitimates' a particular set of intentions and actions. Warspeak's myopic quality provides multiple actors with clarity of focus for action and a convenient shorthand for reinforcing coherent purpose in pursuing a short-term goal. Stephen and Sally present a model to identify the main components of 'warspeak' and show how it animates and orientates parties in the pre-deal phase. However, privileging 'warspeak' as the dominant language in M&A also has consequences. Using the example of the hostile acquisition of PeopleSoft by Oracle, Stephen and Sally show how widespread human misery and significant costs result from a warlike approach and damage value creation post-acquisition. For Stephen and Sally 'warspeak' may be a reason why so many M&A fail to realize value. It obscures more nuanced perspectives and prevents the adoption of other more measured and sensitive approaches. To overcome this problem, they present 'peacespeak' as a currently marginalized language of M&A, and one that has beneficial properties. 'Peacespeak' in the pre-acquisition phase may overcome traditional problems in realizing value in M&A, facilitate the building of common futures and reduce the negative consequences of embedded conflict associated with 'M&A as war'.

The antagonisms and alignments of the protagonist firms highlighted by Stephen and Sally are played out against an institutional backcloth in chapter 5, 'M&A as Power', by Glenn Morgan. Glenn adopts a different level of analysis to prior chapters by focusing on insitutional forces and their effect in setting the context within which M&A are acted out. For Glenn, M&A are broad struggles in society about who controls firms and in whose interests decisions are made. These power dynamics between different social groups are key determinants of the nature and legitmacy of M&A activity. Here the concern is what the rules of the game are and how actors are engaged in social processes of negotiation, on the one hand dominated by, and on the other reproducing, these rules. Glenn draws on a **varieties of capitalism** approach to illustrate the varying contexts within which M&A are acted out and the effects on the conduct and actions of the main actors. Contextual variation raises questions about the role and activities of the state and its interaction with three main groups of actors – employees, shareholders and managers. Drawing on examples of M&A practice in France, Germany, the UK and US, Glenn illustrates how different power structures result in quite different 'games' of M&A. For Glenn there is then no single chess board, but different playing fields, with different rules and actors acting differently to achieve pluralistic outcomes.

The prescriptions of success, actions of top managers and contextual variety raise questions of how to assess the risk or riskiness of M&A in the pre-acquisition phase. In chapter 6, by Matthew Checkley, 'M&A as Risk' is presented as a powerful concept for understanding and managing M&A and a way to help our understanding of why so many M&A are deemed to fail. To begin, Matthew observes that the conceptualization of risk in M&A has been dominated by a financial/economic viewpoint, with risk most commonly defined in terms of the variance in financial outcome from deals. This approach predicts that much M&A activity would reduce overall risk through diversifying actions but empirical evidence struggles to support this contention. This suggests that the conceptualization of risk in an M&A context is inadequate and needs development. Matthew suggests a richer appreciation of risk to include perceptual, experiential, institutional and community-based understanding in analysis and management. He argues 'risk-in-the-wild' is the product of many interacting minds throughout the M&A process and conventional approaches to risk are generally frustrated in 'practice'. Meaningful and workable risk management must engage with the particularities of circumstance that currently elude predetermined abstraction. To convey a richer appreciation of risk in M&A, Matthew identifies three dimensions: 1) directly perceptible; 2) estimable; and 3) virtual risks. These, he argues, need to be managed through social interaction and this perspective requires a shift from modelling financial outcomes to overseeing interactions within and between relevant practitioner groups. Risk managers therefore should occupy a 'middle ground' between detached theoretical views and the particular circumstances, perceptual and local. Managing risk must iterate between extremes and explicitly recognize M&A as process.

Part II: Post-Acquisition

The post-acquisition period is regarded by many as the key time when the potential value from an acquisition can be realized. The statistics on M&A failure have caused many researchers in recent years to focus on this phase as the missing link in the neat prescriptive equations of pre-acquisition characteristics leading 'inevitably' to post-acquisition outcome. If there is widespread M&A underperformance, then maybe the management of the post-acquisition phase is where researchers ought to be searching for explanations.

In chapter 7, 'M&A as Project', Philippe Very and Stephen Gates focus on achieving the financial/economic outcome intended in the post-acquisition plan. They observe that many firms do not rigorously track the post-acquisition integration process and this may lead to value destruction. To redress this weakness, they ask how the integration process might be monitored and how it may be controlled using a monitoring system. They observe that the complexities surrounding each integration are sufficient for each to be regarded as unique and its temporal nature distinguishes it from the day-to-day running of the firm. For this reason, they argue that a project management approach to post-acquisition integration is appropriate. Philippe and Stephen focus on three main themes of project management: the project team, project risk and monitoring project progress. Key themes in the discussion of these elements are the uncertainty and risk of the project due to imperfect knowledge and the need to learn. They therefore suggest that integration is considered as a dynamic and complex process of adjustment which requires flexibility in the design and use of teams, an appreciation of four aspects of risk in the process and the use of multiple measures for project monitoring. These issues are illustrated with a number of cameos of firms managing the integration process. Project monitoring is about tracking events, adapting integration plans, agility and vigilance. Uncertainty is inherent in the process and may bring trouble, but monitoring uncertainty can bring rewards.

M&A as *project* raises significant complexities in how process may be handled as well as how disparate parts of firms may be co-ordinated and controlled. However, failure to realize economic benefit is not the only evidence of post-acquisition malaise. Popular in the M&A literature is the issue of culture clash and the dysfunctional effects this may have on organizational integration. In chapter 8, 'M&A as Boundaries', Derek O'Byrne recognizes that such clashes between organizations occur during the post-acquisition period, but avoids either a purely functional or cultural approach to understanding those difficulties. Instead he shows the centrality of the concept of boundary in understanding intra-organizational clashes; how clashes are the result of different types of boundary, not just 'cultural', becoming significant and how each gives rise to its own particular set of integration challenges. Drawing on an extensive literature on boundaries, he observes that boundaries can both build and reinforce differences, as well as locate contact and connection, across multiple levels. They may also have characteristics of rigidity, flexibility, enactedness and even be created. Using boundaries as a lens for viewing post-acquisition integration, Derek examines the evolution of a horizontal merger in the financial services sector. He observed that multiple boundaries were evident in the merger and arose over time. They were most apparent at the micro level: in his words, '*it is the small and mundane issues that are the causes of major problems*'. It is clear that managing multiple boundaries is critical for successful organizational integration and, from the case study, a dynamic process model for boundary management is proposed. In summary, Derek suggests a multi-pronged approach to enable managers to handle different types of boundary for full organizational integration.

A key way in which value may be created through post-acquisition integration is the transfer and sharing of capabilities. The most prized are the intangible and socially constructed, such as knowledge, which may provide hard-to-imitate and distinctive advantages to an acquirer. In chapter 9, 'M&A as Knowledge', Laura Empson focuses on this most critical of resources and explores why firms seem to struggle so hard to manage this capability. Knowledge sharing between acquired and acquiring companies offers significant opportunities for value creation but empirical evidence suggests that acquirers struggle to realize these gains. Laura observes that knowledge transfer requires an interpersonal communication process but that this is disrupted by fear, distrust and uncertainty. As an example, Laura examines a merger between two knowledge-intensive professional service firms in which knowledge is tacit and proprietary to individuals. She identifies the potential opportunities for knowledge sharing, the impediments that arose, how these problems escalated and how they were finally resolved. The case shows many classic M&A problems but, from a knowledge perspective, the firms did not appreciate fundamental differences in form and content of their technical knowledge bases. Different perceptions of the value and legitimacy of each other's knowledge interrupted knowledge transfer and these differences were perpetuated by two underlying fears about potential damage to firm reputation and personal careers and status: *the fear of exploitation* and *the fear of contamination*. To avoid these difficulties, Laura recommends firms understand the socially constructed elements of knowledge and use entrepreneurial 'integratic' individuals, able to operate throughout the firm in an accurate and timely way.

The actions, activities, perceptions and predjudices of actors in the post-acquisition phase create significant variety in post-acquisition integration. These characteristics of M&A actors are embedded in the histories of the individual persons, their professions, their firms, industries, and social and economic contexts. It is to the latter that Eero Vaara and Janne Tienari turn in chapter 10 on 'M&A as Stereotypes'. They observe a substantial literature on cultural differences and culture conflict in M&A integration and observe its deep embeddedness in the fabric of organizations. In particular, they observe the role that national cultural differences play as a significant part of cultural sensemaking in international M&A. Core to these discussions are national stereotypes that are (re)produced by a wide range of stakeholders, but, as Eero and Janne observe, little is known about this (re)construction. Eero and Janne take national identity-building to mean discourse constructed on the basis of shared understanding of history and continuity. This may be 'banal', with national sterotypes spread around as 'facts' without critical reflection, and can also be used to create or manipulate images of oneself or others, perhaps through humour, for some form of advantage. To illustrate national stereotyping, Eero and Janne describe Finland and Sweden, geographic neighbours, and identify significant differences between the two nations that seem to explain problems encountered in their cross-border M&A. Stereotyping seems to reconstruct particular types of pre-judices and influences actions in anticipation and retrospection. It seems to be used by organizational members to make sense of 'inter-national' encounters and to explain their experiences and problems. However, Eero and Janne warn that this explan-atory power should be viewed with a critical eye, as national stereotypes are often context specific, ambiguous and can overshadow other explanations. Its potential use as a self-serving device to reinforce prejudices also means it should be viewed with caution.

The historical and contextual themes discussed in chapter 10 are continued in Simon Collinson's chapter 11 on 'M&A as Imperialism'. Here he reflects on how these drivers influence the way in which firms engage in post-acquisition manage-ment and considers whether the image of M&A as imperialism is an appropriate characterization for cross-border deals. Simon recognizes that this image resonates strongly with the colonial histories of many European countries and has attracted a negative set of characteristics. For this reason, the spectre of imperialism is often evoked by target firms and societies when faced with unwanted hostile bids by for-eign companies. However, are cross-border acquirers necessarily imperialistic – ethno-centric dominators driven to exploit target firms and their countries? Simon suggests this depends on history and context. In the past, there were few constraints on inter-national acquirers and imperialism was clearly in use. However, today, as contin-gency theory suggests, macro- and micro-contexts influence acquirer approaches to cross-border M&A. Using the example of Kodak's ambitious expansion into China, Simon debates the benefits of the deal to the acquired firms, their employees, com-munities and the wider social and economic well-being of China. It illustrates the critical role of the state in determining the 'rules of the game'.[1] More micro concerns are how the new acquisition should fit into the parent organization, the distribu-tion of power, the decision-making structure and how strategy should be created. To illustrate that there are many different acquisition styles, of which imperialism is just one, Simon presents a typology that suggests there are different styles of cross-border acquisition, they matter, and they should fit with their specific macro- and micro-contexts.

Part III: Integration

Throughout the first two parts it is apparent that many chapters are advocating or forging links between different levels of analysis. Some focus on dynamic links between the firm and its social/institutional context, some on the links between the firm and its actors, and others on links between actors across organizational boundaries. There are also calls for adjustments and reviews of fundamental approaches to M&A as new aspects of the phenomena are perceived to influence outcome. Static, atemporal views are being challenged by more dynamic approaches; assumptions about single outcomes are being confronted with calls for pluralism; single-level analysis is giving way to multilevel analysis. This groundswell has led to calls for greater 'connectivity' in M&A research (Angwin and Vaara, 2005) and the following chapters suggest ways in which an explicit examination of linkages may yield further insights into M&A outcome(s).

In chapter 12, 'M&A as Linkages', David Schweiger, Erin Mitchell, Justin Scott and Caroline Brown recognize that most M&A do not live up to their financial expectations and do not add value to the acquiring firm. The authors observe that many reasons for this can be found in the literature, but argue that looking for single explanations for this underperformance is insufficient. They argue that it is the inter-relationship amongst them that is key. In particular they argue it is the linkage between valuation, pricing, intended synergies, integration and value creation which must be examined. After a brief review of each, they note that most dominate the pre-acquisition phase and are theoretical activities pursued to enable the parties to the transaction to negotiate and arrive at a reasonable price. The challenge, however, begins when the deal is done. The organizations then need to be managed in such a way to enable all earlier assumptions to be converted into reality. Post-acquisition integration is therefore a critical process in the realization of synergies and value creation. By examining in detail a merger between two firms in the retail food industry, the authors then illustrate how the interrelationships between all the key factors can be managed in practice. Through this case study, the authors demonstrate how the key factors identified earlier in the chapter can interact over time, and it is this interaction that is critical for understanding subsequent outcomes.

Chapter 13, 'M&A as Practice', by Duncan Angwin acts as a summary and integrative chapter for the whole book as well as presenting a new approach to understanding M&A. To begin, a 'practice' framework is introduced, which aims to address calls for greater connectivity in the study of M&A. A practice approach makes explicit the multilevel and dynamic nature of M&A, portraying the unfolding of activities and actions by M&A practitioners embedded within several layers of context. The main components of the practice model show how each influences, and is influenced by, others in a dynamic process. Each chapter of the book is then located within the practice framework to show how they have focused on different aspects of the bigger picture and to reveal where the main efforts of the field have been directed. This also serves to highlight areas for further research endeavour. The advantages of adopting a broader practice perspective are then illustrated through the use of a detailed case study. Following the case description, conventional perspectives are used to interpret and explain the data. It soon becomes apparent, however, that these interpretations are limited in usefulness, overlooking significant aspects of the process and providing rather crude explanations for outcome. A practice perspective is then applied to the case, which places greater emphasis on the actual activities and actions of practising managers and reveals how they are constrained and enabled by layers of context, which they also influence to a limited degree. This more nuanced approach enables a better understanding of the evolution and outcome of the case and promises greater insights than traditional approaches towards the creation, evolution and outcome of M&A.

The final chapter, 'M&A as Time', by Duncan Angwin, Scott Dacko and Matthew Checkley, examines a core dimension running throughout all studies of M&A. Whether the effects of time are acknowledged, assumed or ignored, this chapter argues that making temporal assumptions explicit is critical for understanding M&A processes and outcomes. To begin, the previous chapters in the book are reviewed, exposing how time has been treated. From these varied approaches, conclusions are drawn and broader observations made about the role of time in M&A studies in general. A discussion then follows around the different ways in which time may be viewed, recognizing that time has a multidimensional quality of its own. Through making aspects of time more explicit, the chapter argues that it is possible to gain a richer understanding of M&A through a temporal lens. A simulation, presented at an Improvisational Conference on 'time' at INSEAD, Fontainebleau, France, in July 2004 is then described. The audience participated by using multi-time and multi-constituent perspectives to dissect the simulated acquisition process. Their findings illustrate how a temporal approach to M&A can provide new insights and develop a richer understanding of complexities in the phenomena. The chapter then focuses on the opening question of the book – are M&A successful? Through an explicit consideration of time, its multi-dimensionality and multi-constituent nature, insights are achieved which help to explain why competing views on M&A performance arrive at different conclusions. A temporal perspective is therefore critical for enabling a richer understanding of M&A and may well enable core paradoxes and problems to be tackled. A temporal perspective can help to reorient managers and researchers in their understandings of M&A and in the process reveal new horizons to explore.

Alternative Pathways

Although the book has been structured along the lines of an unfolding M&A process, this is just one way in which these chapters can be ordered. The following section suggests alternative ways of navigating through the book, giving dominance to alternative dimensions of M&A research. Table 1.1 draws out a number of these dimensions for each chapter – position in the stream of acquisition events; analytical focus; level of analysis adopted; data source(s) drawn on; treatment of process; and nature of outcomes.

The first four columns of table 1.1 are self-explanatory, but the choice of the latter two requires explanation. They address key approaches to investigating M&A. The *Abstract/Practice* column focuses on the extent to which the perspective takes an objectified, detached view of the phenomena or is enmeshed in rich interactions at a practitioner level. The 'abstract' is associated with calculative, deliberative

Table 1.1   Analytical bases of chapters

Position	Focus	Level of analysis	Data	Abstract/ Practice	Outcome
Pre-acquisition					
2] Success	Performance outcome	Shareholders	Financial	Abstract	Singular
3] Illusion	Achieving a deal	Top management	Dialogue	Practice	Singular
4] Warfare	Negotiation process	Top management	Language	Practice	Singular
5] Power	Firm behaviour	Institutions	Institutional norms and rules	Abstract	Plural
6] Risk	Financial outcome	Firm	Financial/ Behavioural	Abstract	Singular
Post-acquisition					
7] Project	Matching unit performance to targets	Sub-firm performance variation	Unit performance	Abstract/ Practice	Singular
8] Boundaries	How boundaries arise	Employee actions/ perceptions	Boundaries	Practice	Plural
9] Knowledge	Knowledge transfer	Employee actions/ perceptions	Tacit knowledge	Practice	Singular
10] Stereotypes	Stereotyping process/national cultures	Employee actions/ perceptions	National stereotypes	Practice	Plural
11] Imperialism	Firm structure	Institutions and the Firm	Firm structure	Abstract	Plural
Integration					
12] Linkages	Linking key aspects from the whole process	Firm	Valuation, pricing, synergies, integration	Abstract	Singular
13] Practice	Integrating three major constituents of M&A practice	Managers and context	Managerial actions and activities	Practice	Singular
14] Time	Exposing key assumptions about time	Multiple	Multiple	Abstract/ Practice	Singular/ Plural

approaches, which lend themselves to prediction. Common methodological techniques in use are large-scale cross-sectional research designs and quantitative analysis to enable statistical certainty. A 'practice' approach attempts to capture the richness of emergent and messy interactions, of accident and muddle. A 'practice' approach is sensitive to context and history as important influences on events. Common methodologies of this approach are detailed longitudinal case studies, attempting to capture the complexities of 'how M&A is done'. The *Outcome* column focuses on the results of M&A. These may be taken to be singular in nature, such as assessing economic value added (EVA), or plural, with multiple outcomes, such as various results for different stakeholders.

The two columns of 'Abstract/Practice' and 'Outcome' are orthogonal to each other. The richness of practice may result in plural outcomes or be 'managed' to achieve a single outcome. Abstract approaches may also focus on a single outcome or recognize plural results. These two dimensions give rise to a 2 × 2 framework, as shown in figure 1.2. This enables the chapters to be located and grouped into different quadrants and offers an alternative course to the chronological ordering

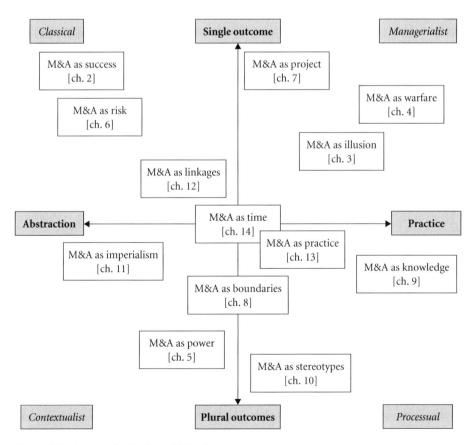

Figure 1.2   A conceptualization of M&A images

of the book. The framework may also enable the reader to begin to make sense of M&A literature in general and open the way for debate on which dimensions should assume dominance in the field, as no 2×2 can fully capture a complex reality. Other ways of organizing M&A literature are also offered later in the book to prevent readers from being too set on just one matrix.

The *Classical* quadrant, contains the chapters on M&A as success, risk and linkages. This quadrant assumes that managers aim to achieve the supreme goal of business, profit maximization, and this is investigated through objectified and detached examination of large data sets and a limited set of key variables. In this approach managers are assumed to act in an optimal manner and their planning deemed to be efficient. Associated with this approach is an armoury of techniques, formulae, matrices and flowcharts. The classical approach has a long lineage in M&A research and is dominated by finance, economic and strategy traditions.

The *Managerialist* quadrant contains chapters on M&A as project, war and illusion. Rather than assume that managers can automatically achieve optimal outcomes, this quadrant recognizes the complexity, on the ground, of managing M&A in the face of organizational, political and contextual pressures. Here managers and their actions are deemed to be vital in shaping M&A outcome. In this quadrant, managers are an explicit focus of analysis and are assumed to be the main explanation for achieving a single outcome, such as profit maximization or the signing of a deal. To capture the complexity of the M&A process, the managerialist quadrant is generally investigated through longitudinal case study designs drawing on qualitative and quantitative data.

The *Processual* quadrant emphasizes the sticky, imperfect nature of all human life, where action is accommodated pragmatically to the fallible processes in organizations and markets. The chapters in this quadrant, M&A as knowledge, boundaries and stereotypes, focus on the evolution of socially constructed approaches to change, where messiness, inertia and accidents all occur to frustrate intentions and outcomes. In this quadrant, outcomes are multiple, complex and often unintended. Common to this quadrant are case study methods that gather longitudinal qualitative data to capture the richness and complexity of multiple interactions over time.

The *Contextualist* quadrant gives dominance to the socio-political systems in which M&A activity is embedded. They set the stage for how M&A take place and determines the actions and activities of managers. In this quadrant, chapters on M&A as power and imperialism show how the cultures and powers of local systems affect the actors involved throughout the M&A process. The actors are not simply detached calculating individuals, as suggested by the classical view for instance, or the prime movers of outcome as suggested by the managerialist view, but are deeply rooted in densely interwoven social systems. These social networks influence their rationalities, their means and ends of actions, defining what is appropriate and reasonable behaviour. This quadrant tends to use comparative case study methods to illustrate differences across contexts, but as the level of abstraction grows, greater reliance is placed on quantification.

The remaining chapters, M&A as practice and M&A as time, are intended to be integrative of M&A research. M&A as practice aims to integrate all quadrants in figure 1.2 and M&A as time aims to make explicit the ways in which time has been employed throughout M&A research. For these reasons these two chapters are located centrally on the figure.

It should be noted that many of the chapters take a dynamic view of their perspective, reflecting shifting currents or suggesting ways in which their perspective might evolve. For instance, the authors on the classical approaches to M&A as success and risk recognize the limitations of highly abstract and static studies and advocate a move towards engaging more with practice, linking valuation to post-acquisition activity, and linking risk assessment more closely with risk management. They also question the overriding dominance of single outcomes and show how their approaches are attempting to address plural outcomes – for instance, option pricing can bring greater flexibility in this respect. In other chapters with a practice orientation, there is also evidence of a move towards greater objectification as academics seek to move from the specific and rich observation towards establishing more generic knowledge. For these reasons, the dynamic nature of research endeavours into M&A needs to be acknowledged.

We also need to remember that M&A activity as a phenomenon is dynamic. Although we began the chapter with commonplace nouns in M&A, we should consider, as many chapters advocate, that the M&A process is not static, and to ignore process is to grievously miss a crucial part of its richness. For this reason, when reading the chapters we should also think of the headings as verbs – as 'actioning' the content, in terms of what M&A actors are doing or should be doing. Table 1.2

Table 1.2   Actioning M&A

Chapter	Noun	Verb
	M&A as . . .	*M&A as . . .*
2	Success	Realizing value
3	Illusion	Suspending reality
4	Warfare	Going to war
5	Power	Exercising power
6	Risk	Managing risk
7	Project	Project monitoring
8	Boundaries	Creating boundaries
9	Knowledge	Embedding knowledge
10	Stereotypes	Stereotyping
11	Imperialism	Socializing
12	Linkages	Connecting
13	Practice	Practising
14	Time	Timing

shows how the chapter headings may have been portrayed to reflect the dynamic nature of their content.

The dialectical tensions of figure 1.1 and the dynamism of table 1.2 allow a rich tapestry to emerge from images that are dominant in M&A practice. This dynamic pluralism is perhaps closer to the reality experienced by practitioners than much of prior M&A research. It highlights less consistency, homogeneity and order than is presupposed by traditional approaches. Coexisting tensions from multiple stakeholders at different times and locations are the norm in M&A and we should recognize the legitimate messiness rather than be lulled into a sense of false security with neat prescriptions that ignore the importance of human agency. This pluralistic approach is deliberately in contrast to the prevailing monist approaches and with it, hopes that some more of the mysteries of M&A can be revealed.

Practitioners leading a firm into an M&A situation do not have the luxury of being able to concentrate on just one stream of activity in a hermetic way. They necessarily have to engage with *all aspects* of these multidimensional phenomena. This requires a broad appreciation of *all* the elements that may influence M&A. They also have to be aware of how all the items of any M&A interact in a series of trade-offs, so that the exercise is one of managing a series of dialectical and tangential tensions. These issues are rarely if ever discussed in the prevailing literature, which tends to offer neat frameworks and clear prescriptions or detailed situation-specific case studies. Figure 1.2 was presented to reveal that there are different approaches to M&A, but this mechanism of categorization is also 'expensive' in distancing categories from each other and denying connectivity, as well as privileging some perspectives over others. The boundaries between categories are less clear cut in practice and their overlaps can offer valuable insights. Some connectivity can be achieved by mapping different trajectories of practice onto figure 1.2, as shown in figure 1.3. These trajectories show that different aspects of M&A are predominantly considered by different quadrants, but do 'blend', sometimes uncomfortably, across quadrant borders.

With trajectory A, firms are influenced by their context, the 'rules of the system' and multiple forces for change. This may give rise to an M&A setting in which the acquiring firm may then investigate targets in the abstract, using classical broad prescriptive frameworks and techniques aimed at a single outcome, such as improving shareholder value. With a target identified often based on publicly available data, negotiations may proceed where richer interaction between the firms and their managements leads to significant complexity and nuancing, although still with a single guiding purpose, such as closing a deal. After acquisition, there are strong pressures from managers on the new organization to achieve an intended outcome. However, over time, this process may begin to fragment into a messy series of processes with increased engagement of disparate parties. Trajectory A follows a rational conceptualization of the M&A process in linking all the quadrants.

Other trajectories are possible, such as trajectory B where the firm may be put onto an acquisition footing through complex social and political interaction within the

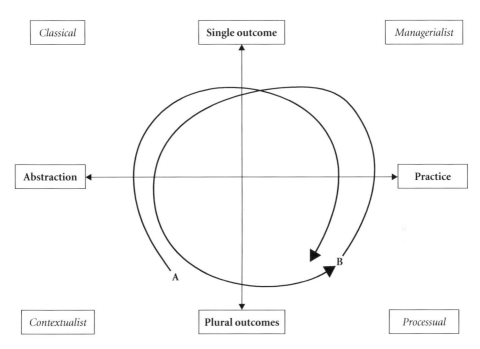

Figure 1.3   Navigating M&A

firm. Although at this stage there may be plural goals from a range of stakeholders, as the process continues by considering constraints and opportunities imposed by context, the application of generic search tools for locating and valuing targets, and organizational routines will rapidly reduce earlier pluralism to a single directed focus. The cycle may then continue back into a pluralist arena of contextual social and political complexity.

These trajectories are simply a device to illustrate how the quadrants may interact as an M&A process unfolds and where there may be greater degrees of emphasis from practitioners and academics alike. In reality, however, there is likely to be an ebb and flow of influences from all quadrants which will vary depending on the companies involved, the types of M&A being engaged in and their specific contexts.

The implication of the trajectories is that all quadrants of figure 1.3 are important in M&A, drawing on a wide range of data and methods to gain a full comprehension of the phenomena. By definition, therefore, an M&A deal that does not appreciate all parts of the figure, or locates part of the process in inappropriate quadrants, may well experience difficulties.

In this introductory chapter, a wide range of images have been discussed to give insight into M&A and demand further enquiry. These images reveal a richness in M&A activity and go further in capturing its complexity than conventional enquiry. The book has organized the images along a process dimension for resonance with practitioners, but this chapter also demonstrates that alternative routes can be navigated, pursing different theoretical approaches. The use of a 2 × 2 framework helps to organize images around key dimensions and suggests ways in which a complete understanding of M&A may be helped by considering different trajectories through its quadrants. Undoubtedly there are perspectives on M&A that are not captured in the book, but its main purpose is to demonstrate that new horizons may be revealed which have been obscured by the domination of a few major areas of enquiry. The images in this book show that there is value in regaining 'the open sea' by extending research efforts into other currents so that 'new horizons' may be revealed.

NOTE

1. Previously China only allowed equity joint ventures. The very small number of earlier foreign M&A was on a limited 'experimental' basis. M&A by overseas companies in China is, today, a much more widely encouraged activity, especially for poor-performing semi-state owned enterprises (SOEs).

Part II Pre-Acquisition

Chapter 2   M&A as Success

Mark Whittington and Ken Bates

Finance has identified 'an elephant' in the M&A domain. The main concern of finance, broadly defined, has been to determine whether mergers and acquisitions are successful. A wide variety of techniques have been employed in exhaustive studies, utilizing numerous criteria for success, to provide an answer. The overall conclusion has been that the majority of mergers and acquisitions are *not successful* for the shareholders of the company that instigated the deal. Where there is evidence of value creation it seems that the shareholders of the target company take the lion's share and the shareholders of the bidding company are, on average, fortunate to gain anything at all. The general explanation for this is that although the acquiring company creates the opportunity for value gain, or synergy, they effectively pass this on to the target shareholders by paying a full price for their shares.

The finance perspective has therefore identified an elephant – why, despite the damning conclusions from studies of five merger waves in the twentieth century, does M&A activity continue to occur, and indeed, in 2006, was beginning another dramatic resurgence? To quote only a couple of examples, Sirower (1997) found only 33% of deals studied added value for acquirer's shareholders and Selden and Colvin (2003) claimed that 70–80% of acquisitions fail. So should we presume that executives initiating M&A activity now believe that their deals will be part of the 20–33% that will succeed? Or is it that executives believe that they have learned from their predecessors' mistakes and hence their deals will buck the past trends? How do they think they can escape 'the winners curse', which dictates that when there is more than one bidder the management team with the most unreasonably high forecasts will outbid all others and win the contest, but lose value for their shareholders?

Why does the acquirer seem to pay too much? Is it because data are inadequate or the valuation techniques used are poor? Are the valuations based on plausible assumptions that break down due to ineffective post-deal implementation? Is the evidence from academic studies itself flawed because it largely relies only on share price movements for a few days after acceptance? We consider the answers to such questions and also discuss the effect on value creation of various factors, such as whether the bid is friendly or hostile, and the size and stock market rating of the acquirer.

For a thorough look at the success of M&A, this chapter will address the role of accounting and finance in each of the stages of a merger or acquisition. While there will be many individuals from the chief financial officer's (CFO's) team involved along with specialist outsiders, the words 'accounting' and 'finance' also refer to a number of approaches as well as to individuals. Accounting generally includes financial accounting and management accounting. Financial accounting is primarily concerned with stewardship, paying bills, invoicing and financial reporting. The management accountants are concerned with management control, operational planning and decision support. Finance, on the other hand, includes concerns with financing the firm and issues connected to the company's listing on the stock market and meeting shareholders' needs. A further area, financial analysis, falls between the two, needing to draw on the knowledge and skills of both accounting and finance; competition and strategy analysts would be in this group. The terms are not tightly defined and the roles of individuals will differ from firm to firm. For brevity the term 'finance' in this chapter will often refer to 'accounting and finance'.

Because mergers and acquisitions involve the functioning of the capital market and are also investment decisions, it is not surprising that finance has said a great deal about such deals down the years. It has had a preoccupation with the level of success of mergers and acquisitions and the factors that might affect the result of the deal positively or negatively. The academic literature focuses primarily on deals that were completed and on whether value has been added through the combining of the companies, usually meaning value for the shareholders of the acquiring firm.

However, the concluding of the deal, and the share price movements from the time of the announcement of the bid through to a few days after its acceptance, is just one part of a much longer story. Figure 2.1 shows the steps in the M&A

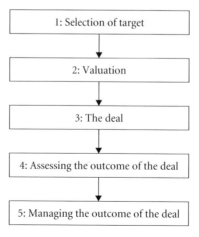

Figure 2.1 Stages in the M&A process

process, and this chapter will consider each stage in turn. Financial analysis of the environment, and potential bid targets, will have been underway from the start of the process. The next stage, how the bid price might be determined, has been the key focus of finance textbooks. The deal itself is an issue for finance because it can be structured in a number of ways, involving cash or shares or a mix of the two. Stage 4, assessing the short-term outcome of the deal, is a key contribution of finance. The final stage is to consider the integration of the acquisition or the management of the new merged entity. This, from our perspective, is primarily a management accounting issue.

After working through each step, the discussion will then consider some key problems and issues in the finance arena relating to M&A, including some of the underlying accounting and valuation issues. The chapter concludes with a comprehensive cash flow valuation case which you are encouraged to attempt *before* you look at the solution provided in appendix 1, which includes a discussion of how the valuations calculated would be utilized to inform the subsequent negotiations.

Key Emphases of the Finance View

Like beauty, success and value are to some extent in the eye of the beholder. There are a number of groups or individuals who may have their own view on the level of success of a particular deal. Governments, shareholders of the acquired firm, shareholders of the acquiring firm, employees, customers, competitors and suppliers may all have differing perspectives when considering a deal to be a success or a failure.

The key question asked by the finance literature is:

'Have mergers and acquisitions added value?'

We need to consider this question carefully before moving on to assess the research findings of the many quantitative studies of value creation.

A natural way for finance to answer the question would be to measure value by comparing the market capitalization (share price multiplied by the number of shares issued) of the new entity with that of the two old companies added together. This approach might just pick up transference of value from other stakeholder groups, competitors, customers or suppliers, rather than value creation for the economy as a whole. The impact of reduced competition and increase in monopoly power from the deal could cause such a transfer. If the gain is in cost reduction from increased economies of scale then value for the economy may have been created. However, the losses sustained by any redundant workers should also be taken into account and even employees of either company that retain their jobs may have their own value levels reduced because of the level of changes imposed on them and the resultant uncertainty and fear (Hapeslagh and Jemison, 1991).

The role of governments is not neutral here and may vary from one nation to another. Governments may regulate M&A activity to avoid undue monopoly power and protect consumers; in both the EU and US, proposed deals may be referred to the regulatory authorities and changed or refused. For instance, the acquisition of the food retail group Safeway by Morrison was allowed *on condition* that certain acquired stores were sold off to avoid undue local monopoly. On the other hand, the French have a policy of encouraging 'National Champions', which implies accepting a degree of monopoly power in the home market in order to enhance international competitiveness. Turkey, and other countries, has encouraged mergers in their finance industry to ensure that some local players are large enough to withstand competition from international banks. A further question is therefore whether any value created in a domestic deal is just a value transfer from other parts of the world economy.

These questions of value are generally reduced in the finance literature to questioning whether shareholders have gained from the deal. The question can be viewed in two ways: has value been created by the deal and, if so, then who has gained? A merger between a and b might be said to have created value (V) if:

$$V_{merged} > V_a + V_b \tag{2.1}$$

The shareholders of the acquired firm will gain because they will have been offered more than the current share price; otherwise they would not have sold. The shareholders of the bidding firm will have gained from the deal if the value of the firm in which they have invested rises over time because of the transaction. The focus of the literature, then, is to assess whether the bidding company shareholders gain from the deal. As we shall see, even this more limited question is difficult to answer.

Stages in the M&A Process

The above section has provided an outline of the finance view of the M&A process. Below we look at each step in detail.

Step 1: Selection of the target

One might legitimately state that this has more to do with strategy than finance. However, behind any investigation of strategic options, there must always be the explicit or implicit thought of financial gain and hence financial analysis is an essential element. The gain might be achieved through cost reduction, perhaps via horizontal merger and the gaining of economies of scale, or margin enhancement, possibly by vertical integration and the acquisition of an immediate customer. Conglomerate deals depend on the exploitation of a particular management approach or of spare resources and again aim to raise profit or reduce risk. The latter may be achieved through diversification as such deals may not be margin enhancing, but might offer the likelihood of reduced volatility of returns and therefore reduced risk for the shareholder, making it more likely that returns will be over the risk threshold.[1]

A recurring question might be, 'where does strategy end and finance begin?' The authors contend that this is the wrong question to ask because there are always numbers, again explicitly or implicitly, behind any strategic initiative (e.g., see Smith, 2003). Here, as in each stage of the process, the accounting and finance specialists will be of most value to their management colleagues if they have a good understanding of the industry, its structure and key parameters for survival and success.

It is also hard to separate step 1 entirely from step 2, the valuation, as there must be some sense of value in mind during the selection process. It may be that a number of potential targets make strategic sense and the choice can only be made once their value to the acquirer is calculated and compared with the current market capitalization.

Step 2: Valuation of the target

The aim of the management team is to create value for shareholders and, in assessing a potential target company, the key aim must be to bid at a price that is less than the perceived future benefit. Clearly the bid has to be above the current share price of the target company – otherwise the bid would be of no interest to the current shareholders. How far above the current share price should the bid be? Obviously a bid only a little above the current market price may well be rejected and, worse still, attract other bidders as the target is now 'in play'. On the other hand a 'knock-out' bid, considerably above the prevailing price, will probably succeed in enticing the shareholders of the target, but may mean paying more than was necessary. Assessing the attractiveness of the target and the worth of the company to the acquirer's shareholders is paramount. If the expected bid premium required to secure the target takes the cost above the forecast value of the acquisition, then good corporate governance would imply that no bid should be made, as the acquirer's shareholders will not gain.

There are many methods of assessing the value, or potential value, of a business. They vary from the simple (and simplistic) to the complex. Here we will briefly summarize the main approaches and later in the chapter we will provide more detail of the approaches we believe to be most useful and demonstrate their application using a case example.

Method (a): Multiples

These approaches can be summarised as:

'How many times the X should we be willing to pay?'

We will use the following information taken from the accounts of Greggs plc, a UK bakery products retailer, to illustrate the meaning of, and the differences between, each of the multiple measures considered.

Greggs plc, key figures
(Extracted from annual report and accounts 2004)

	(£000s)
Turnover	504,186
Operating expenses	−266,463
Operating profit	44,714
Other	0
Profit before interest and tax (PBIT)	44,714
Net interest	1,988
Profit before tax	46,702
Tax	−15,115
Profit after tax	31,587
Dividend	−11,524
Retained profit	20,063
Operating profit	44,714
Depreciation and amortization	21,336
EBITDA	66,050
Decrease in working capital	3,218
Operating cash flow	69,268
Earnings per share (pence)	264.7
Weighted average number of shares	11,931,728
Number of shares at year end	12,141,892
Number of shops at year end	1,263
Share price at 28 February 2006 (£)	46.46

The most well-known X in this context is earnings. The price–earnings (PE) ratio shows the number of times last year's earnings (that is, profit after tax) per share that would need to be paid to buy one share. A PE of 10 would therefore mean that the purchasers would need to be willing to pay ten times the latest year's earnings per share and, in simple terms, would expect to recover their money in 10 years if annual earnings remained static. A small number would imply that profits are expected to be static or falling; a high number would suggest that future earnings will be significantly higher – otherwise no one would be willing to pay such a high price. The total market value of the company (share price multiplied by the number of shares in issue) will be the annual earnings of the firm multiplied by the PE ratio.[2]

Clearly the potential bidder is going to have to offer above the current PE × earnings to interest target shareholders; hence, PE ratios can also be prospective

– based on forecast earnings rather than historic. The current shareholders of the target may base their valuations on reasonable forecasts too, perhaps an average of the forecasts of the analysts following the company, because the benefit of share ownership is future, not past, performance. The bidder would therefore need to predict a higher PE for the target company than the one anticipated by the target's current shareholders for the bid to be seriously considered.

> The Greggs share price on 28 February 2006 was £46.46 and the earnings per share for the year was 264.7 pence.

> Greggs price–earnings multiple was therefore 17.55 times.

One issue with PE ratios is a concern over the earnings numbers as these are clearly affected by the accounting policies of the firm and the accounting standards current at the time. For example, introducing a new accounting standard that forced companies to include stock options offered to employees as a cost in their income statement would reduce earnings. If the market already knew about the options, then one would expect the share price to remain the same and the PE would fall as the declared profit would now be lower. The point is that the underlying economics of the business are unaltered, but the PE would be different. Changes in depreciation policy are a particular problem – especially when two companies in an industry have very similar physical assets, but use quite different depreciation rates. The different cultural context of accounting can often be the reason behind this (Whittington, 2000). In principle, the analyst should be trying to estimate the maintainable earnings figure for a business rather than just accepting the earnings number in the latest income statement, an issue we will consider later.

Price to EBITDA and price to operating cash flow

To deal with the problem of depreciation, and the connected issue of amortization, areas where companies have some choice over accounting policy and therefore the earnings numbers published, these two alternative multiples are used. EBITDA (earnings before interest, tax, depreciation and amortization) is often used not just because of accounting policies, but also because depreciation and amortization reflect historic decisions to buy tangible or intangible fixed assets. These decisions and technical valuations may not be relevant when considering a price to buy the company because they are based on historic transactions rather than the future value to the company of the assets. Price to EBITDA will be closer to the price to cash flow per share ratio, although the latter will also take into account changes in working capital. Care must be taken when choosing the cash flow number to be used in such a calculation and interpretation should take into account whether it is before or after tax payments, for example. One must also consider that these multiples will be of a different order to the PE ratio – for example, a manufacturing firm with significant depreciation will have a far higher EBITDA than profit after tax and therefore the price to EBITDA multiple will be significantly lower than the PE.

Greggs' EBITDA is £66,050,000 in total and hence £5.54 per share.

Price to EBITDA is therefore 46.46/5.54 = 8.39 times.

Greggs' operating cash flow is £69,268,000, more than EBITDA because of a decrease in working capital achieved mainly by an increase in creditors.

Cash flow per share is £5.81 and price to cash flow is therefore £46.54/5.81 = 8 times.

Price to sales

When faced with a company with limited financial figures in the public domain (such as a small private business), or one with figures of limited credibility (for instance, a business with a qualified audit report), this multiple may be the only one that the analyst may be willing to take as meaningful. The multiple times sales approach is commonly used to value professional service businesses, such as accountancy or legal partnerships, where the costs, and hence profits, of the business are affected by the mix of salaried employees and partners rewarded by a profit share, rather than in a manner that would have reduced operating profit.

Greggs' sales is £504,186,000 in total and hence £42.26 per share.

Price to sales is therefore 1.1 times

Price to a particular business attribute

For example, the value of a funeral business might be calculated as a multiple of the number of funerals carried out in a year. This type of multiple is of particular use when the purchaser of the business would expect to be able to manage the acquisition in a manner that might reflect its own experience of running such a business rather than the cost picture of the business being acquired.

For a retail business, a common business attribute to use would be sales area. We are not provided with this figure for Greggs but the accounts do tell us that the number of shops at the year end is 1,263 and hence the share price represents 3.68 pence per shop.

* * *

Multiples are easy to calculate and, in the case of published companies, the PE is readily available from the financial press. Use of this simplistic method may also be extended to unquoted firms by utilising the PE of the most closely related quoted company from the same industry, suitably adjusted for the inevitable differences and the fact that shares in any unquoted business are less marketable and hence relatively less valuable.

Method (b): Dividend discount model

The classic idea behind this approach is that the equity value of a company should be the present value of the investors' income stream.[3] An investor holding shares for only a few years receives income through both dividend and share price growth, but as the share price on sale also depends on future dividends, the value of any share that is expected to be in existence for ever (or at least for a very long time) is dependent only on the future stream of dividend. On the assumption that dividends are on a steady growth path, something many companies would aim for, then the Gordon growth model can be used to value the share:

$$Equity\ value_t = \frac{Dividend_{t+1}}{Cost\ of\ equity - growth} \tag{2.2}$$

Hence, the value of the equity at time t is equal to the expected dividend divided by the excess of the cost of capital over the growth rate. The model depends on being able to assume a stable environment and future growth, in addition to the assumption that growth will be less than the cost of capital. In considering an acquisition the potential acquirer might forecast that the available dividend and the growth rate might be higher under their ownership than under current management. The anticipated higher equity value under new management leaves room for a bid premium.

Method (c): Asset-based valuation

In an acquisition the assets of a company are acquired. Hence it seems reasonable to consider the relative valuation of the assets by the stock market as compared with the value placed on the assets themselves in the company's accounts. The market-to-book ratio attempts to do this by dividing the market value of a company's shares by the book value of equity (shareholders' funds) from the balance sheet. One would anticipate that in most cases the market value should be higher, and hence the ratio should be over one, because the management should have added intangible assets (customer goodwill, for example) to the mainly tangible ones included in a published balance sheet. In principle, one should be concerned about the replacement cost of the assets rather than their book value – the ratio then being referred to as Tobin's q. However, replacement cost will not be readily available, though it could be estimated by an industry specialist.

A 'value' acquirer might seek out firms with a low market-to-book as potentially undervalued by the market. To accept that shares might be undervalued in this way, one would need to reject the notion of market efficiency, perhaps due to thin trading.[4] Many things affect the market-to-book ratio, such as the age of assets, depreciation policies and whether the company has a significant holding of properties that have increased in value but not been re-valued in the accounts. Also note that companies with significant intangible assets, such as brands, that are not shown on the balance sheet, because they have been home grown and not paid for on acquisition, will have high market-to-book ratios. The usefulness of such a simplistic ratio when assessing one particular target company is therefore highly questionable.

Method (d): Cash flow-based valuation

Many would regard this as *the* method of assessing economic gain. Indeed this is the only method used by Brealey et al. (2006) in their chapter on mergers. What is required is a detailed year-by-year forecast of the after-tax operational cash flows that will be generated by the business and the financing that will be required to generate them. These cash flows are forecast for the period over which the company can continue growing (the planning horizon) and subsequently it is assumed that the company will not invest in further growth but will just replace its assets as necessary to maintain a steady state. This means that the years after the planning horizon can be represented by one 'terminal year'. This can then be adjusted by an annuity factor to give the value of the company beyond the planning horizon. This is referred to as the 'terminal value'.

The net cash flows during the planning horizon and the terminal value based on the steady state annual cash generation are then discounted at the company's cost of capital and, after adjusting for net debt, the value of the company's equity is established. Appropriate research is needed, using past strategy and performance in relation to the competitive environment as a base and adjusting for changes in strategy and the environment, to predict future performance. According to Rappaport (1998 – the later edition of his seminal 1986 work), to arrive at the detailed forecast the following key questions need to be answered year-by-year:

1. How long is the company likely to continue growing?
2. By how much each year are sales likely to grow?
3. What is the expected EBITDA margin?
4. What is the expected corporation tax rate?
5. What is the required investment in working capital (stock and debtors less creditors)?
6. What is the required investment in fixed assets (land, buildings and equipment)?
7. At what rate should the company allow for the diminishing value of money over time as investors wait for their cash return (the cost of capital)?

The case at the end of the chapter is of the potential purchase of Greggs by Tesco. This theoretical case (the authors have no knowledge of Tesco considering such a course of action) shows one way in which such a cash flow-based valuation can be carried out. Note that a more detailed description of this methodology is provided by Whittington and Bates (2004).

Method (e): Accounting-based methods

A common fixation with profit as the measure of success means it would be logical to assess a potential target on its profits. The profit measure that needs to be used is economic profit, alternatively called residual income. This is calculated by taking the profit after tax and subtracting a capital charge, which is the required rate of return for the investors (i.e. the cost of capital multiplied by the net asset investment). Any excess is then a true gain for the shareholders, over and above the return that just satisfies their need for a return that matches the risk undertaken. This is similar to the economist's supernormal profit and, in principle, to the well-known Stern Stewart Economic Value Added (EVA™) metric.

The valuation of the equity using this method is, in effect, an expansion of the Gordon growth model and can be summarized as the equity value being the book value of equity plus any after-tax profits over and above the cost of equity, allowing for the timing of the profits – discounting the future expected receipts at the cost of equity. So, when BV is book value and r is the cost of equity,

$$Equity\ value_{t=0} = BV\ of\ equity_{t=0} + \sum_{t=1}^{\infty} \frac{residual\ income_t}{(1 + r)^t} \qquad (2.3)$$

This is often referred to as the abnormal earnings method, because normal earnings would just be equal to the cost of capital.[5] So, in essence, this method discounts the expected excess profits of the company, rather than the cash flows used in the previous method.

Some writers, Penman (2004) for example, prefer this method over the cash flow one. We will discuss the relative merits of these two approaches later.

Method (f): Real options

All the above methods see the acquisition or merger as a single investment. This may be too simplistic as after the deal there will be more decisions to make, for example regarding the level of capital expenditure to undertake and new opportunities that might now be pursued. Effectively the initial deal then gives the acquirer a number of options that might be taken up. These options can be seen as branches of a decision tree, each branch with a net present value and a probability of happening. A complete value of the deal can only be ascertained by valuing all the branches and then weighting the results by the probabilities. This is made more complex if the sequence of the decision nodes is not known and because some of the branches are mutually exclusive and some complementary. This is referred to as the real options approach to distinguish it from financial options (the option, but not the obligation to buy a share at a future date at a set price, for example), though much of the calculation may be similar.

Van Putten and MacMillan (2004) make the point that 'Real options are a complement to, not a substitute for, discounted cash flow analysis. To pick the best growth projects, managers need to use the two methods in tandem.' This comment is in the context of capital projects rather than mergers or acquisitions, but is still relevant here.

It is beyond the scope of this chapter to include a comprehensive example of the use of real options when valuing a target company, so for further insights see Broyles (2003).

Step 3: The deal

Our review of the valuation methods largely ignores the payment characteristics of the deal and the effects of due diligence in adjusting the valuation. Hence we have effectively assumed that once the value is established (or the range of values within which negotiations will take place) the acquisition will be for cash. If all or part of the consideration is to be through the issue of shares, there may be gains or losses in value that will not be reflected in earnings or residual income and would have to be incorporated separately into any cash flow valuation method. According to Penman (2004), in a merger or acquisition the acquirer can add value in three ways:

1. Buying the acquiree's shares at less than fair value,
2. Using its own overvalued shares to buy the shares of the acquiree company,
3. Generating value through synergies reaped by combining the operations of the two firms.

The approaches above only really consider the total value created by the third option.

There will be a due-diligence exercise, which entails the bidder checking over the acquisition target's assets, tax position and other issues that may affect the valuation. This usually takes place after the outline offer has been agreed on. This can involve a number of specialists and will always include lawyers and accountants who will check on the valuations and ownership of the assets. Clearly this is important, as any material differences between the bidder's perception of what is being purchased and the reality of the deal need to be discovered. One of the other aims of this process is to start the assessment of 'fair value' – the appropriate valuations of assets to be included in the acquirer's balance sheet, using its own accounting policies (depreciation periods, for example) instead of those of the target company.

Off-the-record discussions between the authors and a number of specialists who have been involved in due-diligence exercises reveal a tendency for the task to be rushed and always undertaken with undue time pressure. It is not surprising therefore to know of situations where, for example, companies assumed that the acquired company owned the buildings it was using and then found out that this was not the case some time after the transaction was complete and the money had been paid. Another example would be Midland Bank (a UK bank, itself acquired some years ago) buying a small US bank without undertaking a sufficient check of the loan book. Gaughan (2002, p. 465) quotes the president of one company after completing an acquisition: 'We found a surprising number of things about the company that were different than what we anticipated'. In an acquisition, the rule is 'buyer beware' and, whilst in some cases legal action might be possible, money, time and reputation are lost when discovering the purchase was not quite as expected (Angwin, 2001). Needless to say, the best analytic techniques will not undo the damage caused by inaccurate assumptions and incomplete research. The dangers are almost always of underestimating the costs or overestimating the benefits.

Step 4: Assessing the outcome

There is plenty of evidence that mergers and acquisitions create value – see Bruner (2002) for example. The more relevant question, if you are a shareholder of the acquiring firm, is whether the value created was completely included in the price paid. The weight of evidence is that many, if not most, acquisitions and mergers do not add value for the shareholders of the acquiring firm, though many studies suggest that deals may be value neutral. Assuming reasonable corporate governance, the supposed reason for the deal would have been to add value for the shareholders of the acquirer. Eccles et al. (1999) state: 'despite 30 years of evidence demonstrating that most acquisitions don't create value for the acquiring company, executives continue to make more deals, and bigger deals, every year.' Sirower's (1997) own study of acquisition and merger performance looked at 168 deals and found only 33% adding value for the acquirer's shareholders. Selden and Colvin (2003) state a higher rate of failure, claiming that '70% to 80% of acquisitions fail, meaning they create no wealth for the share owners of the acquiring company'.

Acquisition and merger waves

The context can make a difference as acquisitions and mergers happen in waves, meaning a sudden rush of deals followed by a lull and then a further rush. One would expect that the outcome of the deals, in terms of value creation, as well as the importance and influence of the factors that created the deals, and hence their success or failure, could very well change from one wave to the next. Weston et al. (2004) identify five main waves of activity: the period around 1900, fostering primarily horizontal deals; the vertical deals of the 1920s; the conglomerate transactions of the1960s; the big deals of the 1980s; and the period of the strategic deal from 1992 onwards. With such differing types of transaction being predominant, the lessons from one wave through to the next may be limited. Gaughan (2002) presents further statistics and information on each of the waves and also covers deals in the 1970s.

Waves of corporate deal activity can be triggered by a number of environmental factors. Rhodes-Kropf and Viswanathan (2004) accept that deregulation and changes in technology may be factors, but that deal activity will also be affected by the level of stock valuations. At times, when valuations seem high based on fundamentals (referred to as 'overvalued'), acquisitions and mergers are more likely and the bidders are more likely to offer stock than cash in such circumstances.

Moeller et al. (2005) look at the results of US deals through the 1980s and around the turn of the twentieth century. They find that in the 1980s the average loss for acquiring firm shareholders was 1.6 cents per dollar spent, while in the period 1998 to 2001 this rose to 12 cents. However, before assuming the majority of the deals in this latter period were disastrous, a closer look reveals that if a small number of deals with spectacularly poor results are ignored, then acquiring firm shareholders gained rather than lost over this 3-year period. Interestingly the firms that made these large loss deals were active and successful in managing value-creating deals before this point. The firms making the large loss deals then became poor performers on the market themselves.

Finance perspective

In assessing the finance literature it is important to note that the studies differ in a variety of ways. Some look at small 'event windows', running to just a day or two after the deal; others take a longer window. Performance is assessed by the calculation of abnormal returns – a return different from what one would have expected had the deal not taken place. The calculation of what would have been normal is also contentious as there are a number of approaches that might be used. Fama and French (1993) suggest that studies using either of the traditional models, referred to as the market model and the capital asset pricing model, are flawed because they ignore other factors, specifically firm size and the market-to-book ratio, which should have been taken into account when determining normality. Whether the poor performance of deals in these studies would have been reversed is not clear – Fama and French suggest yes, whereas others suggest not.

Jensen and Ruback (1983) carried out an important survey of the literature on acquisitions and mergers, reviewing studies using data up to 1981. Their key finding was that deals had created wealth for the shareholders of the target company and that the shareholders of the bidding company neither gain nor lose. So one could conclude from this that deals had created value, but that, on average, the bid price includes all this value gain (synergy) and effectively passes it to the target shareholders. Mueller (2003) reviews eight studies from the pre-1983 period that looked at both short- and long-term windows. The target shareholders gain about 16% and the majority of studies found a small positive gain for the acquiring shareholders too (0.3%) over the short event horizon. However in the year before the deal, acquiring shareholders had abnormal positive returns of some 11%, supporting Rhodes-Kropf and Viswanathan (2004) in their conclusion that high valuation leads to bids. In the longer post-deal horizon, the acquiring shareholders lose value (−6% abnormal return on average). The standard view, that deals created some limited value for the acquiring company's shareholders, was based on the majority of studies that focused on a short time horizon around the deal. Jensen and Ruback (1983) also conclude that the gains do not come from extra market power of the enlarged company, but from other factors – improved management for example.

Such conclusions fit with the principle of market efficiency – that a well-functioning stock market will correctly price any share based on all information available. This is challenged by those who believe that there are behavioural effects to consider in how investors react in particular situations. These behavioural theories are used to explain stock market 'bubbles', periods of high valuations, which, as we have seen, can lead to intense deal activity. Many studies after Jensen and Ruback (1983) have questioned the assumption of market efficiency and have also questioned the belief that managers act in the best interests of their shareholders – questioning the quality of corporate governance. The introduction of share options for the directors of many companies at least acknowledges that this latter agency problem is at least a possibility unless motivations of managers and shareholders are linked.

Jensen (1986) considered that managers may use funds at their disposal in a manner that could reduce shareholder wealth. Roll (1986) talks of hubris, the expectation of unreasonably high returns, and the fact that, if there is more than one bidder, the management team with the most unreasonably high forecasts will outbid and win the contest – 'the winner's curse'.

There have continued to be many studies drawing on the event study methodology, but the questions asked and the results gained have been more broadly interpreted and, in general, the assumption that there is (on average) a gain for the acquiring company's shareholders is a rare conclusion.

Finance researchers have endeavoured to identify factors that may help to explain variations in the performance of different deals. These are summarized in figure 2.2 and discussed below.

Does the payment method matter? In a large study Andrade et al. (2001) found that when a deal is based on a cash offer, the target shareholders have greater gains than when there is a stock offer. They also find that bidding company shareholders also fare better (or at least less badly) when cash is used in a bid. Other studies, such as Datta et al. (1992), support this conclusion. One should add that it ought to be the factors that management considered in deciding on a cash bid, rather than on a share-based bid, that would lead to this result. To assume that just by bidding cash one could improve future performance would seem like magic rather than good management.

Does the premium size matter? Clearly the higher the premium, usually stated as the percentage increase on top of the prevailing market price before the bid (or before the rumour of a bid), the higher the gain for the target company shareholders. One

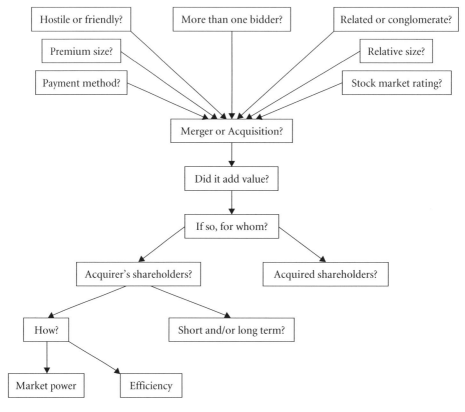

Figure 2.2   Questions about outcomes

of Sirower's (1997) key findings in considering a large number of ways of measuring shareholder performance is that:

> 'The level of the acquisition premium has a strong negative effect on performance across all twenty-eight measures of shareholder performance; the higher the premium, the larger the losses.'

The size of premium over the current share price to offer is a complex decision. A relatively low bid might encourage other bidders and result in a higher final price than an initial higher bid that successfully discouraged any other interest. On occasion it might seem that a competitor counter-bids with the intention that the original bidder will at least pay a full price for the acquisition rather than with the motivation of winning the contest.

Does it make a difference if the bid is friendly or hostile? Sudarsanam (2003) considers a number of US studies and both short- and long-term event windows. He also separates the studies into those where the bid was hostile, unsupported by the management of the target and often referred to as a 'tender offer', and those where the offer is supported by the target's management. In the short-window studies, the acquired firm shareholders gain more under tender offers than under agreed deals, while any gains by the acquiring shareholders are generally statistically insignificant. Sirower (1997) finds no difference in performance between tender offers and agreed bids in his own study, but in his literature review details research with conflicting findings on whether tender offers outperform or underperform. In a review of long-window studies, Sudarsanam (2003) highlights significant variation in the results of the individual studies but finds some evidence that tender offers create more value than agreed deals.

Does it make a difference if there is more than one bidder? It is here where the concept of the winner's curse may come into play. Having entered into a contest, a manager's ego may be too large to contemplate losing. The original bid may have been within the grounds of rational economics, but the need to outbid a rival may push the price beyond a reasonable level, to the joy of the acquired company shareholders. Weston et al. (2004) present a table of studies finding that returns to the target company shareholders are, not surprisingly, larger when there are multiple bidders. Bradley et al. (1988) see a greater transfer of wealth to the target shareholders in a contested battle. Interestingly in an earlier study (1983) they found that firms that lost the bidding war also saw a reduction in shareholder wealth over time.

Does it matter if the target is related in activity or unrelated? In considering the economics of potential synergy, there are more opportunities for gain when the target is related – in the same industry or a supplier or customer, rather than a completely unrelated (conglomerate) deal. Sirower (1997) presents mixed evidence on whether synergies predicted in the bid price are delivered. The measurement problems potentially become even worse here as we consider long-term horizons and firms continually changing shape, possibly selling some of the acquired assets, as well as the changing state of the particular industry and the economy as a whole. The question of what would have happened if the deal had not taken place is also unanswerable. The acquisition of a competitor can be motivated by the desire to avoid it being taken over by someone else; in this case success might be judged not by whether value has been created, but whether there is less value lost than would have been the case if the target had been acquired by a rival. Interestingly, Johnson and Kaplan (1987) predicted that focused organizations would outperform diversified organizations, not least because, for the latter, economies of scale would be dissipated by their inability to respond to competitive pressures from simpler and more focused organizations. They highlight the increased dependence that large, vertically integrated, multidivisional organizations will have on responsive management accounting systems, providing relevant signals on their competitive position in the marketplace – a theme that we will return to when considering the post-acquisition implementation phase.

Does relative size matter? Are results different between acquisitions of relatively large and small targets compared with the bidder? Sudarsanam (2003) finds evidence that relatively small bids are more successful for the acquiring company's shareholders, although Kitching (1967) finds that acquisitions of targets less than 2% of the size of the acquirer perform less well than larger acquisitions. There is also some evidence that acquiring very large firms, in relation to the size of the bidder, may result in worse performance than average. Whilst not relating to relative size, Moeller et al. (2004) find that small acquirers perform better than larger acquirers, producing a small positive return for their shareholders from the average deal rather than an average small negative return for the larger acquirer.

Does the stock market's rating of the acquirer matter? Companies with high PE ratios are expected to grow and improve performance in coming years, necessary assumptions to support such a high valuation compared with past performance. In a result that mirrors US studies, Sudarsanam and Mahate (2003) find that UK companies with high PE ratios, referred to as glamour acquirers, do not perform as well over a three-period horizon as acquirers with lower PE ratios (value acquirers). However, they find that payment method, cash rather than shares, is still the most significant factor in determining post-acquisition returns.

Step 5: Managing the outcome

We believe that the detailed cash flow valuation method that we have described above, and will demonstrate through the Tesco/Greggs case, is the most comprehensive valuation model and if used wisely will lead to better management of the acquisition decision process than alternative methods. One key reason for this contention is that a detailed analysis of value drivers and the preparation of the cash flow forecast will provide sound foundations from which to manage the subsequent implementation. This is because potential synergies have been clearly identified and hence clear targets can be set, thus focusing management attention on ensuring that the synergies are in fact reaped. It is certainly difficult to see how any of the multiple-based acquisition methods provide any useful information to those managing the subsequent integration because they disclose no information on what synergies are expected and how to achieve them. Many writers have said that an acquisition is no different to any other capital investment decision and a common pitfall in managing capital projects is to lose sight of the project justification once the project has started. It is indeed possible to lose sight of the project itself as it is submerged in the aggregated figures of the firm. It becomes difficult to monitor whether what is happening is according to the plan implicit in the initial justification and all too often no post-completion audit takes place. These problems are, if anything, even more of an issue for an acquisition.

With any capital investment project, the estimates in the justification should become the budget for the project implementation and variances to this budget should be monitored and reported on regularly. This is much the same way as the overall management accounting system is used to control the normal ongoing operations. Similarly, with an acquisition, the figures produced by the valuation model should become the budget for the implementation phase and the drivers used in constructing the model should be integrated into the performance measurement system so that they are monitored and reported on regularly. Variances should then be immediately acted upon to keep the integration process on track.

In line with our own experience, mentioned earlier, Haspeslagh and Jemison (1991, pp. 5–6) highlight mangers' frustrations with inadequacies of the analyses on which acquisition decisions are sometimes made with a quote from the chief finance officer of one of the less successful acquiring firms they studied:

> 'The speed with which things took place was mind-boggling. If we had done that sort of quickie analysis for a capital expenditure decision the board's audit committee would have been down around our ears in a minute.'

Such a 'quickie analysis' may not only lead to paying too much, but inevitably also leads to further problems at the implementation stage because there is no detailed budget or performance targets to provide the new management of the acquired business with appropriate guidance. Indeed, as Angwin (2000) notes, the new managers are often not those who negotiated the deal and are often given poor guidance for the future. This is likely to frustrate those responsible for creating the value hoped for when the acquisition was conceived (Haspeslagh and Jemison, 1991).

Additionally, the well-known behavioural implications of budgeting systems are relevant here, with a poorly defined target leading to employees not responding well. Moreover, employees are more likely to accept a target, and be committed to achieving it, if they have been involved in the target-setting process and hence top–down, imposed targets, 'can encourage negative attitudes and result in demotivation and alienation. In turn this can lead to a rejection of the targets and poor performance' (Drury, 2004, p. 665). For example, being given an overall target for value creation, without a detailed breakdown, will probably result in the target being seen as unachievable. It will be argued that any adverse variances arising are due to overpayment for the acquisition, not any inefficiency in subsequent integration. Participation may be important here: if operational managers have worked with the finance team on the detailed cash flow valuation prior to the acquisition negotiations, then they are more likely to accept the task of subsequently achieving those estimates in the post-acquisition implementation period. But note that empirical studies have presented conflicting evidence of the usefulness of participation in the management process. Macintosh (1985) said that the believers have never been able to demonstrate that participation really does have a positive effect on productivity and the sceptics have never proved the opposite.

One of Drury's (2004) limitations to the positive effects of participation is very pertinent to the Greggs/Tesco case at the end of this chapter. Drury argues that where a company has a large number of homogeneous units (such as similar retailing outlets) operating in a stable environment, it is inappropriate for each unit to be involved in target setting and a top–down approach based on benchmarked performance measures can be effective.

Haspeslagh and Jemison (1991) observed that every acquisition changed the established order and pattern of activities at both the acquiring and acquired entities. Consequently the employees, who are expected to create economic value for shareholders, have their own value levels reduced because these changes foster uncertainty and fear. Employees become unwilling to work towards the acquisition's success and they move towards self-preservation and turf protection, reducing the opportunity for the now combined entities to work together. Clearly the entities need to work together if any value is to be created out of potential synergies but Haspeslagh and Jemison point out that even if the managers in acquiring firms have empathy they usually underestimate the depth of the problem of value destruction. When they do recognize it they often react by postponing or even cancelling integration steps that were originally planned in favour of actions that will be 'accepted' by employees. The decision has to be made between recognizing and accommodating employees' needs and pressing ahead with implementation and value creation for the company at the expense of the employee. Jones (1985) found evidence that consultation was linked with post-acquisition success. Any work up front at the target valuation stage, including an awareness of differences between management accounting systems, can reduce the impact of this conflict at the implementation stage.

Obstacles need to be overcome quickly during the post-merger integration phase if maximum value creation is to be realized – including the implementation of changed strategies and the merging of differing cultures. Angwin (2004) discusses the need for introducing change swiftly after the deal has been completed. Whilst the performance review and valuation exercise will have identified the necessary changes in strategy, it is likely that few of the managers responsible for the implementation phase will be immediately aware of the strategic implications. At the acquired entity, few in the original management will be aware of this and their resistance to change may be high. The suggestion to incorporate the figures used in the valuation into budgets and ensure that performance measurement systems include the value driver measures and targets is probably insufficient in itself. This is because it is a common criticism of control systems that the day-to-day budgeting and control are largely divorced from the strategy and hence strategy is devised but never fully implemented. One solution to this which is growing in popularity is the 'balanced scorecard' (BSC), which complements the financial measures commonly used in companies by adding operational measures that are thought to be the drivers of future financial performance (Kaplan and Norton, 1992). The BSC is designed to translate a company's strategy into specific measurable objectives and given that mergers and acquisitions inevitably result in changes in strategy, and post-acquisition implementation is commonly seen as a problem, it would seem to be a useful approach to adopt.

The BSC is unlike traditional measurement systems that have a control bias, where control is achieved by specifying particular actions that employees must adopt and then measuring to see if these actions have been taken. In contrast, a well-implemented BSC focuses not on control, but on communicating strategy and vision to employees, by establishing goals and then leaving employees to take whatever actions are necessary to achieve these goals. This type of approach might be much more acceptable to employees at the target company, who are already feeling vulnerable and are likely to be resistant to an excessive control bias.

Interestingly, Kaplan and Norton (1993) claim to have found from experience 'that the balanced scorecard is most successful when it is used to drive the process of change'. The BSC is particularly well suited for 'defining and communicating priorities to managers, employees, investors and even customers'. In later papers on the BCS, the authors claim that the need for an improved performance measurement system is not a sufficient catalyst for a successful implementation. One example of the necessary catalyst is the need to bring culturally different organizations closer together after a merger. Different managers are often found to interpret their supposedly common strategy in different ways: in one merger example given by Kaplan and Norton (1996), 25 senior executives all agreed on the words of the strategy but had different definitions of the meaning of those words. The BSC implementation forced them to clarify the meaning of the strategy statement and also highlighted gaps in employees' skills and information systems which the merged firms would have to close in order to deliver the selected value propositions to the targeted customers. Granlund (2003) also found goal ambiguity in his case study of a post-acquisition integration.

Discussion

Before reviewing our discussion of valuation techniques, it is necessary to consider the roll of accounting. This is not only because has the use of accounting-based valuations been on the rise, but also because success or failure of a deal can be viewed in terms of the accounting results.

Accounting issues and standards

Are accounting standards relevant? This is a good question, especially if the analyst is using a valuation model dependent on published and forecast accounting figures rather than cash flow figures or on market data. If future earnings per share is thought to be important then any accounting policies, or changes in standards, that influence profit after tax need to be seen as important.

Accounting standards have been in a state of flux over recent years, particularly due to the adoption of the much changed International Financial Reporting

Standards (IFRS) by EU countries for quoted companies from 1 January 2005. One key area of change that will lead to material movements in the level of profit for many companies is the treatment of the goodwill arising from acquisitions. Goodwill is the surplus of payment for an acquisition over the accepted fair value of the purchased assets; 'badwill' is rare,[6] but a possibility. Before 1998 the general preference in the UK was to write off the goodwill against reserves (shareholder's funds). Hence no figure for goodwill appeared in the balance sheet and the value of shareholders' funds diminished, but the profit and loss account was untouched. This treatment improves return on capital and earnings per share by allowing the inclusion of the profits from the acquisition in the profit and loss account without fully accounting for the cost. From 1998 onwards, UK companies had to capitalize goodwill arising on acquisition (i.e. include goodwill as an intangible asset on the balance sheet) and to amortize (depreciate) the goodwill over its expected life of (normally) not more than 20 years. This change, sadly, was not retrospective so analysts considering that this approach was preferable would need to approximate adjustments for past acquisitions. The US had traditionally amortized goodwill but, instead of amortization, switched to impairment reviews – the goodwill on the balance sheet remaining unchanged unless the directors decided that the carrying value was now in excess of the economic value. At first sight the introduction of IFRS, also introducing impairment reviews instead of amortization, would seem to have brought IFRS countries and the US in line. However the Vodafone case below shows the size of potential difference caused by what might be thought to be the minutiae of the standards.

Amortization had the benefit of smoothing and predictability unless there was a clear reason for a major reduction in the carrying value of goodwill. Impairment may lead to many years of no charge at all followed by a significant impairment in one year.

Does this matter? Some would say that a focus on EBITDA (earnings before interest, tax, depreciation and amortization, and, one assumes, impairment) removes this problem and focuses attention on forward-looking numbers rather than the results of past deals. There is certainly some truth in this, but it is not the whole story. The goodwill acquired at the acquisition was as real a spend of the shareholders' cash, or diminution of their ownership, as that for the tangible assets and one could argue that managers should be accountable for the continuing wealth generation from the purchase. Indeed those arguing that future value is based primarily on the sort of intangible assets making up the goodwill, human capital, brand names, patents, etc., should argue that management ought to be held to account. It is also necessary to consider management's reputation and the need for an impairment must question whether the original deal was appropriate or whether the price, at least, was too high. In other words, a focus on EBITDA allows management to avoid answers to potentially difficult questions.

An interesting feature of IFRS is that, in future, acquisition goodwill should be broken into its component parts where possible. Some of the parts may qualify for amortization rather than impairment and, more importantly, management will effectively have to reveal more detail concerning why it was appropriate to pay more than the tangible asset value. Winter, a partner at PwC is quoted as saying:

> 'When a company makes an acquisition, intangible assets that were formerly part of an amorphous blob of goodwill are now required to be identified separately, valued and held on the balance sheet, leaving goodwill as a residual amount.' (Jopson, 2005)

Jopson makes the point that the need for such additional disclosure might make management think twice before bidding because the values of the purchased intangibles will need to be more clearly disclosed.

Much press attention has also been focused on the valuation of pension fund deficits and of other post-retirement obligations that the company may be responsible for. The valuation of these, often significant, liabilities is much disputed. The recent IFRS requires a current market valuation of any deficit. However, key assumptions – for example, life expectancy – behind such an estimate may still be thought optimistic. It is likely that a number of potential deals (e.g. the mooted takeover of the UK retailer W. H. Smith by Permira) have not been pursued because of the pension liability that would be acquired as part of the total package.

Merger or acquisition?

Another accounting issue is whether a particular deal is a merger or an acquisition. There used to be two methods of accounting for a deal – pooling of interests (or merger accounting) and acquisition accounting.

The main differences between the two methods relate to three items in the accounts: *goodwill*, *share premium* and *pre-acquisition reserves*. As there is no significant change of ownership in a merger, the consolidated balance sheet is merely a combination of the two existing balance sheets with all assets remaining at their previous book values (subject to adjustments to bring differing accounting policies into line) and *no* goodwill is created. Shares issued in the share-for-share exchange required for a merger are recorded at nominal value (not at market value, as for shares issued in an acquisition) and hence no non-distributable[7] share premium account is created. A key advantage of merger accounting is that the reserves (pre-combination retained profits) of *both* companies are pooled and any that were distributable before remain available to be distributed as dividends of the new entity.

Under acquisition accounting the pre-acquisition reserves of the acquired company are effectively frozen as permanent capital and hence are not available for distribution. Any excess of the purchase price above the valuation of the assets included in the balance sheet is termed as goodwill and included in the future balance sheet of the acquiring company. In summary, merger accounting has three clear advantages over acquisition accounting. Firstly, no goodwill is created and hence there is no subsequent amortization or impairment testing to worry about and future return on investment will be higher. Secondly, no non-distributable share premium account is created and thirdly the distributable reserves are enlarged, as the pre-acquisition reserves of both companies remain distributable. It is therefore not surprising that merger accounting has proved popular.

This is explained further by taking a brief look at the history of accounting for business combinations in the UK.

The pooling of interests approach was only available if the strict conditions for a merger were met, and initially (under Statement of Standard Accounting Practice 23) the use of this method was *not* compulsory and hence acquisition accounting could be used instead. The choice of method could produce significantly different financial results and from December 1994 the rules were revised (FRS 6) to make merger accounting compulsory if the use of acquisition accounting would not properly reflect the true nature of the combination (i.e. where the parties came together to share in the future risks and benefits of the combined entity). With the introduction of IFRS, merger accounting is no longer allowed.

One might ask whether the above distinction matters now. There are two potential answers to the question.

1. **No,** because under IFRS all business combinations must be accounted for using the acquisition method, and hence, regardless of the actual circumstances, one party must be identified as having the role of an acquirer and the identifiable assets and liabilities of the company acquired are included in the consolidated balance sheet at their fair value while the assets and liabilities of the acquirer are not reviewed and remain at their previous book value. If it really is a merger the directors of new entity will have a choice as to which company is the acquirer and this choice may well depend on which will result in the most favourable set of consolidated accounts. They may wish to minimize the amount of goodwill created and hence reduce the risk of amortization in subsequent years when impairment tests are carried out. They may also wish to maximize the availability of distributable reserves. The US also only allows the acquisition method, though with minor differences that the accounting standard bodies intend to remove over time.

2. **Maybe,** because there is disquiet over the removal of merger accounting on the basis that there are circumstances under which a business combination may be in fact a pooling of interests and all the conditions previously required for the application of merger accounting are met. In such circumstances it can be argued that merger accounting makes sense and is the appropriate method to apply so why should acquisition accounting be imposed? Analysts who truly believe that merger accounting is appropriate could adjust the figures accordingly and anyone planning a big merger of equals might believe it is sensible to hold off for a while and lobby for a change in the accounting rules.

Note that the accounting treatment and terminology may not match the words used in the press releases. One example of this is the creation of Corus by the coming together of British Steel and Hoogovens of the Netherlands. The press releases and company management talk of merger, but the accounting was pure acquisition, with British Steel as the acquirer and Hoogovens as the acquiree. Hence the assets and liabilities of British Steel were brought into the consolidated balance sheet at their previous book value whereas the assets and liabilities of Hoogovens had to be adjusted to their fair value at the date of acquisition and the difference between this value and the consideration paid treated as goodwill.

Vodafone's goodwill amortization and impairment is used to illustrate the potential enormity of difference caused by changes in accounting standards and also that the message behind the movements in the accounts may well be important, even if the numbers themselves appear to be mere slight of hand.

CASE BOX 2.1:   VODAFONE – IMPAIRED ACQUISITIONS?

Vodafone, the international mobile phone operator, is a UK-based company with a listing in the US. Hence it has been reporting using UK GAAP (Generally Accepted Accounting Practices or Principles), now moving to IFRS, as well as US GAAP. Using UK GAAP, the last annual results, for the year ending March 2005, shows group turnover of £34 billion, a loss for the financial year of £7.5 billion and a dividend for the year of £2.5 billion. The loss per share was 11 pence, but when the results were restated using IFRS (with no amortization) this became a positive 9 pence per share. The notes to the accounts reveal that the UK GAAP loss is after an amortization charge of £13 billion and the written parts of the report talk of success and the generation of a free cash flow of £7.8 billion. The carrying value of goodwill, including licences, is £83 billion.

On 27 February 2006, Vodafone issued a press release disclosing the likely outcome of the impairment review required under IFRS. Due to 'lower growth prospects', the impairment is expected to be between £23 and £28 billion, approximately double the amortization charge of the previous year and, inevitably, leading to the largest loss ever reported by a UK company.

Quoting from the press release, the IFRS rules are:

'Under IFRS, Vodafone tests fixed assets, including goodwill, for impairment by compar-ing the carrying value for each operating company to its respective recoverable amount. The recoverable amount is defined as the higher of fair value less costs to sell, and value in use. Value in use is estimated based on discounted cash flows.'

This approach leads to an impairment of over £20 billion. The US accounting requirements are summarized as:

'Under US GAAP, Vodafone tests finite lived fixed assets for impairment using a two step process. The carrying value of each operating company is first compared to its respective recoverable amount. The recoverable amount is determined based on undiscounted cash flows. Secondly, if the carrying value exceeds the recoverable amount, then the carrying value is reduced to its fair value, which is generally determined using discounted cash flows.'

This approach does not, however, lead to any expected impairment under US rules. If underlying performance in the 2006 financial year matches that of 2005 – earnings per share of approximately 9 pence under IFRS – then the amortization per share under old UK standards would be 20 pence; under IFRS the impairment per share will be about 40 pence and no affect under US accounting.

These impairment charges do matter because Vodafone explains that the rationale behind the impairment is that the value in use of the goodwill is now generally forecast to last for only 5 years rather than 10. Such information, complementing that of the lower growth rates, would inform any cash-based forecast and should update any other forecast method too. We suspect, however, that in a complex case such as this one the use of multiples or earnings-based valuation methods would be problematic.

Thoughts on valuation techniques

A key point to bear in mind is that the underlying issues behind any valuation do not change with the method of valuation chosen. Just because a method may be more straightforward does not mean that the questions disappear, they merely become implicit rather than explicit. This then carries the risk that the issues might be ignored. Certainly some methods are more complex than others; some would argue that either the accounting or cash-based valuation models (depending on your viewpoint) introduce unnecessary problems that could have been avoided. We will now review the major valuation methods.

Multiples

The multiples approach is simple and straightforward. However, it is all too easy to forget the pitfalls – for example, that you are buying future earnings, not past earnings, and past earnings may not be a good guide to future earnings. This has been mentioned above but the need to address the issue of earnings quality cannot be over-emphasized. Are past earnings being squeezed out with some less-than-conservative accounting policies; are they propped up by exceptional items such as profits on the sale of properties or even parts of the business? Also, earnings can always be improved for 1 or 2 years by elimination of all expenditure unnecessary for the short term (i.e. discretionary expenditure such as research and development, marketing and brand support, training and even plant maintenance), thus artificially inflating short-term earnings at the expense of long-term prospects. Phrases such as 'In our industry, companies pay a PE of 14', once told to one of the authors, may have merit, but only when applied to an earnings number that is a firm foundation for the forecast of future earnings. Case box 2.2 highlights the practical problems in using the PE ratios of similar companies as a guide.

CASE BOX 2.2:   A CONSIDERATION OF UK FOOD RETAIL PE RATIOS, DECEMBER 2005

The four large quoted UK food retailers had the following PE ratios in mid-December, 2005.

	PE	Market capitalization
Morrison	47.10	£4,999m
Sainsbury	–	£5,200m
Somerfield	27.10	£1,082m
Tesco	17.20	£25,679m

You will recall that the normal explanation of a higher PE is the expectation of a brighter future for the firm when compared with the prospects of its competitors. Here we see Tesco with a much lower PE than the key quoted competitors, but it has market dominance in the UK and not inconsiderable success in other countries. The PE of Somerfield is somewhat higher due to the continuing M&A speculation over the company – effectively pricing in much of the likely premium. Morrison is still digesting the acquisition of the larger Safeway group, which has deflated earnings over the past year, but the expectation would seem to be that the integration will be successfully completed and future earnings will soon be considerably higher. Due to one-off accounting issues, Sainsbury did not post a profit in the last report and hence the PE could not be calculated. Imagine that the owners (Wal-Mart) of the other large food retail group in the UK (ASDA) were considering selling off the UK division due to recent poor performance, would the above table help in deciding on a valuation? In these circumstances, averaging these PEs listed above, or using the distorted food and drug sector weighted average, as some textbooks recommend, would not be helpful.

The review has focused on the PE ratio, but the other multiples can suffer from some of the same problems. The potential bidder needs to adjust for any factors affecting the last available figures – not least the possible avoiding of discretionary expenditures (research and training, for example) that might inflate short-term profits and hence a PE-based valuation. The issue of growth is important, and can be built into the PE model. However, the assumption of one constant growth rate for revenues and/or profits for the continuing future seems straightforward to the point of naivety. Despite this, one should not decry the quickness and availability of multiples. A PE valuation can be a first step and could weed out likely targets from a longer list before a more thorough forecasting method is then employed. But it should not be seen as a final step in the valuation process, not only because it is likely to prove an unreliable valuation but also because it will provide no basis for monitoring post-acquisition creation of value.

Cash flow-based and accounting-based measures

Both of these approaches can be much more comprehensive and while in theory cash-based methods can lead to the same valuation as the accounting-based methods, there are proponents of both approaches that argue superiority of one over the other.

As noted above, we recommend the discounted cash flow approach to valuation. In principle, the accounting-based methods can lead to the same results and Penman's (2004) insistence that 'earnings, appropriately measured, give a better indication of the value generation in a business' and that ' "Buy earnings" is indeed the mantra of investing' (p. vii) is quite persuasive.

Putting aside issues of accounting policy and adjustments (see below), then an accounting-based approach, based on a comprehensive analysis of past and likely future performance in the light of the likely economic environment and plausible strategies, should provide a reliable valuation. It should also provide a detailed budget aligned to the strategy to help take forward the implementation plan.

There are two reasons why we would recommend the cash flow approach. Firstly, Penman's comment that earnings need to be appropriately measured is true; the question is whether earnings can be measured appropriately. Accounts can be complex and, sadly, the standard of disclosure required may not be adequate to undertake the task of appropriate measurement. For example, if a very large company were considering the acquisition of Vodafone, how should the amortization or impairment of goodwill be treated? The logic behind the reduction is a recognition of reduced future cash flows. However, if the impairment is ignored this could be missed; if it is included now, then the timing of the earnings change may be an issue. If Vodafone was a US company, only producing US GAAP accounts, then there would be no impairment at this point and, one assumes, no potential trigger to reduced future profitability. We are not saying that these problems are insurmountable, but a very detailed knowledge of accounting standards and a good knowledge of the industry are required before attempting the 'appropriate' measurement of earnings.

Secondly, we have stated above that an acquisition can be viewed as similar to a capital investment decision. More than this, an acquisition is certainly an alternative to capital schemes and other forms of investment, (research and development, for example). If management is to weigh the options of undertaking capital schemes or making an acquisition, then a similar metric for both would be sensible.

Management accounting texts (e.g. Drury, 2004) cite net present value as the best way of assessing a capital project and detail the defects of accounting rate of return, the earnings-based approach to project appraisal. So, for consistency, one could argue for the cash-based approach to acquisitions as well as for capital schemes. One might also point out that the internal management of most companies are regularly assessing capital schemes, while acquisition appraisal will be a less regular activity. While acquisition appraisal is more complex, including terminal year issues for example, at least the cash-based approach builds on the internal skills already developed. It should not be forgotten that many companies, and analysts, still choose to use cash-based valuation techniques when appraising acquisitions and mergers.

We accept that the earnings-based forecasts lend themselves more easily to a complete financial statement forecast, which has value not just for the forecast itself but also for implementation and auditing of the model. Indeed, the forecasting of income statements and balance sheets should also be best practice when undertaking cash flow forecasts because of the benefits of audit and debt level forecasts, for example.

The fact that cash flow figures are published alongside earnings statements allows the analyst to take on information from both the cash and accruals perspective when putting the valuation forecast together – whether an earnings or cash valuation. Forecasting under either method requires interpretation of all available information. Worryingly, Picconi (2004, p. 88), when assessing the use of published information on corporate pension funds, found that:

> '. . . both analysts and investors are unable to fully incorporate pension information in an expedient manner and that this results in less accurate forecasts and valuation.'

In carrying out a valuation, the questions that need to be addressed concerning the company's prospects are independent of the forecast method chosen. Some methods appear to need less information than others, but this is an illusion because the assumptions are just implicit rather than explicit. Behind a simple PE ratio, for example, there should be a full set of forecast performance parameters, just as required for a full cash flow forecast model.

Real options

The logic of real options has much to commend it and, indeed, it would seem to be used successfully in capital investment decisions in a number of industries, including pharmaceuticals. However, from a pragmatic point of view, there is the danger that this approach is likely to increase the expected gains from an acquisition and we have already seen, when reviewing the surveys of M&A performance, that there is already too great a chance of a takeover being overvalued rather than undervalued.

Where the concept of real options does add value is to highlight that a company has a variety of options when an acquisition has been completed. We have already made the point that implementation of a plan to gain synergies and create value is not given enough attention. The use of real options methodology forces managers to question the alternatives available once the acquisition is complete; indeed, it is difficult to see how a logical decision to bid can be reached before such issues are addressed. It will be clear to the reader that in the Tesco/Greggs case at the end of the chapter, Tesco will have a number of options were the deal to be completed. Some of these will be mutually exclusive and some could be pursued alongside each other.

Further comments

Before announcing a bid many valuations need to be done. One reason for this is to assess the value of choices available to management once the deal has been completed. The second reason is to undertake sensitivity analysis. This involves flexing some of the forecast assumptions to assess the robustness of the forecast – the more uncertain the future, then the wider the range of parameter values that should be considered. The one certain fact of any forecast is that it cannot be entirely accurate; the question is whether this inaccuracy will be material. Some risks, once identified, can be managed and mitigated (currency and interest rate risks, for example).

A target company should also do its own valuation to help decide whether to fight or recommend the bid. Again, we consider the potential response of the Greggs management team in the case at the end of the chapter. A meaningful bid defence may well require the target management to promise to change its approach to financing or, indeed, to the business as a whole. If current management is indeed focused on the interests of its shareholders, then it should consider whether there might be more value for its shareholders if it were to approach other possible bidders or alternatively to seek a partnership with another company.

Finance literature

The finance literature presents a picture of, generally, poor performance of acquisitions and merger activity when viewed from the perspective of the acquiring company's shareholders. The question remains of whether this is due to management having other motives, mis-valuation (i.e. paying too much) or the inability to deliver synergies that could have been material. The one reliable positive result is that deals that have been paid for in cash have, on average, been more successful than those based on share offers. It is important to remember two key points: the studies in the literature highlight poor performance *on average*, but there is always a range of performance across the various deals studied, with some adding less value than average and others actually adding positive value for the acquirer's shareholders. What we have attempted to highlight in this chapter is the steps that need to be taken to ensure that the deal is at the favourable end of the continuum.

Also, the literature is primarily US-based with a significant number of UK studies. There are surveys of other countries, mainly European, but the incidence of deals, especially hostile ones, has been much lower outside the UK and US. While lessons in a particular country can be learned, having a reasonable sample size within a sensible time frame is a problem when seeking statistical significance.

One should also beware of attempting to draw conclusions from the US and UK literature for other countries and cultures. Differing regulatory environments, stock market maturity and cultural attitudes to corporate governance are just three of the reasons for not assuming that what might appear to be true in one country will be true within another. Even within the EU, significant differences clearly exist and it is not clear that the EU itself has established authority over national governments on this issue.

Conclusion

The elephant in the room in this chapter is the large number of deals that do not provide a return for the shareholders of the acquiring firm in the short and, particularly, the long term. This is partly due to the 'winner's curse' – the fact that the winning bid, if the bid is contested, has to be the highest and probably the most optimistic, dependent on the relative levels of assumed synergy of the bidders. This may also be due to 'hubris' (Roll, 1986) – the irrational belief in the likely positive outcome of a deal due to synergy, possibly spurred on by the need to win a battle once it has been started rather than lose to a competitor. History and hindsight can form a better view of who was the real loser. Whether the shareholders of the acquiring firm gained or lost from a particular deal is surely a crucial measure of success. The directors of the acquiring firm instigated the bid and should have done so with the aim of increasing the shareholder value of their company. A failure to create wealth despite a great deal of management time and effort might be due to poor corporate governance, poor valuation of the target or poor post-acquisition management.

The level of analysis required when undertaking a valuation should not be underestimated. For example, watching recent acquisition activity in the food retail sector in the UK, a store-by-store breakdown of cash flow or earnings would seem to be necessary to estimate the value of the acquisition because many of the purchased stores may be sold or closed. A depth of knowledge of the industry is more important than the fine detail of methodology. Wrong assumptions can undermine the best technical model; a slightly flawed model is likely to give less disparity from true economic value.

One should also question the quantity of research directed at some of the issues involved in assessing acquisitions and mergers. The longer the time horizon considered, the more problematic measurement becomes. The implementation of strategy has often been a poor relation of the more exciting decision-focused strategic activity and the same is true here. A greater focus of management accounting techniques, and case study analysis, on the issues and problems of achieving the forecast levels of synergy could produce real insights into either the poverty of the original forecast or the implementation stumbling blocks. Management accounting is, by its nature, a multidisciplinary subject and academics from this discipline could add value to our understanding of the poor performance of acquisitions and mergers.

So, a sensible approach would be to follow up initial broad-brush forecasts with detailed cash-based valuations, drawing on significant industry knowledge either from within or outside the firm. This forecast should contain a number of key performance measures that can be clearly communicated to relevant managers after the deal has been completed and also monitored through techniques such as the BSC.

Economist Robert Shiller is quoted as saying 'One practically has to be a renaissance man (woman) to achieve good work in economics' (Pickard, 2006) and the same should be true of the financial specialists involved in mergers and acquisitions. A knowledge of techniques, by itself, will not ensure success.

Case Example: At What Price Should Tesco Buy Greggs?

Tesco has completed the first step in the M&A process as a considerable amount of research has already been undertaken to identify Greggs as the suitable target. Your task is to complete step two – the valuation of the prey – and armed with this information make recommendations for the remaining three steps of the M&A process.

To avoid venturing too far out of our finance role we will only briefly summarize the rationale for choosing Greggs. We also provide summary financials below to enable you to assess the recent financial performance of Greggs plc, calculate historical value drivers and use these, and your knowledge of the sector, as a basis for estimating likely value drivers going forward and hence future cash flows. To enable you to perform a full analysis we recommend that you supplement the summary information supplied here by downloading Greggs' recent annual accounts available from: www.ir.greggs.plc.uk/greggsplc/report.jsp.[8] This will not only give you more detailed figures but also provide the appropriate context of Greggs' strategy and trading environment.

Greggs plc is a specialist food retailer operating mainly in the UK. It focuses on bakery products and has small outlets in town centres. Its key brand names of 'Greggs' and 'Baker's Oven' are highly regarded. Tesco plc is the leading UK supermarket but is facing limits to its possibilities of expansion in the UK. A combination of nearing saturation point for new supermarkets and new planning restrictions on out-of-town stores forced Tesco to grow through new formats like Metro (town centre) stores and Express (smaller, convenience) stores and in recent years Tesco has made acquisitions of convenience store chains (most notably T&S Stores in 2003). There are limits to the possibility of further appropriate convenience store acquisitions, not least because of the possibility of referral to the Competition Commission, so a little more diversification might be necessary.[9] As well as UK supermarket growth Tesco has three other parts to its overall strategy: expansion into non-food sales, retailing services and international expansion. The latter has to date been mainly in Eastern Europe and Asia but in February 2006 Tesco announced that it will test the Express stores format on the west coast of America. However, overseas expansion might be seen as more risky than diversification in the UK and returns outside the UK continue to be much lower[10] and hence growth through expansion overseas and stagnation in the UK reduces aggregate returns.

Required

a) Prepare an analysis of the recent financial performance of Greggs plc. As a minimum compare 2004 with 2003, calculate key financial ratios and comment on any changes observed.

b) Make a brief comparison of the financial performance of Greggs with that of Tesco using a few key ratios and comment on the potential benefit to Tesco of acquiring Greggs.

Tesco: key ratios 2004/5 results

RONA	PBIT/TA − CL	14.90%
Net margin	PBIT/Sales	6.28%
Asset utilization	Sales/TA − CL	2.37%
ROE	PAT/Equity	15.20%

c) Estimate the total and per share value of Greggs in its existing ownership. (You can use the model provided at www.blackwellpublishing.com/9781405122399 to help you do this but state any assumptions and hence justify the level you set for the value drivers you use in your valuation calculations.)

d) Estimate the total and per share value of Greggs if owned and managed by Tesco (i.e. revise the level of the value drivers in the valuation model to account for the benefits that Tesco can bring to Greggs' operations and the synergies that can be achieved). Again justify your changes.

e) Discuss the two values from (c) and (d) and perform sensitivity analysis as necessary. Highlight how these valuations inform the range for negotiation and hence the possible initial bid price and expected settlement price.

f) Give general advice on how the deal might be structured and how Tesco could maximize the value created, paying particular attention to post-acquisition integration issues.

Summary profit and loss account for the 53 weeks ended 1 January 2005 (comparatives all 52 weeks)

	2004 (£000s)	change	2003 (£000s)	change	2002 (£000s)	change	2001 (£000s)
Turnover	504,186	10.3%	456,978	8.1%	422,600	11.9%	377,556
Cost of sales	-193,009	10.1%	-175,284	7.3%	-163,406	10.8%	-147,468
Gross profit	311,177	10.5%	281,694	8.7%	259,194	12.6%	230,088
Distribution and selling costs	-228,891	9.2%	-209,559	8.7%	-192,790	11.6%	-172,711
Administrative expenses	-37,572	14.0%	-32,968	6.1%	-31,070	20.5%	-25,780
Total operating expenses	-266,463	9.9%	-242,527	8.3%	-223,860	12.8%	-198,491
Operating profit	44,714	14.2%	39,167	10.8%	35,334	11.8%	31,597
Other	0	0.0%	0	0.0%	0	0.0%	0
PBIT	44,714	14.2%	39,167	10.8%	35,334	11.8%	31,597
Interest receivable	2,003	52.6%	1,313	-3.5%	1,361	0.5%	1,354
Interest payable	-15	87.5%	-8	-72.4%	-29	-86.1%	-209
Net interest	1,988	52.3%	1,305	-2.0%	1,332	16.3%	1,145
PBT	46,702	15.4%	40,472	10.4%	36,666	12.0%	32,742
Tax	-15,115	14.2%	-13,235	10.5%	-11,980	20.6%	-9,933
PAT	31,587	16.0%	27,237	10.3%	24,686	8.2%	22,809
Dividend	-11,524	21.6%	-9,476	10.6%	-8,570	11.8%	-7,663
Retained profit	20,063	13.0%	17,761	10.2%	16,116	6.4%	15,146
Depreciation and amortization	21,336	12.0%	19,054	11.6%	17,073	16.5%	14,659
EBITDA	66,050	13.4%	58,221	11.1%	52,407	13.3%	46,256
EBITDA margin	13.10%		12.74%		12.40%		12.25%

Summary balance sheets as at year ends

	2004 (£000s)		2003 (£000s)		2002 (£000s)		2001 (£000s)
Fixed assets	163,110	1.5%	160,704	5.9%	151,745	18.8%	127,686
Current assets	83,833	48.3%	56,521	21.0%	46,705	-4.1%	46,708
Current liabilities net	-74,811	9.1%	-68,558	5.6%	-64,943	6.9%	-60,762
Net current assets	9,022	175.0%	-12,037	34.0%	-18,238	-51.3%	-12,054
TA less CL	172,132	15.8%	148,667	11.4%	133,507	15.5%	115,632
Shareholders' funds	157,158	17.2%	134,150	11.8%	119,965	15.8%	103,554
Creditors > 1 year*	14,974	3.1%	14,517	7.2%	13,542	12.1%	12,078
	172,132	15.8%	148,667	11.4%	133,507	15.5%	115,632

* Includes provisions for liabilities and charges (deferred tax)

	2004 (£000s)		2003 (£000s)		2002 (£000s)		2001 (£000s)
Net expenditure on fixed assets (from cash flow statement)	23,742		31,574		41,134		25,497
Current assets:							
Stock	7,283		7,126		6,330		6,275
Debtors	13,949		13,037		11,740		12,406
Cash at bank and in hand	62,601		36,358		28,635		30,027
Additional information: number of stores	1,263	2.60%	1,231	2.41%	1,202	5.07%	1,144

NOTES

1. In the capital asset pricing model it is assumed that the greater the volatility of returns (measured by a company's beta) the greater the risk premium that shareholders add to the risk-free interest rate to arrive at their required rate of return. Hence if volatility is reduced, the required rate of return is reduced and shareholders could be satisfied by lower returns.
2. The latest annual earnings may be adjusted to exclude exceptional (non-recurring items) and an average of several years may be used instead of 1 year's earnings.
3. This chapter will assume knowledge of net present value techniques. If a revision of this topic is required, many texts, including Brealey et al. (2006), cover this area well.
4. This term refers to a share that is infrequently traded and implies that the current share price may not reflect all available information.
5. The logic of this is that if a company earned above the required rate of return to satisfy the shareholders' risk, then other companies would be attracted into its markets and compete profits down to the point where returns just matched the risk level.
6. But one recent UK example (2004) is the acquisition of Safeway by Wm. Morrison, who paid a consideration of some £321 million below the fair value of the assets acquired.
7. A reserve is distributable if it meets the criteria for being available for shareholders as a dividend, it is non-distributable if it is regarded as part of the core capital of the business.
8. Note that the year 2004 was the latest full year report available to us at the time of writing.
9. Among other possibilities we considered were Thorntons and Café Nero. Thorntons has a useful portfolio of high street shops plus an online business but its performance over recent years has been relatively poor, with low returns and lacklustre growth. The low PE reflects the market's view that future growth prospects are poor and the price could be cheap. Introducing some Tesco Express products into Thorntons shops would increase footfall and sales and would reduce seasonality. There could be synergies through linking the online businesses. The downside is that current shops might be too small for the range expansion and would Tesco want to take over the manufacturing side of the business, especially as chocolate has a questionable future in these health conscious days? Café Nero has had a much more favourable past performance, with higher growth and returns and a high PE indicating that the market is expecting continued rapid growth. However, the fit with Tesco is less clear, there would be the problem of franchisees and the price could be high.
10. Tesco's return on net assets for the UK segment was 18.3% in 2005 compared with 9.9% for both Asia and the rest of Europe.

Chapter 3 M&A as Illusion

Chris Smith

> Why might not whole communities and public bodies be seized with fits of insanity, as well as individuals? Nothing but this principle, that they are liable to insanity, equally at least with private persons, can account for the major part of those transactions of which we read in history.
>
> Bishop Joseph Butler (1692–1752)

Bishop Butler might just as well have been writing about modern mergers and acquisitions (M&A) as about the strange happenings of his own times. Two seemingly contradictory findings continue to emerge from empirical data on M&A:

1. Most acquisitions destroy value for the shareholders of the acquiring firms. These shareholders almost inevitably become a victim of the 'winner's curse' (i.e. all potential gains from the acquisition are hopelessly over-capitalized in the purchase price).[1]
2. Acquisitions continue apace as soon as senior managers have free cash flow 'burning a hole' in the corporate coffers.

Something is wrong here. Surely, wouldn't any sensible manager knowing about point 1 desist and hence, over the long term, M&A activity would diminish not increase? This of course depends of what 'sensible' means and, as I plan to illustrate in this chapter, once the acquisition process has begun, 'sensible' does not get a look in. The inevitable processes of individual and group cognition create a shared *illusion* – an illusion of certainty and reward that masks the reality of risk and loss . . . but first a personal anecdote to set the scene.

Illusory Value . . . A Bird in the Bush

In my managerial career I was involved in four acquisitions/mergers. In two of these I was part of the conquered and in the other two a part of the conquering team; and those readers aghast at my use of such stark winner–loser terms have clearly never been part of an acquisition. One of my 'conquered' episodes was in fact close to the ideal of a win–win, both in process and outcome. I had initiated the idea to my corporate headquarters of the sale of Steelbilt,[2] the stand-alone strategic business unit (SBU) for which I was the General Manager. The business needed significant cash injections to remain viable but was not even closely related to other businesses in the corporate portfolio in terms of markets, products or processes. The corporate centre agreed and let me loose as salesman-in-chief.

This was a particularly easy job because the CEO (and owner) of my largest competitor, Unicraft, had indicated on several occasions that, should the opportunity arise for a trade sale, he would be a potential buyer. From his perspective he was able to gain significant additional distribution, relatively cheap capacity and the removal of his chief competitor (Steelbilt and Unicraft vied for market leadership). From 'our' side we were able to sell off a non-core asset at a gain to its book value, free up cash flow for more heartland businesses and do all this while maintaining ongoing employment for the workforce in a region where regular paid work was not easy to find at that time. (Again some readers might be surprised to learn that the prime motivation for this latter point was more moral than economic – even managers have feelings!)

Charles, the CEO of Unicraft, and I, through meeting at trade fairs, regulatory committees and so on, had become friendly and had often enjoyed a meal and a convivial drink after meetings, in airports or other places where our paths had crossed. Due to this high level of interpersonal goodwill and the fact that both sides had access to all necessary information the 'negotiations' proceeded smoothly and swiftly to an agreed pricing formula and a draft 'heads of agreement'. As we listed the items to be included in the sale, I suggested that we exclude 'debtors' – i.e. that LeMali (the parent body of Steelbilt) be responsible for collecting all outstanding debts incurred up to the point where Steelbilt ceased to be a LeMali business.

Charles sensed an opportunity and, with more suspicion than our 'friendship' warranted, wanted to know why. My reasons were simple and, what's more, honourable. LeMali (and hence Steelbilt) were ferociously efficient at managing debtors. Where our peer companies tended to average 50+ days of outstanding debt, 'we', through structured discounts, a zero tolerance of lateness and a pathological pursuit of defaulters, averaged 13 days.[3] This corporate obsession with debtors was forced on the business units by 1) being made a component of the performance bonus of the business managers and 2) by influencing monthly business profits, because a significant proportion of any debts that were overdue had to be written off against the income statement – *everyone* paid attention to debts and debtors!

In the books at the time of sale, Steelbilt had approximately €1.0 million in debt. The actual debtor figure was more like €1.2 million but the aggressive write-downs produced the lower book value. Charles insisted that he buy the debts for their book value. I argued and pleaded with him that this was a mistake. LeMali would be able to collect the debt as it stood but Unicraft would have far greater problems. Charles figured that buying €1.2 million of debt for €1.0 million was good business and, even allowing for some slippage, he would make a profit. The more I argued, the more convinced he became that he was onto something and the more obdurate he became. Even when I was able to demonstrate the 'facts' of his company's past problems collecting from some of the customers whose debts he was about to buy, he refused to see any problems. You will have guessed by now the ending of the story. Although most of his purchase made sense in the way that Charles had planned, he made a mistake with the debtors. A year later he had managed to collect just under 60% of the book value and was resigned to not collecting the remainder.

This episode intrigued me. Charles was, and remains, a hardheaded, analytical, risk-averse businessman. Despite this – and in the face of disconfirming 'facts', contrary 'evidence' and strong alternative counsel (i.e. from me and my team) – he undertook an illogical course of action, taking risks he had no need to take that eventually cost his business a substantial amount of money, not to mention the ongoing hassle and ill-will engendered in the process of chasing recalcitrant debtors. He and his team had come to believe in the reality of a mirage, an *illusion* of profits in a large desert of loss.

Illusions and Delusions

The small episode described above captures the essence of one of the basic dynamics inherent in most mergers and acquisition – rational, risk-averse people deluding themselves into believing in an illusion of riches, in comparison with which the premium price they are paying pales into insignificance. Even those automotive engineering types from BMW and GM, renowned for their 'hard-headedness', went out and confidently acquired Rover and Fiat respectively – and what value illusions those acquisitions turned out to be!

Illusions are a perceptual 'trick'. Hence, although no water really exists, a *mirage* gives the appearance of water due to the 'trick' of the sun's rays being distorted by atmospheric conditions. Mirages appear real even to those who do not need water, but offer cruel and false hope to the desperately thirsty. So too do all illusions appear real, but are only 'dangerous' to those who believe them to be real and then take risks because of this belief. Figure 3.1 illustrates a classical visual illusion. While both horizontal lines are the same length, the fact that they are set within two converging 'tramlines' makes the upper line appear longer than the lower. We are fooled

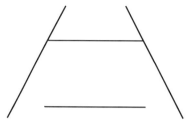

Figure 3.1 The tramline illusion

by the relativity of the lines. Interestingly, despite 'knowing' this 'fact', it is not possible to convince our brains to 'see' the horizontal lines as the same without removing the tramlines. (Try it if you don't believe me.)

Now this is a harmless trick played by our brain – harmless, that is, unless you are in the business of buying lines and you pay a higher price for the upper line than the lower one because you believe are getting 'more' line. What you will have done is paid a premium price that will return you negative value in the line 'industry', as you will have paid a premium for . . . nothing! The original owners of the upper line will be very happy to have met you of course.

Illusions, which are false perceptions, can become closely associated with *delusions*, which are false (but firmly held) beliefs. The philosopher-psychiatrist Karl Jaspers, in his book *General Psychopathology*, first differentiated delusions from beliefs through three criteria:

1. *Certainty* (i.e. held with absolute conviction),
2. *Incorrigibility* (i.e. not changeable by counter-argument or contradictory proof), and
3. *Impossibility or falsity of content* (i.e. the belief is implausible, bizarre or untrue).

These criteria carry through in today's psychiatric definitions where the most recent *Diagnostic and Statistical Manual of Mental Disorders* defines a delusion as:

> 'A false belief based on incorrect inference about external reality that is firmly sustained despite what almost everybody else believes and despite what constitutes incontrovertible and obvious proof or evidence to the contrary. The belief is not one ordinarily accepted by other members of the person's culture or subculture (e.g. it is not an article of religious faith).'

It takes little pondering to realize that the difference between a 'true' belief and a 'false' belief (i.e. a delusion) can often depend on who is doing the labelling. As Thomas Kuhn demonstrated, old scientific 'paradigms' typically hold sway in their communities for a long time after disconfirming evidence has begun mounting[4] (i.e. group delusion). For example, the scientific belief that combustion was due to the release of *phlogiston* held sway for nearly 100 years after being initially propounded in the late seventeenth century by Johann Becher. On the other hand, to change an existing delusion ('paradigm' in Kuhn's language), a single pioneer has needed to be 'delusional' in holding and espousing beliefs from which he/she will not be swayed by argument or 'evidence' and in the face of mockery, vitriol and hostility from his/her subculture. Some of the greatest thinkers in our history have been labelled 'heretic', 'mad' or 'delusional' and forced to recant, sent into exile or put to death for their beliefs – unless, of course, they did the sensible thing and just kept quiet, in which case no one has heard of them.

This is not to say that 'scientists' are any less susceptible than the rest of us to a form of 'magical' thinking that causes them to see the world as they believe it to be rather than how it is. An example of this comes from the domain of homeopathic medicine.[5] One of the tenets of homeopathy is the 'law of infinitesimals' wherein the action of a drug is inversely proportional to its concentration (i.e. the less drug, the more effect). The dilution of some homeopathic medicines is such that one molecule of the drug exists in an amount of water greater than the volume of all the world's oceans. But what the sceptics fail to understand, according to one scientist of homeopathy, is that water has a 'memory' for the health-giving properties of the medicinal molecule that overcomes the need for the molecule to be in the dose that the patient receives. Moreover this memory can be transferred from already therapeutic water to new water sources by playing the new source a soundcard of the electromagnetic extraction of the therapeutic memory from the original homeopathic treatment (i.e. water). Is this a delusion or a new scientific paradigm? Remember they also scoffed at Galileo.

Delusions are not new in the corporate world either, as an anonymous executive attested when writing after the Wall Street Crash of 1929:[6]

> 'In these latter days, since the downfall, I know that there will be much talk of corruption and dishonesty. But I can testify that our trouble was not that. Rather we were undone by our own extravagant folly, and our delusions of grandeur. The gods were waiting to destroy us, and first they infected us with a peculiar and virulent sort of madness.'

The problem, however, with differentiating a 'truth' from a 'delusion' in corporate dealings, and in mergers and acquisitions in particular, is the fact that 'proof' can only be gathered over time, and in the case of M&A after the event. We end up with what Latin users refer to as *post hoc* or (for Latin economists) *ex post* verification. In this sense the M&A process is akin to gambling. The punter places his/her bet and awaits the outcome to find out whether s/he is 'out of pocket' or 'in the money'. As a backdrop to the examination of M&A as illusion, I will use the case of a major takeover battle in Australia in 2004. During the different stages of this (and any) acquisition, corporate illusions and delusions of value develop and grow as the process unfolds.

CASE BOX 3.1:   THE BATTLE FOR ALH[7]

Coles Myer vs. Woolworths in Packaged Liquor

At the beginning of 2004, the Australian packaged liquor industry (comprising alcoholic beverages sold for consumption off the premises) had a total retail value of around 10 to 12 billion Australian dollars.[8] The industry had been consolidating over several years, with the major supermarket chains Coles Myer and Woolworths having made gains to 18% and 22% of the market respectively. Both retailers had pursued an aggressive acquisition strategy in the quest for increased sales and lower costs through increased buying power.

Unlike other countries, such as the UK, liquor is not sold directly from supermarket shelves in many parts of Australia. Only two states, the Australian Capital Territory (ACT) and Victoria, allow this practice but even here it does not happen as a general rule. This is due partly to tradition, but partly due to the fact that, under licensing laws in Australia, only people over 18 years of age are allowed to sell liquor – supermarket check-outs are often operated by younger people, particularly in peak holiday periods (e.g. Christmas) when much liquor is sold. In the other states (representing 74% of the population), legislation mandates that liquor must be sold from stand-alone premises. Shoppers are permitted to have access to these premises from the supermarket but only after they have exited the supermarket. The liquor sites operate separate tills and are more constrained in opening hours. Because of the separation of liquor from other consumables many liquor sites owned by the major supermarkets are not associated with supermarket premises and it is chains of such outlets that the big two had been buying up.

In June 2004 the major protagonists faced off in terms of liquor outlets as shown below:

Coles Myer (total 626) *(Including 485 Liquorland,* *90 Vintage Cellars,* *56 Theo's, 5 Quaffers')*	**VS.**	**Woolworths (total 523)** *(Including 331 Woolworths* *or Safeway liquor shops,* *125 BWS, 28 Dan Murphy,* *15 First Estate, 13 Bailey &* *Bailey, 11 Cheapest Liquor)*

Coles Myer and Woolworths' predatory attentions now turned to the liquor outlets of ALH.

Australian Leisure and Hospitality (ALH)

The Foster's Group is one of Australia's largest suppliers of packaged beer from its wholly owned Carlton and United Breweries. However it had been struggling and had not managed to increase shareholder value over the three accounting years 2001/2 to 2003/4.

In November 2003, as part of a strategy to increase cash and pare back to core businesses, Foster's floated a property trust for A$650 million and its wholly owned subsidiary Australian Leisure and Hospitality (ALH) for A$850 million. ALH, a pub and liquor company, had 4% of the packaged liquor market which it served through 263 outlets including some drive-in bottle departments attached to hotels (see breakdown below).

> **Australian Leisure and Hospitality (total 263)**
> *(Including 105 drive-ins, 109 detached bottle shops, 34 liquor barns, 15 walk-ins)*

It had been reported that both Coles Myer and Woolworths had been left out of a trade sale process that ran in parallel with the float (although this was disputed by the chairman of Foster's at the company's annual general meeting (AGM) in October 2004). ALH declared a net profit after tax of A$61.5 million for the year ending 30 June 2004, with directors confidently forecasting an 11.9% improvement on this figure for 2004/5.

The Battle

The table below outlines the stages in the battle for control of ALH from 1 July to 25 October 2004. Both major players used different structures and tiers for their offers (i.e. prices based on levels of acceptances) during the bidding process but these nuances are not relevant to the main issues and have been omitted in the table (although one detail is discussed below as it pertains to the value of the offer). Both retailers had partners in their bids: publican Bruce Mathieson cooperated with Woolworths and Macquarie Bank with Coles Meyer. Again for the sake of clarity/simplicity the bidding vehicles are referred to as Woolworths and Coles Meyer throughout the following.

June 30	ALH shares close at A$2.48
July 1	Woolworths launches an on-market raid for ALH shares.
July 8	Having acquired 15.8% of ALH stock, Woolworths lodges a formal bid at A$2.75 a share.
Aug. 12	The directors of ALH urge rejection of the Woolworths offer, stating that 'the mid-point of the Independent Expert's control valuation for ALH shares is 20% higher than the (Woolworths) offer price, and this is before taking into account the potential synergistic and strategic benefits that (Woolworths) could extract'. (Australian Stock Exchange Announcement 15/05, 12 August 2004)
Sep. 28	Newbridge Capital, an investment company, bids A$3.05.

Sep. 30	Woolworths lifts its bid price to A$3.15.
Oct. 13	Coles Myer enters the fray and bids A$3.35.
Oct. 18	Woolworths makes a conditional, tiered offer of A$3.40–3.50 (basically, the higher the acceptance level, the higher the price).
Oct. 22	Coles Myer lifts its bid to A$3.75.
Oct. 25	Woolworths counters with A$3.76.

At this stage independent financial analysts were united regarding the main strategic issues with respect to 1) the acquisition battle and 2) the industry consequences of a takeover, but were divided on 3) the price/value at $3.76.

1) Acquisition

Due to the different structures of the offers, the acceptance by the ALH board (and the hedge funds who owned 40% of its stock) of the Woolworths offer would ensure payment in 5 days whereas Coles Myer payment would be delayed for 3 months. Analysts calculated that the time-value of money added A$0.05 to the Woolworths offer (more like A$0.09 claimed Woolworths – naturally!). What this meant in strategic bid terms was that Woolworths could play tit-for-tat with small counter bids over any Coles Myer offer whereas Coles Myer needed to jump the bidding in larger increments.

2) Industry

The major supply industries for packaged liquor – i.e. beer and wine – are highly concentrated and undergoing similar consolidation to their retailing customers. In the wine industry in 2004, for example, five out of a total of about 1,070 wineries accounted for over 80% of production, with the bottom 1,050 (boutique) wineries supplying less than 8%. In 2002/3, Southcorps, the leading winery (with 30% of the market through brands such as Penfolds, Seppelts and Seeview), implemented a policy of discounting in an attempt to gain retail shelf space commensurate with its overall market share. This coincided with a push for market share growth by the two major retailers, whose aggressive buyers forced other wineries to match the Southcorps discounts. The end result was cheaper wine for consumers, lower margins for an increasingly beleaguered wine industry (also beset by grape overproduction) and an increase in the retailers' power over their wine suppliers (and a new CEO but no market share or shelf space gain for Southcorps).

ALH, being a smaller player, had less clout with suppliers and hence was paying more for its liquor (how much more has not been revealed). Whichever of Woolworths or Coles Myer gained control of ALH would immediately achieve cost savings from suppliers as well as some cost savings by rationalizing outlets with overlapping territories – some analysts suggested that such savings would fund the acquisition over the medium term. As well as its 263 outlets ALH had a number of undeveloped sites considered suitable for big-format liquor stores. Hence, on top of immediate market share benefits, the winner of the ALH tussle could look forward to added growth from new sites.

3) Price/value

As with all acquisitions, herein lies the major issue. The 25 October A$3.76 offer was 52% higher than ALH's close of trade share price on 30 June. The offer valued the company at A$1.325 billion – a 56% increase on the stock market valuation at floatation only 11 months earlier and a multiple of over 19 times the forecast 2005 earnings. The offer price was also 14% higher than the valuation provided by ALH's 'Independent Expert'.

Despite this, some analysts argued that for Coles Myer a price of A$4.00 was affordable and the acquisition would still be positive for earnings at that price and, because of its larger size in the market and hence with more to gain, Woolworths could afford A$4.20 and still reap financial benefits over its costs. Naturally all this depended on the size of the 'synergy pie' and how well the diner could digest it.

* * *

On the morning of 26 October, Woolworths announced that it had picked up 5% of ALH's share capital from the investment fund 'Investors Mutual' before the market had opened. This placed 21.7% of ALH stock under Woolworths' control and so ALH asked Coles Myer for its response – i.e. would there be an increased offer?

So what should Coles Myer do?

Pathways to Value Illusions (i.e. Overpayment)

In the following I will take the perspective of Woolworths. However, all bidders go through similar processes in all such decisions. The fact that one bidder drops out does not mean that that bidder is any less deluded, only that reality (often in the form of the unwillingness of others such as banks or shareholders to fund the delusion) finally encroaches.

The pathway to final payment proceeds through two major phases entailing several common overlapping and mutually reinforcing processes:

1. *Setting the scene* – the target company and its benefits are assessed using sophisticated financial tools and an initial bid price is established.
2. *The chase* – through the various formal and informal mechanisms of takeover activity, a competition on price and outcome takes place between predators and prey.

1. Setting the scene

Rational numbers

According to the efficient market hypothesis,[9] the value of a listed company is its market capitalization, which, in turn, is captured in its share price. The share price, then, is the total discounted cash flow of the corporation into perpetuity (i.e. its net present value (NPV) divided by the number of shares on issue). A formula for the NPV of a company is shown in equation 3.1 where the value is the sum of the firm's discounted free cash flows (FCF) in the forecast periods 1 to n added to its terminal value (TV).[10] So if we take n to be 10 years, the TV is the cash flow in the 11th year discounted by the return rate (r) minus the growth rate (g).

$$\text{NPV}_s = \sum_{t=1}^{n} \frac{\text{FCT}_t}{(1+r)^t} + \frac{\text{TV}_n}{(1+r)^n} \quad \left(\text{where } \text{TV}_n = \frac{\text{FCF}_{n+1}}{(r-g)}\right) \tag{3.1}$$

Now isn't that an impressive algorithm? With some variations this is the underlying, rational model used by analysts for valuing companies when they make recommendations about share prices to their clients. The company value divided by the number of shares gives a 'target price' and, if this is higher than the current market price, a 'buy' recommendation is made while if it is lower then 'sell' is suggested. Note that this value incorporates all the known or speculated plans, improvements, synergies or shocks that current management and the market have identified, hope for or fear. If future 'negative influences' on earnings outweigh positive ones then the share price derived from the NPV will be low relative to current earnings (i.e. a low price–earnings (PE) ratio) and, conversely, if optimism about the future has led to a high NPV a high PE will result.

These days, of course, there is no need for laborious calculation, as even the most basic PC is programmed with such calculus and hence, in the case of an acquisition, all the predator's managers need to do is to plug in their estimates of FCF, r and g for n years. What could be simpler for a group of clever, motivated, successful managers?

But that is not all. Unfortunately for acquirers, they are rarely able to gain control at the market price. A 'premium' must generally be paid and hence, if no other gains are available, the acquiring company always pays more than current market value of the stand-alone entity. Enter 'synergy' (S)! If synergies, as decreased costs or increased sales revenue, are extractable *due to the merger* then the NPV of the target plus the value of these synergies is greater than the target's stand-alone NPV and hence a higher purchase price is justified. So there are two values for the target company: its value as a stand-alone business – captured in its current share price – and its (increased) value as part of the acquirer's stable. So now we have the final term of the pricing equation. For an acquisition to make sense to the shareholders of the acquiring firm:

$$P \leq \mathrm{NPV}_s + (S - C) \tag{3.2}$$

That is, the price paid (P) must be at least equal to (and ideally less) than the sum of the current value of the target (NPV_s) plus the hoped-for synergies (S) minus any operational costs (C) incurred in creating synergy. More specifically, if the current share price does reflect the current value of the company, then the premium paid for control must be, *at worst*, equal to the net synergies ($S - C$) that the merger will liberate or else, by definition, value is being destroyed.[11]

So, armed with their laptops programmed with some formula equivalent to that in equation 3.1, the managers of Woolworths now set about estimating the necessary FCF, r and g, and for equation 3.2, the S and C parameters, to arrive at a P value for AHL. From these quasi-rational beginnings the dreams, delusions and illusions of value grow as managers, despite being in an arena shot through with uncertainty, act with overconfidence, particularly when in a herd (group) of other like-minded confidants.

Overconfidence under uncertainty

By definition, each parameter the managers are attempting to estimate will be a *guess*. As an Arabian proverb tells us, 'those who pretend to know the future lie, even if they accidentally speak the truth'. Each manager in the acquisition-planning group (and keep in mind that it is groups that generally make such decisions – more of this later) knows that no one can forecast the future. He or she is as able as anyone to regale an audience with the fallibility of any group that purports to forecast any economic eventuality beyond the (very) short term. Professional economists are unable to forecast GDP, unemployment figures, inflation or even recessions; stock analysts are unable to forecast movements in share prices; and sales managers are unable to forecast sales. Nor does expertise offer immunity to being woefully wrong: the prestigious and expert Harvard Economic Society reassured investors that 'a severe depression like that of 1920–1921 is *outside the range of possibilities*' (my emphasis – remember this for later) in its publication on 16 November 1929.[12]

Notwithstanding this set of empirical hurdles our managers must now apply a rate of return (r) guess, to guesses about FCF, growth rates of FCF (g) and synergies (S) for the next *10* years and then to perpetuity. The final value (i.e. P) is acutely sensitive to the smallest changes in any of these parameters. Table 3.1 shows the results for a mythical company that has FCF of 1,000 in its first year and alternative growth rate scenarios of 5% and 6% for the next 10 years. Discounting these cash flows at 12% or 13% gives the alternative final values shown. Note that with small changes to initial assumptions the variation in the final value can be significant. In this case the largest value (17,503) is nearly 31% greater than the smallest (13,335) – a big increase from varying each of the growth and discount assumptions by only one percentage point.

Despite the uncertainty and the large differences from even small variations in initial assumptions, our managers are *superbly self-confident* . . . and herein lies a

Table 3.1   The effect of varying g and r on 10-year FCF and final valuation

	$g = 5\%$		$g = 6\%$	
r	12%	13%	12%	13%
Year 1	1,000	1,000	1,000	1,000
Year 2	938	929	946	938
Year 3	879	863	896	880
Year 4	824	802	848	825
Year 5	772	745	802	774
Year 6	724	693	759	726
Year 7	679	644	719	681
Year 8	636	598	680	639
Year 9	597	556	644	600
Year 10	559	516	609	562
10 year total	7,609	7,347	7,903	7,626
Terminal value	7,486	5,988	9,600	7,529
Total value	15,094	13,335	17,503	15,155

problem. Human beings (and yes, managers, this means you) are consistently over-confident when asked to make estimations for parameters *about which they demonstrably know nothing.* When people are faced with questions like 'what is the population of Kenya?' or 'how long is the Amazon River?' and are asked to give a range in which they are 90% confident, they tend to offer narrow ranges, and miss the correct answer, rather than hedging their bets with a wide range that is more likely to incorporate the right figure. In one study using nine such questions, less than 1% of a sample of over 1,000 executives achieved nine correct ranges ('answers') with most getting four to seven wrong.[13] Remember the confident Harvard Economic Society's 'range of possibilities' excluded a depression. The average correct score for words that spellers are '100% confident' they have spelled correctly is . . . 80%.

Even when people accept absolutely that an outcome is driven by chance alone, their behaviour reveals that their direct involvement in the process breeds confidence that they favourably influence that random outcome. For example, individuals bet more on the roll of a die if they see the die rolled than if they don't see it, and bet even more if they roll the die themselves.[14] To help with their final guess at P, the Woolworths management use sophisticated skills and tools (i.e. computer spreadsheets). In using these tools the managers become involved and committed to the process and this very involvement promotes further confidence and commitment. Empirical evidence points to such overcommitment by management teams involved in acquisition processes[15] and to a relationship between the premium paid for an acquisition and the 'hubris' or 'exaggerated self-confidence' of the CEO.[16] The sense of being able to control outcomes extends to the managers' views of their capabilities to appropriately manage the new company once it is in the corporate stable.[17]

Not only does direct involvement of managers boost confidence in this way but the fact that the final figures emerge from the computer give them an authenticity they would not have if scrawled on the back of a beer coaster. Even in universities, supposed bastions of rationality, we fall for this. Professional academic assessors give higher grades to student reports or essays that are word-processed than to the same essay that is handwritten. The printed number/word is somehow more impressive, more real – it inspires more confidence.

But is this confidence necessarily misplaced? Well, the reality is no one knows; but what we do know is that when people are operating under uncertainty, and seeking a number that they do not know, their (confident) sense of that correct number is influenced by any number that happens to be 'available' to them. If they do not know the population of a country, for example, the fact that people are asked to write down the last few digits of their telephone number before making a guess influences their estimate. After this phenomenon of availability[18] is explained, the number that comes up from the random spin of a wheel still influences the guesses of those who watch the spin – forewarned is not forearmed! Even in courts, judges give different sentences for exactly the same case depending on the sentence the prosecutor asks for (i.e. the sentence that is made 'available').[19]

Hence one of the most powerful influences on any such guesses managers make is the *anchoring effect* displayed by any credible number they are given to start with. If we ask (for example) 'is ALH worth more or less than $1.0 billion?' the answer is a simple 'yes' or 'no'. Now if we ask the same manager the question 'what is ALH worth?' his/her answer tends to be around that $1.0 billion mark. The answers from other managers will also tend to cluster around whatever value we have indicated to start with (e.g. $1.2 billion). The Woolworths managers are not only subject to unknown, random influences in their development of an illusionary value, but they also start with a credible anchor that contextualizes their calculations. That anchor is the current share price of the company and, as we know, the eventual 'price' that will be paid will always be more than that starting point. According to the efficient market hypothesis this starting point is a rational reflection of the value of the company. According to another influential set of theorists, this value is a random number – equivalent to spinning a wheel![20]

So what about critical analysis and reflection on evidence during the pricing process? Unfortunately when creating an illusion of wealth and well-being we need to dispense with such killjoy processes. In all studies of peoples' response to evidence the results are depressingly consistent – we see what we believe. We seek evidence to support our views and ignore, belittle, suppress and/or distort data that brings them into question. For example, when shown two studies, one in support of and the other questioning the effect of capital punishment, individuals rated the study in line with their own beliefs as 'more convincing' and 'better conducted' than the other. The same two studies were shown to those who were for and those who were against capital punishment. On reading the study contrary to their views people did not change their intensity of belief but on, reading the supporting study, they believed even more so in their original view.[21] Hence the investment banker's report recommending an acquisition will be well received by those bent on acquisition (who will now believe even harder) while the cold water thrown by other analysts will be consigned to the waste paper basket 'where it belongs'.

Money in potentially large quantities seems to have a particular propensity to promote illusionary thinking, as John Kenneth Galbraith[22] noted when he wrote:

> 'Nothing has been more remarkable than the susceptibility of the investing public to financial illusion and the like-mindedness of the most reputable of bankers, investment bankers, brokers and free-lance financial geniuses. Nor is the reason far to seek. Nothing so gives the illusion of intelligence as personal association with large sums of money. It is, alas, an illusion.'

So thank goodness that one human being never makes such important decisions as acquisitions alone. A management team (group) is always involved and this must ameliorate the fallibilities of the individual . . . surely?

The herd mentality

All of the illusion-creating cognitive and perceptual processes we have discussed so far have pertained to individuals. But that's why we make such decisions in groups, right? Managers in groups can steady each other; apply the blowtorch of rational inquiry to their colleague's fanciful daydreams and have their own feet kept firmly on the ground and their heads out of the clouds. Unfortunately, for such things as acquisition pricing, it is more likely a group will make things worse and not better, as Charles McKay[23] warned us over a century and a half ago:

> 'Men, it has been well said, think in herds; it will be seen that they go mad in herds, while they only recover their senses slowly, one by one.

This is firstly because groups tend to gravitate to a common set of beliefs to which all members subscribe and, secondly, because individuals in groups become less responsible and less 'knowledgeable' than when they act alone.

People in groups, and in particular those who work together in successful, cohesive groups like management 'teams', tend to share the same values, beliefs, norms, stereotypes, perceptions and general way of viewing the world. This outcome results from far more than what psychologists might term 'authority' effects (and others might term 'sucking up to the boss') or conscious desires to belong. Most of us have, on occasion, gone along uncomplainingly with a group decision that was contrary to our own view, because it was not worth 'rocking the boat' over an issue we perceived to be relatively unimportant. This kind of conscious conformance (*compliance*) is a common and necessary part of group functioning. However, we like to think that if we believed the issue to be important enough, and we disagreed, then we would stand our ground and fight the cause against group opposition. The problem, however, is that group members tend to conform to shared perception of the world (*conversion*) to the extent that dissent from the mainstream group view is not only discouraged but, more often than not, is not actually present. In groups we do tend to see the world in the same way as our group members – we share the same illusions.

The term 'groupthink' is often used to describe this situation where groups of intelligent, educated and appropriately motivated (i.e. not self-serving) managers can come to believe in an illusion of reality that to incredulous outsiders is crazy. Most readers will be familiar with such examples as the Bay of Pigs fiasco, when an attempted invasion of Cuba (approved by President Kennedy) was designed to tap into supposed popular discontent and bring down Fidel Castro.[24] Despite a disagreement between groups about reality, 'norming' led to the launch of the ill-fated Challenger in 1987. The Shuttle exploded shortly after lift-off killing all on board. The cause of the explosion was traced to the failure of a rubber component, called an O-ring, to properly seal a joint due to the fact that the O-ring had become brittle in the low temperatures. Prior to the launch, the engineers at Morton Thiokol, a NASA supplier, had argued that the documented evidence precluded a launch in conditions with temperatures markedly lower than any previous launch (i.e. 27°F) because O-ring problems were correlated with lower temperatures. NASA engineers, viewing exactly the same data, argued vehemently that no such conclusion was warranted. The data are presented in aggregated form in table 3.2[25] – so, would you have launched the Shuttle at 27°F?

Such egregious episodes tend to blind us to the fact that it is the norm for groups to exert unremitting, unconscious influence on their members' views of the world. It has been suggested that the last thing a goldfish understands is water, and similarly the 'water' of social influence is not consciously registered by group members and is hence is rarely understood by them. These influence processes impact on every decision a group makes and as people make a lot of decisions in groups this process has been extensively studied.

Group polarization, first named 'shift-to-risk', is one well-established phenomenon that directly pertains to acquisition pricing. Groups tend to be more gung-ho than

Table 3.2   Launch temperature and O-ring failures for shuttle launches

Launch temperatures (°F)	Number of flights	Number of O-ring failures
73–83	9	2
63–72	11	2
53–62	4	6

individuals when it comes to taking risks and evaluating financial outcomes. In an early experiment revealing this tendency, jurors were asked to individually assess the amount of compensation they would award to an injury claimant. The award they made, as a group, was 32% more than the average of the assessments that they had made on an individual basis prior to group discussion.[26]

Many other field and laboratory studies consistently confirm that groups make decisions that are more extreme than individuals would make but there is no consensual view on why this is so. We do know that people (managers) in groups lose a sense of personal responsibility for group outputs and behaviours (*diffusion of responsibility* – hence we get lynch *mobs*) and, relying on some mystical sense of group knowledge, tend not to check facts for themselves but rely on the actions of others to guide their own action and thinking (*pluralistic ignorance*). We also know that confidence increases in groups and, as discussed above, individual managers are already overconfident in their ability to predict the unpredictable and manage the unmanageable. Hence, in pricing a potential acquisition, the price that a group of managers will decide on will almost inevitably be higher than the price obtained by averaging their individual estimates before their first team discussion – the illusion is strengthened when we all see it!

So, through a process of quasi-rational individual and group processes the Woolworths managers (aided by input from advisers and bankers whose fees depend on action rather than inaction) arrived at a price at which they would go to market in their bid for ALH. That price of $2.75 per share (case box 3.1) represented a premium of some 11% over the prevailing market price a week before. Was this the right price? Well, as you can infer from the foregoing, the answer to that is 'who knows?' In this case the consensual view of analysts and commentators was that the price was low with respect to their valuation models but was as good a starting point as any. All players recognized that it was a preliminary price, an opening bid that would almost surely have to be increased as Woolworths engaged in battle with the directors of ALH and in all probability other predators – but the chase had begun.

2. The chase

The directors of ALH are legally bound to pursue the best interests of shareholders. On this basis, if another firm offers to buy at a price 11% over the prevailing share price, the response should be a speedy 'Yes – thanks'. Clearly the 'market', privy to all necessary information, has made its judgement on the value of ALH and this is reflected in a share price of $2.48. Hence any price above this should be accepted. However, it is understandable that the ALH directors might see an opportunity to boost the price even further, by bargaining hard and hoping that other interested parties might join in and make it an auction rather than a negotiation. This has a rational ring to it but even here we have evidence of an illusionary process. When people 'own' something they put a higher price on it than if they do not own it and are asked to buy it. Hence students given a commemorative mug from their university asked a much higher price than those without the mug were prepared to pay. (I am using the sense of 'ownership' loosely here with respect to the directors of a firm although experience suggests that directors' use of language like '*my/our* company' reflects a possessiveness that is more than figurative.)[27] Research by the strategy consultancy McKinsey shows that CEOs are reluctant to divest parts of their empire, even if the value argument to do so seems compelling to outsiders.[28]

After a decent pause of 5 weeks or so, the directors of AHL come back and, unsurprisingly, say: 'You must be joking! Our experts say the company is worth 20% more [i.e. $3.30] than your derisory offer and anyway you have not priced in the benefits of your synergies so go away . . . and think again.' This response fails to answer the questions of why the market disagrees with the 'expert' and why the purchaser's potential synergies have got anything to do with it, but in reality, of course, it boils down to 'our illusion of $3.30 is better than your illusion of $2.75'. A few weeks of stalemate is ended when a rational investor, Newbridge Capital, enters the fray and bids $3.05. Rational, you say? Investment companies and hedge funds are well aware of the M&A dynamic that the share price of the acquiring company tends to dip on acquisition and that the premium paid for the acquisition is always well above market. Hence investment firms will sell the acquirer's shares and buy early into the target. Hedge funds go 'short' on the acquirer and 'long' on the target and hence profit from the illusion without buying into it. That's rational in anyone's language. Newbridge Capital had no intention of buying AHL but the managers were sure (in their own minds) of being bought out by either Woolworths or Coles.

Woolworths immediately respond by offering $3.15 and the nuisance bidder Newbridge Capital has its profit ensured. Finally Coles Myer joins in and bids $3.35. At this point the directors of AHL can sit back, watch the fun and get ready to count the loot. Their 'expert' valuation of $3.30 has been reached and hence their fiduciary duty is clear: to accept the highest bid forthcoming above that price. Over the next month the action hots up with Woolworths finally offering a price some 36% higher than its opening bid. Naturally the Woolworths managers were aware that an auction would develop and it is highly unlikely that they put in their 'real' valuation as their first bid. It is conceivable that they had a valuation higher than their final price (we are, after all, talking illusions here) but the evidence is clear that most acquirers overpay. This suggests that acquirers end up paying more than their own valuation models suggest they should. What happens during the process of bid and counter-bid that makes the illusion even more alluring and valuable? What happens is that, as with all illusions and delusions, reality becomes distorted. Money, and the risks associated with spending it, takes on different meanings.

The meaning of money and value

The first thing that happens when a new bidder appears is that the new price confirms the previous offering as being a 'real' price. With no other buyer in the picture the only interaction is between potential buyer and seller, and this negotiation of 'price' is the same haggle that goes on in markets around the world. The buyer has no real idea of whether he/she is being 'ripped off' as the true 'value' of the item being bought is unknown. However, once another buyer is prepared to bid higher than you are for the same item, your last bid is acknowledged as undervaluing the prize and in this way every bid, bar the final one, is validated. Reality is shared illusions.

But what happens as buyers begin to reach the ceiling of their value 'comfort zone'? Rarely do buyers at house auctions or acquisitions drop out of the bidding at some pre-arranged limit despite the fact that they may have fixed one at the outset. The perceived value of the purchase increases as others put a higher value on it. There is a sense of 'I must have got it wrong; look how much others are prepared to pay'. This escalating illusion of value is one of the dynamics underpinning the asset and stock price bubbles that periodically reappear despite the warnings from previous bubbles. In the last Internet stock bubble, many brokers confessed to having stayed out of the process in the early days because they could not see the value in the stocks but succumbed to the hysteria later in the belief that 'all those others can't be wrong'. Hence most homeowners buy a home above their pre-arranged limit, and 'stretch' themselves financially, and most acquirers buy companies above the valuation limits set by their first modelling and often stretch themselves into serious financial difficulties as a result.

Added to this is another illusionary twist. A dollar is a dollar, right? Wrong! Under 'mental accounting' (i.e. 'the inclination to categorize and treat money differently depending on where it comes from, where it is kept, and how it is spent'), the value of a dollar varies. Just as gamblers who lose their winnings tend not to feel that they have lost anything, so executives feel that money spent, for example, as (someone else's) salary is different to the same amount spent on machines or acquisitions.[29] Even the terminology is different; salaries are 'expenses' (negative) while machines or acquisitions are 'investments' (positive) and whereas expenses are 'controlled' investments are 'managed'. Hence the same Woolworths executives who will query an expense claim of an extra night in a hotel will agree with colleagues to up the ALH bid from $2.75 per share to $3.15 with equanimity, as this is a 'strategic investment' and, as such, 40 cents is not much extra to pay. The shibboleth 'strategic' deflects those who show an inclination to explore the financial sense of the move. (In one company I worked for, once the 'strategic investment' had lost money for a sufficient time to require further mystification, it became known as 'patient money' – another example of an illusion when needed.)

The fact that the 40 cents 'does not sound much' underpins the process whereby executives lose sight of the implications of the total expenditure when they focus on small increases over their original amount. This is related to the well-known sunk cost phenomenon where managers continue to pour money into large projects that have having already absorbed more cost than originally planned. Because $100 million has already been spent, this encourages managers to throw more money on the pyre because 'we've gone this far, so for the sake of another $5 million we may as well go on – besides what's another $5 million compared with what we've already spent?' Of course, this line of reasoning leads to vast over-expenditures over the long term as each $5 million becomes even smaller in relative terms.[30] The amusing, salutary tales of perpetual overspending on fanciful military hardware by the US Pentagon is at least partly to do with this pathological incrementalism.[31] The fact that the project, in terms of total spend, may have long ago passed the point of (rational) economic viability fails to deter the impulse to throw good money after bad. This tendency to overcommit is exacerbated if the orientation becomes one of avoiding a certain loss (as opposed to making a potential gain), as we shall see later.

And so an incremental increase over an earlier bid in an acquisition auction seems, somehow, a lesser amount than if this incremental sum was spent as a stand-alone expenditure. This is particularly the case when the other bidder has offered a price that you must match. The last bid becomes 'what is on the table' and bid increases tend to be judged relative to this amount. Before commencing hostilities in earnest, Woolworths had acquired 15.8% of its target's stock. For the sake of argument, let us assume the average price for this to have been at around the final market value of $2.48, which means this has cost Woolworths a total of $138 million. Table 3.3 shows the various prices bid (from case box 3.1), the cost for Woolworths to buy the outstanding 84.2% of stock at that price (and the total value of AHL) and the incremental amount over the previous offer.

So, having initially bid $2.75, the Woolworths team must first deal with the nuisance bid of $3.05 from Newbridge capital. Now we are back to the problem mentioned earlier that the *available* bid figure has become $3.05 and not $2.75, no matter how 'sensible' $2.75 may have seemed. AHL is now worth at least $3.05 per share (or nearly $1.1 billion in total) because a potential purchaser has offered that amount; $3.05 is the new *anchor*. To better this offer Woolworths has to add 'only' 10 cents which, in total, is 'only' $30 million more than it would have to pay if it matched the Newbridge offer. Gone are all those clever formulae working out NPV

Table 3.3 Bid share prices and total amounts for AHL acquisition

Share price ($)	Value of outstanding stock (total AHL[32]) ($ million)	Increment over previous bid ($ million)
2.75	814 (967)	–
3.05	903 (1,072)	89
3.15	933 (1,108)	30
3.35	992 (1,178)	59
3.50	1,036 (1,231)	44
3.75	1,110 (1,319)	74
3.76	1,113 (1,325)	3

and *S*. The question now is: 'Are we going to lose the prize, worth $1.1 *billion* (in total) for the sake of a mere $30 *million*? Of course not!' In a sense, the Woolworths managers see themselves as now paying $30 million and not $1.072 billion plus $30 million. (Of course, their sense of well-being is bolstered by the fact that they have secured 15.8% of the stock at what now seems to be bargain basement prices.)

Notice that this relativity problem gets worse as the bids increase. The final Woolworths bid needed to top the $3.75 bid by Coles Myer is a trifling 1 cent ($3 million). Whereas the lines in our visual illusion in figure 3.1 are the same length in absolute terms the lower one appears shorter due to its relativity with the diverging tramlines. Hence, while $3 million seems derisively small compared with $1.1 billion, it would seem less paltry if you tried to sneak it through as an expense claim. In the same way as the tramline illusion is difficult to counter with rational logic, so too is the value illusion of the incremental relativity of bid prices. Go on, confess: you too would have difficulty missing out on AHL for a 'mere' $3 million more.

The meaning of risk

Not only can the perception of money change meaning during the acquisition process but so too can the perception of risk and its consequences. The discount rate (r) applied to the forecast cash flows of the target incorporates the estimated degree of risk in the venture. As has already been noted this is a guess but, in general, the use of the percentage weighted average cost of capital (WACC) of the firm is as good a guess as any. This is particularly so if the acquisition (as in the Woolworths/ AHL case) is related to other businesses in the portfolio. Logic dictates that the risk perception of the executives should remain constant during the acquisition process and, as our finance texts remind us, risk and return are related in that higher risk demands higher returns or, in the case of a risky acquisition, a lower price. Naturally if, by some magical process, the Woolworths executives became aware that risk was lower than they had estimated, or that risk should be seen in a new light, then this would mean that they could confidently go forward with an even higher price. That magical change in risk perception takes place as the acquisition changes from being viewed as making a potential gain to being viewed as avoiding a certain loss.

It is well established that the propensity of human beings to take risks is changed by the way in which they perceive the situation or how that situation is 'framed'. Specifically, we tend to take more risks to avoid a loss than we will take to make a gain of the same size (in economist-speak we have 'asymmetric risk functions').[33] Findings on the importance of 'framing' are based on asking people such things as which of two incompatible treatment programmes they would support in fighting a deadly disease that is expected to kill 600 people:

Programme A: 200 people saved with certainty, or

Programme B: 600 saved with a probability of 0.33.

Given these choices most subjects opt for programme A. However, if asked to choose between exactly the same options worded negatively, i.e.

Programme C: 400 die for certain, or

Programme D: 600 die with a probability of 0.67

most people choose programme D. The 'objective reality' that programme B and programme D are identical means nothing when subjected to human perception (the font of all illusion).

Bringing this back to money (i.e. acquisitions), which of the following two options would you choose?

Option A: Receive $100,

Option B: Toss a coin to receive $200 or nothing.

If you are like most people you will have taken option A. But what about the following?

Option C: Give over $100

Option D: Toss a coin to give over $200 or nothing

In this case most people choose to take the coin toss (Option D) – i.e. they are more risk-averse when it comes to possible gains than possible losses. This is reflected in the well-documented tendency for punters who are losing to bet more heavily in the last race (the 'get-out stakes') and on horses at longer odds (i.e. a higher risk of losing) in an attempt to recoup their losses. McKay (1841) noted this tendency at even higher levels.

> 'Money, again, has often been the cause of the delusion of multitudes. Sober nations have all at once become desperate gamblers, and risked almost their existence on the turn of a piece of paper.'

So how does this come into the AHL acquisition? In the beginning the Woolworths team is focused on buying the target as a potential gain and hence is relatively risk-averse in terms of the final price that might be negotiated. Now when Coles Myer enters the bidding, reality changes. The options now include a certain loss (i.e. option C above) of the AHL business (and its benefits) to a fierce rival and so both teams become less risk-averse and overcommit in order to avoid losing the prize to the other. Although it is doubtful that either side actually lowers the risk (discount) rate in their formal valuation models, the price for AHL increases as the implicit risk rate in the illusory valuation model is reduced.

In the End M&A Are Always Based on Illusions

At noon on 26 October, Coles Myer formally ended its battle for AHL. Chief Executive John Fletcher was quoted as saying that, at $3.75 a share, ALH was 'a responsible proposal from both a strategic and financial perspective' but above this price the costs of the takeover would 'swamp the benefits'. By the end of the day, Woolworths/Matheson owned almost 41% of ALH and was on its way to nearly 27% of the packaged liquor market. At the close of share trading its share price had dropped 16 cents to A$13.43 with Coles Myer gaining 9 cents to A$9.30.

Is $3.76 a good 'price' or an overpayment for AHL, a 'true' valuation or an illusion for the shareholders of Woolworths? No one knows and, in all probability, no one ever will. Compared with the average market price prior to the bid, Woolworths needs to extract net 'synergies' of some $400 million to break even on the premium it has paid. Given annual profits for AHL of the order of $62 million, this seems an ambitious goal in the medium term. The ground rules may also be changing in the industry. At the end of 2004, Coles Myer announced the start of a major sales campaign for its liquor business, with suppliers being 'invited' to subscribe to marketing costs. It also announced a trial run of putting liquor on its grocery shelves in one of its Melbourne (Victoria) stores, with observers expecting this to eventually be rolled out in all of its stores in Victoria and the ACT. Over the long term it could be that the battle for liquor sales moves inside the supermarket walls, as in other countries, in which case $3.76 will then seem a value illusion indeed.

Whatever the eventual outcome in this particular case, all prices for acquisitions are 'real' in being what must be paid for the acquisitions to go ahead. Price in this sense is a 'hurdle' to be cleared as part of the acquisition process. However, all prices for acquisitions are also illusions. They are illusions of the value of the target company to the shareholders of the acquirer. Managers, delusionally overconfident in their abilities to estimate and forecast uncertain parameters, are further bolstered by group support during the acquisition process to become ever more insensitive to uncertainty and risk to create the necessary value illusions for the acquisition to go ahead.

Hence, given the illusionary dynamics of people and process in M&A there should be no surprise that most acquisitions are overpriced; surprise should be reserved for those few that are not.

NOTES

1. One of the most egregious examples of the 'winner's curse' was the vast overpayment that the British government was able to acquire from competing telecommunications companies for 3G licenses. Most of the cost of these had to be written off with no value obtained for the £ millions spent. Richard Thaler (1992) offers more examples.

2. Details have been changed to preserve anonymity.

3. Debtor 'days' is a way of expressing debt owed in terms of the number of days' sales (e.g. if the average daily sales is 100 and the firm is owed 400 this is 4 debtor 'days'). There are nuances to this that the interested reader can look up in any accounting text. To look up the excuses that debtors come up with for not paying, the interested reader is referred to all of the well-known fairy tales based on fantasy and make-believe.

4. Kuhn's (1962) classic book looks at issues of scientific revolution.

5. This example and the opening quote for the chapter are taken from Francis Wheen's (2004) bitingly satirical paperback *How Mumbo-Jumbo Conquered the World* wherein he demonstrates that illusion is alive and well (and fully subscribed to) across all domains of public and private life including academia and science – i.e. where the 'experts' live.

6. 'The Royal Road to Bankruptcy, By One Who Took the Ride', *Atlantic Monthly*, January 1993.

7. Data and information about this case came from various public sources, including newspaper, magazine, television and Internet-based reports, as well as company announcements from all the protagonists.

8. All reference to dollars in the chapter are references to Australian dollars.

9. The 'efficient market hypothesis' (EMH) traces its roots to Adam Smith's 'invisible hand' of the market. With respect to a stock price it asserts that the current market price of widely traded stock is an unbiased predictor of the future value of that stock. It does not claim that the price is in any sense the 'right' price but that, due to the interplay and competition between investors for market information, it is 'about right' on average. Three forms of the EMH have been proposed: the *weak form* suggests that the stock price incorporates *all past information*; the *semi-strong form* that the price captures *all current and past public information*; and the *strong form* that the price captures *all current and past public and private information*. Of the three, the semi-strong form has garnered most empirical support although the EMH in any form has many critics.

10. The terminal value after *n* years can be regarded as growth perpetuity with *g* being the growth rate of free cash flow in perpetuity. This particular variation is taken from Mark Sirower's (1997) critique of acquisitions and their supposed synergies.

11. Technically, of course, value is neither created nor 'destroyed' by the simple transaction of acquisition but is, rather, transferred from the shareholders of the acquiring company to the shareholders of the target company. However here we are taking the perspective of the shareholders of the predator firm.

12. For a recent confirmation of the perpetual fallibility of experts in forecasting in political, economic and social spheres, see Philip Tetlock's (2005) extensive research, which shows that experts are no better than non-experts at forecasting but they are more confident!

13. See Russo and Schoemaker's (1989) book.

14. There is a long history of research into overconfidence. Sutherland (1992) summarizes the main issues in chapter 17.

15. Haunschild et al. (1994) write on overcommitment in acquisitions.

16. Hayward and Hambrick (1997) discuss the issue of CEO hubris and the premium paid.

17. Duhaime and Schwenk (1985) engage in conjecture on the role of various cognitive biases in the acquisition and post-acquisition phases.

18. For discussions on availability, anchoring and a variety of other cognitive biases and heuristics, readers can do no better than to start with Tversky and Kahneman (1974) – after all, Kahneman was awarded the 2002 Nobel prize for his work in this area and only Tversky's death prevented him from being a co-recipient.

19. Englich and Mussweiler (2001) showed that judges gave sentences on average 8 months longer for exactly the same case if the prosecutor asked for a 36-month verses a 12-month term.

20. An informative and engaging exposition of share prices as random events is Burton Malkiel's (1990) classic caveat for value-based investors, *A Random Walk Down Wall Street*.

21. The paper by Lord et al. (1979) discusses this tendency in detail.

22. 'The 1829 Parallel: Modern Stock Market Speculation', *Atlantic Monthly*, January 1987.

23. Charles McKay's book (1841) highlights how group behaviour reinforces delusions.

24. Irving Janis coined the term 'groupthink' and those not familiar with his work should read his (1982) book.

25. This data is from the case 'The launch of space shuttle flight 51-L' in Corbett (1994) p. 136.

26. This finding is from Davis (1982).

27. Thaler (1992) discusses the part 'ownership' plays in the winner's curse.

28. This research is presented in Dranikoff et al. (2002).

29. Richard Thaler (1985) came up with this concept.

30. See Belsky and Gilovich (1999).

31. The movie *The Pentagon Papers* (based on the book of the same name) is an amusing and/or horrifying (depending on your viewpoint) story of these excesses and the extent to which intelligent, 'sane' people will go to protect the pathological processes involved.

32. The figures vary slightly from exactness due to rounding.

33. In their paper on 'prospect theory', Kahneman and Tversky (1979) investigate decision making under risk.

Chapter 4   M&A as Warfare
Warspeak in Mergers and Acquisitions

Stephen Cummings and Sally Riad

Merger processes and challenges are often described with expressions like 'battle', 'raid', 'feint', and 'keeping the powder dry'.[1] And yet if the purpose of a merger or an acquisition is to secure, preserve, maintain and add value (admittedly not always the case), one would have thought that the language of peace might be more appropriate. Words such as 'friend', 'mutual', 'communal', 'harmony', 'unity', and 'accord', however, are much less frequent in merger discourse (and, when they do arise, seem to jar or appear misplaced). The language of war is a far more 'natural' bedfellow. In this chapter, we examine merger 'warspeak' – a term we introduce to encompass a wide range of war-related terminology and respective practices.[2] In doing so, we discuss how warspeak has become common in various merger contexts and comment on its implications.

The chapter first investigates the dynamics that make warspeak such a prominent metaphor in merger discourse and practice. It then examines whether this is constraining or enabling, and whether it is likely to add or destroy value post merger. The chapter concludes by exploring how an understanding of the dynamics of warspeak (and its binary counterpart 'peacespeak') might enable us to engage with mergers more effectively.

Why Warspeak?

> A picture held us captive. And we could not get outside it, for it lay in our language and language seemed to repeat itself inexorably.
>
> *Ludwig Wittgenstein*

This book focuses on 'images' of mergers and acquisitions. Following Wittgenstein, our chapter examines mergers through warspeak, a language with which merger accounts are imbued and which generates the images that hold us 'captive'. Such language has power to mobilize people in a specific way, according to the rules of its game (Wittgenstein, 1958). Images generated in language are commonly associated with 'metaphor'. The metaphors employed in or associated with an event say much about how we understand it. Yet the dilemma is whether metaphors are specific *features* of language or whether *all* language is inherently metaphorical. This notion is addressed by Robert Chia (1996), who reviews metaphors as 'appreciators' and as 'metaphorizers' – both notions relevant to this chapter.

- *Appreciators* are terms that, if taken literally, would be nonsensical but which when taken metaphorically excite the imagination (e.g. 'kill' in merger warspeak). These offer useful ways of perceiving the world; imagery that efficiently adds colour and movement to describe somewhat statically perceived events, states, entities and attributes. A merger or acquisition event, for example, can be somewhat bland until inspirational metaphors such as those embedded in war are applied to conjure more colourful and dynamic images and meanings. This notion of metaphor becomes relevant when we discuss the 'myth' of war later in the chapter.
- *Metaphorizers*, on the other hand, are terms that become literal, and seemingly 'natural', as a result of the stabilization of a term initially used metaphorically (e.g. the warspeak word 'target' in merger discourse). Through repetition, metaphorizers become convenient linguistic devices that efficiently pull together, and legitimate, many ideas.

While metaphors allow for economical expression, offering a 'shorthand' way of directing attention to various facets of experience (Chia, 1996), the language in which they are embedded reinforces certain structures; hence, when accepting circulating language uncritically, we reinforce existing power relations (Wittgenstein, 1958). This resonates with Jeffcutt's (1994) argument that 'an understanding of organization comes to organize our understanding'. Specifically, in relation to war and organization, Monin and Monin (1997) state that rather than master metaphors, metaphors master us. Hence, it is relevant that we attempt to challenge and deconstruct stabilized terms, re-examining taken-for-granted concepts and revealing their inherent contradictions.

The Extent of Warspeak

The central tenet of this chapter is that warspeak is pervasive in mergers – at times to the detriment of those engaging in it. In the first instance, this statement on the overwhelming extent of warspeak in mergers may come as something a surprise – but consider the following. First, war is broadly defined as active conflict that results in casualties and claims lives. Approached in this way, one can quickly recognize that 'conflict' has always been a central theme in mergers. Second, consider the word 'target'. Perhaps one of the commonest in merger vernacular – across both friendly and hostile mergers – this term has its origins in warspeak. Indeed, over the past two decades, many leading academics in the field of mergers have described how notions of war pervade merger accounts and are central in mergers (Boyd, 2003; Hirsch and Andrews, 1983; Schneider and Dunbar, 1991; Vaara et al., 2003). The business press's merger commentaries are rife with warspeak (Koller, 2005) – a dynamic to which we return later in this chapter.

Even academic work reinforces warspeak. Here it is either used to describe combative merger events or deployed by the authors themselves in discussing mergers, as the following examples (where we have emphasized the warspeak terms) illustrate. For example, in one of the earliest papers on the role of culture in mergers, Buono and his associates (1985) describe a situation where:

'Each parent organization was seen by employees of the other bank as an "*invading enemy*", rather than as a co-equal partner . . . there were distorted perceptions about the *feelings of hostility toward this "enemy"* . . . [then] came what might be described as the "*arm wrestling" phase* . . . The layoff, which occurred in mid-December, quickly became known as the "*Christmas massacre*".'

In a similar vein, Marks and Mirvis (2001) discussing the psychological dynamics of mergers in a more recent but also seminal paper, state that:

'One way executives cope with their shock is by a *defensive retreat*. This allows acquired executives to *regroup and reformulate a battle plan for countering the enemy* . . . Even in mergers of equals, perceived fears of losing status or ways of doing things lead executives *to dig in and protect their turf*.

In table 4.1, we demonstrate the occurrence of the terms 'merger' and/or 'acquisition' in combination with terms of war in the abstract or title (using the ProQuest search engine and a data set of all available publications up until 2005). Initially, we

Table 4.1   War and Peace in non-academic and academic merger literature

Word	All articles	Academic papers	Word	All articles	Academic papers
War	6,342	235	Unity	367	100
Battle	2,103	57	Concord	294	1
Fight	1,370	47	Love	501	22
Hostile	2,500	361	Accord	144	12
Conflict	1,045	198	Harmony	185	26
Kill	410	11	Peace	104	5

include all articles that feature this combination, and then only academic articles. We also contrast occurrences of peace-related antonyms to war-related words together (with 'merger' and/or 'acquisition'). The contrast, particularly given what we might expect as outlined in this chapter's opening paragraph, is stark.

Academics and our students, the media, practitioners: we are all implicated in the spreading of warspeak in merger discourse.

The Salience of Warspeak

In elaborating on warspeak and the impact of its conceptions toward some pragmatic propositions, we begin by canvassing some of the dynamics that join warspeak and mergers. While our discussion is by no means exhaustive, we have compiled the following nine interrelated propositions on the association of mergers with warspeak. These are summarized in figure 4.1.

1. Warspeak resonates with foundational language in management and strategy

If one were to consider mergers' location within the broader domains of strategy and management, one would note that 'war' is already deeply ingrained in the language of these fields. The Western roots of 'strategy' are often (and proudly) traced all the way back to the word *strategos* (literally 'leader of combined troops') in Greek, while Eastern lines of strategic practice generally begin with great military philosophers like Sun Tzu. His often-cited *The Art of War* (*Bing Fa*) translates literally

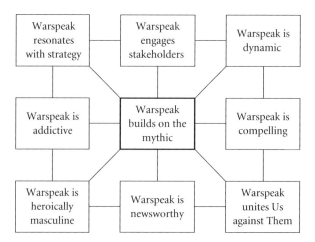

Figure 4.1   The dynamics of warspeak

as 'soldier doctrine'. Both histories of management (George, 1972; Wren, 1994), and critiques of these histories (Cummings, 2004), make much of the intertwining of military practice and the emergence of management as a civilian profession. Within organizational theory, warspeak is core to economic competitive models (Rindova et al., 2004) and the strategic management literature. Indeed, there is also a plethora of books that theorize organizational strategy and marketing as military warfare (Garsombke, 1988). Little wonder then that people come to relate to mergers, such salient strategic events, with warspeak at the forefront of their 'armoury' of language; and no surprise that *Joining Forces* should be such a convenient title for discussing mergers and acquisitions (Marks and Mirvis, 1998).

2. Warspeak engages capital markets and stakeholders

Capital markets often become focal in merger events or rumours, and the language in which they operate is one of 'winning' and 'losing' – often framed as combat; the crossing of the threshold that gives control, or losing control by failing to 'hold enough ground'. Such language fuses merger activity and the capital markets with the exciting qualities of power and glory. It joins them in a spectacle that grabs the attention of even those not normally interested in the ramifications of business transactions.

However, shareholders are but one group of stakeholders, many of whom are mobilized through warspeak. People involved in mergers and acquisitions also engage in warspeak towards vivid and emotive communication with a variety of parties external to the organization. The role of warspeak in effectively interacting with stakeholders has been underlined in strategy generally, and in acquisitions specifically. More broadly, Rindova et al. (2004) argue that the language of war tends, in many circumstances, to increase stakeholder involvement and improve performance. Through its thematic consistency, warspeak can affect stakeholders' interpretation of a firm's strategic activity, enabling firms to engage stakeholder support. Focusing specifically on acquisitions, Boyd (2003) argues that framing an acquisition as 'war' stirs up organizational communication internally and externally to effectively engage stakeholders with the organization's identity. In this way, and ironically, warspeak itself becomes a 'weapon' of corporate persuasion. It productively conveys to these interested parties a sense of direction and confidence. To shareholders and other industry observers it says that this company is 'on the march'. It is going places.

3. Warspeak is dynamic

> Let me have war, say I. It exceeds peace as far as day does night. It's spritely walking, audible and full of vent. Peace is a very apoplexy, lethargy; mulled, deaf, sleepy, insensible; a getter of more bastard children than war is a destroyer of men.

Shakespeare's lines above, taken from *Coriolanus* (Act 4, Scene 5), resonate with the dynamics that often drive merger settings.

Warspeak provides dynamic images that are convenient for organizations and managers who, in turn, confront normative expectations to be active, dynamic, making change, 'thrusting forward'. Claiming – at a performance review or before shareholders or the board – that one has 'maintained the peace', 'smoothed the waters', or kept things as they were, is generally unlikely to inspire much respect. Far better to speak of 'battles won', new 'territories conquered', advancing on a number of 'fronts'. Or even, if times are tough, a planned 'retrenchment' to preserve energies for the next 'thrust', or defend against the 'barbarians at the gate'.

Mergers and acquisitions are usually a context of change. And when considering change management prescriptions more broadly, advice consistently centres on efforts to 'rally and mobilize the troops'. The widely cited change framework developed by J. P. Kotter (1995) sets the first crucial step in any change process as 'creating a sense of urgency'. Such urgency is often framed in terms of crisis, in which warspeak is central.

In keeping, Miller and Beck's (2004, p. 159) analysis of crisis metaphors presents 'war' as a dominant category. They present the following syllogisms, metaphorical structures that illustrate the relationship between events and people:

Wars require heroics;   Soldiers fight;
Crises require heroics;   Employees fight;
Crises are wars.   Employees are soldiers.

Armies mobilize;   Generals order;
Companies mobilize;   CEOs order;
Companies are armies.   CEOs are generals

4. Warspeak inspires a compelling mission

> Compared to war, all other forms of human endeavour shrink to insignificance.
> *General George S. Patton*

In his book, *War Is a Force That Gives Us Meaning*, renowned war correspondent Christopher Hedges (2003) explains the enduring attraction of war, despite the obvious concurrent desire for peace, is that: 'Even in its destruction and carnage, [war] can give us what we long for in life. It can give us purpose, meaning and a reason for living.'

Linking back to the first of our nine dynamics described here, so much of the strategic management and associated literatures sees the development of a sense of purpose, mission, strategic intent, and shared meaning as a key to effective progress (Campbell et al., 1993; Cummings and Davies, 1994). It is not surprising then, that the dynamism of crisis and urgency instigated by warspeak, described in point 3 above, can lead to organizational militarism which, in turn, facilitates decisive, efficient and productive strategic action. During war, leaders can invoke 'special powers' and defer the normal internal political process that may lead to dissent. Garsombke (1988) underlines the role of a militaristic culture in legitimating managers' attempts to control the situation and people through discipline. Productive discipline becomes particularly relevant in situations where time is commonly considered to be a crucial factor – such as mergers.

Framing mergers in war terms adds to the sense of purpose of those who like to be at the forefront and provides their leadership with an authority that is difficult to question. The resulting focus can be related to Robin Wensley's 4-M matrix, in which he uses an 'x-axis' of high versus low 'strategic intent', and a 'y-axis' of high versus low 'strategic anticipation' to outlines four strategic modes (Wensley, 2003). 'Meandering' indicates an organization with low intention and low levels of anticipating the future. A 'meditative' organization is also low on intent, but high in terms of anticipation. 'Myopia', on the other hand, refers to being high in terms of a clear intention, but low with regard to sensing or anticipating change. And, finally, the 'Manoeuvring' mode characterizes an organization high on both intention and anticipation dimensions.

Warspeak enables merging or acquiring parties to operate in a *myopic* state, with an integrated and focused strategic intention leading to a high degree of clarity in the near or short term. While this can lead to problems, particularly in the medium term and beyond (of which more is discussed in the next section on the constraining effects of warspeak), in many situations myopia is a very productive thing, as Wensley (2003) points out. For example, where the industry environment is stable and relatively certain, valuable time and resources can be wasted on the scanning and self-analysis implied in a more thoughtful and anticipative, or less 'gung-ho', approach. Or, in environments where competitors are 'losing their heads' (often the case in the tense climate brought about by an impending merger or takeover), having an unshakeable sense of intention or purpose can be a source of comparative advantage.

In the recent address, George Bain, former dean at Warwick and London Business Schools and more recently President at Queens University in Belfast, outlined some of the best things he ever learnt. He noted that: 'People will march for a phrase; they will not march for a paragraph and, even less, for a page.' A particular attraction of warspeak in mergers is that it provides such a call to 'arms': it helps outline what is to be done in environments where further steps may not be immediately obvious. And, for 'good' managers, knowing what should be done, and then to be seen to be doing it, is very important. Warspeak furnishes compelling metaphors and images that clearly mark out where people stand and how they should move forward. The language of peace, on the other hand, is much more nuanced, much less certain. It requires more meditation. Its character takes longer to understand, its lines are not clearly marked and it takes longer to explain. A declaration of war need only be a slogan, while peace can involve complex treaties, chapters and appendices.

5. Warspeak unites 'Us' in opposition to 'Them'

> War makes the world understandable: a black and white tableau of them and us.
> *Christopher Hedges*

Hedges' words echo those of David Hume's *A Treatise on Human Nature*, written some 250 years earlier:

> When our own nation is at war with any other, we detest them under the character of cruel, perfidious, unjust and violent: But always esteem ourselves and allies equitable, moderate and merciful . . . It is evident that the same method of thinking runs through common life.

Warspeak tends to reduce intra-organizational conflict, jealousy and points of difference, facilitating internal solidarity. Through the creation of a greater sense of 'Us' and 'Them', warspeak makes 'Us' feel good about, and proud of, being 'Us'. In so doing, it makes certain groups care about their actions and respective consequences and take sides where they might otherwise hesitate or mull. In an organizational context, the role of the language of war in creating internal unity premised on us/them distinctions has been underlined by both Garsombke (1988) and Rindova et al. (2004).

Focusing on cross-border mergers, Vaara, Tienari and Santti (2003) investigated the use of metaphors in building cultural identity. Specifically, they examined how metaphors help construct the important images of 'Us and Them' and images of a 'common future'. The first ('Us') category is particularly relevant before an acquisition or merger; the second ('Them'), particularly (although not exclusively) important during and after such an event. The authors found war and battle metaphors to be very salient in this context. Yet, while it is easy to see how war images can lead to 'Us and Them', it is just as easy to see that such images might lead away from the construction of a 'common future' (an issue that we address in the next section). But it is important to remember that us/them categorizations in mergers are not fixed; they are fluid, depending on who makes for the opposition at a particular time (Riad, 2007). So it is important to note that us/them warspeak is not always about opposition to the potential merger partner; ironically, merger partners can at times unite as 'us' to confront another entity altogether. As case box 4.2 at the end of this chapter illustrates, merger partners can unite through warspeak to confront other entities opposed to the merger, as in proxy 'battles'. Either way, while empowering in some ways, the polarization of us/them can also be detrimental to the creation of shareholder value (a point also noted by Boyd (2003)).

6. *Warspeak is newsworthy*

As established in the previous passages, warspeak is traditional, dynamic, compelling and unifying – therefore, it works well in media communications. The media, and particularly the business media, engage with it because it succinctly adds drama and, hence, gives heightened importance to what could otherwise be perceived as a dry event. This elevates such news from the back pages of the business section of a newspaper to the front of the business pages or even into the general news sections (Dunford and Palmer, 1996). Yet, this salience of warspeak with the media sits within the wider milieu by which the media engages the public in 'war' communication or 'the media-tion of violence' in Cooke's words (1993, p. 181) – a context for '. . . wars fought by the media but also, in a very important way, *for* the media'.

   In reviewing the key narratives concerning the role of mainstream media in communicating conflict, Thusu and Freedman (2003) point to three themes or roles played by the media: critical observer, publicist, and finally, the theme of most interest to us here, 'battleground'. In this 'battleground' role, media conflict communication becomes the surface or game-board on which war is imagined and executed. The media thus comes to constitute the spaces in which wars are fought, and this constitution becomes the main way through which most people experience war.

   Later in this section, we underline how merger warspeak builds on the 'mythic' attributes of war. Specifically focusing here on the role of the media in merger warspeak, we draw on work by Fursich (2002) on the appropriation of mythic categories by journalists. In elaborating on 'myth' as an explanatory device explaining media production and consumption of merger accounts, he cites the following from an article in the *New York Times Magazine*:

> 'When you add to the emotional ingredient of the DaimlerChrysler merger the fact that the companies represent the winners and losers in the last world war, you have an almost perfect drama, a grand epic for the age of globalization . . .'

   Indeed, extensive systematic research by Koller (2003; 2005) analyzing the use of a wide range of metaphorical expressions in mergers and acquisitions across four business publications – *Businessweek, The Economist, Fortune* and the *Financial Times* – found that the four most popular metaphors, by quite some distance, were war-based: 'target' (used 92 times across all four publications); 'hostility' (71); 'battle' (49); and 'war' (36). By contrast, friendly or non-violent metaphors were far less frequent or non-existent: 'suitor' (11); 'love' (5); 'flirt' (3); 'mate' (3); and 'affection' (1). Further, in these non-war metaphors, what is represented is romantic, individual relationships, rather than love, friendship or peace in a broader communal sense.

   The business news media, however, does not operate in isolation. At the level of individual business organizations, the media's use of warspeak feeds, and is fed by, organizational public relations management (Boyd, 2003; Fursich, 2002). And significantly, sometimes particular organizational members become implicated in the warspeak that riddles public accounts (as illustrated in case box 4.2 on Hewlett-Packard at the end of the chapter). At a broader level, the media's warspeaking accounts of mergers interplay with beliefs reinforced by popular culture. It is perhaps little surprise that of the very few successful movies or novels about the business world in recent decades many (e.g. *Wall Street* and *Barbarians at the Gate*) have drawn upon the drama of merger 'wars' (Angwin, 2003). And, it is easy to see why, given what has been said about the power of war above, the *Illiad* might furnish a script for a Hollywood blockbuster, whereas the *Odyssey* (a much more nuanced tale about an individual journey away from war) or *The Trojan Women* (a tale of traumatic aftermath) would not: an issue that bleeds into our seventh category.

7. *Warspeak favours heroic masculinity*

'Is a soldier a soldier if he is afraid, weak, and vulnerable? Is a mother a mother if she is fearless, strong, and politically effective? . . . most cultures' war myths – of men in arms and of women at home – are a fiction . . .'

Miriam Cooke

While there appears to be something noble about the pursuit of mergers in warspeak, this is generally couched in terms of heroic masculinity. On the one hand, warspeak tends to appeal to the egos of those driving mergers who enjoy such forceful and heroic status (e.g. 'hero managers', 'dragons' and 'captains of industry'). They are spurred on by the competition, determined to win and to be seen to win. Yet, on the other hand, the understanding of leadership and heroic masculinity has been tightly interwoven, to the point that the two are uninspected, an argument made by Sinclair (1998). She underlines how physical combat becomes a common metaphor for leading change in organizations – as in merger situations.

Such leadership (displays of courage, physical and emotional toughness, unflinching attitudes) is generally defined by the presence of something women do not have (by implication). Wilson (1992) further argues that the use of 'war' in management generally is associated with a predominantly 'male' language with which women may feel uncomfortable; over centuries war has not only been typically represented as a masculine activity, but has also been represented as a test of manhood. This sets in place a pattern by which the leader's path is one of establishing himself as 'a hero against culturally and mythically resonant criteria' that leads to the stereotyping of women and the rejection of the feminine (Sinclair, 1998, p. 37; see also Calas and Smircich, 1991, for related ideas on the masculinity of strategic management discourse in general – something which connects us back to the very first of our nine categories).

This is asserted by Tallman (2003), who states that despite advances in women's leadership roles, the majority of organizational leaders are still men. He reviews masculine archetypes – a key one of which is 'warrior' – and how they affect how leadership is represented and enacted. 'Warrior' is a model of courage, discipline and self-control, with an alert mind. He is also loyal to a cause and vision, to which he perseveres single-mindedly and decisively. The shadow side, however, is that he can be cruel and merciless and compromising of ethical principles so as to 'win'. Another significant implication of a 'warrior' model, according to Wilson (1992), is that women become linguistically excluded in organizations since warspeak reproduces specific power relations. An example of the early reaction to such power dynamics can be seen in Betty Harragan's (1977) classic guide, *Games Mother Never Taught You*, for women who want to make it in a man's corporate world. Centred on 'war', the guide's central aim appears to be the 'enlistment' of women. The contents section, a veritable 'minefield' of warspeak, features pages of headings like, 'You're in the army *now*', 'Line jobs are the action arena', 'Chart offensive and defensive formations'. It also explicitly features four pages of military metaphors (pp. 99–103). Yet, ironically, even when at times perpetuated by women, warspeak creates an unequal reality, its metaphorical construction male-dominated, with codes and practices that reinforce patriarchy in organizations (Wilson, 1992). This renders the chapter title, 'An uneasy coupling', on women and top management in mergers, very appropriate (Tienari et al., 2003).

That merger dynamics are gendered is a notion that is becoming increasingly salient to the analysis of mergers (Collins, 2005; Riad, 2007; Tienari et al., 2003; 2005). Specifically relevant to the discussion of warspeak in mergers is Tienari et al.'s (2003, p. 239) analysis that elaborates on assumptions in the work/family binary that marginalizes women and excludes them from an increasing number of key management tasks during merger integration. Reinforcing the now contested notion of work and family as separate spheres, the premise is that 'women cannot deliver (because women deliver and take care of babies)'.

This resonates with the broader dynamics of warspeak in societies. Both Meyer (2002) and Cooke (1993: 162) discuss how 'war' is constructed as a predominantly 'masculine' endeavour represented through binaries: '. . . "war stories" in this context are slotted into gendered categories defined by the iconic dichotomies of "homefront"/"battlefront", "warrior"/"nurturer", "protector"/"protected" and the differential value assigned to each.' Such notions can further constrain gendered roles in mergers, by confining women to keeping the 'home fires burning', undertaking more mundane tasks, while men go into the 'battlefront'.

8. *Warspeak is addictive*

Christopher Hedges (2003) describes war as 'an enticing elixir'. His experiences in reporting war led him to describe it as an anodyne, but highly seductive, narcotic. And, linked to points previously covered here, he explains that: 'It [war] gives them [the participants] purpose, resolve, a cause. It allows them to be noble.' Indeed, the main thesis presented by Le Shan, a former military psychologist, in *The Psychology of War* (2002) is that war is easy to kick off, but difficult to bring under control

– not only because it is an integral aspect of human behaviour, but moreover because it fulfils psychological needs and eases tensions by creating an alternate reality structure, one that makes the lives of its participants seem more intense, more meaningful, and more noble. This addictive window into an alternative reality means that warspeak – including its images and its respective conduct – tends to perpetuate itself (as noted by the reference to Wittgenstein early in the chapter).

The effect is not unlike that described by Duncan Angwin (2003) where he likens the acquirers to explorers in order to better understand their motivations. Angwin uses the explorer metaphor to highlight what recent writing on mergers overlooks: that those who drive mergers and acquisitions become addicted to the journey or the quest toward the target far more than the achievement of the target itself. Thus, merger behaviour is often driven by a similar lust. (There is no such thing as 'a rational army', claimed Montesquieu: 'it would run away.')

Once the target has been achieved and the celebrations have died away, the explorer or the acquirer becomes restless and unfulfilled. The only way to rekindle their souls is to strike out again. This 'need' to explore and conquer rather than find and settle creates a perpetual exploration cycle which, Angwin argues, goes a long way to explaining why much more senior management emphasis is generally placed on 'winning the war' (and then the war after that) rather than 'winning the peace'.

But warspeak plays a further role in the creation of 'serial acquirers'. For the primary actors in mergers, the 'battle' to take over or assimilate another company never creates the security or the harmony desired or attained – there is always another potential 'target', or a range of fears: for example, the fear that somebody else might undermine 'Us' by beating 'Us' to that potential 'target', or the fear of becoming a 'target'. In fact, what is found after the act of acquisition can be especially *unlike* the harmony we experienced among 'Us' during wartime (Hedges, 2003, p. 22). Thus, acquirers are drawn, or feel lured, to return to the siren-song of a war footing over and over again.

9. Warspeak conjures up the 'mythic' and undermines the 'sensory'

> It is well that war is terrible – we would grow too fond of it.
> *Robert E. Lee*

Lee's famous quotation indicates a difference between the perceived or 'mythic' elements of war and the brutal pragmatic reality or 'sensory' elements. The mythic elements of war, the dynamism, the nobility, the compelling stories, the camaraderie, the heroism, all conspire to feed the addiction described above.

Le Shan makes much of this distinction between the mythical and the sensory effects of war. He and others before him, claim that humans are largely drawn to the point of killing through the heady mythical effects of war often laid out by the media. However, humans confronting the sensory terror can help temper the myth, and hence the perpetuation of war. In 'real life', when people are experiencing the actual horror of being in battle, it generally cools their ardour for war. Young soldiers come face to face with gruesome slaughter, horrifying and dehumanizing images, smells and sounds. It is literally (not just metaphorically) sickening. But while merger practice hitches its wagon to the mythical effects of warspeak, those who perpetrate it are often spared – or at least distanced – from the sensory results.

Le Shan (2002) outlines the difference between the state of mind of those in peacetime in contrast to those on a 'war footing'. Some of the dimensions of the table that summarizes his findings are abbreviated in table 4.2 and provide a good way of recapping and connecting some of the themes developed earlier in this section. For example, the table indicates why warspeak is more dynamic, more compelling and more internally unifying than its opposites.

What keeps the wheel of warspeak in mergers spinning freely is the fact that it appeals to all of the mythical elements that make war seem more desirable than a state of peace. In many cases, those who engage in merger warspeak hardly ever confront the traction provided by the grim sensorial horror instigated by their corporate 'warfare' (let alone actual 'real' war). The traumatic sensory elements of merger warspeak are kept at an arm's length. Sure, some customers may find

Table 4.2 An abbreviated version of Le Shan's 'peacetime versus wartime'

Peacetime	Wartime
1. Good and Evil have many shades of grey. Many groups with different ideas and opinions are legitimate.	1. Good and Evil are reduced to Us and Them. There are no innocent bystanders; there are only those *for* and *against* Us. The crucial issues of the world are divided into black and white.
2. Now is pretty much like other times . . . the differences are qualitative.	2. Now is special, qualitatively different from all other times. Everything is cast in the balance; whoever wins now wins for ever.
3. When this present period is over, things will go on pretty much as they have in the past.	3. When this war is over, everything will be vastly different. It we win, it will be much better; if we lose, terribly worse. The world will be deeply changed by what we do here.
4. There are many problems to be solved . . . life is essentially complex, with many foci.	4. There is only one major problem to be solved. All others are secondary. Life is essentially simple. It has one major focus.

their favourite products 'wiped out'; some employees may be 'stood down', but they will be sent letters, fruit baskets and redundancy packages, while the devastating effects of their dismissals are rationalized as part of the necessary pains of change. Mergers also instigate many other traumatic experiences that are often glossed over. Indeed, one of the most widely cited early papers on mergers, 'The merger syndrome' by Marks and Mirvis (1985), underlines the stress and anxiety that affects merger participants. Such negative experiences affect not only those who lose their jobs, but also other staff, who often take their cues of management through how their colleagues were treated. People's lives can be ruined through redundancy or stress, but often senior executives turn a blind eye. What continue to be reproduced in merger warspeak are the mythical elements, while the sensory painful elements are undermined. Hence, the cycle of warspeak in mergers becomes a rolling stone.

The Enabling and Constraining Effects of Warspeak

> Men are interested in the outcomes of wars, not their causes.
> *Seneca*

Warspeak (and the way in which the nine elements outlined in figure 4.1 reinforce one another) provides a far more compelling language than its alternatives in merger discourse. Peace, neutrality, détente – they don't seem to stand a chance. But what are the effects of this deeply rooted warspeak?

Having outlined the pervasiveness of warspeak in merger discourse and examined its salience, this section investigates the enabling and constraining effects of warspeak. By 'enabling' we mean whether warspeak enables value creation or whether it is more likely to erode value. We recognize that this warrants broader social commentary on warspeak in mergers: however, space limits the full exploration of these dynamics. Further, we do not provide the definitive answers to the scenarios that we raise (the field is too nuanced and each case too individual to do so in any instance); rather, we offer some thoughts, develop some thinking approaches and a couple of illustrative cases. Our purpose is to provide material that enables readers to contemplate and think differently about how they might approach warspeak in merger settings.

The enabling effects of warspeak can be easily gauged from the paragraphs in the previous section. Warspeak exhibits a good 'fit' with other related language games; it indicates and helps engender dynamism, focus, unity and momentum toward closing a deal; it appeals to and thus motivates key players; and it makes the whole merger process appear dramatic and even heroic. These effects are summarized in the left-hand column in table 4.3.

Table 4.3   The constraining effects of warspeak presented against its enabling effects

Enabling	Constraining
1. Easy/'natural' to use. Good fit with other business language games (e.g. capital markets, strategy);	1. Can lead to boundedness that prevents more imaginative and individualized language being developed.
2. Indicates action, thereby creating an impression of good leadership and management. Helps build momentum.	2. Makes is difficult to consider a more measured or 'do nothing' strategy – even though this might be more sensible.
3. Provides focus and certainty in environments that might otherwise be chaotic. Helps 'get the deal done'.	3. Blinkers out wider or more nuanced perspectives that might be prove better in the medium to long term.
4. Unifies and builds energy among internal 'forces' by creating 'in' and 'out' or 'Us' and 'Them' groups.	4. Aggression gets taken out in other ways against 'out' groups. This can create a spiral of ill-feeling, diminishing trust, reprisals and counter-reprisals.
5. Motivates high ego-orientation or masculine types who gravitate to senior positions or engage in merger processes.	5. Can tie an organization to the ego, characteristics and addictions of its leaders, which may not be based on clear business logic.
6. Makes mergers appear dramatic, interesting and heroic. Creates publicity and high expectations.	6. Glosses over the fact that people can and will get hurt. Failing to prepare for this can lead to demoralization and feelings of betrayal that undermine post-merger cooperation.

The book that in some ways created a template for this one, *Images of Strategy* (Cummings and Wilson, 2003), started by putting forward a broad view of what a good strategy does (rather than getting too caught up on defining exactly what a good strategy is). It claimed that a good strategy both oriented and animated an organization. There seems little doubt that warspeak and the associated imagery of war has a large capacity to both animate and orient in the merger process. But what of the potentially constraining effects of such animation and orientation? In many ways these can be seen as the other side to the enabling factors. They are outlined in the paragraphs to follow and summarized in right-hand column of table 4.3.

First, while using warspeak comes easily and appears a natural fit with merger environments, this ease of use can lead to management becoming blinkered, preventing more imaginative and creative language being developed and promoted to fit the particular merger or acquisition proposed (of which we shall say more in the next section).

Second, warspeak creates an impression of action, thereby creating an impression of good leadership and management. This often becomes self-fulfilling, which helps build the momentum necessary to get things done. However, this dynamism can take on a life of its own, making is difficult to consider a more measured, 'softly, softly', or 'do nothing' strategy – even though this might be more sensible given the particularities of the case at hand.

Third, warspeak can provide focus and certainty in environments that might otherwise be chaotic. This helps build confidence and gets people moving forward. But this can shut out wider, more nuanced perspectives or manoeuvres that might be prove better in the medium to long term.

Fourth, unity can come from the creation and increasing definition of 'in' and 'out' or 'Us' and 'Them' groups that warspeak promotes. The downside of this is that pent up aggression then often gets displaced, or taken out in other ways against 'out' groups (most often the 'acquiree', but sometimes within the acquirer itself as differences of opinion are brought to a head). This aggression generally creates a spiral of ill-feeling and escalating reprisals and 'tit-for-tat' counter-reprisals.

Fifth, although warspeak can be highly motivational, particularly to those high ego-orientation types who often gravitate to senior positions or engage in merger processes, it can further tie an organization to the ego, desires and addictions of its leaders or strong personalities. These aspirations, while they may appeal to the masculine orientation outlined in our previous section, are often not based on the clearest or most explicit of business logics that would justify a merger.

Finally, while warspeak can make mergers appear dramatic, interesting and heroic (which in turn creates publicity, fervour and high expectations), this can gloss over the fact that people can and will get hurt. Failing to prepare for this can lead to demoralization and feelings of betrayal that undermine post-merger cooperation.

Indeed, as the previous section of this chapter explained, while the effects of war are mythic and sensory, the harsh sensory effects are often underplayed in a pre-merger environment because of the fact that they will probably not have to be faced directly. So, although it is well recognized in the merger literature that a history of hostility is problematic for effective post-merger collaboration, this hardly features while organizations are in the throes of pre-merger 'war'. However, warspeak soon becomes constraining in a post-merger environment as participants seek to reconcile the legacy of territorial and ideological battles, and as the pragmatic, painful effects of war (anxiety, stress, redundancies and closures) come to surface.

Placing these constraining effects alongside the enabling effects of warspeak allows us to see fairly clearly that while its consequences are often positive, pre-merger, toward 'doing the deal', these positives may turn into negatives once the merger or acquisition has been achieved on paper – negatives that diminish the ability to create value for the medium and long term. Table 4.3 demonstrates this divide between enabling and constraining effects pre and post the act. In a way, those aspects on the left drive forces to conceive of and complete a merger deal, whereas those negative effects on the right are precisely the sort of things to be avoided once the deal is done. Hence, while the result of wars may excite us, we would do well to understand the causes of warspeak outlined in earlier in this chapter and be ready to attempt to mitigate the negative effects that these causes will provoke.

The table, and our discussion to this point, suggests that consciously framing and communicating a union in terms of peaceful images and language ('friend', 'mutual', 'communal', 'harmony' or 'accord', for example) may be one way to preserve and develop value in the post-merger environment. However, table 4.3 also makes a distinction that suggests, on the one hand, that framing a proposed union pre-merger in peaceful terms may be both possible and useful in terms of reducing the post-merger negatives that warspeak can provoke when the deal is between companies who share friendly relations, or at least an indifference or non-competitiveness. On the other hand, though, given that a history as foes will have already set off a spiral of ill-feeling and escalating reprisals and counter-reprisals, and that pre-merger speculation and uncertainty will not create an environment conducive to 'burying the hatchet', it may work well for the acquirer to benefit from that war-footing and develop a plan as to how the peace can be quickly won and the negative effects of warspeak diffused after the deal is done. Our next section explores this binary relationship, between war and peace, in more detail.

Discussion: From Warspeak to 'Mergers as War and Peace'

> Only the dead have seen the end of war.
> *Plato*

> We know more about war than we do about peace – more about killing than we do about living.
> *General Omar Bradley*

> Lest we forget . . .
> *anon.*

In the 1890s, as Alfred Nobel developed the concept that was to become the 'Nobel Prizes', he and his confidants debated the proper form of a 'Peace Prize'. Nobel came to believe that offering the prize for efforts at disarmament would be futile and that it should instead reward efforts at arbitration and ending the prejudices that caused war. In a similar vein, our chapter does not advocate 'killing off' warspeak with regard to mergers and acquisitions. As Plato suggests, only the dead will no longer encounter this pervasive event and the images that it provides. As figure 4.1 at the outset of this chapter outlined, warspeak, in relation to mergers, has at least nine positively reinforcing lives. As the middle sections of our chapter explain, despite the fact that warspeak brings with it many negatives, it is also a prime mover with many positive effects. To paraphrase Christopher Hedges' thesis on war: warspeak is a force that gives meaning to merger and acquisition processes.

However, we do want to conclude by advocating greater cognizance of the pervasiveness, power, strengths and potential weaknesses of warspeak in M&A contexts and greater cognizance of the value of warspeak's alternatives: peacespeak or love-speak or arbitration-speak or reconciliation-speak. In this way, managers may begin to actively engage in greater dialogue with regard to warspeak and its effects and thus begin to develop strategies for mitigating warspeak's potentially constraining or negative effects.

A theory for enhancing greater cognizance and questioning

Greater cognizance can be aided by reviewing the ideas already put forward in this chapter. In addition, useful insights can be gained by drawing on Jacques Derrida's notions of difference and deconstruction. Derrida (1978) highlighted the inability of concepts to have meaning without the presence of opposites. The relationship between terms, he argued, is one of mutual definition, so opposites must be always already present in language. This calls into question the way in which a group of people will privilege one term (e.g. masculine, war) above another (e.g. feminine, peace) by seeing, often inadvertently, one as an advance on the other, as such privilege is not linked to any objective truth but to contingencies and traditional precedents.

The starting point of Derrida's 'deconstructive' approach is thus that moral and social beliefs are constructed on the basis of such objectively undecidable and undividable conceptual oppositions (e.g. white/black, masculine/feminine, us/them, war/peace). Hence, an existential ambivalence and uncertainty pervades our experience. To makes things more certain we structure meaning so that one half of each pair of binary oppositions is *privileged* and the other *marginalized*. Over time, such relationships become ingrained and go unnoticed in our everyday experience until we 'dig them out' and question them. Derridean deconstruction involves two steps toward this.

Firstly, Derrida seeks to highlight the halves that are marginalized as a consequence of the unquestioned privileging of their opposite, his aim being to show that: 'we are not dealing with the peaceful co-existence, but rather with a violent hierarchy. One of the two terms governs the other or has the upper hand. To deconstruct the opposition, first of all, is to overturn the hierarchy,' or reverse their meanings. This can be achieved by substituting what are seen as positive terms with negative ones in a dialogue or text. So, we might reflect on being 'white-balled' rather than 'black-balled', or a 'black knight' instead of a 'white knight' being a saviour.

Secondly, Derrida brings into play a further step: his notion of 'differance'. 'Differance' also builds from an appreciation of writing being based on binary divisions. According to Derrida, there are two ways of thinking about such divisions. One may emphasize the two separate terms, thinking in terms of hierarchical binary oppositions as described above. Alternatively, one can emphasize the actual process of division itself. The latter view enables us to see that division is not just an act of separation but is also a way in which terms are connected. In other words, divisions are both separations *and* joins. It is this alternative view, seeing division as the sharing of a 'whole' in a continuous cycle of differentiation or alternation, that Derrida wishes to emphasize here.

'Differance' means that no hierarchy can be conceived of as decided and settled as objectively true or progressive. Firstly, different communities can view the hierarchy differently. Secondly, as meanings are shaped by particular customs – and customs change – privilege can change too. Thirdly, there is a perpetual double movement *within* each opposition so that the positively valued, or privileged, term (e.g. war) is defined only by contrast to the negatively valued, or marginalized, second term (e.g. peace or reconciliation or love).

The relationship between the apparently opposing terms is therefore one of mutual definition in which the terms 'inhabit' one another to the extent that without one, the other does not exist. The noun 'normal' is a good example. The concept must incorporate the existence of the 'abnormal' in order for it to make any sense, as norms can only be recognized as such through infractions. Consequently, the claim that 'normal' or 'civilized' can be objectively seen as a later development, better, or progressive cannot be supported by appeals to logic. Each 'half' must have always co-existed, and must always be co-joined and 'competing' with one another.

It is in this sense that one can understand the thinking behind Derrida's 'differance'. His misspelling of difference is an attempt to capture not only a meaning in terms of the traditional meaning of the word as 'to differ from', but also a meaning 'to defer', as in 'to postpone'. Privileged terms, claims Derrida, not only *differ* from the terms they marginalize they also *defer* them. Yet the deferred term is only postponed, not cancelled. Consequently, no term can be conceptualized apart from its 'other': a marginalized term is always a central feature of the privileged. It can never be overcome and, as such, the tension will always be provoked, particularly if we use the terms 'un-questioningly'.

In summary, Derrida's thinking provides us with a useful theoretical understanding as to: why there is no necessary fundamental reason for the privileging of warspeak by particularly influential communities such as business journalists, academics and managers; why people can, and should, therefore, substitute warspeak for other more peace-like language and think through what the effects of this reversal might be; and why one would need to be aware that it would make no sense to think of permanently doing away with warspeak – to consider peace in mergers necessitates considering war. But, by the same token, when talking in warspeak in M&A we should also be actively considering peace.

Practical effects

Perhaps the most obvious approach to utilizing Derrida's thinking in the practical world of mergers is for academics, students, journalists and managers to take the binaries and privileged terms described in this chapter and begin to subvert and circumvent them. As Cooke (1993, p. 178) notes, perhaps one way to move beyond the masculine dynamic that advances warspeak is to parody and reverse binaries such as masculinity/femininity, so that: 'we begin to question the myth: the mystique of the unquestionable masculinity of soldiering, of the essential femininity of peace advocacy'. Similarly, we might take the fifth constraining effect outlined in table 4.3, and deconstruct the notion that privileges the type of masculine hero-leader whose ego can come to constrain an organization. Perhaps it is better at this point to think of, or look for, a leader at this point in a merger who is 'post-heroic' to use Charles Handy's term (Handy, 1989). Rather than rely on Herculean personal efforts, they seek to achieve through developing the capability of others. A view of leader sees more join than separation in the traditional leader/follower binary, seeing leadership as more about 'constellations than stars' (Procter-Thomson, 2005).

Indeed, given that it is more habitual than foundational, we can take the whole of the dynamic outlined in figure 4.1 and overturn it, by playing up the opposites that it defers. This anti-warspeak 'wheel' is shown in figure 4.2 and described in the list below. This wheel, by deconstructing the privilege unthinkingly afforded to

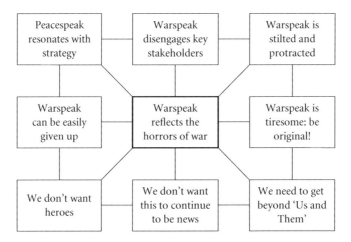

Figure 4.2   Toward 'peacespeak': an anti-warspeak dynamic

warspeak, can help engage a mindset that should aid the development of peacespeak or other metaphorical alternatives.

1. *Peacespeak resonates with strategy*   To begin, we might simply overturn the notion that warspeak resonates with strategy. Indeed, while much is often made of strategic management's military origins, it is worth noting that the position of Strategos, identified as the source of our word strategy, was as much a political position as a military one. In this respect it required subtle manoeuvring, compromise and delicate negotiation skills as much as might.

2. *Warspeak disengages key stakeholders*   While we discussed how the excitement of warspeak engaged important stakeholders, it is also useful to remember during any merger process that the conflict and uncertainty that it often musters can also disengage good employees and customers and lead them to go eleswhere. This may be a problem when it comes to realizing and building value. Hence, it might be better to frame discussions in terms of peace, continuity and reconciliation.

3. *Warspeak is stilted and protracted*   While warspeak can create a sense of dynamism, it can just as easily create slow and stilted progress, protracting and drawing out events that could be developed far more quickly through metaphors of détente and conciliation. If you are prone to seeing things in warspeak, think of World War I. Through this lens it is easy to see how warspeak can also lead to small issues becoming overblown, becoming bogged down, and endless resentment and reprisals. Case box 4.1 at the end of this chapter provides a good example of this.

4. *Warspeak is tiresome: be original!*   Warspeak may be compelling, but it is overused. Try to open up merger discourse and practice by developing different metaphors that speak more directly to exactly what you want to achieve.

5. *We need to get beyond 'Us and Them'*   While warspeak unites Us against Them, which can motivate people to attack and acquire, it should be fairly obvious that extracting maximum value from a merger requires getting beyond the us/them binary. So it might be useful to think twice before continuing to use it.

6. *We don't want this to continue to be news*   War is newsworthy; generally more newsworthy than peace. However, as somebody involved in a merger, it might be worth reflecting on whether you want this merger to continue to be in the media spotlight.

7. *We don't want heroes*   Warspeak is heroically masculine, but it is likely that at some point in a merger we would need to beyond being driven by this characteristic and substitute in other types.

8. *Warspeak can be easily given up*   War is addictive, or at least difficult to move beyond, for those actively engaged in fighting. While warspeak brings with it some of these addictive characteristics, it is always worth thinking that it could be dropped at any time. There are alternative metaphors and we are not

physically or psychologically connected to warspeak in the same way that a seasoned soldier is to war.

9. *Warspeak reflects the horrors of war*   Warspeak builds on the mythic appreciation of war in society. However, it should always be remembered that war is horrific and that, as such, it can evoke the negative sensory horrors of war (certainly for those most gravely affected) in addition to positive mythical effects.

We suggest that good managers or journalists or students should be able to be conscious of, think through, and utilize where appropriate, both of the dynamics outlined in figures 4.1 and 4.2. Indeed, they should be used in combination in attempting to mitigate against some of the worst potential effects of warspeak while not losing completely many of the positive of productive effects of its associated metaphors.

In summary, while warspeak has utility, particularly pre-deal – it seems to come 'naturally', it motivates and focuses minds, it creates energy that helps get deals done, and so on – in many situations, warspeak actually diminishes the ability to create value for the medium and long term. Therefore, by being more cognizant and able to see how we might begin to put warspeak into reverse and privilege peace-speak or anti-warspeak, we may be able to mitigate warspeak's negative effects. Case box 4.1 below, which examines the 'war' that ensued as the information technology company Oracle sought to acquire PeopleSoft, provides an opportunity to think through or debate the pros and cons on war imagery and language in a merger setting.

Conclusion

While it is impossible to provide definitive hypotheses about such a new area of research, we hope that our proposition – namely that M&A processes could be better understood were we to be more cognizant of the images conjured up by warspeak, and the alternatives, and consequently increase dialogue about its effects ('lest we forget') – has some resonance and inspires further research. As Hedges (2003) notes, one of the main reasons for the relative success of South Africa's 'Truth and Reconciliation Commission' is its will to pursue the truth about the prejudices and effects of apartheid to enable them to be aired, moved on from, but never forgotten, while not seeing its purpose as apportioning blame and prosecution (as its strategic intent makes clear: 'the conflict resulted in violence and human rights abuses from all sides. No section of society escaped these abuses.'). While we should never trivialize apartheid by making simplistic comparisons, it is true that if more were said about the pain of merger processes rather than who targeted who and who won out, this would serve to curb the glorification of warspeak and encourage the incorporation of 'the other' as quickly as possible: peacespeak and reconciliation.

Perhaps we might also be aided by what we read: in reality, while tales like *Barbarians at the Gate* and the *Illiad* get the blood up for battle, mergers, in practice, may be better thought of as an *Odyssey* – a series of difficult and nuanced challenges toward a state of peace.

CASE BOX 4.1:   ORACLE TAKES PEOPLESOFT

Oracle finally struck a deal to buy PeopleSoft on Monday, 13 December 2004. This ended an 18-month hostile takeover battle, one of the longest in history. Oracle paid US$10.3 billion, or $26.50 a share, to acquire more than 70% PeopleSoft's outstanding shares, nearly 11% higher than PeopleSoft's then share price. The transaction created a company with more than 22,750 customers and more than 53,800 employees, and vaulted Oracle to 'number 2' behind SAP in the $13.8 billion market for business applications that track inventory, management accounting and process payroll.

'This has been a long, emotional struggle,' said PeopleSoft director George Battle. The prolonged fight pitted PeopleSoft against its investors, led to the ousting of its long-serving CEO, Craig Conway, and undermined almost a billion dollars in sales according to some analysts. PeopleSoft had rejected all five of Oracle's previous bids since its first offer in June 2003. The bidding began at $16 and reached a $26 peak in February 2003 before Oracle began to reduce its offer. Conway, a former Oracle employee, fought the bid 'tooth and nail', until he was ousted from PeopleSoft in October 2003, accused of misleading investors.

On 6 June 2003, Oracle's CEO Larry Ellison announced his intention to launch a hostile bid towards PeopleSoft. Ellison's move surprised many commentators. PeopleSoft had totally different practices from Oracle. Said one observer: 'PeopleSoft is, like its products, considerably more people-centric and "soft" than Oracle's notoriously edgy and cold corporate culture, where winning matters most and where one of the industry's most aggressive sales cultures has thrived for decades.' It was thought that Oracle's culture would destroy the PeopleSoft approach to business, which was built by its founder Dave Duffield and his successor Conway. Moreover, hostile bids are uncommon in the technology sector because bidders are usually afraid that valuable technical staff will flee the target company if they don't like the new management. The timing of the bid certainly seemed to catch PeopleSoft off guard: it came just 4 days after PeopleSoft celebrated the acquisition of J. D. Edwards, an acquisition that moved it to number 2 in the market by some counts – just ahead of Oracle.

But to those who knew him, Ellison's move was totally in keeping with his character. Marc Benioff, a long-time Ellison protégé, said in *Fortune* magazine that: 'Larry's the SunTzu of the software industry. He's all about the software war. This is typical Larry Ellison Sun Tzu move. This could be real, it could not be real, but it is clearly defocusing for PeopleSoft.' In any event, according to Larry Ellison the deal was not out of blue. He claimed that he had signalled his intentions to Conway a year earlier.

'It's always possible, however,' continued Benioff, 'that Conway, himself a long-time Ellison student as a top executive at Oracle, may come up with a clever counter-strategy: like, say, a white knight bid from IBM, or maybe a successful lawsuit.'

Conway made it clear that he would fight the hostile takeover with everything he had because, in his words, 'Ellison is a brilliant tactician and a heartless one'. And indeed what ensued was a 'battle royal'.

Conway furiously refused Oracle's first offer, calling it 'diabolical' and 'atrociously bad behaviour from a company with a history of atrociously bad behaviour'. He went on to describe Larry Ellison as a 'sociopath'.

'Almost from the moment you start working [at Oracle] you learn never to let the truth get in the way of a good marketing campaign or a strong proclamation', claimed Conway – who had been an Oracle executive, remember. 'It's uncanny how quickly you get corrupted into that ends-justify-the-means mentality. They have an incredible propensity to declare things as fact, which just aren't.'

Ellison bit back. In early July 2003, he said that 'If Craigee [Conway] and Bear [supposedly Conway's dog] were standing next to each other and I had one bullet, trust me, it wouldn't be for the dog.'

Both sides carried the war into court. PeopleSoft filed a lawsuit on 13 June 2003 contending that Oracle was interfering with PeopleSoft's contracts with customers and engaging in unfair trade practices. Conway complained that: 'by making an offer with the acknowledged intent of eliminating PeopleSoft's business, Oracle seeks to disrupt PeopleSoft's efforts to complete new sales, thus effectively damaging PeopleSoft's business even if Oracle never buys a single share of PeopleSoft stock.'

Indeed, the mere threat of the deal did seem to make many existing or potential PeopleSoft customers hesitate before committing to PeopleSoft's long-term software licensing programs. In the months since Oracle first made its hostile bid, PeopleSoft's fortunes changed dramatically. The company's second quarter earnings for 2004 dropped to $11 million, a decline of 70% over the same period in the previous year. PeopleSoft's licence revenue from application software – the only specific arena in which Oracle and PeopleSoft competed directly – fell 36% to $69 million by the last fiscal quarter of 2004.

Oracle reacted by upping its offer from $5.1 billion to $6.3 billion and filed a counter-suit against PeopleSoft management for misrepresenting Oracle's efforts and unlawfully blocking the transaction.

The media were enthralled by the spectacle. *The Economist* gushed that: 'Fans of the raw-meat variety of capitalism are finding much to admire in Oracle's hostile bid for PeopleSoft, a big rival in the software business. There is the theatre: two sworn enemies slugging each other senseless.' Some called the bidding: 'Larry's art of war'.

Not to be outdone, CNN reported that: 'The fight may have become less public while the two sides wait for the Justice Department's antitrust division to figure out whether it'll let Oracle proceed, but behind the scenes this battle has only gotten nastier. The sniping has become vicious (and entertaining – a good Silicon Valley squabble is always fun to watch).'

However, Oracle's continued tactics of 'upping the ante' and 'divide to conquer' saw cracks appear within PeopleSoft, and Oracle's confidence grew as time went by. On 1 October 2004, PeopleSoft's board dismissed Conway as CEO, citing 'a loss of confidence'. He was replaced by founder and Chairman Dave Duffield.

On 25 November 2004, Oracle provocatively announced its candidates for PeopleSoft's board of directors – a plan that would allow Oracle to quickly finalize a takeover deal and take control of PeopleSoft's board once a majority of shareholders indicated they were willing to sell, even though PeopleSoft was still rejecting Oracle's offers. This had the effect of making many feel that it was just a matter of time.

After Oracle extended its fifth bid for PeopleSoft's outstanding shares, and with an escalating proxy war within PeopleSoft threatening to do further harm, Oracle finally secured a majority shareholding on 13 December 2004. PeopleSoft founder Duffield, who had replaced CEO Conway, quietly resigned on 21 December, and on the 29th Oracle announced that it had received offers of more than enough shares to take full control of PeopleSoft. Two days later, Oracle fired PeopleSoft's Co-president and Chief Financial Officer, Kevin T. Parker, and three other top executives.

The war had done plenty of damage, much of which would continue to have repercussions for many years to come. Beyond the wounds inflicted on sales over the previous 18 months, the *Wall Street Journal* reported that PeopleSoft's forecast earnings for 2004 had badly mislead Wall Street and that Oracle management was already worried that PeopleSoft's 'sucking business forward' (a kind of scorched-earth retreat), could have damaged the company's long-term viability. Charles D. Bona, analyst at Sanford C. Bernstein & Co, claimed that 'The deal [has been] a big distraction [to Oracle] and I think they overpaid.' One group delighted with what had ensued was SAP: 'The prolonged uncertain period during the takeover war between Oracle and People-Soft has helped increase customer interest in products from SAP,' said Henning Dagermann, CEO of the German company. As the dust on the Oracle–PeopleSoft deal was still settling and the outcomes uncertain, SAP rolled out a plan that let PeopleSoft customers maintain their current PeopleSoft application's support while switching to SAP products.

After winning the fight, Oracle management faced the difficult task of integrating not just PeopleSoft, but also Peoplesoft's acquisition, J. D. Edwards. It named its integration plan: 'Project Fusion'. Its first action was to announce, on 14 January 2005, the termination of 5,000 people – 9% of the combined company's workforce. When pressed by the media to break down how many of the 5,000 people were PeopleSoft employees and how many were Oracle staffers, Oracle officials declined to comment.

Questions

1. *What might the costs of Ellison and Conway's warlike approach to this acquisition be, both before and after the deal?*
2. *What forces escalated the war-like behaviour between Oracle and PeopleSoft?*
3. *What might the benefits of Ellison's bold war-like approach to mergers and acquisitions be?*
4. How would you have managed the acquisition differently if you were Oracle's management? Outline how you could have used the anti-warspeak wheel shown in figure 4.2 to think differently?

This case is written by Stephen Cummings, Sally Riad and Nathan Zhang. It contains elements of D. Kirkpatrick, 'Larry Ellison and the art of war', *Fortune.com* (12 June 2003); 'PeopleSoft Files Suit in Fight with Oracle', *New York Times* (14 June 2003); 'Barbarians in the valley; Oracle versus PeopleSoft', *The Economist* (28 June 2003); M. L. Songini, 'Oracle Makes Hostile Offer for

PeopleSoft', *ComputerWorld* (29 June 2003); D. Dirkpatrick, 'PeopleSoft CEO Fires Back', *Fortune.com* (23 July 2003); A. Dolbeck, 'Software Wars: Oracle Continues the Fight for PeopleSoft', *The Weekly Corporate Growth Report* (29 November 2004); M. Friedenberg, 'Oracle-PeopleSoft Battle's Side Effect', *Information Week* (29 November 2004); 'PeopleSoft ends fight, accepts $10.3 billion Oracle Bid', *Boston Herald* (13 December 2004); J. Pallatto, 'PeopleSoft CEO Duffield Resigns', *Eweek* (29 December 2004); 'Oracle assumes control of PeopleSoft, names directors', *Boston Herald* (29 December 2004); J. Pallatto and L. Vaas, 'Oracle Firings Bring Black Friday for PeopleSoft Staffers', *Eweek* (14 January 2005); R. B. Ferguson, 'SAP Buy Targets PeopleSoft Migration', *Eweek* (19 January 2005); L. Vaas, 'Analysts: Project Fusion Is the Death Knell for PeopleSoft Apps', *Eweek* (19 January 2005).

CASE BOX 4.2:   HP, THE OTHER HP, AND COMPAQ

On 18 March 2002, after a protracted period of 'peace' and 'war', shareholders of Hewlett-Packard voted in favour of a merger with Compaq.

The Chairman of HP, Carly Fiorina, had attempted to see the proposed merger in unusual terms. Drawing on her background in medieval history, she chose 'Heloise' as her code name for HP during the acquisition process. She named Compaq 'Abelard'. Heloise and Abelard were two twelfth-century historic figures joined in a troubled romance: Abelard, a teacher, and Heloise, his student, had a secret relationship that angered Heloise's uncle. The lovers had a child and were later married, but Abelard decided to keep the affair secret. However, eventually, Heloise's uncle learned the truth and hired helpers to castrate Abelard.

HP was founded in 1938 by two electrical engineers, William Hewlett and David Packard, in the Packard's backyard garage. It became one of the pioneers in the IT industry. In 1985, HP introduced the LaserJet printer, which quickly became (and probably still is) the company's most successful product.

HP is famous for its 'HP Way' (a set of values and principles to guide the company beyond simple financial measures initiated in 1956 by Bill Hewlett and Dave Packard). But after a long period of sustained growth, the IT industry had stumbled in late 1990s. As a result, HP was forced to cut jobs and asked employees to take unpaid leave – something that seemed to run contrary to the HP Way principles.

Although HP was a model company in many ways, some believed that it had become inbred, sluggish and out of step. In 1999, Carly Fiorina was appointed as Chairman and CEO of HP, becoming the first outsider to take charge of the 62-year-old company. Fiorina brought big changes to HP. She consolidated operating units, sheared away layers of bureaucracy, and engineered a new marketing campaign featuring a simplified '*hp*' logo. In her words: 'We set out on a process to preserve what was best about HP and reinvent the rest.' By 2001, Fiorina had realized that printers were carrying far too much of the profit load for the company. Growth had to be cultivated in other directions. In May 2001, Fiorina hired consultants to look at possible acquisition opportunities. On 3 September, Carly Fiorina announced HP's plans to acquire Compaq in a stock transaction valued at US$25 billion.

The relationship had emerged peacefully. It had grown out of a phone discussion between HP's CEO Carly Fiorina and Compaq's CEO Michael Capellas in late June 2001, and talks between the two companies appeared amicable to say the least.

'From the start, the two sides were intent on getting the deal done,' claimed Larry Sonsini, HP's leading attorney and a key player in the negotiations. Unlike many other mergers, HP wasn't looking to squeeze Compaq for the best price and send its executives packing. The talk was of HP wanting something akin to a 'merger of equals'. To protect the deal, lawyers added a number of clauses to make it hard for either side to walk away: there would be a $675 million break-up fee if either side terminated talks without a better offer; and no matter how much either stock rose or fell, there was to be no renegotiating price.

After the merger announcement, Fiorina travelled extensively around the country in an effort to win support for the merger from analysts, investors, and HP employees. Indeed, it was suggested that HP and Compaq had put together 'by far the most detailed, comprehensive merger plan the industry had ever seen'. Right from the beginning they had planned the post-merger integration process – labelled the 'Clean Room Operation'. The operation comprised 23 separate teams organizing every merger detail, from computer system to human resource.

But at 10 a.m. on 6 November 2001, a phone call from Walter Hewlett to Fiorina turned the proposed union upside down. The co-founder's son, and a member of the HP board, informed her that he and his family would publicly oppose the planned merger between HP and Compaq. Then, just hours later, David Packard Jr., the oldest son of the other Hewlett-Packard co-founder, issued a statement announcing that he would also vote against the merger.

According to Walter Hewlett, Fiorina had exaggerated the importance of scale in the computer business. In addition, Hewlett believed that rather than make the company more competitive, the merger would expose HP to the brutal, low-profit PC business. Finally, Hewlett believed that the merger would significantly dilute the value of the company's lucrative printing business. Hewlett started his own advertising campaign to convince shareholders that they should vote against the deal. His main thrust was that: 'no large-scale high-tech merger has ever worked – ever'.

David Packard used his opposition of the deal to question Fiorina's leadership of HP. He believed that Fiorina's high-handed management and her efforts to reinvent the company ran counter to the company's core values as established by the founders, citing the recent layoffs as an example. Packard commissioned and publicized a survey that showed that 63% of HP employees in the Corvallis, Oregon, area opposed the merger.

Fiorina knew that if the merger was to fail, her career at HP would certainly be in jeopardy – she would be seen as a 'lame duck' CEO. Analysts were declaring that: 'Fiorina, who had initially won accolades both inside and outside the company, had so fallen from grace that she was in danger of losing her job.'

So she fought back, going to work calling investors and planning a new round of meetings immediately. She attacked Hewlett with harsh words: when Hewlett first approached the board with his opinion of being against the merger, Fiorina called his intrusion 'an insult'. Fiorina and HP issued a letter to shareholders, calling Hewlett an 'academician and a musician', 'a man without a plan'. They stated that Hewlett did not know the business, so that he did not know what he was talking about. They asked if HP's future should rest in the hands of people 'who had never wanted an active role in their fathers' company'. It was also put about that another reason for the families being against the deal was that the incentive to preserve wealth rather than to create it was strong for the Hewletts and Packards: their HP stocks financed donations to numerous worthy causes, such as Packard Humanities Institute. A survey was done which showed that 76% of workers in Corvallis and in Vancouver, Washington, supported the merger. The Chairman of Compaq even entered the fray in support of Fiorina, using phrases like 'the battle lines are drawn' and stating that Hewlett should be forced to resign from the HP board.

The 'proxy war' was fuelled by media reports and it was claimed that the media interest became far more intense after the 'fighting broke out'. The merger was portrayed as: 'a civil war in Palo Alto'; 'the last gasp of the Bubble Economy'; and 'the triumph of a crass newcomer – HP CEO Fiorina – over the company's traditional values as embodied by director Walter Hewlett'.

After 9 months of intense internal fighting, the merger was approved. On 18 March 2002, HP shareholders voted in favour of the merger, but only by the slimmest margins: just over 2%. The war was described as 'the biggest, most costly proxy battle in American corporate history'; a battle that had exposed HP to 'a divisive, destructive public fray'. However, HP attorney Sonsini commented afterwards that: 'If anything good came out of the proxy contest, it was the time that it gave the[m] to build [their] integration plan. It also gave time for the respective management teams to get to know each other and look each other in the eye and say that they accomplished this goal and are truly committed to make the deal succeed.'

Beyond the merger there were differing views of whether the union could be called successful or not. On 11 August 2003, *Forbes* magazine wrote: 'One year into the US$19 billion purchase of Compaq Computer, HP CEO Carly Fiorina has cut US$3.5 billion in annual costs – a billion dollars more and a year earlier than promised. Despite erasing 17,000 jobs since the merger, HP has gained market share in key categories, scored 3,000 new patents, and debuted 367 new products . . . Pre-merger, HP and Compaq had more than a thousand locally set policies on such things as rebates for customers and dental coverage for employees. These they unified into a single set of rules for 160 countries. HP's post-merger PC manufacturing costs are down 26%.'

However, on 7 February 2005, *Fortune* claimed that: 'The irrefutable evidence on how wrong the [merger was] is contained in the two companies' own merger proxy, which precisely laid out the healthy operating margins that the combined company expected to be earning in its 2003 fiscal year on its computer operations. The margins weren't earned then, and in 2004 they weren't either-not by a long shot. Only the prodigious, money-coining strength of HP's star business, Imaging and Printing, has kept the company looking respectable . . . Ever since September 2001, when the Compaq deal was announced, HP shares have been a dead-in-the-water asset. Recently, at about $20 per share, HP was 13% below its price just before the merger news hit the market.'

On 9 February, Carly Fiorina announced her resignation from HP. Afterwards she commented that 'I think I was treated differently [as a woman in my role at HP]. I thought we had gone beyond that. But I think it did make a difference during the proxy battle and it does make a difference still.'

Questions

1. Do you think that Fiorina's non-war metaphor for the proposed relationship with Compaq – Heloise and Abelard – was a good and/or useful one?
2. What forces led to a war breaking out in this case? Does a merger or acquisition inevitably create an environment for war (either between or within companies)?
3. Do you think the potential for generating value was diminished by HP's internal proxy war? What advantages might have accrued had the process been entirely peaceful?
4. Would this situation have developed differently if Fiorina was 'one of the boys'?
5. Did the war within HP have any positive effects?
6. Do you think this merger could have been managed any better? If so, how would you have gone about it?

This case is written by Stephen Cummings, Sally Riad and Nathan Zhang. It contains elements of M. Williams, 'HP's Deal for Compaq Has Doubters as Value of Plan Falls to $20.52 Billion', *Wall Street Journal* (5 September 2001); 'Survey: HP employees oppose merger', *CNN.com* (20 February 2002); B. Etzel, 'H-P's Hard-Fought Victory', *The Investment Dealers' Digest* (12 August 2002); D. Tait, 'Analysis of the Hewlett-Packard Proxy Battle', *Mediate.com* (2002); A. Vance, 'HP–Compaq Merger Still Causing Discord', *PC World* (14 March 2003); Q. Hardy, 'We Did It', *Forbes* (11 August 2003); B. Shearer, 'Carly's creation: New rules in M&A proxy battles', *Merger and Acquisitions*, vol. 38, no. 7 (2003); C. L. Hoopes, *The Hewlett-Packard and Compaq Merger: a Case Study in Business Communication*, Provo: Brigham Young University (2003); P. Burrows, *Backfire*, New Jersey: Wiley (2003); C. J. Loomis, 'Why Carly's Big Bet Is Failing', *Fortune* (7 February 2005); and A. Maitland, 'Carly Fiorina', *Financial Times* (20 November 2003).

NOTES

1. In this chapter, we use the heuristic term 'merger' to discuss both mergers and acquisitions rather than to imply 'a union of equals'.
2. In developing the term 'warspeak', we were inspired by Ulf Hannerz's 'culturespeak' and George Orwell's 'newspeak'.

Chapter 5   M&A as Power

Glenn Morgan

Introduction

In this chapter, I wish to look at mergers and acquisitions from the point of view of power. My interest is not so much in what may be termed the microdynamics of power (i.e. how individuals assert their will over others; how one side of an M&A deal overcomes another), it concerns more what authors (such as Lukes (1974) and Clegg (1989))[1] have referred to as 'structural power'. By this is meant how the institutions of society (the underlying patterns of political power, authority, trust, ownership, labour relations and skill formation) pre-structure the game that individual firms and actors play. The 'game' is an appropriate analogy because games have rules defining who can constitute a 'player', how the player is constrained to act 'within the rules' and how 'victory' in the game is determined. We can see these rules as predetermined before any particular set of players begins to play. Power is already distributed by the rules themselves. Thus, in a game of chess, a queen is more powerful than a pawn. In a football game, the goalkeeper has the power to pick the ball up within his/her own penalty area, which no other player can do. In games where the players are theoretically equal, they can come into the game with significantly different powers because of natural ability, training, diet etc., though even here there are rules about what constitutes proper preparation and what constitutes 'cheating'. Of course, ultimately rules are human constructions (even the rules of chess) and they can be changed, but if the game is to proceed there must be a relative stability in the rules. The argument here is that rules are not 'neutral'. They reflect a process of social negotiation arising from social conflict between actors with differential power. The rules reflect and reproduce power differences. They are a temporary but sustainable compromise in a situation of unequal power. Fligstein (2001, p. 28)[2] has described the implications of this approach in the following terms:

> 'Rules are not created innocently or without taking into account "interests" . . . In order to get analytic leverage on real systems of rules and power, it is necessary to think

systematically about how government capacity and the relative power of government officials, capitalists and workers figure into the construction of new market rules to define the forms of economic activity that exist in a given society.'

Games are characterized by two features. Firstly, some actors are more skilful than others in playing the game and this skill can in certain circumstances counteract or neutralize more structurally powerful (but less skilful) actors. Secondly, some actors bend and stretch the rules more effectively than others. Powerful actors may bend the rules further in their favour but so may less powerful actors. In fact less powerful actors may develop this over time as another mechanism for equalizing their chances against the more structurally powerful. The bending and stretching of rules, indeed the 'cheating' in which some actors may engage, is important for the evolution of rules. It means that there is likely to be a continuous process of reinterpretation and clarification of rules that may result in changing the power relations or reinforcing them.

In relation to mergers and acquisitions, therefore, my interest is twofold. First, I want to understand how the rules of the game of M&A reflect broader social processes of power, conflict and negotiation. By the rules of the game, I am less interested in detailed legal and informal regulation of M&A processes (though these are obviously crucial) and more interested in what may be termed the level of 'meta-rules'. By 'meta-rules', I am referring to rules that structure the possibilities of specific legal regulation. These meta-rules set the limits to what is possible in terms of specific rules and their evolution. Secondly I want to reveal how these 'meta-rules' structure patterns of mergers and acquisitions in different societies. In other words, I am interested in how rules emerge in particular national contexts that then shape how the game of M&A is played within that arena.

What image of M&A emerges when we start from this point? Essentially my argument is that mergers and acquisitions are a crucial mechanism of power in the restructuring of firms and societies. Mergers and acquisitions are political phenomena. They are not just matters of concern between managers but are issues of importance for society more generally. They reflect broader struggles in society about who controls firms and in whose interests decisions are made. The argument of this chapter is that it is important to bring these political and power dynamics to the surface because they reflect real tensions in society. Managers need to understand this level of 'meta-rules' in order to understand what is possible, how this relates to power and the politics of mergers and how this is changing in the light of globalization. They need to understand that the politics of M&A differ across countries and that the key actors who can influence these processes also differ.

The chapter proceeds in the following way. Firstly it locates the analysis of mergers and acquisitions within broader theories of power and the development of capitalism, in particular linking it to discussions about 'varieties of capitalism'[3]. Secondly it provides an analysis of how the meta-rules of mergers and acquisitions can be understood in different societies and illustrates these processes with a range of examples showing that mergers and acquisitions reflect politically constituted conditions for the development of particular modes of firm development. The nature of power and conflict between different social groups is a key determinant of the factors that structure the nature and legitimacy of M&A activity in different contexts.

Discovering a Critical Approach to Mergers and Acquisitions

The starting point for my argument is the 'varieties of capitalism' approach (VoC). For these authors, modern industrial societies have evolved along distinctive paths. Although they are all 'capitalist', in the sense that the core mode of economic organization is based on the operation of markets, in their particularities, they are distinctive and divergent. A simple example of this divergence would be in terms of the role that the state plays in relation to the economy. Table 5.1 illustrates this.

From a VoC point of view, these high-level differences generate questions about the role that the state plays in these different societies. In France, for example, the high level of public expenditure reflects the important role of the state in funding healthcare, pensions, education and unemployment benefits as well as its continued participation in many core industries. The low percentage in the US reflects exactly the opposite.

Why do these differences exist? From the VoC perspective, this leads to an analysis of how different groups in society fought over the issue of the relative significance of the market and the state in determining the life chances of groups and individuals as capitalism emerged and became integrated with democratic political processes. High state expenditure generally reflects a victory of some coalition of social democratic forces, the aim of which was to limit the role of the market and instead create a common platform for welfare that is due to all members of society by virtue of their 'citizenship'. This means that the state takes on a redistributive role, taxing people to ensure that all citizens have basic rights to education, health, pensions

Table 5.1   Public sector expenditure as % of GDP

France	46.2
UK	35.9
Germany	32.7
Japan	23.2
US	19.5

Data from World Bank website: relates to public accounts around 1998–9 etc. Hall and Soskice (2003) broadly refer to this as a 'coordinated market economy' (hereafter CME). The emphasis on 'coordinated' draws attention to the way in which key actors in society (in particular, trade unions, employers' associations and the state) participate in developing institutions that limit the impact of the market in many areas of social life. These actors impose certain patterns of action on the society as a whole (e.g. in terms of state-coordinated collective bargaining, state-coordinated training, state-led investment in research and development and high-technology industries). Coordinated market economies depend on a broad societal consensus that the market leads to high levels of uncertainty and inequality which have to be ameliorated and controlled by the state and what is often called in the European context, the coordinated actions of the 'social partners'. The problem for such systems is balancing these requirements with the benefits of a market driven system (e.g. efficiency, entrepreneurialism and innovation). CMEs can take a variety of forms depending on the degree to which the state is the most powerful actor in the process of coordination. For example, France is traditionally seen as highly state coordinated. In Germany, coordination occurs more through negotiation between the social partners, with labour and capital represented through strong trade unions and employers' associations respectively. In Japan, coordination occurs within and across firms in alliance networks known as *keiretsu* and supported by the state (rather than dominated by it).

Low state expenditure generally represents the victory of social forces support-ing the market as the predominant means whereby individuals ensure for them-selves and their families their standard of living. Hall and Soskice refer to this as a 'liberal market economy' (LME), emphasizing the role of the market in the provi-sion of goods, services, labour and capital. Thus individuals have to build their own skills and careers, selling them on the labour market to the highest bidder in a con-text where the collective setting of wages and salaries through trade union bargaining is of limited significance. Similarly, they have to save for their own pensions, pos-sibly fund their own healthcare through insurance and buy their own education. Capital is provided to individuals and firms at market-based rates and there is no central direction of investment. Clearly, there are variations among LMEs, with the UK having a stronger tradition of 'citizenship' and welfare state rights than the US, though underlying both is the centrality of the market as a determinant of life chances for the individual.

Most analysts tend to agree that while there are only a few liberal market economies in the world (the US, the UK, Australia are the most obvious) and many coordin-ated market economies (e.g. most of continental Europe in various ways fits this model), the powerful trend in the battle of ideas over the last three decades has been towards a heightened legitimacy for the liberal market model. This is increasingly reflected at the international level where regulatory bodies (such as the World Bank, the IMF, the WTO) are much more likely to establish standardized practices based around a liberal market model than around a coordinated capitalism model.

Although it might be thought that M&A activity is not a 'political' issue in the sense that support for the welfare state might be, my argument is that it is nevertheless entwined within the same forces and is in effect part of the same game. For example, a brief examination of the empirical facts reveals that CMEs and LMEs have very different patterns of M&A activity and it is therefore fruitful to ask why.

In Germany (a classic example of a CME), for example, there were barely any hostile takeovers until the 1980s and very few mergers and acquisitions as a whole. Even since then, there have been very few and an even fewer number which have involved a non-German company. In the US and the UK (both LMEs), however, mergers and acquisitions are common and hostile and contested bids occur frequently. From the VoC point of view, these differences are likely to reflect distinctive underlying social and economic processes. The question is, what mechanisms of social conflict and power can explain these differences? What meta-rules of social and economic action have emerged in these societies to structure these patterns?

Varieties of Capitalism and M&A: Stating the Problem for Analysis

The starting point for our analysis is therefore relatively simple. Patterns of M&A activity varied significantly across the world's major economies up into the late 1990s. In Japanese, the word for 'takeover' means 'hijacking'. This reflects the fact that mergers and acquisitions were very rare in Japan in the 1990s and 'hostile' bids non-existent. A similar situation prevailed in Germany. The first hostile takeover bid launched in Germany occurred in 1997, when the steel producer Krupp-Hoesch made a bid for its competitor Thyssen. This raised considerable alarm and eventually resulted in an agreed merger.

CASE BOX 5.1:   THE FATE OF A HOSTILE TAKEOVER BID IN GERMANY: KRUPP'S BID FOR THYSSEN, 1997

In March, 1997, Germany's second largest steel producer, Krupp-Hoesch, made a bid for its main competitor, Thyssen, which was the largest steel producer in Germany. Krupp-Hoesch offered 25% more than the then current market price for Thyssen. Workers at both companies opposed the plans and their union backed this with the threat of industrial action. Thyssen managers also opposed the bid, as did local politicians and media. The Minister of Labour at the time declared that 'hostile takeovers are not part of the "language of a social market economy but of the language of the Wild West"'. The trade union, IG Metall, organized a demonstration of 30,000 workers in front of the headquarters of Deutsche Bank (which was one of a consortium of investment banks supporting and advising on the offer) to protest at the bank's involvement. Eventually, the regional government of North Rhine-Westphalia brought the two managements together. After an initial meeting, Krupp agreed to withdraw its hostile bid and the companies then began talks on a merger, which was rapidly agreed. Although one of the key objectives had been to restructure the German steel industry, the new management signed a joint agreement with IG Metall to the effect that there would be no compulsory redundancies during the period of restructuring of the new company. Instead there would be generous offers of early retirement, voluntary departure and transfers to other parts of the company.

In their 1998 paper, Franks and Mayer[4] state that there were only three hostile takeovers in Germany in the whole of the post-WWII period up to 1997. Two years later another notable hostile bid was launched by the UK company Vodafone for Mannesmann. What distinguished this bid was not only that it was 'unfriendly' but that it was also cross-border and involved the purchase of a long-established pillar of the German industrial establishment (i.e. Mannesmann) by a British company with less than 20 years of independent existence (this case is discussed in more detail later).

In terms of friendly mergers and takeovers, too, the numbers have remained small in Germany. For example, in the period from 1995 (when the German Takeover Commission was first founded) to the end of 1998 there were only 65 friendly mergers.

In comparison, the UK had been familiar with hostile takeovers since the early 1950s, when a small number of entrepreneurs (such as Charles Clore) and financiers (such as S. G. Warburg) had gone against the City establishment and founded the principle that such bids were an acceptable part of City life. As City historian, David Kynaston states, 'in the City of the mid to late 1960s, nothing quite caught the imagination like a juicy takeover bid, with its attendant glamour and prospective fat fees' (Kynaston, 2002, p. 327). In his study *The Rise of the Corporate Economy*, Leslie Hannah stated that between 1960 and 1969, 5,635 UK firms disappeared by merger and in the following 10 years to the end of 1979, another 3,166 firms went (Hannah, 1983, p. 178). From this period onwards, even through economic downturns, UK mergers have always totalled above 400 per year.

It is interesting to note that the US followed the UK somewhat later into the era of hostile takeovers. Goldman Sachs, for instance, one of Wall Street's premier investment banks, refused until the 1990s to advise hostile bidders, preferring instead to build its reputation and business on the basis of defending incumbent management (see Endlich, 2000[5]). O'Sullivan (2000, p. 162) states that in the US 'until the mid-70s, hostile takeovers were regarded as beyond the bounds of reputable business practice for established corporations and were largely the preserve of speculators'. However, this changed rapidly in the early 1980s as the leveraged buyout (LBO) movement got under way, driven by financial deregulation and the emergence of new forms of financial engineering, increasing shareholder activism and more aggressive investment banking firms. Although the LBO movement collapsed under the weight of its own debt and legally dubious practices in the late 1980s, the US had irrevocably

Table 5.2   UK mergers by number and by value (£millions)

Year	Number of M&A	Value of M&A
1981	452	1,144
1982	463	2,206
1983	447	2,343
1984	568	5,474
1985	474	7,090
1986	842	15,370
1987	1,528	16,539
1988	1,499	22,839
1989	1,337	27,250
1990	779	8,329
1991	506	10,434
1992	432	5,941
1993	526	7,063
1994	674	8,269
1995	505	32,600
1996	584	30,742
1997	506	26,829
1998	635	29,525
1999	493	26,163
2000	587	106,916
2001	492	28,994
2002	430	25,236
2003	558	18,679

Source: Office of National Statistics

shifted to a context where the market for corporate control was highly active and legitimate. It recovered dramatically in the 1990s through to the collapse of the dot.com boom, when M&A activity shrank down again, though by 2005 there was some recovery in the market for corporate control.

From the VoC perspective, therefore, it is clear that patterns of M&A vary significantly across national contexts. In the following section, I develop an argument about how to account for these differences by focusing beneath the firm level on the power relations between social groups.

Accounting for National Differences in M&A Patterns

In his recent book entitled *Political Determinants of Corporate Governance*, Mark Roe provides a framework for analysing corporate governance and its determinants that I shall develop in relation to the sphere of M&A.[6] Roe (2003, p. 3) states that 'how social conflict has been settled powerfully affects how firms are owned and how authority is divided'. He argues that in societies characterized by strong social democratic institutions, traditions and actors (i.e. in CMEs), employees within firms tend to be relatively powerful with extended rights and powers making them difficult to remove or change in terms of their work practices. This is augmented by broader social values and governmental strategies that tend, in Roe's terminology, to 'demean shareholder primacy, pushing firms to stabilize employment, to expand, whether or not expansion was profitable for shareholders, and to avoid change that would disrupt the quality of the workforce' (ibid., p. 27).

Roe's analysis develops what is known as the 'agency' approach to the firm but modifies it considerably in order to understand how broader issues of social conflict emerge. The agency model emphasizes that as firms grow, there is an inevitable separation of ownership from control. The issue then arises as to how the owners (the principals) ensure that their agents (the managers) act in their interests. The answer is that they have to establish forms of governance, control and monitoring that align the interests of managers with those of the owners. The problem is that managers do not necessarily share the same interests as shareholders. Managers may be more interested in the stability of their own employment, the growth in their own level of material rewards, power and status, whereas shareholders are going to be more concerned about the value of returns to their shares. The question that stems from this is obvious. What mechanisms of governance most efficiently and effectively achieve this alignment and ensure that the interests of managers and shareholders do not diverge?

In this model, the firm is basically reduced to a two-way relationship between principals and agents, as represented in figure 5.1.

Roe's argument is that the dynamics of firm governance cannot be contained along this single dimension. He introduces employees into the model as an active participant (figure 5.2). In this way, at the theoretical level, the conflict becomes triangular in nature. Employees are interested in stability of employment and high rewards for the least effort. Between shareholders and employees, therefore, there is a major conflict of interest.

As employees, managers share with the rest of the employee body an interest in stability of employment and high rewards for least effort. This is reflected in figure 5.2 by the shorter distance between employees and managers. In turn, this increases the importance to shareholders of creating mechanisms that align the interests of managers with their own because if they do not it is likely that managers

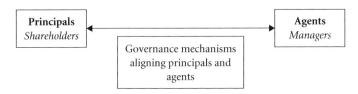

Figure 5.1 The principal–agent model of the firm

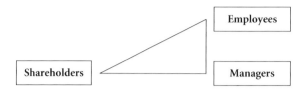

Figure 5.2   Introducing the employees into the model

and employees will form a powerful alliance against shareholders. They need to both maximize the interests of managers in supporting shareholder goals and minimize the power of employees to interfere in this process.

How do shareholders achieve this? Clearly this is fundamentally affected by the outcome of broader social struggles between capital and labour. In LMEs, as previously described, the outcome of these struggles has been to render employees weak (e.g. the collective institutions of labour are weak, legal rights to stability of employment, representation and consultation are limited, and the political power of labour's representatives in the legislature and government is weak). In such contexts, the pressure on managers to align with employees is also weak. This does not mean that managers will automatically act in the interests of shareholders but it does mean that with the development of various sorts of incentive systems (linked to the value of shares) and board-level monitoring, the gap between the interests of shareholders and those of managers can be narrowed (figure 5.3).

In such a system, shareholders (potential and actual) can in the main trust that the firm is being run in their interests and not those of employees or managers as a separate group. On this basis, savers are willing to invest in firms, confident that even if they themselves are not closely monitoring their 'agents', the system works to do this. This 'trust' expands the market, brings many savers into the market and facilitates the liquidity of the market. Dispersed share ownership facilitates 'exit', so

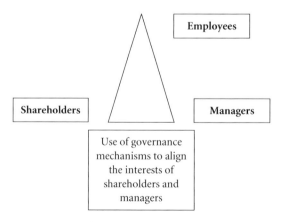

Figure 5.3   The revised model in liberal market economies where labour is weak

that shareholders know that except in exceptional cases they need not be locked into a particular company. The key point here is that this is not a 'natural' evolution of capitalism per se but the specific outcomes of the defeat of labour.

This becomes clearer when we consider contexts where employees are powerful. Employee power can be seen in the existence of strong trade unions and collective bargaining institutions at national and industry level that are dominated by concepts of occupational wage (rather than firm-level bargaining, where wages are determined more by what the firm can pay). It can also be seen in legal rights to consultation and participation in decision making. It can arise from the centrality of social democratic parties with strong trade union links to the political process. It is often reflected and reinforced in health and welfare benefits that are not punitive (in the sense of aiming to force employees back to work) but based on strong notions of the rights of the citizen. Finally, employee power can be increased by the acquisition of skills that are necessary to production and not easy to replace by acquiring new employees on the labour market. This in turn is related to the provision by the state and the social partners (of labour and capital) of strong training facilities. These characteristics, of course, appear in various combinations in different examples of coordinated market economies. The result is a discourse and set of practices about business which emphasize the rights of the employees (and society more broadly) to be taken into account. Shareholder rights have limited legitimacy and are not accorded the primacy that they have in LMEs.

What follows from this for shareholders and managers? In the first place, managers have to accommodate to employees in some way. The system cannot work without some forms of cooperation and coordination between managers and employees. How can shareholders ensure that this cooperation is not against their interests? There are limited mechanisms that they can use. The law indeed may militate against the use of some mechanisms that appear perfectly normal in LMEs but are seen as distorting the priorities of the firm in CMEs. For example, share option schemes for senior managers have only become possible in Germany the late 1990s and are still seen as somewhat disreputable in a context where the collective effort of all the social partners is seen as the essential determinant of firm performance. Similarly, in Japan, differential individual performance bonuses lack legitimacy in a context where heavy emphasis is placed on teamwork and collective effort. Thus the process of aligning the interests of shareholders and managers through the use of performance bonuses related in particular to share price is opposed and undermined by the broader social context.

So how can shareholders respond if they cannot simply implant these sorts of incentive mechanisms? Generally speaking the answer seems to be that they become more involved in monitoring what goes on inside the firm than would be the case in the US–UK model. Not all potential shareholders wish to incur the cost of this. If a shareholder has a spread of small investments, the time and effort required to engage in monitoring is not worth it. Such systems in effect discourage dispersed shareholding because potential small shareholders do not have the time or expertise

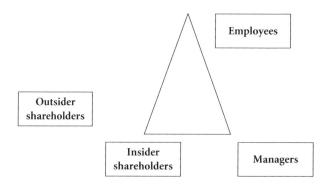

Figure 5.4 Extending the model as shareholders counteract employee power in CMEs

to engage in this monitoring. As a result, these systems tend to be characterized by a small number of investors with large shareholdings for whom it is worth engaging in the monitoring process. These shareholders become, in effect, 'insiders', engaging closely with the firm and the management in its overall direction and performance. As will be discussed, shareholders who are not part of this inside group cannot assume that this group will act in the interests of all shareholders. Therefore, we can distinguish between insiders and outsiders in these systems. This is not just a split in function but also has an impact at the level of interests. The insiders look after their own interests and not those of the outsiders. Insiders achieve private benefits from their control. Outsiders have little power and may indeed find themselves taken advantage of by the insiders. The result of this in broad terms is that shareholding tends to be concentrated in large blocks of owners who closely monitor what is going on inside the firm to ensure that their interests are being followed. These blocks tend not to be traded on the open market. Indeed, in such systems there is a tendency not to go for public listings at all, as this can potentially disrupt the insider control. The market itself has limited liquidity as a result. Outsiders are reluctant to buy in to the market where they might find themselves locked into firms where insiders are making the key decisions without reference to other shareholders. This reinforces power and control in the hands of the blocks.

The dynamics of these relationships have a fundamental impact on how the firm is organized and how it relates to broader social forces. In the following sections, I illustrate this and link it to M&A activity. For purposes of exposition, I concentrate on comparing Germany, France, the US and the UK.

CMEs, 'The German Model' and M&A

In post-war Germany, employee power has been deeply established most obviously in the system of co-determination.[7] This consists of two parts – the works councils and the two-tier board system. The German board system differentiates between a 'management board' and a 'supervisory board'. The role of the supervisory board is to monitor the decisions of the management board and take ultimate strategic responsibility for the direction of the firm. The personnel of the two boards is distinct; executives do not appear on the supervisory board, nor do non-executives appear on the management board. The link is the Chair of the Management Board who effectively is the CEO of the company[8] and represents management decisions to the supervisory board. Under the Co-determination Act of 1976, the supervisory board of any company with more than 2,000 employees must contain 50% representatives of the shareholders and 50% representatives of the employees. The Chair of the Supervisory Board, who is nominated by the shareholders' representatives, has a double vote in the event of the tie. This board structure gives employees considerable blocking power, which is supported by the existence of 'works councils' under the Works Construction Act of 1952. Works councils are elected by all the employees in a particular plant and have co-determination rights over issues such as working hours, piecework rates and bonuses, working conditions, transfers and dismissals. Works councils also have rights to be informed and consulted about any personnel issues, financial matters and major strategic changes, such as the implementation of new technology or the relocation of jobs. These rights are embedded in a broader national context where 'labour' is a social partner legitimately represented in many arenas that are coordinated through joint meetings between trade union associations, employers' associations and the state (e.g. the dual training system).

All of these features balance the relationship between shareholders, managers and workers in a particular way. Employees are powerful – they can challenge, delay and in some cases overturn decisions that are contrary to their interests. Their interests have to be taken into account. Roe (2003, p. 24) argues that this creates:

> 'pressure on the firm for low-risk expansion . . . the pressure to avoid risky organizational change is substantial and the tools that would induce managers to work in favour of invested capital . . . are weak.'

What happens to shareholders in this context? Roe's argument is that such a power structure militates against dispersed share ownership and in favour of blockholding. To counteract these effects, shareholders have to undertake a high degree of monitoring of firm-level activities. If shareholding were widely dispersed, it would not be in the interests of any particular shareholder to engage in this level of monitoring given its potential cost. However, if shareholding is concentrated, it is worth while for the shareholder to engage in this monitoring.

In Germany, this is reflected in two ways that are significant for patterns of M&A. Firstly the need to monitor closely is a disincentive to widening the shareholding base of a company. Instead, many firms remain private and family run. For example, Germany has a substantial sector of middle-sized firms (the *Mittelstand*) that avoid going public. Their capital requirements are met either out of retained earnings or through the German banking system, where long-term lending relationships with particular companies have been standard practice (the '*hausbank*' system, facilitated by a diverse banking system in which regional and local savings and cooperative banks have played a central part). This is reflected in the fact that in 2000, the stock market capitalization of German firms as percentage of GDP was just 68%, while in the US it was 181% and in the UK 201% (see Jackson, in Yamamura and Streeck (2003), p. 279). Thus there are simply not the numbers of public companies available for merger and acquisition as there are in the UK and the US.

Secondly, even in public listed companies, ownership tends to remain concentrated. In Germany a series of studies based on data from the early 1990s found similar results in terms of the concentration of ownership into blocks. Edwards and Nibler, for example, found that more than half the firms (87 out of 156) in their sample of the biggest non-financial firms in Germany, and 47 of the 105 listed firms, had a single owner holding over 50% of the equity. In the German system, holding 50% or more of the voting shares gives management control of the company, though it is worth noting that 75% of the votes are required to amend the charter of the company, change the supervisory board and alter profit transfer and control arrangements. In Jenkinson and Ljungqvist's study of all German listed companies in 1991, they found that 72% of companies were majority controlled (i.e. 50% or more of shares were held by a small number of blockholders). Another 15.4% of firms had a blocking minority and only 9.8% of firms had no significant blocks.

In itself, the block system does not, of course, negate the power of employees but it does have an important impact on where as well as how power is exercised. Basically, according to Roe, many key decisions are made outside the supervisory board by private negotiations between the blockholders and managers. Supervisory boards only meet two to four times a year. When they meet they are often presented at the last minute with the documentation for the meeting and then this may be removed from them at the end of the meeting on the grounds of confidentiality. Shareholder representatives tend to be reluctant to criticize management for fear that employee representatives will use this as a weapon. Thus, supervisory boards are very weak forms of monitoring of management behaviour because information flow is constricted and discussion and debate curtailed. One positive outcome for shareholders is that employee involvement and knowledge about the firm is minimized. The relative weakness of the supervisory board does not mean that shareholders are not consulted, but rather that they are consulted in other, less formal ways (e.g. through separate meetings between managers and the block shareholders). What emerges, therefore, is a strong alliance between the block shareholders and the management, and an attempt to keep crucial information and decision making away from employees.

This is reinforced by a more general attitude towards the release of information in the public domain. Germany has traditionally had an opaque system of financial disclosure, which has continued to allow the existence of hidden reserves and highly aggregated accounts. Both of these features mean that the exact financial position of the company and its different activities tends only to be known to the insiders. Roe (2003, p. 40) explains this as follows:

> 'Business owners in social democracies may have preferred that employees not know how well the firm was doing, fearing that when profits were high, employees would demand higher pay. They may accordingly have preferred that the publicly available information be opaque. But when information is poor, the demand rises to have owners closer to the enterprise, owners who can see through the smoke and monitor managers as well.'

The block system creates private benefits of control, which reward the insiders and discriminate against outsiders as well as neutralizing or reducing the power of employees. Edwards and Nibler (2000, p. 242) state that 'the controlling owner can secure an exorbitant director's fee, induce the firm's manager to trade with another firm (which he or she wholly owns) at prices that transfer profits to the latter or run the firm in any other way advantageous to that owner but not to general shareholders'. In cases where full control of companies has changed hands, differential prices have been paid and minority shareholders generally have received much less than major blockholders. In the past, this has been partially legitimated by the existence of different classes of shares (e.g. between non-voting shares and voting shares or by identifying a certain class of share which has greater voting weight than another class).

The dominance of the blocks within the German system means that potential bidders cannot gradually build up shares by purchases in the stock market. Instead they have to negotiate with existing blockholders to purchase existing stakes at premium prices. Koke demonstrates that this does happen on a regular basis, stating on the basis of his research that 'a new shareholder purchases a block larger than 10% in 9.9% of listed firms, on average in any given year'. He also notes that in 41.5% of the cases in his sample, a majority block is purchased and in 24%, a minority block is purchased. From this he concludes that 'new shareholders come in because they want to take over control of the respective firm' (Koke, 2004, p. 64). Until recently, such holdings could be built up in Germany with very little public disclosure. The UK rule of public tender at a fixed price once the holding went to 30% was not followed. In effect, a purchaser paid above-market rates to the majority blockholder to secure control and then offered below market rates to minorities, or even, in some cases, offered nothing, preferring to hold control without necessarily purchasing 100% of the stock.

For any shareholder not on the inside, therefore, the risks were high. They are discouraged from buying shares in the first place because their rights from share ownership may be limited. This in turn dampens the demand for shares in the marketplace. In such systems, share prices move only slowly and dividends are also limited. Insiders tend to take gains privately, balancing the requirements for industrial peace (and therefore employment stability and growth-oriented strategies) with those of serving shareholders as a whole.

Who are these blockholder shareholders? In Edwards and Nibler's study, the largest owners in 42 of the 105 listed companies were individuals/families with a mean of 57% of voting equity held in their hands. In the unlisted firms in their study, individuals/families were the largest owners in 21 of the 51 cases with the mean of their equity holdings being 82% and the median 93%. Clearly in most cases, these holdings reflect the historical origins of the firms and the unwillingness of families to lose control. Banks were the largest owners of 13 of the listed firms and second largest in 19 others. Often these holdings are part of a broader set of relationships. Thus the *hausbank* will traditionally expect to provide all money transmission services for the company as well as meeting much of its lending requirements, its corporate broking requirements for bonds, shares and rights issues, its foreign exchange and treasury needs etc. This is another private benefit of control that traditionally banks have been reluctant to give up.

The final main important category of blockholders consists of non-financial firms. These shareholdings are generally established between firms that have business connections with each other in terms of being suppliers or customers. Originally emerging as ways to pay off debts during cash shortages in the immediate post-war period, cross-shareholdings became ways of cementing alliances and cooperation between firms in closely associated regions or sectors. Thus they link together firms that are also linked by production arrangements in supply chains. As pension obligations in Germany are funded by companies, holding the assets in an interdependent network is a way of maintaining control. Again these networks offer private benefits of control to those participating in the network. For all these groups, therefore, shares are not held for their market value but for the private benefits of the control that can be achieved. It is difficult to persuade these blockholders to give up control, and, without their cooperation, M&A activity cannot occur.

Again, these sorts of features have an impact on the extent of the stock market and, more generally, its dynamics. In a recent paper, Hopner and Jackson[9] collected corporate performance data on the 19 largest UK firms and the 20 largest German firms (see summary in table 5.3). The result provides for fascinating reading in relation to the dynamics of the capital markets and M&A.

What is striking is that in terms of key indicators of real returns to capital, there is not much difference between the UK and Germany. Where the difference lies is in terms of market valuation, which is much lower in Germany even though turnover is higher. Also of significance for the argument presented here is the massive difference in terms of the number of employees in these large firms, with the German ones being much higher, reflecting the power of employees in this system. Hopner and Jackson (2001, p. 14) describe the German context as a 'low level equilibrium – low earnings and dividends corresponding to lower share prices. By contrast UK firms have higher share prices but require higher payments to investors to maintain comparable returns to capital.'

Table 5.3   Corporate performance in Germany and the UK, 2000

	Germany	UK
Price–earnings ratio	17.8	21.5
Dividend yield	2.7%	2.6%
Return on equity	18.2%	20.4%
Market valuation (€ million)	20,754	42,337
Ratio of market value to turnover	0.51	2.14
Market value per employee (€ million)	0.14	0.97
Price–book ratio	2.5	4.6
Turnover (€ million)	38,122	22,015
Return on sales (EBIT to sales)	9.4%	19.2%
Employees	138,072	60,676

Market value is depressed in Germany, as there is no significant market for corporate control, while book value is also artificially constrained by concealing information. This in turn means that companies find it less easy to become acquirers through some of the moves that are characteristic of US and UK companies. They are less likely to offer share swops (partly because their share price is not particularly high relative to underlying assets, partly because a share swop dilutes the control of the inner group and partly because the German legal system militates against this and favours cash offers). Companies tend to have to use a combination of retained cash and some borrowing for growth, thus militating against a policy of high returns to shareholders. However, as their key large shareholders are receiving the private benefits of control and are involved in the central decisions, this does not generate investor dissent or investor activism. Long-term shareholders interested more broadly in the growth of the company are able to shape decision making in ways that avoid confrontation with a strongly unionized labour force while still serving their own interests.

This German example demonstrates that in societies where labour has traditionally been powerful, both within the workplace and in terms of government and political discourse more generally, this has a particular impact on M&A activity. Firstly, mergers and acquisitions in general (and particularly hostile takeovers) are discouraged as there is an expectation that there will be negative consequences for employees. Secondly, the inevitable restructuring of capital therefore takes place in other ways. In particular, it takes place through the intervention of the core group of shareholders and, in some contexts, the state. The tendency to become a public firm with shares quoted on the stock exchange is inhibited in such societies because it is seen as opening the firm up to all sorts of potential conflicts that are best settled behind closed doors through negotiations between the founding individuals and families, their banks, their network partners and employees. Therefore these societies have a smaller level of stock market capitalization than do countries like the USA and the UK. Even in the case of firms that do go public, their ownership tends to be concentrated and these core groups of owners are highly involved in monitoring management activity. Hostile takeovers are risky because they may simply lead to high levels of conflict and politicization that make it impossible to achieve any economic gains. Agreed takeovers may occur but they are generally organized behind the scenes between core shareholders.

CASE BOX 5.2:   THE VODAFONE–MANNESMANN TAKEOVER

For many decades, Mannesmann had been a 'typical' German firm based in the engineering sector and controlled by insiders, among which the most important was Deutsche Bank (the largest bank in Germany with multiple cross-shareholdings in many of the largest German companies). Traditionally, the Chief Executive of Deutsche Bank was the Chair of the Supervisory Board of Mannesmann. Historically, employee representatives had been very powerful within the supervisory board of Mannesmann. Because of its interests in iron, coal and steel, Mannesmann was governed by a different set of co-determination laws, which gave employees even greater power than in normal German firms. Firstly, the Chair of the Board was not elected by the shareholders but had to be agreed between employee and shareholder representatives. Secondly, the Labour Director of Mannesmann had to be appointed with the consent of employee representatives. As its interests in coal and steel declined in importance, the management of Mannesmann tried to argue that it should no longer be subject to these rules. However, it was not until 1999 that the courts finally agreed that Mannesmann no longer had to follow these rules. Despite this, the Labour Director elected under these rules remained in place up to and including the period of the Vodafone takeover bid.

In the 1990s, Mannesmann expanded into mobile telecommunications. Its success in this area brought in new investors and led to it having one of the most dispersed and international ownership structures of any major German company: 60% of its owners in 1999 were from overseas and 40% from the US and the UK. This was in spite of the fact that the company was, in a number of respects, not very shareholder friendly. It did not have a listing in New York. In accounting terms, it stuck to the German system, which was very opaque and allowed the company to keep reserves hidden from its shareholders. Managerial compensation was not tightly coupled to share prices. Few shareholder value performance criteria, such as discounted cash flow, had been implemented. What attracted investors was the company's growing importance in mobile networks, particularly in Germany but also elsewhere (e.g. Italy).

It is important to note, however, that as a company, Mannesmann was a conglomerate. While 28,400 people were employed in its telecoms operations, nearly 100,000 still worked in its engineering subsidiaries in 1999. Because of the vast expansion of the telecoms business, turnover was 9 billion euros in telecoms and only 14.3 billion in the engineering businesses (even though employment was three times greater).

In 1999, its ownership structure changed again when it purchased Orange, which had been set up by the Hong Kong conglomerate Hutchison Whampoa. Orange was internationally owned, with many US and UK institutional investors having substantial shareholdings. As a result of this, Mannesmann had become very different from most other German firms in one key respect. It no longer had concentrated German ownership. On the contrary, its ownership was dispersed and international. This made it potentially vulnerable to an outside takeover in a way that most German firms were not.

Vodafone, which had been in an alliance with Mannesmann, saw the purchase of Orange as a direct attack by a supposed ally on its home market. Within weeks of the Orange takeover being completed by Mannesmann, Vodafone responded by making a hostile bid for Mannesmann. Its offer was based on a share swop. Vodafone's shares had rocketed in the previous few years as the mobile market had taken off. So too had Mannesmann's but the differential between the two had grown because of the faster rates of growth of the British stock market compared with the German one, reflecting the difference between the low-value and high-value equilibria as described by Hopner and Jackson. In 1992, Mannesmann's price–book ratio was 1.4 and it grew to 10.2 in 1999. In the same period, Vodafone had gone from a PBR of 7.7 to one of 125.5, giving Vodafone a much higher valuation relative to its real assets than Mannesmann.

Immediately, both the German government and the employees inside Mannesmann responded negatively to Vodafone's bid. Politicians at regional and federal level expressed their opposition. Trade unions that represented the engineering side of the business were particularly concerned. Vodafone made it clear that it would sell these on to other companies but from the employee point of view this was seen as likely to lead to redundancies, closures and, at the very least, uncertainties. The works council and the union cooperated to oppose the takeover. In many respects, therefore, the German system closed ranks to try to prevent the takeover.

The Mannesmann management (led by the recently appointed Klaus Esser), however, did not align themselves with these 'nationalistic' and 'job protectionist' arguments. Instead, they argued a business case, claiming that their combination of fixed line and mobile businesses had a stronger future than Vodafone's dependence on mobile networks. Esser proposed a gradual negotiated disposal of the company's engineering sections, working with the unions to find buyers for the businesses who would sustain current employment levels. The cash released from these sales would help further develop a telecoms company that spanned fixed line and mobile networks. The use of this business case was in some ways a recognition of the obvious fact that the company's owners were not traditional German institutional blockholders but dispersed international investors more concerned with shareholder value than the maintenance of the 'German model'. Esser's arguments, however, depended on a long-term perspective. They failed to convince the shareholders who were offered an immediate substantial reward for accepting the Vodafone offer. In the short term, shareholders gained some 100 million euros, constituting a 120% rise in share price between mid-October 1999 and 3 February 2000, a classic short-term gain familiar to Anglo-American shareholders but totally alien in the German context.

So alien was this that certain key managers from Mannesmann ended up in German federal court for acting against the interests of the company as a whole. Klaus Esser, the CEO, received DM31 million as an 'achievement award' on the successsful completion of the takeover. Other senior managers also received large bonuses. Esser, Joseph Ackermann (Chair of the Mannesmann Supervisory Board and CEO of Deutsche Bank) and a number of other senior executives were taken to criminal court for their actions on the basis that they had been more interested in the personal gain arising from the success of the takeover than the general interest of the company and its broad network of stakeholders. There was a serious possibility that these leaders of German industry could be sent to prison for actions that in the Anglo-American context would only have brought them praise. Although the case was eventually dismissed in 2004, it revealed the continuing deep hostility of the German public, its politicians and employees generally to the idea of takeovers. The fact that, as predicted, the engineering businesses that were sold on to other companies underwent substantial restructuring and many employees lost their jobs reinforced this hostility.

Questions

1. Why did this hostile bid succeed?
2. Did Klaus Esser do anything wrong?
3. What lessons should other British companies take from the Vodafone takeover?
4. Is there anything hypocritical about German attitudes to takeovers in their own country?

Case adapted from Hopner and Jackson (2001).

Changes in the German System

It is important to note that the German model that I have described is not static. Over the past decade, there have been substantial changes emerging, which are beginning to change the situation. In summary, these can be described as follows:

1. Employee power is being increasingly challenged by managers. The increasing problem for German firms has been that of sustaining their high costs and still making a profit when firms from other countries are catching up. As new potential sites for production with lower costs have opened up (in Eastern and Central Europe, Asia and Latin America), German companies have threatened to, and in many cases have, set up overseas production facilities. They have challenged their workforces and trade unions to change their practices and demands if they want plants to remain sited in Germany. This use of what are termed 'coercive comparisons' has led workers to accept employer demands for restructuring. Because these demands tend to be focused on particular firms and particular plants, this has undermined the traditional industry-wide collective bargaining system. Although the works councils and the supervisory board membership

of employees has not been directly challenged, there has been overall a diminution of employee power. For example, in November 2004, after six rounds of negotiations and a number of warning strikes involving about 100,000 employees, the bargaining parties at Volkswagen (VW) signed a new package of agreements on pay and job security. The compromise, which ended the 2004 bargaining round at Germany's biggest car manufacturer, included a number of concessions by the IG Metall trade union, in particular a pay freeze until 2007, in exchange for a company promise to safeguard employment until 2011 and make further investments to secure the future of German VW plants. It is estimated that the deal will save the company €1 billion per year in labour costs.

2. German companies have become increasingly internationalized. As part of this process, they have engaged in many international mergers and acquisitions (e.g. Daimler–Chrysler, Deutsche Bank–Bankers Trust (and Morgan Grenfell) and the BMW–Rover takeover). This has undermined nationalistic claims for protection against overseas predators and this argument, which was common in the Vodafone–Mannesmann takeover, is now rarely heard. This process of internationalization has also meant that the 'German-ness' of the shareholders has reduced. Over 40% of shares on the main German markets are now held by overseas investors.

3. Block shareholding is gradually diminishing in importance. Changes in tax laws mean that block shareholders can now sell their shares without being liable for the huge capital gains taxes that had previously inhibited such sales. Financial institutions such as Deutsche Bank are particularly affected by this, as they want to turn these assets to different uses and follow a more US-based model of investment banking, where shares are either managed on behalf of others or are bought and sold on the bank's own account by reference to profits that can be taken in the market. Shares in companies are not long-term assets in this model.

4. Transparency of accounts is being gradually forced on large German companies, particularly as they become more linked into international capital markets, which expect adherence to international accounting standards.

5. Reform of takeover legislation in the Securities Acquisition and Takeover Act has introduced an obligation on firms to launch a mandatory public offer for stock once they hit the 30% level. Companies are increasingly discouraged from two-tier share structures (i.e. one class of shares holding voting rights (and held by insiders) and the other class having no voting rights). Under this legislation, managers have little access to techniques such as 'poison pills' to kill off a hostile bid (in contrast to the situation in the US as discussed in a later section). However, effective control of the corporation does still require more than a simple majority: 75% of shares must be cast in favour of what is termed a 'domination agreement', which terminates the bid target and enables the merger to legally occur. At 50%, a dominant shareholder may sack the management board but cannot effect a legal merger.

Many of these changes arise from international pressures. Some of these are economic, such as the need to respond to heightened competition, the need to access US capital markets and the need to attract international investors into the German stock markets. Other international pressures are more political (e.g. the increasing EU involvement in cross-border M&A has led to standardization in a number of areas, which has undermined the distinctiveness of national systems such as Germany). There are intense debates among researchers, commentators, policy makers, shareholders, trade unions and others about the depth of such changes and their implications for the balance of power within German society.

Questions

1. What M&A activity has occurred in Germany in the last six months?
2. What role, if any, have employees and politicians had in the M&A activity?
3. Do you think the German system of M&A is basically converging on the US/UK model? If so, what factors are speeding up this change and what factors are inhibiting it?
4. If you worked in the M&A part of a US/UK investment bank, would you advocate deeper involvement in the German capital markets? What risks would you be taking?

M&A in France

It is worth just briefly considering another example of a coordinated market economy. France has some similarities with Germany but also many differences.[10] In France, employee power is less easy to define than in Germany or in the UK. Trade unionism has been significant in many large firms, though in 1995 only 10% of the employed population were members of trade unions (below even the US, with around 15%, and well below Germany with around 30%; France was the lowest in all the OECD countries). However, as Rubery and Grimshaw (2003, p. 152) state, 'trade unions occupy an important place in the economic, social and political life of France. French unions (jointly with employer bodies) administer unemployment insurance and pension funds; they participate in policy-making bodies and have seats on the boards of nationally owned companies'. French trade unions have also been split along political lines reflecting political party divisions. Hancke (2002, p. 41) states that 'organised labour never thought of itself as the representative of working class interests *within*, but always *against* capitalism instead. The resulting situation was therefore always ridden with strife.' Reforms in the early 1980s designed to introduce works councils on the German model weakened unions further as they lacked the coordinated organizational capacity to make an impact. As a result the works councils were dominated by non-unionists and rapidly became incorporated into management's views rather than providing any real opposition. In broad terms, French employees have been weak in power at the workplace level but significant on the broader political scale. While for much of the time, French workers are quiescent, they retain the old French tradition of occasionally bursting onto the streets of Paris and elsewhere in protest at changes that will undermine their power. Employers and politicians cannot afford to ignore their broader social power even if their influence in the workplace is limited.

French managers, on the other hand, are very distinctive and very powerful. A central element of this comes from the highly elitist system of education. In France, the top positions in government, industry, finance and the civil service are in effect reserved for the graduates of what are termed the *grandes ecoles*. These schools were set up in the Napoleonic era to train the most gifted pupils in the whole of France in aspects of administration and engineering. More lately, there have been a number of such schools set up specifically in the area of business. While university entrance is based on successful completion of the high school diploma and is therefore relatively open, entrance to the *grandes ecoles* is much more limited. A rigorous entrance exam has to be passed; preparation for the entrance exam requires that students study for a further year after the completion of the high school diploma. At the *grandes ecoles*, a great deal of the curriculum (beyond the particular specialism of the school) is concerned with logic and reasoning using philosophical and mathematical techniques. Graduates leave the school with a very high status, a network of contacts that will be useful throughout their lives and an approach to others that is based on a view of themselves as the meritocratic elite of French society. The graduates of the *grandes ecoles* may move between government and industry frequently – a process referred to as *pantouflage* (spinning doors, as the individual spins from one high-status position to another). Their main reference group always consists of other graduates of the system, and they are expected to support each other through good times and bad. This is a system that creates high power distance within the organization. The *patronat* (boss) of the large French company expects to make decisions in a logical and rational way and for these decisions to be followed by others. There is little consideration for the participation of others in the system. Because the *patronat* is part of the elite network, decisions are often made on the basis of broader political objectives, a fact that is reflected in the support given by the French state to many of the largest firms (treated as 'national champions').

This elite runs the government, the major financial institutions and the large companies in France. As with Germany, share ownership in large companies has in the past tended to be held by a combination of the state and the largest financial institutions. The individuals at the top of these organizations constitute a tightly knit network and conceive of themselves in terms of '*la gloire de la patrie*'. In other words, they see themselves working together to enhance France itself. Part of this task involves managing the workforce and ensuring that potential conflicts can be avoided as far as possible, while not allowing employees any direct influence on company strategy.

In terms of M&A, the state had a major role. Roe (2003, p. 67) states that:

> 'Ministry approval historically had usually been necessary, sometimes as a formal requirement, sometimes as an informal understanding, and the Ministry rarely approved a takeover without a social plan in place, one that had the offeror appropriately renouncing laying off employees. . . . Even when the state withdrew from active involvement in takeovers in 1999, it continued to condemn those takeovers that would yield "a social massacre" with "massive layoffs".'

French companies tended to protect themselves from takeovers in two ways. Firstly, many of the largest companies have blockholders, who control between 20 and 30% of the company. Bloch and Kremp's data for the late 1990s states that around 40% of the CAC 40 (the top 40 firms on the French stock exchange) had a large shareholder that possessed more that 33.3% of the shares of the company. In non-listed forms, the figure is even higher at 66% (Bloch and Kremp, 2001, p. 112). In fact, concentration is even higher than in Germany, partly because in the major privatizations of the early 1990s, the government sold shares primarily to a small group of financial institutions whom it could trust to act in the broad interest of modernizing French industry. This was known as the policy of creating a *'noyau dur'*, a hard core of owners who could be guaranteed to provide the stability to build the new companies and not pressurize them for high returns. Secondly, and associated with this, was the way in which holding company structures were built, which, through certain core cross-shareholdings, enabled a small group of individuals to control the a large number of publicly quoted companies. In terms of the models previously presented, France can be seen as illustrated in figure 5.5.

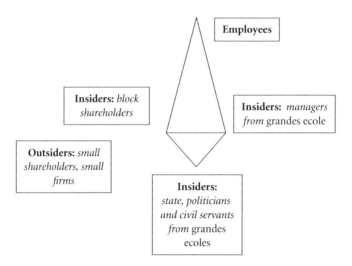

Figure 5.5   The French system: the centrality of the state and the *grandes ecoles* networks

As a CME, therefore, France shares some similarities with Germany. Employees cannot be considered powerless but their potential outbursts of opposition are counteracted by the strong unified nature of the elite. This is reflected in case box 5.3, which looks at the M&A activity of the French company Vivendi.

CASE BOX 5.3:   COMPAGNIE GENERALE DES EAUX'S CONVERSION INTO VIVENDI UNIVERSAL

The rise and fall of Vivendi Universal reveals both the strengths and weaknesses of the French system in relation to M&A. Compagnie Generale des Eaux (CGE) was founded in 1853. It was a private company that supplied initially water and sewerage. Through this it built up a wide range of political contacts at local and national level and expanded into many other areas that were funded by the state but run by private industry (e.g. cable TV, hospital and clinic management, schools and hospital catering, park management and public housing, land and property development). For many years, CGE was run by the well-connected Guy Dejouany but, at the age of 73, in 1993 he was looking for a successor.

The man he chose was Jean-Marie Messier. Messier had worked hard to become a member of the French elite, progressing from a middle-class background in Grenoble through the most prestigious of the *grandes ecoles*, Ecole Polytechnique. From there he went to another of the *grandes ecoles*, Ecole Nationale D'Administration created by De Gaulle in 1944 to provide the French civil service with an elite group of potential administrators. One hundred and twenty of France's brightest students go to ENA each year for a 27-month course. In the 1990s, the prime ministers and presidents of France were mainly ENA graduates (Chirac, Balladur, Jospin and Juppe). As a civil servant, Messier was instrumental in organizing the privatization of French state firms in the late 1980s, pushing particularly the idea that shares should be sold in large blocks to trusted members of the elite (the *noyau dur* policy) rather than dispersed among the public more generally. Following this, Messier joined Lazard Freres, the dominant investment bank in France at this time, where he further enhanced his reputation for deal-making. When he reached CGE, Messier, at the age of 37, was known as one of the brightest and most well-connected of the younger generation of the French elite.

The French elite in government and finance supported each other in the building up of their companies. This meant there was likely to be very little opposition within France to the plans of chief executives such as Messier. This had already caused problems in France in the experience of Jean-Yves Haberer, who ran the state-owned bank, Credit Lyonnais, during the 1980s. Haberer had been put in charge of the bank by the French elite and had developed grandiose plans for its development. He went on a purchasing spree across the US and Europe buying at inflated rates a whole range of companies. When these companies failed to produce the expected profits, like Messier later, he turned to his friends in the elite to support him and cover up the problems. For some time this was achieved but gradually the scandal broke and Haberer's position collapsed.

Like Haberer, Messier inherited a very powerful company in CGE that had a steady and strong balance sheet. Like Haberer, however, Messier wanted more – for himself, for his company, for France. Messier was not much interested in the core water businesses except for the cash they could supply for his planned diversification into the media industry. In terms of the French elite, establishing a global media conglomerate based in France would certainly be to '*la gloire de la patrie*' in its continuing battle with Hollywood and other Anglo-Saxon forces that were seen as threatening the French language and, through this, French culture itself. This increased, therefore, the willingness of the French elite to back Messier as he changed the name of CGE to Vivendi and began to make deals to enter the new media markets.

Vivendi established its new media identity by buying into Canal Plus, a broadcasting station that was first of all renowned for its sponsorship of the French film industry. Canal Plus also ran broadcasting channels in France and elsewhere. Vivendi also developed its mobile telecom network, Cegetel. In the midst of the broader global stock market boom, Vivendi also benefited, with its share price tripling in the 3 years up to mid-1999. The mirage of a group that spanned telecoms, the Internet, the news media and entertainment was particularly powerful at this time. In the US, the merger of AOL and Time Warner was seen as presaging a new future along these lines. Messier was gradually putting together something equivalent, though he wanted to add into that an integration with mobile phones. After discussing possibilities with Klaus Esser in the midst of the Vodafone–Mannesmann takeover battle, Messier suddenly switched sides and united with Chris Gent of Vodafone to create Vizzavi (in the process contributing to the final scuppering of Esser's defence against the Vodafone bid). Vizzavi was to be the platform whereby Vivendi's media products could be downloaded via Internet-linked mobile phones. In the wake of these announcements and the 'new economy' still surging upwards, Vivendi's share price continued to rocket – up 40% in the first 3 months of 2000.

Messier's biggest coup was his merger with the Canadian family owned group Seagrams, which in turn owned Universal Studios as well as the major record labels MCA and Polygram. This deal would give Messier a huge boost to the content he could provide on his phone, Internet, cable and TV portals. Vivendi's stake in the diversified entertainment industry globally would be secure. Again the French elite was happy to support Messier. The French flag was being planted on American soil. This was the high point of Messier's power and popularity.

In the following months, however, the tide began to turn. Firstly, the markets began to crash and 'new economy' firms that had failed to turn a profit lost value dramatically. Messier, however, continued on, paying way over the odds to seal the Universal deal and then proceeding to purchase the US cable company USA Networks, just as the markets were beginning to turn downwards. In the early stages, Messier had been able to fund his purchases through his existing cash mountain and then effectively borrowing against the expectation of the continued upward surge of his own company's shares. By 2000, he had used his cash mountain, his shares were falling, his debts were increasing and his new investments were not providing him with the returns required.

Even then, the French elite did not turn against Messier. It was only when he made two fatal mistakes that undermined his claims to be supporting '*la gloire de la patrie*' that his support began to crumble. Firstly, he moved himself, his family and the head-quarters of the firm to New York. This was seen as a drastic betrayal of his and the company's French heritage. Personal ambition and pride were luring him beyond his natural base. Secondly, and associated with this, he criticized the idea of the 'French exception' (the government policy that limited the number of foreign films which could be shown in French cinemas and on French TV – a policy which was essential to the survival of French cinema, one of the jewels in the crown of a distinctive French cultural identity). He then sacked the head of Canal Plus, Pierre Lescure. Lescure had been a champion of the 'French exception' and was seen by the French cultural elite as their main supporter in Vivendi-Universal. Employees in Canal Plus took over the TV station and broadcast messages critical of Messier – a typical example of the sort of 'direct action' that tends to happen in France when employees or other interest groups feel that they have not been consulted.

French public opinion turned against him, as did other key actors. In particular, Edgar Bronfman Jr, the scion of the Seagram family owners, who retained a seat on the board of Vivendi-Universal, saw his investment shrinking as the company's share price declined. Between the conclusion of the merger in June 2000 and December 2000, the share price fell from $115 to $75. By March 2001, the Vizzavi venture was deemed to be worthless by analysts. Following the reopening of the markets after 9/11, Vivendi's shares were down to $40. Messier was using all sorts of financial tricks to push the price up, such as buying back shares through borrowing money short-term in the hope that this would push the shares up or at least keep their price from falling for the time being. However, the situation failed to improve.

Only now did the French establishment really abandon Messier. Claude Bebear, who ran the huge insurance and investment company AXA, and who was Chair of the Vivendi-Universal board, began to use his connections to establish a coalition against Messier. Messier, however, continued to resist until eventually a personal emissary from President Chirac told him that he must go.

Many of Messier's investments had turned worthless. The only profitable ones were those that he had started with and had not managed to sell off or destroy. In the years following his resignation in 2002, the Vivendi board tried to gradually slim down the company and receive some sort of price for the assets left.

Questions

1. Why did Messier have so much power to make M&A decisions with very little accountability?
2. Why was Messier not removed earlier as his empire began to crumble?
3. Looking at large French companies with which you may be familiar, do you think they resemble Vivendi-Universal under Messier? If so, in what ways?
4. Could a British CEO ever act in the way Messier did?

This case has been adapted from the book by Johnson and Orange (2003) on Messier.[11]

The Anglo-American Model

In general terms, we can say that in both the UK and the US, labour is weak, particularly at the societal level in terms of a legitimating discourse for the participation of unions in company strategy-making but more broadly in terms of power in the workplace. Employment rights are limited and labour market flexibility and the mobility of employees is taken for granted. Trade unions can, of course, seek to ameliorate this through industrial action but this too tends to be tightly circumscribed and not supported by law or government. Employee representation in strategic decision-making (i.e. at board level) is nonexistent. At plant or workplace level, there is no equivalent of the works council system. Jacoby, a noted commentator on employee relations in the US states that 'efforts to increase employee voice in US companies confront a variety of barriers' (in Gospel and Pendleton, 2005, p. 47). These included legal restrictions in both the arena of labour law and corporate law. In general, restrictions on employees' rights are less in the UK given its long tradition of trade unionism, though changes in legislation, as well as in the conditions of employment (away from large-scale factory settings to diverse, white collar service work) have reduced trade union membership and undermined the use of strike action compared with earlier periods.[12] Compared with Germany and France, employees exert very little impact on corporate governance or M&A processes.

This weakness of employees implies that managers are potentially powerful in such a system. Thus the 'agency' problem in these systems is very different from that in the social democratic systems analysed earlier. In those systems, it was the pressure on managers from employees to provide continued and sustained employment that created the agency problem for investors and it leads to concentrated ownership to act as a counterweight. In the Anglo-American system (figure 5.6), the problem is that managers may act in their own interests and focus on growth of the business for its own sake rather than what is now labelled as 'shareholder value'. The key power struggle is not between labour and capital so much as within 'capital' (i.e. between managers and shareholders). This creates a distinctive dynamic in these societies that has profound implications for M&A activity.

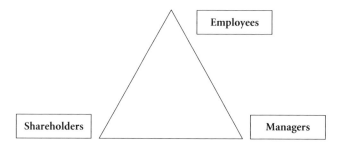

Figure 5.6   Power relations in the Anglo-American context

In the past two decades, as shareholder value has become a more dominant ideology, this power struggle has intensified. Firstly, the discourse of shareholder value has become more diffused. The reasons for this are varied but one essential element is the spread of shareholding itself. This has two elements that help differentiate the US and the UK. The first element concerns the growth of personal share ownership. Although this boomed in the UK in the 1980s and early 1990s – thanks to the massive give-aways associated with the privatization of public utilities and later the shift of financial institutions (particularly building societies) into private ownership – there has been no significant increase since then. In fact personal share ownership has slipped back. In the US, on the contrary, personal share ownership has continued to expand. Briefly during the dot.com boom, it expanded into a new cohort of 'day traders' – drawn by the low commission of online brokers and the seemingly inexorable rise of share prices – trying to beat the market by devoting themselves to multiple small trades almost on a minute-by-minute basis. The second element concerns the larger question of changing demographies and pensions for old age. In the US, individuals have increasing responsibility for managing their pension funds either on their own account or through institutional investors. This makes for a great vulnerability to stock exchange movements on the personal level. People's dependence on stock market performance has drastically increased in this environment. They have to be more conscious of stock price movements, a fact that also faces those who save in more collective funds. In the UK, the switch over to personal pensions, based on a fund invested in the capital markets, away from occupational pension schemes based on a final salary settlement, has been slower in coming than in the US. Residual expectations of state provision remain, even when governments over the past 20 years have tried to reduce these. In the UK, even with personal pension schemes, these are likely to be managed by the institutional investors who also manage occupational pension schemes and individuals are less likely (than in the US) to involve themselves in detail in managing their pension portfolio. The demand for shareholder value is driven primarily through these institutional investors in the UK, which compete against each other for business.

This demand for shareholder value has empowered shareholders in their struggle with managers. Three interconnected processes can be considered – transparency of information, management compensation systems and the market for corporate control. In each of these areas, what one can observe is that with labour absent from the picture, a broader dependence on shareholder returns for pensions and the growth of shareholder value ideology, the power struggle between shareholders and managers has increased. Arguably it is more intense in the US than in the UK for reasons that will be explored later.

Transparency of information and accounts is crucial for shareholder decision-making, both on a day-to-day basis and at moments when M&A proposals come to the shareholders. In principle, this is a foundation stone of the US and UK systems expressed in systematic external auditing and regular release of information to the markets and to regulators. Recent events in the US with Enron, Worldcom, Tyco and a number of other companies reveal that this cannot be taken for granted. Managers have been shown to conceal both suspect business dealing and the use of company funds for private benefits. Auditing firms have failed to question these areas in company accounts sufficiently strongly because they have arguably become increasingly dependent on senior managers for other more lucrative consultancy business, as was the case with Arthur Andersen and Enron. If information is not accurate and available, shareholders may be reluctant to support M&A bids. Thus in the US where this has become particularly difficult, the Sarbanes-Oxley reforms were introduced to bind managers and auditors more strongly into the accurate representation of company accounts. Similarly, pressure has been placed by US regulators on the surviving Big Four accounting firms to divest themselves of consultancy arms that might compromise the independence of the auditing function.

A second key element in this power struggle has been linking management compensation schemes to shareholder value, thereby addressing the principal–agent problem. This has generally been managed through stock option schemes, though again major problems have arisen in the practicalities of this process. Firstly, stock option schemes themselves have not been classified as expenses against company earnings. Their issuance has in effect been a charge against the capital of the company, inevitably diluting the ownership stake of the existing shareholders. Secondly, the terms of issuance of stock options have been very weakly controlled. It has been common to simply renew stock options at a lower price when existing options have been 'below the water' – in effect, rewarding failure. This relates to the fact that there is no downside risk for the stock option recipient, unlike the shareholder. They cannot actually lose money; they just do not gain it. Tight measures of performance that are capable of controlling for general trends in the market have proved difficult to enforce, once again leading to a sense that failure is being rewarded.

Interestingly, these problems have been rather differently articulated in the US and the UK. In the US, the problem has been primarily an increasingly clear understanding that stock options have become a means of robbing existing shareholders and that this can only be overcome by properly expensing them. The fact that the share option system generates massive internal inequalities in the firm (between those with the options and those without) has been of limited political interest. This reflects the broader US context in which a high level of inequality is accepted as reflecting the consequences of a society (ideologically, at least) based on achievement and meritocracy. In the UK, more concern has been on the 'fairness' of 'fat cat' bonuses where the inequality itself is an issue (reflecting British values such as 'fair play' and a lingering, if declining, sense of social democratic egalitarianism). This has been made even more political by the looseness of the performance criteria for these rewards. The sense that a relatively small coterie of top executives and institutional investors were rewarding each other by granting generous stock options has become highly political. This has led to changes in UK company law, requiring a public vote on the approval of top management compensation packages at a firm's annual general meeting. For example, in November 2002, the board of GlaxoSmithKline proposed an increase in the annual rewards package of the Chief Executive, Jean Pierre Garnier, from £6 million to between £11 and £19 million. This was in spite of the fact that Garnier had presided over a slump in share values of the company of 30% in the previous 12 months and a fall in profits over the same period of 25%. Following harsh public criticism of this proposal, institutional investors refused to support it at the AGM and the package had to be renegotiated.

These issues re-emerge within M&A contexts. In the UK, the sight of target firm managers, who have clearly underperformed the market, benefiting from a takeover as their share options increase in value and being paid large exit bonuses, creates a political backlash, undermining the legitimacy of M&A activity more generally. Such issues are less likely to occur in the US where the sense of 'looking after Number 1' is more generally accepted.

These tensions between shareholders and managers are most clearly seen in the market for corporate control. In these systems, shareholders exercise their most important power through the stock market. Moves in share price reflect expectations about future performance as well as responses to current performance. The gap between current performance and expectations provides the framework for M&A activity. Where existing managers fail to meet market expectations of what their business can deliver, share prices will fall. The wider the gap between the existing share price and market sentiment about what the business might be worth under a different management provides the space into which acquirers can insert themselves. Conversely, firms and managers consistently delivering above and beyond what their investors expect find their share price rising. This provides them with a panoply of extra weapons in the M&A business. Two, in particular, are important. Firstly, borrowing becomes cheaper – though too much borrowing obviously undermines the share price and may create a downward spiral. Secondly, because its shares are attractive to the market, it is able to build deals on share swops rather than using cash (either borrowed or in hand).

This goes together with a context in which both supply and demand are driving up the markets. In contrast to social democratic systems, there are fewer inhibiting factors holding firms back from the market. On the contrary, being quoted on a stock exchange is essential to building a profile and position that will encourage outsiders to invest in the company. On the demand side, the growing number of pensioners and those saving for their pension is continually increasing the capital available to institutional investors searching for profitable outlets. This was one of the factors driving the stock market boom of the late 1990s, pumping share prices up to previously unimaginable levels and enabling the successful companies to use their new price to develop M&A bids.

Even here, however, one needs to be careful of assuming too easily that managers and shareholders have an unequivocal shared interest in a dynamic M&A market. Strangely enough, this is particularly the case in the USA. For example, John Plender (2002, p. 113)[13] states that:

> 'American law is very friendly to the management at the expense of shareholders. A majority of jurisdictions in the US, including that of Delaware in which more US companies are incorporated than anywhere else, have enacted "stakeholder" statutes that allow managers to frustrate takeover bids at will. The deterrent vehicle . . . is the right to issue poison pill securities that make hostile takeovers prohibitively expensive. Explicit consent is not usually required from shareholders for the issue of these value-destroying securities.'

Although managers can supposedly only employ these tactics in cases where it benefits shareholders (and not just where it protects managers), Ferrarini states that 'many argue that a board can now use the poison pill to implement a "just say no" defence against a takeover' (Ferrarini, 2003, p. 243; see also Davies, 2003, pp. 279–83; see Wasserstein, 2000, for a sophisticated practitioner's account of these dynamics). Recent court decisions in Delaware have widened this latitude.

WHAT IS A POISON PILL DEFENCE AGAINST TAKEOVER?

'The poison pill makes an unfriendly takeover prohibitively expensive. The idea is simple. A corporation issues a new class of securities to shareholders that have no value unless an investor acquires a specified percentage of the company's voting stock (typically 10 to 20%) without prior board approval. If an investor crosses the threshold, the securities activate in a way that devalues the investor's stake in the company. A poison pill serves two possible purposes. First, it is a vehicle to slow the attack and provide directors and shareholders a reasonable period of time to consider a takeover bid and, if appropriate, develop alternatives . . . Secondly, the pill might be used as a means to preclude takeovers altogether. In *Household International*, the Delaware Supreme Court expressly confirmed the authority of a board to issue a poison pill as a preventive defensive measure.'

Wasserstein (2000, pp. 801–2).[14]

Plender argues that the federal system in the US is a significant factor. As company incorporation in the US is a state-level activity, states compete against each other for this business. To win the business, they basically have to convince incumbent management to come to register in their state. Increasingly, therefore, laws have been implemented at state level that benefit incumbent management against shareholders and thereby act as an incentive for the managers to register the firm in a particular state. The state of Delaware, for example, has a population of only 783,600 and ranks 45th among US states. However, it has built a new business area by encouraging managers to register their firms in the state of Delaware. It now earns a fifth of its total tax revenues from company incorporations and its laws and processes of judicial decision-making reflect this by making it easier for incumbent managers to hold out against hostile takeovers. Incumbent managements are also bolstered by laws in most US states that make it impossible to call an extraordinary meeting of shareholders or to vote out directors unless there is evidence of criminal wrongdoing in the carrying out of their role. Interestingly enough, there are also what are known as 'constituency statutes' in many US states, 'which, at least in the context of takeover bids, permit the incumbent board to abandon their exclusive consideration of the interests of the shareholders and to give equal consideration to a wide range of additional interests' (Davies, 2003, p. 282). Other tactics that incumbent managements can use include 'shark repellents' (rules embedded in the corporate charter than make an unfriendly takeover difficult and costly) and 'golden parachutes' (large contractual compensation payments to management, triggered on a change in control).

Conversely, the UK has few of these protections. 'Stakeholder' interests, even as narrowly defined as the interests of incumbent management, are not brought into consideration in the UK context. The tactics management can use to delay or deflect a takeover bid are limited to putting the alternative case in front of shareholders. Extraordinary meetings can be called by 10% of shareholders and 50% of those attending can replace any or all the directors (as happened in the case of Eurotunnel in 2004). Poison pills are generally barred in the UK. Davies states that the UK Takeover Code is 'based on "the non-frustration" rule designed to place the decision on the fate of the bid exclusively in the hands of the shareholders of the target company and to reduce the target-management to an information-providing and persuading role' (Davies, 2003, p. 280). Contested takeovers are conducted in the full glare of the market, with extensive press publicity and comment about both the business case and the personalities involved (as happened in the bid for Marks & Spencer by Philip Green).

Arguably, one of the other things that differentiates the US and the UK is that in the UK the investment banks (or the merchant banks as they used to be known) have traditionally dominated the voluntary regulatory institutions that manage the M&A process.[15] These institutions have been City-based and dominated by a concern to sustain and expand deal-making by removing constraints that might reduce shareholder enthusiasm for this (e.g. by criminalizing insider trading and stopping incumbent managers from frustrating M&A bids). Bebchuk and Ferrell (1999, p. 1192) have produced a variation on this argument:

> 'The British procedure for producing a set of take-over rules (via the City Panel) gave institutional shareholders in the UK an advantage over the representatives of management because the rule-making process was delegated by Government to the City institutions, led by the Bank of England. UK regulation is not imposed from the outside by a detached governmental body but rather by a group that has strong connections to the interested parties and that group gives less weight to managerial interests because of the close connection at least some of them had with the interests of shareholders.'

In conclusion, the argument is that in LMEs like the US and the UK, the primary issue is the relationship between managers and shareholders. In the US, although there is a powerful market for corporate control and many ways in which shareholders try to align the interests of managers with their own, there are also a number of ways in which managers can subvert this in terms of concealing relevant information and enacting 'poison pills', which inhibit the operation of the market for corporate control. By contrast, in the UK, it has proved more difficult to produce a consensus for standard forms of managerial alignment because compensation schemes have been ill thought out and have often seemed to benefit executives in poorly performing companies. The result has been that the British press, politicians and, increasingly, investors have become increasingly sceptical about the role of share options schemes and have sought to evaluate them much more carefully than previously. However, because managers do not have the same protection as their US colleagues through poison pills, they are not able to protect themselves against the market for corporate control to the same degree. As a result, the market works more effectively to discipline managers than it does in the US. This reflects the different balance of power in the two contexts. In the UK, the investment banks and their allies in the City of London have been able to impose rules facilitating an open market for corporate control on managers in stock exchange quoted companies. In the US, the balance of power of these two groups is actually more even. This is a consequence of the continuing power of the top industrial corporations in the US to set a legislative agenda favourable to themselves, particularly at local state level, where many issues are decided but also in Congress where links between local politicians and local industries are very strong. The investment banks on Wall Street, powerful as they are, are not sufficiently dominant at state and federal level to undermine the continued constraints on merger activity that can arise from 'poison pills' and other forms of takeover defence.

Conclusions

The aim of this chapter has been to consider mergers and acquisitions from the point of view of power. I have concentrated particularly on what I have termed structural power, the power in society that is shaped by the clash between dominant social groupings. I identified three main groups – employees, shareholders and managers – and argued that these groups have different degrees of power to influence the M&A process. To return to the game metaphor, actors appear on the field of play in M&A with different characteristics determined by the broader social context in which decisions about the dominance of the market and the role of the state have been taken. Indeed, it is the case that different actors appear according to these national contexts. In Germany, the difference between insider and outsider shareholders is crucial, whereas in the UK this distinction is not really meaningful and, for most purposes, shareholders can be treated as a single category. In France, on the other hand, it is important to distinguish not just insider shareholders but also their allies in management and in the state because in social terms these groups are integrated through their membership of the French social elite. So, there is no single 'chess board' or single set of rules. Depending on the context, there are different pieces on the board and the powers that these pieces have is distinctive. In Germany, employees are a significant player in M&A activity; they have to be involved and won over. In France, employees are potentially disruptive but they lack the capability to sustain a high level of involvement or influence over M&A. In the US and the UK, these actors are neither disruptive nor powerful or involved in M&A. These are different playing fields with different actors and the processes and outcomes of M&A activity vary accordingly.

To summarize, in coordinated market economies, the market has been subordinated to the interests of various groups in society. In Germany, the power of employees has had a fundamental effect on how the stock market has grown and how shares are held. This has meant that generally the social order is hostile to takeovers. This in turn leads to the system of block shareholding as the only means whereby shareholders can ensure that their interests are upheld. M&A activity is limited as share ownership is concentrated and long-term. The French example reveals that there are different forms of power that can be exerted by employees and that there are different ways in which shareholders and managers can coordinate their interests against employees. In the French context, two factors are crucial. Firstly, the state supports management as part of a broader vision of sustaining France as a distinctive cultural, economic and social system. Secondly, this vision is particularly propounded in the *grandes ecoles* and, through their education in these institutions, the French elite, across politics, civil service, finance and industry, establishes strong cooperative networks reinforced between firms by interlocking share ownership. This means that hostile mergers and acquisitions are generally avoided and the restructuring of industry occurs through coordinated action among the elite. Occasionally this process can go drastically wrong, as it did with Credit Lyonnais in the 1980s and Vivendi more recently, but it is the elite that eventually steps in and resolves the issues. Shareholders per se are ineffective, as Bronfman found with Vivendi. It is the combination of political, economic and social power that needs to be brought to bear.

Where labour is weak, the key conflict is between shareholders and managers. Here the contrast between the US and the UK revealed that there is no one structural solution to the issue of aligning shareholder and management interests. In the US, managers have retained some autonomy even though there is a very active market for corporate control. This power derives from various sources but is particularly affected by the political structure of the US and the division between federal and state level responsibilities. Corporate managements have exploited this division to provide themselves with some protection against the market for corporate control even though Wall Street investment banks are very powerful in growing and destroying companies and the careers of the executives who run them. In the UK, the investment banking community is very powerful within the economic system and company executives have little ability to shelter from the demands of the stock market, the institutional investors and the investment banks. The rules of the takeover game have been predominantly made in the City of London. In this way, it has ensured that there are no 'artificial' barriers in the market for corporate control.

In conclusion, the argument is that the underlying structure of power in a society shapes the context of M&A activity. It determines the actors who are likely to be involved and the powers that they can bring to bear on any merger or acquisition process. In many discussions of M&A, we are encouraged to see them in terms of their economic and efficiency causes and consequences. By adding the power dimension, we can see much more clearly how the underlying social structure and the political mechanisms of different societies affect a range of aspects of M&A – how often, how many, how contested etc. M&A activity has its own logic and its own specificities. Once the actors and their powers are constituted, the game can be played with varying degrees of skill and cunning, leading to varying outcomes. However, the argument presented here is that underneath the surface game, there are more permanent and long-term structures produced through politics and power. The more we understand these relationships, the better we can hope to judge future patterns in M&A activity and future debates on its purpose, significance and contribution to wider social welfare.

Questions

1. Can mergers ever be non-political?
2. What role should an understanding of political risk play in decisions on M&A?
3. Is merger regulation becoming more technical and less political?
4. Is there likely to be an equalization of M&A activity across CMEs and LMEs in the foreseeable future?
5. Examine two recent M&A deals involving firms from France and Germany buying into overseas markets. How much employee and shareholder involvement was there?

NOTES

1. The underlying link between these arguments and the theory of power emerges from a reading of Lukes' (1974) short but masterful book *Power: A Radical View*. Clegg (1989) builds and further develops Lukes' argument.
2. Fligstein (2001) develops a broader argument about how rules become institutionalized and with what effect.

3. Although within this field there are a number of different ways of referring to this phenomenon, I will use the term 'varieties of capitalism' in a generic way to refer to this approach (rather than specifically meaning the particular approach used by Hall and Soskice (2003)). For a more elaborated model of different forms of capitalism, see Whitley (1999).

4. Specialist journal articles on German corporate governance that are referred to in the text include the following (in chronological order): Franks and Mayer (1998); Edwards and Nibler (2000); Jenkinson and Ljungqvist (2001); Koke (2004). An important book is Edwards and Fischer (1994). Two edited collections that have important articles on the corporate governance of Germany as well as the other societies discussed in this chapter are Hopt and Wymeersch (2003), (particularly the chapters by Ferrarini, Davies and Hopt) and Barca and Becht (eds) (2001), (in particular the chapters by Bloch and Kremp, Becht and Bohmer, Goergen and Renneboog – on France, Germany and the UK respectively).

5. The book about Goldman Sachs by Lisa Endlich (2000) is a fascinating insight into this major player in M&A both sides of the Atlantic.

6. Mark Roe's (2003) book has been very influential in helping me frame the debate in this chapter. It includes a series of short portraits of corporate governance in different societies. See also Gordon and Roe (eds) (2004) for similar arguments. The book edited by Howard Gospel and Andrew Pendleton (2005) contains a series of very useful studies on different countries, emphasizing the relationship between ownership structures and the power of labour.

7. On Germany, the edited collection by Yamamura and Streeck (2003) is the best source of papers which show both how Germany has worked as a system in the past and the challenges it currently faces.

8. In what follows, I use the anglicised term CEO to describe this position in the German firm.

9. This information is adapted from the 2001 paper that Martin Hopner and Gregory Jackson have written on the Mannesmann takeover. Entitled 'An emerging market for corporate control? The Mannesmann Takeover and German Corporate Governance', it is available as Discussion Paper 01/4 from the German Max-Planck Institute for Research on Societies, the homepage for which is www.mpi-fg-koeln.mpg.de.

10. Bob Hancke's (2002) book provides an excellent account of the French context. Vivien Schmidt's (2002) excellent book provides more detail on the politics and economics of France as well as Germany and the UK. A good selection of chapters that describes in clear and concise terms particular national systems including France is available in Crouch and Streeck (1997).

11. A book by Jo Johnson and Martine Orange (2003) is available in Penguin paperback and is excellent reading for anybody who wants a clear and fun account of how the French elite works.

12. For more details on employment systems generally, see Rubery and Grimshaw (2003).

13. *Financial Times* commentator John Plender in his book also offers an insightful and highly critical account of the capital markets, which touches on issues of M&A at many points.

14. Bruce Wasserstein's (2000) book is full of interesting material from a practitioner who built and sold his own investment bank and has since been CEO of Lazards.

15. On the history of M&A activity in the UK, Hannah (1983) is the classic source. David Kynaston's (2002) massive four volume history of the City of London is the ultimate resort for anybody interested in the personalities and practices of finance in the UK in the modern era. (Volume 4 is referred to here.) Both of these books relate to the broader question that has preoccupied many historians and commentators: how did manufacturing capital in the UK become so subordinated to the demands of finance and the City of London, even compared with the US? A classic discussion of the issue appears in Ingham (1984).

Chapter 6   M&A as Risk
Gambling with Minds

Matthew Checkley

Chance favours the prepared mind.
Louis Pasteur

M&A activity is, at best, a gamble. On Monday, 10 January 2000, America Online (AOL) announced its purchase of Time Warner for $163 billion. This was, for its time, the largest ever merger. A young Internet company, AOL, had bought one of the world's great media firms. Two years later, $200 billion of equity value had been lost in the merged entity. Many top managers had quit. Steve Case, the inventive head of AOL, was ejected from the business he had launched. Just after 2 years from deal consummation, Ted Turner resigned as vice-chairman of AOL-Time Warner, several billion dollars poorer.[1] With hindsight, the risk had outweighed the returns.

The M&A process is near unique in strategic management for the size and speed of the *transformational* change it can bring to organizations. There is a wealth of evidence that much of this change is risky. Risks lie in wait for profitability, for employees, for buyers and suppliers, for shareholders, for competitors and for legislators.

> 'Of all the strategic planning and decision-making a corporation undertakes, a merger or acquisition of another company is one of the most important and complex.' (Schniederjans and Fowler, 1989)

The unsteadying cocktail of vast complexity, rapid execution and large stakes makes M&A fraught with risk. It is risky from – and perhaps because of – the many, disparate perspectives of actors and onlookers. Yet, poor risk management in M&A is a common source of underperformance.

I argue in this chapter that, to date, risk has been narrowly conceived in M&A. I take the position that exploring various perspectives on risk can help us to better interpret the outcomes of M&A. Furthermore, broadening our thinking might help us to appropriately avoid, control, or, *importantly*, take advantage of risk.

Figure 6.1   M&A can be a gamble

To view M&A through the lenses of risk, I explore the current state of know-ledge of risk in M&A. I then suggest how risk can be defined more broadly, and highlight where significant risks, seen broadly, appear in M&A. Next I consider what ideas are applicable to risk management in M&A. I conclude by examining how risk management might be reconceived at a foundational level.

Perspectives on risk are discussed from the literatures on philosophy, the decision sciences, chaos theory, financial economics, accounting, sociology, venture capital fin-ance, psychology, organizational science and strategic management. Illustrations and insights are drawn from M&A case studies, as well as mountaineering and boxing.

The Current State of Understanding of Risk in M&A

Part of the fascination of risk is its breadth of relevance. In common with such con-cepts as social power, knowledge, rational choice, or strategy, it is relevant or implicit to a huge range of thinking and research on M&A, and beyond. This breadth also presents a challenge. Arguably, *any* research on such important M&A topics as, for example, deal negotiation, financial performance or intergroup conflict, has risk as an implicit element. Nevertheless, this research review focuses on studies that tackle risk explicitly. The following discussion shows some of the depth and breadth of research into risk in M&A. The literature tends to be strong on highly quantified and detached analyses of the outcomes of industry-wide M&A activity. It perhaps has less to say to assist the practising M&A strategist or manager.

Risk in M&A has been modelled by researchers in financial economics, accounting, organizational science and strategic management. However, a financial market-view of risk prevails. The financially based literature is itself dominated by one theory, which, in turn, leads to one conception of risk. *Modern portfolio theory* centres on the realization that a combination of risky assets is less risky than the sum of the riskiness of individual assets. Risk is defined as the variance in asset values over time (Brealey and Myers, 1981). A young Internet company, for example, is considered to be of higher risk than a large incumbent utility company; the value of an Internet stock will typically vary more than a utility stock. To complicate matters, some financial economic literature employs more than one definition of risk. Occasionally, risk defined in terms of the variance of financial outcomes is combined with risk seen as the likelihood of some negative outcome, or 'hazard'.

Consistent with modern portfolio theory, the framework commonly employed in examining risk in M&A is the *capital asset pricing model* (CAPM) (Markowitz, 1952). Investors can eliminate some sorts of risk (i.e. '*diversifiable*' or '*unsystematic*') risk, by holding a diversified portfolio. This is because increasing the number of assets in a portfolio, the contribution in terms of risk, of each asset, measured by its standard deviation or variance, becomes less significant. Indeed, at some point it is insignificant. Other risks, such as the risk of a recession, cannot be eliminated. These are '*undiversifiable*' or '*systematic*' risks. Thus, a basket of all of the shares in an equity market will still be risky. Investors must be rewarded for investing in such a risky basket by earning returns, on average, above those that they can get on safer assets, such as government bonds. Such assets are 'safe' because there is virtually no possibility of a government defaulting on its due payments, or 'coupons'.

For each particular asset, the way it is valued depends crucially on how much the asset's price is affected by the risk of the market as a whole. This is measured by *beta*. Risky assets should earn a premium over the risk-free rate. This is equal to: beta × (market return − risk-free return). Hence the CAPM equation is:

$$\text{Return on asset} = \text{risk-free return} + beta \times$$
$$(\text{market return} - \text{risk-free return}) \qquad (6.1)$$

Much of the literature on risk in M&A has been concerned with extending the CAPM beyond stock purchases, and into corporate acquisitions. The idea is simply that if stocks or bonds can be considered as asset classes, then so are entire corporations. Companies can have a risk rating, just like their equities. On this view, diversifying the elements of a corporate conglomerate *should* be conceptually parallel to diversifying a stock portfolio. Indeed, mergers have long been seen as motivated by risk reduction via diversification (Steiner, 1975).

The CAPM provides an influential model of risk, yet research reveals findings that sit awkwardly with its predictions. The CAPM is consistent with diversification reducing overall risk. Yet, in some studies no relationship is found between mergers and reduced risk for the acquiring firm (Lewellen, Loderer and Rosenfeld, 1989). Similarly, doubt has been cast on risk *reduction* as a motive for diversifying mergers (Thompson, 1984). Mergers have even been interpreted as motivated to *increase* risk (Langetieg, 1978).

All types of merger have been shown to increase unsystematic risk. However, systematic risk can be reduced where firms are 'related'. For example, two firms in the same industry (such as car manufacture) would be considered as *related*. A firm in retail cosmetics would be considered as *unrelated* to one in engineering. However, it has also been shown that through acquisitions firms can diminish both systematic and total risk (Lubatkin, 1987). Risk can be minimized by diversifying into similar rather than identical or very different businesses (Lubatkin and Chatterjee, 1994). So-called 'related diversification' can be engineered to provide both differential responses to business cycle shifts and to minimize *operational* risk (i.e. the chance of operational underperformance) (Amit and Livnat, 1989). Generally, research suggests that some relatedness is better than none for performance (Ramaswamy, 1997).

Mergers have often been studied in terms of the 'relatedness' of the relevant firms, but a particular type of *related* merger is that leading to vertical integration. Vertical mergers are found to reduce systematic risk, especially when the acquiring firm competes in a concentrated market (Chatterjee, Lubatkin and Schoenecker, 1992). Yet, being fully vertically integrated produces higher systematic and *bankruptcy* risk (the *chance* of bankruptcy) in turbulent product-market environments (D'Aveni and Ilinich, 1992).

M&A activity creates risks not just for stock- and bondholders, managers and employers, but also for society. Mergers might be claimed to be 'anti-competitive' (i.e. not in the public interest), for example, where a firm gains a near-monopoly position through merger. This risk of M&A being *socially inefficient* falls to regulators to check. Research debates – with mixed findings – the extent to which regulation can and does meet these aims (Schnitzer, 1995).

It is argued that corporations should not focus on diversifying shareholder risk via corporate action. This is because shareholders can achieve that for themselves, simply by manipulating their stock portfolios. But there are other challenges to the mapping of the CAPM from asset classes such as stocks onto corporate entities (Chatterjee and Lubatkin, 1990). Mergers may be value creating because they can reduce *systematic* risk in a manner that stockholders cannot achieve on their own. Research has also explored the idea that managerial agency is the main point of difference between the (managerial) corporate world and simple stock purchases. Managers might act to reduce their undiversifiable *employment* risk (the *chance* of losing suitable employment) through unrelated mergers (Amihud and Lev, 1981), although these findings are disputed (Lane, Cannella and Lubatkin, 1998). Moreover, top managers' stock holdings in their employing firm are found to be associated with corporate risk taking. Here, researchers defined risk as the variance in equity analysts' forecasts of earnings per share (thereby acting as a proxy for the unpredictability of cash flows) (Wright et al., 1996).

For some firms, acquisition might also be seen as a risk-*avoidance* strategy; it can serve as a substitute for innovation. In a parallel to a 'make-or-buy' decision, firms can be motivated to acquire innovative firms, because internal innovation is risky; prone to failure, costly and slow in coming to fruition (Hitt, Hoskisson and Ireland, 1990).

Risk in M&A has been seen as variance in financial outcomes from the deal. Less common is research on the risks of M&A negotiations and deal-preparation, or post-deal integration. When analysis shifts from corporate-wide financial outcomes, so the definition of risk also shifts. More common in non-financial analysis is the use of risk as the likelihood of some negative outcome, or 'hazard'. The likelihood of being acquired has been conceived as a risk. This risk of takeover has been shown to *increase* with organizational slack, the age of the firm and having a financially trained CEO. The risk decreases for family controlled firms and firms with higher market-to-book value returns (Davis and Stout, 1992). Risks also vary with the financing terms of the deal. Paying in stock, rather than cash, for example, can push more risk onto the stockholders of the acquired firm.

But it is not just being bid-for that has been seen as a risk. With a notable symmetry, *bidding* for a firm is also conceived as a risk. Unsuccessful bids have been shown, on average, to increase the profitability of the target and reduce the profitability of the bidder (Hviid and Prendergast, 1993). Furthermore, the employment risks of M&A to managers are notable; management turnover is elevated within 4 years post merger (Haveman and Cohen, 1994). Mergers tend to destroy jobs (Nahavandi and Malekzadeh, 1988). It is not just jobs that are shed in the post-deal phase. There can also be cultural shift. Merger integration success and risk is affected by the level of 'acculturative stress'. This stress is a function of how easily each side of the merger can adapt to cultural change as a result of the diffusion of cultural elements from the other side (ibid.). Despite the challenges of organizational change, there is evidence that employees are helped by clear communications and forewarning of impending changes in the post-deal phase. A merger 'preview' can help employees (Schweiger and DeNisi, 1991). And advisers to a deal might exacerbate – rather than mitigate – risks. Investment bankers may be encouraging premia for target firms, thereby attaining higher fees. This is consistent with a conflict of interest between bankers and bidders (Kesner, Shapiro and Sharma, 1994).[2]

In summary, the conceptualization of risk in M&A has been dominated by a financial economic view. M&A activity has been seen as an artefact of modern portfolio theory, with risk most commonly defined in terms of the variance in financial outcomes from a deal. Such theory would predict that much M&A activity would *reduce* overall risk, due to a diversifying effect. Yet the M&A process is, generally, found to be a poor choice for reducing risk, with related diversification a less risky choice than unrelated diversification. So far the predictions of financial theory sit awkwardly with the evidence from M&A activity. This suggests that the conceptualization of risk in a M&A context is inadequate and needs development. I have noted that a few recent strands of literature have begun to address this need by examining the complexities of context. This stream of research, although less voluminous, has tackled a broader range of topics, including deal preparation, communication with staff, and the challenges of post-deal integration. Noteworthy is that many of these studies suggest new approaches to the conceptualization of risk. In the following section I examine in more detail the limitations of the dominant model of risk in the study of M&A.

Some Limitations to the State of the Art

Thinking about risk can unlock deep characteristics of M&A. The review of research on risk in M&A suggests as much. For example: M&A tends to increase overall risk; merely the act of bidding for a deal can change risks for both bidder and target; and many risks appear to be in the post-deal phase. But there are limitations to the view taken to date.

Much research is based in the CAPM. But the CAPM has itself come under critical review, in the context of M&A research (Harrington, 1993) and beyond (Roll and Ross, 1994). More generally, theories of risk are argued to fail to account for much of managerial behaviour (March and Shapira, 1987). Furthermore, one might ask of *some* theory that it assists practitioners. Yet there is scant evidence of M&A strategists using the M&A research literature to assist in their work. While financial outcomes are investigated, with some contradictory results, less is known about the *processes* of risk management in M&A.

There is little in the literature that engages with the relevance of corporate history or memory to risk and its management. This point is addressed in research on new models of risk behaviour (Sitkin and Pablo, 1992). The proposed model claims that risk behaviour is best understood as an outcome of risk propensity (which is itself influenced by outcome history) and risk perception:

> 'By drawing attention to historical patterns of organizational risk activity and the values of key organizational decision makers (and of the organization's culture) with respect to risk, the proposed model could form the basis for useful departures from past strategic management research, which has emphasized objective measures of risk . . . and has neglected the impact of behavioural or processable aspects of risk. One of the most prominent topics of concern to strategic management researchers in this area has been to understand the determinants of merger and acquisition activity. For example, risk propensity has been largely neglected as a predictor of how an organization approaches the potentially risky merger and acquisition process.'

Moreover, almost all research on risk examines aggregated, quantified M&A outcomes or, in contrast, it examines a few deals in great detail. But one deal might influence another (Strearns and Allan, 1996). It is possible, for example, that one deal precipitates a trend towards consolidation. The research literature understandably focuses on the risks *inherent* to M&A activity. Yet presumably the risks of doing a deal have to be weighed against the risks of *not* doing a deal. There could be an opportunity cost (and risk) to *not* engaging in M&A. (The case study on Grant Thornton at the end of this chapter discusses these points.) The analysis of M&A purely as *unitary* events – whether highly aggregated or individuated – appears, from a risk perspective, to be overly atomized.

There has been support for the hypothesis that financial synergies are a motive for mergers following negative capital shocks to that industry (Chamberlain and Tennyson, 1998). This resonates with *prospect theory* (Kahneman and Tversky, 1979) in suggesting that firms facing the prospect of below-expectation returns will become increasingly risk-seeking. If M&A activity is conceived as a *deliberate* strategic risk, prospect theory would predict that it is disproportionately favoured by troubled firms. This, in turn, could go some way to explaining the 'performance conundrum' of M&A (Angwin, 2000), in which *most* deals are shown to have been value destroying. A risk-seeking interpretation of M&A is further bolstered by the evidence that some firms are motivated to acquire businesses that generate (risky) innovation (Hitt, Hoskinsson and Ireland, 1990), although, again, there is counter-evidence (Stoughton, 1998).

The prior research on M&A focuses on outcomes. The view promulgated by most financial economic analyses can be seen as one of '*information processing*'; get the data and put them into a model (such as the CAPM) to calculate the outcome of some action. Yet, within the pre- and post-deal phases, there is human intention and politics at work (Vaara, 2003). This might involve ambiguity, deception or malfeasance. In this context, *missing* or *distorted* information is significant to the creation and management of risk. Similarly, an *institutionalized* understanding of risk (Short, 1984) is an interesting – yet largely overlooked – feature of M&A.

CASE BOX 6.1:   BLOATED OR WEIGHT-DRAINED?

I was discussing the risks of boxing with Paul, my boxing trainer. In his view, the big risks (which are not inconsiderable, given that they feature permanent brain damage and death) originate not so much in the fight itself, but from 'preparation'. Paul's point was that if being punched hard really is the cause of the worst injuries in boxing, one would expect that heavier – and harder hitting – boxers would suffer most. Yet, almost all of the tragedies have been in the middle and lighter weight divisions. Paul explained that boxers, particularly in the lower weight classes, come under considerable pressure to be at a precise weight for their class at the time of the pre-fight weigh-in. It is not uncommon for fighters to mismanage this process badly and still be overweight a few days prior to the fight. They need to lose weight quickly. This can be achieved by

Figure 6.2   Deal making and boxing

sitting for hours in a sauna, avoiding food and drink, and taking diuretics. However, dehydration leads not just to weight loss, but also to a general weakening of the body and to a change in the state of the brain – a condition known collectively as being 'weight-drained'. It is these (pre-fight) hard-to-detect alterations that amplify the risks of brain damage.

Perhaps this process of needing to *appear* in a certain 'condition' for a big event – yet dangerously mismanaging the preparation – is not exclusive to boxing. A friend working for a mid-sized engineering firm learned that his company might be acquired by a large utility company. The potential acquirers sent over a team to perform 'due diligence', with a focus on the finances. Because his job involved overviewing the management of major projects, the billing systems, and the financial accounts, my friend believed this was a troubled firm, financially, strategically and managerially. He guessed most of this negative potential would become evident to the potential buyers through the due diligence process. Some of it became so. However, it quickly became apparent that the acquirers had already decided what an excellent purchase the firm would be. What he saw as acute risks were glossed over. The deal went ahead, to the great relief of his management team. They had spent almost all their energy for several months in making the prospective deal appear as attractive as possible, chiefly by tightening cost controls and accelerating the billing process. Yet, the next few years saw deep regret from the acquirers. They missed almost every financial target for the enlarged group, due largely to the profound underperformance of this acquisition. My friend's interpretation as an 'insider' was that the utility company management did not care to examine the downside risk of their prospective purchase. The thrill of doing the deal, and a desire not to rock the boat once the due diligence had been launched, caused a costly error of judgement.

As in boxing, preparation for the big (M&A) event can make contenders appear to be in better condition than they really are. Preparation can involve deceiving ourselves, as well as others. Perhaps the more 'objective' measures of readiness to perform – such as body weight, or financial outcomes – are only a small part of the whole story.

The financial economic view of risk is explicit in linking risk taking to value creation. But, in common with most risk analyses, it deals in historical data. Yet, for the strategist, value creation means taking a future-looking view of risks and their management. Risk *management* deals with future scenarios, yet most risk *analyses* deal with historical data.

To conclude, the dominant financial economic models of risk (used in most M&A risk research) have come under critical review. Moreover, most prior conceptualizations of risk in M&A fail to account for both corporate history, and how that influences risk and its management. Prior research on M&A also has little to say about how strategists must anticipate *future* possibilities to manage risk. Prospect theory engages somewhat with 'history' and might be used to explain the oftentimes negative relationship between risk and returns from M&A. Furthermore, prior models of risk analysis have tended to emphasize an 'information processing' methodology. Yet, where managerial intentionality meets organizational complexity, there can be ambiguity, politics and even deception. Risk and its management, in this context, cannot be reduced to pure information processing. Finally, M&A activity has been seen in atomized terms – deals have been studied as unconnected to other deals. Yet evidence from M&A research and case studies suggests that deals *are* interrelated. This must have implications for the risks of M&A.

A Broader View of Risk

The restrictions in the prior conceptualization of risk suggest the introduction of some alternatives. Risk can be seen more broadly, without losing traction with what 'matters' in M&A. Research on risk in domains other than the finance and strategy of M&A has employed a range of definitions and models.

> 'A review of risk models in other academic fields indicates that variance, size and nature of outcomes, probability of loss, failure to attain targets, ruin, and lack of information are common ways to conceptualize risk. In strategic management, variance, innovation and ruin concepts of risk have been used.' (Baird and Thomas, 1990)

The broader literature tells us that risk can be variously defined; it shows 'pluralism'. But its meaning is not thereby insipid. There are common themes in the definitions. All characterizations are ultimately tied to notions of probability. Risk concerns balancing possible gain against potential loss. All notions connect us with a *future* we might wish to influence. Risk is linked to the value we place on conceivable 'states of nature'. Outcomes might be cash flows, business won or lost, or, more subjectively, pride, shame, revenge or glory.

The picture of how people perceive risk is elaborate. There is evidence that different people perceive risks differently, and differently over time, and that individuals' risk perceptions do not fit purely rational models (Kahneman and Tversky, 1979). There is also evidence of risk perception becoming institutionalized. Institutions can be seen as producing risk, or, in contrast, reliability (Short, 1984).

Risk is implicit to many other ideas, each of which is itself basic to interpreting and managing M&A. Skill, adventure and exploration, creativity and innovation, excitement, trust, fear, hope, competition and strategy are all unintelligible without underlying risk. As John Adams (1999) put it, 'The number of different kinds of risk is as great as the number of adjectives that might be applied to behaviour in the face of uncertainty.'

Risk is reflexive. Risk management is always concerned with the future. Yet risk assessments are historic. When risk is managed, the future differs from the past. Put another way, the act of managing risk involves, typically, changing the nature or outcomes of risk. In the field of risk, measurement and activity changes what is later measured and acted upon.

Resonating with much of Western philosophy, research into risk has been preoccupied with dualisms. We can learn of the risk seeker and the risk averse, the risk taker and risk bearer. Risks can be objective or subjective. Risks might concern binary outcomes, such as deals won or lost. Or risks could concern outcomes that are distributed over a spectrum, such as cash flows, which can be positive or negative and also take many different values. We can read of damaging risk (a source of inertia or ruin), or beneficial risk (a source of vitality or opportunity).

In summary, risk analysis connects us with differently valued futures in which we weigh-up (quantitatively or otherwise) the likelihood and nature of outcomes. It can be as dynamic and as plural as people; their states of mind, traits, values, interactions and contexts. Risk critically underlies much of M&A activity. There is risk in M&A seen as exploration, seen as political development, or as psychological change. Risk underlies many other concepts, such as innovation, fear and strategy.

What risk is not

There are limitations to the prior treatment of risk in M&A. These have been used as a springboard to a wider view. However, having explored a bigger picture, it is worth considering how broad the expanded canvas *could* be. What are the boundaries of risk as a concept? Clearly, risk has discriminatory analytical value. It *cannot* be applicable to *everything* in M&A. This section briefly considers what risk, conceptually, cannot be.

Risk cannot be understood purely as impending misfortune. Disaster that is inevitable cannot be said to be a risk. Nor can risk be understood purely as lack of knowledge of 'how things work'. Mathematical models of some financial market systems are said to be 'chaotic' or indeterministic. Even when all the 'laws' and initial conditions of chaotic operations are known, they still produce unpredictable outcomes.

Research has focused on the quantification of risk. It might be said to have been seen as 'calculable'. Yet, all risks cannot be wholly detached from subjective values.

Not all conceivable outcomes from M&A – such as changes in status or job satis-faction – are easily quantified or objectified. Indeed, most risks seen in the strategic management of M&A are dynamic and *incalculable* (following precedent (Knight, 1921), the term *'uncertainty'*, rather than *'risk'*, might be applied to much of M&A activity; I maintain the commonplace use of the term 'risk'). Risk, despite being virtually omnipresent in any strategic analysis of M&A, is unyielding to *compre-hensive* description. Certainly, the risk we *feel* when faced with the career and organ-izationally endangering or enhancing events of M&A is worlds apart from what we could read in a text. *'Risk in the wild'* eludes total explication.

Finally, risk analysis is not the 'golden bullet' for managing M&A. Thinking about it is engaging insofar as it unlocks value, however 'value' might be defined. It is impossible to wholly detach the idea of risk from other fundamental ideas, such as trust, power or knowledge (Nooteboom, Berger and Nooderhaven, 1997). Risk analysis must, at a minimum, be married to the constitution of strategic value in M&A. Risk is just one complex image in a larger montage.

To conclude, risk is not inevitable misfortune. Nor is it reducible to a lack of information. It is not wholly explicable, static; nor is its 'control' a managerial panacea. But its value as a concept lies at the heart of M&A.

Three Ways of Seeing Risk

I have argued that risk can be seen as a richer idea than is typical in most prior analyses of M&A. Exploring a fuller conception might, in turn, enrich our under-standing of M&A. To highlight risks that are under-represented in the literature, and by way of temporary expedient, I now categorize risk in three ways (follow-ing John Adams' (1999) work in this area – see figure 6.3). Each category is largely distinct, yet overlapping. I will later argue that fixed and predetermined categories of risk analysis can be as much part of the 'problem' as the 'solution'. But for now I want to emphasize how risk *in M&A* might be seen afresh.

Firstly, some risk can be seen as directly perceptible, or *'objective'*. For example, it is objectively risky (to life, limb and vehicle) to attempt to drive a car around a sharp mountainside bend, in icy conditions, at 120 miles per hour. Similarly, it is object-ively risky (to career, cost control and data integrity) to attempt to fully integrate two large corporations' IT systems within one day. Objective risk provides research and analysis with a limited role. The risk is clearly apparent to the risk-taker (by definition) and no amount of semantic nuance or calculative refinement makes that risk appear materially different.

Secondly, some risk can be seen as *'estimable'* through systematic investigation or research. For example, infectious diseases might only be perceptible through scientific investigation. We might use microscopes and biochemicals to test for the presence, absence or alteration of infection. The record of reducing many diseases,

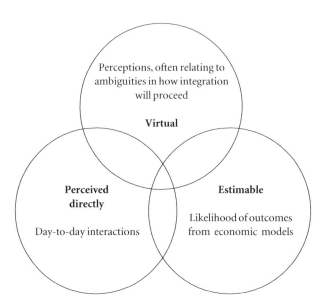

Figure 6.3   Three kinds of risk, with examples
Source: Adapted from John Adams (1999)

such as cholera, attests to the success of science in identifying and reducing certain risks (hazards, in this case). Similarly, vertical integration in turbulent product-markets is estimably risky relative to mergers in general. Knowledge of such a relation presumably has *some* benefit to those exposed to M&A risks. These risks are, in some sense, estimable; that is, perceptible via science, study and research.

Thirdly, risk can be unknown, inestimable, or '*virtual*'. Where 'experts' fail to agree on the nature of a risk, interested parties put a meaning on the uncertainty. Hence, whether the risk is real or not, it can have real consequences. People will respond to their meaning or interpretation of risk. Virtual risk is perceptual and, as such, comes via 'cultural filters' and is influenced by social interaction (Adams, 1999). It might be said to be 'socially constructed'.

Obvious examples of worldwide virtual risks can be found within the topics of BSE, global warming, the use of the contraceptive pill, the threat from terrorism, the consumption of fat, sugar or salt, the use of many vaccines, and even exposure to the mass media. Each of these virtual risks has had widespread consequences for the choices people make; what they eat, how they vote, where they travel, what they spend, who they associate with, and even their state of mind.

In the world of virtual risk, we are left with the unnerving realization that almost any kind of novel and unquantifiable challenge might be perceived as deeply risky by some parties, and not at all by others. Perhaps some middle managers of a newly merged entity have heard a rumour that they are to be made redundant. Moreover, how they respond to the perceived threat can affect its likelihood. They have little basis for estimating their risks yet, within the managers' domain, and for the success of the entire deal, such perceptions can be of vital importance.

Virtual risk is more prevalent than might at first be believed. In studies of post-deal integration (Vaara, 2003), for example, we learn of highly complex political, personal and cultural reasons for difficulties. These affect outcomes; they influence the success or failure of the deal. And yet the individuals concerned are not quantifying outcomes and their probability. They are dealing with ambition, frustration, fear, hubris or anxiety. These emotions often relate to the uncertainties of the interactions with the 'other side' of the integration effort. And, just as the risks of driving a car are increased by other drivers, so risks can become magnified by *interactions* with other risk-takers. One experienced post-acquisition integration manager put it this way, 'My management beliefs are driven out of social concerns . . .'. M&A managers have to deal with inestimable risks. I next explore the hitherto submerged intuition that *virtual* risk is central to M&A management.

Sources of Risk in M&A

Research on M&A is clear – it is risky. Over half of deals lead to value destruction (Angwin, 2000). Some lead to bankruptcy; some lead to social trauma for participants (Angwin, 2000). Prior research is also consistent in relating risk to a few dimensions of M&A activity. These dimensions tend to emphasize *pre-deal* conditions. For example, risks vary with the level of relatedness, 'cultural difference', and innovativeness of the participating firms. Furthermore, risk is significant in post-deal integration. Research has discussed high management turnover, psychological stress and operational risk. This section focuses on *why* M&A is risky, with an emphasis on *sources* of virtual risk. These sources are drawn from the defining characteristics of M&A. Virtual risk is fostered by the special nature of M&A. M&A activity tends to create uncertainty through its high stakes, vast complexity, conflicts of interest, and rapidity of organizational change. I now elaborate on these themes.

M&A has been described as the market for managerial control (Jensen and Ruback, 1993). It is highly illiquid. There is in many prospective deals a risk of foreclosure. Secrecy and speed is paramount. This causes a rapid acceleration in the numbers of advisors hired to help close the deal. And once a deal is signed, there is then a rapid acceleration in the size and variety of the communities of practice – such as operations, marketing, sales or accounting teams – affected.

CASE BOX 6.2:   NO TURNING BACK

'To the climb the world' was how two young British mountaineers – Joe Simpson and Simon Yates – described their driving ambition. That passion had brought them to the Peruvian Andes in the spring of 1985, to climb the remote 21,000 ft (6400 m) peak of

Suila Grande, using a new route – the West Face. The compelling tale of their misadventure, *Touching the Void* by Joe Simpson, is now famous as both a best-selling book and a critically acclaimed film docudrama.

The pair had an aggressive strategy for the climb. They planned to climb 'Alpine style'. This involves no preparation of multiple camps, each higher than the last, in the manner of climbs in the Himalayas. Instead, Suila Grande was to be climbed with minimal equipment, in three or four days, in a single push from their camp at the foot of the range. They described it as, '. . . a very committing way of climbing . . . you have no line of retreat . . . there's no margin for error'. This style of climbing also brings, '. . . an element of risk back . . . it takes you out of the humdrum, and makes you feel more alive'.

The two friends were successful, reaching the summit on the third day of the ascent. This is the point at which climbers can allow themselves feelings of triumph, and relief. Portentously, however, they knew that, '80% of accidents happen on the way down'.

After beginning the descent, Joe crashed through unstable ice, to be left with an agonizingly broken knee. The already nerve-grating descent was made even more challenging by the injury. This contributed to another accident. Joe later fell again; within seconds he jarred to a halt, separated from a fall into the void – and oblivion – by just the single climbing rope linking him to his partner. Simon was, in turn, slowly being dragged off the steep icy slope by Joe's weight, towards the edge. Simon's terrible choice, after

Figure 6.4   Risks can come after the 'high point'

hours of struggle in the darkness, was to remain bound to Joe and risk falling with him to his death or to cut the rope and – in all probability – kill Joe. The rope was cut.

The next few days saw an incredible tale of survival. Miraculously, Joe fell on an ice bridge within the huge crevasse below. With the horribly smashed leg, shock, exhaustion, frost bite, and little hope of ever climbing up and out of the crevasse, he later – extraordinarily – managed to discover, and inch towards, an escape hole closer to the base of the crevasse. A tortuous 3-day crawl back to camp, over harsh terrain, and suffering extreme dehydration, finally brought safety. Joe and Simon were reunited 4 days after the lifeline had been severed. Joe had lost one-third of his bodyweight during the climb, and required six operations on his knee.

The glorious moment of reaching the summit is the stuff of dreams for mountaineers. They are on top of the world. That event is most celebrated by climbers and the public alike. Something similar might be said of the signing of the deal for a large merger or acquisition. There is fanfare. The press gathers and announcements are made. Almost invariably, chief executives make statements of how this is an historic moment, heralding a brighter future of growing opportunities.

Despite the panoply, where do the greatest risks of the deal lie? Research shows us that certain pre-deal conditions – such as the premia paid to acquire firms – have some bearing on longer term financial success (Sirower, 1997). But considerable evidence points to difficulties in the post-acquisition phase as being the main cause of merger underperformance (Haspeslagh and Jemison, 1991). Ominously, mountaineers experience their moment of glory just prior to the greatest risks of serious misfortune. Could M&A be similar? We can have plans, hopes and dark fears for both M&A deal-making, and the final ascent of a summit. Both endeavors are risky. Mistakes for climbers can mean incredible suffering. M&A post-deal integration can lead to culture clash, psychological distress, commercial disruption, loss of corporate memory and managerial talent. Yet, in both endeavors, the greatest dangers come after the high point, when there is no turning back.

Much of this early-stage planning is top–down. The deal is conceived in the minds of the acquiring management team or their advisers. Decision making is by the few, on behalf of the many. This engenders risk. Research has shown, for example, that smaller groups are more prone to error than larger groups (List, 2003). Groups might also be more risk-taking than individuals. Studies (Kogan and Wallach, 1966) report the phenomenon of 'risky shift', which suggests that groups choose riskier decisions than individuals in isolation.

Once a target is selected, the team of advisers grows, and then interacts with the soon-to-be acquired management team and their advisers. But advisers can be both 'disconnected' from the context of the deal, and they might have incentives at odds with those of the deal managers (Kesner, Shapiro and Sharma, 1994). Following the 'signing off', announcements can be made to the equity markets, staff, suppliers and buyers, and the business press. But most of these interactions are unidirectional. The deal originators are essentially *telling* relevant parties how things will change.

Yet, even in good acquirers, there are two common weaknesses. These are risk analysis (especially of downside risk; the chance and scale of hazard) and external communications to interested parties.

A further defining characteristic of M&A is the scale and speed of *change* that it brings to participants (Angwin and Savill, 1997). One M&A manager described how 'It's important to remember that most real changes are made by people who don't like change . . . we even had a founding manager of an acquired firm doing his best to wreck the integration efforts.' Seen by these lights, M&A activity is risky *because* it imposes substantial, rapid organizational change on communities of practice, yet it can come without a matching level of social interaction between those affected (Vaara, 2003). Without much time, knowledge or guidance, participants are left to stare into the lacuna between themselves and the future. In this context, virtual risk is rife. And, because virtual risk can grow with *interactions* within and between other virtual *risk-laden* practitioner groups, it also balloons at each inflation of the number and type of affected parties.

In summary, risks are known to be high in many areas of M&A; certainly post-acquisition integration can entail major operational, financial and strategic risks. But virtual risk is argued to be prevalent because M&A activity is special. It is privately conceived and planned by small numbers of top managers, along with 'external' advisers. The resulting organizational changes can be deep and rapid. But the changes required of practitioner groups are rarely matched to a suitable level of guiding social interaction with managers and other relevant parties. Communities

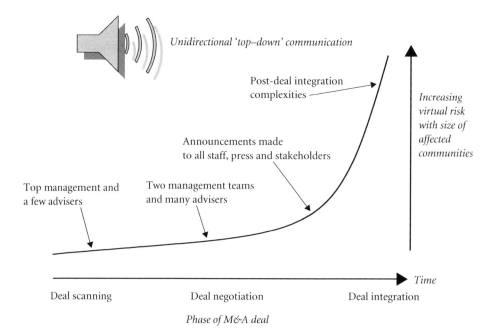

Figure 6.5   M&A increases virtual risk

of practice can be left not knowing how or why to adjust to change. All of this, in turn, results in incalculable, virtual risks, as evinced by the loss of managerial talent and 'corporate memory', demotivation and malfeasance.

The Basis of Risk Management in M&A

Risk and its sources in M&A can be reinterpreted. M&A risk management can therefore *also* be reinterpreted. I have argued so far that risk management (in general, and in M&A research) has traditionally centred on quantification and control. This is related to the prior focus on *estimable* risk. 'Standard' rationalist models, using, for example, the historical probabilities of some hazard, are commonplace. For example, the view underlying the CAPM is one of calculating financial outcome variances. The 'optimal' balance of risk and reward for a company can be achieved by increasing or decreasing M&A activity (or its inverse, 'divestments') in target businesses that show appropriate financial metrics. There is scope for refining this 'measure-and-control' approach. There is also scope for changing it.

Refinements to the traditional approach to risk management might come from adapting the methods of other, high-risk environments. For example, the use of performance-contingent contracts is commonplace in venture capital (Sahlman, 1990). This is regarded as a particularly risky sector of business activity, with venture capitalists described as risk managers above all else. M&A proffers fertile ground for extending contractual risk-management techniques. Similarly, ideas can be adapted from other risk-focused sectors, such as the insurance industry. This sector might be seen as redistributing (or 'sharing') risk in society in order that policy holders are better able to take 'healthy' risks (Arrow, 1965). On this view, insurance becomes a kind of societal lubricant. Perhaps rethinking risk management in M&A can, in parallel, support the transformation of industries and technologies. Businesses will be able to shift their boundaries and explore new possibilities – via M&A – with greater ease.

The measure-and-control approach can be refined. Or it might also be fundamentally re-thought. Following my prior line of argument, the management of virtual risk must engage with the cultural biases or *perceptions* of those who create value in M&A. Value is often created by *experienced* communities of practice, such as sales teams or research and development staff. It *might* be possible to measure and control risky behaviours, but the perceptions and biases underlying them can only be inferred. The lone means to managing risk created perceptually is to work with perceptions. The only individuals qualified to anticipate how perceptual risks might be managed are the individuals themselves. Yet, like the ability to create value, risk perceptions are known to be partly based on hard-won experience (List, 2003). Therefore, and notwithstanding some managerial leadership and intervention, risk management, on this view, must be *grounded in the hard-won experience* of practitioners relevant to realizing value in M&A. Insofar as virtual risk and value are created collectively by institutions or communities of practice, so these *shared meanings* become significant.

The subtle challenge for M&A managers is that the control-orientation of contractual, financial or statistical techniques could *counteract* attempts to manage risk, and especially virtual risk. Contracts are said to be 'incomplete'. The result is that a contractual or financial measure is rarely, *in the wild*, wholly detached from perceptions and unknown risks. And where virtual risks are more prevalent, there is likely to be less managerial 'traction' via contracts or financial manipulation. Put directly, when human intentionality interacts with risk-management techniques, there is potential for an undesired outcome.

For example, in the domain of road safety, it has been found that road signs warning of forthcoming hazards are prone to make drivers *less* risk-averse where such signs are absent. Similarly, statistics from UK roads suggest that the use of driver safety belts tends to successfully decrease in-car risks (the chance of death or injury), but the resulting feeling of security for drivers makes them *less* careful in their interactions with other road users. Safety belt legislation has pushed traffic-related injury from inside to outside the vehicle (largely onto pedestrians and cyclists). There has been little or no overall reduction in accident rates. And in venture capital finance, contracts can be overly restrictive, causing problems for investee-entrepreneurs in highly unpredictable businesses (Sahlman, 1990). An example from M&A management is that of using a 'stay-bonus' – a measure to motivate important managers to remain with the newly merged entity. Potential outcomes of this measure are that managers who would be better to quit will stay, merely to receive the bonus, and those that stay may distort firm performance to ensure the bonus is paid. Each of these cases provides an example of how *a detached view of risk can remain suspended in practice*.

In summary, there can be virtue in both the quantified, control-style approaches to risk management engendered by estimable risk *and* the socially constructed, interactive approaches engendered by virtual risk. More sophisticated approaches to estimable risk might be adapted from other sectors, such as venture capital or insurance. But, risk management *in the wild* is ultimately tied to virtual risk. To ignore this fact is to chance producing polices with either no benefit, or undesired outcomes. On this view, the emphasis in risk management should shift from its measure-and-control origins to find a new balance. This could come via working with the perceptions of individuals, institutions and communities of practice. Risk management becomes more about relying on *practitioners' experience* to anticipate, choose and manage risk.

New Foundations for Risk Management

I have argued so far that established conceptions of risk in M&A offer insights. Prior research has been dominated by the pursuit of calculable risks, which are then susceptible to rational decision-making responses. The CAPM provides just such an approach. Because these approaches emphasize 'objective' data, they might be described collectively as '*objectivist*'. But they are limited. Other, less commonly discussed ways of seeing risk also offer insight. Most of these 'newer' ways are socially constructed, particular, incalculable and dynamic. The concept of *virtual risk* captures much of what is little evident in the broader risk literature. Virtual risk is argued to be both significant and to have been largely overlooked in prior discussions of M&A management. To reason for virtue in all these ways of seeing risk is to argue for – some kind of – *pluralism*. To reason that different views of risk are more powerful when combined into one analysis is to argue for – some kind of – *connectionism*.

There is a gulf between models of risk in M&A, and what practising managers can usefully *apply* to the particularity of their circumstance. Prior models offer little on narrowing the chasm between *abstraction* and *located* action. Moreover, the prior research emphasis on abstraction can – when applied – *do violence* to the integrity of practice. For example, safety belt legislation in the UK resulted in the most vulnerable, most health-conscious, most eco-friendly road users – pedestrians and cyclists – becoming even *more* vulnerable. Largely predetermined venture capital contracts have resulted in entrepreneurs being hampered in pursuing new markets and technologies, due to contractual restrictions on their 'emergent' entrepreneurial context. The use of the CAPM in determining M&A strategy would likely fail in its own terms – research suggests that such a policy could result in an *inverse* relationship between risk and reward. In the huge merger of Compaq and Hewlett-Packard in 2002, the 'numbers' made sense, and risk analyses were performed, but many critically important managers departed.[3] Something *fundamental* is missing from standard approaches to risk.

To take seriously the argument that decades of work on risk analysis has *not* worked well for M&A practitioners is to need to ask *why?* This chapter has suggested an underlying explanation: the established understanding – of what *kinds of risks* are important – is in error. Attempts to apply established models of risk will be *frustrated in practice*. I have argued for the importance of perceptual, experiential, institutional and community-based understanding in risk analysis and management. Ultimately, M&A activity is a product of the mind; its risks are the products of many, interacting minds. These embodied elements of risk in M&A are *as important* as objectivist factors. Objectivist analyses emphasize abstraction, the quantification of large-scale outcomes, rational choice and control. But discrete and theoretical viewpoints on risk can remain suspended in practice.

Meaningful and workable risk management must therefore engage with the particularities of circumstance in a way that can elude predetermined abstraction (including the categories of risk presented in this chapter). Pluralism and connectionism imply that M&A risk managers are most strategically effective when *moving plastically* between different approaches to risk. Risk managers should occupy a '*middle ground*'. (This expression of a 'middle ground', and related ideas of a 'successor foundation' and 'experiential groundedness', owe much to Brian Cantwell Smith's (1996) work.)

For example, suppose that value creation from a deal depends on retaining certain R&D personnel. The risk of losing disaffected staff has been identified. An incentive-based 'approach' to this risk is devised: provide 'stay-bonuses'. However, using 'local' knowledge, it is believed that some staff will leave in any case, and, furthermore, some are happy to stay under likely circumstances. This leaves a portion of managers who might be usefully incentivized to remain in their current roles. The risk then appears that those who receive the 'stay bonus' will – consistent with 'equity theory' (Adams, 1963) – make the others appear disfavoured, and so de-motivate them. In the face of more *located* knowledge, the original *detached* plan is recast to provide stay-bonuses to the entire R&D team, but to tailor the size and nature of the bonus to each case. This simple example illustrates how risk might be managed by *combining* levels of knowledge. It suggests the value in working back and forth, between *detached, theoretical* views, and *particular, perceptual, 'local'* understanding, in order to combine them. I argue that this approach to risk – in the middle ground – has been largely absent, both in prior research, *and* in the practice of risk management in M&A.

To summarize, there is virtue in the enmeshing web of risk-management practice. However, alone, this can engender a stunted parochialism. There is *equal* virtue in the withdrawal of abstraction. However, alone, this can engender a rootless cosmopolitanism. Managers are made most effective by blending these approaches; by working in the *middle ground*. Fixed or predetermined categories of risk analysis or action would make this plasticity unworkable. This chapter has attempted to broaden the discussion of risk in M&A, and to focus on approaches grounded in experience, perception and dynamic communities of practice. The argument has been for a *balance* and a *connection* between practical, *in the wild* risk management in M&A, and abstract models relevant to risk. Whether M&A risk is found in financing terms, staff retention, IT systems integration, or customer care, *more* of the management of risk should be grounded in *practitioners' hard-won experience.*

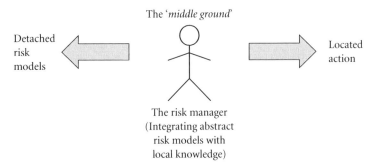

Figure 6.6   Risk is best managed from the 'middle ground'

Summary and Recontextualization of Risk in M&A

This chapter has maintained that risk is a powerful concept for understanding and managing M&A. Prior analyses of risk in M&A have focused on a financial market view, and largely interpreted M&A as an exercise in portfolio management. Studies have centred on variances in stock market returns as the dependent variable. The variation of this risk has been associated to pre-deal conditions, such as the relatedness of the merging companies, or their financial slack.

I have reasoned for the benefit of many kinds of risk analysis, including those that play on rational-choice models. However, I have focused on *'virtual risk'*; risk that is inestimable. The management of virtual risk is argued to have been largely overlooked in prior research, to be significant in determining M&A success, and to be influenced by social interaction. M&A can be interpreted as highly risky because the process often imposes substantial, rapid change on individuals, communities of practice, and institutions, yet without a matching level of social interaction between those involved.

Communities produce risk, and communities produce reliability. Approaches to risk management that explicitly control financial or operational risk – such as the contingent, contractual methods of venture capital finance – might have a greater role in M&A. But if virtual risk is prevalent, the relevant 'culturally filtered' or perceptual risks can be managed only via social interaction. The emphasis in managing risk thereby shifts from modelling financial outcomes to overseeing interactions within and between relevant practitioner groups.

Past attempts at risk management in M&A have been frustrated by misinterpretations of risk. Instead, M&A, and many of the associated risks, can be seen, fundamentally, as products of the mind. A 'successor' foundation for risk is therefore described. This commends pluralism, and a need to integrate approaches, but also the grounding of risk analysis and management in the hard-won experience of practitioners. Risk management is argued to be most effective when it operates in the *'middle ground'* – interactively between located practice and detached abstraction. Polarized approaches lead to either irrelevance or unwanted outcomes. Much understanding of 'what matters' to risk management can only come via direct involvement and experience. It is by working in the middle ground that the risk manager can pay adequate respect to both formal models of risk, and the particularity of circumstance.

The new emphasis on risk in M&A portrayed in this chapter does not seek to diminish prior research. It is precisely the insights and contradictions of narrower, deeper, more calculative risk analysis that highlight the appeal of alternatives. But broadening the interpretation of risk comes with its own traps. It would be all too easy to rubbish practical M&A policies as employing 'limited' risk analysis, where managers are operating under pressurized conditions. However, a broader conceptualization can only sensitize managers to their particular risk-laden challenges. Many risks are created by the interaction of pluralistic minds. They can be managed by the interaction of pluralistic minds. Fuelling discussion around multiple interpretations of risk is therefore central to mindful risk management.

Case Study

The case study in case box 6.3 below explores the idea that risks apply to both action *and* inaction. Merging is risky, but perhaps so is *not* merging. Prior discussion of risk in M&A has sometimes implicitly explored it as an occasional, discrete, deal- and choice-driven phenomenon. But risk might also be seen as a continuous, yet radically varying, undercurrent. Seen by these lights, firms must *always* navigate risk in M&A.

Moreover, typically, M&A activity has been considered as a unitary event. Yet, one deal (and its risks) might also be better understood as interacting with other deals (and their risks). This case asks the reader to consider the scenario of a firm that *might* have merged during a critical period in its industry's development, but did not.

CASE BOX 6.3:   GRANT THORNTON – A CASE OF THE RISKS OF *NOT* MERGING?[3]

We had eight, then six, five, and finally four. There has been, since the 1980s, intense media coverage of the consolidation of the largest accounting firms. The glories and tribulations of these 'mega-mergers' have been closely monitored. But what has it all meant for those players just too small to be swept up in the merger mania; firms such as Grant Thornton? In 1996, Grant Thornton was the eighth largest auditor in the US, yet it was growing notably slower than its larger peers. (See table 6.1.)

Since the late 1980s, the accounting and consulting sector in the US had been dominated by the 'Big Six': Arthur Andersen & Co.; Coopers & Lybrand LLP; Deloitte & Touche; Ernst & Young; KPMG; and Price Waterhouse. In sum, they made fees of almost $49 billion in 1996, which constituted over 92% of the revenue of the top nine firms.

Mergers were nothing new in this sector. In the mid-1980s we had the 'Big Eight'. The merger in the late 1980s of Deloitte Haskins & Sells with Touche Ross & Company formed Deloitte & Touche. Next, there was the merger of Ernst & Whinney with Arthur Young & Company to form Ernst & Young, giving us the 'Big Six'. Price Waterhouse tried to join with Deloitte in 1984, but talks faltered. Price Waterhouse once more was set to merge, this time with Arthur Andersen in 1989, but again the deal fell apart.

Price Waterhouse next announced in September of 1997 that it intended to merge with Coopers & Lybrand. This would create a firm with combined worldwide revenues of $12 billion, over 130,000 employees and more than 8500 partners. Onlookers speculated that, without this deal, and as the sixth largest firm, Price Waterhouse risked becoming a 'niche' player. Shortly after the Price Waterhouse and Coopers & Lybrand announcement, KPMG and Ernst & Young declared that they too would be combining. Yet, by early March 1998, and following 4 months of negotiations, the $18 billion merger had been abandoned.

Table 6.1   Performance of the accounting companies

Company	1996 fees ($ billion)	% increase 1995–1996
Arthur Andersen	9.5	16.8
Ernst & Young	7.7	13.0
KPMG Peat Marwick	7.4	8.0
Coopers & Lybrand	6.8	9.7
Deloitte & Touche	6.5	9.5
Price Waterhouse	5.0	12.6
BDO Seidman	1.3	8.1
Grant Thornton	1.3	7.1

Source: 1998 US Industry and Trade Outlook.

Merger Motives . . .

So, what was driving this merger frenzy? The desire to create a larger consulting practice may have been a main motivation. The sector was undergoing some basic changes. In 1996, for example, the top 100 US accountancy firms earned, for the first time, more from consulting ($8.3 billion) than either auditing ($7.9 billion) or tax services ($5 billion). Yet, according to the US General Accounting Office (GAO), the mergers of the 1980s and 1990s happened for three major reasons:

1. The largest accounting firms wanted to match the growing scale and global reach of their customers (e.g. firms such as Pepsi Cola and Ford).
2. They wanted to achieve greater efficiencies. On average, Price Waterhouse's 3300 partners charged $1.5 million each in 1996, with Coopers & Lybrand's 5200 partners making fees per head of $1.3 million. Yet, Arthur Andersen's 2611 partners made $3.6 million each.
3. They also needed to develop technical and industry-specific capabilities.

There was evidence of these mergers delivering benefits to customers. The competition between big firms has kept audit fees stable, and technological advances, mainly through the use of software and related IT, enhanced the efficiency of audits. Tellingly, however, the revenue gap between the largest accounting firms and the next four firms widened between 1988 and 2002 (see table 6.2).

Reasons Not To Merge . . .

These huge mergers appear to have conferred benefits on the enlarged accounting firms, and upon their customers. But perhaps not everything bigger is better. On top of the challenge of combining different cultures, enlarging can mean taking on the risks of more complex operations. A prime cause for concern has been legal liability. All Big Five US

Table 6.2   The gulf between the big and the rest

Accounting company groups	Average revenue* ($ million)	Average no. of partners	Average no. of non-partners	Average no. of quoted clients
1988				
Big Eight	1,566	1,126	10,991	1,359
Next tier**	288	364	2,118	234
Difference	1,278	762	8,873	1,125
2002				
Big Four	4,468	2,029	15,664	2,046
Next tier**	290	292	1,532	245
Difference	4,178	1,737	14,132	1,801

* Average revenue figures have been adjusted for inflation.
** In 1998, the 'next tier' included Laventhol & Horwath, Grant Thornton, BDO Seidman, and McGladrey & Pullen. In 2002, the 'next tier' was identical to that of 1988, but for Crowe Chizek and Co., replacing Laventhol & Horwath.
Source: Public Accounting Report, 1989 and 2003, US General Accounting Office.

accounting firms became limited liability partnerships (LLP) to help protect the partners from litigation. There is also the intrafirm conflict between accountants and consulting colleagues. Some clients were troubled by one-stop firms, as conflicts of interest appear when they are independently audited by the same firm providing consulting services. Indeed, Andersen Worldwide voted to separate off its consulting arm, with effect from 2000. This separation occurred not long before the high-profile Enron scandal and the subsequent demise, through regulatory litigation, of Andersen's accounting practice.

Since Andersen's suspension, fees reportedly climbed again. Still, audit fees began to rise only after new legislation took effect. The Sarbanes-Oxley Act of 2002 prohibited companies in the US from using the same firm for auditing and consulting services.

The Move To Second Tier . . . ?

With the new millennium, some client companies apparently started thinking that bigger is not always better. Auditor-Trak, a database tracking this sector, informed that in 2003 all of the Big Four lost, on net, audit clients. More than half of those clients switched to smaller auditors. Second-tier firms, such as Grant Thornton and BDO Seidman, gained over 21% of the migrating clients, who claimed they were charged lower fees by the second-tier auditors. Some 34% shifted to more local firms, and the remainder churned within the Big Four.

Although Grant Thornton engaged 60 partners and about 500 employees from Andersen, a gulf still marked it from the Big Four. Following the Andersen debacle, the GAO surveyed 147 public companies – 88% stated that they would *not* contemplate using a non-Big Four company for their audits. This perception is evinced by the data in table 6.3.

Table 6.3   The transfer of Andersen's clients

	Number of former Andersen's clients	% of Andersen's total clients	Average assets of transferred clients ($ million)
The Big Four	938	86	2,508
Grant Thornton	45	4	644
BDO Seidman	23	2	54
Other	79	7	193

Source: 'Who Audits America, 2001–2002', US General Accounting Office.

How Things Shaped Up . . .

By the end of fiscal year 2003, Deloitte was the largest of the Big Four. It was also the last Big Four firm to retain its entire consulting division. Around $1.8 billion of the firm's US revenue came from consulting work. But in terms of growth in revenues for the year, Grant Thornton topped the league, at 21.2%. Among the Big Four, Ernst & Young led US revenue growth, with 17.4%. Grant Thornton also enjoyed the largest growth in audit practice, at 26%.

Plus Ça Change . . .

While the psychological scars from Enron were still healing, a new corporate scandal came to light in January 2004. Parmalat – a huge Italian dairy producer – collapsed under billion dollar debts. The media speculated over the role of two accounting firms: Grant Thornton, whose Italian operation was Parmalat's main auditor until 1999, and Deloitte Touche Tohmatsu, which took over the auditing task in the subsequent 4 years. Almost immediately, chiefs of Grant Thornton International in London and Grant Thornton LLP in Chicago were distancing themselves from their Italian affiliate. Weeks later, the entire Italian operation was expelled from Grant Thornton's global network. The potent effect of risk on accounting firms had become ever sharper.

Discussion Questions

1. How might a 'financial economic' risk analysis of Grant Thornton's prospective merger with a Big Four firm contrast with a risk analysis based on ideas of virtual risk? Specifically:
    (a) Briefly, what, in each case, would be the 'variables' of interest to a risk analysis?
    (b) In overview, what might be an appropriate managerial response to your 'virtual' and 'financial economic' risk analysis?
    (c) Is there any synergy or conflict between your two classes of managerial response?
2. Might we conclude that the strategic risks of Grant Thornton *not* merging in the 1980s or 1990s with a larger firm were in fact greater than the risks of merging? What can this tell us about the nature of risk in M&A?

I would like to thank Dr Mark Ashton Smith for his assistance in formulating an interpretation of Brian Cantwell Smith's concepts of the 'middle ground' and experiential embeddedness. I would also like to thank Dr Sofiane Sekioua for his help with the exposition of the CAPM.

NOTES

1. The material on AOL-Time Warner was adapted from a précis of Nina Munk's recent book on that merger, *Fools Rush In*. The précis can be found at: www.ninamunk.com/bookPage.asp.
2. The details are from the following website: www.businessweek.com/technology/content/aug2004/tc20040813_4553_tc120.htm.
3. The case study on Grant Thornton employs material derived from the following four websites: 'Bolting from the Big Four', www.cfo.com/printable/article.cfm/3012773?f=options; 'Auditor Consolidation: Few Choices, Big Implications', www.businessfinancemag.com/magazine/archives/article.html?articleID=14106&pg=4; 'Price Waterhouse and Coopers & Lybrand: A Mega-Merger'; www.johnwiley.com.au/highered/ob/studentresources/cases/pricewaterhouse.htm; www.stevedenning.com/SIN-25-Parmalat&Deloitte.html.

Part III Post-Acquisition

Chapter 7 M&A as Project

Controlling the Integration Progress With a Project Monitoring System

Philippe Very and Stephen Gates

According to a recent study conducted by The Conference Board (2000),[1] only 45% of acquirers use a formal plan or process for tracking integration performance and for reporting activities. Moreover, only 44% of the interviewed acquirers declared that they measure the success of the integration.

These are surprising findings. Though the research has limitations due in particular to the sample size, it could help explain why a majority of acquisitions fail. After closing the deal, the acquirer must implement the changes in processes and organizations that are required for exploiting synergies and for realizing forecasted cash flows. Integrating can be a very challenging task when it implies major modifications at both firms' organizations. When required changes are not made, or not made to deadline, the expected value will not be created or, even worse, the acquirer's value can be destroyed. These considerations militate for careful organization and supervision of the integration. Consequently, if acquirers do not rigorously track integration progress, it is not surprising that they have difficulty fulfilling their acquisition objectives. As Jemison and Sitkin (1987) and Very (2004) have shown, a key success factor lies in the ability of the acquirer to appropriately manage the integration process.

In this chapter, we focus our attention on M&A integration and propose answers to the following question: how should this process be monitored? For that purpose, we will first examine the characteristics of acquisition integration and show that it can be viewed as a specific project. This exploration will help us recommend to acquirers how to organize the management of this phase, and how to control integration progress with a monitoring system. Lastly, our developments will also show that integration success requires specific behaviours from project leaders.

M&A Integration as a Project

It is clear that there is not one best way to integrate an acquired company. The integration design and plans depend greatly on the context of the deal: the acquirer's strategy, the past performance of the acquired firm, its size, the extent of forecasted synergies, the friendly or hostile nature of the acquisition etc. Consequently, the integration design should match deal contingencies (Hunt, 1990): each deal is definitely unique.

Moreover, as Angwin (2004) and DePamphilis (2001) explain, speed of integration is presented as a key factor to achieve the cash flows expected from the acquisition. Financial markets wait, not only for integration plans, but also for rapid integration results. One survey by Andersen Consulting (1999) indicates that successful acquirers complete most integration activities within 6 months to 1 year. Therefore, acquirers generally plan an accelerated pace of integration that is intended to deliver cash flows prior to a precise deadline. This emphasis on speed can be found in many deals, even if the influence of early integration actions on acquisition performance has not yet been clearly demonstrated (Angwin, 2004).

These observations suggest that M&A integration possesses two essential characteristics:

1. It is unique, thanks to deal contingencies, and deserves a unique outcome; it creates a new – more or less different – organization and new management systems.
2. It is a temporary endeavour, with a definite beginning (deal closing) and a definite end (deadline for integration). Integration will cease once the declared objectives have been attained.

These two characteristics constitute the basic distinction between projects and current operations of a firm: while projects are temporary and unique, current operations are ongoing and repetitive. This explains why an acquisition can be assimilated to a project and why more and more acquirers use a project management approach to monitor integration.

With the exception of Angwin (2000), very few management tools and methods are generally discussed in the literature about M&A. Applying methods of project management to deal with the integration offers an acquirer the possibility to rely on managerial techniques that have been extensively tested and developed by companies and that often have already been used within the company itself to manage other projects: building a new facility; designing a new product; renovating the information system. Consequently, integrating an acquired firm can be seen as an opportunity to apply methods already mastered by the firm.

Moreover, project management allows the acquirer's top executives to give over leadership of an integration to a team of company managers. Top executives are generally exhausted once they leave the negotiation table, where they fought hard to buy the target at fair conditions. If they choose to carry out the integration themselves, their health will suffer. Remember that, after the announcement of a deal, top managers are forced to ensure the communication with the diverse stakeholders. Therefore, it becomes difficult to manage simultaneously the day-to-day integration tasks. On the contrary, top managers using project management methods give responsibility of integration to a dedicated integration team; they organize clear systems and rules of coordination between the top management and the team. Each party knows which decision is his/her own responsibility. In such cases, top executives can concentrate on the communication task and have more free time to manage the whole corporation.

From a knowledge perspective, it is also worth noting that acquiring is a learning process. During the negotiation phase, acquirers are constantly seeking, gauging and verifying information about the target and synergies. Once the deal closed, they continue to learn about their partner and sometimes modify their integration plan to cope with the new knowledge accumulated. Similarly, project management methods assume that, at project launch, you do not know exactly what will happen: as a project is unique, it presents risks that more or less threaten its completion. Therefore, these methods are appropriate for managing any learning process like an integration.

The above reasons explain why experienced acquirers like GE Capital (Ashkenas, Demonaco and Francis, 1998) or Cisco (Killick, Rawoot and Stockport, 2001) adopt project management methods for integrating acquisitions. Our own experience with top executives suggests that these methods are increasingly used by acquirers.

CASE BOX 7.1:   PRAXAIR'S MULTIFUNCTION PROJECT APPROACH

Praxair's senior management strongly believes that a multifunction project approach is needed for successful integration. The integration project team generally includes relevant business units: finance, IT, marketing, production, environmental, logistics, tax, human resources and communications. These diverse experts are in more or less temporary roles throughout the integration. The integration process then receives high-level attention and sufficient resources to address issues quickly. Project milestone schedules are set to achieve operations and business improvement targets such as operational productivity, product quality, logistics efficiency, safety standards, and customer retention. Praxair's integration team specifically tracks, among other performance indicators, end points: when the target's old system and organization go away.[2]

Project management can be interpreted as a combination of initiating, planning, executing, controlling and closing processes. Project leaders look to optimize resources and time in order to reach the expected project objectives. This means that they must mobilize the necessary financial and human resources, set plans, tasks, targets and milestones, then control progress throughout the whole project implementation.[3] In this chapter, we will essentially focus on three main constituencies of project management: project team, project risk and monitoring of project progress. Applied to the case of integration, project team means integration team; project risk corresponds to risks of value destruction or value leakage; monitoring of project progress consists of controlling value drivers. Let's examine successively these key features of project management.

Project Team

CASE BOX 7.2:   INTEGRATION TEAM OR TEAMS?

When the German Daimler-Benz merged with the US automaker Chrysler in 1998, project management was used to monitor integration. Two leaders, one in Michigan and the other in Stuttgart, were nominated as heads of the post-merger integration (PMI) team. They organized 12 sub-teams called IRTs (issue resolution teams) to track synergies and put in place the new organization. These teams cooperated on 98 main projects, under which 1200 specific projects were identified and organized. For each project, the PMI members could review documented progress according to fixed criteria. They could look at presentations documents or minutes of meetings. The PMI Infobase allowed for daily monitoring of any project advancement thanks to a classical project management tool: the 'traffic light' system, with its green, yellow and red signals. 'Green' light meant that the project was in line with forecasts. On the other hand, a project flashing 'red' meant that the project was not progressing as expected in term of costs, timeline and production of outputs.

Adopting project management means that the acquirer creates a team for the purpose of performing integration. This team as a whole does not outlive the project: it is disbanded once integration is complete and its members are reassigned within the company. The team can be large, as in the Daimler-Chrysler example, or rather small, for instance when it essentially plays a gate-keeping role (Haspeslagh and Jemison, 1991) aimed at preserving the autonomy of the acquired firm. When the acquirer buys a company operating in a new business or country, the team's mission can consist of transferring a few competencies between the companies while at the same time ensuring the managerial independence of the acquired firm. The French hotel chain company Accor gave much autonomy to the acquired US company Motel 6. As building materials and habits were different between countries, the French standardized system of construction could not be transferred to the USA. Moreover, French and US clients do not share the same conception of an economic-class hotel: in the USA, more people-based service needs to be offered. Synergies were also weak in this area. Consequently, only a few managers were involved in this integration, which preserved a great deal of autonomy for the target firm.

The team is generally composed of full-time and part-time members. While some leaders spend all their time on the integration, many experts join the team for a limited period. The full-time team leading the acquisition includes at least financial, legal and business skills. A recent study suggests that an integration entrusted to a financial manager presents the risk of too much focus on pure economic outcomes; a business unit manager as leader is likely to better monitor integration progress because he/she is more experienced with tracking performance alongside many dimensions like people retention, customer satisfaction and transfer of skills. Temporary team members work to exploit specific synergies and go back to their former positions once their tasks are completed. For instance, a sales manager can be hired for 2 months to help eliminate redundancies between sales forces. A production manager can spend 1 month to help upgrade manufacturing equipment. Some managers can also work partly for the integration, partly for current operations.

'No team can make a bad deal good, but a bad team can make a good deal bad' (Aiello and Watkins, 2000, p. 103). Team members can be recruited either from the acquirer or from the target firm. It depends on the deal context and objectives. Researchers have found that acquirers rely heavily on the executives of the acquired company when they enter a new and unknown country (Very and Schweiger, 2001). Recruitment of team members is based on diverse characteristics: technical skills required for the project, motivation, acquisition experience, individual qualities like leadership, openness to multiculturalism or curiosity. Carlos Goshn, CEO of the carmaker Nissan, responsible for Nissan's turnaround after its acquisition by Renault, gave the following answer to a question about team selection: 'Personal qualities are the most important element; the way you are and the way you handle things is much more important than experience. That said, I wouldn't say it's an absolute requirement for success to have multicultural experience, but it is value-added. You really just feel more comfortable with someone who has a strong international or global experience' (Emerson, 2001, p. 7).

Integration as a project can require the constitution of two different teams. For instance, when the type of integration chosen is symbiosis (Haspeslagh and Jemison, 1991), a new organization is set up, built on the best practices of each partner and the efficiency systems that should be appropriate to reach the acquisition objectives. In such a case, the acquirer must simultaneously maintain uninterrupted service to customers of both companies while designing and implementing required changes to the organizational structure. The task is quite difficult: when important changes are forecast, employees tend to focus on the resolution of internal issues, particularly those that affect their own future. To overcome such problems, experienced acquirers often create two teams; the first one is in charge of integration, concentrating on how and when to implement organizational changes (project team) while the second one ensures the continuity of current operations with customers (business unit leading team). These two teams work jointly on the introduction of changes to avoid disruption of current operations. To facilitate coordination between the two teams, one or two managers can be appointed members of the two teams.

CASE BOX 7.3:   DECISION-MAKING PROCESS WITH TWO TEAMS

The Dutch Company Philips Semiconductors acquired the Californian electronics company VLSI in 1999. Two teams were created: the integration management team (IMT) and the operations management team (OMT). The head of the OMT was also the co-leader of the IMT. A steering committee was also created with top executives from Philips Semiconductors. Relying on formal functional procedures, this committee gave its agreement on any change content proposed by the IMT after coordination with the OMT. This decision-making process allowed top executives to maintain a clear vision over structural modifications, human and technical issues, or the level of synergy implementation at any time during the integration phase.

Project Risk

While any project contains its own uncertainties about what the end-product will look like, the M&A integration project is far riskier than many other undertakings. Making an acquisition means welcoming a company you have scarce information about. Most of the time, the acquirer has its first perception of the target thanks to published information and to the products and/or services sold. Then, in the case of friendly deals, due-diligence procedures help in getting a better understanding of its strengths and weaknesses, and of its compatibility with the acquirer's strategy. Whatever the extent of time and effort spent on due diligence, the buyer gains only limited access to the soft characteristics of the target, like its culture or its informal decision-making processes. It can hardly predict which human reactions will be provoked by the change of ownership and the implementation of the integration plan. In brief, the level of knowledge accumulated prior to deal closing cannot give complete assurance that strategic expectations will be reached within the forecast deadlines.

The acquirer obviously lacks information about its target prior to the marriage, despite due-diligence efforts. After deal closing, it should continue to learn as much as possible about the acquired firm in order to validate or modify the implementation plan. Consequently, integration should be considered as a dynamic process of adjustment in a context of intricate and incomplete information. As target knowledge improves, mid-course corrections to the integration process will be made according to the occurrence of new events, to the rise of human reactions, or to the discovery of unrevealed facts. According to researchers, such adaptation should increase chances of creating value. Throughout the integration, there is a need to track project progress, to identify and manage identified risks, and to stay vigilant to signs of unexpected problems. This is why risk management and measurement-based monitoring of integration should help realize the expected value.

Managing Risk

Classical project risk management[4] includes four main processes: 1) risk identification; 2) risk quantification (how the emergence of identified risks can influence the final outcome); 3) risk response development (solutions that enable the acquirer to respond to threats and to seize opportunities); and 4) risk response control (how to monitor changes in risks all along the project).

Risk identification

As we said earlier, it is impossible to get an overview of all the risks inherent in an integration, because of the low level of knowledge accumulated about the target and the realization of synergies. However, some risks can be anticipated. Following initial work by Hunt (1990), Bower (2001) and Schweiger and Very (2003) have explored the heterogeneity within the so-called M&A wave, primarily from a strategic point of view. These researchers have then built typologies and described, for each type, the main synergies, the major integration changes and the potential sources of value destruction. For instance, Schweiger and Very distinguished five strategic types of activities: 1) consolidate within a geographic area; 2) extend or add new products/services/technologies; 3) enter a new market; 4) vertically integrate; or 5) enter a new line of business. Risks differ according to the type considered. When 'consolidating within a geographical area', acquirers need to implement strong integration changes and are likely to deal with individual fears, organizational politics, cultural resistance, departure of talented employees and loss of customers. In contrast, when 'entering a new line of business', acquirers will introduce slighter changes and have to manage fewer human issues: individual fears and departure of business experts at the target constitute the principal risks of value leakage. In addition, it is worth noticing that the integration design itself raises specific challenges that need to be monitored. For instance, the full absorption of an acquired firm might not be seen as a winner–loser game that could generate resistance to change and departures. In symbiotic acquisitions, where both firms create a new organization using each partner's best practices, selecting managers for filling positions in the new structure can destroy a cooperative atmosphere. This is why acquirers should identify not only the risks attached to the deal strategy and synergies, but also those that could arise from the integration plan itself.

Consequently, using previous work done on M&A types, the acquirer should be able to identify, early in the process, important risks associated with a targeted acquisition. Moreover, if it has made similar strategic moves in recent times, it can use the experience accumulated to more precisely assess the issues that could threaten the integration project and its outcome. It is worth signalling that using acquisition experience must be done with much care. Haleblian and Finkelstein (1999) found that the appropriate application of lessons learned from past acquisitions clearly depends on the level of similarity between the new and former deals.

Risk quantification

Once potential risks are estimated, acquirers can proceed to risk quantification. The objective is to analyse the influence of risk occurrence on the outcome of the integration process: potential changes in the nature of the outcome, in integration costs and in integration duration.

Project managers generally calculate economic consequences by combining the probability of occurrence and the estimate gain or loss attached to a particular risk event. Decision trees and simulations are also used for elaborating scenarios and evaluating the impact of risk occurrence on the timelines and costs associated with the project. If the initial objectives of the project could be threatened, some slight differences in the end product of integration could be considered as acceptable. Therefore, risk quantification helps clarify which events and reactions need to be managed and what extent of variance in outcomes is agreed on by the top management.

Risk response development

Once the main risks and their consequences are identified, acquirers can elaborate solutions to respond to the occurrence of unfavorable events. Preventive and reactive action plans can be set up, depending on the nature and importance of the risk. For instance, when cultural resistance has a strong probability of occurrence and could thwart acquisition objectives, the acquirer can attempt to prevent the emergence of such a clash. Actions to promote mutual understanding of both staffs, to develop in-depth cultural learning, or to create a new organizational identity can be designed, announced and implemented as early as possible in the process. Anticipation can help avoid the occurrence of a particular risk.

CASE BOX 7.4:   ANTICIPATING THE DEPARTURE OF KEY PEOPLE

When companies like Lucent, Oracle, or Cisco buy small or medium-size technology firms, they identify as early as possible the key experts within the target and prepare plans for retaining these employees once the deal closed. Increased responsibilities, authority, salary, stock options, stay-bonuses in cash or stock and task-completion bonuses are among the diverse means and tools that are studied, then budgeted and tracked to avoid a significant loss of company value due to the departure of key people.

Acquirers can also prepare contingent action plans to respond to a risk event if it happens. In such a case, the integration managers develop a comprehensive view of what they will do if an event threatens the project. They are ready to react and undertake actions that should ensure an acceptable integration outcome.

Risk response control

Once solutions have been decided upon, the last step, risk response control, consists of:

- executing anticipated actions for avoiding the occurrence of some risks;
- identifying the occurrence or non-occurrence of other risks that should be managed;
- controlling so that the extent and nature of negative events correspond to what has been forecast and, thus, elicit the proposed solutions;
- implementing the plans to overcome the issue once a risk event happens.

'Risk response development' and 'risk response control', as defined by project managers, are sometimes considered as a whole and called 'integration interventions' by merger specialists (Schweiger, 2002). Managing risks prudently requires committing additional financial and human resources to meet potential increased costs or delays encountered when the diverse risks occur.

   Whatever the initial effort of the acquirer, the most thorough analysis cannot ensure that all risks have been identified, given the low level of knowledge accumulated about the target prior to deal-closing. Consequently, while acquirers should prepare themselves to fight or avoid possible threats, they should also prepare themselves to work around and react to unexpected events. This is why integration managers generally gain from carefully elaborating a process-monitoring system that should help them to track signs of surprises and unforeseen problems. Moreover, as we will see in the next section, such a system also helps monitor that the integration is progressing in line with expectations and is delivering the forecast performance.

Value Drivers

Monitoring means measuring progress and implementing mid-course corrective actions when required. Therefore, a first task of the integration team consists of elaborating a set of measures that will allow adequate control of the integration process.

The acquisition risks described in this chapter show how most measures for tracking integration progress are deal-specific. These metrics should be developed from the main value drivers that characterize a particular acquisition. Two types of value drivers must be considered:

1. First, the acquirer seeks for value creation, which relies upon the actual exploitation of synergies and the organizational changes needed to reach strategic goals; increasing revenues and cost savings can come directly from the strategy. As Bower (2001) clearly showed, not all M&A are alike and measures of performance should include the overall strategic objectives of the acquirer. Moreover, the increase in the firm's size thanks to its acquisitive strategy can have direct advantages: for instance, the acquirer can improve its negotiating power with stakeholders like bankers or suppliers. Value creation is also built on synergies. Each deal is characterized by its specific synergies. Resource sharing is a first source of benefits: for instance, the consolidation of sales forces in some acquisitions can provide cost economies while simultaneously producing revenue enhancement by product cross-selling. Administrative functions are often pooled together for eliminating redundancies and reducing costs. Tangible as well as intangible resources, like a brand, can be shared. Another source of value creation is the transfer of functional skills, like technological expertise, that can increase revenues thanks to the improvement of product competitiveness. A third source of benefits resides in the transfer of management skills for organizing the turnaround of a target and improving its economic performance. A last source of value creation resides in the sharing of financial resources, when one firm provides financial support to allow its partner to increase its growth rate and enhance its revenues.

2. Second, the acquirer must avoid value leakage, defined as the dissipation of the potential value of combining the two companies or the negative impact of the acquisition on the intrinsic value of either firm. Value leakage stems from the occurrence of identified risks or unexpected events. Appropriate measures for controlling value leakage depend on the risks identified by the acquirer as early as possible in the process. The mismanagement of these risks can have dramatic consequences (Schweiger and Ivancevich, 1987): inability to exploit synergies, departure of key people, loss of productivity, loss of commitment, etc. In the banking sector, for instance, departures of well-known investment bankers after a merger can prevent revenue growth, and, even worse, they are likely to decrease the intrinsic value of the acquired company.

In sum, the elaboration of metrics and milestones for monitoring progress should rely on the identification of the main value drivers pertaining to each particular transaction.

CASE BOX 7.5:   IDENTIFYING VALUE DRIVERS AS EARLY AS POSSIBLE

At GE Capital, acquisition integration is a process that begins with due diligence and runs through the ongoing management of the new enterprise. As soon as possible after the deal is signed – within days if possible – decisions about management structure, key roles, reporting relationships, layoffs, restructuring and other career-affecting aspects of the integration should be made, announced and implemented.

A successful integration melds not only the various technical operational aspects of the businesses but also the different cultures. The best way to do this is to get people working together quickly to solve business problems and accomplish results that could not have been achieved before.

CASE BOX 7.6:   LAUNCHING INTEGRATION

At closing, the GE Capital business leader and acquisition integration manager organize orientation and planning sessions for the management team of the new acquisition and themselves (Ashkenas, Demonaco and Francis, 1998). During these sessions, participants create an initial period plan for acquisition integration. The plan addresses such issues as the need for integrating functions, taking any steps necessary for financial and procedural compliance, making any shifts in compensation and benefits, and managing customer contacts. This timetable creates a sense of urgency, challenge and energy while at the same time forcing the management team to move into action. Distributing the initial plan widely sends the message about the course of the integration process and its performance measurement.

Measures for Project Monitoring

We will use case study illustrations to show how performance measures apply to acquisitions. Since it would be too complex to describe the whole set of measures pertaining to an acquisition, we will describe examples of measures attached to a particular risk and how acquirers use them. For that purpose, we listed two synergies – eliminating redundancies and increasing product development timeline – and three domains of risks that could prevent value creation – loss of key people, cultural resistance, and loss of clients.

Measures used when eliminating redundancies

In a recent acquisition at Aegon, the cost savings target was 25% of the acquisition's cost structure. A total of 60% of the cost savings came from headcount reduction, namely, reducing the direct field agents selling whole life insurance door to door. Typically, two-thirds of a life insurance company's cost structure relates to personnel's compensation and benefits. The remaining 40% of savings came from consolidating head offices, data centres and investment divisions. In Aegon's experience, most cost savings are delivered during the first 18 months, and all within 2 years. Since it is so incremental, cost savings must be explained to investors every quarter.

At BP Amoco, the overall cost savings performance goal engaged many people in the process of generating personnel reduction targets. Personnel reduction needed to be balanced between the two companies and also at various levels of employees in both companies. Quarterly reporting of progress against targets forced managers to take action or to explain why the targets were not met. On the other hand, business leaders strive to overachieve so setting personnel reduction targets can lead to more cuts than optimal. In some cases, the CEO needed to balance business leaders' tendency to outperform by questioning them about how they could maintain capability and company value.

Measures used for monitoring product development timeline

Increasingly, acquisitions are made to acquire new technology. Since the target companies may have little or no revenue, the main performance milestones focus on new technology or product development. At a large American information technology firm, the main goal of recent acquisitions has been to acquire new technology and to position the company in a new market. New product development and product development cycles were of great importance, both to the operating business head as well as to the product development director. These measures were similar to those already in place within the division making the acquisition. The technology development measures included product schedule, product content, employee retention/turnover and product cost.

- *Product schedule* – adherence to major committed milestones within the development lifecycle.
- *Product content* – committed functionality meeting the agreed client requirements at the committed quality and performance levels.

- *Employee retention/turnover* – retention levels of critical management and technical staff assigned to key projects.
- *Product cost* – product costs within committed cost targets.

In addition, since the acquired technologies were well defined, market share information could be provided by industry market research groups. Nevertheless, a new binary (yes/no) measure was created to track whether the acquired company did or did not position the company to enter the new market. At the completion of the acquisition integration, the binary measure reported whether the functionality, schedule and costs of product and solution set under development met the requirements for a successful new market entry.

Measures used to control the loss of key employees

The common denominator for selection of management, key contributors and the general employee population is that the processes should occur as early and quickly as possible. Several company examples illustrate management selection during the integration process.

At Eastman Kodak, the single most important task accomplished during one recent integration was selecting the leadership team on a proportional basis based on a comprehensive review of talent in both organizations. This lent enormous credibility to the entire integration process. The leadership team was announced the day after closing.

BP Amoco's CEO set three clear management selection principles for the first four management levels. First, during management selection, business operations should not be disrupted. Secondly, management selection should reflect the relative shares of the two companies. In other words, 60% of management should be from BP and 40% from Amoco. Any exception to this principle needed to be explained to the CEO, sometimes leading to changes to fit the relative shares. Third, diversity in the management ranks would not be diminished.

At Science Applications International Corporation (SAIC), a balanced scorecard for senior managers measured performance in terms of revenue and sales, but also included elements such as retaining key people and keeping resignation rates down. In this way, senior management compensation was linked to management and employee retention during acquisition integration.

At Abbott Labs, retaining the sales management team and its sales force was a key goal during acquisition integration. The measure was simple: compare the turnover rate among these people prior to the acquisition versus their turnover rate after the acquisition. The integration team spent a lot of time speaking to the sales management team about the key issues for their sales people. The vast majority of their key 'hot buttons' were retained, such as incentive plans, car policies and pay structure, even though these were different than the rest of the Abbott sales force.

This strategy was a success: the acquired company sales force and management have lower turnover than prior to the acquisition.

Measures used to control cultural resistance

Differences in corporate culture can be just as significant as differences in national cultures. For example, when SC Johnson acquired DowBrands, it brought marketing and distribution while the target provided product technology and engineering. Consequently, Dow's manufacturing plants and research and development facilities were left untouched in the beginning. SC Johnson management, inexperienced with the products made by the acquired company, told DowBrands' people: 'We never made a bag.' While that statement made Dow's people feel secure, they then resisted changes all the more when SC Johnson tried to inculcate more of its marketing culture in a traditionally production/engineering-oriented DowBrands' culture.

A cultural integration survey instrument helped identify when it was time to hold a 'building the bridge' meeting, where people from both sides came to explain their points-of-view. Provided by a consulting group, the survey instrument helped profile the two companies' differences and similarities on such cultural values as achievement, approval, conflict avoidance, risk aversion, centralized/hierarchical, conventional, controlling, competition, among others. DowBrands is very capital-intensive, where production is king and engineering processes take priority, while at SC Johnson, managing inventory tightly, yet producing to customer demand, created start/stop production conditions that required more frequent changes. This was a change for the DowBrands processes and people. It was during this cultural integration session that the two groups really understood their differences. SC Johnson learned that consciously introducing a marketing culture into an acquisition is a critical integration activity.

Measures used to control the loss of customers

Since Lucent's acquisitions largely focus on delivering revenue synergies, customer retention is essential. Lucent monitors closely how well customers accept the integration. The sales force reports particularly on the frequency of customer calls for assistance and changes in the length of time to respond to customer needs. Tracking customer response time can be one of the most powerful measures for evaluating how the integration is able to keep the business running at the same time.

Early in the integration, a list of all customers is prepared and matched against Lucent's current customers. With this information, Lucent does the following:

- incorporates into the customer account plan any new requirements of the customers that both Lucent and the acquisition serve;

- monitors monthly how acquired customers are responding to the Lucent/new company combination, using especially information from sales people and executive visits;
- develops an account strategy for new customers to Lucent;
- reports at the 6- and 12-month review how acquired customer accounts have performed and what new customers have been landed.

Mid-Course Corrections

Despite the amount of time and effort provided in the early stages of the acquisition process, acquirers cannot imagine all the risks and events that could negatively affect the integration. Therefore, they are unable to design the perfect accompanying measurement system that will ensure that the project is progressing as expected. This is particularly true in hostile takeovers, where the acquirer suffers from the lack of unpublished information about its target, but must anyway prepare the integration. Even in friendly deals, acquirers have to learn after the marriage. Therefore, the measurement system is likely to be modified with the increase of knowledge acquired about the target transaction.

Changes to the plan made during the integration can also generate reactions among employees. Consequently, integration adjustments and the way they are managed and controlled could generate new sources of value leakage. This is why the elaboration of measures and progress control remain ongoing processes for the integration project management team.

CASE BOX 7.7: MID-COURSE CORRECTIONS TO MONITOR EMPLOYEE TURNOVER

Mary Jane Raymond, Merger Integration Vice-President at Lucent, explained (The Conference Board, 2000, p. 25):

'Employee retention is the most universally monitored performance measure at Lucent for every acquisition. Our acquisitions are all about growth and talent: we are buying the intellectual power of the people. To understand the dynamics, we first look at the historical retention. In fact, we discuss this during initial discussions with the new company. We then monitor new hires and losses in every one of our weekly integration meetings after announcement. We discuss the losses, the reasons, the efforts to keep the people (discussion of opportunities, financial packages, equity, "getting to know Lucent" talk etc.) and what we may need to do differently with the next person. The new hires and losses are reviewed with the senior management every 2 weeks.

'After the first several months, or after the management team is fully in place, whichever is later, the management team assumes all aspects of people management, including attraction and retention of talent. Management teams share information on new hires and losses every month with the merger integration team. With this information, we are able to monitor new hires and losses in all acquisitions on a running basis. We compare how we are doing and take steps to correct issues.'

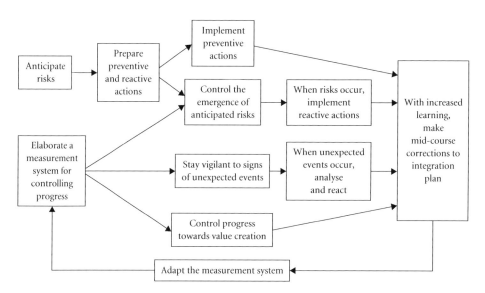

Figure 7.1   Monitoring, acting and reacting

Figure 7.1 illustrates how project monitoring applied to acquisitions can help manage the integration phase. Nonetheless, possessing the right organization and the right measurement system is not enough for guaranteeing the overall integration success. The right attitude and behaviour of integration managers is also required.

Integration Manager Behaviour

As the Lucent example described above shows, integration managers should constantly be attentive to what is happening. They should carefully listen to the core and periphery of their company. In other words, the way they behave and manage the project influences integration output.

There are four reasons to be vigilant:

1.   Since integrating can be conceived as a learning process, a learning behaviour is required for effectively accumulating knowledge. This means that managers

should pay attention to new information from or about the acquired company, to the labour climate at the diverse sites of the new group, to reactions of employees, etc. Moreover, while a well-elaborated measurement system can help in identifying the occurrence of risks and the progress towards value-creation objectives, initial information asymmetry inhibits anticipating all the risks associated with the project. In addition, external events like an economic down-turn or a technological revolution within the industry can lead integration project managers to modify the integration plan. Being attentive to what is chang-ing inside, outside, and around the two companies is essential for developing adequate corrective actions.

2. As research findings about cultural issues tend to show (Schweiger and Goulet, 2002), the influence of cultural differences on acquisition performance is not statistically proven. Larsson and Risberg (1998) argued that the problem is not posed correctly, and introduced the concept of cultural awareness as a proposi-tion to explain performance. To manage cultural differences, you first need to be aware of the existence of differences. Once and only once you have a clear picture of value and style differentials, you can act to create a common denominator – if needed. Thus, this stream of research sustains the idea that acquirers should pay attention to differences and consequently adapt their integration actions.

3. The relationship between the experience of acquisitions and the performance of a target deal has been found to follow a U-shape curve. Researchers (Haleblian and Finkelstein, 1999) inferred that inexperienced acquirers tend to reproduce lessons from their first deals, even if the context of the new transaction is dif-ferent. Acquirers start to capitalize on past deals once they become aware of differences and similarities between former acquisitions and the target one.

4. Researchers have often complained that arrogance in the way the integration was handled often leads to poor outcomes. Overconfidence, arrogance and too much determinism have been associated with integration failure. In particu-lar, the temptation to dominate and impose when acquiring must be resisted and a more comprehensive behaviour should be adopted to avoid unexpected and negative reactions in the target firm (Haspeslagh and Jemison, 1991).

These four arguments explain why integration managers should benefit from heigh-tened vigilance. When the acquirer's management team detects a sign of change, it is alerted to the need for immediate diagnosis and for possible corrective actions. When a problem is identified in its emerging phase, it is then possible to respond quickly. The route to value creation through acquisition can be redesigned if neces-sary. In other words, the vigilance of the acquirer's management team is likely to influence the overall performance of the acquisition.

While not specifically dealing with acquisitions, Lampel and Shapira (2001) dealt with judgemental errors in response to strategic surprises that take place in inter-actions between partners. Strategic surprises emerge when there is a conjunction of speed and contrast. Speed allows little time for warning and response. Contrast reflects differences between the assumptions made by one partner before the action and the intentions of the other. The authors insisted on the role of interactive norms in estimating the probability of strategic surprises. They argued that vigilance decreases with overconfidence due to past relationships: 'If historical evidence is systematically collected, it is not a guarantee against potential changes in partners' intentions' (Lampel and Shapira, 2001, p. 610). They also recommend:

- maintaining vigilance over time,
- not relying extensively on history in predicting intentions,
- collecting more information when a sign is detected to validate the judgemental model managers use, so far as it does not become too costly.

These implications can easily be translated to the context of acquisitions, where two partners are combining their efforts, and where surprises often arise. When integrating, the members of the integration team must not only possess the adequate tools and measures for tracking project progress, but also adopt an adequate behaviour for avoiding the emergence of unexpected human reactions and for quickly responding to surprises.

Conclusion

M&A integration could be improved if managed as a project. Utilizing project management means that specific resources are dedicated to the preparation and implementation of the changes required to create acquisition value. It clearly separates the management of current operations from the management of changes. Project management offers a number of advantages in comparison with direct handling by top executives or managers supervising current operations:

- Many companies already have gained experience in project management through specific endeavours like an organizational change or a new product development. Consequently, at least some managers inside the organization possess the skills required for implementing these methods.
- The creation of an appropriate project team in charge of integration enables the acquirer's top executives to concentrate on their top decision tasks. At the same time, it involves leaders from both companies in the change process.
- Project management increases chances of maintaining most employees' focus on their current tasks and preserves service quality, customer relationships or internal efficiency. The employees report to a team in charge of current operations, while the project team works on changes. Such an organization ensures service continuity with the past.
- Project management ends with a review of what happened during the monitoring of a project, in order to capture lessons learned. As the content of an

integration plan depends on the target and the deal context, acquirers can essentially accumulate experience about the handling of the integration. In this respect, project management review can identify tools for strengthening useful experience about integration.

- Project management methods incorporate the management of risks. Since each acquisition is unique, every integration is full of unexpected events.
- Project management relies on the elaboration of targets and milestones that are necessary to plan and control integration progress.
- Project management introduces a deadline for project completion. Under pressure from stakeholders, acquirers need to achieve value creation according to the declared deadline for integration.

For all these reasons, using project management techniques is useful for organizing the integration task and monitoring progress through completion. However, the high level of uncertainty that surrounds the firms' combination makes tools and methods insufficient for ensuring integration outcomes. Vigilant behaviour of integration managers is required to track signs of unexpected events and implement mid-course corrections to the integration plan.

Maybe the best metaphor for illustrating behavioural issues is the one of the doctor who does not exactly know what his patient is suffering from. The patient has undergone various examinations at hospital; now he is lying in his hospital bed, with a monitoring system to detect some possible organic trouble. The doctor asks every day for results and wonders about his patient. Once the monitoring system signals some trouble, he knows that he will run to his patient's room to analyse what is happening. The diagnosis made, he will probably be able to identify the disease and design the right treatment. Part of the job of integration managers is to act as such doctors: choose the right monitoring system, be attentive to the signals it provides, analyse the nature and importance of the problem and then elaborate and implement corrective actions. Uncertainty can bring trouble, but monitoring uncertainty can bring rewards.

CASE BOX 7.8:   HILL-ROM'S PROJECT MANAGEMENT FOR M&A INTEGRATION

With 6000 employees, Hill-Rom is an operating subsidiary of the US holding company Hillenbrand Industries, Inc. Hill-Rom provides healthcare facilities worldwide with integrated care process and environment solutions, including facility assessments, high-quality and advanced products, and professional programmes and clinical services that can help improve asset productivity, operational efficiency and patient outcomes.

Hill-Rom's acquisition integration process focuses on the first several months to get the acquired company re-positioned rapidly. During this critical period, the management structure is put in place, acquisition tasks are completed and the most important synergies are commenced. Responsibility for the performance measurement process during integration is shared between the business unit manager, who sets business objectives for the acquired company, and the integration team, which executes the integration plan. At closing, managers from the acquired company are recruited onto the integration team.

In the beginning, the acquisition team can be very large and then it reduces in number for the integration phase. The roles of the team members may change throughout the process. For example, legal and business development staff are very active during the negotiation and contracting phases, but their roles may diminish when the deal is closed and integration begins. All key functional areas are represented on the acquisition integration team to the extent that the business considers their participation important. Typically, marketing, human resources, regulatory, information technology, finance and continuous improvement representatives make up a core part of the team. According to the nature of the acquisition, staff from other functional areas – like sales, customer service, distribution, manufacturing, or engineering – may be full- or part-time members of the team.

The acquisition team performs budgeting just like an operating unit. As the acquisition team goes through its initial valuation process, it creates a high-level 5-year financial model. Then during the due-diligence process, the acquisition team gets a much clearer picture and outlines an operating budget that becomes the acquired company's operating budget until the next planning cycle. At that time, the business unit and the new management team engage in a vision-creation exercise and develop forecasts that are segmented into annual plans. Objectives behind the purchase of the company would be reflected in the plans. For example, the objective to double sales in 3 years would set the parameter for the first year's revenue target.

As for the initial period acquisition implementation plan, Hill-Rom starts by identifying where it can create value with the target company and then sets out specific steps to achieve it. These steps then get the highest priority. The full integration plan is completed and approved prior to closing. All the steps have an owner, a start date, a milestone completion date and resource names and time estimates. The resource time estimates are used to sequence the steps. Hill-Rom stresses that it is just as important not to start steps early as it is to finish them on time.

Hill-Rom tries to identify management value and talent prior to closing. At the beginning of the initial integration period, there are weekly updates on these people. At the end, the integration team reports, to corporate senior management, which target managers it succeeded in keeping. Figure 7.2 describes the internal process of the company.

Hill-Rom tracks both monthly business performance and weekly milestone progress during its acquisition implementation phase. The steps that are implemented during the first 100 days require time to take effect and may not show up in the financial statements by the third month. Consequently, the integration team will use localized measures to ensure the improvements are working as intended. For example, the customer service area might track the length of time customers are on-hold while the purchasing area might track the value of the price reductions it has arranged. Manufacturing might install hourly and daily measures to sustain the improvements gained

Initial valuation process	Due diligence and integration planning	Announce to close	Close + 100 days	End of 100-day period
• Create a high-level 5-year financial model	• Define an operating budget for the acquired company • Identify where Hill-Rom can create value within target company	• Business unit manager sets objectives for acquired company • Set out and finalize full integration plan prior to close. Plan steps have owner, start date, milestone completion date, resource names, time estimates	• Managers from acquired company recruited onto integration team • Management structure put in place. Weekly updates on management selection and retention • Acquisition tasks completed and most important synergies commenced. Weekly progress meetings; monthly progress report sent to corporate headquarters	• Report to corporate senior management on which target managers were retained. Training given on Hill-Rom's performance management system • Long-term measures cast in cement and tied to performance-based bonuses

Figure 7.2 Hill-Rom's merger integration process

through *kaizen* events. Some examples would include output per line per hour, quality performance – such as number of defects – shipping performance, safety, work-in-process, etc. The measures tracked during the first few months of the integration period are simple, focused and few. They may or may not become permanent measures.

The business unit and the integration team track progress weekly and review issues in a weekly teleconference. A summary report is sent to corporate headquarters monthly. If the acquisition team reports that it is falling behind the number of milestone completion dates, it is expected to have counter-measures arranged to remedy the situation. The integration team is responsible for ensuring that all steps in the plan get completed. For example, if a product-testing project is falling behind, the team may arrange additional resources from Hill-Rom or use an outside test lab.

At the end of the initial integration period, training is given on the Hill-Rom performance-management system. In a formal process, the new company's business strategy is cascaded and deployed. The strategic goals are passed down to each level of the organization, where measures are selected, objectives are set and responsibilities assigned. The key long-term measures are agreed upon and tied to the company's incentive compensation plan.

Discussion Questions

1. How and when does Hill-Rom determine the performance measures to avoid value leakage? To control for value creation?
2. How does the acquisition team make mid-course corrections?
3. Which performance measures does Hill-Rom find most important during the first 100 days? Which ones are likely to be long-term measures?
4. Does Hill-Rom consider cultural integration? If not, what measures might help monitor the cultural integration of its acquisitions?
5. Keeping in mind the tasks performed by Hill Rom's integration team, describe the individual behavioural qualities that an integration manager should ideally possess.

Acknowledgement

The authors appreciate the contribution of The Conference Board, for which interview material was compiled in preparation of a research report on this topic.

NOTES

1. The Conference Board is a not-for-profit independent business research and membership organization that creates and disseminates knowledge about management and the marketplace to help businesses strengthen their performance and better serve society. Working as a global, independent membership organization in the public interest,

it conducts research, convenes conferences, makes forecasts, assesses trends, publishes information and analysis and brings executives together to learn from one another.

2. Most examples come from interviews with large companies made by Stephen Gates during his research for The Conference Board on integration management. A few examples arose from the authors' experience.

3. For a detailed description of project management, consult the reports published by the Project Management Institute www.pmi.org. This organization aggregates and diffuses knowledge from many companies about project management. See also Turner (1992).

4. See the reports published by the Project Management Institute www.pmi.org. See also Turner (1992).

Chapter 8   M&A as Boundaries[1]

Derek O'Byrne

Introduction

Post-acquisition integration has received considerable attention in recent years as an explanation of the poor record of achieving acquisition objectives. An oft-quoted explanation for this poor record is the occurrence of 'cultural clash'. Some cultures, the literature tells us, just do not match and cannot be expected to merge (Love and Gibson, 1999; Cartwright and Cooper, 1997; Siehl et al., 1988; Sales and Mirvis, 1984). Accordingly, the expectations of achieving integration objectives might be assessed by the likelihood of cultural clashes occurring. Unbundling the concept of culture clash draws attention to the importance and role of boundaries. A clash involves conflict arising from two or more groups differentiating themselves from each other along some key dimensions. Two conditions must be met for this to occur. Firstly, it requires the groups to be bounded from each other along one or more dimensions and, secondly, it requires that each group is motivated to maintain the boundaries that divide the groups. These two assumptions suggest that the focus on achieving integration can be conceptualized in terms of the boundaries that might exist between groups and the motivation of the combining groups to maintain those boundaries.

Understanding Boundaries

A concept of boundary is common to disciplines as diverse as geopolitical theories (Paasi, 1999), communication (Petronio et al., 1998), transactions cost economics (Williamson, 1994; Barney, 1999), psychology (Puddifoot, 1997; Tajfel and Turner, 1986), sociology (Hawley, 1995), leadership (Gilmore, 1982) and strategy (Barney, 1999; Brooks, 1995; Jemison, 1984). In recent years, the concept of boundary management or boundary maintenance has entered into the lexicon of management and organization theory. It has developed to mean the ways in which the organization balances the external instability in the environment with the internal need for order (Llewellyn, 1994). It recognizes the important role that organizational boundaries play in filtering and interpreting environmental clues in an effort to maintain identity (Llewellyn, 1994) and sustain the balance between 'autonomy' and 'dependence' (Clegg, 1990). Issues of identity, dependence and autonomy are central to much of the emerging literature on M&A integration (Hogg and Terry, 2001; Stahl and Mendenhall, 2005) as they represent the potential for intergroup conflict to occur within the integration process. In this regard mismanaged boundaries may represent potentially significant impediments to the creation of a unified group post integration.

A Framework for Organizational Boundaries

Yan and Louis (1999) presented one of the first systematic attempts to draw together and discuss a variety of perspectives on organizational boundaries. They identified four distinctive conceptualizations of boundaries that they classified as demarcations, perimeters, interfaces and frontiers for transactions. Conceptualizations of boundaries as demarcations reflect the need to distinguish one aspect of a social system from another. The boundary between organizations represents the conditions that serve to separate one from another. This separation usually relates to a physical defined space, whether territory, technology or time (Miller and Rice, 1967), that distinguishes the organization from others – for example, different customer markets, different products or different location in the supply chain. Accordingly, focusing on boundaries as *demarcation* addresses primarily the link between the organization and its environment (Scott, 1998) and has application in defining the parameters of organizations vis-à-vis that environment. Conceiving boundaries as *perimeters* emerges from system theory (Thompson, 1967) and views boundaries as a mechanism to close off a system from undue external disturbance. System designers established boundaries to buffer the organization from interference. Boundaries were seen as a protective mechanism that close off the organization so that it could be free from disturbances originating outside of the system. Considering boundaries as *interfaces* focuses on boundaries in terms of interconnections. Boundaries serve to create flows of communication and transactions between systems as they interact with one another. This approach to studying boundaries focuses on the interaction at the boundary interface in terms of the exchanges of inputs/outputs and communication flows. Finally, conceiving boundaries as *frontiers* extends the interface perspective. It relates boundaries to the transactional nature of the environment and considers the boundary as the 'marketplace' in which transactional activities takes place.

Both the demarcation and perimeter concepts create an image of boundaries as building and reinforcing differences between the focal unit and others. This emphasizes internal order and cohesiveness based on separation and distinctiveness from other units. It assumes the need to maintain stability and order by regulating and controlling the flow of inputs into the system. Boundaries accordingly become a management tool that offers protection and creates stability. Organizational units will create buffering strategies to cut off their units from unwarranted disturbance. These themes are well supported in institutional theory (Meyer and Rowan, 1977), resource dependency theory (Pfeffer and Salancik, 1978) and rational systems theory (Scott, 1998). In contrast, interface and frontier images suggest the boundaries are a place of contact and connection. Creating a boundary around an activity also creates a set of interactions that occur at that boundary, which, by definition, will necessitate dealing with those that are different (i.e. outside the boundary). In this respect the boundary becomes the 'space' where the system interacts with others. These themes are central to open systems theorists (e.g. Thompson, 1967).

Independently, the work of Paulsen and Hernes (2003) and Hernes (2004) and O'Byrne and Angwin (2003) has developed similar frameworks for discussing and understanding boundary effects at the organizational level. Paulsen and Hernes (2003) categorized boundaries along physical, social and mental effects and described how the nature of these boundaries exert influence on organizations and groups. These influences affect the ordering of internal interactions; they demarcate the internal and external spheres and create a threshold that regulates flows between the internal and external spheres. In contrast O'Byrne and Angwin (2003) discussed boundary influences along physical, behavioural and cognitive dimensions. They drew distinctions between boundaries as physical manifestations, interactions and values and belief systems and proposed how particular management interventions influenced the saliency of boundaries in a merger. They found that management interventions such as pre-merger contact, the involvement of leaders in socialization processes and the creation of vision all helped to create more unified boundaries post amalgamation.

Defining Boundaries

Leading from the above discussion the most common approach to defining boundaries is to consider what is within or without the organization or group and the way inside and outside are differentiated. Aldrich and Herker (1997) consider the distinction in terms of members and non-members of the group, while Scott (1998) talks about the criteria used in determining whom to admit or reject. This is closely linked to a view of a boundary as a protective device that limits the external influence on the organization (Thompson, 1967; Leifer and Deldecq, 1978). Organizations must manage dependencies that arise from their need to acquire resources from and dispose of outputs to the environment (Pfeffer and Salancik, 1978). A boundary exists at the point between the organization and its environment and serves to reduce or eliminate the power others may potentially hold over the organization by regulating the flow of information, people and resources. Thompson (1967), for instance, reviews the mechanisms by which internal operations may be closed off from external variations, and Pfeffer and Salancik (1978) considered how boundary spanning and linkages might reduce the influence of outside interest groups on the organization. The common characteristic of these views is the presence of a clear definition of the differences that distinguish between inside and outside the organization, through the identification of physical entities, people, technology or products that reside in a defined space relative to the organization.

In addition, boundaries can be considered as the created or enacted (Ashford et al., 2000) difference between the organization and its environment. As well as physical elements, a boundary will also have cognitive elements and can be created through social construction processes. For instance, Bacharach et al. (2000) suggest that boundaries are 'limits of self' while Nippert-Eng (1996a; 1996b) have shown that they are 'idiosyncratically constructed'. Boundaries are ways in which individuals (or organizations) can simplify and order their environment (Michaelsel and Johnson, 1997; Zerubavel, 1991) by building 'mental fences' (Zerubavel, 1991) around domains that make sense to the individual. Membership of a group, for instance, may lead a member to define for him or herself what is important and what behaviours are acceptable based on his or her notion of what that group represents. This notion of boundary is closely related to identity and identification. Placing cognitive limits around the group roles and responsibilities that exist within domains greatly eases individual sense-making as it defines the relevance of clues to that particular set of roles and responsibilities. Similarly, the existence of demarcated domains facilitates a clearer understanding of the relationship between domains and reinforces expected behavioural characteristics of individuals or organizations situated within different domains. Ashforth et al. (2000) considered how individuals construct role boundaries within organizations to understand the way in which they cross from work to other domains of activity. They argue that the existence of domains enables groups to evolve and differentiate within those domains along physical, cognitive and relational dimensions.

Boundaries as Ever-Shifting

The notion of boundaries as difference may however imply a degree of rigidity that may not be present. Some group differences – for example, gender or nationality – may be permanent and unchangeable. Even though the difference is permanent it does not imply that it will differentiate all social situations. In may be relevant in some cases, for example a social discourse, but not in others, such as a work context. For any given social context, therefore, there may be a number of possible dimensions on which groups can be divided but that is not to suggest that the division is one that the groups themselves enact as a difference in that social context. In this respect the existence of boundaries per se will not have any influence on events; it is the group's definition of that boundary as salient in the given context that counts. In M&A terms, integration problems can be expected not because of the existence of differences, whether actual or perceived, but when the differences become defined as important and salient. A critical question, therefore, is how do boundaries become salient within M&A and how do changes in boundaries subsequently occur? Little in the literature fully explains how boundary changes occur in social contexts. Hawley's (1995) explanation of the Amish entrepreneur who continually redefined her boundaries with her community provides some explanation of boundary changes. In this instance the entrepreneur continually 'pushed the limits' of acceptable behaviour until she was refused permission to continue. In this way the boundary was tested by being physically challenged. A key element of the challenge was the manner in which the boundary extension was justified and positioned by the entrepreneur and its alignment with the interests of the community. Similarly, Gilmore (1982) has considered the leader as a creator of environments through the negotiation of boundaries and the regulation of transactions across those boundaries while Bacharach et al. (2000) have discussed boundary setting as a managerial device used to manage relationships. Central to these works is the importance of intersubjective assessments to understand both the existing boundaries and the logic in why those boundaries are changing.

A Model of Boundary Management in M&A

The discussion to date has identified a number of dimensions to boundaries and how they might operate. These can be collated together and considered under three headings, consistent with O'Byrne and Angwin (2003) and O'Byrne (2001):

1. the physical boundary,
2. the behavioural boundary,
3. the cognitive boundary.

The physical boundary

There are often tangible and visible divisions between an organization and its environment. These tangible differences arise from clearly demarcated rights to ownership of physical aspects of the business. The most obvious of these is the core operating technology, tasks and products within the firm and the relevant resources underpinning them. It is most often these physical aspects of the business that generate the value-creating potential of the acquisition. There are, however, other aspects of the organization that create physical boundaries. These might include the buildings, products, procedures, or even the name of the company. A distinguishing feature of these is that they are bounded by physical space. Accordingly it is physically clear when one is inside or outside of the boundary (e.g. in the office or outside the office). Significant attention has been paid to these physical aspects of merger integration (Birkinshaw et al., 2000; Marks and Mirvis, 1997; Pritchett, 1997; Haspeslagh and Jemison, 1991; Kitching, 1967; 1973).

The behavioural boundary

As well as considering organizations as physical systems they can also be considered as behavioural systems. Membership of an organizational or social system brings with it norms of behaviour. The position within an organization defines not only the tasks to be completed and the relationship with others but also the expectation of how one should act within those relationships. Different firms have very different behavioural expectations. Some emphasize supportive actions while others emphasize competition and debate. Many behavioural boundaries may however operate on a very subtle level, such as dress code, approach to problem solving and managerial styles or cultural behavioural patterns. The distinguishing characteristic of the behavioural boundary is that it reflects the taken-for-granted actions that are normal for that firm. It is the pre-selected response to a given situation or stimulus. Again this area has received considerable attention in the M&A literature, usually in terms of the human aspects of mergers (Buono and Bowditch, 1989; Ivanancevich et al., 1987), cultural compatibility, (Cartwright and Cooper, 1995; 1997), retention of key staff (Hayes and Hoag, 1974) or stress (Marks and Mirvis, 1985).

The cognitive boundary

Cognitive issues in mergers have attracted significant attention in recent years through research on issues such as social identity (Hogg and Terry, 2001; Terry, 2001; van Kippenberg and van Leeuwen, 2001), psychological responses (Puddifoot, 1997) and emotions (Kusstatscher and Cooper, 2005). Cognitive boundaries result from the way organizations make sense of the world around them. The world we live in is too complex to understand in its entirety so we must accordingly bound the information and stimuli we receive to facilitate making sense of it. This is the third type of boundary that may exist, a cognitive boundary that defines for the organization what information is important, why it is important, and how to interpret it. Soft system methodologies (Checkland, 1993; Checkland and Scholes, 1990; Wilson, 1990) suggest that human activity can be viewed in different ways. How it is viewed depends on the perspective of the viewer. These methodologies draw on the concept of 'Weltanschauung' or world-view. It is used to represent the way in which real world events are filtered and given meaning in the eyes of those experiencing the event (Wilson, 1990). Individuals have a unique development in terms of their beliefs, background, interests and environment and hence develop different Weltanschauungen of the world (Yolles, 1999). Within each individual, there emerges a means of structuring and ordering knowledge which provides them with what appears a natural way of looking at the world. Understanding an action, event or situation is therefore a function of what Weltanschauung is being used to view it. Yolles (1999, p. 32) also argues that groups have a shared 'world-view' and, thus, common models of reality. Accordingly each merging unit will have a unique way of understanding the actions and events surrounding a merger.

Applying Theory to Practice

While the above discussion does highlight that 'boundary' is an abstract construct, a number of key factors are highlighted that allow the construct to be used in practice. On a basic level, boundary is concerned with perceived differences in physical, behavioural or cognitive terms. A boundary can only exist when a demarcation between two sides of that boundary is possible. Furthermore the boundary can only be sustained when that demarcation is sustained. The task of managing boundaries therefore becomes one of identifying potential areas of perceived difference and working to eliminate the sustainability of that perception. Case box 8.1 and the following analysis demonstrates how a firm tackled differences in the amalgamation of its organizational units and managed the differences that occurred.

CASE BOX 8.1:   BOUNDARIES IN ACTION – THE ACQUISITION OF RETAIL COMPANY BY CONTRACT & CAPITAL[2]

Retail Company (Retail), a reasonably small company in the financial services sector within a medium-size European country, was acquired by Contract & Capital Sales in early 1999. Retail specialized in a consumer sector of the market. It had a head office structure and 82 branches throughout the country, with a staff well in excess of 1000. The business concentrated on day-to-day products and services used on a frequent and regular basis by the customer. The company resold some of the products of Contract & Capital but also resold many competing offerings. Retail had been aware that it needed greater scale and scope to compete in an ever more competitive market and had been the target of several suitors prior to the acceptance of the Contract & Capital deal.

   The Contract & Capital group emerged from the merger of Contract Ltd and Capital Ltd some years previously. Both firms were market leaders in their segments of the market. While Capital had some retail operations, it still remained focused on capital (long-term) products. The firm had a national coverage, with 70 branches. A major hindrance to developing its retail operations was the lack of direct access to some parts of the distribution system. This access was a critical factor in the delivery of effective services to the customer. Indeed Contract & Capital was using a competitor to provide these services resulting in longer work-cycle times, slower services to the customer and greater cost.

The strategic logic behind the acquisition of Retail was reasonably simple yet very powerful. By merging the Capital operations and the Retail operations into one large retail force it would enjoy full access to the distribution system and have the necessary scale and product ranges to compete effectively within the industry. This new force would also be a tied agent for Contract's products, increasing the capacity to cross-sell services and products. While there would be some cost efficiencies from the elimination of duplicate head office and support functions, and from the rationalization of the branch networks, the real value in the deal was the capacity to offer an extended range of products to a wider customer base. This extended range of products would emerge from combining the best products and processes from each firm.

The Organizational Cultures

On the surface the cultures of the two combining organizations looked similar. Both organizations espoused the importance of customer service and their commitment to providing quality services. Capital was, however, very focused on achieving volume and aggressively selling its product ranges. In contrast, Retail focused more on the long-term relationship with the customer and was more service-orientated and facilitating in the way it sold its product range. It was more risk adverse and procedural driven than Capital. The general feeling toward the merger was that Retail staff were more favourably positioned than the Capital staff: they had substantial benefits from an employee share option scheme, had better terms and working conditions and were likely to dominate the amalgamation given the focus on retail operations. The integration management allocated considerable resources to the development of cultural understanding through significant investment in communication and intra-organizational contacts. These contacts took the form of training in products/services, pre-branch amalgamation meetings and forums, and local social events. Many additional events were also organized by local branch managers.

The Branch Network

One of the major challenges in achieving the strategic goals was designing and implementing an effective branch network. Combined, Capital and Retail operated a total branch network of 150 branches. The new organization, Capital & Retail, was to reduce this figure by about 40 branches to 110. Many of the branches were located in close proximity to one another and were easily identifiable as potentially mergeable. The product range adopted by the new firm built on the strengths of each partner, with the main products of each being selected as the new firms offering. Both organizations therefore retained what they would have seen as their key products. Decisions regarding the technical infrastructure such as IT systems also logically followed from the key strengths, with IT system selection reflecting the merging partners competencies. Key technical issues had to be resolved to facilitate this technology combination and dual systems using both Retail and Capital systems operated for several months before a unified IT system was adopted. Branch amalgamations were undertaken on a phased basis, commencing in November and ending in the following May. A key element of this phased process was the ability of the integration team to 'learn' about the issues and problems on a phased basis and adjust their preparation for each additional branch amalgamation in the face of this experience.

The State of the Merger

Sixteen months after the acquisition had been approved, and almost 2 years after the initial offer, the new organization had amalgamated its branch network and its support structures. Its success was summed up in a press interview by the director who headed the new firm when he stated the merger was 'as close to a textbook merger as you can get'. Difficulties were acknowledged, however, especially around the nature of customer service, which, given the demands on staff, may not have been as good as it should have been. But generally the integration of the two organizations as a whole had gone broadly according to plan and the financial outlook for the firm was very positive.

An Analysis of Practice: Boundaries and Tensions

Post amalgamation the individual branches enjoyed varying degrees of success in terms of the level of integration that had occurred. However, the type of boundary issues that emerged had a striking degree of similarity across branches. The heritage of each of the combining branches created strong affinities to certain aspects of the work and organization environment. From early on in the merger each branch sought to preference its physical environment over the other. Decisions needed to be made on several aspects of the new organization, including which product would be sold or eliminated from the new branches, which branch would remain open and which would close, which manager would manage the amalgamated branch and what information system would be selected. The central management tackled these issues by creating a central integration office. Adopting a work-stream model, each decision became the responsibility of a dedicated task force made up of representatives from all parties. The role of this task force was to identify 'best practice' and to select a model of 'the best of both'. Each aspect of work structure in the new organization became the responsibility of one dedicated work-stream task force. Notwithstanding the workgroup contributions to creating a logical decision framework for the selection of key components of the new organization, a number of issues surfaced at the branch level.

Emergent physical boundaries

Clear problems arose in relation to the terms and conditions of work, as differences existed in the practices of each firm. While work terms were centrally negotiated between the various staff unions and the management, they impacted strongly in the particular branches. A primary issue was the hours of work. In Retail the branches remained open late on a Thursday until 7.00 p.m. for which staff received 'schedule days' amounting to an additional 2 days' leave a month. In contrast, Capital worked a standard week. A temporary solution was that the Capital staff worked the additional time and claim time off in lieu. However this resulted in Capital staff getting 1 day a month leave rather than the 2 given to the Retail staff, creating some feelings of inequity. Branches were affected differently by the problem, with some sets of staff accepting the need to compromise while in other branches staff refused to work the overtime. This created a level of uncertainty for staff, as it was unclear what the long-term working conditions would be and how this would affect the individual. Ultimately the Thursday working hours issue and the schedule day was resolved through the elimination of the late-night working. However, this solution was only agreed approximately 18 months after the first branches began to merge.

In addition to the schedule day, there were also other aspects of the terms and conditions that differed, such as starting times, lunch times and holiday arrangements. This created a huge degree of uncertainty as staff struggled to become familiar with their new work environment. This was particularly evident in respect of the informal conditions of working within the branch such as tea break protocol, smoking protocols and car parking. While these were often small and mundane issues, they nonetheless created a significant number of problems for the branch managers as staff took time to familiarize and accustomize themselves with their changed environment.

Similarly, terms and conditions differences in the range of products and services offered by the branches also created tensions. There was a close relationship between the product and the daily duties of the staff, with each organization identifying strongly with its product set. While there was a degree of overlap in the product sets, this was reasonably minimal. Capital was very proud of its heritage and its position as market leader in its field. It identified strongly with its sales offerings and defined itself in terms of its capital-based products. On the other hand, Retail provided a retail service and felt it had far better products in the retail sector than Capital. This actually facilitated the decisions about the products that would be sold in the new organization, as product decisions reflected the perceived competencies of each organization. The suite of long-term products was selected from Capital and the suite of retail products was selected from Retail. This allowed the integration management to reinforce the best-of-both concept and extol the virtue of the organizations along product set lines, creating clearly demarcated product territories. This product differentiation however was also re-enforced in other areas of the process, such as IT systems choices, which again followed closely along the product set lines. The IT system represented a core tool of the daily operations and was a central activity in the daily duties of all staff. Indeed the IT system provided the most physical and tangible representation of the activities of staff, given staff spent almost all their day interacting with the IT system. Changes to the system therefore represented a fundamental change to the actual work practice of the staff and created a substantial tension for staff in having to learn about and become familiar with the new system. There was strong ownership of the system from the staff point of view and a great sense of loss when it was being changed.

Two other issues of great concern to staff were the amalgamation of premises and the issue of who would manage the amalgamated branch. The amalgamation of branches took place in approximately 40 locations around the country. A process of evaluating each location and deciding whether the Capital or Retail branch would be selected as the amalgamated branch, based on the business case, was completed. Given the retail focus of the new organization, the Retail branch was selected in most cases as the new sales outlet. The branch presented a strong physical symbol for each organization and staff spoke affectionately about their premises. Moving from the branch meant the staff had to get to know a new office layout, while those that remained in their branches had a large number of additional people now working among them. Each branch saw itself as a team, with a 'family' ethos; accordingly, the significant increase in size of the branches required the formation of a new team within the amalgamated branch and challenged the existing family relationship. However, a strong desire emerged to maintain this family effect and staff shared a sense that it could be maintained if the staff could quickly get to know one another and get on. The corollary of this family effect was the sense of loss that was felt with the changes in the team constitution and the strong feeling that the fabric of the team was being torn asunder by the changes. The importance of this sense of loss was to drive the existing teams more tightly together and strengthen the old team.

One of the strongest physical manifestations of the branch and its boundary with its amalgamating partners was the branch manager. The branch manager appeared to represent a strong symbol of leadership. Branch staff perceived the manager as the person who united the branch and provided the support necessary for sustaining the branch heritage. The loss of the branch manager was a key issue for all staff. Losing the manager meant losing a mentor, reducing support to the branch team and a loss of knowledge about the staff performance and branch operations. There was a significant feeling of loss when the branch manager was replaced and a great sense of uncertainty in getting to know how the new manager would lead the branch. An important aspect of the manager's role appeared to be the direction and leadership, on an individual level, that the staff derived from the manger. There was a familiarity with and clear awareness of the expectations of the manger and the manager was looked upon as a mentor and sponsor for the branch.

The ownership structures of the two organizations presented another problem, with Contract, and more relevantly its shareholders, becoming the new owners post merger. This created a slightly unique boundary problem in that it represented a difference not between the two combining organizations but between them and a head office or shareholder-orientated management. This was particularly evident in the case of Retail, which had enjoyed a governance structure based on a semi-state style ownership. The company's management reported to a board of trustees rather than a profit-focused shareholder-based body. In the new merged structure Capital & Retail were now a trading arm of Contract & Capital, a large stock company. This shift to shareholder accountability was a huge issue for the Retail staff and had major perceived implications for the type of job the branch would be required to perform, shifting the focus onto a profit-focused footing. There was a general sense that the new symbols of ownership, the shareholders and the head office management, were impersonal and distant and had altered the family structure of the branch through their interventions, which in turn reduced the loyalty and commitment of staff. The second effect of the change of ownership was that the Contract group and the shareholders, while accepted by Capital and Retail, became the focus of criticism for their values and beliefs. In a very direct way Contract became an enemy of what both Capital and Retail stood for prior to being acquired by Contract.

Emergent behavioural boundaries

A second wave of problems emerged as the branches became more closely intertwined and had amalgamated their branch operations. As time progressed, problems began to emerge from the relationships the staff engaged in during the course of their duties. The branches amalgamated at a time of great changes in the legislative requirements within the industry and consequently the staff faced into an incredibly busy period of activity. This created a difficulty for all individuals as they tried to balance their desire to integrate into a new work environment and new work teams while simultaneously coping with significant changes in work practice brought about by the merger and by legislative change. To make matters worse, the difficulty in agreeing the terms of condition of employment for the new organization created even greater uncertainty about the future. At the initial stages of the merger, the staff were highly motivated to invest personally in creating an appropriate work environment; however, as time progressed this personal investment began to be questioned. Generally, both sets of staff accepted the need to invest time over and above their standard day and tolerated perceived inequalities (such as the schedule day) to facilitate the creation of the new branch and staff were working significantly in excess of their usual work time. People believed that by putting in the required personal effort, there would be a favourable outcome in the longer term. However, as time progressed, issues remained unresolved and staff began to question the sense of their commitment. In branches where the amalgamation was not running smoothly, this confusion created conflict over who was and who was not contributing the required level of personal commitment. Some staff members were seen as not caring and only doing enough to get by. The workload was seen in comparison to what the other group was doing and perceived inequalities in commitment levels between the groups began to emerge. Differences in the relationship of the person to the work process in the branches also facilitated the emergence of intergroup differences. It became evident that while the work and culture of the organizations appeared similar, differences in the way the groups tackled their work varied. For example, in Capital, staff targets were set on volume of activity while in Retail it was based on overall branch profitability. Capital staff had great difficulty in understanding how Retail staff could get away with such small targets and felt that they would get a wake-up call when more strenuous targets would be set. However, the primary difference was not the volume of activity but the type of product on sale. Capital sold high-value capital products and Retail sold low-value retail products. Strongly linked to the differences in targets is the difference in approach to achieving these targets. Both organizations described themselves as customer-orientated prior to the merger. In work process terms, however, this meant very different things in each organization. Capital's work process identified the once-off long-term needs of the customer and then sold to them the appropriate products from a predefined list and range. In this respect, Capital was primarily a sales-driven organization. In Retail, the work involved repeat transactions and standardized interactions. Customers consumed large volumes of standard products. The design of work process in Retail was accordingly service-orientated. The effect of the differing sales or service orientation was to confuse staff about how they should approach a given customer interaction. In Capital, the sales focus had emphasis on the sales interface with the client and the concentration of time was spent on the sales process. In contrast, Retail focused on the client interaction and support, so activities such as administrative support and queue handling were important activities. This was evident in the relative importance each branch placed on certain tasks. To Capital staff, for instance, the cashier's role was among the lowest jobs in the branch while to Retail it was a senior job. Structures within the two head office organizations also supported the differences in sales versus service orientation, with Capital having centralized administration (frees the branch to sell) while Retail had a decentralized administration system (locates records and information at the local level).

The expected relationship with the customer also created potential confusion. Each branch had different behavioural expectations of what constituted effective customer service. Differences existed for each organization in the interactions between staff and customers, and the relationship that was built and managed between staff and customers. Variations in services included the speed of response to customers, the manner in which selling took place (i.e. immediate consumption of a product versus longer term consumption) and the interface between the customer and the branch (i.e. in the length of time a customer interaction would last).

While both organizations espoused strong customer values, each held strongly negative views of the capacity of the merging partner to meet their level of customer service, arising from the differing approach to sales and service. In Retail, the focus was on servicing the customer where the customer needs tended to be of an ongoing daily nature, while in Capital, the customer had more complex demands with many different product types and ancillary products possible. Capital took the opportunity to sell the widest range of products during an encounter with the customer and had developed a strong sales-focus in customer service. Indeed, the performance measures emphasized the volume of sales and defined customer service in terms of delivering the right product. In contrast Retail delivered a short-term product that was delivered speedily and there were regular interactions between customers and staff.

A clear example of the application of the behavioural difference arose in the approach to queue management. The nature of the two task environments created two very different customer-flow demands. Retail, in particular, had large volumes of customers frequenting the branch. Customer service was therefore defined in terms of the ability to keep the customer's time in the branch to a minimum and to maintain a fast-moving queue. In contrast, Capital's focus on longer term discussions with the customer resulted in a smaller amount of higher maintenance traffic in the branch. Retail staff complained bitterly about the lack of concern that Capital staff showed in keeping the queue moving and the impossibility of managing the new numbers in the branch while Capital staff complained bitterly about the waste of time and resources in having so many people visiting the branch and the lack of Retail's ability to sell effectively.

The importance of team membership and structure for each of the combining groups had been identified at the outset of the amalgamation process as a core concern. As the groups began to merge and more interaction occurred, the concern about the physical aspects of the new group receded to concerns about the interactions and relationships that were being formed in the new group. Initially each branch was wary of each other and unsure about how they should interact with, or interpret actions of, the other group. Stories about groups being social or unsocial, or helpful or unhelpful, began to emerge and be discussed. In branches that integrated quickly, the manager often took the responsibility to bring staff together at the earliest opportunity and build a team environment. In many branches, this team-building effort started prior to the actual physical amalgamation. The benefit of this interaction became evident later in the process, as staff had formed relationships and expectations in terms of acceptable behavioural interactions prior to the formal coming together of the amalgamated branch.

Emergent cognitive boundaries

As interactions created visible differences in behavioural patterns, these differences themselves also stimulated a cognitive cycle. The confusion over how things should be done began to challenge the values and belief systems of the combining groups.

The physical and behavioural aspect of the work was underpinned by very different philosophies about how work should be conducted. For example, there were strong and divergent feelings about aspects of work, including the interpretation of 'being busy', of what products should be sold, how they should be sold and finally of the role of the people within the branch, including promotion and advancement criteria.

Perhaps the strongest indicator of a cognitive boundary arose in the definition of what 'being busy' actually meant. The shorter customer service cycle in Retail created multiple customer interactions throughout the day, while in Capital the focus on large volume items and multiple cross-selling as part of one transaction created a longer customer interaction cycle with less immediate customer demands. In terms of the flow of customers, therefore, Retail had a significantly larger number of daily customer visits than Capital. The lower amount of customer visits in Capital, however, was often translated in the eyes of Retail as meaning the staff in Capital were not busy. In contrast, Capital looked at the volume target being achieved in Retail and considered Retail staff as not having been 'busy' and that they would get a shock when they were asked to reach the volume Capital was achieving. Linked to the notion of being busy, there were clearly different values on how time was best spent servicing or selling to the customer or what was a reasonable time for responding to customers. These time differences related again to the context of the two organizations' prime activities (retail services or capital items) and the time orientations that underpinned these activities. Retail defined effective working and good customer service in terms of getting the customer serviced as quickly as possible and spending the minimum time with the customer. This is in contrast to the idea of identifying and diagnosing customer requirements and selling the maximum range of products within an interaction that permeated within Capital.

A second challenge arose from changes in the identity and sense of belonging of the groups. The heritage of each group was well respected and created a strong sense of loyalty within each of the branches. This sense of belonging and identity was formed both at the level of the organization (i.e. Retail or Capital) but also at the level of the branch, with each branch unit being perceived as unique in the eyes of the branch staff. Staff reported a sense of family, sense of pride, sense of unity and loyalty to their old unit and felt proud about its reputation. There was a strong feeling that these qualities had been lost in the new structure. Uniqueness took on many forms but was often expressed in terms of family loyalty and unity. A second aspect of uniqueness was the pride felt by the staff in relation to the customer's perception of the service provided and the sense of reputation in the community. This presented a sense of identity to the staff and a belief in what they were doing. An outcome of this boundary was the sense that the staff member did not yet belong in the new organization with a concomitant loss in the sense of loyalty and pride in the new organization. However, this was set against a backdrop of a potential positive image moving forward with a clear vision for the organization; that of being a significant player in the market.

Developing Theory on Boundary Effects in M&A

Drawing on the theoretical framework of boundary discussed earlier and having explored the differences that exist within the Retail case, this section sets out to theorize how the different boundary types have latent potential to hinder integration in an amalgamation and how they might be managed.

Managing physical boundaries and surroundings tension

Physical boundaries occur from differences in the physical environment of organizational members. They represent the physical component parts of the work environment, from the work structures through to the products, people, tools and other important symbols that represent key components of work. Where changes were perceived to occur to the physical surroundings of the staff, then the staff appeared to feel a sense of 'loss of familiarity' and a need to get comfortable with the new surroundings. This was evident within the study, with examples such as the sense of uneasiness about the layout of buildings, the tension of getting to know more staff because of the increase in staff numbers or the sense of starting a new job because of the need to learn a new IT system. The relationship of each boundary type to the creation of a type of surrounding tension is outlined in table 8.1. All of these tensions were closely related to the surroundings of the staff and the move from a familiar surrounding to a changed surrounding.

The impact of the changes in the familiarity of the tangible aspects of the work environment results in the comfort of the traditional surroundings being lost and a sense of disorientation occurring. Boundary issues that are likely to arise as a result of the unfamiliar surroundings will most likely be attempts at reasserting familiar surroundings. Preferences over product sets, IT systems or buildings may emerge and will typically take the form of a debate about one set of surroundings being better than another. Such conflicts concern disagreements *about* physical aspect of the work.

Physical boundaries have the potential to create problems for integration if the boundary disputes result in one or other group disengaging from the change in the surroundings and rejecting the new. This could occur, for instance, if one side fails to accept new work practices, fails to change to a new IT system or fails to accept the new directions set by the leader. The effect of these problems is likely to result in the staff disengaging from a particular boundary issue. A physical boundary dispute is, however, likely to be an isolated event, as it concerns a particular tangible aspect of the surroundings that can be resolved by the reduction or elimination of the unfamiliarity associated with that aspect.

Resolving physical boundary problems or eliminating the potential for them to emerge involves management of the physical surroundings in the amalgamation.

Table 8.1   Types of and tensions created by physical boundaries

Type of boundary	Cause of boundary	Tension created by boundary	Example from case
Work requirements	Differences in the context of work (i.e. terms and conditions)	*Unfamiliar structures*: What are the structures to which staff are working?	The schedule day versus overtime for working late on Thursday
Product set	Differences in the range of product and services offered by the firms	*Unfamiliar products*: Understanding the new products	The 'skills gap' in product knowledge between the two organizations
Location	New premises or altered premises (comparison of old versus new)	*Unfamiliar location*: New or different building	Not knowing the layout of the building or the unsuitability of the building
Team constitution	Alteration to the existing team structure through the addition of a number of new members	*Unfamiliar people*: Need to get to know new people	The concerns of the team size and getting to know the new members
Owners	New ownership structure	*Unfamiliar demands*: What is required by the new owners?	Shareholder objectives
IT system	Selection of one IT system over another	*Unfamiliar tools*: Need to get to know how systems operate	Difficulty in adopting to new IT systems
Branch manager	New manager, which represents loss of gatekeeper and symbol of leadership and power for one group	*Unfamiliar direction*: What does the new manager value and how does he/she operate within the new power structure?	Personal loss over the departure of the manager and to the need to get to know how the new manager operates

Specifically, if the potential for physical boundaries to create boundary issues revolves around the need to reassert a familiar environment for staff, then management can reduce the potential conflicts by making the surroundings more familiar and more accessible to staff. There were many examples in the case of how the branches achieved this effectively. There were a number of centrally managed initiatives, such as staff swapping, that engaged each set of staffing and allowed staff to see how the other branch operated and to engage with one another. There were also integration meetings organized where the amalgamating branches came together to prepare and plan the amalgamation. There were also initiatives at the local level, such as social events and informal meetings. Comparing branches that integrated well and poorly suggests that better performing branches invested heavily in pre-amalgamation contact and awareness building while far less contact and awareness was evident in the poorer performing branches.

Managing behavioural boundaries and interaction tension

Behavioural boundaries occur from expectations of the relationships that occur between the staff and others in the work environment, notably through customer interaction, team interaction, work processes and the extent to which staff members are willing to commit themselves to the work. These boundaries emerge from the different actions that form the basis of group interactions and set the norms of behaviour for the group as a whole. When behavioural boundaries come into contact, confusion arises as to how tasks should be completed, with a corresponding mismatch between the action and the needs of the action recipient. A clear example of this in the case data was the mismatch in dealing with the immediate requirement of daily transactions for Retail customers and the longer-term requirements of Capital customers. Staff members were effectively asked to interact with customers in a new manner that was at odds with their previous behaviour pattern. Indeed, interactions could occur that appeared to meet the perceived needs of the customer but failed to meet the actual needs. This was particularly evident in the sales versus service issue. Queues were kept moving rather than each interaction being seen as a sales opportunity. This boundary clearly creates a tension for staff in the interactions between staff within the branch and between staff and their customers. The particular types of interaction tension for each of the potential boundaries within this category are identified in table 8.2.

The potential for behavioural boundaries to create problems will be highest when the behavioural differences go unchecked and the staff continue to operate under the behavioural norms applicable to their previous organization. In such case it might be expected that the differences in approaches will heighten the confusion between staff. A breakdown in the social process of interaction will result in fragmentation among the combining groups and the formation of distinctly separate groups that will interact with each other poorly. In general, the behavioural boundaries merged effectively within the case example. This perhaps can be put down to the very effective centrally managed programmes of training, development and support that the organization initiated. All staff received training in new systems, procedures and products. Supporting staff were seconded to branches for the first weeks of the amalgamation to assist staff and to advise them based on previous experience. In addition, at the local level, staff exchanges and individual managers' initiatives in discussing the working and social relations with new staff facilitated individual staff

Table 8.2 Behavioural boundaries: types and tensions

Type of boundary	Cause of boundary	Tension created by boundary	Example from case
Personal investment	Level of personal commitment that an individual is willing to invest in the work/group	*Commitment confusion*: Creating balance between self and work	Working 'unrealistic' times and working extra to facilitate group cohesion
Work processes	Differences in how work is performed and tasks completed	*Task confusion*: Matching tasks and the way they are performed to meet new work requirements	Servicing versus selling to the customer
Team behaviour	Expectations of behaviour within the team	*Social confusion*: Operating in new emergent social order and determining the position within that social order	Importance of being a team player and the desire to have good social relations in the new branch notwithstanding 'being wary' of each other
Customer service	Changing customer requirements and interactions	*Translation confusion*: Translating the products and procedures into meaningful customer interactions	The queue management emphasis in each organization

to link the new work surroundings to the necessary behavioural expectations and smooth the transition.

Resolving or eliminating the potential of behavioural boundary problems is based on producing a mechanism for the resolution of the interaction tension that the boundary creates. Providing awareness of these new surrounding and relationships is insufficient, as this will only tackle the awareness of the new surroundings. In addition a new repertoire of behaviour responses is required and this can only occur when the staff are shown and trained effectively in the new requirements. There are four distinct aspects to this in the particular case and these relate to the four boundary types. Staff must be confident in their investment in the organization by understanding the relationship of their inputs to the potential rewards they might receive, both organizationally and socially (building motivation). There must be clarity on the work requirement and how to deal effectively with the products or service (product training); there must be a consistent expectation as to the role and performance of the team (team building and norm formation); and there must be clear guidance as to service requirements (customer sales and service training).

Cognitive boundaries and affective tension

Cognitive boundaries arise from beliefs and values. They represent the potential for differences that arise from the underlying assumptions that individuals take for granted within their work. The case indicates two types of cognitive boundaries, work beliefs and belonging, arising within the amalgamating organizations. These boundaries arise from a common set of values individuals assign to the work and the organization and which creates a predefined schema for understanding the work and the individual's place within the work structure. For example, the definition of work within Retail revolved around the completion of transactions initiated by the customer whereas, to Capital, work entailed the initiation of sales by staff. While there is a behavioural focus to the difference in work practices, there also exists a significant cognitive effect that translates into what each set of staff value as being productive work. A behavioural boundary might be eliminated through effective training but a cognitive boundary arises as staff reject the underlying logic of the changed behaviour. This is evident here as the drive by the parent company to focus on a sales approach to customer service was in some cases seen in Retail as being inappropriate and inconsistent with their previous philosophy. Retail staff were not willing to 'flog products to the customer' even if that is what the parent company required. The tension created from this type of boundary contact is 'affective' in nature. It challenges the value and belief set of the staff and makes them question the link between 'why' they are doing things and 'what' they are doing.

Two types of challenge arise from the boundaries. First is a sense challenge, questioning the belief that the operation is in some way better than the old and that the values underpinning the activities are valid. This is clearly evident in Retail's reluctance to accept a sales orientation – if it meant flogging goods to the customer – because it challenged Retail's underlying values. The second challenge arises from the loss of identity felt by staff when their old organization is lost and the subsequent need for them to recreate a new identity within the new organization that accepts both them and their partner firm. Again this was very evident in the references to pride and the loss of pride resulting in the formation of a new organization that failed to mirror the old organizations' values and beliefs. The types of tensions created by cognitive boundaries, and the two types of challenge that arise, are identified in table 8.3.

Boundary problems that occur from cognitive boundary clashes are most likely to be severe. They will arise from the emotions and values staff hold about the organization and accordingly differences will be manifest in terms of rights and wrongs. These problems will be affective in nature and may emphasize feelings of trust, pride or justice. In contrast to physical boundaries, that will create conflict about an issue, or behavioural boundaries, that will create a conflict with actions taken, cognitive boundaries will create conflict *because* of an affective reason.

To manage cognitive boundaries, either to resolve emerging conflict or to prevent conflict in the first instance, requires an attempt to resolve the challenges to sense

Table 8.3 Types of and tensions created by cognitive boundaries

Type of boundary	Cause of boundary	Tension created by boundary	Example from case
Work beliefs	Differences in the underlying logic of why the work is performed in a given manner	*Sense challenge*: Understand the validity of the other's way of conducting activities	The need to accept that 'being busy' included sales and service. The Retail vs. the Capital way
Belonging	Importance of group membership and identity	*Identity challenge*: Motivation to feel part of the combined organization/let go of the old and accept the partner organisation	Sense of pride felt in the branch and organization achievements

and identity. Contact and training will bring to the fore the types of physical and behavioural differences that emerge in the amalgamation but will not specifically address the logic and understanding of staff. These activities may show what needs to be done but not necessarily why or why the staff should feel a sense of belonging to the new organization. The key activity in the reduction of cognitive boundaries in the study appeared to be the sense of vision created for the new organization. The branch with the least level of integration was focused very strongly on the daily operations and on short-term goals. In contrast, the branches showing the greatest integration had clear images of the future, of the benefits the new group would have and how they would be better off as a result. Although in many cases there were existing problems to be resolved, the potential for the future was seen as a worthy cause for the suffering. Several activities build this vision. Through the head office interventions, the level of information and communication coming from the central integration office and the variety of communication meetings present a vision of the company being a major force, a company to be proud of and a leader in its industry. At the local level, the branch manager, in branches that integrated well, spent considerable time talking about the future to staff and explaining to them the potential going forward. This was done through the manager spending time with branch staff on a group and individual bases discussing the changes and what they meant. In the case of these branches each staff member was met individually by the manager for discussions on the future and his or her role within it. In these branches, managers were seen to support team integration and foster discussions in an open manner. This gave a context for staff in which they could deal with the affective challenges and make sense more readily of the work changes facing them.

It also served to bond the team under a common banner and create a more cohesive unit that aids identity formation.

A Model of Boundary Management

Drawing together the tensions created by the different boundary types, the effects these tensions create and the manner in which they were managed creates a model of how interventions might influence the potential for a boundary to become salient. Table 8.4 sets out the model.

Three types of broad interventions occurred in the case: contact and awareness building, training and support, and vision building. Each one of these interventions has a separate but distinct effect on a boundary type as outlined in the earlier discussion. However, what is also evident is that the tension created by each boundary type requires a specific type of intervention to reduce or eliminate that tension. For instance, building awareness of the products on offer by each branch will allow staff to understand the range of products and not to feel unfamiliarity in handling or discussing them. However, when it comes to interactions with the customer they may be incapable of understanding the way in which they are expected to sell the products. In addition, the awareness of the products does nothing to help in resolving the potential challenge to the staff's value set on what types of products should or should not be sold. Similarly, training the staff in sales or supporting them in their sales efforts will help resolve the confusion on how to interact but fails to provide any help in building familiarity with the products or in understanding potential shifts in value sets. Finally, broad approaches in building a vision will motivate potential changes in value sets and identity but fail to address either the actions required or build familiarity in surroundings.

This model explains why so many problems can occur within a merger integration. A coherent set of interventions is required if all potential sources of boundary differences are to be managed. Furthermore these interventions must be tightly focused on achieving a particular goal of building awareness, building a repertoire of actions or building a vision. Failure to tackle all of these areas leaves the organization open to a set of boundaries becoming salient and creating intergroup conflict. It is also worth considering the impact of failing to address each boundary type effectively and to consider the relationship between each boundary category. It is possible to consider the boundaries in terms of an inverse pyramid, with physical integration at the apex only being the beginning of full integration (see figure 8.1).

People progress from resolving physical boundaries through behavioural boundaries and onto cognitive boundaries in sequence, with the focus and intensity of the boundary importance increasing at each level. Where a boundary becomes salient in a given context, however, it is not possible to progress to the next level.

Table 8.4   The impact of interventions on boundaries

	Physical boundaries	Behavioural boundaries	Cognitive boundaries
Type of tension created by boundary	From: Surroundings	From: Interaction	From: Cognitive attachments
Potential for boundary conflict where boundary becomes salient	Boundary arises *about* an issue due to *unfamiliarity*	Boundaries arise *with* an action that creates *confusion* over its appropriateness	Boundaries arise *because* of a *challenge* to the value set or identity
Effect of management interventions on each boundary			
Contact and awareness building	Builds awareness and familiarity	Staff are aware of surroundings but confused on how to interact within the new surroundings	Staff are aware of surroundings but not how it relates to their values
	Reduces saliency of boundary	*No effect on boundary*	*No effect on boundary*
Training and behaviour support	New repertoire of actions but unfamiliarity remains as to how they link to the surroundings	Builds repertoire of actions that can reduce confusion	New repertoire of actions but not how they relate to values
	No effect on boundary	*Reduces saliency of boundary*	*No effect on boundary*
Building of a vision	New vision but unfamiliarity remains regarding changes in the surroundings	New vision but confusion in translating vision into actions	Builds vision that allows a new identity and value set to be accepted
	No effect on boundary	*No effect on boundary*	*Reduces saliency of boundary*

If intergroup conflict occurs, the non-resolution of the boundary issue might stimulate staff to justify their positions by seeking to extenuate the perceived difference, which in turn is likely to influence not only the boundary category at which the conflict occurs but also boundary categories at lower levels. In this respect a cycle of regression may be experienced, resulting in new conflicts emerging. This might be depicted diagrammatically as in figure 8.2.

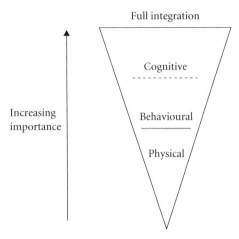

Figure 8.1 Hierarchy of boundaries

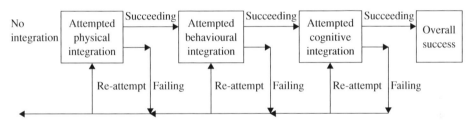

Figure 8.2 A stage model of integration disruption

Conclusion

The model presented in this chapter presents a new way of looking at the potential conflicts that might occur in merger integration. It moves attention away from static issues, such as a predefined cultural fit, and emphasizes a dynamic process model of boundary management. Dynamic, because it draws attention to different types of boundary and their potential to create salient differences over time, causing integration problems, and how different interventions can be used to mitigate these difficulties. Paying attention to differences and building bridges to commonality are important elements in achieving integration objectives in a merger. The case clearly shows that this is a multifaceted task.

While the chapter has focused on achieving post-acquisition integration outcomes, it is clear that integration approaches need to be considered long before the actual date of unit amalgamation. Many of the boundaries and their potential for problems occur very early in the merger process. In this respect the model presented offers significant guidance to those who are planning to unite organizational units. The actions identified can be initiated in a planned, phased way to aid pre-integration planning. For instance, contact and awareness building can occur at the earliest opportunity, possibly immediately after merger announcements; similarly, training and vision re-enforcement can be commenced rapidly. More importantly, however, the framework provides guidance to managers on how to distinguish categories of boundaries, identify potential differences and anticipate the nature and likelihood of problem creation. The model of dynamic boundary management provides a systematic approach for identifying, managing and eliminating interorganizational post-acquisition clashes.

NOTES

1. This chapter is an extension of O'Byrne and Angwin (2003).
2. All names of companies, persons and dates have been altered to provide informants with anonymity. The help of the case company and its staff is very gratefully acknowledged.

Chapter 9   M&A as Knowledge

Laura Empson

It is more than 15 years since Haspeslagh and Jemison (1991) published their landmark book *Managing Acquisitions: Creating Value Through Corporate Renewal.* Their innovative premise was that value is created post merger as a result of the transfer of capabilities between the merging firms. Knowledge sharing represents a particularly significant source of potential value creation. Managers should, therefore, pay particular attention to the management of the integration process and not simply focus their energies on pre-merger negotiations.

Haspeslagh and Jemison's perspective has become established wisdom among management writers over the past 15 years (see Angwin (2000) and Sirower (1997), for important studies that build on this perspective). It is far from apparent, however, that mergers and acquisitions have shown substantially improved performance during this period, as Pablo and Javidan (2004) demonstrate.

Arikan (2004) finds that, when the value of the target firm is based primarily on intangible assets such as knowledge, buyers on average experience an economic loss of 12% over a 5-year period post acquisition. Schoenberg's (2001) study of knowledge transfer by European acquirers confirms that the ability to transfer knowledge consistently falls short of acquirers' expectations.

There are many possible reasons for this poor performance, but probably the most convincing explanation is the simplest. In mergers and acquisitions, managers often fail to create value from transferring capabilities (i.e. sharing knowledge) because it is very, very difficult to do so. When seeking to exploit existing knowledge and create new knowledge, managers are wrestling with the intangible. They are often beaten.

This chapter explores the opportunities that mergers[1] and acquisitions present for sharing knowledge and examines the process by which knowledge sharing takes place. Based on a case study of a consulting firm merger, the chapter identifies the problems that arise and suggests ways in which these problems can be prevented or overcome. Professional service firms, such as consulting firms, provide an interesting context in which to study knowledge sharing because their technical and client-based knowledge represents their key income-generating assets. At the same time, the knowledge-sharing process is likely to be particularly difficult in this context because knowledge in a professional service firm is often tacit and proprietary to individuals. If these individuals are unwilling to share knowledge, or choose to leave the firm altogether, the merger may fail. Lessons learnt in such a complex and risky context can, therefore, yield valuable insights about how to create value by sharing knowledge in mergers and acquisitions more generally.

Before presenting the case study, the chapter briefly explains what is meant by knowledge in professional service firms, some of the problems that arise when attempting to share knowledge *within* organizations, why mergers and acquisitions can be viewed as valuable opportunities for sharing knowledge *between* organizations, and problems that are likely to arise in the context of mergers between professional service firms.

Knowledge in Professional Service Firms

There is no simple answer to the question 'what is knowledge?' For the purposes of strategic and organizational management, it is perhaps easiest to understand knowledge in terms of what it is not. It is not data and it is not information. Data are objective facts, presented without any judgement or context. Data become information when categorized, analysed and placed in context. Information, therefore, is data endowed with relevance and purpose. Information develops into knowledge when it is used to establish connections, make comparisons and assess consequences. As Davenport and Prusak (1998) argue, knowledge can, therefore, be seen as information that comes laden with experience, judgement and values.

The primary activity of a professional service firm is the application of specialist technical knowledge to the creation of customized solutions to clients' problems. Technical and client-based knowledge are, therefore, the key income-generating assets. The form and content of knowledge in professional service firms is explained in detail in Empson (2001) but is summarized briefly below.

The technical knowledge of a professional service firm encompasses sectoral, organizational and individual forms of knowledge. Sectoral knowledge is generic, widely shared by all firms in a specific sector, and may be formally codified through the syllabus of professional exams. Organizational knowledge is firm-specific and consists of distinctive products and processes that have been developed and disseminated within a firm, either through formalized knowledge-management systems or through ad hoc methods of apprenticeship and socialization. Individual technical knowledge is proprietary to each professional and is derived from his or her previous work experience, education and unique mix of client assignments.

Client knowledge may also be categorized into three broad categories: a general understanding of a particular industry, detailed knowledge of a specific client, and personal knowledge of key individuals within the client firm. This kind of relationship-based knowledge is particularly valuable for professional service firms as their 'products' cannot be inspected in advance and are created through interaction with clients after the initial purchase decision has been made. A strong relationship between the individual professional and the client is, therefore, a precondition for a successful sales and delivery process.

This defines the 'content' of knowledge in professional service firms, but what 'form' does the knowledge take? We each have a limited stock of explicit knowledge that we find easy to codify and articulate to others, such as books we have read, reports we have written and advice we have given to colleagues. The primary goal of formal IT-based knowledge management systems is to identify the valuable knowledge that resides within individuals, present it in some easily understandable form, and disseminate it throughout the organization. But most of what we know is not tacit but explicit. Tacit knowledge in its purest form cannot be codified. A successful salesperson cannot explain to a junior colleague exactly how to close a sale. This kind of knowledge is best transferred through observation and practice, and many professional service firms still employ the traditional craft-based apprenticeship model for transferring knowledge between partners and trainees.

The distinction between tacit and explicit knowledge is not absolute. As Nonaka and Takeuchi (1995) explain, much of our knowledge remains tacit simply because we have not attempted to make it explicit. It is this unarticulated yet codifiable knowledge that presents the greatest opportunity for knowledge sharing within organizations. As outlined below, this process of knowledge sharing is far from straightforward.

Knowledge Sharing Within Organizations

Knowledge represents a source of power for individuals, particularly within a professional service firm. By sharing valuable knowledge with a colleague you run the risk of diminishing your value to your firm. Potentially you are no longer indispensable. Davenport and Prusak (1998) argue that you will only agree to share your knowledge with a colleague under three conditions. The first is *reciprocity*. Your time and energy are finite; you will only take the time if you think you are likely to receive valuable knowledge in return at some future point. The second is *reputation enhancement*. It is in your interests to be viewed as an expert within your organization; if you do not have a reputation for expertise your knowledge cannot represent a source of power. The third is *altruism* (or *self-gratification*). There will be some subjects you care passionately about and you will seek opportunities to discuss them with others. Davenport and Prusak suggest that an internal market for knowledge exists within organizations. Knowledge is exchanged between 'buyers' and 'sellers', with reciprocity, reputation and altruism/self-gratification functioning as payment mechanisms.

Davenport and Prusak highlight some of the personal reasons why an individual might be reluctant to share his or her knowledge, but there are also numerous organizational factors that can impede knowledge sharing. In large and complex organizations, the lack of an appropriate knowledge-management infrastructure will pose problems. Where technologically based knowledge-management systems do exist, their effectiveness will depend on an appropriate combination of individual incentives and cultural norms of trust and cooperation. Without trust the 'internal market' for knowledge will not function effectively because individuals cannot be sure that they will be rewarded appropriately for sharing their knowledge. Given the considerable difficulties of sharing knowledge *within* organizations, sharing knowledge *between* organizations is likely to be even more difficult.

Knowledge Sharing Between Organizations

Until the 1990s, management writers emphasized three main reasons for undertaking mergers and acquisitions: 1) to turn around poorly performing firms through the introduction of superior management; 2) to increase potential markets through diversification; and 3) to secure competitive advantage through increasing monopoly power. It was only in the early 1990s, with the development of the resource-based view of the firm by writers such as Barney (1991) and the increased emphasis on knowledge as a core resource, that mergers and acquisitions came to be widely regarded as an opportunity to create value through gaining access to new sources of knowledge (see Greenberg and Guinan (2004) and Ranft and Lord (2002) for studies of this phenomenon in technology-based industries).

According to the resource-based view, a company's competitive advantage derives from its ability to assemble and exploit an appropriate combination of resources. Sustainable competitive advantage is achieved by continuously developing existing (and creating new) resources to respond to changing market conditions. Writers such as Grant and Spender (1996) argue that knowledge represents an organization's most important value-creating asset; the primary function of a firm is to create conditions under which many individuals can integrate specialist knowledge to produce goods and services.

In mergers between professional service firms, bringing together the technical knowledge base of two firms may lead to the creation of an entirely new service offering. The process of innovation will require a high level of cooperation between merger partner colleagues, as individuals from each firm will need to develop an understanding of each other's expertise to create an entirely new basis for conceptualizing or delivering the service. It may not, however, be necessary to 'merge' the knowledge bases in this way. Professional service firms often undertake mergers to gain access to a related source of expertise that clients may wish to purchase alongside their own. An extreme example is the opportunity for 'one-stop shopping' created by the Big Five professional service firms of the 1990s. In these diversified professional service firms, the emphasis is on sharing knowledge about clients rather than sharing technical knowledge. Professionals in these cases do not need to understand exactly what their colleagues do. They only need to know enough to spot opportunities for cross-selling. They also need to trust their merger partner colleagues sufficiently to introduce them to their clients.

Impediments to Knowledge Sharing in Professional Service Firm Mergers

In merging professional service firms, management's attempts to encourage knowledge sharing are likely to run into particular difficulties. In any kind of organization, the announcement of a merger can create a highly stressful environment of uncertainty, fear and distrust, as demonstrated in studies such as Buono and Bowditch (1989), Cartwright and Cooper (1992) and Mirvis and Marks (1992). Even if redundancies are not planned, individuals may fear loss of status and changes to their working habits. They may resist senior management's initiatives to encourage cooperation between the combining firms and may ultimately resign.

These negative reactions will be particularly troublesome when sharing knowledge is an explicit merger objective. Sharing knowledge is above all an interpersonal process. Explicit knowledge may be shared relatively easily, but the experiences and insights required to interpret and apply this knowledge reside within individuals. Individuals cannot be compelled to share knowledge, so the managers of merging organizations in general, and professional service firms in particular, are highly constrained in their ability to bring about knowledge sharing.

Consequently, mergers between professional service firms represent an interesting context in which to study knowledge sharing. The opportunities to create value from accessing new knowledge will be considerable, but so too will the obstacles. These issues are illustrated in the following case study of a knowledge-based merger between Sea Consulting and Land Consulting (names and dates have been disguised to preserve anonymity). The case is presented in four parts. The first explores the opportunities for sharing knowledge and presents a brief description of the two firms prior to the deal. The second examines the initial impediments to sharing knowledge that arose. The third explains how these problems escalated and the fourth describes how they were ultimately resolved.

In reading the case study it is useful to focus on three main themes. First, what are the opportunities to create value from sharing technical and client-based knowledge? Second, what are the key differences in the form and content of the firms' knowledge bases? Third, what realistically can be done during the pre-merger planning and post-merger integration phases to facilitate knowledge sharing? These three issues will be discussed in detail in the conclusions section.

Table 9.1 Sea and Land at the time of formal alliance

	Sea	Land
Size		
Fee income	US$110m	US$150m
Offices outside USA	11	1
Total staff	470	570
UK staff	85	90
Governance		
Legal structure	Partnership	Privately owned
Largest single shareholding	7%	75%
	(Philip Short, founder and MD)	(Bob Porter, founder and MD)

Sea and Land Merger (Part A): Opportunities For Sharing Knowledge

Sea Consulting

Sea was a strategic management consulting firm, founded as a partnership in the 1960s by a Harvard Business School professor. Although relatively small (see table 9.1 for further details), Sea regularly won business from larger, 'big name' strategy consulting firms such as McKinsey and the Boston Consulting Group. It sought to differentiate its service offering by becoming expert in what was then the emerging field of change management consulting. Another basis of differentiation was Sea's worldwide network of faculty associates from leading business schools. They provided access to current research, often worked closely with consultants on projects, and were an important source of sales contacts.

Consultants were expected to perform highly complex analysis to develop innovative solutions to client problems. Recruits were selected more for their analytical skills than for their relevant work experience. The majority of consultants had MBAs but their knowledge differed considerably according to their previous careers and the unique combination of project experiences they had gained while working at Sea. Knowledge transfer occurred on an ad hoc basis on projects, as senior consultants worked closely with junior consultants to help them develop the skills relevant to specific projects. Consultants also relied upon more widespread informal networking amongst peers. Sea consultants made very little effort to codify and disseminate this knowledge formally.

The culture and values of Sea were shaped by the academic origins of the firm. Intellectual ability and creativity were prized over all other qualities, including interpersonal and organizational skills. Psychometric tests conducted on Sea consultants concluded:

> 'Consultants show an extremely strong preference to avoid structure, order and planning. They are creative and very flexible . . . While Sea consultants have outstanding analytical skills, people skills are somewhat lacking. Sea consultants are on the whole very autonomous and would prefer a working environment where they did not have to be part of the team, but could instead be an individual contributor.' (*Report on results of psychometric tests on Sea consultants*)

The intellectually elitist and exclusive atmosphere of the firm was reflected in its office accommodation. The London Sea office was located in a Georgian town house in Mayfair, decorated to reflect the eighteenth century origins of the building. The partners sat together in one large room at antique leather-topped desks. The walls of this room were lined with books and decorated with paintings commissioned by Sea to reflect the history and development of the firm.

Land Consulting

Land Consulting was also established in the USA in the 1960s but was a privately quoted firm specializing in operational improvement, with a developing business in change management (see table 9.1 for further details). The premise of Land's consulting offering was that, in order to achieve lasting change, Land consultants needed to work closely with individual clients over an extended period, coaching them in specific skills and helping them to identify operational problems and develop and implement recommendations. Land developed the 'pilot project' sales process whereby Land consultants spent a few weeks working with a potential client, identifying the most important issues, developing a potential project plan, and quantifying the potential financial benefits. When the project was finally sold, the client relationship passed to the 'results delivery' manager, whose primary role was to facilitate clients' progress through a series of core processes that would enable them to develop their own solutions. These core processes provided consultants with a very clear set of guidelines about what they should do with their clients at each stage.

Because consultants were primarily concerned with the process rather than the content of a project, they were recruited on the basis of their relevant business experience and good interpersonal skills rather than their analytical abilities. Few Land consultants had MBAs and most were older than their counterparts at Sea. The highly prescribed recruiting and training process was designed to produce uniformity. On joining the firm, all consulting staff received training at Land's New Jersey headquarters. As well as learning about the core processes they were trained in the Land 'language', which they were expected to use when communicating with clients and with each other. Problems were called 'issues' and issues were expressed in positive rather than negative terms, such as 'how to . . .' (or 'H2 . . .' when writing on flip charts). Concerns and criticisms were phrased in terms of 'I wish I knew . . .' (or 'IWIK . . .' on flip charts).

> 'In Land there were 20 brilliant guys at the top, with this huge pyramid under them of guys who didn't ask too many questions but knew how to implement. Land codified its skills because it knew the skills gap between the top and the bottom of the organization was so great.' (*Manager, Land*)

The need for intensive client interaction meant that Land consultants worked full-time at the clients' offices and rarely visited their 'home' office. While Land's London office was in the same Mayfair street as Sea's, it was different in style and atmosphere. Land's offices were in a 1970s office block and furnished with modern desks and equipment. The rooms were light and relatively stark, and some of the modern artwork supplied by the New Jersey head office presented 'inspiring' messages. Bob Porter recognized that it was difficult to create a sense of corporate affiliation among consultants who rarely visited their offices and who worked together in temporary teams at a series of client sites. His solution was to create a codified set of values, to recruit consultants who were capable of embodying those values, and to penalize consultants who failed to do so.

Working together and in competition

Philip Short, Managing Partner of Sea, and Bob Porter, Managing Director of Land, had a long-standing professional and personal relationship. Philip Short was a board member of Land and head of its remuneration committee. When Land consultants established an office in London, Philip Short introduced them to many of Sea's clients and allowed them to use Sea's office facilities.

Competition between the two firms developed gradually during the next 3 years. When one client simultaneously bought the services of both firms for two separate projects, there was considerable conflict between the consulting teams.

> 'Sea seemed very different to us. They were very knowledgeable and confident. They were full of bar charts. We didn't understand them.' (*Consultant, Land*)

> 'Land was trying to fix the processes of a massively loss-making operation. As the Sea manager, I recognized that something fundamental had to be done on the strategy side, but the Land manager refused to accept this . . . He made my life hell.' (*Manager, Sea*)

Three years after establishing the London office, Bob Porter sold Land to Cosmos, a global information management consulting firm. Porter's decision to sell

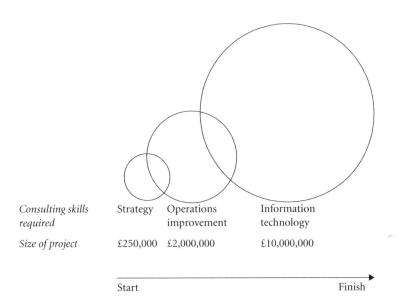

Consulting skills   Strategy   Operations   Information
required   improvement   technology

Size of project   £250,000   £2,000,000   £10,000,000

Start   Finish

Figure 9.1 Land: Bob Porter's vision of an integrated consulting firm

was motivated by two factors: his desire to realize the value of his 75% stake in the firm and his belief in the concept of 'one-stop shopping' as a means of expansion. Bob Porter outlined his one-stop shopping concept of consulting to the Land staff (see figure 9.1), showing how a strategy capability could generate sales of operations-improvement projects, which would ultimately lead to large-scale information technology projects. At the time he developed this plan, no consulting firm was offering this kind of 'one-stop shopping', though many firms attempted to do so in the years that followed. To achieve his plan, Land needed access to an established consulting capability.

The day after concluding the sale of Land to Cosmos, Bob Porter approached Philip Short and proposed that the partners of Sea Consulting also sell their own firm to Cosmos and then merge with Land Consulting. Philip Short strongly supported Porter's proposal and encouraged Cosmos to make an offer for Sea.

Philip Short presented the proposal to the partner group as an opportunity to 'play in a different league' and to 'reshape the competitive space' within the consulting industry by combining strategy, operations and information management into a new service offering. He described his vision of the future using the graphic shown in figure 9.2.

'Philip drew these three interlocking circles. His idea was that, where the circles over-lapped represented a "propeller" that would drive the business forward.' (*Partner, Sea*)

The Sea partners initially rejected Philip Short's proposal but over the next 6 months, the vast majority of Sea partners came to recognize the benefits of the deal. Many

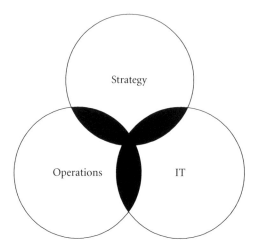

Figure 9.2   Sea: Philip Short's vision of an integrated consulting firm

Sea partners were concerned about the implications of abandoning the partnership structure but were attracted by the substantial payments available.

'The cash was more or less attractive depending upon our personal levels of wealth and our personal levels of greed. I would not have voted for the merger if it had not been for the money. I liked Sea just the way it was. I liked being able to control my own destiny.' (*Partner, Sea*)

Philip Short and a small group of partners began to develop plans for integration. They described the overall objective in a document to partners as follows:

'We should let the market success drive the necessary degree of integration in all areas . . . Operational integration in the US and the UK would occur gradually over a few years . . . it might never be complete so long as many clients continue to want to buy strategy services . . . We would expect over time that each firm would begin to understand and to participate in the opportunities created by the other distinctive channel, but the two firms would remain reasonably separate for a period of time.' (*Memo to Sea partner group*)

The intention was for both Sea and Land to retain their separate legal identities for a while longer and to operate as a formal alliance in the short term with a view to moving towards a full merger in due course. Timescales were deliberately vague. No statement was made of an intention to work more closely with the IT parent company. Indeed Cosmos honoured its informal commitments at the time of these negotiations and retained an entirely arm's-length relationship with Sea and Land for several years.

Sea and Land Merger (Part B): Impediments To Knowledge Sharing

The senior executives of Sea and Land announced their intentions to the press as follows:

> 'Sea and Land will collaborate on a growing number of opportunities but, for some time to come, each firm will also have many clients which are not shared . . . We have a well-crafted management plan that gives us 3 years to train, develop, recruit, and support the staff we will need to deliver the integrated product.' (*Joint press release*)

The 'well-crafted management plan' was not apparent to the staff and vice-presidents of Sea and Land.

> 'Sea and Land had no specific merger plans. The idea was "Let's just get on with it and see how it works."' (*Vice-president, Land*)

> 'There was no apparent architecting at the top. It was a case of "Thou shalt go out and work together."' (*Manager, Sea*)

Immediately following the sale of Sea to Cosmos, eight task forces of Sea and Land vice-presidents were established to consider how Sea and Land would work together. One related to the development of an integrated service offering, three related to internal organizational issues, and four related to sales and marketing.

> 'There was no explicit statement of an intent to transfer knowledge. It was somehow assumed this would happen by osmosis.' (*Manager, Sea*)

Conflict and attempts to cooperate

In the USA, Land was considerably larger than Sea and quickly began to dominate the combined firm. This did not happen in London, as the two offices were relatively evenly matched in terms of revenue and staff. The head of Land's London office was keen to pursue 'full integration', but Sea consultants were concerned that full integration would, in effect, mean a takeover of Sea by Land.

> 'Sea was such a heterogeneous culture and Land was so homogeneous. It seemed clear that Land's homogeneous culture would prevail unless we fought hard to preserve our own.' (*Vice-president, Sea*)

The conflicting visions of the future were manifested in the interpersonal conflicts between the leaders of the firms' London offices, Jonathan Aldridge (Sea) and Gene White (Land).

'It was fairly open warfare between Jonathan and Gene. They fought over everything, from the allocation of profit between the two practices to the artwork on the walls of the partner room.' (*Manager, Sea*)

'Gene and Jonathan had worked all their lives to become office head. Suddenly they got their wish but realized that they had no real authority. They had to share power with each other. It was disastrous for both of them.' (*Vice-president, Land*)

With the leaders of the London office unable to work together, it was not surprising that their colleagues were generally reluctant to cooperate. A limited number of joint projects were attempted, some with disastrous consequences. However, in a few cases, vice-presidents of Sea and Land were able to form good working relationships with each other. These people recognized the opportunities the alliance presented for making money and were keen to take a chance on working together, by sharing client relationships and developing a more coordinated service offering.

'During the first year there was very little communication going on between the two firms. I started talking to Joe (from Sea) about how we could sell work together. We decided I should move my desk into his office and just get on with it.' (*Vice-president, Land*)

Three joint projects undertaken during this time highlight the problems and opportunities offered by closer cooperation. In the first project, there was intense conflict between the Sea and Land managers.

'It is very hard to separate out the personal conflict from what was occurring at the business level. Two inexperienced strategy people were on the pilot project and it became clear that the Land people designing the project did not understand what strategy was . . . When I was brought in I was told by the Sea vice-presidents, "Don't accept their brief." They told me that I was co-managing with Michael Holmes (of Land) but Michael's perception was that he was running the project. He greatly resented me being there. He felt that they could do the strategy without us. He would not let me see any of the clients on my own.' (*Manager, Sea*)

By contrast, the Sea and Land managers on the second project eventually developed a close working relationship.

'Initially Sue [the Sea manager] and I were fairly hostile with each other. We didn't trust each other. I was junior to her so she wasn't going to work for me. But I had the relationship with the client so I wasn't going to work for her . . . So after about a week we decided to co-lead the project. We spent hours talking to each other about really trivial things, just getting to know each others' ways of working, and realized that there were a lot of things that our firms did the same. We just called them different things . . . We started off wary but we soon came to respect and like each other.

It was a very visible project within our firms so it was in both our interests to make it work.' (*Manager, Land*)

In the third project, the Land manager described one particular incident:

'On one occasion I had to physically restrain one of my team from hitting a Sea consultant at the client's offices. Throughout the project this Sea associate and one of the analysts had systematically denigrated everything that my operations guys were doing. My guys were slogging their guts out and these Sea people were insulting them at every possible opportunity. The Sea guys assumed they knew how to do the things that we did. It made us feel as though our skills were cheap and worthless. They said our work was just grease monkey work.' (*Manager, Land*)

As consultants from both firms came into greater contact with each other, they became increasingly concerned about fundamental differences in both the form and content of their knowledge bases and the scope and basis of their client relationships. Because the knowledge base of the Land consultants was highly codified, their colleagues in Sea looked down on them. Because the Sea consultants lacked a codified knowledge base, their colleagues in Land wondered if they knew anything at all.

'Some Sea people were almost hysterical. They were saying, "Who are these hairy-arsed guys? Is my reputation as an elite strategy consultant going to be sullied by contact with these labourers?"' (*Manager, Sea*)

'We viewed the Sea consultants as intellectual butterflies. What exactly was it they were doing with their clients? These business school types didn't seem to understand what was going on in the real world.' (*Manager, Land*)

Geneva meeting

Fifteen months after the formal alliance, Philip Short and Bob Porter brought the European vice-presidents together for a meeting at the Rococo hotel in Geneva for their first ever joint management meeting. The day began with Philip Short and Bob Porter delivering up-beat speeches about the progress that had already been made towards integration. The day continued with presentations from various vice-presidents about integrated projects they had worked on, which drew upon the skills of consultants from Sea and Land. Halfway through the afternoon, and in the middle of one of these presentations, Fausto Pescatore, a vice-president from Sea Consulting's Rome office, suddenly jumped up.

'This is completely ridiculous. We have sat in this room obediently all day listening to speeches. We have nodded politely. Yet as soon as we break for coffee, we huddle together with people from our own firms and talk about how much we hate the other guys. All this talk about global visions and integrated projects is bullshit. There are serious conflicts between our two firms and we have to face up to them. If we don't do it now, today, Planet Consulting will never be anything more than just a fantasy of Philip and Bob's.'

Sea and Land Merger (Part C): Escalating Problems

Following Fausto Pescatore's outburst, Philip Short broke up the formal meeting and held an impromptu 'Town Meeting'. This was a change management technique that Sea consultants used with clients to surface emotional issues and resolve conflicts.

> 'This was the first time that the issues were acknowledged in public and we started to work together to try and address them. At the end of the 3 days we all signed the Geneva Commitment. I can't even remember what it said anymore. What mattered was that we all acknowledged that there was a problem and that we made a commitment to do something about it.' (*Vice-president, Land*)

The Geneva Commitment was perceived to be a turning point in the integration process. Attempts to keep the two firms separate were finally abandoned.

> 'At Geneva, Philip Short decided, "To hell with it. We can't carry on like this. We've just got to ram the two firms together and see what happens."' (*Vice-president, Land*)

Drive toward integration

Eighteen months after the formal alliance, the legal merger between Sea and Land was completed. The Sea and Land brands were replaced by a new name, Planet Consulting, and a significant marketing programme was commissioned to heighten the profile of the 'new' firm.

In London, some of the Sea and Land vice-presidents moved into each others' offices. As part of the move towards greater cooperation, David Young replaced Gene White as head of operations in the London office. However, to facilitate integration, Jonathan Aldridge and David Young redefined their responsibilities, removing the disinctions between strategy and operations and instead taking responsibility for sales and service delivery respectively in both the strategy and operations practices. The two men described how they set about achieving a good working relationship.

> 'Jonathan and I both wanted to make it work, but we still had a very different view of things. We debated issues extensively but, ultimately, we made our own decisions about our respective areas of responsibility. It was not about consensus. We tried to

persuade each other but, when we did disagree, we made sure we supported each other in front of the rest of the organization.' (*David Young, Joint Managing Director of Planet Consulting, London*)

'It was a real pleasure working with David. I enjoyed our public appearances together. It was an opportunity to demonstrate to the firm that we worked well together. I knew the rest of the organization was watching us carefully for signs of conflict but we genuinely did like each other.' (*Jonathan Aldridge, Joint Managing Director of Planet Consulting, London*)

Staff from both Sea and Land praised the progress David and Jonathan made toward overcoming conflicts.

'It was a real turning point when Jonathan got involved in the pilot projects. We had rammed the pilot project process into Sea and brooked no opposition. This sales process was responsible for the phenomenal growth of Land and we weren't going to compromise . . . But the strategy people thought the quality of work we did during the pilot project phase was heinous . . . So it was incredibly important to get Jonathan alongside us, adapting our processes to suit the needs of strategy projects, and giving us a bit of credibility with the Sea consultants.' (*Manager, Land*)

'David was very important to the integration process. He made a real effort for the firm. He picked up all the shit that no one else wanted to deal with. He gained a lot of respect among the Sea consultants for doing that.' (*Manager, Sea*)

Miserable managers

By developing a consensus between themselves, David Young and Jonathan Aldridge established a foundation for building a consensus within the vice-president group. But as relations started to improve among the vice-presidents, many Sea managers felt a loss of support. Their morale deteriorated even further.

'The vice-presidents were going through a conversion process. They became very disconnected from what was happening on the ground. We Sea managers felt our vice-presidents had deserted us, were lying to us. You could tell from their body language that they didn't believe what they were saying. They were being politically correct in front of us and fighting like hell in private. All the time we were getting bruised at the client site.' (*Manager, Sea*)

In an attempt to replicate the Geneva experience, the managers of Sea instigated an off-site meeting with the managers of Land. At this meeting, Sea and Land managers spoke about the problems they had encountered when working together on joint projects and discussed how these might be overcome. Sea and Land managers were encouraged to discuss their stereotypes and prejudices about each other.

Figure 9.3   A Sea consultant as seen by Land consultants

Figures 9.3 and 9.4 show cartoons of a 'typical' Sea and a 'typical' Land manager which were drawn by a cartoonist within Sea and are based on comments made at the off-site meeting.

Jonathan Aldridge encouraged Sea staff to join pilot project teams, thereby making it easier to incorporate strategy into the supposedly integrated project. Land and Sea consultants began to talk to clients about 'organizational transformation' (OT) projects, in which the strategy and operational activities were not simply combined but fully integrated to develop programmes of fundamental change. Clients showed considerable interest in this concept and several large integrated OT projects were sold. At this stage, OT existed only as a marketing concept and there was very little detail to guide consultants about what the concept meant in practice. Gradually, through a process of trial and error, results delivery staff on a series of projects began to operationalize the concept and to develop tools and techniques for delivering the service to clients.

Figure 9.4   A Land consultant as seen by Sea consultants

Some Sea and Land staff had positive experiences of working together on these projects.

'The project I was on was described as a "model integrated project" but the truth was it worked because neither I nor the Land manager gave a toss what the other was doing. We just trusted each other to get on with it. It was important to stop trying to take control of the project and just accept that both of us had a joint responsibility to deliver.' (*Manager, Sea*)

'It was really neat. It wasn't particularly difficult to work together. We had a nice feeling on the project; we were making it work and we were well perceived by the rest of the firm. There were rumblings of disasters on other projects but I didn't understand why they were having problems.' (*Manager, Land*)

Others were less fortunate.

> 'I almost resigned on two occasions while working on integrated projects. I was work-
> ing horrendous hours and under acute stress. I was getting crucified every day on the
> project. My marriage came close to breaking up. I stayed because I got so much sup-
> port from the Sea people. They were saying "You can't quit. You are fighting for all
> of us."' (*Manager, Sea*)

Leadership vacuum

By the second anniversary of the formal alliance, and 6 months after the creation
of Planet Consulting, considerable progress had been made. As shown in table 9.2,
revenue in the London office increased by 130% over these 2 years, in spite of a
tough economic climate. The number of consultants had risen by 75%. Despite
the relatively strong financial performance, consultants were frustrated by various
factors: the continued pressure to develop an integrated service; the structural
impediments to integration which remained; and the ongoing lack of clarity about
the future direction of the firm. For the most part, the market-facing aspects of
the firm, including brand name and sales processes, had been integrated. But two
sets of internal systems still coexisted. For example, the strategy and operations practices maintained separate recruitment and training processes, as well as separate
terms and conditions of employment and separate promotion structures.

Staff had begun to blame senior management for failing to resolve the ongoing
difficulties. The consensus-based and visionary management style of Philip Short,
by now European Managing Director of Planet Consulting, was perceived to be inappropriate for the current environment.

> 'Philip leads from behind. He tries to avoid appearing too directive. He has this vision
> but there is a huge void underneath.' (*Vice-president, Sea*)

David Young and Jonathan Aldridge were also beginning to be criticized for
their apparent reluctance to act decisively. These tensions bubbled up during the

Table 9.2 Planet Consulting: London office

	Beginning of formal alliance (Sea plus Land)	End year 1	End year 2
Fee income	£30.5m	£51.3m	£70.5m
Total staff	175	287	300
– Consultants	134	225	232
– Support	41	62	68

office Christmas party. After several drinks, two consultants from Sea and Land approached David and Jonathan and told them how they felt.

> 'You are eating up your loyalty reserve. No one is listening to the staff's concerns. The final retention bonuses will soon be paid. People will start to leave.' (*Manager, Land*)

> 'We are fed up with all this involving of everyone in the integration decisions. We just want someone to stand up and say "This is what is going to happen."' (*Manager, Sea*)

Sea and Land Merger (Part D): Creating Value Through Knowledge Sharing

Responding to the pressure for change, David Young and Jonathan Aldridge launched a major in-house project in the New Year called 'Self Transformation'. The consultants at Sea and Land finally began to apply the change management techniques they used with their clients to themselves. The project established office-wide Town Meetings at which staff could raise their concerns with senior management; it commissioned a staff attitudes survey to determine the state of morale; and it attempted to define the desired values of the new firm. As well as such cultural issues, the project dealt with a range of structural and systems-related issues (including organizational redesign to eliminate the distinction between the strategy and operations practices) and systems reconfiguration to standardize recruitment and promotion practices.

To facilitate knowledge sharing, a unit known as 'Innovation' was established to capture and disseminate technical knowledge. The staff within the Innovation area established an extensive programme to identify and codify the knowledge developed at the project site and a full-time role was created to manage the process of knowledge sharing throughout the firm. Manuals were created and used in the training of Land and Sea consultants, but staff from both firms recognized that the manuals were only a partial representation of the required technical knowledge. As the Sea consultants spent more time observing the Land consultants with their clients, they came to recognize the tacit interpersonal expertise the Land consultants deployed in order to deliver their codified procedures effectively. Land consultants also began to recognize the legitimacy of the tacit dimension of the Sea consultants' knowledge base.

> 'I realize now that strategy is about the way you think, not just a tool kit.' (*Consultant, Land*)

> 'It's not until I start talking to people from other strategy consulting firms that I realize how much I have learnt in the last few years about managing client processes. I am able to do so much more for my clients than I could have done when Sea was just a strategy boutique.' (*Manager, Sea*)

Staff were particularly encouraged by Planet Consulting's success in winning an integrated project worth over £20 million in fee income. This project drew upon the skills of both the operations and the strategy disciplines and was seen to have resulted in the development of entirely new skills as a result of integrating the two service offerings. Some of the staff who had resisted the merger most strongly came to accept it when they began to see evidence of how both disciplines could work together effectively. But, as one consultant bemoaned:

> 'Why did it have to take so long and why did it have to hurt so much?' (*Manager, Sea*)

Conclusions

Many of the problems that arose in Sea and Land are common to mergers and acquisitions in general and have been examined in previous merger process studies referred to earlier in this chapter, such as Angwin (2000), Buono and Bowditch (1989), Cartwright and Cooper (1992), Greenberg and Guinan (2004) and Haspeslagh and Jemison (1991). For example, the fact that it was a merger rather than an acquisition meant that power structures were ambiguous, which made it difficult to resolve conflicts. Other problems were associated specifically with attempts to share knowledge and this final section focuses on these specific knowledge-related issues. It ends by recommending how such problems can be minimized and avoided in mergers and acquisitions more generally.

Knowledge sharing in Sea and Land: what went wrong

The management of Sea and Land had vague and inconsistent visions of the opportunities for knowledge sharing that the merger presented. Partly because of this, they had vague and inconsistent plans about the process by which value could be created from sharing knowledge. They did not appreciate the fundamental differences in the form and content of the technical knowledge bases and did not understand the extent to which these would inhibit knowledge sharing. Similarly, they did not appreciate the important differences in the scope and basis of client relationships. Finally, management expected consultants to develop opportunities for ad hoc knowledge sharing on a project-by-project basis, but failed to develop structures and systems to facilitate these initiatives. Each of these problems is examined in more detail below.

1. Inconsistent visions of opportunities for knowledge sharing

Figures 9.1 and 9.2, which outline Bob Porter's and Philip Short's visions of the integrated firm, help explain the problems inherent in the merger from its initial conception. Porter recognized that small-scale strategy projects often initiated large-scale operations improvement projects. His vision of the future was, therefore, about creating the conditions for seamless handovers of projects from strategy to operations consultants. This was more about sharing client relationships than sharing technical knowledge. To sell the integrated service offering, consultants would need to understand each other's work in general terms but they would not need to work closely together on project delivery. Philip Short, by contrast, had a vision that was simultaneously far less detailed and far more challenging. Short's vision simply highlighted the possibility that opportunities existed at the intersection of strategy, operations and IT areas, whereas Porter's vision implied causality and even attempted to quantify the impact of cooperation. Short was, in effect, implying that a new kind of service offering could be created by bringing these areas of expertise together. This would require consultants to work closely together, suggesting a high level of organizational integration. His colleagues at Sea did not appear to recognize, and certainly did not accept, the implication of Short's vision.

2. Poorly specified plans for knowledge sharing

At no stage, either before or after the merger, were detailed plans developed about how value could be created. Both Sea and Land were professional change management consultants, with experience of advising clients on mergers and acquisitions, but their management paid considerably less attention to managing their own firms than they did to managing their clients. This may in part reflect the fact that both firms were relatively small and were used to operating in a fairly entrepreneurial manner. Their reluctance to engage in detailed planning may also have been a means of avoiding conflict. Consensus could be achieved between Short and Porter because they were never explicit about how their alternative visions could be achieved. Conflict was intense, however, amongst the people who were trying to handle the day-to-day problems of managing the London office and delivering client service. Because there was no overarching integration plan, consultants were expected to work out how to cooperate on an ad hoc basis. This frequently gave rise to intense conflicts. Because the management of Sea and Land were obliged to share power, consultants had no recourse to an ultimate authority to resolve their conflicts.

3. Fundamental differences in form and content of knowledge bases

Why were consultants so reluctant to share knowledge? To make sense of these intense and emotional reactions, we need to understand the fundamental importance of perceptions – specifically, how consultants perceived the legitimacy and value of each other's knowledge base.

The way in which knowledge was conceptualized in the combining firms differed fundamentally. Whereas Sea consultants emphasized the inherently tacit nature of their knowledge, Land consultants emphasized the more routinized and codified aspects of their knowledge. The comments and criticisms cited throughout the case suggest that Sea consultants assumed that the codified knowledge of their new colleagues in Land was simplistic and unsophisticated. At the same time, the consultants from Land appeared not to have recognized the legitimacy of the tacit knowledge of their new colleagues in Sea, dismissing it as insubstantial or unreal.

Davenport and Prusak's (1998) model of the internal market for knowledge, outlined earlier in this chapter, sheds light on this phenomenon. Knowledge sharing could not proceed on the basis of *reciprocity* because the consultants perceived their own knowledge to be more valuable than their new colleagues' knowledge. This phenomenon has been termed a *fear of exploitation* (see Empson (2001) for a more detailed explanation). Fear of exploitation reflects the anxiety that individuals experience under the stressful merger conditions when they perceive that they are being asked to give away valuable knowledge while being offered little of value in return. Managers of knowledge-based mergers need to understand the subjective and highly personal context within which individuals evaluate and legitimize each other's claims to knowledge and the effect that this can have on the functioning of the internal market for knowledge.

4. Fundamental differences in scope and basis of client relationships

In developing an integrated service offereing, the intention was to share client relationships as well as technical knowledge. Whereas consultants did not recognize each other's technical knowledge to be valuable or legitimate, when it came to sharing clients, they were more concerned about the value and legitimacy of each other's image. The fear of exploitation was exacerbated by a *fear of contamination*. (see Empson (2001) for a more detailed explanation). Applying Davenport and Prusak's framework, consultants were reluctant to share knowledge and client relationships because they saw no opportunities for *reciprocity* and were concerned it would damage their *reputation*.

The strategy consultants at Sea perceived themselves as more 'up-market' than the operations consultants at Land (the so-called 'grease monkeys' and 'hairy-arsed labourers'). In a professional service firm, association with a 'down-market' colleague may have a direct impact on the fee rate a professional is able to command. The personal image of a professional is integral to the clients' perceived value of the service he or she is offering. In the case of Sea and Land, however, the fee rates and the salaries paid to the professionals were broadly similar, which suggests that a full explanation may lie beyond purely commercial considerations.

Various writers, such as Alvesson (2001) and Ashforth and Mael (1989), have highlighted the close relationship that can exist between organizational identity and an individual's self-concept. Changes to that organizational identity, for example as a result of a merger, can prove highly threatening at an individual level (Empson, 2004). The problem may be particularly acute in professional service firms because the images of the firm and the individual professional are so closely associated with the client's perception of the quality of the service. Consequently, while professionals may articulate their fear of contamination in terms of the negative impact on their reputation among clients (and the negative impact on revenue), their concerns may also derive from a more fundamental anxiety about their sense of self-worth. In this context, therefore, visiting a client with an 'inappropriate' colleague potentially threatens an individual's self-concept, as well as his or her potential fee income. As with the fear of exploitation, the fear of contamination combines objective and commercial concerns with highly subjective and personal considerations.

5. Lack of support for 'integration entrepreneurs'

It is important to remember that not all consultants were so reluctant to share knowledge. The twin fears of exploitation and contamination were not universal. Some consultants recognized the opportunities that the merger presented from the outset and others were able to set aside their personal concerns and accept the challenge to make their specific projects successful. These 'integration entrepreneurs' represented the foundations of management's implicit intention to allow integration to be driven by ad hoc initiatives from the ground up. However, they received little support from management, either at a practical or personal level. They tried to develop integrated ways of working with teams of consultants who often lacked the appropriate skills and temperaments to work together effectively. They operated within the confines of structures that remained deeply divisive and with systems that sustained the differentiation of the two practices.

Sharing knowledge in M&A: getting to grips with the intangible

As the Sea and Land case demonstrated, it is extraordinarily difficult to create value by sharing knowledge in mergers and acquisitions. Managers are indeed wrestling with the intangible when they try to 'manage' a resource that is inherently ambiguous and amorphous. The commercial logic for sharing knowledge may be unassailable, but that is not the point. Knowledge resides in people and people, especially when threatened by a merger, will respond according to their own internal logic, which may be far removed from the commercial logic of the firm. Because knowledge sharing is inherently complex it is unwise to look for a simplified set of solutions to the problem. Nevertheless, there are a few basic questions to bear in mind and a simple workplan that may help you to establish priorities and sustain you throughout the process (see figures 9.5 and 9.6).

When considering a knowledge-based merger it is important to attempt to understand certain aspects of your own firm and your merger partner firm. The most important of these are: 1) the form and content of the knowledge base and; 2) the scope and basis of client relationships. The questions in figure 9.5 will help you to clarify what you do and do not know about these issues. (For further guidance, refer back to the earlier section of this chaper – Knowledge in Professional Service Firms – which explains in more detail about both the form and content of technical and client knowledge.)

Objective: To assess technical knowledge in both firms

How would you describe the *content* of your firm's knowledge base?

- What knowledge is essential to the creation and delivery of your core product or service?
- How is your knowledge distinctive from your competitors'? To what extent does it represent a basis for competitive advantage?
- What do you need to know more about?

How would you describe the *form* of your firm's knowledge base?

- To what extent is your essential and distinctive knowledge formally codified or easily communicable?
- To what extent is this knowledge associated with specific individuals and their team? What would cause these individuals to remain or resign?
- To what extent is this knowledge taken for granted and embedded in organizational processes? How could you articulate this knowledge to your merger partner colleagues?

To what extent can you answer these questions about your potential merger partner?

Objective: To assess scope and basis of client relationships

How would you describe the scope and basis of client relationships in your firm?

- Which of your client relationships must be protected at all costs?
- What do your clients value about you? What might cause them to value you less highly?
- To what extent are these valuable client relationships owned by specific individuals and their team? What would cause these individuals to remain or resign?
- What new client relationships would you like to develop?

To what extent can you answer these questions about your potential merger partner?

Figure 9.5   Key questions to consider in knowledge-based mergers

Learning about your own firm will be just as important as learning about your merger partner firm. There is, in many cases, a limit to how much you can learn about your merger partner colleagues prior to the merger, unless they are willing to work closely with you during the planning phase to enable you to explore these issues jointly. A long-established habit of cooperation may be helpful, but not necessarily, as the Sea and Land case demonstrated.

Focusing on the questions outlined in figure 9.5 will help you to develop a more realistic sense of where the key opportunities for value creation lie and the kinds of problems that you are likely to encounter. Prior to the merger, you should at least be able to identify the key knowledge and client relationships that you need to preserve in both firms (and the individuals who are most closely associated with these). However, it is unlikely that you will be able to engage in much detailed integration

Phase 1 Discovery (Pre merger)	Phase 2 Preservation (First year post merger)	Phase 3 Integration (Years 2 to 3 post merger)
Assess content and form of knowledge base Assess scope and basis of client relationships		
Identify opportunities for sharing knowledge and clients Define objectives and develop high-level work plan		
	Focus on: • Preserving key technical knowledge • Preserving key client relationships • Retaining key individuals	
	Identify/support integration entrepreneurs Facilitate pilot projects	
		Reassess opportunities for knowledge sharing Formalize knowledge-management systems Roll out integrated projects Begin to remove structural impediments to integration and to standardize systems

Figure 9.6 Integration workplan for knowledge-based mergers

planning pre merger as the real process of discovery can only begin after the merger is complete, when you start to try to work with your merger partner colleagues.

More detailed integration planning is best attempted gradually, through a series of small-scale pilot studies. The management of Sea and Land were right to recognize that the knowledge-sharing process cannot be structured and driven by senior management but instead takes place on an ad hoc basis between like-minded individuals who are most closely engaged in the delivery of the work. Some people in merging firms will be keen to seek out the opportunities that the merger presents. Greenberg and Guinan's (2004) study of technology-based mergers and acquisitions identified the qualities of these 'entrepreneurial' individuals who take a major role in promoting knowledge sharing. They are able to act quickly under pressure, think creatively about new products and services, and are flexible in their response to competitive threats. Above all they are opportunistic, able to identify and evaluate opportunities objectively and able to avoid the more territorial and risk-averse behaviours of their less entrepreneurial collegues.

A key role for management during the early stage in the post-merger process is to identify potential integration entrepreneurs and to bring them together to facilitate their initiatives. As the successes of the integration entrepreneurs are recognized and celebrated, more recalcitrant individuals will begin to recognize the opportunities that the merger presents and will begin to feel less personally threatened. This is the time to reassess the opportunities for value creation in the light of what you have learnt about your own firm and your merger partner post merger. This will also be the time to roll out the successful pilot initiatives more widely across the firm. By now you will have a clearer understanding of what knowledge is key and codifiable and which individuals will be willing to cooperate with the process. This more receptive environment may also represent a good opportunity to remove remaining structural impediments (such as departmental boundaries) and adapt existing systems (such as differentiated reward structures).

Bresman, Birkinshaw, and Nobel (1999) have demonstrated that knowledge transfer is not likely to occur in the first few months following acquisitions in general. Depending on the extent of difference in the knowledge base and client relationships at the start of a merger, and the extent of integration you are planning to achieve, the process may take many years to develop successfully. In the case of Sea and Land, 3 years elapsed before individuals were willing to accept such a degree of change. Studies of mergers in other professional service firms indicate a similar timescale (Empson, 2000). In organizations that rely upon a more strongly codified or explicit knowledge base, it may be possible to accelerate the process because such firms are not so dependent on the cooperation of individuals in the knowledge-sharing process. However, wrestling with the intangible will never be simple. As one of the consultants at Sea said:

> 'There is no easy way to manage a merger, only pain. But there is quite a bit you can do to manage the pain.'

NOTE

1. The terms 'merger' and 'acquisition' are often used interchangeably. In this chapter the term 'merger' is used when referring to both mergers and acquisitions in the specific context of professional service firms. This reflects the conventional practice among managers of professional service firms, who often seek to de-emphasize imbalances in the power relationships between the two firms.

Chapter 10   M&A as Stereotypes

Banal Ideas and Self-Serving Explanations

Eero Vaara and Janne Tienari

Introduction

Recent cross-border mergers and acquisitions have received a lot of attention and triggered vibrant research activity. Such cases include the merger between Asea (Sweden) and Brown Boveri (Switzerland) in 1998, the German BMW's acquisition of Rover (UK) in 1992, the merger between Daimler (Germany) and Chrysler (US) in 1998, the strategic alliance of Nissan (Japan) and Renault (France) in 1999, the merger between the pharmaceutical companies Astra (Sweden) and Zeneca (UK) in 1998, and Hoechst (Germany) and Rhône-Poulenc (France) in 1999, and the merger between the airlines Air France and KLM (Netherlands) in 2004. Notions of national cultures and cultural differences, their consequences and integration efforts to resolve cultural conflict have been enthusiastically discussed in relation to all these cases. This has often meant the (re)production of national stereotypes by the managers and employees, industry experts and business analysts, journalists and also by us researchers.

As readily accessible discursive resources, national stereotypes are a significant part of cultural sensemaking in international mergers and acquisitions. Despite vast political, anthropological, sociological, socio-psychological and linguistic literatures on national identity-building, we do not know much of the (re)construction of national stereotypes in the context of international mergers and acquisitions. This is theoretically problematic in the sense that we thus lack an understanding of an essential part of the multifaceted cultural sensemaking and identity-building processes in this context. For practical purposes, this lack of attention is particularly unfortunate given the harmful consequences of national stereotyping in merging organizations. In brief, stereotypes are self-constructive: they sustain and even reinforce simplistic and in many ways problematic cultural conceptions. Stereotypes

are also self-serving: they promote one's self-image at the expense of the other –
and thus reinforce prejudice.

This chapter therefore concentrates on national stereotyping in international
mergers and acquisitions. We focus on the Finnish–Swedish setting, which provides
a particularly interesting context for such analysis. To begin with, reflections on
Finnish–Swedish cultural idiosyncrasies and differences manifest a paradox. On the
one hand, due to geographical proximity, in the international scene Finns and Swedes
are usually considered very similar. Both are classified as Scandinavian or Nordic
people who share particular traits and traditions. This is also the picture that is
provided in mainstream comparisons of cultural difference in management and
organization (Hofstede, 1984; Calori and de Woot, 1994). On the other hand, a closer
examination of Finnish–Swedish encounters points to significant differences. These
differences seem to explain many of the problems and disappointments encountered
in mergers and acquisitions between Finnish and Swedish companies (Laine-Sveiby,
1987; 1991; Vaara, 2002; Risberg et al., 2003; Vaara et al., 2003c).

The Finnish–Swedish setting provides rich and entertaining examples of national
stereotyping. However, this setting also gives us an opportunity to exemplify tendencies that can also be found in other contexts. More specifically, we aim at illustrating how stereotypes are convenient means to make sense of international
encounters. We maintain that using stereotypes as 'explanations' should, however,
viewed with a critical eye. Furthermore, we argue that stereotyping tends to reinforce inbuilt prejudices and (re)construct particular kinds of power relationships
in the international merger context.

The remainder of the chapter is structured as follows. We begin with a brief
theoretical discussion on national stereotypes, and argue for a discursive perspective on stereotyping. We then proceed to examine the Finnish–Swedish setting. After
an illustration of commonly used stereotypes on self (auto-stereotypes) and the other
(hetero-stereotypes), we focus on Finns and Swedes as decision-makers. We examine how stereotypes can be served as explanations but argue that this explanatory
power is at best superficial. We then single out inherent problems related to stereotyping and, finally, suggest means to alleviate these problems in the international
merger context.

National Stereotypes as Discursive Resources

National identity-building is a topic that has been examined in different ways by
political scientists, anthropologists, sociologists, social psychologists and linguists.
Without engaging in an in-depth review of these varied literatures, it is important to emphasize that all national identity-building is based on nationalism as a
discourse and ideology, that such identity-building involves the reconstruction of

'us' vs. 'them' relationships, that the specific identities created are always contex-specific, and that discursive resources such as national stereotypes play a central role in these constructions.

Nationalism can be conceptualized in various ways. For example, it can be understood as a social movement, institution, discourse or ideology (e.g. Gellner, 1983; Anderson, 1983). For our purposes, it is meaningful to view nationalism as a discourse constructed on the basis of shared understandings of history and con-tinuity. This echoes Benedict Anderson's (1983) idea of nations as imagined com-munities rather than stable a-historical institutions. In this context, it is particularly interesting to note the central role of what Michael Billig (1995) has called banal nationalism in contemporary society. According to this view, the construct of nation is often accepted and reproduced mindlessly and uncritically, rendered possible by mundane habits of language, thought and symbolism in everyday life.

While the basis of national identity-building lies in nationalism, the (re)construction of specific identities develops around self-categorizations. According to social iden-tity theory (Tajfel, 1981; Turner, 1985), people in social groups construct a social reality through dividing the world into 'us' and 'them'. This is linked with various processes of inclusion and exclusion, usually leading to preferring one's own group over others. In particular, in-groups tend to give themselves more favourable judgements than they would to out-groups. They create a positive self-image and thereby boost their self-esteem. At the same time, they define their boundaries to other groups, which are often considered inferior or less developed.

Recent sociologically inspired reflections on identity-building have concentrated on the social definition of identities. Accordingly, national identities are also con-structed through social negotiation, that is, both through self-definition and ascrip-tion by others (e.g. Breakwell and Lyons, 1996). For our purposes, post-colonialism, developed on the basis of Edward Saïd's (1978) ideas, is a particularly interesting perspective. According to this view, most of Western-driven anthropological and other analyses around national characteristics and differences involve problematic assumptions concerning normality, morality, legitimacy, progress or development (e.g. Westwood, 2001; Prasad, 2003). In *inter-national* settings, it is important to note that a colonial attitude can also often be subtle and visible mainly in the norm-alization of one's own practices and values and rendering the other as inferior, strange, exotic or deviant (e.g. Westwood, 2001). In these settings, it is often the case that the asymmetrical power relationships are particularly visible in the discourse of the colonized themselves (Saïd, 1978).

The discursive perspective on national identity-building then emphasizes that there exist discursive resources, such as national stereotypes, that can be activated in specific contexts (e.g. Wodak et al., 1999). As noted above, such discourse can be 'banal' in the sense that commonly held national prototypes and stereotypes are spread around as 'facts' without critical reflection (Billig, 1995). The activation of discursive resources such as national stereotypes can be subconscious in the sense of not pausing to think clearly how the specific linguistic resources are used.

However, this discursive activity can also involve particular discursive strategies that are more or less intentionally used for various purposes. Without going into detail, such strategies can involve, for example, macro-functions such as construction, preservation, transformation, demontage/dismantling or micro-functions such as singularization, autonomization, assimilation or dissimilation (e.g. Wodak et al., 1999). The point to be made here is that there exists a variety of means to create or manipulate images of oneself and others, of the nations and nationalities in question as well as particular political organizational issues at hand.

Such discursive strategies are frequently used in the media. In contexts such as sports, it seems natural to assert national sentiments with stereotypical images of others (Boyle and Haynes, 1996). The English tabloids covering Euro 1996 in football present a banal example. The European Championship was held in England. After German newspapers had rejoiced their victory over England in what they termed the English national sport, English tabloids immediately replied that the UK had already twice that century beaten the Germans in the Germans' national sport. However, the popular press can be effective in reinforcing nationalism in contexts where its naturalness is not self-evident (see Brookes (1999) on the British press covering 'mad cow disease').

Such discursive strategies are also common in international mergers and acquisitions. Tienari et al. (2003) studied the media coverage of a Swedish–Finnish company acquiring a state-owned Norwegian company. The acquisition process was prolonged due to the tussle in the Norwegian parliament over the acquisition offer. In one of their examples, Tienari et al. (2003) describe how the CEO of the major Norwegian competitor of the acquisition target (and a potential acquirer) drew explicitly on nationalistic discourse in his public comments when he advised 'the State not to sell the bank for silver coins', referring to the price offered with a biblical metaphor. 'Besides, it is not right that Stockholm shall become our financial capital,' he added. It was clear for the audience who the 'we' are. The intentional reference to Stockholm (capital of Sweden) constructed a particular 'them'. The Swedish–Finnish acquirer was portrayed as a Swedish company, and this Swedishness an apparent problem for Norwegians.

The discursive construction of national identities and stereotypes can also involve humour. According to *Encyclopaedia Britannica*, humour is the only form of communication in which a stimulus on a high level of complexity produces a stereotyped, predictable response on the physiological reflex level. Humour is manifest, for example, in particular joking relationships between nations (Gundelach, 2000). In order to work, the relationship between the two nationalities has to be relatively close because humour usually requires some common ground (or perceived knowledge of the two sides) to make sense. Such humour can be banal, and jokes often reconstruct commonly held prototypes and stereotypes of one's own and the other's community. Stupidity-based jokes are a universal phenomenon: 'why do the Irish have potatoes and Arabs the oil? . . . because the Irish had the first choice' will be told by an Englishman and 'why do Finns have forests and Arabs the oil?

. . . because Finns had the first choice' by a Swede. For the purposes of our argu-mentation, however, it is the more nuanced and contextualized humour that will be of specific interest.

It should be emphasized that in the cross-national context, humour can also be 'colonial' in nature and tone. This may be inherent in joking relationships between nations with a mutual colonial past; of colonizer and colonized. This can involve imperialism, hegemony or domination in the sense that one party's essential superi-ority is clearly expressed vis-à-vis the other, often subtly, and without a specific awareness of such reproduction. Often, it is the 'colonized' in particular who reproduce their inferior but resistant position in the relationship. Humour can also involve irony and become a counter-force challenging commonly held banal views. Self-irony is an example of this. When used by someone not belonging to the imagined collective being ironized, the same expressions and jokes may turn offensive.

What is then specific about national stereotypes as linguistic resources? As with any linguistic resources, their existence depends on their enactment. By definition, stereotypes are, however, widely held conceptions around specific nations and nationalities. They tend to be related to specific (common) national histories, or, more accurately, conceptions, myths and legacies around specific historically import-ant events. As stereotypes are relational, particularly important in this respect are relationships between nations, especially those plagued by colonialism or conflict such as war. Stereotypes are also easily accessible. This means that over time there exist not only oral expressions but also written documentation around the concep-tions in question. In this respect, particularly interesting are conceptions spread as 'true history', 'research findings' or 'common experience', as they easily legitimate and naturalize the use of specific stereotypes.

Contrary to common belief, national stereotypes are not, however, a clear-cut discursive category. What may pass as an observation or an experience in one con-text may be seen as a stereotype in another. Consider, for example, the difference in long-term quality versus short-term profit orientation in decision making in German versus US parts in the Daimler–Chrysler merger case. It should also be noted that the existing repertoire of stereotypes is usually extremely large and varied, although naturally some stereotypes are better known or more commonly used than others. Consequently, in specific speech acts one can easily find varied, ambiguous and even contradictory stereotypes. Finally, it should be emphasized that the auto- (own) and hetero- (others) stereotypes can and often do vary signific-antly. For example, as noted above, there is a tendency to construct positive images or attribute positive values to the conceptions regarding oneself.

Unfortunately, studies of stereotyping are scarce in the organizational context. In her insightful study on national stereotyping in (and around) a transnational bank in the City of London, Moore (2000) provides intriguing examples of how employees locate (and are located by) others by means of stereotypical character traits. The bank in question was German, which brought a distinct flavour to interpersonal relationships, for example, in humorous interactions between the English and Germans. In general, the English–German relations seem somewhat uneasy, as Warner and Campbell's (1993) jocular description of German business style as 'Technik über Alles' demonstrates. On the one hand, when referring to military operations, the stereotype of German efficiency and reliability is likely to carry negative connotations. On the other, the appropriation and strategic use of stereotypes such as efficiency and reliability can take on positive meanings in a context such as banking or selling automobiles.

In the City of London, Moore (2000) concludes, it is crucial to present oneself (with the help of stereotyping) in a way which involves a complex strategy of shifting identity in time. While being German can at one time be considered advantageous, at another it may turn to a disadvantage. The context – or *Zeitgeist* – shifts. According to Moore, national stereotypes take on a powerful role in the expression of identity, and the ability to present oneself using symbols that evoke several identities is essential. Stereotype-based humour may play a crucial role in such contextual identity-building.

Studies focusing on stereotyping in the merger context are, however, almost non-existent. We have in our analyses tried to highlight the role of nationalistic discourse, and these analyses have also touched on stereotyping (Hellgren et al., 2002; Tienari et al., 2003; Vaara et al., 2003a, b and c). To go further in this reflection, we now focus on the Finnish–Swedish setting, which is arguably a particularly fruitful case for this kind of analysis.

The Finnish–Swedish Setting

From 1323 to 1809, Finland was part of the Kingdom of Sweden. Finland adopted its judicial system, governmental administration and basic political structure from its Western neighbour. However, the origins of the Finnish language, for example, allegedly come from the East. Finland was also a part of Czarist Russia from 1809 until 1917. That year, Finland finally gained its independence. There is thus a postcolonial type of relationship between the Swedes and Finns, which tends to be reproduced when making sense of Finnish–Swedish encounters. In such sensemaking, Swedes tend to emerge as the 'Big Brother' and Finns take the role of 'Little Brother'.

As a remnant of the colonization period, there is still today a considerable Swedish-speaking minority in Finland, amounting to approximately 6% of the population. The Swedish-Finns, as they are called, typically carry a well-off image. This group of people often finds itself in a complex position between Swedes – that they are not – and the 'real Finns'. Alongside Finnish, Swedish is an official language in Finland. All Finnish-speaking children must learn a certain amount of Swedish at school. Many Finns are reluctant to use Swedish, however, and obligatory Swedish for Finnish-speaking school children remains a contested issue in the society.

Like any nations, both Sweden and Finland have a rich mythological and historical basis to draw from when making sense of national identity and identification. Sweden has a long history as an important Nordic – or Scandinavian – nation. This history can be traced back to the Vikings. During specific periods, like in the seventeenth and eighteenth centuries, Sweden could even be considered a major European power. The Kingdom of Sweden ruled over most of the Baltic Sea region and Poland. Historical legacies of this 'Great Power Period' (*Stormaktstiden* in Swedish) still seem to play a role in shaping Swedes' self-images.

Swedes have also excelled in international arenas more recently. A significant number of Swedish companies had already begun to internationalize in the nineteenth century. From Nobel prizes to Abba, Swedes have played a salient role on the global scene. This role is far more important than the size of the population (around nine million) would indicate. For some 200 years, Swedes have avoided wars. This has developed into a tradition of political neutrality, which is nowadays being re-evaluated. However, it is especially the development of the welfare state – 'The People's Home' (*Folkhemmet*), to a large extent based on social democratic ideas – that the Swedes are famous for. Democrary, equality, solidarity and consensus can be seen as the cornerstones of contemporary Swedish auto-stereotyping and national identity-building.

In contrast to Sweden, Finland is a relatively new nation. The Finnish auto-stereotypes draw on specifically important national myths, many of which relate to the emergence of the Finnish nationalist movement in the early nineteenth century. (In the nationalist revival of the time, Finns resemble Czechs, Poles, Greeks and Norwegians.) It is, however, especially the experiences of the World War II and achievements in sports that seem to play a central role in shaping contemporary Finns' self-images. In brief, Finns consider World War II – and especially the Winter War in 1939–40 – as a heroic period, when the young nation stuck together, succeeded in countering the attacks of the mighty Red Army of the Soviet Union, and managed to stay independent.

Throughout recent history, military-related metaphors have survived in images of Finns, especially when it comes to comparing the Finns with the Swedes. An image of toughness and endurance is (re)constructed. As to sports, the legends of the Flying Finns and other sportsmen (usually not women) have provided a basis on which to draw when building auto-stereotypes. In terms of the discursive construction of such images, it is irrelevant that the Finns referred to – for example, Paavo Nurmi as The Flying Finn in the 1920s – are actually seldom known abroad. It is the discursive construction of a strong, enduring nation and people that is of importance here. Paavo Nurmi also provides an example of how Finnish sports-related imagery often has a link with Sweden. Many Finns still recall that Nurmi, who won nine Olympic gold medals in long distance running, was denied participation in the 1932 Olympics. This was due to a protest by Swedes, accusing him of professionalism. Back then, the Olympics were strictly for amateurs.

On both the Finnish and Swedish sides, but especially in Finland, international matches in popular sports such as athletics and ice hockey have kept banal nationalism alive. Sports tend to provide a rich metaphorical basis also when it comes to examining contemporary events such as Finnish–Swedish mergers and acquisitions (e.g. Vaara et al., 2003b and c). This close relationship is reflected not only in specific literatures or media coverage but also in areas such as joking relationships. In fact, jokes about Finnish–Swedish relationships remain extremely popular, especially in Finland. Swedes typically make jokes about rowdy and barbaric drunken Finns, while Finns joke about soft, 'queery' Swedes (e.g. Haltsonen, 2001). Analogies to relations between the English and the Irish, for example, are evident here.

Finally, against the background of colonization, it is not difficult to understand that for the Finns, Sweden is on the whole the most important reference point when it comes to inter-national comparisons. For the Swedes, in contrast, Finns appear as far less important. As a result, Finnish–Swedish encounters often result in much more intensive cultural sensemaking on the Finnish than on the Swedish side. This is reflected, for example, in the media coverage around Finnish–Swedish relationships, and contemporary events such as cross-border mergers and acquisitions. We now turn our attention to recent Finnish–Swedish merger and acquisition cases.

Finnish–Swedish Mergers and Acquisitions

Economically, Finland and Sweden have always been close. During the past 30 years, we have, however, witnessed an unprecedented wave of Finnish–Swedish mergers and acquisitions. This has led to a significant restructuring of the Finnish and Swedish corporate and industrial structures, with far-reaching implications. These dramatic events have also triggered a great deal of discussion around Finnish–Swedish relations and cultural differences. These discussions have in many ways reproduced specific images of Finns and Swedes.

However, mergers and acquisitions have also per se shaped the imagery and created new myths around Finns and Swedes. For example, 'management-by-perkele', a label associated with stereotypical Finnish management, was created by Swedish journalists in the late 1980s. The label emerged in association with large-scale Finnish acquisitions in Sweden. 'Perkele' is a Finnish swear word meaning devil. The Swedish press came up with the term 'management-by-perkele' when reporting on the way Nokia's Vice-President Kalle Isokallio managed the acquisition and subsequent integration of Ericsson Information Systems. His sturdy and ruthless behaviour was something that the Swedes, apparently used to a more consensual style, did not appreciate. The Finn was bossing around unnecessarily, giving orders instead of listening to the Swedes' viewpoints, and perhaps even cursing at times. In contrast, since the 1980s, Finns have come to use the concept of 'management-by-perkele' in a humorous and even positive light. The concept refers to tough decisions in difficult circumstances, especially when contrasted with the image of ambiguous and undecisive, stereotypical Swedish management.

We have studied several cases of Finnish–Swedish mergers and acquisitions from different theoretical and methodological perspectives (e.g. Vaara, 2002). Most of our analyses have focused on the merger between the Finnish Merita Bank and the Swedish Nordbanken in 1997, which later led to the building of the pan-Nordic financial services group called Nordea. We have studied cultural sensemaking and identity-building both within the organization (e.g. Vaara et al., 2003a and c; Tienari et al., 2005; Vaara et al., 2005) and in the media (e.g. Risberg et al., 2003; Tienari et al., 2003; Vaara et al., 2003b).

We have also examined other cases, such as the forest industry merger between the Finnish Enso and the Swedish Stora in 1998, and touched on the telecom sector merger between the Finnish Sonera and the Swedish Telia in 2002 as well as the Finnish Sampo's acquisitions in the Nordic insurance business (e.g. Tienari et al. 2004). The material on Nordea and other cases has provided us with an extensive textual database on cultural sensemaking and identity-building. In addition, while carrying out research projects, we have participated in several kinds of workshops and meetings, and had informal contacts with Finnish and Swedish top managers. We have also cooperated extensively with Finnish and Swedish researchers interested in Finnish–Swedish mergers and acquisitions. In all, this social interaction has provided a great deal of opportunities to observe Finnish and Swedish stereotyping – in action.

The Finnish–Swedish cultural comparisons provide us with examples of stereotypes, some of which are summarized in table 10.1 (see Laine-Sveiby, 1987; 1991; Jönsson, 1995; Ekwall and Karlsson, 1999; Säntti, 2001; Risberg et al., 2003; Vaara et al., 2003c; Smith et al., 2003). However, in the following, we shall concentrate on those auto- and hetero-stereotypes that characterize Finns and Swedes as decision-makers, because this is a particularly central area in organizations in general and in merging organizations in particular.

Stereotypes as Superficial Explanations

National stereotypes are by definition widely used conceptions, and people can draw freely from a number of discursive resources in stereotyping. In the Finnish–Swedish setting, the stereotypes used tend to be based on widely shared myths. For example, stereotypes depict Finns as action-oriented decision-makers and Swedes as consensus-oriented. Finns are often portrayed by Swedes as more introvert and less talkative than their Swedish counterparts. Swedes, in turn, are depicted to value extensive formal and informal discussion before a decision can be reached.

Like other stereotypical conceptions, these are discursive resources that tend to be circulated in various forms. At the one end we can point to jokes. For example,

Table 10.1 Images of Finns and Swedes

	Finnish self-image	Finns' image according to Swedes	Swedish self-image	Swedes' image according to Finns
General features	• Honesty • Equality • Rationality • Practical orientation • Duty • History 'lives on'	• Honesty • Trustworthiness • Determination	• Honesty • Equality • Rationality • Practical orientation • Security • Modernity	• Honesty • Trustworthiness • Self-righteousness
People and social interaction	• Openness • Frankness • Individual orientation • Spontaneity • Action • Flexible directions • Personal autonomy • Readiness for change • Endures conflict • Difference • Short time = efficiency	• Quietness, stiffness • Forcefulness • Aggressiveness • Difficult to understand	• Openness • Informalness • Group orientation • Planning • Participation • Organizing; orderliness • Common rules • Anticipation • Avoids conflict • Equality • Long time = quality	• Loudness, softness • Self-confidence • Internationality • Difficult to understand
Management	• Who is responsible decides • Sturdy decisions • Individual responsibility • Results count	• Authoritarian (the boss decides) • Formal • Bureaucratic (centralized power) • Emotional	• 'Anchoring' decisions • Consensus • Individual and group responsibility • Process and results count	• Vague and slow • Formal • Bureaucratic (slow decision making) • 'Slippery'
Relationship with the 'other'	• Nationalistic • Conscious of uniqueness • Comparing		• Rational • Modern and developed	

the souvenir shops in Brussels sell postcards depicting reverse stereotypes of all nations in the European Union. Examples include 'organized as a Greek', 'talkative as a Finn' and 'flexible as a Swede'. The following are example of numerous jokes that we have encountered in the Finnish–Swedish context:

> A Finn and a Swede decided to have a good time and drink. After a day of serious drinking the Swede raised his glass and said 'Cheers!'. The angry Finn replied with a question: 'Have we come here to talk or to drink?' (*A joke circulated in many encounters*)

> What is the difference between an introvert and an extrovert Finn? The introvert Finn looks at his shoes when speaking to you. The extrovert Finn looks at your shoes! (*From an interview of a top manager*)

> Two Danes, two Finns, two Norwegians and two Swedes are shipwrecked and cast upon a deserted island. By the time they are rescued the Danes have formed a co-operative, the Finns have chopped down all the trees, the Norwegians have built a fishing boat, and the Swedes are waiting to be introduced. (Connery, 1966, p. 18, in Gundelach, 2000, p. 113.)

At the other end, we can see the management literature reinventing and reinforcing such stereotypes. This is the case with researchers (e.g. Laine-Sveiby, 1987; 1991; Säntti, 2001; Vaara et al., 2003c) but even more so with the popular management literature. For example, Staffan Bruun and Mosse Wallén, two Finnish journalists, write in their popular book on the success of Nokia (1999), the global telecommunications giant with Finnish roots:

> 'It is management-by-perkele – direct communication between managers and employees, and quick, unemotional decisions. The organization is flexible. There is readiness to confront change . . . It consists of countless small guerrilla units that carefully plan an attack and strike although the risk for failure is high. It is easier to be forgiven in Nokia than to get a permission to do something. The important thing is that one does not make the same mistake twice.'

Significantly, stereotypical images are reproduced when they seem to explain real-life experiences for organizational actors. For example, in Merita-Nordbanken, our top management interviewees frequently referred to their management group meetings. When chaired by a Swede, these meetings that started in the morning often 'lasted so long that lunch had to be postponed. However, when a Finn was the chairman, the lunch had to be called earlier than planned. Such experiences tended to show for Swedes not only that Finns are less eager to discuss issues but also brought with them conceptions that Finns are therefore often less democratic leaders than the Swedes. For the Finns, in turn, these experiences confirmed the hetero-stereotype of discussion-prone Swedes. Finnish top managers at Nordea also gave examples of how they were aware of the stereotypes Swedes held of them, and how they at times tried to tone down their 'overly Finnish behaviour'.

Media is another area where stereotypes often serve as means of sensemaking. For example, when reporting on the dismissal of two Finnish senior managers in TeliaSonera in 2003–4, both the Finnish and the Swedish media frequently referred to the cultural differences between Finns and Swedes and to the consequent incompatibilities. This is how *Svenska Dagbladet*, a leading Swedish daily newspaper, explained the dismissal of the Finnish chairman of the board in an article entitled 'It is inevitable that there are cultural conflicts' (30 April 2004):

> In recent years the differences between Swedish and Finnish management styles have been discussed, and what has come out is that we Swedes have noticed that Finnish managers use the whole hand (not just one finger) to point to things and thump on the floor if that is necessary to get things moving. In Finland, in turn, people look at the Swedish business as something that is led by the weak who cannot order anything without asking for the opinion of the people working in the storage house.
>
> It is inevitable that there are two cultures and that at times there are conflicts. Yet it is important that we at both sides accept the differences and adjust our behavior. Tapio Hintikka [the Finnish chairman of the board] could not do that and had to face the consequences.

It is yet important to note that national stereotypes provide, at best, superficial explanations for specific experiences in inter-national encounters. First, stereotypes are extreme generalizations. While it is usually not difficult to find examples that reinforce stereotypical images, it is not too difficult to find counter-examples either. In all of the Finnish–Swedish mergers and acquisitions we have studied, we can easily point to Finns who are more extrovert or talkative than most of their Swedish colleagues, or to Swedes who are more authoritarian decision-makers than their Finnish counterparts.

Second, national stereotypes are usually ambiguous. In fact, even the same images can be interpreted in very different ways, for example, as positive or negative. The image of Finnish action-orientation is often seen as a virtue from the Finnish perspective when implying decisiveness and effectiveness. For the Swedes, this same stereotype can trigger negative images if action-orientation implies a lack of analysis and discussion among relevant stakeholders. Similarly, the Swedish tendency to discuss may be considered a virtue if it means careful preparation and winning the support of all those involved. Yet it can also imply weakness and slowness if contrasted with decisiveness. Interestingly, the same stereotypes can also be used on different sides, based on different reasoning. For example, in the Finnish–Swedish context, the Finns can depict the Swedes as bureaucratic, especially when referring to the Swedish tendency to discuss issues to the extent that this seems to impede effective decision making. The Swedes, in turn, can view Finns as bureaucratic when referring to their apparently undemocratic and athoritarian decision-making tradition.

Third, stereotyping tendencies seem to vary according to the context of their enactment. Finns and Swedes in the Nordea case provide an interesting example of changing views (Vaara et al., 2003a). While the top managers interviewed often pointed to fundamental differences between Finns and Swedes in the Merita-Nordbanken phase, these differences seemed to become far less important when Merita-Nordbanken merged with the Danish Unidanmark. As a Swedish top manager put it: 'I believe Swedes and Finns feel that one does not only understand each other professionally, but one can also trust each other, so to speak. There is a kind of Japanese honour mentality among the Finns, which says one cannot break one's promises. A Danish manager in the same position is more, if the expression is allowed, a merchant. . . .' Another Swedish top manager put it more bluntly: 'In Denmark, they have more of a Latin negotiation culture. I mean in Sweden and Finland we build it up logically.' A Norwegian interviewee described his perception of the relationships between the four nations at Nordea: 'It is a fight, with Danes on the one side, and Swedes and Finns on the other.'

Fourth, when using stereotypes, we often tend to overlook other explanations for observed behaviour. For example, the fact that Swedes and Finns at times end up speaking Swedish together means that the one (Swede) is using his/her mother tongue while the other (Finn) is communicating in a foreign language. This would be an obvious explanation for the Finns' tendency to speak less – or more briefly or more blunt comments. Stereotypes also offer very convenient explanations that shift attention, for example, from conflicts or managerial mistakes. For instance, in the case of the dismissal of Finnish managers in TeliaSonera (see above), there seemed to have been serious conflicts between the senior managers that had more to do with personal chemistry than national stereotypes.

Fifth, stereotypes often confuse specific institutionalized practices with imagined cultural 'characteristics' or 'traits'. For example, in Sweden, there is a tradition to discuss organizational decisions in various organs before announcing the official decision. Among other things, this practice is anchored in the Swedish co-determination law, which must be respected in all organizations. This practice may actually not be that different from the practice usually followed in Finland, but still at times the differences are visible. The problem is that Finns, like many others, often misinterpret such practices and prefer the stereotypical explanation for the observed behaviour of the Swedes. The point is that such practices that tend to be followed in Sweden or Finland should not be seen as stereotypes, that is, as essential characteristics of Finns or Swedes as decision-makers.

The Problematic Consequences of Stereotyping

While stereotypes provide superficial explanations for people's behaviour, they can still be 'lived real' in inter-national encounters such as mergers and acquisitions. The point is that stereotypical conceptions can make people adjust their own behaviour according to the imagined traits or patterns. Charles and Louhiala-Salminen in Kangas and Kangasharju (2005) studied everyday communication in two major Finnish–Swedish mergers. They illustrate in an interesting way what happens when people from two apparently different cultures interact. For example, Finnish 'reticence' may in meetings produce Swedish 'discussion'. Charles and Louhiala-Salminen show how Swedes interpret the Finns' silence in a way different from how it was intended, react according to their own cultural frame (i.e. silence is problematic and must be filled with discussion), and in this way provide further evidence for the Finns' stereotypical image of Swedes as indecisive chatterboxes. In this sense, stereotypes become self-serving and self-constructive.

Importantly, these stereotypes most often involve tendencies to promote one's self-image at the expense of the other – and thus reinforce prejudices. For example, Swedes tend to expect and value discussion. Apparently, Swedes celebrate the ability to come up with well-thought-out decisions that everyone involved can subscribe to. In Finnish–Swedish encounters, the Swedes therefore tend to criticize the Finns for being hasty, undemocratic, patronizing and old-fashioned. When dealing with the Swedes, Finns, in turn, often make action-orientation a virtue and emphasize the value of straighforwardness and effectiveness. At the same time, they tend to label Swedes inflexible and unable to make decisions.

These self-serving stereotyping tendencies are closely related to the historical relationship between the nations. In the post-colonial Swedish–Finnish setting, the result often is that the stereotyping on the Swedish side tends to reinforce an image of Swedish superiority over the Finns. In Finland, in turn, the stereotypes are often means to resist the image of inferiority by harsh criticism of the Swedes. Risberg et al. (2003) present an example from an article in *Dagens Industri*, the major Swedish daily business newspaper, (20 November 1997) on the Swedish tendency to (re)construct images of superiority:

> **The end of management-by-perkele**
> *Finnish managers are listening to their employees*
> A wind of change has blown over the industrial life and its outstanding figures in Finland. Whisky and cigars in dim lighted cabinets are out and management-by-perkele belongs to the past. . . . The new generation of Finnish managers are taking care of their health, playing ball with their children and demanding an open dialogue with their subordinates. And little by little they are beginning to learn about openness; press conferences are no longer arranged for the top management to show off and glitter; now it is about answering questions as far as possible. Jorma Ollila, the CEO of Nokia, is leading the development. He has managed to implement a totally new corporate culture among his employees.

Many readers of *Dagens Industri* are likely to recognize the Swedish stereotype of Finnish management style, coined in the Finnish swear word *perkele* ('devil'). As pointed out above, 'management-by-perkele' is a term that became famous in Sweden in the mid-1980s. According to Risberg et al. (2003), the tone in the text above indicates that the Finnish managers are now making progress as they are working for 'open dialogue' and 'little by little they are beginning to learn about openness'. What is interesting here is that this progress is described as moving from the stereotypical Finnish management style (as perceived by Swedes) towards the archetypal Swedish style characterized by egalitarianism, cooperation and consensus; that is, the 'open dialogue' (see Ekwall and Karlsson, 1999; Zander, 1999; Berglund and Löwstedt, 1996). For the Swedish audience, the obvious underlying message in the text is that the Finns are now 'little by little' reaching a more advanced and modern stage in management and managing, which Swedes have mastered for quite some time.

Tienari et al. (2004) present an example from the Finnish media. They analysed (yet another) short burst of public discussion around Finnish and Swedish management styles. This time, the discussion was triggered by a remark by Björn Wahlroos, the outspoken CEO of the Finnish financial services company Sampo (and, interestingly enough, a Swedish-speaking Finn). An article based on Mr Wahlroos' speech was titled 'Sampo's Wahlroos: Nerds Prevail in Swedish decision making' in *Helsingin Sanomat* (7 May 2003), the most widely read daily newspaper in Finland: 'According to Björn Wahlroos, the management style in Sweden, which emphasizes consensus, is catastrophic for managerial work in practice. This is especially the case in the boards of companies where board members should be able to distinguish between line management and collegial decision making.'

Mr Wahlroos was also quoted to have remarked that 'it is a major advantage that in Finland most managers are reserve officers who are used to the fact that line management has its time and place, and the same goes for collegial decision making' (*Helsingin Sanomat*, 7 May 2003). For at least a male Finnish audience, the message is clear. The reference to reserve officers brings to mind the fact that the Reserve Officers' School (as a voluntary and competed-for part of the obligatory military service in Finland) has traditionally served an important role for the male Finnish elite. It testifies to the fact that in Finland (in contrast to Sweden), military management can be drawn on discursively as a positive reference. 'According to Wahlroos, collegial decision making, which emphasizes consensus, results in a situation where the nerds win the discussion. After collegial discussion, most often the alternative with the least risk is chosen.' The auto-stereotype of Finnish management is thus based on the (masculine) ability to take (individual) responsibility and risks in difficult and challenging situations. A clear contrast is built to a stereotypical image of the Swedes.

As the case above show, stereotyping seems to reconstruct particular kinds of prejudices that should be taken seriously. For example, seeing the Swedes as colonizers imposing their own practices on the Finns or viewing the Finns as old-fashioned and stubborn obviously hinders and even prevents open-minded cooperation in Finnish–Swedish settings. Moreover, this kind of stereotyping may also have far-reaching implications for individual people in international organizations. For example, if a Finn is seen as authoritarian because s/he is a Finn (e.g. by Swedish decision-makers), this is not likely to enhance his/her career. The same applies to a Swede who is seen as bureaucratic because s/he is a Swede (e.g. by Finnish decision-makers).

How To Go Beyond National Stereotyping?

We are probably forced to live with some form of national stereotyping. However, in contexts such as cross-border mergers and acquisitions, there is every reason to try to go beyond the most superficial and problematic images. While there are obviously no magical solutions, we have come to value four practical methods in international merger settings: 1) investing in socio-cultural learning, 2) organizing communication training, 3) creating special fora for cultural sensemaking, and 4) focusing attention on a new joint culture and identity.

First, socio-cultural training provides a means to learn about the cultures of the specific nations and organizations in question. In brief, studying the history and society of the nation in question helps to understand many important cultural practices but also makes it possible to comprehend where certain stereotypes come from. In concrete settings, such education should, however, be carefully planned so that it does not itself reproduce prejudices or involve cultural imperialism.

Second, when dealing with inter-national interaction, it is important to invest in communications training. In international contexts, the choice of common medium is at times a complex question (as was discussed above vis-à-vis the use of Swedish language in a Swedish–Finnish organization), but clearly foreign language skills are needed to be able to understand each other and express ideas as effectively as possible. Language skills specifically help to avoid misunderstandings that are often linked with stereotypical conceptions. Such training should also focus on communication practices and differences in traditions; for example, what kind of communication is considered appropriate in particular settings.

Third, to pay attention to the problematic aspects involved in cultural sensemaking and stereotyping, it is also useful to organize special occasions such as joint discussions. In Merita-Nordbanken, for example, managers underwent a series of cultural seminars. At best, these seminars triggered in-depth discussions concerning the Finns' and Swedes' perceptions of themselves, the others, and their joint future (Säntti, 2001; Vaara et al., 2003a). Such seminars were also carried out in some units when Merita-Nordbanken later merged with Unidanmark (Björkman and Vaara, 2004). Using humour when making sense of cultural differences seems to be a particularly effective means to be able to go beyond stereotypical conceptions. It should be noted, however, that humour is a potentially risky form of communication. A basis of mutual trust is necessary for using humour as a tool of cultural integration.

Fourth, and finally, it is useful to direct attention towards a joint future culture and identity. In settings such as international mergers and acquisitions, cultural sensemaking tends to concentrate on national differences. In the worst cases, this reinforces national stereotypes and hinders cooperation. It is therefore also important to focus attention on the organizational culture and identity of the new post-merger organization. This should not be seen as something involving only naive corporate culture or value programmes but a challenge to be taken seriously at different levels of the organization and in different locations. The Nordea case is an interesing example of both the pros and cons of investing in the creation and development of a joint Nordic identity (Søderberg and Vaara, 2003).

Conclusion

In this chapter, we have focused on national stereotyping in cross-border mergers and acquisitions. We have argued that it is useful to regard stereotypes as discursive resources in making sense of inter-national encounters. These discourses are readily available in literature, folklore, media and, for example, organizational gossip. This allows us to understand, among other things, their widespread and uncritical use. As we have shown, stereotypes are (re)produced when they help organizational members to explain their experiences and the problems they encounter. However, this apparent explanatory power should be viewed with a critical eye. This is because stereotypes are extreme generalizations that at best help us to look at some overall patterns of behaviour. Also, they are most often context-specific and ambiguous. They overshadow other explanations for observed behaviour, and confuse specific organizational practices with essentialist cultural 'traits'. Furthermore, as stereotypes tend to be used in self-serving ways, stereotyping is likely to reinforce prejudices. These prejudices hinder social interaction but may also have more far-reaching implications, for example, for people's careers.

We have focused on Finnish–Swedish mergers and acquisitions. Our examples are obviously context-specific but we believe that the tendencies analysed here characterize also other settings. Nevertheless, it would be interesting to study stereotyping in other contexts to be able to compare both the content of the stereotypes and their use in more detail. For example, it would be intriguing to explore stereotyping in the recent mergers and acquisitions between British, German, French, US, Japanese and Chinese corporations. These settings would probably reflect complex (re)constructions of identities and stereotyping due to the strong national identities involved.

Our analysis of the Finnish–Swedish setting emphasizes the importance of the historical relationships of the nations in question. It suggests that a post-colonial lens may be particularly useful in understanding the 'wider context' of (symbolic) power relations in inter-national mergers (e.g. Prasad, 2003; Risberg, 2003). It would therefore be intriguing to examine other post-colonial as well as neo-colonial types of settings and explore the reproduction of specific kinds of supeririority–inferiority relationships in national stereotyping. In this sense, the recent waves of foreign acquisitions in the former Eastern Europe and the Far East would be fascinating cases. In contrast, it would be exciting to compare such cases with others where, for example, Eastern European or Far Eastern companies have acquired European or US corporations.

CASE BOX 10.1:   M&A AS STEREOTYPES – 'THE SIMPLE WAY FORWARD'*

> **Bengt**: We have this great system that we'd like to introduce in Finland as well. Maybe we should sit down and discuss this. We can go to the sauna afterwards and have a few Kosken, too, if you like, ha ha ha . . .
> **Virpi**: Yeah, sure, more discussion is exactly what we need.

Bengt is the Swedish CEO of NORDCORP, a newly merged Swedish-Finnish company with operations in both countries. Virpi is the Finnish COO in NORDCORP. Bengt is puzzled. The Finns in the new organization seem resistant to implement some of the most crucial procedures that are needed to make the merger a success. The merger negotiations went relatively smoothly but now there seems to be little momentum on the Finnish side. The Finns are doing a good job results-wise but they are reluctant to change.

Bengt introduced the system to Virpi and other key people in the Finnish organization. He offered to discuss the issue before implementing it, and even joked about going to the sauna and having a drink afterwards. That's what Finns like to do. But the reaction was unsettling. What is the problem here?

Eventually, Bengt found out. The 'personal chemistry' with the top Finnish managers did not seem to be working at the time so Bengt first decided to call an old friend. Lars is a management consultant who has a lot of experience working with Finns. Lars used to be the CEO of a Swedish company that acquired a couple of Finnish firms back in the 1980s. As far as Bengt could remember, Lars did a good job in integrating the Finnish companies.

Bengt and Lars agreed to meet. In the end, it only took two sessions with Lars for Bengt to make sense of the situation. The first meeting added to Bengt's anxiety but the second one proved an eye-opener. Bengt began the first session by explaining the situation in the merged company, and Lars started to ask him questions:

> **Bengt**: Take the example of the new system. Some of the key people in Finland do not make an effort to introduce the system in the organization. How can it be adequately introduced if the key people are not behind it? Top management commitment is crucial in a situation like this.
> **Lars**: Why should the Finns comply?
> **Bengt**: It's not a question of Swedes and Finns, and it's not a question of complying. It is about implementing an advanced system for the purposes of a multinational organization. And standardizing systems is paramount in a multinational such as ours.
> **Lars**: What makes you think that the Swedish system is the most advanced?

Bengt: Eh? We've developed this system for years. It has stood to test, and everyone's behind it. It took me and my colleagues a lot of time and effort to implement it in the first place.

Lars: But didn't you agree on a merger of equals?

Bengt: What do you mean? Of course we did, and that's what I'm talking about. We're helping them out.

Lars: How much do you know about the Finnish system?

Bengt: It seems outmoded. Or, er, I don't know the details but that's my impression. And Finns are so quick-and-dirty in their management anyway. They are authoritarian: it's the boss that decides. They want to do things fast, and that's what I'm offering here. Well, now that you mention it, perhaps we should do a bit of benchmarking just is case there are features in their system that we can use. Identifying and adopting best practices is extremely important in a situation like this.

Lars: How can you benchmark between systems embedded in two totally different contexts?

In Bengt's view, the discussion was turning a bit odd. Why did Lars insist on talking about Swedes and Finns? Multinationals such as NORDCORP don't work on a national basis – or at least they shouldn't. And what was wrong in taking advantage of features of the Finnish system if the overall system could somehow be improved in this way?

Lars: Who exactly are the key people on the Finnish side?

Bengt: I don't like the expression 'Finnish side'. We're all one organization. But it must be Virpi and Matti. Virpi is the Chief Operating Officer and Matti is head of sales. Funny names, right?

Lars: What are they like? I mean, as individuals?

Bengt: Both are very competent. They're real professionals. That's not the problem.

Lars: What is the problem then?

Bengt: Everything has happened so quickly. We've introduced the merger at a fast pace because the owners expect this. I haven't really had time to get to know anyone personally . . . And you know the quiet Finns – they're difficult to interact with.

Towards the end of the first discussion, Lars wrote down a few additional questions for Bengt to ponder on as a basis for their second meeting. First, Bengt was to find out more about Virpi and Matti and the functioning of the Finnish organization. Second, Bengt was to find out more about their system. Third, he was to learn more about the Finnish legislation and institutional environment, particularly vis-à-vis the system he wanted to be introduced in Finland. Bengt and Lars got together a few days later:

Lars: So what did you find out about Virpi and Matti and others?

Bengt: That was a bit weird. I called Mats, one of my nearest colleagues in the Swedish organization. He has been interacting with the Finns ever since the merger announcement. Mats said that they had perceived me as too authoritarian, dictating stuff that they would need to negotiate in their organization before making any decisions. Virpi, in fact, has an MBA from Uppsala University in Sweden. According to Mats, Virpi's management style is very decentralized. She is a good communicator. The same seems to apply to Matti.

Lars: What about sauna and drink?

Bengt: Virpi and Matti are both teetotallers. It seems that my joke about going to the sauna and having a few drinks didn't really resonate. I admit that the sauna thing was a bit much, especially in front of a lady. But I was just trying to ease the tension. In Sweden, we refer to the Finnish Koskenkorva as 'Kosken' for short. The word is so damned long and difficult.

You've no doubt heard about this drink, which resembles vodka. I thought it's real popular in Finland. Apparently, my joke didn't really make sense, not in that situation anyhow. The word 'Kosken' is incomprehensible for Finns and, according to Mats, they don't drink much of the stuff anyway.

Lars: How did the Finns interpret your behaviour?

Bengt: Mats said that I'd just confirmed the Finns' stereotype of a patronizing Swede when I pushed our Swedish way as best and most advanced.

Lars: What did you find out about the Finnish system?

Bengt: That was curious, too. It seems that they had put a lot of effort in streamlining their system a few years back, and they were in the middle of revising it further when we merged. It's working fine. And Mats said that he always speaks English with the Finns. Perhaps I should try that as well. It seems that the Swedish word 'diskutera' [to discuss] carries particularly problematic connotations here. For Finns, it seems to refer to endless and meaningless debate: the Swedish strategy of getting their own way. Overall, I didn't realize that this could be such a complex and sensitive issue.

Lars: What did you find out about the institutional and legislative environment?

Bengt: Don't rub it in, old friend. I found out that the Finnish legislation actually doesn't allow for some of the features we have in the Swedish system. And because of my apparently pushy behaviour, they played a joke on me. They let me boil in my own juices for a while. Only now, I can see the sarcasm in all this.

Lars: So what's the bottom line?

Bengt: The bottom line is that we're taking a timeout with standardizing the system. I need to talk to Virpi and her team again very soon. And after that, if they agree, we might want to introduce some kind of cultural sensitivity programme in NORDCORP, which would give Swedes and Finns an opportunity to meet and grasp the situation together. We really can't afford any more of these misunderstandings. On a personal note, I need to tone down my authoritarian behaviour. What irony!

After the meeting, Lars sent Bengt a list of questions to pin on the wall of his office:

1. What are typical stereotypes concerning Finns and Swedes?
2. Do they make sense in this setting?
3. Do the Finns behave like the stereotypes would indicate?
4. Do I behave like a stereotypical Swede?
5. What are the issues that are particularly sensitive for the Finns?
6. What about us Swedes?
7. Are there 'real' difference in organizational practices or institutional systems that I should pay attention to?
8. How can I together with others learn to overcome stereotypical conceptions?

* This case is entirely fictional although its elements are based on observations and insights related to real-life mergers and acquisitions between Finnish and Swedish companies.

Chapter 11   M&A as Imperialism

Simon Collinson

Introduction

In March 2000, a quintessentially English brand, Tetley Tea, was acquired by Tata
Tea Limited, owner of 54 tea estates and the second most popular tea brand in
India. Coming more than 50 years after the end of 200 years of British colonial
rule had supported British-owned tea estates in India, this shift of power is an
appropriate symbol for the twenty-first century. But the takeover was barely
noticed by the British public. In stark contrast to the imperialist approach of the
British in India all those years ago, Tata took a hands-off approach, allowing the
existing management, with its local knowledge and experience, to continue running Tetley.[1]

   Is cross-border merger and acquisition a form of imperialism? Given the general definition of imperialism as 'any instance of aggressive extension of authority'
(*Chambers Concise Dictionary*), the term could be applied to both national-level
colonization and corporate-level cross-border M&A. Similarly, imperialism as a
'policy of extending your rule over foreign countries' could be a description of corporate internationalization strategies.[2]

   In this chapter we shall argue that imperialism provides a useful lens through
which to examine cross-border M&A. It leads us to focus on two key dimensions
– context and practice – that determine how power and control are exercised during such M&A activity. As emphasized by contingency theorists (such as Donaldson,
2001), macro-level context is important because it determines the conditions
(political, economic, legal and social) under which ownership is permitted. Context
also strongly influences the conditions of ownership, the distribution of power and
control and the key issues of who benefits and who is exploited. To explore this
theme, we will examine a series of mergers and acquisitions through which Kodak
gained a dominant position in mainland China in the late 1990s.

Practice is important because, in our view, generic 'best-practice' does not exist. On the one hand, different strategies and different forms of organizational structure and human resource management are appropriate for different contexts. The strategic options and the tactical degrees of freedom for international managers are the result of the political, social and economic conditions of the time and place in which they operate. On the other hand, however, within very similar contexts different styles and approaches have different performance (and other) consequences. There is no standard solution. In some cases, an imperialistic style of M&A is the most efficient and effective form; in others, more democratic decision-making and federalist structures will reap more rewards. We will examine the Nissan–Renault deal as an example of a highly interventionist, arguably ethnocentric, yet highly successful takeover.

Finally, these dimensions of context and practice, which combine macro- and micro-level approaches to cross-border M&A, are not only relevant for international managers. We believe that sensitivity to both dimensions is important for policy-makers seeking to control or influence M&A activity to progress national or international agendas. They are also relevant for activists (including antiglobalization lobbyists) seeking to influence the actions of multinational firms.

This chapter is structured in three main parts. We examine the macro-level first, looking at changes in patterns of M&A and governance. The second part focuses on the management and organization of international M&A. Finally a framework is presented for comparing various kinds of cross-border M&A, with imperialistic approaches placed alongside other forms of governance and management.

The Big Picture: The Changing Global Context for M&A

The mercantilism that began in the sixteenth and seventeenth centuries provided the starting point for international economists to examine exchange and transactions across national borders. Theories of 'absolute advantage' proposed by Adam Smith (1776), 'comparative advantage' by David Ricardo (1817), Heckscher-Ohlin (1933), Leontiev (1953); the names and frameworks are reeled out in lectures the world over. Such trade theories provide the backdrop for examining the strategy, organization and tactics of international business, the aim of which is to understand the competitive advantages and disadvantages of using different approaches in different geographic, cultural and business contexts.

The motivation for firms to engage in cross-border M&A has remained largely unchanged since this early period. Major strategic drivers, for example, include: 1) *vertical integration* – the acquisition of overseas buyers or sellers to extend the boundaries of the firm up or down the supply chain (sometimes termed *internalization*, following Dunning's work (1980; 1993)); 2) *horizontal integration* – buying out competitors in the same industry; 3) *product extension M&A* – to enhance one's economies of production or distribution; and 4) *market extension M&A* – the acquisition of firms located in different geographic markets.[3]

Although all of these types were practised in the mercantilist period, vertical M&A dominated because the major trading activity in developing countries was the export of commodities to supply emerging firms and evolving consumers in the newly industrializing regions in Britain, the USA and parts of Europe. But rather than 'legitimately' acquiring existing businesses, the earliest multinational enterprises (MNEs) either forcibly acquired or actively developed large-scale primary industries in colonized parts of Asia, Africa and Latin America.

Imperialism explains much of M&A throughout this part of history. Superior military power was the basis for the acquisition of local assets and (mainly natural) resources, and the exploitation of local labour during early colonialism. Royal families headed the hierarchies that ran empires, backed by their armies and armadas. These established the governance structures, institutional infrastructures and legitimacy under which trading companies exploited the endowments of other countries and repatriated profits as well as commodities to the home economy. It was not, however, simply military might and expansionist monarchs or governments that underpinned the various periods of colonization throughout the past four centuries. Broader social acceptability was a strong ally, supporting domination and subjugation in the name of cultural superiority as well as economic growth. Companies had the same set of objectives as they have today, to expand into other markets, tap into cheaper sources of materials and labour, create economies of scale and grow in size and power to reduce risk and maximize profits. They were able to pursue these goals more directly because of the relative absence of social and political constraints on their activities.[4]

Theoretical traditions around the issues of international ownership, power, control and exploitation have been underpinned by a variety of implicit or explicit moral philosophies. Economic development thinking crystallized into two broad camps in the 1960s: the 'modernists' and the 'dependency theorists'. The former saw development as a linear, follow-the-leader path (see Rostow, 1960): 'trickle-down' of resources and opportunities would take care of the poor in societies; economic and social inequality was a necessary stage of development. There was some support for this view from (ethnocentric) psychologists, who saw countries as having varying levels of 'cultural predisposition' towards development (see McClelland, 1961). This extended an age-old theme – the need to civilize or, specifically, 'Westernize' laggard countries and cultures. Unequal power structures were legitimized on the basis of this thinking and there are clear parallels with ethnocentric styles of M&A we examine later in this chapter.

As a reaction to the modernist perspective, critical dependency theorists saw economic relationships between developed and developing countries as innately exploitative, rather than mutually beneficial. The global economic system served advanced Western nations at the expense of the underdeveloped through unequal terms of trade and through the activities of multinational firms. This is similar to the perspective adopted by the antiglobalization activists more recently. (See Cardoso and Faletto, 1971; Amin, 1974.) This view gave rise to the emergence of development policy approaches including the 'basic needs' and 'appropriate technology' movements. A central tenet of dependency theory was that developing countries needed to 'de-link' from the West in order to develop. The success of 'newly industrialized countries' (NICs) in the 1960s and 1970s, however, indicated the exact opposite.

Recent growth in cross-border M&A

Real-world changes in the where, why and how of cross-border M&A have altered the emphasis placed on power and exploitation in theoretical approaches. Studies of rapidly developing Latin American and Asian countries, including the 'four Tigers' (Hong Kong, Singapore, Taiwan and South Korea), show that multinational firms were responsible for transferring significant technological capabilities to acquired firms, subsidiaries and joint-venture partners in these countries. This eventually resulted in their new levels of export competitiveness. Despite inequalities of ownership and power, firms at the periphery of the global system learned to compete via these unequal relationships.

There may be disproportionate benefits to the owners of capital but the knock-on effects to non-owners who receive foreign direct investment and evolve into owners are now better-understood. Over the long term, social welfare improvements as well as economic development and wealth-creation pointed to the benefits of becoming integrated into an unequal global system. (See Amsden, 1992; Hobday, 1995; Lall, 1996.)

Recognizing the benefits of integrating into the global economy, governments have become very involved in attracting inward investment, including 'out-in' M&A, but with particular conditions. Moreover, MNEs are competing more actively to get access to growing markets outside the 'triad' regions and are willing to make compromises and fulfil requirements placed on them by these host governments.[5]

For a time these drivers underpinned a strong rise in cross-border M&A activity, in line with other indicators of globalization. Average annual growth rates, by value, were 26.4% in the period 1987–90, 23.3% in 1991–95 and 49.8% in 1996–2000. Between 1995 and 2000 the deal volume totalled more than $12 trillion. Growth rates then dropped dramatically in 2001. The number of M&A deals fell from a high of 7,894 cases in 2000 to 4,493 cases in 2002 and their average value fell, from $145 million in 2000 to $82 million in 2002. The number of M&A deals worth more than $1 billion declined from 175 in 2000 to only 81 in 2002, the lowest since 1998.[6]

On average for the decade 1989–99 about a quarter of all mergers and acquisitions were cross-border, in terms of both value and number of deals. M&A in developing countries, which accounted for around 10% of total foreign direct invest-ment (FDI) in these countries at the end of the 1980s, grew to account for over 30% at the end of the 1990s. These were driven particularly by changing policies in emerging and developing countries relating to FDI and foreign equity shares. The privatization of state-owned firms in energy, telecoms, construction and pri-mary industries in the developing and emerging countries of Eastern Europe, Latin America, Africa and some parts of Asia was also significant.

We should, however, keep the growing involvement of developing country firms in perspective. In a list of the 81 cross-border M&A deals (over 10% of equity) in 2002 that were worth over $1 billion there are only 13 firms from non-OECD countries. Eight of these were the subject of acquisitions by developed-country firms. Just five non-OECD firms feature in the entire list of acquirers, and just one from Asia – the Hong-Kong grocery firm A. S. Watson bought $1.2 billion-worth of Kruidvat Holding, a drug store firm from the Netherlands. Most M&A activity, including cross-border activity, is between developed countries of the triad regions.

When considering the 'M&A as imperialism' argument it is interesting to note that minority acquisitions (10–49% of equity) account for one-third of acquisitions in developing countries and less than a fifth in developed countries. Although 70% of cross-border M&A in terms of value (50% in terms of numbers) are horizontal, and could therefore be seen as a means of removing the local competition, the World Trade Organization (WTO) characterize over 95% of acquisitions (in terms of deal value) as 'non-hostile'. It suggests that long-term economic and strategic motives dominate, rather than short-term financial motives, which were more prevalent in the 1980s.[7]

The highs and lows of cross-border M&A and global FDI in general follow the broader economic cycles of growth and recession in the major economies. The boom in cross-border M&A from 1995 to 2000 has important parallels with the boom in the USA, which peaked between 1898 and 1902. Both were linked to significant changes in technology, financing mechanisms and regulatory and legislative con-ditions that led to the emergence of new markets for goods and services and new configurations of production and distribution networks.

A range of general factors have driven triad-based firms (in North America, Europe and Japan) to internationalize over this period, including the double-pull of grow-ing markets outside the triad and cost advantages, in the form of cheaper materials, labour and expertise abroad. The double-push of maturing home markets and ris-ing costs, particularly for Japan, has added impetus.

The growing sophistication of information and communication technologies (ICTs) and the Internet in particular have facilitated this globalization process. Adding to these, specific drivers have made cross-border M&A a more popular mode of inter-nationalization. The liberalization of trade and investment regimes and the relaxation of controls over cross-border M&A by national governments have been especially important in the three giant economies, China, India and Brazil. The privatization of state-owned enterprises and deregulation of the service sectors in these economies has also helped accelerate FDI alongside portfolio investment. An essential facilitator of this growth has been the evolution of global capital markets, making billion-dollar acquisitions feasible. Both the development of international financial instruments and the increasing cross-border cooperation of financial institutions underpin the 'money-go-round'.[8]

Changing context: new rules of the game

The context in which M&A activity takes place consists of the economic, political, social and cultural conditions that determine the local 'rules of the game'. This encompasses both what is acceptable legally and what is acceptable in terms of the values and norms of the dominant business culture. Important associated trends are the growing attractiveness of emerging markets, increased market liberalization and the greater power of host governments who are governing the liberalization process. Because countries like China and India combine the cost advantages of cheap labour and expertise with growing consumer markets they have a greater choice of suitable investors and more power in negotiations with foreign entrants. Multinational firms have always wanted to invest in local manufacturing and marketing in these countries but were not allowed to.

Table 11.1 illustrates the growing number of regulatory changes made between 1991 and 2003 that were favourable to FDI, partly explaining the above-mentioned trends.

Table 11.1   Removing the constraints on foreign direct investment

Item	1991	1992	1993	1994	1995	1996	1997	1998	1999	2000	2001	2002	2003
Number of countries that introduced changes in their investment regimes	35	43	57	49	64	65	76	60	63	69	71	70	82
Number of regulatory changes,	82	79	102	110	112	114	151	145	140	150	208	248	244
of which:													
more favourable to FDI[a]	80	79	101	108	106	98	135	136	131	147	194	236	220
less favourable to FDI[b]	2	–	1	2	6	16	16	9	9	3	14	12	24

[a] Including liberalizing changes or changes aimed at strengthening market functioning, as well as increased incentives.
[b] Including changes aimed at increasing control as well as reducing incentives.
Source: UNCTAD, *The World Investment Report* 2004.

At the firm-level, there is a growing awareness by managers of the need to adapt both their strategic approach and their organizational structure to the requirements of host country governments, as well as to host country factor conditions. This can be a complex process. For example, in April 2000 the US electrical firm AES launched a public takeover bid for 51% of Grupo Electricidad de Caracas (Grupo EDC) in Venezuela. It was considered hostile by the Grupo EDC board and a battle for control followed, involving Venezuelan state agencies such as the National Securities Commission (CNV), tribunals, unions and local companies. The US Securities and Exchange Commission (SEC) and Enron, among others, joined the fray on behalf of AES and it evolved into an international contest, with the USA portrayed as the imperialist aggressor by some observers. Other commentators, how-ever, noted the entrenched self-interests of both private- and public-sector parties supporting Grupo EDC.

As mentioned above, the newly industrializing Asian countries developed weal-thier economies and improved social welfare conditions through careful manage-ment of the market liberalization process. China is now attempting to follow the same process, channelling FDI into targeted areas of the economy and using foreign firms' capital, technology and knowledge to advance its own indigenous firms.

China attracted more FDI than any other country in 2003 and the conditions for any M&A agreements are set by regional and national government agencies. Their remit goes well beyond that of governments in developed economies and they have the necessary power and control to push multinational firms to fulfil at least part of the broader economic agenda for the country. Foreign managers' awareness of the government's agenda and the evolving rules of the game are of paramount importance to any market entry. The need to understand ever-changing govern-ment objectives and the variety of forms of market intervention by various levels of public-sector agency add greatly to the usual complexities of establishing part-nerships with local firms in a foreign business context.

When multinational firms negotiate with host governments, there is a range of factors that strengthen or weaken the bargaining power of each side. Kobrin (1982) terms these 'power resources' and 'constraints' and lists them for multinational firms and host country governments. A high level of competition in an industry, for example, constrains a multinational firm in negotiations with host governments because there are rivals vying for preferential market-entry conditions. Governments can play competing firms off against each other. Power resources encompass the kinds of things the firms can offer and local governments want, such as employ-ment, capital investment, technology, training and access to export markets to earn foreign exchange. In return the governments can offer certain kinds of access, given their control over foreign equity levels, taxation and subsidies, and their influence over local customers and aspects of pricing and competition.

The following case study of Kodak illustrates the central role of government for investors and the need for managers to be aware of, and adapt to, the local polit-ical agenda at any particular point in time.

CASE BOX 11.1:   KODAK IN CHINA – CHANGING THE RULES OF THE GAME

'Fewer than one Chinese household in ten owns a camera today. And that camera exposes about four rolls of film each year. If only half the people in China shot a single 36-exposure roll of film a year – a fraction of usage rates in other countries – that would swell the number of worldwide "clicks" by 25%. Each second, 500 more photos would be taken. That's the equivalent of adding another US or Japan to the world photographic market. China offers more potential for photography than any other market in the world.' George Fisher (Kodak CEO), 23 May 1998 (Kodak press release at: www.kodak.com/US/en/corp/pressReleases/pr19980323-01.shtml).

In 1997 Kodak faced growing competition in its domestic US market and was struggling with the impending technological and market shift towards digital imaging, away from its traditional stronghold in film-based products. It was also losing a long-running battle with regulatory authorities in Japan, challenging what it saw as anticompetitive practices that protected its key rival Fuji's hold on its own domestic market. At this time it had a 'limited' presence of 600 people in the fastest-growing market, China, importing, distributing and selling $250 million-worth of film. It was competing head-to-head with Fuji and local manufacturers, but falling behind; Fuji had the greater market share.

The options open to foreign investors in China then were far more restrictive than they are today. Outside-in M&A activity or even majority foreign-owned joint ventures were not allowed under highly protective government regulations. Kodak needed more than a change of strategy; it needed a change in the local 'rules of game'. Kodak's overall aims were: 1) for exclusive rights to produce and sell locally (shut out rivals); 2) to establish distribution, retailing and marketing operations to tap into the growing consumer market in China; 3) to establish production facilities for China and the Southeast Asian region; and 4) to use a combination of M&A and joint ventures to tap into local film business knowledge and resources.[9]

Surprisingly, it achieved all of these objectives. Under the direction of CEO George Fisher, who had led Motorola's developments in China, the firm engineered what is now considered to be a very successful series of mergers and acquisitions. These resulted in an investment of $1.2 billion and a massive expansion in its local production, sales and marketing operations.

The key was an agreement with the Chinese government orchestrated from the very top, between Fisher and Prime Minister Zhu Rongji. This gave Kodak exclusive rights to the local market by placing a moratorium on other foreign investment in the industry (blocking Fuji and Agfa) and forcing all but one of the existing Chinese competitors to close or be acquired. Kodak was allowed to purchase majority control of three local film companies in Xiamen, Shantou, and Wuxi. Two of these had supplier relationships with Fuji, which were severed, leaving Fuji to rely on a Hong Kong company, China-Hong Kong Photo Products Holdings, to distribute its products on the mainland. Three other failing local film companies were forced to close.

The two companies formed under Chinese Company Law, Kodak (China) and Kodak (Wuxi) in figure 11.1, are Kodak-controlled Chinese companies. The government

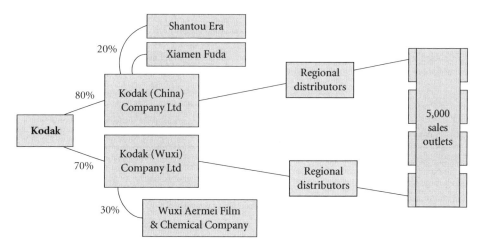

Figure 11.1   Kodak's structure in China

agreement allowed Kodak a greater proportion of ownership and more management control than any other foreign company had ever been granted in China up to that point. It gained a 70% share in Kodak (Wuxi), which manufactures and sells chemical products for photographic processing, and an 80% share of Kodak (China), which manufactures film and paper. The corporate structure adopted, a limited liability shares company, represented a radical departure from traditional equity joint-venture structures allowed previously by the Chinese authorities.

Kodak introduced a new system of management control, topped by a Kodak-controlled board of directors. Shantou Era and Xiamen Fuda were limited to the appointment of one director each to Kodak (China) Company's ten-person board. Key objectives were to introduce best-in-class management practices and processes, invest in local training programmes, create a performance-based culture and establish core Kodak values, 'with local characteristics'.[10]

The overall investment has paid off for Kodak. It now controls the entire indigenous Chinese photo film industry and has a market share of around 60%, from 40% in 1998. The only remaining local competitor is the aptly named 'Lucky Film Corporation', which has about 20% of the market and with whom Kodak signed a US$100 million 20-year cooperative agreement in 2003.[11]

Although the relationship between Fisher and Zhu Rongji set the all-important tone for the negotiations, the so-called 'Grand Plan' was a massive initiative, stretching over several years. It involved seven state-owned enterprises, six provincial governments, ten city governments, five Ministries and Commissions, local tax authorities and several banks and trust companies. All of this was under the umbrella of the Central Coordinating Committee designated by the Chinese government.[12] The critical key though was Zhu Rongji's broader, long-term ambitions for the liberalization of the Chinese economy and his immensely powerful position at the pinnacle of a steep, complex government hierarchy.

Foreign funds and employment were major attractions for the Chinese side. Shantou Era Photo Materials and Xiamen Fuda Photographic Materials (with 2,000 employees) were in debt to the tune of $843 million prior to the takeover. According to the *People's Daily* newspaper, the tax paid by the Xiamen joint cooperative venture just one year after it went into operation surpassed the total taxes paid by the old factory over the previous 14 years. Kodak also donated funds to community initiatives, including the Shanghai Children's Medical Centre in Pudong and Project Hope School under China Youth Development Fund, and established scholarship programmes with five top universities in China. These benefits came alongside the direct and indirect employment created by the new ventures and the inflows of technology and expertise from Kodak.

* * *

Beyond the above references, additional insights into this case, and particularly into the relationship between Zhu Rongji and Fisher, come from interviews conducted with Ira Wolf, Vice-President of Kodak Japan during this time.

Discussion Questions

1. Why did Kodak want to invest in China?
2. Why was there a 'window of opportunity' for Kodak created by both the situation in China and by the broader geopolitical context at that time?
3. Who benefited from Kodak's investments in China?
4. Who, if anyone, lost out and/or was exploited?
5. Could we characterize this M&A activity as imperialistic?

Stepping back from the Kodak case it is useful to revisit some of the above themes. The Chinese government wields enormous power and control over its own economy and businesses and over the 'rules of engagement' for foreign firms wanting to invest (see Nolan, 2001; 2004). It had a specific local industry development plan and some fear of the economic and socio-political destabilizing influence of high unemployment and indebted local firms. These continue to be relevant issues today. Kodak also had considerable 'power resources' as one of the two key players in a global industry: its financial muscle, its technological capabilities and its brand. In the resulting M&A process, Kodak was granted dominant shareholder status but the conditions of ownership were strongly influenced by the political agencies involved in the takeover.

From the perspective of the local firms, the nature of the deal and the subsequent imposition of a predominantly 'Western' organization style and structure by Kodak could very well be seen to be imperialist. However, in an 'average' market economy these local loss-making firms would have had to adapt or die out long before this point. The question as to whether Kodak is reducing local debt, saving jobs and developing indigenous wealth-creating capabilities or exploiting the people and the situation to improve its own profitability is not straightforward. It is probably doing both, in collusion with the Chinese government, so should this be considered imperialism?

The Micro-Level: The Organization and Management of Cross-Border M&A

At the micro-level we can compare and contrast different styles of M&A in terms of the actions of the dominant firm during the transaction and as the merged organization evolves over time. An imperialistic M&A deal would tend to be associated with a degree of ethnocentricity. The top tier of management would be dominated by home-country nationals and procedures; management styles would be 'transferred' from head office and 'imposed' on regional subsidiaries in place of local 'ways of doing things'.

Many firms rely on a highly centralized system where HQ managers are responsible for monitoring and responding to changes in markets and business environments that are far away. In such cases a top–down, bureaucratic organization structure enforces a limited remit on subsidiary managers, stifling what Birkinshaw (2000) terms subsidiary initiative. Detailed reporting mechanisms and frequent visits become even more important than normal to promote information flows between the centre and the periphery and ensure compliance. In these kinds of company structures, all divisions and subsidiaries tend to be required to participate in the 'internal market' for products and services as opposed to sourcing these from outside the organization. This reinforces the use of the internal hierarchy over external markets.

When Upjohn of the US acquired Pharmacia AB of Sweden in 1995, the highly interventionist, ethnocentric approach of the American firm created significant problems, pushing restructuring costs from an anticipated $600 million to an estimated $800 million. The US firm imposed a more centralized, bureaucratic and hierarchical style of organization onto the newly acquired Swedish and Italian parts of Pharmacia. It moved the R&D HQ to London, introduced a new management layer and tried to establish standard mechanisms for divisional accountability and reporting. This clashed with the egalitarian, team-centred style of the Swedes, resulting in a decline in staff morale, inefficiency, delayed projects and, more significantly, the loss of key R&D staff (Belcher and Nail, 2001; Frank and Burton, 1997). The initial structure and work practices imposed by the US firm were inappropriate for the new combination of cultures and anticipated synergies failed to materialize. This example provides a contrast to the Renault–Nissan case below, where cross-cultural and organizational differences were equally marked, yet a highly interventionist approach proved very effective.

At the opposite end of the spectrum, polycentric firms with 'federal' structures are characterized by devolved decision making, where subsidiary performance may be monitored and maintained at arm's length with a range of simple financial controls to ensure subsidiaries stay profitable. Holding companies and conglomerates like the once-powerful Hanson and GEC in the UK, which grew largely through M&A, showed some of these characteristics. Nestlé, Philips and Unilever have also preferred such structures in the past. Subsidiaries or newly acquired organizations are able to reflect the local cultural norms and HQ appreciates the need for different organization designs, procedural norms and rewards systems as long as profits flow to the centre.

The Fujitsu–ICL acquisition in 1990 showed how a less-interventionist, hands-off approach could work very well. When Fujitsu bought 80% of ICL from STC, its core strategy was to build a series of global alliances, both as technology sources and as locally recognized entities, through which to sell group products. ICL was allowed to remain firmly European for two main reasons: 1) because the political environment in Europe in the late-1980s was relatively hostile to Japanese products and investment; and 2) because local customers and suppliers had developed good relationships with the firm and these would be threatened by changes in personnel and organization. Fujitsu could also benefit from ICL's ongoing involvement in European R&D programmes in the IT area.

A year later ICL and Nokia Data merged to become a stronger European force in the evolving IT hardware and systems industry. This was a much more complex merger. Although it was dominated by the UK-side, led by Ninian Eadie and Peter Bonfield, the two organizations became much more fully integrated with a merged structure, shared senior management and joint decision making. This process also involved Ericsson Data Systems, which had merged with Nokia Data 3 years previously and had a characteristically egalitarian, team-based Swedish culture. An internal study contrasted the 'fast moving, non-bureaucratic, non-strategic, directive' Nokia Data with a 'more coordinated, systematized, strategically directed, consensus organization' ICL (Mayo and Hadaway, 1994).

Most MNEs are somewhere in between the imperialist and federalist extremes. Geocentric firms are often seen as 'ideal types' characterized as meritocratic, collaborative networks. An equal sharing of power and responsibility between headquarters and subsidiary; senior management promoted according to ability rather than nationality; and subsidiaries that share worldwide objectives, with managers focusing beyond national market interests, are all indicators of what Nohria and Ghoshal (1997) term a 'differentiated' global network. ABB and Unilever have both been put forward as examples of this in the past.

To leave key decision-making responsibilities with local managers of newly acquired companies to ensure their commitment and harness their knowledge requires HQ managers to relinquish power and control. For many firms, this proves the most difficult aspect of becoming a 'transnational' corporation. Even when the fallacy of the all-seeing, all-knowing central hub has been debunked, long-term managers based in MNE home divisions are often reluctant to leave decision-making power with foreign managers (Child, Faulkner and Pitkethly, 2001; Birkinshaw and Hagstrom, 2000; Bartlett and Ghoshal, 1987; Ghoshal and Bartlett, 1998). Newly acquired firms may also be treated differently according to the relative size of the acquisition, the importance of the host market, the relationship with the parent company's operating divisions and the respect cultures (corporate and national) involved (Stahl and Voigt, 2004; Lubatkin et al., 1998).

A fairly cursory look through a range of cross-border M&A examples shows a range of the above kinds of approaches and mixed post-M&A performances. We would argue that success or failure cannot be attributed to managers adopting either an interventionist or a non-interventionist approach in configuring post-M&A organizations. The difference comes down to the *appropriateness* of one approach compared with another in each particular context. The effectiveness of strategy, structure and management practices is *contingent* on circumstances.

CASE BOX 11.2:   RENAULT AND NISSAN – 'NO PAIN, NO GAIN'?

By definition, in Japan any 'takeover' is seen as hostile. M&A activity is referred to as *'tekitai teki baishu'* ('bid by the enemy') and, partly because of the destabilizing effects on long-standing interfirm networks and *'keiretsu'* structures, remains relatively unusual. One study quoted by the *Financial Times* estimated that the value of M&A activity as a percentage of national or regional GDP is around 18% for Europe, 14% for the USA and 6% for Japan. Certainly prior to the mid-1980s inward M&A by foreign firms was largely unheard of because of the political and social as well as the economic resistance they would encounter.

The long, drawn-out economic recession in Japan has prompted some changes in these patterns and we now find three of the big-five car firms are in effect controlled by foreign firms: Nissan by Renault, Mazda by Ford and Mitsubishi by DaimlerChrysler. The two top-performers, Toyota and Honda, have escaped this fate and survived the extended domestic market recession better than their competitors mainly because they were more internationally diversified (Rugman and Collinson, 2004).

In terms of M&A, the Renault–Nissan alliance was highly interventionist and ethnocentric in style, yet it has been one of the most successful of its kind ever (Economist Intelligence Unit, 2002). The explanation lies in the nature of the problems being experienced by Nissan, which Renault's intervention was able to address precisely because of its foreignness.

At the time of the alliance in 1999, Nissan was Japan's second largest automobile manufacturer and the world's fifth, with annual global sales of 2,568,000 vehicles. It had 131,260 employees and 203 consolidated subsidiaries and was firmly part of the 'Fuyo' *keiretsu*. Renault had 138,321 employees and was a strongly home-region oriented firm, heavily dependent on its home economy, France. Alone it was relatively small, holding just 4.2% of the global market, but vied with Volkswagen for European market leadership (holding 10.7% of this market in 2002). Together Renault and

Nissan now account for 9.1% of global auto sales, placing them jointly among the top five auto companies.[13]

The alliance began in March 1999 with Renault taking a 36.8% stake in Nissan; this has now increased to 44.4%, with Nissan having a reciprocal 15% stake in Renault. The alliance has deepened following the far-reaching changes put in place by Carlos Ghosn, installed as President and CEO of Nissan and now revered for having engineered a radical turnaround in the firm's fortunes.

For Nissan, the years leading up to the alliance were characterized by declining sales in all markets, contributing to 6 years of losses and mounting debt in the 7 years to 1999. This period was particularly marked by a drastic decline in unit sales in Japan, from 1,131,000 units in 1996 to 733,000 in 2000. Factory utilization in Japan was down to 53% and Nissan was in debt to the tune of $19 billion at the time of the alliance (Kelts, 2003). By the end of 2002, as the restructuring imposed by Renault began to take effect, it had posted interim half-yearly profits of $2.3 billion, massively reduced debt and a rising share price.

Carlos Ghosn, the Brazilian-born French CEO, has been credited for much of this turnaround. His nickname in business magazines is 'le cost-cutter' to signify his main mechanism for improving the bottom-line in acquired companies (Burt and Harney, 1999). But he has also been called the 'ice-breaker', allegedly by DaimlerChrysler Chairman Jurgen E. Schrempp, for his takeover approach, which ignores local business practices that stand in the way of profitability (Gold, Hirano and Yokoyama, 2001).

The changes that he orchestrated at Nissan following its alliance with Renault illustrate the organizational and structural factors that had become sources of weakness and failure at the firm in the face of the domestic market recession. These measures included cutting costs through plant-closures and layoffs (21,000 worldwide) and substantial changes to Nissan's human resource management practices. The action also involved reducing dealerships to break down the 'downstream' *keiretsu* affiliations in the domestic distribution and marketing networks. More importantly it resulted in a halving of the number of suppliers to Nissan in Japan, dismantling parts of the local supply *keiretsu*.

The firm had been deeply embedded in unprofitable external relationships and inflexible internal organizational structures that had become inefficient and costly in the recessionary environment. The lifetime employment principle in particular, backed by the social contract between management and labour and linked to the age-related hierarchy, strong unions and strong labour laws placed a set of obligations on senior management that made the radical restructuring initiated by Renault very difficult for an insider to instigate.

Poor performance and rising debt had been accepted by institutional and *keiretsu* shareholders, exacerbating the inertia. An inward-looking group of directors and senior management was locked into a system of socially and politically reinforced obligations towards employees and external stakeholders who resisted change. The composition of the firm's board prior to the alliance is symbolic of this inward-looking perspective, with 37 Nissan insiders, out of a total of 40 board members, each having spent at least 27 years with the firm. The three 'outsiders' came from the Fuji Bank, the Industrial Bank of Japan (IBJ) and the Japan Development Bank (JDB).

The imposition by senior Renault managers of a range of internal and external changes was only possible alongside a shift of power (through ownership) to the French firm and, arguably, a shift in (or shock to) the cultural beliefs and norms that underpinned the Japanese organization. The series of layoffs, a revised governance structure and a much less 'Japanese' system of human resource management, including performance-based pay and meritocratic promotion systems, were part of a more fundamental change in the formal and informal aspects of the organization.

Discussion Questions

1. Why did Renault want to invest in Nissan?
2. What broad economic and specific corporate pressures resulted in the need for a radical shakeup of Nissan?
3. In the context of traditional Japanese employment and working practices and interfirm relationships, why were the changes pushed by Renault's Ghosn considered 'radical'?
4. Who benefited from Renault's investment in Nissan?
5. Who, if anyone, lost out and/or was exploited?
6. Could we characterize this M&A as imperialistic?

A key difference between the Renault–Nissan and Kodak cases lies in the contexts in which the agreements took place and the agencies or constituencies involved. For Kodak, the government's policy objectives and evolving approach towards foreign investors was central; the Chinese film companies, their managers and employees were largely peripheral. In the Renault–Nissan case, the senior management at Nissan and the problems they faced were central. But the wider intrafirm and interfirm structures and relationships within which Nissan was embedded were also very important components. The Japanese firm's irresistible path-dependency and the resulting inertia in the face of an increasingly adverse external competitive environment made Ghosn's interventionist 'style' of M&A activity appropriate for the circumstances.[14]

Different perspectives at the micro-level

Returning to our contrasting approaches to understanding M&A and reflecting on some of the above case studies, it is important to note that the above 'versions' of events largely reflect a normative, mainstream or prescriptive approach. The main focus is the performance implications of different styles of M&A organization and the macro-level or micro-level factors that affect success or failure. A more critical appraisal of international M&A would ask different questions. For example: who has the power? Whose culture (national or corporate) and associated norms and values are imposed on whom and come to dominate the post-M&A organization? Who benefits most from the relationship? It would also bring a different perspective to bear on the central question of 'M&A as imperialism'. Exploring these issues requires different frameworks and measures, but there is insufficient space here to explore all the relevant options, so we will briefly look at some possible starting points.

Organizational socialization processes, within institutional theory, would be one possible focus. These are the processes by which individual actors learn and adapt to the beliefs, values and behaviours required to fulfil new roles in an organization (Schein, 1978; Van Maanen and Schein, 1979). They are also the main mechanisms by which such values and norms are transmitted and maintained (Bauer, Morrison and Callister, 1998). Institutional theory examines how rules, requirements, values and standards are built into societies and are taken into account or changed by individual actors.[15] Scott (1998) describes three pillars of institutions within organizations:

1. *Regulative*: rule setting, monitoring and sanctioning;
2. *Normative*: reflecting beliefs, norms and values, often inherent in standards and operating procedures and accepted 'ways of doing things';
3. *Cognitive*: shared social knowledge, taken-for-granted symbols, signs, jargon.

Studies in this field show how various socialization strategies and practices relate to individual job satisfaction, commitment and effectiveness and to overall organizational culture, teamwork and efficiency (Chow, 2002; Evans, Pucik and Barsoux, 2002). In practice socialization takes place through formal and informal induction activities, training, mentoring and general meetings and interaction. Individual work roles, organizational goals and values, people, 'special languages', politics and organizational history, are seen to be key socialization domains (Chao et al., 1994).

Both formal and informal, unwritten or tacit rules and principles are involved and the exercise of power to assert one set of principles over another (for example, after a merger) will take place via both channels. Establishing a formal hierarchy denoted by lines of command, salary, office, power over budgets and power over the sanctions and rewards affecting others takes place alongside the creation of new organizational relationships (the 'people' domain) with tacit distinctions of authority and power.

These elements of a particular organizational culture will, in combination, tend to either reflect a balanced mix of national cultures and norms of all employees, or to reflect those of the dominant group, normally the owner. This relates not just to organizational efficiency (the focus of normative interpretations) but also to power and legitimacy within a particular context (Boons and Strannegard, 2000).

In the Renault–Nissan case, for example, the initial catalyst for change came from a radically new strategy, widespread restructuring and the imposition of a range of non-Japanese work practices. It would be difficult to label these work practices as entirely 'French' but the initial changes were characterized by a strong move towards 'de-Japanization' and the 'imposition' of more European ways of doing things. Were we to focus on the processes of organizational socialization to analyse this M&A example, we might well gain a better insight into the imperialistic nature of

Renault's style of takeover during the initial period of the merger. The approach would allow us to identify particular processes and mechanisms by which a new set of norms, values and accepted practices was enforced or evolved in the newly merged organization. We might also be able to monitor how the structure of the M&A and the relationship between the two organizations became much less imperialistic as mechanisms like the exchange of engineers, designers and other personnel between facilities have prompted the development of a joint-organizational culture.[16]

In summary, we are arguing here that different perspectives may well not alter our view as to whether any particular M&A could be characterized as imperialistic or not. Alternatives to the normative or mainstream approach followed earlier in the chapter can, however, provide greater insights into the processes at work inside newly merged organizations, the evolving balance of power and the underlying set of norms and values that come to dominate.

Discussion and Conclusions

A central aim of this chapter has been to examine issues of ownership, power and imperialism at both the international (macro-) and individual organization (micro-) levels. Imperialism literally refers to 'the power or authority of an emperor' or 'the policy of making or maintaining an empire'. Whether legitimacy comes from royalty, government or the senior management of a multinational firm via ownership, some might say it carries it the assumption of superiority and will normally be contested.

Here we argue that at the macro-level there has been a shift in the international balance of power politically and economically. This is reflected at the micro-level in the changing 'rules of the game' for multinational firms in emerging markets. Moreover, multinational competitors from non-triad countries, like Tata, will be a significant force in the global economy in the near future.

At the micro-level, despite the risks, M&A have become a dominant international expansion strategy (Hitt, Harrison and Ireland, 2001; Davis, Desai and Francis, 2000). Firms are choosing to extend their boundaries overseas to 'internalize' parts of the value chain, trusting internal hierarchies rather than external markets. The aim is to reduce risk and improve profits by increasing direct control over sources of key inputs, accessing new markets or creating technical alliances, or simply by diversifying geographically. But M&A require firms to engage with the organizational and cultural differences of the acquired firm more immediately than is demanded by an organic, gradual (Uppsala model) style of expansion.

In this chapter we have proposed that some mergers and acquisitions can be characterized as imperialistic and ethnocentric in that decision making is centralized and the values and norms of the dominant owner are imposed on the resulting organization. Others are more polycentric, reflecting a mixed range of values and

Table 11.2   Types of international 'M&A': at the macro- and micro-levels

	Type of 'M&A'			
	(1) Imperialist	(2) Interventionist	(3) Arm's-length	(4) Non-interventionist
Organization	Ethnocentric	Single culture dominates	Geocentric	Polycentric
Structure	Steep hierarchy	Flat hierarchy	Federation	Network
	(hierarchy) ◄———	(heterarchy)	———►	(market)
Strategy creation	Dictated	Centrally decided	Jointly specified	Locally specified
Decision making	Centralized	Allocated	Shared	Devolved

norms and with power more equally distributed. Either of these approaches can lead to success or failure, depending on the political, economic, social and cultural context in which the M&A take place.

The framework in table 11.2 bridges the main themes and the various levels of analysis referred to in this chapter. It presents a typology for comparing various kinds of cross-border M&A in terms of their organizational structure, allocation of decision-making responsibilities and distribution of power.

In 'imperialist' M&A, decision-making power is centralized at the corporate level with the aim of furthering the strategic objectives of the firm. This can be an effective or ineffective approach, depending on the context. At this level, the framework draws on the work of Bartlett and Ghoshal (1998) and other mainstream international business approaches. There are also links with the Williamsonian markets-versus-hierarchies framework at all three levels (Nohria and Ghoshal, 1997; Hedlund, 1986).

There are clearly strong parallels at the macro-level when we think of the relative balance of power between nation states. The British Empire (and others before it, though few after it) was highly imperialist and had a steep organization hierarchy, with centralized decision making and policy dictated to the periphery. There was a centralization of power to build and control a global empire. An ethnocentric belief in the superiority of the cultural norms and values of the British provided much of the rationale for this structure and the underlying socialization processes.

In terms of the theoretical approaches adopted in examining both macro- (international) and micro-level (intra- and interorganization) relationships, two common and very broad camps take contrasting perspectives in relation to the above framework. A 'normative', functionalist or mainstream approach would see economic efficiency and performance improvement as the dominant focus in analysing such relationships, with organization structure and the distribution of decision-making power as simply the means to these particular ends. At the macro-level, solid economic growth, a trade surplus or positive balance of payments would indicate success, justifying the power structures that underpinned this success. Similarly, at the micro-level, revenue growth, cost-cutting or enhanced profitability might be the main indicators of success, justifying the structures and strategies that underpinned this performance. A 'critical' approach would focus more on the underlying structures and relationships themselves, often seeing unequal distribution of power, or the imposition of a set of cultural norms as an objective in its own right.[17] This is an oversimplification in view of the complex array of studies and theories that exist, but it is a useful one for our purposes.

Those taking a normative or mainstream perspective would ask: what style of M&A, in the range of options in table 11.2, would optimize efficiency and effectiveness of the newly merged organization? What balance between imperial and federal; ethnocentric and polycentric; steep hierarchy and network structure; dictated or locally specified strategy; centralized or devolved decision making, would create the most profitable way of managing and leveraging the merged assets, systems, expertise and capabilities of the two firms?[18] They should also ask: what balance would be *feasible* and/or *appropriate* in the specific political, economic, social and cultural context, the time and the place, of the M&A?

At one level, the message here is that beyond the financial analysis normally driving M&A, there is an increasing need for 'cultural and organizational due-diligence', as proposed by Angwin (2001). This increasingly insistent message, coming from a range of strategy analysts, reflects the realization that the high failure rates recorded for cross-border acquisitions are a result of poor cultural and organizational alignment.[19] The anticipated synergies following mergers are often not realized because of the problems associated with integrating different organizations and different corporate and/or national cultures.[20] For this reason, among others, well over half of all acquisitions fail.[21] But, going beyond this message, this chapter emphasizes the need to better understand the context in which M&A take place to guide this decision.

Both the Kodak and the Renault–Nissan cases examined in this chapter are considered outstanding success stories. The performance improvements following the respective takeovers for both the acquired and the acquirer justify the structure and style of takeover – for those taking a normative approach.

Yet both cases could also be seen as imperialistic M&A in some sense. Change was dictated through the power of ownership. In the Kodak case this was made possible by a change in the politically controlled legal and institutional conditions governing foreign M&A in China. In the Nissan case there was an acknowledged need for change despite the business structures and political and cultural norms that underpinned the inertia at Nissan. In both cases, arguably, the acquired firms did not want to be acquired and the changes that were initiated were ethnocentric, yet these firms benefited greatly from the resulting partnership.

Those taking a critical approach might suggest that: 1) the resulting benefits were unequal, and 2) the performance improvements should not justify the degree to which one cultural group imposed its 'way of doing things' on another. If we were to sympathize with the Japanese and Chinese that lost their jobs as a result of these mergers we might conclude that these were not 'fair', democratic or ethically justifiable business activities. Irrespective of the many benefits, the change took place against their will. Western multinational firms expanded their power and control over assets and people that we might argue they have no 'legitimate rights' over (calling into question ownership rights).

In cross-border M&A, as in all kinds of business activity, there are innate contradictions between the business outcomes and the ethical outcomes. Whether you consider any M&A to be 'imperialistic' depends largely on the perspective and priorities you choose to adopt.

NOTES

1. Tata Tea is part of the Tata group, one of the largest publicly quoted conglomerates in India, with a $9 billion turnover in that year. The profitability of its rapidly growing software division, TCS (Tata Consultancy Services), the largest software exporter in India, provided the financial boost for this unrelated acquisition. It represents the beginnings of a growing trend of more powerful firms from developing and emerging countries engaging in global M&A activity. However, the vast majority of cross-border M&A still involve either two firms from the triad regions (Europe, USA and Japan) or a triad-based multinational acquiring a firm from outside the triad.

2. Note that Lenin saw imperialism as the 'monopoly stage of capitalism' – the point at which there was the ultimate concentration of resources and power in the hands of a few (Lenin, 1916). More recently, some in the antiglobalization movement have adopted a similar stance, focusing on the exploitative actions of multinational firms (e.g., see Klein, 2000).

3. Derived from Walsh (1988).

4. It might be argued that there are parallels between historical periods of colonialism and the current geopolitical situation. It is clear that ethnocentric perspectives and economic, corporate and military power are all connected in ways that reflect some aspects of the past. Although this has the makings of an interesting debate it is not the focus of this chapter.

5. The inability to attract much investment – because of small markets, poor infrastructures and high-risk socio-political systems – is increasingly seen to be one of the key differentiators of LDCs (less developed countries), which receive less than 2% of world foreign direct investment. Most sub-Saharan African countries, for example, remain unattractive to MNEs and have developed little 'bargaining power' to benefit from this growth process. See Narula and Dunning (2000).

6. UNCTAD (2003) *The World Investment Report.*

7. UNCTAD (2000) *The World Investment Report* (and subsequent reports in 2003 and 2004).

8. See: Chunlai Chen and Findlay (2003); UNCTAD (2000) *The World Investment Report* (and subsequent reports in 2003 and 2004).

9. The details are from: Vanhonacker (2000); Holstein (1998); Kodak Company website at www.kodak.com/.

10. The details are from 'Kodak in China – Growth and Localization', a 2003 speech by Henri D. Petit, Chairman and President, Greater Asia Region, Eastman Kodak Company (www.kodak.com/).

11. *China Daily*, 24 October 2003: www.chinadaily.com.cn.

12. From Henri Petit's 2003 speech, op. cit.

13. See Rugman and Collinson (2004) and company annual reports.

14. The causes and consequences of this inertia in Japanese firms have been examined elsewhere. See: Collinson (2001); Collinson and Wilson (2006).

15. This kind of approach has been used, though not often, in analyses of international and internationalizing firms. See Kostova and Roth (2002).

16. Van den Berg and Wilderom (2004) define organizational culture as 'shared perceptions of organizational work practices within organizational units that may differ from other organizational units'.

17. Although there are many articles that provide definitions of these two approaches, Clark (2004) and other essays in a special edition of the *Journal of Management Studies* provide what could be termed a review and an update of these respective positions, reflecting on the work of Karen Legge.

18. These trade-offs sit within the standard 'integration versus responsiveness' framework that lies at the heart of much international business research. Global economies of scale and scope, and greater efficiency for MNEs, can result from the centralization of resources and decision-making responsibility, from standardizing products, services, processes and brands and from creating a uniform organization and corporate culture, as far as is possible. On the other hand there are benefits from adapting products and processes to suit local endowments, conditions and preferences; from managing resources at the local level to reflect changing local opportunities and threats; and from configuring the organization to suit local cultures and business practices. This integration-responsiveness trade-off varies by firm, host and home country and time. See: Bartlett and Ghoshal (1998); Rugman (1979).

19. See, for example: Marks and Mirvis (2001); Morosini, Shane and Singh (1998); Olie (1994).

20. See, for example: Ashkenas, DeMonaco and Francis (1998); Carey (2000); Marks (1991); Schuler and Jackson (2001); Very et al. (1996).

21. See Seldon and Colvin (2003). DePamphilis (2001) more specifically lists: 'overestimating synergy', 'the slow pace of integration', 'poor post-merger communication' and 'conflicting cultures' as commonly cited reasons for failure, as well as 'poor strategy', 'use of stock as payment' and 'overpaying'.

Part IV   Integration

Chapter 12 M&A as Linkages

The Critical Link Between Valuation, Pricing, Synergy and Integration

*David M. Schweiger, Erin P. Mitchell,
Justin L. Scott and Caroline D. Brown*

Introduction[1]

In their effort to sell the idea and the price paid for an acquisition to both share-holders and employees, executives often articulate the numerous synergies that will result from the deal and how they will create value for all those involved. Yet, in spite of such optimistic pronouncements, both practical experience and research evidence clearly demonstrate that most mergers and acquisitions have not yielded the proclaimed synergies, have not lived up to the financial expectations of those transacting them and have not added any additional value for the acquiring company's shareholders (Bruner, 2002).

Many reasons have been advanced to explain the poor M&A results. They have included inaccurate valuations, inflated prices, poor due diligence, excessive optimism, exaggerated synergies, and failed integration. Although each reason has merit, it is the interrelationship among them that ultimately determines whether value is created or lost (Schweiger and Very, 2003). In this vein, it is the purpose of this chapter to illustrate the relationship among valuation, pricing, intended synergies, integration and value creation and to do so through a comprehensive case analysis. We begin by discussing what we mean by value.

Perspectives on Intrinsic Value

Value is a function of cash flow. For an investment such as a merger or an acquisition to truly create value, it must produce more cash flow on a risk-adjusted basis than that which could be achieved by investing in the next best alternative of similar risk. Discounted cash flow models are built on the fundamental belief that the intrinsic value of an investment is the present value of future free cash flows. Present value is determined by estimating cash flows associated with the acquisition strategy over some reasonable period of time (e.g. 5 years), calculating a terminal value, and then discounting these two elements back to the present using a required return consistent with the risk undertaken. The required return, or discount factor, may be the weighted average cost of capital of the acquiring firm, of the firm being acquired, a combination of the two, or a higher return, if warranted by the risk factors and characteristics of the transaction.

From a financial economist's perspective, value is created when the return on the investment exceeds the required return. Since the majority of M&A transactions employ a discounted cash flow model (Bruner et al., 1998), value creation would be defined as a positive net present value from the investment. Value destruction occurs when the return on the investment is less than the required return or the net present value is negative. Value is maintained when the return on the investment is equal to the required return, implying a net present value equal to zero and an investment that met the expectations of the investor.

Price Versus Value

The price paid for a target and its intrinsic value to a particular acquirer can be quite different. M&A pricing is driven by a number of factors, and it may or may not be consistent with value as defined above. Perceived synergies, supply and demand, negotiation position, emotions, hubris, market conditions and other factors influence the price of the transaction. Throughout much of the 1990s, many transactions occurred at prices that were greatly in excess of what discounted cash flow models using reasonable assumptions could justify. Market measures of valuation based on comparable transactions (e.g. price–earnings multiples and market–book ratios) reflect what companies have been sold for in the marketplace, not what a particular target may be worth to a specific acquirer.[2] Exorbitant multiples and inflated pricing often result in the acquiring company exaggerating potential synergies.[3] This exaggeration creates unrealistic expectations and essentially commits the organization to a doomed strategy of trying to capture cash flows that do not exist. Therefore, while realizing synergies in terms of tangible cash savings or cash generation creates value, flawed pricing limits the success of even the most effectively executed integration strategies.

The fundamental driver of value in the M&A process is the stream of free cash flows that the target and/or combined firms will produce after the combination is completed. Target firms recognize this potential value and attempt to extract a premium from the acquiring firm that approximates the present value of the improved cash flow stream that results from realizing synergies. Consequently, value creation, destruction and maintenance are driven by the price paid relative to the intrinsic value of the target and the degree to which synergies are realized. The extent to which synergies are realized is dependent on how well the integration process is managed.

Identifying the Sources of Synergy

Essentially, there are four basic categories of synergy: cost reductions, revenue enhancements, increased market power, and intangible benefits. Reducing costs is the most reliable way to realize cash flow from synergies. Fixed-cost reductions are typically achieved through the elimination of redundant personnel in support areas, sales and administration, headquarters reductions, a reduction in fixed assets, increased utilization of existing assets, distribution optimization and overall economies of scale. Variable costs can be reduced through increased productivity and increased purchasing power.

Enhancing revenue growth opportunities is one of the most cited, but least successful, synergies put forth by companies in the midst of an acquisition or merger. These revenue growth initiatives typically surround cross-selling opportunities of new or complementary products and services through sales organizations or distribution channels that call on different geographic regions and customers. The success of this strategy is inherently dependent on the degree to which markets demand these diverse product and services.

Market power synergies accrue to firms that survive a market consolidation. This type of synergy is common in industries or markets suffering from long-term overcapacity, deeply deflated margins, and diminishing opportunities for organic growth. Market power may provide opportunities for increasing price, more favourable terms for the seller, or increased negotiating power over suppliers.

Intangible synergies encompass everything else that has not been previously addressed. They typically are difficult to quantify and even more difficult to realize. Intangibles such as brand equity and knowledge management are not only difficult to capture, but are also difficult to transfer across organizational and geographic extensions.

The success of a company realizing multiple synergies lies in management's ability to define and quantify what the synergies are, and to devise a concrete strategy to realize the cash flows associated with them. Successful integration plans must prioritize synergies in terms of impact and achievability to ensure that the highest impact synergies with the greatest probability of success receive the most attention. Similarly, negative synergies (e.g. defection of key employees and customers; redundant facilities, personnel and assets; unnecessary cannibalization of existing market share with lower margin products; poor morale) must be managed to min-imize value leakage and destruction.

Integration

Why is integration so important? As the discussion above suggests, most of the elements in the M&A process take place prior to the closing of a deal. They are theoretical activities to help arrive at and negotiate a 'reasonable' purchase price. Once the deal is closed the challenge first begins. Now the organizations and the people of the combining organizations have to be managed in such a fashion that all of the assumptions about synergies, cash flows and earnings are converted to reality. Due to the nature of the different types of synergies, each one has a vary-ing probability of success and a different level of impact, necessitating a different level of integration. Thus, the integration method will vary with the strategic intent of the acquisition, the synergies to be captured and the types of assets and personnel involved.[4]

Enamoured of the excitement of doing deals and the preoccupation of financial and strategic issues, integration has not, historically, been an area that has received much attention by executives. Increasingly, however, that has been changing. Burned by a lack of results, many executives have come to appreciate the import-ance of the roles integration and people play in the success of the M&A and their ability to create value for investors. Growing research in this area has also demon-strated many disappointing mergers and acquisitions may be attributed to failure to plan for and execute integration.[5]

Based on the previous discussion, we attempted to see whether any firms suc-cessfully linked valuation, pricing, synergies, integration and value creation. Below is an example of one such case that defied the risks of failed expectations so pre-valent with other mergers of its era.

Case Illustration: The Merger of Kroger and Fred Meyer[6]

In the late 1990s, there was tremendous pressure to consolidate in the retail food industry. Larger grocery stores were reaping strong benefits from greater economies of scale, forcing some suppliers to charge below cost in certain cases.[7] This scale advantage became fully evident in 1998, when Wal-Mart rose to the top in market share for grocery stores. Its success in this sector was a result of its Super Centers, which helped the company squeeze prices to the extent of being able to offer lower prices than any other competitor. As a result, Kroger Co. saw the necessity to expand its operations. A Kroger official stated, 'You can't squeeze costs forever. You only get revenue increases by merging or opening stores, and new construction is a risky operation.[8] Rather than moving into new markets with a brand name that was not established, Kroger sought to merge with an existing business, minimizing the risks involved. Kroger was rumoured to have looked very hard at acquiring Shaw's, an established grocery store in the East with annual revenues of $2.6 billion, and American Stores, an established chain in the West with annual revenues of $19 billion, which was subsequently acquired by Safeway.[9] Safeway, it was rumoured, was to have been considered by Kroger as a potential merger partner, which prompted Ron Burkle, Chairman of Fred Meyer, to take notice. With the potential for his primary rival to merge with one of the larger Eastern chains, Burkle decided the best defence was a strong offence, and contacted Kroger about the possibility of a merger. Pursuant to those conversations, in October 1998, Kroger announced plans to acquire Fred Meyer, Inc.

Execution of the merger was planned for spring 1999. Federal approval was granted on 27 May 1999 and required the closing of only eight store locations. That same day, Kroger proceeded with the purchase of Fred Meyer and commenced formally integrating that company as a wholly owned subsidiary, which would retain its historical brand name in its markets of operation. This merger rendered Kroger the largest national grocery chain in the United States with over 2200 supermarket stores in 31 states, significantly augmenting its market position.

The remainder of this chapter will analyse the relationship among valuation, pricing, synergies and the integration processes associated with this transaction, and will evaluate the success of this merger in creating value for Kroger Co. and its shareholders. This will then be linked back to the framework presented earlier in the chapter.

Valuation and pricing

Purchase price

Per the merger agreement, which was to be based on pooling – of interests, Kroger was to issue one of its shares for each of the 156,036,181 outstanding shares of Fred Meyer common stock. (No Fred Meyer preferred stock had been issued.) The value of the Kroger shares was to be set as the value on the day the merger was executed (27 May 1999). Kroger common stock traded at a price per share of $54.69 that day, bringing the value of the shares purchased to $8.53 billion. In addition to the common stock purchase, Kroger assumed around $4.8 billion of long-term debt from Fred Meyer; thus, the total price paid by Kroger to acquire Fred Meyer was roughly $13.33 billion. In evaluating whether or not this purchase price was reasonable, and whether or not any premium was paid, a valuation approach using a variant of discounted cash flow (adjusted present value – APV) has been employed, as well as an analysis of market multiples exhibited in grocery consolidations at the time surrounding the merger.

Valuation

In using an APV approach to value Fred Meyer at the time of the merger, expected Fred Meyer future cash flows at the time of the merger yield a baseline present value of $10.97 billion. (See figure 12.1, which shows results derived using assumptions described in figure 12.2.) The baseline value of $10.97 billion (significantly less than the $13.3 billion paid), along with the company's quantification of its expected synergies from the transaction, indicates that a premium of around $2.3 billion was included in the purchase price. Kroger stated expected synergies from the merger to be $40 million in FY1999, $115 million in FY2000, $190 million in FY2001 and $225 million in FY2002 and each year subsequent.[10] (This equates to $75 million in the first 12-month period, $150 million in the second and $225 million in the third.) In addition to the synergies anticipated to result from the Kroger–Fred Meyer transaction, the company further expected to reap benefits from synergies associated with previous Fred Meyer mergers that were still in integration. These additional synergies were stated at $115 million for FY1999, $145 million for FY2000, and $155 million for both FY2001 and FY2002. Once discounted, the present value of the combined total expected synergies equates to $2.37 billion. Adding this to the APV standalone value yields a total estimated value of $13.34 billion, which lends support to the reasonableness of the purchase price paid by Kroger.

Market value based on multiples

There was a flurry of merger activity going on in the services industry in the late 1990s, particularly within the grocery segment. Several grocery acquisitions were identified that took place around the time of the subject acquisition. Based on a compilation of EBITDA (earnings before interest, tax, depreciation and amortization) multiples for these mergers that was prepared by The Food Partners, Inc. (figure 12.3), it is evident that although Kroger's acquisition of Fred Meyer was done at a higher-than-average multiple, it was still within the normal range for mergers occurring during that year. Given the size and substance of the acquisition, plus the specific 'fit' of Fred Meyer's operations with Kroger's structure and goals, the above-average multiple is not too surprising. Market activity EBITDA multiples for grocery acquisitions during 1997–9 ranged from 5.5× to 12.5×. The year of Fred Meyer's acquisition by Kroger, the higher end of this range was evident, with multiples between 7× and 12.2×. The multiple for this transaction was approximated at 10.6×, near the centre of that range, but, again, higher than the average that year. Given the variances that can occur with multiples based on the size of transactions, along with the transaction-specific factors cited previously, this positioning within the market is considered to evidence support that the price paid by Kroger was reasonable.

Discount rate	9.00%			Estimated tax rate			34%	*
Annual growth rate		7.00%	6.50%	6.00%	5.50%	5.00%	4.24%	
	1999	2000	2001	2002	2003	2004	2005+	
EBIT	562,652	889,711	947,543	1,004,395	1,059,637	1,112,619	1,159,794	
Taxes	(191,302)	(302,502)	(322,165)	(341,494)	(360,277)	(378,290)	(394,330)	
EBIT (1 – t)	371,350	587,210	625,378	662,901	699,360	734,328	765,464	
Amortization	92,268	94,783	94,783	94,783	94,783	94,783	94,783	
Merger costs	268,854	0	0	0	0	0	–	
Depreciation	323,039	151,177	174,532	189,855	205,177	220,500	235,823	
Operating cash flow	1,055,511	833,170	894,694	947,539	999,321	1,049,612	1,096,070	
Change in net working capital	50,178	33,333	33,333	33,333	–	–	–	
Net capital expenditures	(637,374)	(711,000)	(464,000)	(475,000)	(475,000)	(475,000)	(475,000)	
Free cash flow	468,315	155,503	464,027	505,872	524,321	574,612	621,070	

Base case value 10,146,633

Terminal value 13,044,946
Sum year 5 13,619,558

Financing side effects	2000	2001	2002	2003	2004	2005
Principal amount debt	4,968,677	4,821,635	4,569,842	4,197,918	3,725,231	1,624,217
CMLTD	147,042	251,793	371,924	472,687	2,101,014	1,624,217
Fixed	1,952,767	1,923,228	1,893,205	1,878,453	1,873,720	1,620,564
Average interest rate	6.75%	6.30%	8.97%	7.16%	7.54%	7.54%
Variable	3,015,909	2,898,428	2,676,658	2,319,486	1,851,532	3,674
Average interest rate	5.97%	6.08%	6.18%	6.30%	6.45%	6.45%
Total average interest rate	**6.28%**	**6.17%**	**7.34%**	**6.68%**	**7.00%**	**7.54%**
Interest paid	311,862	297,386	335,236	280,623	260,701	122,426
Interest tax shield	106,033	101,111	113,980	95,412	88,638	41,625

Terminal value of tax shield 594,555
Total 636,180

Discount factor: financing	**7.50%**
Growth rate	2%
Present value	**823,286**

Discount rate calculation: base cash flows

Beta	Kroger	0.461
	Winn-Dixie	0.588
	Safeway	0.614
	Albertson's	0.309
	Average	0.493
Risk-free rate		5.55%
Market premium		7.00%
Discount rate base C/FI		**9.00%**

3/1/1998**

Adjusted present value (APV) calculation	
Equity portion	10,146,633
Debt portion	823,286
Baseline APV	**10,969,919**
Baseline APV	10,969,919
NPV of expected synergies	2,370,339
Total APV	**13,340,259**

Figure 12.1 APV Base case cash flows and terminal value to present value ($000s)

Net present value of synergies	2000	2001	2002	2003	2004	2005+
Expected synergies this merger	40,000	115,000	190,000	225,000	225,000	225,000
Expected synergies former FM mergers	115,000	145,000	155,000	155,000		
Less tax expense	(52,700)	(88,400)	(117,300)	(129,200)	(76,500)	(76,500)
Total synergy benefit	102,300	171,600	227,700	250,800	148,500	148,500

	Terminal value
	3,119,093

Present value	2,370,339
Discount rate	9.00%
Growth rate	4.24%

Depreciation expenditure calculation

	2000	2001	2002	2003	2004	2005
Beginning balance PPE	3,975,500	4,686,500	5,410,500	5,885,500	6,360,500	6,835,500
Capital expenditure	760,000	760,000	500,000	500,000	500,000	500,000
Disposals	49,000	36,000	25,000	25,000	25,000	25,000
End balance PPE	4,686,500	5,410,500	5,885,500	6,360,500	6,835,500	7,310,500
Property plant and equipment @ depreciation rate 1/31	151,177	174,532	189,855	205,177	220,500	235,823

Amortization calculation

	2000
Goodwill	3,791,334
Amortization expenditure	(94,783)
	3,696,551

Changes in net working capital

	1999	2000	2001	2002	2003	2004	2005
Accounts receivable	(17,819)	0	0	0	0	0	–
Inventories	5,513	33,333	33,333	33,333	33,333		0
Accounts payable	44,665	0	0	0	0	0	–
Net change in w/capital	50,178	33,333	33,333	33,333	33,333	–	–

Capital expenditures

	1999	2000	2001	2002	2003	2004	2005
Purchases of PPE	(722,188)	(760,000)	(500,000)	(500,000)	(500,000)	(500,000)	(500,000)
Sale of PPE	65,673	49,000	36,000	25,000	25,000	25,000	25,000
Other assets	19,141	0	0	0	0	–	–
Net CapEx	(637,374)	(711,000)	(464,000)	(475,000)	(475,000)	(475,000)	(475,000)

* Compound annual growth rate taken from page 13 of 'Growth through single and multi-unit acquisitions: the opportunity and process in independent retail', 5 May 2003, Mary L. Burke, Principal, The Food Partners (www.fmi.org/events/may/2004/handouts/growth.pdf).
** http://web.ask.com/

Figure 12.1   (cont' d)

- Fred Meyer's EBIT, which had grown at around 7.8% for the previous year, would grow at 7% for FY2000–2002, and which growth rate would decrease by 0.5% per year until FY2005, when it would level off at 4.24% (a compounded annual growth rate of the grocery industry for the years 1999–2001). These numbers were considered reasonable, due to Kroger's historical growth of the preceding years while integrating acquisitions of 8%, plus Fred Meyer's expectations of operational savings from a number of initiatives that had been put into place over the previous few years.
- A corporate tax rate of 34%.
- Depreciation and amortization expenses calculated using the straight-line method over 31 years and 40 years, respectively.
- Exclusion of the FY1999 costs of Fred Meyer's previous merger activity in calculating earnings from operating activities for that year (as base year zero).
- Inventory reductions of $100 million realized in equal shares over the forthcoming 3 years. This was based on the fact that management of Fred Meyer believed that, as a result of previous merger activity, it would be able to lower the level of inventory held over the coming years.
- 77% of Fred Meyer's stores 'had been opened or remodelled in the past seven years'. (1999 10-K). Capital expenditures for FY2000 of $760 million were planned to assist in completing the planned renovation of the remaining 23%. These were then projected to drop to a maintenance level of $500 million beginning in FY2001.
- Dispositions, which had dropped at a 29% compounded rate from 1997–9, were projected to continue to drop at 25% per year until they reached a constant level of $25 million for FY2002 and beyond.
- No significant changes in accounts receivable or payable were expected.
- A cash flow discount rate of 9.00%, composed of:
  - A risk-free rate of 5.55%, the 30-year treasury rate as of 1 April 1999,
  - A beta of 0.493, the average of the current betas of Kroger, Safeway, Albertson's and Winn-Dixie, and
  - A market risk-premium of 7%.
- A financing discount rate of 7.5%, which approximates the expected average interest rate for 2005 and beyond as stated in the FY1999 10-K. This represents a nearly 1.25% premium over the FY1999 average interest rate, included for potential fluctuations in interest tax synergies associated with operational debt strategies.
- Kroger-estimated synergies from the merger of $40 million in FY2000, $115 million in FY2001, $190 million in FY2002, and $225 million per year in FY2003 and in each subsequent year.
- Synergies from previous Fred Meyer mergers still being integrated of $115 million in FY2000, $145 million in FY2001, and $155 million for both FY2002 and FY2003.

Figure 12.2   Assumptions used in Kroger-Fred Meyer APV

Planned synergies

Financial perspective

Because of the premium paid for Fred Meyer, Kroger needed to realize synergies within the newly formed company to validate the purchase price. Purchasing and merchandising synergies were expected to account for about 50% of the savings,

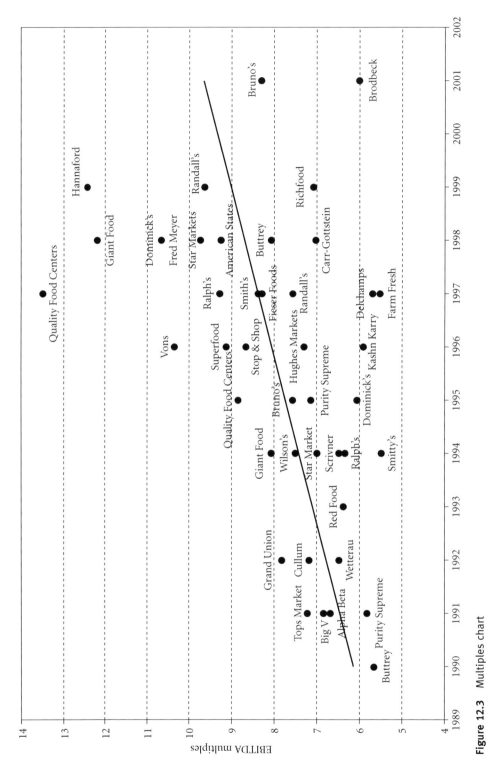

Figure 12.3 Multiples chart

Source: from page 15 of 'Growth through single and multi-unit acquisitions: the opportunity and process in independent retail,' 5 May 2003. Mary L. Burke, Principal, The Food Partners.

and in-market synergies and general and administrative cost reductions were expected to each account for about 25% of the synergy amounts. This was in addition to the synergy savings that Fred Meyer already anticipated from its own recent acquisitions.[11]

In terms of purchasing, Kroger planned to leverage its size in procuring retail products.[12] This merger increased Kroger's size by about a third, making it a much larger player in the marketplace. Kroger anticipated its size would promote a more competitive environment for its suppliers, leading to lower prices, which would reduce Kroger's overall costs and give it a better competitive position.

Much of the merchandising synergies were expected to emerge from the combination of the companies' strong private-label programmes. Both companies had successful programmes and anticipated adopting the best practices of each programme to fully realize the benefits in this area.[13] Kroger perceived a large opportunity for expansion in the private-label market, striving for a three-tier brand structure to widen its offering to a broader consumer base. This would benefit Kroger by allowing it to offer a larger selection of private-label items, as well as more than one private-label item of a certain product. By segmenting the market in this way, Kroger would be able to reach a broader customer base.

In Arizona, where there was geographical overlap between the two companies, Kroger planned to take advantage of in-market synergies. Some of these synergies were expected to come from the consolidation of distribution or manufacturing centres serving the market. Several of the store names in Arizona were to be changed to one of the more dominant brands within Kroger's portfolio to attract more customers.[14] In addition to bringing in more customers, this was expected to help reduce the advertising and merchandising expenses in these markets.[15] It further planned to streamline distribution and realize benefits of economies of scale both in that arena and in its manufacturing operations, through combining supply chains.[16]

From an administrative viewpoint, the company intended to reduce overhead expenses and consolidate its support services to effect synergies at the corporate level. As with any merger, there was duplication in certain areas. Kroger planned to make these functions as efficient as possible by eliminating any unnecessary services or expenses.

Strategic perspective

Geographical coverage was one of the major strategic drivers behind the Kroger–Fred Meyer merger. Kroger held a dominant position in the Midwest and the Southeast and Fred Meyer could supplement this with its strong presence in the West. There was very little overlap in the markets that each company independently served,[17] which made Fred Meyer a very attractive purchase candidate.

An additional strategic synergy Kroger planned to leverage was the solid brand equity offered by Fred Meyer. In order to take advantage of this brand image, Kroger intended each store to maintain its own name and location. Fred Meyer CEO Robert Miller commented, '[t]here is unquestioned value in preserving the names and unique operating characteristics of the divisions.'[18] Kroger planned to incorporate these stores to help in leveraging its size, but also wanted to give the stores the freedom to respond to local customer needs.[19] 'It will be important for customers to see the same familiar Fred Meyer stores that they have become accustomed to,' according to David B. Dillon, Kroger's then president. This represented a standard part of Kroger's acquisition strategy, evidenced by the fact that it was already operating stores under nearly 25 different names, believing that grocery stores have strong local followings and brand-loyal customers.[20]

Another expected strategic benefit of the merger was the assimilation of new product lines into the company's portfolio. Fred Meyer was the fourth largest jewellery retailer in the US, with several stand-alone jewellery stores. The company also operated multidepartment stores, similar to Wal-Mart's Super Centers, which presented a new format for Kroger.[21] These new markets offered new avenues of growth for the company and gave the supermarket chain a more diversified portfolio of operations. In addition to these different stores, Fred Meyer also had experience in non-food merchandising.[22] Kroger wanted to use this expertise to expand into new product areas in its own stores, potentially using new private labels.

Finally, Kroger's merger with Fred Meyer was also a competitive move against Wal-Mart and its Super Centers. It was beneficial from a defensive standpoint, providing Kroger with operations throughout the country and allowing the company to achieve a better competitive position by reaching new markets immediately and attaining economies of scale.[23] By acquiring instead of building, Kroger had immediate access to these markets, giving it a first-mover advantage in the Western states that did not yet have Wal-Mart Super Centers. Not only was the merger going to increase the size and number of stores in Kroger's portfolio, but Fred Meyer's multidepartment stores would place Kroger in a new market in which it could directly compete with Wal-Mart and similar companies. This would give customers another 'one-stop-shop' option, and allow Kroger to remain competitive, even with Wal-Mart cutting into the grocery market.

Realized synergies

Financial perspective

Kroger was actually able to achieve its anticipated synergies ahead of schedule. It exceeded even its own expectations by achieving synergies of $160 million in fiscal year 1999.[24] At the end of the second quarter of 2000, Kroger had already realized $257 million in synergy savings. At this point, it was well positioned to exceed the $260 million in expected savings for that year.[25] By the beginning of 2001, Kroger had already achieved its ultimate goal of synergies amounting to $380 million, an entire year before these results were originally projected.

Kroger centralized its purchasing function to take advantage of its larger size.[26] Kroger's purchasing and distribution power have doubled due to its merger activity.[27] Kroger's increased purchasing power played a large role in the realization of these synergy savings. The suppliers were forced to provide goods at a lower price and to deliver them to stores more quickly. The increased purchasing power has allowed the grocery giant to obtain lower prices, allowing it to better compete with the 'falling prices' of Wal-Mart. Additional economies of scales were achieved not only through the improvement of leveraged purchasing, but also through the development of information technology and the coordination of the manufacturing and distribution across a larger store base. These, too, added to the realized synergy savings.

The merchandising synergies from the combined private-label programmes allowed Kroger to introduce more than 1,100 new private-label items in fiscal year 1999, boosting earnings for the year.[28] Kroger also adopted a three-tier merchandising approach to the private labels. Kroger already had its own mid-priced brand, but supplemented this with a value brand and a premium brand. Kroger adopted the *Private Selection* premium brand from Ralph's and repositioned Fred Meyer's value brand as *For Maximum Value*.[29] This strategy allowed it to position the private-label products to meet the needs of all of its customers, providing a basis for augmenting sales in this segment.[30] Although private-label products are typically priced 20–30% lower than equivalent national brands (except for the premium brand items), Kroger's margins on these items are generally 10% higher. Therefore, despite the fact that increased volume in private-label products may have served to suppress sales growth from a dollar perspective (due to lower retail prices on those items), it actually added to Kroger's overall profit.[31] As a further benefit, the additional manufacturing capacity from Fred Meyer allowed Kroger to reach a level of manufacturing 50% of its private-label products itself, giving it even larger margins on these items.

As for in-market synergies, Kroger decided to close a dairy in Phoenix in order to streamline its operations and improve efficiency.[32] Substantial savings were also realized by closing a pharmaceutical warehouse in Salt Lake City, with a nearby warehouse able to take its place. The company also changed the names of some of the Smith's and Fred Meyer stores to the better-known Fry's Food and Drug Stores.[33] These changes allowed the company to market one brand name in those areas and to consolidate distribution and some manufacturing and merchandising.

Strategic perspective

Due to its merger with Fred Meyer, Kroger became the nation's first coast-to-coast integrated grocer, achieving its geographic goal of nationwide presence. At the end of 2002, Kroger operated in 48 major markets (defined as a market where Kroger operates at least nine stores), and held the number 1 or number 2 position in 41 of those markets.[34] Undoubtedly, retention of the strong existing brand name equity in most of the acquired markets was a key factor in this.

As anticipated, Kroger also benefited from Fred Meyer's experience in various domains – from its knowledge of operating different formats (including warehouse stores and supercentres), to its extensive non-food merchandising experience, and particularly its premium private-label line.[35] Kroger took advantage of this knowledge, using the opportunity to expand horizontally and vertically – including more pharmaceutical and food suppliers in its supply chain, and operating more types of stores to sell its food and drugs.[36] Kroger also used lessons from its now more extensive private-label offerings to expand into a fourth tier in that segment, by introducing natural and organic foods under the name *Naturally Preferred*. As an emerging market with no dominant national brand, this product line provided major growth opportunities.[37]

From a competitive standpoint, Kroger succeeded in positioning itself as more of a peer with Wal-Mart's grocery operations, by virtue of its national reach, economies of scale and increased variety of store types. Furthermore, as a perhaps-unanticipated competitive benefit, the expanded private-label products also helped Kroger steal market share from national food brands for its own products. In the pre-merger Kroger stores, private labels held more than 25% market share in terms of sales. Since the merger, the legacy Fred Meyer stores' private-label market share increased from 16–18% to almost 20%.[38] Accordingly, the newly combined company's competitive position was enhanced on multiple fronts from this transaction.

Integration process

To capture the synergies between Fred Meyer and Kroger, Kroger commissioned integration teams prior to Federal approval of the merger. As of October of 1998, Robert Miller (CEO of Fred Meyer) and David Dillon (President of Kroger) had already started to lead teams that were 'responsible for identifying significant synergy opportunities.'[39] Kroger opted to retain much of Fred Meyer's staff, relocating them from Portland, Oregon to Cincinnati, to help with its expansion to the West. Miller was named Kroger's Vice-Chairman and Chief Operating Officer. As an added incentive to its top managers responsible for integration, Kroger also issued restricted stock awards tied to the synergies being attained.[40] This provided focus and incentive towards realizing the values projected in the valuation.

To integrate operations between Fred Meyer and Kroger, the new Kroger was restructured into 20 divisions in three regions. The Eastern region had 11 divisions operating under the Kroger name; the Central division operated primarily under the banner of King Soopers; and the Western region's six divisions operated as Fred Meyer. Each operating division had the authority to make pricing and merchandising decisions to take advantage of local demographics, and the competitive nature and economic condition of the region. However, with centralized purchasing and the consolidation of accounting, data processing, logistics and related support functions, these divisions were still able to attain economies of scale. Therefore, management would be able to make decisions on a local basis, yet still have the economies of scale of a large conglomerate. Shared best practices were also an important part of the integration plan, as well as negotiating for lower costs for raw materials for the manufacturing division, which produces the private-label merchandise.[41]

In addition to geographic segmentation, the new Kroger was also divided into several different types of store format groups as part of the integration. These included: 1) a combination store, which includes a mix of food and general merchandise; 2) superstores, which are similar but slightly smaller than the combination store; 3) a multidepartment store, which has a diverse mix of food, apparel and general merchandise, including electronics; and 4) price impact warehouse stores, which offer lower prices for greater quantities. While Kroger had developed expertise with the combination store, it had not yet developed the expertise in running a multidepartment store, which Fred Meyer had done successfully in the Western United States. Thus, it relied on expertise from that entity to guide the operations of those formats.

Kroger's integration plan to achieve proposed synergies also included elements of distribution consolidation, systems integration, store conversions, reduced transaction costs, store closures and administrative integration. The integration plans for distribution consolidation called for divesting some warehouses made obsolete by the merger and closing overlapping dairy operations. These changes were handled by communicating early with the workers, as well as with corresponding severance payments. System integration called for integrating the computer systems between Fred Meyer and Kroger, as well as divesting some obsolete computers.[42] One of the primary problems with this aspect was the fact that the Fred Meyer computer systems were designed for multidepartment stores, which could be overly cumbersome for a grocery store.[43] Store conversion called for changing the banners in the newly acquired stores, as well as some advertising adjustments and reconfiguration of the store merchandise layout. As for store closures, four underperforming stores were closed, and three stores were divested to comply with a ruling from the State of California. Administration integration charges resulted from a write-down of obsolete training materials and severance costs for Fred Meyer executives who did not want to become a part of Kroger.[44] It also included charitable contributions of $20 million dollars that Kroger was required to make due to an obligation of Fred Meyer.[45]

With the relative size and scope of such an undertaking, it is not surprising to note that Kroger's integration plan bore a significant cost. Integration-related expenses reached a high of $304 million in FY1999, dropping to a still substantial $13 million in FY2000.[46] These charges were a combination of cash expenditures, asset write-downs and accrued charges. The financial impact of integration continued beyond the first few years, as well. An example of this is Kroger's 2002 adoption of the item cost method from the former Fred Meyer Company. This change increased merchandise costs by $91 million and reduced net earnings that year by $57 million.[47]

Integration process effectiveness

Despite early commencement of integration efforts to avoid difficulties, the acquisition faced some problems during the course of integration. Some of the problems can be attributed to a breakdown in due diligence, as Kroger did not properly assess the relationship between Fred Meyer and local labour groups, leading to a labour standoff that devolved into a public relations situation. Also, Kroger was also unable to maintain much of the key personnel from Fred Meyer, making it more challenging for it to capture some of the synergies which had been hoped for. Finally, the newly formed company faced some unanticipated financial consequences as a result of the integration.

As mentioned earlier, one of the key potential synergies that drove Kroger to acquire Fred Meyer was a reduction in operational expenses. Consolidating some of its warehousing and distribution operations would allow Kroger to generate savings. In the early 1980s, as part of its acquisition of Fry's (a Western-based food market chain), Kroger had acquired two Arizona warehouses run by expensive unionized labour. The Fred Meyer acquisition left Kroger with another distribution centre in the area – one operated by non-union labour. As a part of the integration process, Kroger chose to close the Fry's warehouses in favour of the non-unionized location and laid off the entire workforce of 450 workers in a tremendous cost-cutting measure.

A 21-week strike ensued, which had reached beyond Arizona, as Teamsters in Southern California began picketing lines in support of the Teamsters in Phoenix.[48] On 30 November 1999, a ruling by the National Labor Relations Board stated that Kroger had engaged in unfair labour practices, stemming from accusations that they had intimidated non-union workers to cross picket lines.[49] The Teamsters said that this ruling would become the standard for all subsequent Kroger–Teamster contracts, making the existing Arizona Teamsters' contract binding, despite the ownership of a facility changing hands.[50] Strong pressure from the Teamsters prompted Kroger to hire back 207 workers, though at diluted wages and benefits. Kroger clearly was not able to attain the savings it expected from this move, as it was forced to pay severance packages to employees with whom it had severed ties before the strike. Additionally, by starting a conflict with an organization as far reaching as the Teamsters union, Kroger weakened its leverage with that organization throughout the country – an action that could have future implications for the company.[51]

The Kroger–Fred Meyer integration faced another surprise when Fred Meyer's long-time CEO, and then Vice-Chairman and Chief Operating Officer of Kroger, Robert Miller, was named Chairman and CEO of Rite Aid in December 1999. A 30-year veteran in food retailing, he was integral in Fred Meyer's rise to prominence, having been named 1998 Mass Market Retailer of the Year. Along with Miller, Rite Aid lured other members of the former Fred Meyer's top management, including Mary Sammons, who was named President and Chief Operating Officer. Sammons had been the head of 135 Fred Meyer's large department stores in the

West. Other Fred Meyer staff following them to Rite Aid included David Jessick, who was named Senior Vice-President and Chief Administrative Officer, and John Standley, who was named Executive Vice-President and Chief Financial Officer.[52] They were also followed by Marty Tassoni, a 29-year Fred Meyer veteran, who was named Senior Vice-President over category management.[53]

From an investor's perspective, it appears these moves were not anticipated. This is evidenced by the fact that Kroger stock dropped 26% to $15.31 once news of the leaders' departure hit investors.[54] It is evident from statements made before the acquisition that Robert Miller was to be a key member of the integration process. In addition, one of the main reasons for Fred Meyer's attractiveness to Kroger was its diversity of product lines into non-food items. It seems likely that Mary Sammons could have been crucial to this movement, since she had been the head of non-food operations. The departure of these executives represented a loss of knowledge and experience in those key areas that would be difficult to replace quickly.

The post-merger entity has also faced its share of financial challenges since the acquisition date. At the end of FY2001, Kroger suppressed 1,500 jobs (less than 0.5% of the workforce) due to its poor results for the third quarter of FY2001, which showed a 33% drop in profits. These weak results were due in part to the recession in the US economy, but were also affected by some expenses potentially related to ongoing integration of stores, including $10 million for system conversion, $110 million for store closing and related costs and $81 million on energy contracts. Furthermore, almost 2 years after its merger with Fred Meyer, Kroger discovered improper accounting practices at one of the companies that Fred Meyer had acquired not long before its merger with Kroger (namely, Ralph's). The practices at Ralph's were believed to have begun before Fred Meyer acquired the company. Not only did Kroger not uncover these practices during due diligence, but it did not learn of them until a couple years after the merger was completed. Because these misstatements were not uncovered, Kroger was forced to restate its earnings for 1998, 1999 and the first two quarters of 2000.[55]

Value creation

In determining whether Kroger's acquisition of Fred Meyer Stores, Inc. succeeded in creating value, two categories of value criteria were designated: *financial performance enhancement* and *stated goal attainment*. The sections that follow contain an analysis of Kroger's performance in each of these categories.

Financial performance

The first criterion considered in terms of financial performance was whether or not the price paid became justified by the post-merger performance of the company. As mentioned earlier, 1 year after the acquisition, Kroger was ahead of schedule on its planned synergies, with all $380 million being achieved a year before the planned attainment date. This would appear to indicate that Kroger's purchase price would be justified.

However, to demonstrate a value that supports that price, the merger impact would also have to at minimum sustain, and not hinder, overall financial performance of the entity. Pre-merger, the combined sales were projected to reach $43 million.[56] Actual results for FY2000 show sales in excess of that amount, at $45.3 million, with steady overall sales growth evident in subsequent years. Furthermore, until difficulties in 4Q2001 related to the recession in the US markets, identical stores and comparable stores (those expanded or relocated) continued to show internal growth, albeit at somewhat declining rates, which was not evidenced as being attributable to the acquisition.[57]

From a profitability standpoint, in regarding the pre-merger 1% net margin of Fred Meyer for FY1999, along with the pre-merger 1.60% net margin of Kroger Co. for FY1999, it would appear that profits have also improved since the merger, due to the fact that the combined entity has posted steadily increasing net margins since the acquisition (with the exception of the 1.41% shown for initial merger year of FY2000, which was affected by significant integration costs), rising to 2.33% for FY2003. The financial performance figures for Kroger are outlined in tables 12.1 to 12.5. Despite a slight drop in profitability as a percentage of sales for the initial fiscal year of the merger, this growth in profitability from both a dollar and percentage standpoint, combined with the sales growth and the acceleration of synergy realization, would seem to indicate that some of the strategic and financial value expected was indeed attained.

An additional concern evident at the time of the merger was the impact of assuming Fred Meyer's debt of $4.8 billion.[58] With Kroger's existing debt levels, this left the emerging entity the most highly leveraged of any major supermarket chain.[59] However, since the time of the merger, Kroger has been able to easily service its debt obligations, and has continually been able to increase its capital, reducing overall leverage. Its return on equity has also continued to rise (see table 12.5), which mitigates any concern about the impact of the debt burden.

The second financial criterion considered was whether the acquisition created an attractive return for shareholders. Due to debt taken on in the late 1980s to thwart a previous hostile takeover, Kroger had been in a negative equity position up until

Table 12.1   Kroger's revenue 1998–2003 ($ million)

	2003	2002	2001	2000	1999	1998
Q1	15,058	15,102	14,329	13,493	6,389	6,139
Q2	11,927	11,485	11,017	10,289	6,442	6,232
Q3	11,696	11,382	10,962	10,329	8,024	7,687
Q4	12,470	12,129	12,692	11,240	7,349	6,510
Year	51,760	50,098	49,000	45,352	28,203	26,567

Table 12.2   Earnings per share for Kroger 1998–2003 ($)

	2003	2002	2001	2000	1999	1998
Q1	0.47	0.36	0.12	0.24	0.10	0.17
Q2	0.34	0.31	0.25	0.06	0.18	0.21
Q3	0.32	0.16	0.24	0.15	0.24	0.18
Q4	0.50	0.43	0.44	0.29	0.34	0.28
Year	1.56	1.26	1.04	0.77	0.85	0.85

the time of the Fred Meyer merger. It had made significant strides in reducing this debt, but likely gladly embraced the positive post-merger equity position attained by the end of FY2000. This undoubtedly assuaged shareholders as well. In addition, with the aforementioned increases in net margin, return per share also benefited. As evidenced by table 12.2, earnings per share (again with the exception of a small decrease for FY2000) has shown significant growth since the merger, nearly doubling from a pre-merger level of $0.85, to a FY2003 level of $1.56. Since earnings per share were projected to grow between 16 and 18%[60] in the 3 years following the merger (meaning by the end of 2001, which equates to FY2002), this growth far outpaced expectations. If measured at the FY2002 date, the $1.26 earnings per share that year represents 48% growth over FY1999 performance, still well beyond the anticipated return.

Noteworthy as well, in a measure of return, is the company's stock performance. As shown in figure 12.4, Kroger's stock performance has declined since the time of

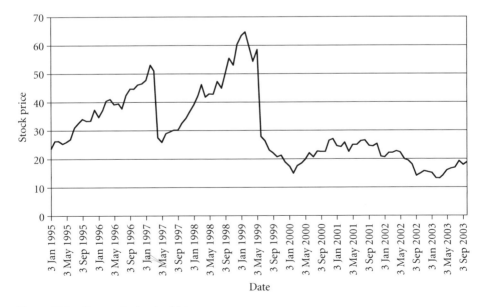

Figure 12.4   Kroger stock price history

Table 12.3   Kroger's income statement analysis ($ million)

	2002	2001	2000	1999	1998	1997	1996	1995	1994	1993
Revenues	50,098	49,000	45,352	28,203	26,567	25,171	23,938	22,959	22,384	22,145
Operating income	3,567	3,397	3,125	1,410	1,377	1,212	1,134	1,027	954	889
Depreciation	973	907	961	430	380	344	311	278	253	241
Interest expense	648	675	652	267	285	300	313	331	392	475
Pretax income	1,711	1,508	1,129	713	712	568	510	421	284	173
Effective tax rate	39.0%	41.6%	43.5%	36.9%	37.6%	37.9%	37.4%	36.2%	39.8%	41.7%
Net income	1,043	880	638	450	444	353	319	269	171	101
Net margin	2.08%	1.80%	1.41%	1.60%	1.67%	1.40%	1.33%	1.17%	0.76%	0.46%

Note: FYE is January of the following year; thus FY2000 covers results from January 1999 to January 2000.

Table 12.4 Kroger's balance sheet ($ million)

	2002	2001	2000	1999	1998	1997	1996	1995	1994	1993
Cash	161	161	281	122	65.0	Nil	Nil	27.0	121	104
Current assets	5,512	5,416	5,531	2,673	2,641	2,353	2,107	2,152	2,226	2,168
Total assets	19,087	18,190	17,966	6,700	6,301	5,825	5,045	4,708	4,480	4,303
Current liabilities	5,485	5,591	5,728	3,192	2,944	2,713	2,565	2,395	2,251	2,174
Long-term debt	8,412	8,210	8,045	3,229	3,493	3,479	3,490	3,889	4,135	4,473
Common equity	3,502	3,089	2,683	−388	−784	−1,182	−1,603	−2,154	−2,460	−2,700
Total capital	11,914	11,299	10,728	3,042	2,874	2,629	2,040	1,908	1,858	2,051
Capital expenditures	2,139	1,623	1,701	923	612	734	726	534	395	245
Cash flow	2,016	1,787	1,599	880	824	697	614	547	424	342

Table 12.5   Other financial data for Kroger

	2002	2001	2000	1999	1998	1997	1996	1995	1994	1993
Current ratio	1.0	1.0	1.0	0.8	0.9	0.9	0.8	0.9	1.0	1.0
% long-term debt of capitalization	70.6	72.7	75.0	106.1	121.5	103.2	171.1	203.8	222.5	218.1
% net income of revenues	2.1	1.8	1.4	1.6	1.7	1.4	1.3	1.2	0.8	0.5
% return on assets	5.6	4.9	3.7	6.9	7.3	6.5	6.2	5.8	3.6	2.4
% return on equity	31.6	30.5	27.7	NM	NM	NM	NM	NM	NM	NM

the merger. Initial market reaction to the acquisition announcement was indeed negative; however, once Wall Street further analysed the deal, positive reactions were seen and the stock recovered.[61] This reaction, combined with the previously discussed increases in sales and margin performance, would indicate that the reason for the decline in Kroger's stock is not a consequence of the Fred Meyer transaction. In fact, when regarding the stock's 10-year stock performance in comparison to the S&P and a peer group (see figure 12.5), it is evident that the market as a whole, and in particular many grocery stocks, experienced significant declines. Furthermore, after Kroger's acquisition of Fred Meyer, the gap between its performance and that of its peer group widened, with Kroger outpacing the pack (witness 2000–2002 performance). Although the gap has narrowed somewhat from the initial boost witnessed in 2000, its current position is still greater than what it was in the 3 years prior to the transaction.

From an internal perspective, Kroger states a desired rate of return on investment of 11–13%, and states that all of its acquisitions have met this expectation, with the exception of Fred Meyer, which it states to have exceeded the cost of capital.[62] Given the lack of negative Kroger commentary concerning the results of the merger, plus the attainment of projected synergies and solid financial performance shown, it is likely that the lower-than-hurdle rate of return was anticipated by the company in entering the deal. Assuming this to be the case, this would lend credence to the strong strategic reasons behind this consolidation event, as opposed to it being a purely financially driven transaction.

Stated goal attainment

One of the primary strategic aspects of this merger was to fend off erosion of market share. The primary emerging competitive threat at the time of Kroger's decision to buy Fred Meyer was Wal-Mart, which Kroger saw as a concern – not only due to its rapid growth in the grocery sector in 1998, but also due to its size and reach, which posed the potential threat of further market share erosion. Thus, the Fred

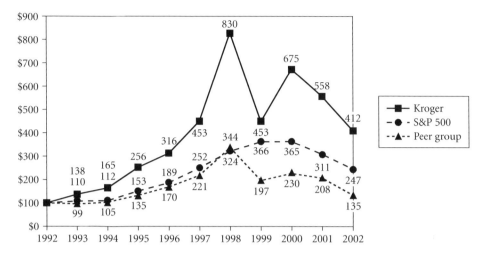

Figure 12.5 Comparison of 10-year cumulative total returns* of The Kroger Co., S&P 500 and peer group**

Prior to fiscal year 1999, the company's fiscal year ended on the Saturday closest to December 31. Beginning in 1999, the company's fiscal year ends on the Saturday closest to January 31. Performance for 1999 includes the 28-day transition period resulting from the fiscal year change.

* Total assumes $100 invested on 3 January 1993 in The Kroger Co., S&P 500 Index and the peer group, with reinvestment of dividends.

** The peer group consists of Albertson's, Inc., American Stores Company, Fleming Companies, Inc., Giant Food Inc. (Class A). Great Atlantic & Pacific Tea Company, Inc., Safeway Inc., Supervalu Inc., The Vons Companies, Inc., and Winn-Dixie Stores, Inc. The Vons Companies, Inc. was acquired by Safeway Inc. on June 16, 1997. Giant Food Inc. was acquired by Koninklijke Ahold N.V. on December 14, 1998. American Stores Company was acquired by Albertson's, Inc. on June 23, 1999. As a result, Vons, Giant Food and American Stores are excluded from the performance graph beginning with the year of their acquisition.

Source: Annual Report 2003, www.kroger.com

Meyer merger for Kroger provided an important 'offensive' defence against this threat, given the increased national scale it afforded the company, and the competitive expertise derived from the fact that the structure of many of the Fred Meyer stores was similar to that of a Wal-Mart Super Center. In this respect, Kroger gained a stronger competitive position against Wal-Mart's threat. However, Wal-Mart has still succeeded in garnering a strong market share in the grocery industry and is a leader in that respect. Accordingly, the Fred Meyer merger did not give enough competitive capital to Kroger to allow it to entirely overcome its foe. Nonetheless, it is evident with the substantial amount of consolidation and price pressures that the pre-merger Kroger would have likely had a much more difficult battle in order to continue to compete in the grocery industry had it not acquired Fred Meyer. In that sense, one can say that this strategic goal (which encompasses geographic diversity and economies of scale for operations) was attained.

Additional goals of this transaction included the opportunities for growth that were expected to be afforded through Fred Meyer's non-food item merchandising expertise and its private-label products. With the discussion earlier concerning the private-label expansion and market share growth that has occurred (see 'Realized synergies'), strategic goals related to acquiring Fred Meyer's private brands appear to have been met. However, non-food item merchandising is more difficult to evaluate. Kroger has not exhibited a substantial increase in the number of multi-department stores in its portfolio since the merger, and instead continues to focus the predominant amount of its operations on more grocery-oriented formats. One potential reason for this may be the fact that although Fred Meyer had expertise in merchandising non-food items, its marketing philosophy was to operate with lowest-cost pricing for food items, but with a 'promotional' pricing strategy for non-food items.[63] Consequently, its price positioning against the major non-food competition (mainly Wal-Mart) was likely higher, and it may not have been able to garner the deep supplier discounts that would position it more favourably. Kroger therefore may have recognized that it would not be able to compete in this price-driven segment of the market and thus shied away from expanding the multi-department store format.

Key challenges

Although the acquisition of Fred Meyer by Kroger created value, the case demonstrates that numerous challenges that potentially militate against value creation often arise. These challenges were with respect to strategic planning, due diligence, management retention, union involvement, and corporate communication.

Strategic planning

Even with clear strategic goals being evident in Kroger's reasons for acquiring Fred Meyer, it appears that additional benefits could have been pursued with this opportunity that were not evident in the assimilation of this company. For example, Kroger could have used Fred Meyer's marketing segmentation strategy in its types of stores to create national store banners that served different economic markets with different strategies, such as the high-end Ralph's and the low-price Fred Meyer, while developing an intermediate positioning for the Kroger name. In applying such banners/brands nationally to stores with similar marketing and merchandising positions, Kroger could have potentially realized deeper cost reduction and sales penetration, as well as more nationwide brand awareness. Although it is not clear whether or not such a strategy was considered, given Kroger's acquisition philosophy of trying to preserve the local value associated with existing names, this is unlikely to have occurred. Regardless of its philosophy, examination of the potential benefits of this structure would have been worth while.

An additional strategic opportunity that does not appear to have not been considered is the chance to upgrade or overhaul entire systems to become more efficient and leading-edge. Markets and employees expect change and disruption with merger integrations anyway, so taking advantage of this expectation to implement things such as better information systems corporate-wide, manufacturing upgrades, or conversions such as a potential just-in-time delivery system for a fast-turning item, would result in lesser change impact than implementing them post-merger, after the dust settled. While Kroger appears to have worked to integrate existing systems to gain efficiencies, no mentions are made in terms of structuring the new entity with enhanced systems, which could have proven to benefit the company from a long-term perspective.

Due diligence

Kroger should have been more thorough in conducting its financial due diligence of Fred Meyer. Fred Meyer had recently acquired several companies, and the financial statements and practices of these companies should have been fully investigated. Although Fred Meyer assumedly performed due diligence before originally acquiring Ralph's, this proved not to have been enough. Had Kroger fully undertaken the burden of performing due diligence on all aspects of the target company, including any issues that may have been present in prior-assimilated entities, it could have avoided this surprise.

Management retention

Kroger's management should have worked harder to keep Fred Meyer's top management involved in the Kroger organization. Even though it is not known to what extent these managers' expertise was needed by Kroger, it still hurt the company's reputation with investors, causing a significant drop in stock value when their resignations were announced. Kroger had touted these individuals as being an important part of the integration process and therefore should have made every effort to keep them, including routine check-ups on their satisfaction within the new organization.

Union involvement

The battle with the Teamster's union was not good for Kroger's image, particularly in Arizona, where it was trying to seamlessly change the ownership of Fred Meyer without causing much notice in the general public. In retrospect, it would have been a better idea for Kroger's management to work directly with the Teamster union during the due-diligence process, since it appears the warehouse closing surprised many. It would have been more effective for Kroger to have communicated to the labour unions what its intentions were, allowing the groups to possibly negotiate some kind of a compromise. It is clear that the Kroger management underestimated the resolve of the union, whose 21-week strike hurt Kroger's public image. The company's eventual settlement also hurt its reputation and its ability to deal with labour unions throughout the United States.

Corporate communication

Another thing that Kroger could have done to better manage the integration process involves its customer communication plan, particularly in Portland, Oregon,
where Fred Meyer was headquartered. Several newspaper articles quoted local
shoppers expressing their apprehension that their 'Freddie' would be changed, which
arose in part from the fact that Fred Meyer was one of the most visible corporate
citizens in Portland (both as an employer and a community contributor). From
press releases, it seems that the communications coming from both headquarters
were aligned and that the message was clear: there will be little impact felt at the
store level. However, this had apparently not trickled down to the final customer,
which is something that could have been addressed more thoroughly.

As a means to accomplish this, Kroger could have used its own workforce as mes-
sengers. Since front-line employees are in touch with the customer daily, they are
primary means of communication with customers. Consequently, these employees
represent a convenient vehicle for conveying the company message. After the
merger became certain, Kroger could have issued the news as part of a monthly
newsletter from corporate to store mangers, updating them on the state of events.
Managers could have then passed this information on to employees, who could have
in turn shared it with customers.

In addition to communicating with employees, Kroger-Fred Meyer could have
made additional efforts to communicate with the community at large. Given that
Fred Meyer was so well recognized and respected in the community, the public relations arm of the acquired company should not have had too much trouble getting
coverage in the Portland press. Representatives from Kroger should have been present to reinforce the message that customers should feel minimal local change or
disruption, since this was indeed their plan. Should the Portland media have been
less than cooperative about writing an article, an op-ed piece or advertisement letter could have been written by Fred Meyer's CEO.

Conclusion

The case presented in this chapter suggests a clear linkage between valuation, pricing, synergies, integration and value creation. In particular, it demonstrates that
when a premium is paid for an acquisition, synergies must be realized and that
the integration process is critical to the realization of these synergies. Despite
some unforeseen difficulties, the continued success of Wal-Mart and rough domestic market performance over the past several years, this company has persevered
as a leader in the industry, with market capitalization of $10 billion and earnings
performances ahead of many competitors (see table 12.6). It is highly unlikely
that the regional, $28 billion sales company with negative equity that was Kroger

Table 12.6 Peer comparison financial statistics

Description	1-day price change (%)	Market capitalization	P/E	ROE (%)	Dividend yield (%)	Debt to equity	Price to book	Revenue quarter vs. year ago	EPS quarter vs. year ago
Services	1.331	3,979.55bn	24.696	14.328	2.237	0.952	3.736	14.958	12.152
Retail (Grocery)	1.299	129.42bn	20.28	18.509	2.975	1.235	3.16	4.73	-6.03
Ahold (ADR)	1.266	9.68bn	41.6	3.408	N/A	2.803	1.705	5.824	41.704
Albertson's, Inc.	2.402	7.66bn	10.931	13.354	3.638	0.995	1.448	1.253	-25.926
AMCON Distributing Co.	0.673	14.23m	10.793	8.032	2.673	2.95	0.832	13.159	-18.561
Arden Group, Inc.	-3.772	209.62m	16.498	12.705	1.613	0.023	1.975	2.566	-4.818
BAB, Inc.	11.628	3.09m	8.727	9.338	8.333	0.332	0.672	7.677	183.333
Blue Square-Israel Ltd.	3.106	318.72m	N/A	5.942	18.855	0.385	1.045	1.341	N/A
Casey's General Stores	1.667	759.85m	18.462	10.327	0.918	0.432	1.818	10.644	13.061
Delhaize Group (ADR)	3.535	4.03bn	24.852	3.913	1.769	1.172	1.002	12.538	-80
Distribucion y Servicio D	5.114	1.70bn	42.923	8.662	0.87	0.895	3.6	8.272	27.949
Foodarama Supermarkets	0	25.17m	15.819	4.411	N/A	4.473	0.663	12.333	-50.607
Fresh Brands, Inc.	1.586	70.87m	9.282	14.182	2.555	1.153	1.246	3.574	-9.945
Great Atlantic & Pacific	-0.234	328.54m	N/A	41.036	N/A	1.622	0.589	3.557	N/A
Gristede's Foods, Inc.	8.571	22.39m	N/A	39.782	N/A	6.338	2.675	14.727	N/A
Ingles Markets, Inc.	0.498	231.21m	16.694	5.847	6.535	2.751	0.967	4.282	1.961
Kroger Co.	3.063	14.04bn	12.155	30.397	N/A	1.951	3.347	3.555	-23.939
Marsh Supermarkets, Inc.	0.81	89.04m	53.589	1.227	4.643	1.701	0.678	1.858	-71.105
Nash Finch Company	1.335	199.65m	7.389	12.191	2.156	1.635	0.867	2.164	-22.108
Pantry, Inc.	1.23	223.63m	22.495	8.613	N/A	4.246	1.842	4.425	47.321
Pathmark Stores	0.693	218.31m	14.816	4.155	N/A	1.73	0.598	0.841	77.391
Publix Super Markets	0	14.60bn	23.522	21.323	N/A	0	4.752	7.466	20.445
Ruddick Corporation	1.366	753.92m	12.691	12.665	2.206	0.395	1.549	2.803	-1.695
Safeway Inc.	0.433	10.25bn	33.3	7.638	N/A	1.876	2.504	3.072	-28.09
SUPERVALU Inc.	1.676	3.33bn	13.178	12.581	2.331	1.008	1.612	3.216	-3.175
Synergy Brands Inc.	2.107	6.34m	N/A	49.806	N/A	1.422	2.135	31.102	N/A
Uni-Marts, Inc.	-2.597	10.79m	N/A	1.217	N/A	4.15	0.561	9.291	25
Village Super Market, Inc	-1.697	82.27m	6.849	12.228	0.976	0.408	0.776	2.275	-18.733
Weis Markets, Inc.	1.792	957.77m	15.915	10.938	3.18	0	1.688	3.277	1.807
Whole Foods Market, Inc.	0.977	3.40bn	34.689	15.801	N/A	0.224	4.558	15.457	25.905
Wild Oats Markets, Inc.	-1.257	328.70m	38.596	5.32	N/A	0.361	1.897	2.567	24.138
Winn-Dixie Stores, Inc.	0.711	1.40bn	5.833	26.061	2.018	0.327	1.357	4.547	19.677

before this transaction would have ever reached this status without the help of Fred Meyer.

NOTES

1. This section was adapted from Schweiger and Lippert (2005).
2. In the midst of bidding wars executives may forget that a target is worth more to some than others.
3. Sirower (1997) proposes that this is typically a result of the synergies being exaggerated by the buyer, the synergies not being present to begin with or the synergies not being fully realized during the integration process.
4. For a complete description of the integration process, see Schweiger (2002).
5. A continuing stream of research by practitioners and academics points to the importance of integration in M&A value creation. These include several studies by major consulting firms, such as Coopers & Lybrand, Mercer Management Consulting, A. T. Kearney and Hewitt Associates, which are reported in 'J. R. Cultural due diligence', *Training*, November 1997, pp. 67–75 and J. S. Lublin and B. O'Brien, 'When disparate firms merge, cultures often collide', *Wall Street Journal*, Eastern Edition, 14 February 1997. A 1999 *Forbes* study by Schmidt of Forbes 500 executives on the main reasons why synergies are not realized cites five organizational issues as among the top ten. Comprehensive reviews of academic research identifying integration as an important element in M&A value creation are presented in Schweiger and Walsh (1990) and Schweiger and Goulet (2000). Also see Chatterjee, Lubatkin, Schweiger and Weber (1992).
6. This section includes portions contributed by Sylvan Prunet and Jeffrey Millings in the paper 'Kroger Co.'s 1999 Acquisition of Fred Meyer Stores, a Study of Value Creation,' Moore School of Business, October 2003.
7. J. Seiberg, 'Fruit of the Boom', *The Daily Deal*, 5 July 2000.
8. G. De Lombaarde, 'Kroger Eyes New Markets', *Courier*, 6 June 1998.
9. Ibid.
10. 'Kroger and Fred Meyer Merger Approved', Press Release Archives, 27 May 1999, www.kroger.com.
11. 'Still King Kroger', *Supermarket News*, 26 October 1998, vol. 48, no. 43, http://home.earthlink.net/~tsalesinc/Kroger1.htm.
12. Terry Kinney, 'Kroger Merger Spurs Stock Split', May 1999, www.mailtribune.com/archive/99/may99/52199b2.htm.
13. Ibid.
14. Cliff Peale, 'Kroger–Fred Meyer Deal Brings Changes in Arizona', *Cincinnati Post*, 13 April 1999, www.cincypost.com/business/1999/kroger041399.html.
15. Robert Goldfield, 'AZ Store Decision Offers Glimpse of Kroger Plan', 21 December 1998, http://portland.bizjournals.com/portland/stories/1998/12/21/story3.html.
16. 'Still King Kroger', op. cit.
17. 'Kroger to Merge with Fred Meyer to Create the Nation's Largest Supermarket Company with Annual Sales of $43 Billion', Press Release Archives, 19 October 1998, www.kroger.com.
18. 'Kroger and Fred Meyer Shareholders Approve Merger', Press Release Archives, 13 April 1999, www.kroger.com.

19. 'Kroger and Fred Meyer Merger Approved', op. cit.

20. 'Kroger Co.'s 1999 Acquisition of Fred Meyer Stores' op. cit.

21. 'Kroger and Fred Meyer Merger Approved', op. cit.

22. 'Still King Kroger', op. cit.

23. 'Fred Meyer Sold to Kroger Co.', Press Release Archives, 19 October 1998, www.kroger.com.

24. Compared with $155 million expected savings. 'Kroger Reports Record Earnings, Before Merger Costs, for Fourth Quarter of 1999', Press Release Archives, 9 March 2000, www.kroger.com.

25. Ken Coons, 'Kroger Reports 17% Earnings Gain', 13 September 2000, http://new.seafood.com/archives/0009/sfdpriv/news1/20000913KR1G.html.

26. Jack Neff, 'Kroger's Private Label Power Drives Performance', *Food Processing Magazine*, 5 July 2001, www.foodprocessing.com/Web_First/fp.nsf/Contentframeset?openform&MainSrc=$$search.

27. Kroger Online Case Study, http://oak.cats.ohiou.edu/nz330198/esp/casestudy.htm.

28. 'Kroger Reports Record Earnings, Before Merger Costs, for Fourth Quarter of 1999', op. cit.

29. Neff, 'Kroger's Private Label Power Drives Performance', op. cit.

30. *Revue de Presse*, 15 December 2000, www.leleux.be/leleux/JLCHome.nsf/0/98F1DB06C5A16A3EC12569B600368F31?opendocument&NL.

31. www.enquirer.com/editions/2001/06/21/fin_kroger_strategy.html.

32. Angela Gabriel, 'Kroger Merger Creams Dairy', *The Business Journal*, 11 October 1999, http://phoenix.bizjournals.com/phoenix/stories/1999/10/11/story4.html.

33. Bob Driehaus, 'Kroger sees 16–18% annual growth', 17 February 2000, www.cincypost.com/business/2000/kroger021700.html; 'Metro Phoenix Fred Meyer Stores Becoming Fry's Marketplace Stores', Press Release Archives, 20 June 2000, www.kroger.com.

34. Ebscohost.

35. www.quicken.elogic.com/sec_mgmt.asp?ticker=KR.

36. Kroger Online Case Study, op. cit.

37. Neff, 'Kroger's Private Label Power Drives Performance', op. cit.

38. Ibid.

39. 'Kroger and Fred Meyer Merger Approved', op. cit.

40. Kroger Co. website, 'Merger Related Costs', under Corporate Plan.

41. Kroger Co. 8-K, 21 October 1999.

42. Kroger Co. 10-K, 27 April 2000.

43. Kroger Co. 10-Q, 6 December 1999.

44. Kroger Co. 10-K, 27 April 2000.

45. Kroger Co. 10-Q, 20 December 1999.

46. Kroger Co. 2002 Annual Report.

47. Ebscohost.

48. 'Teamsters Strike at Kroger Ends, Members Gain Unprecedented Job Security', 16 February 2000, www.teamster.org/00news/nr_000216.2htm.

49. D. Holthouse, 'Strike Two', 9 December 1999, www.newtimes.com.

50. C. Mack, 'Facing New Challenges', *Secretary Treasurer's Report*, www.teamsterslocal70.org/secretary%20report%20-%20apr-may%202000.htm.

51. G. Creno, 'Arizona Grocery Chain Revises Layoffs', *The Arizona Republic*, 7 June 1999.

52. 'New Team Has Food, GM Roots', *Racher Press*, vol. 17, no. 10, 8 May 2000.
53. 'Rite Aid Stock Soars by 40 Percent as Former Kroger Exec Takes Helm', *Bloomberg News*, 7 December 1999.
54. Ibid.
55. 'Kroger Announces Strong Preliminary Results for Fourth Quarter and Restatement of Prior Earnings by Minor Amounts', Press Release Archives, 5 March 2001, www.kroger.com; Stephen Taub, 'Kroger to Restate 1998–2000 Earnings', 6 March 2001, www.CFO.com.
56. Cliff Peale, 'For Kroger, Fred Meyer is the Future: Customers Loyal to Northwest Store', *Cincinnati Post*, 16 November 1998, www.cincypost.com/news/1998/fred111698.html.
57. Corporate Plan, www.kroger.com.
58. Ursula Miller, 'Freddy's Pioneered One-Stop', *Cincinnati Enquirer*, 20 October 1998, www.enquirer.com/editions/1998/10/20/bus_fred20.html.
59. Ibid.
60. Lisa Biank Fasig, 'Kroger holders expected to OK Meyer merger', *Cincinnati Enquirer*, 11 April 1999, www.enquirer.com/editions/1999/04/11/fin_kroger_holders.html.
61. 'Kroger buys Fred Meyer', http://portland.bizjournals.com/portland/stories/1998/10/26/weekinbiz.html.
62. The Kroger Co., 'Capital Expenditures', page 43 of Corporate Plan, www.kroger.com.
63. Fred Meyer 1999 10-K.

Chapter 13   M&A as Practice

Duncan Angwin

There has been over half a century of research into understanding M&A. This is a reflection of the importance of the phenomena to a wide variety of stakeholders as well as an indication of its complexity. Many inroads in understanding M&A have been achieved by economists, strategists, finance and organizational behaviour academics. Each has focused on particular aspects of the phenomena, identifying important features and relationships from the perspective of a single discipline. However, for the level of research effort expended, the amount of unequivocal findings remains disappointingly small (Grant, 2002) and many are so broad as to be of little value to practitioners. Indeed, despite all of these research endeavours, there is evidence that the failure rate of M&A, already in excess of 50%, is increasing.

Reasons for the lack of consistent findings include the practical difficulties involved in researching M&A and the complex nature of the phenomena themselves. Practical difficulties in researching M&A (see the M&A 'Primer' following chapter 14) have too often resulted in convenience-led research (i.e. researching issues where secondary data are readily available rather than tackling questions that require engagement with primary data). The complexity of M&A as a process phenomenon, involving all aspects of business and multiple levels of organizations across many interfaces, has rarely been embraced. M&A research has tended to focus on a single disciplinary approach, just one level of analysis and a particular stage in the M&A process (Javidan et al., 2004). This has elicited some important insights but has also served to fragment understanding of M&A, resulting in large amounts of disparate unconnected information and, importantly, dividing M&A formation concerns from implementation. The failure of disciplines to interrogate other perspectives and the lack of interdisciplinary research may be a reason why so many 'results' from M&A research are inconclusive or unhelpful.

There is now a critical need to adopt a more integrative view of M&A. A richer appreciation is necessary if we are to go beyond fragmented and partial views. A more holistic approach can bring new insights and perspectives on core questions and may also challenge researchers to adopt new methodologies. In this chapter,

'M&A as Practice' is offered as an integrative approach to understanding M&A. It has the virtue of being able to draw upon a diverse set of established research traditions to achieve richer understanding than can be achieved by a single disciplinary perspective alone.

The following section describes the 'M&A as Practice' framework in detail. It adopts a sociological view of M&A as a set of social practices and examines the intimate connections between institutions, practitioners, practices and processes (Whittington, 2002). The integrative and holistic nature of 'M&A as practice' provides a broad tapestry against which the contents of this book can be displayed, showing where these contributions focus their energies, how they may be viewed in relation to one another and where there are areas for future research. Following this discussion a detailed case study of a merger, from inception to conclusion, is presented and then interpreted through the 'M&A as practice' lens. This illustrates how an integrated processual perspective can uncover dynamic linkages, across different disciplines, to provide a more nuanced and informed insight into the case data than would have been possible otherwise. In particular, the 'M&A as practice' lens highlights, rather than ignores or downplays, the dynamic interconnections between layers of context.

A surprising feature of M&A literature is that it tells us very little about who the practitioners are in M&A, how they interact and what they do throughout the process. There is a great deal more to know about M&A practitioners and the skilfulness of their work. For this reason, 'M&A as practice' places practitioners at the heart of its framework. Surfacing which practitioners are involved, what activities they engage in and how these affect the course of M&A is critical for going beyond broad characterizations of M&A and getting closer to the ground (Bower, 2004) to produce more valuable and insightful research.

The 'M&A as Practice' Framework

The 'practice' approach to management is a new take on key issues in the domain of strategic management that may affect firm outcomes. Its newness means that the 'practice' approach is currently evolving with a number of frameworks in circulation attempting to crystallize the essence of what a practice approach might be (see www.strategy-as-practice.org). Central to the orientation of the 'practice' group is a greater emphasis on vertical interactions, a downplaying of the organizational boundary across which these interactions take place, and an emphasis on the actual activities and actions of practitioners (see Johnson et al., 2003) which lead to strategic outcomes.

One widely cited conceptualization of strategy-as-practice adopts an explicit focus on strategy as a social practice. It has three main foci: **practitioners; practices; praxis** (Whittington, 2002). The focus on **practitioners** is to identify who the key practitioners are in the strategic process in question. So often these practitioners are assumed to be top management, rather than it being made explicit. However, from a practice perspective, practitioners may include middle managers in an organization as well as practitioners from other firms. These firms may be in a horizontal alignment with the focal firm, as competitors for instance, or vertical in a value-chain sense, as suppliers and customers, or vertical in a hierarchical sense, as institutional investors and professional advisers for instance. The **practices** focus is on the tools and techniques 'in use' by practitioners. These may range from codified tools and techniques to rules of thumb and from generic to customized. Practices in use will show varying degrees of overlap between the practitioners involved. **Praxis** focuses on what practitioners actually do – their 'work'. This would include how they spend their time, what actions, activities and routines they engage in and how they prioritize them.

While the '3Ps' conceptualization is attractive in giving weight to the work of practitioners, it tends to downplay the role of institutional forces, which can have a very significant role in M&A. For this reason, a different version is used in this chapter, which highlights the constraining and facilitating role of the institutional context. In this model of strategy-as-practice, proposed by La Ville and Mounoud (2003), the practitioners involved are known and distributed around the framework. The focal practices are the result of institutional forces, tools and techniques in use and actual practitioner activities. The model is described here as an 'M&A as practice' framework as it is applied to M&A.

The 'M&A as practice' framework is shown in figure 13.1 and is organized around three components: **text; tools; talk**.

Text consists of structures/discourses of strategy as embodied in institutions, fads and fashions. It is the institutional and social context within which M&A activity is conducted. This 'text' dominates the M&A domain and drives 'tools' used to

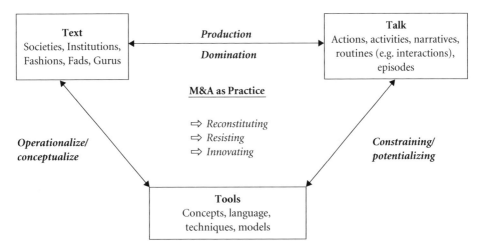

Figure 13.1 An integrative framework for M&A as practice
Source: Adapted from La Ville and Mounoud (2003)

operationalize the M&A process. The text also bounds the activities of practitioners by means of explicit legal requirements as well as less explicit social rules and norms. **Tools** consist of techniques, concepts, models and language. They are a primary means by which the demands of 'text' are conceptualized and operationalized. Such 'tools' serve to potentialize and constrain the actions and activities of practitioners. They may also cause aspects of the 'text' to be revisited. A new financial technique, for instance, may require adjustments to legislation and monitoring procedures. 'Tools' potentialize the ability of practitioners to act and craft a deal. They also limit their activities by framing the ways in which they perceive M&A. **Talk** is about the actions, activities and narratives involved as practitioners enact M&A. What practitioners talk about and focus on is influenced by the tools they use, although in facing unusual situations practitioners may need to be creative and adaptive or develop tools for their own purposes. Practitioner's 'talk' is also influenced by the societal context in which they are located, which privileges some information and activities over others. However, practitioners through innovative activities may also influence the 'text' and cause adjustment to what is legitimate and possible. Through practitioner actions and activities the strategic 'text', and its 'tools', maybe subverted, mastered or transformed.

At the core of the model is *practice* as an intimate interplay between text, tools and talk. This allows the practice of M&A to show routine as much as innovation, structure as much as restructuring, acceptance as much as resistance. In the consumption of M&A through practice there is potential for reconstitution, resistance or innovation at multiple levels of activity. The practitioner actively interprets, criticizes, learns and experiments with the implications of M&A initiatives.

Although the La Ville and Mounoud (2003) orientation is towards the middle managers embedded within the focal organization, this ignores the critical role of other practitioners in M&A, such as top managers. They are also enmeshed in a series of opposing forces, both internal and external to the firm, and are part of the unfolding of strategic initiatives forged by complex stakeholder pressures. 'M&A as practice' focuses on the interaction between discourses of 'grand-strategy' and 'everyday actions'. Top managers stand at a pivotal point between the macro-drivers of context and shifting coalitions of interests in organizations. The La Ville and Mounoud (2003) framework also focuses on just one organization. However, by definition in M&A, a minimum of two organizations are involved, which adds an additional layer of complexity to the 'M&A as practice' approach.

'M&A as Practice' Perspective on the Book Contents

The 'M&A as practice' model allows the varied chapters in this book to be located within an integrative model. Some chapters focus on key legs of the practice model, some on the interplay between its dimensions and the remainder are

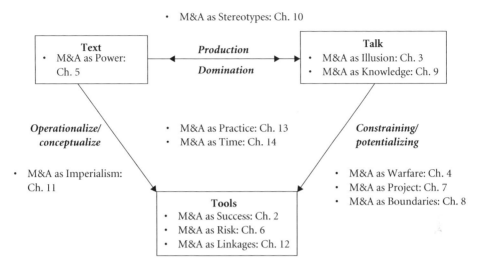

Figure 13.2   M&A as practice – chapter orientations

integrative. For the reader interested in navigating a strategy-as-practice route through this book, figure 13.2 shows the location of the chapters in these terms.

Chapter 5, *M&A as Power*, focuses on **the text**, which frames the legitimate arena in which M&A activity takes place. This chapter shows how power determines the rules and conditions for M&A, the practitioners involved, the tools and techniques used and the conduct of a deal. It deals with power as 'domination' of 'talk' and also suggests how 'talk' may help (re)produce 'text' in terms of game playing. The chapter also shows how 'text' leads to, as well as game-playing legitimates, the use and acceptability of certain tools and actors in specific contexts.

Chapter 11, *M&A as Imperialism*, focuses on the interaction of **text** and **tools**. Attention is drawn to the socio-economic context as a way of assessing the ways in which acquisitions are integrated. Here, *text* is determining the techniques used and structures decided upon.

Chapter 2, *M&A as Success*, focuses on **tools**. It offers a battery of tools and techniques for assessing M&A performance and the conduct of M&A valuation. Its methods are determined by a profit-maximizing context, which in turn acts as a facilitator and constraint on the efforts of practitioners. Chapter 6, *M&A as Risk*, focuses on *tools* as a series of tools and techniques for assessing the viability of M&A. Although much of the work in this area has a deterministic quality over what managers do, and is constraining in nature, the chapter argues for a closer link with managerial practices for more sensitive and valuable insights into risk in the M&A process. Chapter 12, *M&A as Linkages*, recognizes the substantial variety of tools and techniques in use throughout the M&A process and the lack of integration among them. It highlights the need for an integrated approach that draws on outputs from key techniques and models to enable profit maximization.

Chapter 4, *M&A as Warfare*, focuses on the interaction along the **tools and talk** dimension. Here practitioners are influenced in their actions by the language, or 'tool' of warfare, which causes them to act in particular ways and draw on particular techniques. The chapter's message is that the language of warfare is constraining in the actions and activities of practitioners and not always in the best interests of the affected parties. A new language would have the effect of altering practices and activities. Chapter 7, *M&A as Project*, focuses on creating more flexible techniques for monitoring managerial practices. Here the use of tools is sensitized to the vagaries of managerial practice, showing that they are not purely constraining but also receptive to uncertainties in the process. Chapter 8, *M&A as Boundaries*, also focuses on the interplay between **tools** and **talk**, showing that while tools and techniques may be designed to improve change, it is practitioner actions and activities that create boundaries and influence their significance and longevity.

Chapter 3, *M&A as Illusion*, focuses on how top executives actually negotiate a deal. This focus on **Talk**, the narratives, actions and interactions between these executives displays their manoeuvrings and psychologies against a faint background of shared tools and text. It is their rich interactions on several planes over time that affects outcome, rather than the dominance of tools and text. Chapter 9, *M&A as Knowledge*, also deals with the nature of managerial work. Although there is an overarching intention to transfer knowledge, this chapter focuses on the minutiae of day-to-day interaction to show how interpersonal tensions, agendas, personalities and histories all interact to interrupt an outcome determined by tools.

Chapter 10, *M&A as Stereotypes*, examines the interaction between **talk** and **text** to illustrate how practitioners may engage with the fabric of text in their attempts to make sense of, and influence, a complex M&A situation across national boundaries. Drawing on their national contexts these practitioners are both influenced by, as well as manipulating of, deep-seated social/historical conditions. In this chapter, as well as chapters 3, 4, 8 and 9, we can see the practitioners as able to shape and influence their contexts. Their everyday interactions on multiple levels, dealing with interacting and conflicting forces, can lead to a creativity that may drive change through the 'M&A as practice' model. Here, agency matters.

Figure 13.2 also has the virtue of showing where the chapters are making significant assumptions about aspects of practice. For instance, those chapters in the 'tools' part of the figure tend to assume that the 'text' is set and immutable. They can also assume that the models will inevitably lead to intended outcomes in a prescriptive way. Chapters towards the 'text' part of the figure are sensitive to different 'texts' but perhaps downplay the 'craftiness' of actors in being able to circumvent rules and prescriptions and being able to influence 'text' through their actions. Chapters in the 'talk' part of the framework can assume away the 'text' and also take for granted the organizing, legitimating and constraining effects of 'tools'. While it is important and perhaps practical for research into practice to focus on parts of figure 13.2, it is also necessary to remember to ensure that an integrative perspective is achieved.

Chapter 14, *M&A as Time*, observes that time runs through all our chapters on M&A, but in different guises and in different ways. Conceptions of time vary between text, tools and talk as well as within each of these categories. In a number of instances it is the different conceptions of time(s) that cause difficulties in the M&A process for all practitioners. By making 'time' explicit, it's integrating and fracturing characteristics become clear.

In the current chapter, *M&A as Practice*, the framework aims to integrate key dimensions of M&A to enable a more holistic and integrative picture than is common in the literature. The advantages of this approach are shown in interpreting the following case study.

The Merger Case

This case study – in which the players are anonymous to protect the identity of the firms – is about the merger of two large European manufacturing firms. Key to understanding how value is gained or lost is analysis of the activities of practitioners. To collect this data, close fieldwork and thick description (Rouse and Daellenback, 1999) in a single rich case study is essential (Mintzberg, 1973; Pettigrew, 1985; Johnson, 1987) to enable the unpacking of complexity (Melin, 1986; 1989). For this case, the data collected was real-time and involved a mixture of observation, monitoring and face-to-face discussion with all practitioners involved in activities and actions specific to the merger, and which could be construed as having strategic impacts, throughout a 2-year period. When the data collection began it was uncertain that the deal would actually be consummated, and there were no preconceptions about how the process would unfold.

The context for merger

The merging companies are located in a very fragmented declining European industry. Advances in technology have driven overcapacity and there has been 'capacity creep' from generic learning and operational improvements. Some non-European governments subsidize domestic firms directly or indirectly (through subsidizing energy costs, for instance), allowing cheap exports into the European markets and they also operate protectionist measures, which can harm European exports. At the same time, in some European countries, governments have been reducing subsidies, which has made domestic industry less competitive. Volatile exchange-rate movements have caused considerable difficulties and the recent strength of pound sterling and the euro have hit European export sales hard.

Industry-level dynamics have also been forces for decline and have led to persistent aggressive competition. Major customers have grown globally and used their greater bargaining power to drive down prices. Their relative negotiation power has grown over fragmented incumbents where even the largest players account for only 3% of world production. Even though higher disposable incomes and improved living standards of the populace have led to rising end demand, this is not feeding through to the manufacturing industry due to the strength of intermediate customers. On the supplier side, the industry has faced rising energy costs from national or very large suppliers, with whom the industry has little bargaining power. Industry mentality is one of maximizing throughput and perpetually cutting costs as a means of survival. There is no incentive to cut manufacturing production because other manufacturers will take up the slack with ease and the firms reducing output will have both lower volumes and lower prices.

To avoid this vicious circle, industry consolidation has appeared attractive because it would improve asset utilization rates, purchasing and market power as well as raising returns on investment.

The protagonists

The two merging companies are pure players in the same industry. Company A has a fully integrated process, which is widely regarded as one of the most efficient in the world. Their strategic emphasis on cost efficiency is well illustrated by their pre-merger website: 'We must continually improve our cost efficiency', 'We aspire to achieve the best productivity in the world'. Despite being able to increase capacity substantially, it was doubtful pre-merger whether Company A had sufficient marketing resources to fully utilize the new capacity. Company A emphasized automation and so, even with doubling its throughput, would not increase the numbers of employees.

Company B has traditionally struggled against larger plants because its investment in efficiencies was inadequate and incremental cost reductions insufficient to keep its unit costs competitive. However, Company B did possess a number of attractive niche products and an extensive distribution network. Its approach to sales was to sell direct to users, which is people intensive. The business employed nearly three times the number of Company A.

The deal

The deal was planned during record levels of M&A activity, when mega-mergers and cross-border deals were in abundance. The strong stock market supported enthusiasm for mergers in industrial sectors of this type among financial institutions as well as investors. Even so, to proceed with the merger, for local regulatory reasons, Company B management had to win over 90% of its shareholders. Working closely with investment banks, lawyers and accounting firms, both companies had frequent meetings to hammer out the terms of the deal. Attention focused on the merger document as the primary means of addressing key issues necessary to win approval from institutions. From the announcement to the merger completion, both management teams also embarked on a communications campaign, arguing why the merger was a good deal. This included an exhaustive programme of road shows in major European capitals as well as New York and Boston. The following comments from both CEOs show their view that there was good strategic fit between the two companies. 'The strategic and synergistic fit of the two companies is excellent, and our intention is to deliver to our shareholders the inherent value in a focused . . . company' (CEO, Company A). 'The merger combines the cost leadership position of Company A with the wide product range and extensive distribution network of Company B to create further opportunities in the fast-growing markets' (CEO, Company B).

Anticipated benefits of the merger

The merger prospectus identified synergies of €100m+ per annum. These were expected to be mostly realized in 2 years. The synergies were anticipated in economies of scale in production, efficiencies in sales and distribution, improved logistics, economies of scale in purchasing, and efficiencies in R&D and administration. Many of the efficiencies would be through de-duplication of activities and assets. An additional benefit was perceived to be greater market presence, which would reduce earnings volatility and overall business risk. The strategic rationale for the merger can be summarized as follows:

1. *Production economies of scale* – through volume consolidation.
2. *Market power* – by becoming the dominant producer in the market, potentially giving market control and higher margins.
3. *Administrative savings* – efficiencies in sales, distribution, purchasing and R&D.
4. *Financial savings* – capital investment sharing in this capital-intensive industry is helped by reducing duplicate investments.

The potential benefits of the merger were well communicated to stakeholders but, for the anticipated value creation to occur, intentions had to be realized in the post-acquisition phase.

Post-acquisition approach

The top management was aware of post-acquisition process frameworks by Haspeslagh and Jemison (1991) and Angwin (2000). The framework by Haspeslagh and Jemison sets out three distinct conceptual approaches to managing acquisitions based on the extent to which the business needs strategic interdependence and the extent to which the acquired business requires organizational autonomy. The framework had received empirical support and refinement from Angwin, who confirmed a fourth type of integration approach and also identified a range of actions and their timing for each integration style.

Top management saw the merger as *absorption* (Haspeslagh and Jemison, 1991) or *subjugation* (Angwin, 2000), on the basis that there would need to be high inter-dependence between the two companies to allow de-duplication of production facilities, sales and distribution companies. These intended consolidations across the group implied that autonomy of business units would be low and individual managers' idiosyncrasies removed in favour of centralized control. As the deal was a merger, a new entity would emerge from the combination.

Following Angwin (2000), top management saw the implications of the subjugation style as creating overnight change in the businesses in terms of presenting a new identity to the world through new emblems, logos, and stationery. Excellent communications were viewed as essential from the outset to stabilize the organization and to convey the vision for the future. Teams were set up immediately to plan and implement integration in depth in all major functional areas, as well as addressing cross-functional issues such as corporate and national cultural compatibility.

The intended post-merger management actions were:

1. Developing a new corporate identity.
2. Considerable use of communications to stabilize the companies and set the vision for the future.
3. Exploit dominant market position.
4. Maximize production efficiency for economies of scale.
5. De-duplicate positions and activities to reduce costs.
6. Create integration teams to bring about cultural and organizational change.
7. Achieve early control of financials such as budgets, cash flow.
8. Use purchasing power to reduce supplier costs in raw materials.

The identification of the merger as a potential subjugation style suggested to management that very substantial changes in the early stages of post-merger integration were necessary. High levels of meticulous planning would be necessary to cope with the complexity of this integration style and the speed with which changes would need to be made. Despite this awareness, there was no evidence of any detailed post-merger plan. Indeed, post-completion, the chief financial office stated that the business plan was being reviewed and would be verified 120 days into the post-merger phase!

Post-merger activities

Corporate identity

Very early attention was paid to the new identity of the business and many decisions and actions were taken prior to the first 100 days so that the first action of rolling out the new image could occur on day one. A new logo was launched; videos were distributed; brochures, flags, stationery etc. were all coordinated with launch-day presentations. This was a massive task and was achieved with military precision. The positive effect on employees was tangible. After this flurry of activity, communications quickly became single medium, through the company intranet.

The right senior managers

As a merger, implicit in the agreement was a balance in top management posts. The CEO and four top executives were from Company A and five top executives from Company B.

On day 7 of the merger, the senior executive in charge of sales and marketing, drawn from Company B, left unexpectedly and was replaced by a more junior non-commercial executive from Company A. The consequences were no commercial voice on the executive committee, despite being a key strategic area for the new group, a dramatic increase in workload for the new appointee, who was also keeping his other responsibilities, the loss of tacit knowledge about how Company B operated in this, their core area of expertise, and the altering of the balance of power at the executive level.

In the production area, executive management preferred appointing younger managers to production units. Two new managers of production units were appointed but both subsequently left along with another manager from a different unit. These changes hindered executive management in gaining control and being able to make any changes to these units.

Market face

A major strategic intent of the merger was to present a unified identity to the marketplace and to rationalize sales/distribution. The importance of the image was such that at the launch seminar for the merger, the number of slides explaining the significance of the logo was only four less than the CEO's presentation on the vision for the whole group!

Rationalizing sales/distribution required the amalgamation of sales offices across Europe. While early actions in this respect seemed coherent, implementation was more difficult in some geographic areas than others. In Sweden, amalgamation was accomplished in less than 70 days, and in Italy not at all. In Sweden, merging the offices proved straightforward, as Company A's presence had been small and its MD was happy to take a less prestigious position in a larger unit. In his view: 'titles are meaningless and I am too old to worry about such things'. He was able to maintain the motivation of his employees and the two business units had developed a good relationship over time and found working together straightforward.

In Germany, the largest market in Europe, the merger was complicated by Company B's unit being in the middle of a substantial business reorganization prior to the merger. This reorganization was aimed at regionalizing central European sales to reflect varied demands of major customers. At this stage there was clear evidence that the new approach was bearing fruit. The manager then had many frustrations throughout the first 100 days because his intended reorganization was being questioned by new management. This led to significant uncertainty amongst employees. The support for his new model had been from the senior executive who had left seven days after the merger. The German manager was now reporting to the senior executive appointment, who was so busy that, in effect, he was reporting to a regional manger. This signified a loss of prestige and made the German manager more remote from a key decision maker. In addition, the regional manager style was from the power culture of Company A, where it was the norm to give instructions and expect them to be followed, whereas the German manager was from Company B, where there was a more person-oriented culture and dialogue was the norm. The German found his merger partner's attitude infuriating: 'The Company A people don't listen and are not prepared to change'. The relationship between the two executives was very strained, with the German MD questioning whether senior managers really understood how much value they would lose through their suggestion of combining direct sales forces. To add to his frustration, towards the end of the 100 days, these senior executives visited him to insist he find ways to reduce his costs by 30%. This had become an unexpected priority of top management, who realized that cost reduction in sales was easier than elsewhere in the group.

In Italy, with the second largest market in Europe, the two operations from both companies were of comparable size. The managers could see the advantages of combining their operations and simplifying their supply arrangement. However, they were told not to take any actions. Initially this was met with disappointment but after three months this disappointment turned to bitter criticism of top management. There had been poor communication and there was no clear information on plans for the future. There was considerable uncertainty amongst employees and key staff were considering their positions.

Streamlining sales operations

In addition to rationalizing sales businesses, it was intended to streamline vertically through the production to sales process. This would reduce what was perceived as an unacceptable cost of administration. Wherever possible, standard product should be supplied direct to market. Additional processing and stockholding activities would have to focus on more value added activities and act as true profit centres. The model (shown in figure 13.3) was presented on day 10 of the merger and issued as a formal document on day 31.

A framework was developed for the alignment of sales and distribution with production (see figure 13.3).

Large numbers of employees in the sales companies were worried, understandably, and many questioned the logic. One of the strengths brought by Company B to the merger was the market power provided by being close to the customer. This network allowed the company to penetrate most of the main markets and took away

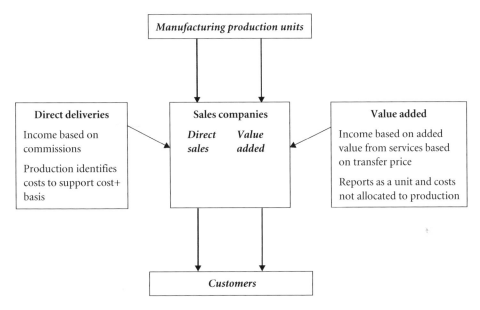

Figure 13.3   Path of actions for de-duplicating sales/distribution and presenting a unified face to market

some of the power of large stockists. Moving towards the proposed model would mean greater reliance on independent stockists as well as losing proximity to customers. The model showed management intended to move towards Company A's 'lean and simple' production-led approach. It sent the message that cost efficiency was king. The problem for Company B was that it was a complex organization of multiple production units, with local invoicing and credit controls. Managing directors in the countries understood the new model, but couldn't see how it could be implemented without very serious change, particularly in information technology.

Key product area

The key product area represented 65% of the new company and had been identified as one with excellent opportunities for exploiting economies of scale through more efficient use of resources. However, management paid little attention to it during the first 100 days, with the first discussion taking place on day 92! The integration manager felt that early swapping of products might confuse customers and, as the production units were quite full, swaps might upset balances in production. This cautious approach is at odds with stated synergy intentions. The effect of the delay was for unit managers to create defences to resist swapping of their most profitable products to other manufacturing units. In the meeting, which took place 92 days post-merger, cost information was not made available and units were unable or unwilling to compare costs. Progress was slow and few decisions were made. It was clear there would be local resistance in the future to product swaps.

Establishing financial control

Day 1 of the merger, the chief financial officer's message was to control finance while there was high capital spend on production. Fifty-two days into the merger, all unit managers were instructed to prepare and update the year's forecast as well as prepare a 5-year plan within a month. This instruction was greeted differently around the group. The Italian managing director felt he couldn't see 6 months ahead, let alone 5 years, whereas his Swedish counterpart saw it as an opportunity to put forward his growth intentions. This request had a heavy impact on management time when significant changes were expected. In the words of one manager: 'the 5-year plan work has detracted from the daily operational change and may have slowed the pace in the first 100 days'. The wisdom of requesting such a plan has also to be questioned because it assumed autonomous units when the situation was for many units to move towards merging.

The most difficult area

The most problematic area was information technology (IT). Only two actions were taken to address this. One, a study detailing its complexity was presented after 55 days and revealed there were 450 different computer systems in operation, costing around €65m per annum. Senior management realized this was a large project, but underestimated significantly its complexity.

Local management was reluctant to authorize further expenditure on IT without being clear on the company vision for IT. Even the smallest changes met with strong resistance. For instance, throughout the 100-day period there were debates on which e-mail system to use and no agreement was reached. Getting information from this vast range of systems was also problematic and top management found it incredibly difficult to operate without coherent information in a common format. In the words of a senior executive: 'Major changes in IT are needed to allow product swaps and direct invoicing to happen as well as for management information to be obtained. This is a missing key ingredient when looking at change. All information requires a massive effort to compile.'

Areas of inaction

Company A and B are in the same industry but are headquartered in different countries and are organized differently. They differ in national and corporate cultures and yet no actions were taken to manage culture shift. They were also organized very differently and had quite different values about how to operate in this industry. No actions were taken to make these differences explicit or to manage some form of transition.

While a great deal of information was transmitted to the employees over the 100 days, at the end of the period an internal review concluded that communications had not been very good. The dominant channel for disseminating information was the company intranet, but only 65% of employees had access on their own desks. In a group survey, 62% of employees felt the intranet was not good enough. In addition information was not well controlled with any senior person apparently acting as editor. As a consequence, unit managers often found themselves unprepared for questions from staff. In one instance an analyst's report from a major bank had been included, which predicted the closure of a major manufacturing facility! The communication was also one-way with the exception of an interactive part of the website. Only six questions were registered from a workforce of 16,000! Having had their review, it is surprising that actions were not taken to improve communications.

Merger review

After 1 year, a formal update of merger synergies was presented. Expectations for the first year had been revised down 60%. Product swaps were still 30% of revised savings but this was expected to be achieved through transport cost reductions rather than through economies of scale savings.

Sales and marketing savings showed the biggest variance, being scaled down 70%. The sales operational model remained the favoured way of operating but had still not been implemented 18 months post-merger. This simpler, lower cost method of operation was not achieved, computer systems had not been changed and there were important markets where management had still not addressed the issue of more than one channel to market. Nevertheless sizeable cost reductions were still demanded. This led to game playing among sales company managers in working with commodity producing units for greater savings and neglecting non-commodity units. The non-commodity units were beginning to realize they could no longer expect the same level of market-based resources to sell their volumes or promote new products.

Lack of strategic direction, in terms of manufacturing unit product programmes, continued. Eighteen months post-merger, managing directors of production plants presented their current and intended programmes to sales company executives. There was an obvious overlap of current programmes, with different plants targeting the same market segments. In the words of the group marketing manager: 'I now see that I can get product A from at least two producers and I can get product B from everywhere!'

This continued lack of clarity, and top management not acting decisively, allowed production units to continue to develop their own programmes. This was contrary, and detrimental, to achieving better economies of scale.

IT continued to be a difficult issue post-merger. The complexities and the cost of changing major systems led to existing systems being maintained. In fact, some system changes intended prior to the merger were reviewed and a number of plans were either put on hold or scrapped. Management directed its attention to conserving cash. If there was no urgency to modify or change systems, they favoured maintaining the status quo. This made it more difficult to integrate the company and left sales companies having to work in a number of different systems when they loaded orders remotely onto individual manufacturing centres.

Face to face communication between management and employees deteriorated as the cost pressures began to build. Travel restrictions were imposed and visits between sites reduced. The intranet continued to be the main distribution channel for information.

The macro-context had also deteriorated. At the merger, European consumption was forecast to grow at 5.5% but the reality was an unexpected fall of 6.3%. Variation in raw material prices also had the effect of reducing inclusive prices by 10%. This led to lower prices in the market and underloading of plants during the summer months. Management was forced to issue a profit warning for third quarter results and pressure for cost reduction throughout the business intensified.

The deteriorating business situation caused management to bring in a number of unintended measures, aimed at stemming cash flow from the business. 'The Group is far away from the cash position in the original business plan.' Initiatives to generate cash internally from reductions in work in progress or finished goods stocks became a priority. Large-scale investments were on hold for at least 3 years and there was increased possibility of plant closures and divestment of non-core activities. Forecasts for future synergies were optimistic but as the merger integration manger remarked: 'Synergies are often forgotten after 2 years of a merger'. The difficulties in realizing fundamental synergies raised serious questions about the shape of the future organization.

At this time the deputy CEO announced he was leaving, despite his insistence, at the merger launch seminar, that he was 'on board' for the long term. His replacement came from Company A, further swaying the balance of top executives. It then became known that the firm's largest two competitors were to merge and then, shortly afterwards, the company itself received a takeover bid, which was ultimately successful.

Case Interpretation

When researchers became involved with the case companies, it was unknown how the merger, if completed, would work out. Although the deal was consummated to widespread approval of markets and investors, it is clear that on a number of levels the merger was later unsuccessful. The new company failed to achieve its stated aims, began making losses and was subsequently acquired itself. Insights into this strategic outcome can be achieved using different perspectives on M&A, namely the 'classical', 'processual' and 'practice' approaches.

The 'classical' approach to M&A rests on the rationality of finance and economics, the supremacy of the grand plan and a profit maximizing outcome. As a merger there was no premium payable to shareholders who had their original shares can-

celled and new ones issued in the enlarged firm. The markets viewed the transaction favourably; indeed, over 90% of shareholders in Company B approved the
deal. The strategic logic of the merger, as expressed in pre-merger communication
from the firms and their top management as well as in merger documentation,
stressed the vital significance of achieving economies of scale and increasing market
power to continue competing in an increasingly hostile industry. Scale advantages
were to enable greater bargaining power over suppliers. Developing differentiation
in products and sales were presented as crucial for extracting higher margins in an
increasingly price competitive industry. This 'classical' approach is predicated on a
strategic logic leading inevitably to enhanced profitability and shareholder returns.
It assumes stated intentions will be acted out in strict accordance with the plan and
anticipated gains will be realized.

The case shows that almost none of the original financial and strategic expectations were realized and yet there was nothing in the 'classical' perspective that
suggested there could be difficulties that might result in underperformance. The
'price' of the deal was not perceived by the markets as being unreasonable and its
structuring was not unusually complex. The strategic logic seemed sound and the
horizontal and friendly nature of the transaction boded well for synergy gains.
Neither firm was in poor financial condition and there was not a great disparity
between them in size. However, strategic outcomes were quite different from those
anticipated. The classical school lacks a mechanism for understanding these variances and can only infer deviant behaviour on the part of managers.

The 'process' approach in M&A attacks the rationality inherent in the classical
tradition and raises awareness of the post-acquisition phase as a powerful mediator
in the relationship between stated intentions and strategic outcomes. The process
approach identifies complexities and irrationalities that interfere with simple performance relationships. The case shows how, despite clear statements of intended
synergies between the two organizations, very few were realized, or were in the process of being realized, and few actions taken which would allow them to be realized.
Two areas of focus from the 'process' approach are resource-based and cultural
differences.

The processual models by Haspeslagh and Jemison (1991) and Angwin (2000)
focus on ways in which two organizations can combine to allow additional value
to be achieved. An appropriate combination is determined by the tension between
the need for integration to create or capture value, and the need for the acquired
organization to remain distinct. In the case, the companies believed that full integration along *absorption/subjugation* lines was appropriate to achieve economies of
scale, and so greater efficiency in all aspects of the business. However, it is also clear
from the case that the two firms involved had different bases for their competitive
advantages. Company A competed on costs through scale efficiencies and was production led. Company B was differentiation based and focused on gaining margin
through niche products and customized marketing efforts. While, superficially, full
integration seemed to offer the best of both worlds, the organizational structures,
resource allocations, capabilities and competencies were fundamentally different.

For these reasons other integration styles, such as *symbiotic/collaborative*, might have been preferable to avoid structural and operational clashes. Bringing these two organizations together in an absorption/subjugation style led to immediate conflict over the fundamental logics of the businesses and the relative importance of manufacturing and sales and how they might work together.

The processual frameworks, which focus on cultural aspects of mergers, do not give indications of whether transactions make sense financially, economically or strategically, but do show whether cultural clashes are likely. In the case, the location of the merging firms in different national contexts and variations in beliefs, values and norms due to different organizational power structures were likely to cause integration difficulties. Models such as those by Nahavandi and Malekzadeh (1988) and Cartwright and Cooper (1992) would have surfaced how the organizational culture of Company A – based in a highly centralized structure with a top–down, directive style of management, permitting little individual autonomy – was likely to clash with that of Company B, where the organizational structure was much flatter, participative management the rule, and greater individual autonomy allowed. These frameworks would have raised awareness of potential problems with full integration and the need for mechanisms to address these difficulties.

The processual frameworks provide insights into how strategic intentions can conflict with organizational differences and give rise to post-merger tensions and stress. However, their high level of analysis is limited to broad organizational differences, leaving considerable room for translation into 'strategic activities on the ground'. The case shows all too well the many variations within the integration process, both horizontally, across geographic territories and across functions, and vertically in different power plays between levels of management. There are also major tensions managing interfaces between critical parts of the business. This led to parts of the merger process with some integration aspects proceeding as planned, some being partially implemented, some not beginning at all and some initiatives being taken which were not in the original plan. These variations and complexities are not captured in existing process models. For example, using Haspeslagh and Jemison's (1991) typology for the sales outlet mergers, we can see an *absorption* approach between sales offices in Sweden, a *symbiotic* relationship being fought out in Germany between the two companies and a *preservation* style in Italy where the two sales companies continued to exist independently of each other. The Haspeslagh and Jemison (1991) framework allows only for one approach. The framework also fails to cope with vertical variations within the merged company. For instance, it does not address the links between manufacturing and sales, where manufacturing operations may merge for efficiency and sales remain distinct for differentiation reasons (see Cummings and Angwin (2004) for an alternative framework to cope with this problem). The organizational level of the framework ignores other levels of analysis and interaction as well, such as interfaces with the macro-context and links with outcomes. None of the process models can cope with this sort of complexity, either in a prescriptive sense or as a technique for analysis. There is a need for a framework that can link the complexities of managerial activities with more local, organizational and broader contexts.

'M&A as practice' seeks to address these issues. It examines the interactions between macro and micro as strategic activities unfold. In so doing, it recognizes the importance of sub-organizational analysis as well as its interplay with different levels of organization and environment. The framework shown in figure 13.1 enables a more complete understanding of the case by being more comprehensive in nature than other frameworks, more focused on practitioner activities, and making explicit interlevel interactions.

Text

The 'text' of the merger is set by the bull market in the financial world and the largest wave of M&A activity ever seen. In so far as M&A can be seen as 'fad or fashion', this was where M&A activity was at its peak. Particularly in vogue were consolidation type mergers in mature industries, driven by globalization pressures and cross-border M&A. For these reasons, the merger in the case study was the 'right' type at the 'right' time and received widespread support from financial institutions and investors.

The stock markets on which the merging firms were listed subscribed to businesses maximizing profits for shareholder benefit. This principle is enshrined in finance and economics and is widely disseminated by business schools, consultants and gurus. Any public deals being launched had to satisfy the markets that this was a primary objective of the transaction.

Throughout the whole merger process, this part of the institutional text remained constant, anticipating the merger would increase shareholder value. When this failed to materialize, the markets down-rated the shares and welcomed the company's eventual takeover by another firm.

Throughout the merger process other aspects of text began to assume importance as the numbers and diversity of practitioners, who were in a position to influence strategic outcome, increased. Post-merger, a far more diverse range of practitioners were directly involved in the merger process. Within the company, a large tier of directors and senior managers across 14 countries were involved, as well as different customers and suppliers. The texts behind these practitioners in these countries underpinned different approaches to business and social relationships. Some of these variations were enshrined in laws and codes, such as employment laws; others reinforced by socio/cultural norms.

Text/tools interaction

Strong institutional norms, often codified in law, govern the way in which management and advisers must argue their case for merger. The 'acceptable' languages of 'strategic' intent are finance and economics and the concepts in these disciplines offer legitimate arguments. In this case, the merger appeared to be financially sound and the proposed exchange of shares was uncontroversial. The strategic case for the merger was 'operationalized' by resorting to the most commonly cited rationales for merger, namely enhancing economies of scale and increasing market power (Trautwein, 1990). This 'efficiency' rationale was widely accepted within the financial community and fitted the dominant 'text' – that the merger should generate value for shareholders.

The strategic text remained in place throughout the merger process although other aspects of text began to assume greater importance. The issues of national variations were not operationalized, even though there appeared to be some awareness of their existence.

As the commercial context of the firm deteriorated, there was intensifying pressure from the text for evidence of improved financial performance. In particular, profit figures and forecasts were scrutinized.

Tools

Institutional laws regarding the launching of M&A state that intentions have to be declared in a merger document that meets certain strict reporting criteria. The issues to be covered and language used are clearly established in laws and codes of conduct and advisers are compelled to act in appropriate ways to satisfy these requirements. For instance, the investment bank needs to produce a fairness opinion to indicate that the terms of the merger are fair and not prejudicial to shareholders.

In the case, the merger document focused on the rationale and justification for the merger, the opinion of the financial adviser, and the verifiable financial and legal information relating to the two companies. This included audited balance sheets, earnings statements and asset valuations. The strategic case for the merger was operationalized in a number of ways: financial modelling based on logical deduction of how financial statements would look if economies of scale and enhanced market power were achieved; powerful statements from the chief executives about the soundness of the merger, employing efficiency and market arguments; letters from financial advisers attesting to the robustness of the numbers.

To convey to investors and to employees how efficiency gains would be achieved, a new tool, driven by the strategy text, was the introduced (see figure 13.3). This showed how vertical linkage from manufacturing production to customer for low differentiated products could be organized. This tool/concept shows clearly the potential for improvement in the firm.

The top management team also used process integration frameworks (Haspeslagh and Jemison, 1991; Angwin, 2000), which indicated how value could be enhanced post-deal. They classified the merger as absorption/subjugation, as this is predicated on achieving greater efficiencies through improved economies of scale and greater market power.

As the merger progressed beyond completion into post-merger integration, a great deal of emphasis was placed on senior managers producing 5-year plans for their business areas. Otherwise, no further tools or concepts were employed for integration. As the company's performance continued to decline, there was an increased emphasis on the financials, in particular cost reduction.

Tools/talk interface

The clarity of tools for conveying the reasons for the merger allowed practitioners in the pre-merger phase to cohere on a tight focus for the transaction. The language of these models fitted the text, and was one the practitioners were very comfortable with. The merger document offered a convenient and undisputed framework within which this small body of practitioners could operate efficiently.

Post-merger, the strategic imperative of achieving economies of scale through rationalizing production and simplifying the production–marketing interface were clear indications to institutions, the firms and their stakeholders of the 'potentializing' outcome sought from the merger. The process models gave more detailed indications to employees of the likely levels of post-merger change such as rebranding/renaming the company, communicating broad intentions, stabilizing the business, and adjusting top management positions. These concrete prescriptions allowed clear direction on some post-acquisition changes. The new tool (see figure 13.3) for conceptualizing more efficient links between manufacturing and customers was intended to 'potentialize' senior managers' actions to achieve these ends. However, its abstract quality did not lend itself to easy interpretation on the ground.

The lack of other tools and concepts had the effect of 'constraining' employee actions and activities. This was the case with the Italian sales offices, wanting to act, but not having had explicit instructions to do so.

As the performance of the firm deteriorated, cost targets assumed dominance over all other tools throughout the group. These targets focused the attention of business managers and severely constrained activities.

Talk

Pre-merger, a small team of practitioners – top management within the firm, financial and legal advisers – was able to focus clearly on their task of conveying forcefully the benefits of the merger to the institutions through the merger document and exhaustive road shows in major financial centres of the world. The narrow set of issues required of them by the text, in a legitimate language of finance and law, allowed focus. The smallness of the team had the advantages of efficient communication, high levels of flexibility, speed of action and considerable secrecy (essential for not disturbing the share price). Multiple meetings took place, often at the offices of the merging companies, and were frequently convened at short notice. These positive characteristics allowed tight interaction between specialists and rapid interpolation between their inputs to the merger document. This speed and flexibility allowed all the required conditions set by the text to be met in an appropriate time frame.

Immediately the merger was announced, there was a massive communications programme to all employees about the vision for the firm and intended post-merger integration actions. This involved communication through the intranet, letters, memos, brochures, videos and meetings. Meetings ranged from stadium style, where the firms' senior management addressed thousands of employees, to small group meetings as well as one-on-one for key employees. With this barrage of communication in the first few days of the post-merger period, employees were clear on overall strategic intentions, but the main focus was on actions to be taken during the first 100 days. More medium-term plans were largely absent from these communications.

Renaming/rebranding the company, changing top management and communicating the visions to employees were achieved with military precision. Employees were motivated and the merger 'potentialized'. While communications continued throughout the first 100 days of integration, other explicit activities began, with teams researching where integration savings might be made, such as in IT alignment. The financial officer also demanded forecasts and 5-year plans from all unit managers. This was widely perceived to involve a great commitment of time and energy.

Even though the broad strategic intentions for the merger were clear, beyond immediate and somewhat superficial changes (i.e. no changes to the basic business model and organizational structure), there was no post-merger plan about how these should be enacted. There was little attempt to connect high-level organizational strategic initiatives with the complexity of the firm and how these initiatives should be enacted in practice. Broad directives were issued from head office and communications were mainly unidirectional. In the manufacturing side of the business, junior managers were appointed into senior positions, and then the integration task delegated to them. Often the situations in which they found themselves were complex. They could not perceive how to translate the high-level demands into local actions. They also had a steep learning curve to understand their new positions. Several left the company shortly afterwards, unable to cope with such pressures.

Longer serving senior managers in the sales part of the business also did not receive any translation of high-level organizational strategic demands from the corporate centre. They were forced to interpret what these might mean for their areas of responsibility. Their actions were to adopt in full, in part, ignore or mutate the demands. For instance, implementing mergers between direct sales forces was achieved without difficulty in Sweden, as the two offices had been working together beforehand, relationships were good and one senior manager was happy to make way for the other. In Germany, the employees in one office were part way through a reorganization and the strategy model proposed from the corporate centre was perceived to clash with this new approach. There was stiff resistance from the German operation, which was compounded by the quality of reporting relationships. The MD of Germany, the most important sales operation in the group, had reported at board level prior to the merger and was to report directly to a senior executive on the board of the new group. However, this senior executive left within days of the merger being consummated. The new appointment was too busy to communicate with the German MD who therefore had to work through a lower ranking executive. This was a loss of prestige and status for the German MD. There was also a clash in management styles, as the new appointee coming from Company A had a directive style, demanding cost reductions without consultation, that conflicted with the German's normal style of participative management, characteristic of Company B. The German MD felt no one listened and he had great concerns over the damage that the new model might cause. His energies were therefore directed at resisting further change.

When the German MD was eventually visited by senior executives, it was not to reinforce the integration model or to look for ways in which it might work, or to discuss how communications could be improved, but to demand 30% cost reductions. The way in which he was to achieve this was his problem.

In contrast with Sweden and Germany, Italy, the second largest market, was not asked to merge its large sales companies for fear of confusing and losing customers. This was a 'constraint' on the Italian managers, who were very keen to make changes. They became increasingly critical of headquarters executives, who barely communicated with them. In frustration, a number of key personnel left the firm.

In other areas of the business there was also inaction in terms of integration. The key product area represented the majority of the company's business and was to be a major source of efficiency gains. However, there were no explicit plans and nothing was discussed for the first 3 months. During that time, managers came up with ways of avoiding anticipated change initiatives by failing to provide cost information, which prevented comparisons between units.

Inaction also resulted from the discovery that earlier high-level assumptions about integration were based on gross simplifications. In the area of IT, a post-merger report revealed phenomenal complexity. With no clear view of how to proceed, managers throughout the business would not commit to spend on IT, so preserving complexity. The consequences were serious. There was a lack of coherent information at the highest levels of the firm and many areas of business integration could not begin to consider other changes, such as aligning billing information, when it was not clear what 'new' IT system might be used.

While passive resistance was the main characteristic in many key areas during the integration, top management became increasingly assertive about the need to cut costs. The response of many business unit managers was to engage in game playing, to avoid integration changes in their area but also to attempt to meet these demands. As the pressure on group finances intensified, communications within the group deteriorated, so that 18 months into the merger it was apparent in a large

meeting of managers that the company still operated a very fragmented organization. The pressure on cost reduction also had the effect of dramatically cutting travel
expenses, greatly reducing the richness of inter-unit communications.

The issuing of a profits warning made the drive for cost reduction the major focus
of the firm. Large-scale investments were halted and question marks raised over
which parts of the business might be sold off. At this point, the deputy CEO left
the firm. Shortly afterwards the firm was acquired.

Talk/text interaction

Throughout the merger process, 'talk' was dominated by the 'text' in its requirement for improved profitability to achieve higher shareholder returns. In the pre-
merger phase, there was strong and clear alignment between the contextual demands
and the activities of a small group of key practitioners. In presenting the merger
proposal and documentation, they accorded with the demands of the text, demonstrating how the merger would benefit the firm and its shareholders.

In the immediate post-merger stage, the broad financial and economic demands
of the text were apparent to all practitioners but there was little translation into
actions on the ground. In addition, other aspects of text, embedded in the practice
of managers, assumed importance. Local and national variations in socio-cultural
variables along with different types of pressures from suppliers and customers
hindered most attempts at organizational integration. As these efforts stalled, the
industry environment continued to deteriorate and the demands for improved financial performance remained strong. The textual conflict could not be resolved with
inaction on the ground. 'Window dressing' activities, such as cutting costs piece-
meal, were entirely inadequate in the face of these mounting pressures. The text
demanded resolution and a new team of managers was encouraged to acquire the
firm for this purpose.

Despite the clarity of textual demands, the myriad actions of many practitioners
were sufficient to be an opposing force. Practices throughout the firm at all levels
served to prevent synergies from materializing and ultimately caused the firm to
fail against its merger targets, being forced to issue a profits warning and ultimately
being acquired itself.

The Merger as Practice

While all the elements of the M&A as practice framework are well represented in
the merger case, one insight achieved through this integrative approach is the way
in which the components are interacting effectively along some dimensions and not
others over time. These 'connections' and 'disconnects' offer explanation for merger
outcome.

Pre-merger stage

In the early stages of the merger it is clear that there was a tight connection between 'text', 'tools' and 'talk'. The textual requirement of profit maximization was 'conceptualized' through legitimate 'tools', such as merger documentation, using the acceptable language of standard financial techniques and legal prescription. These 'tools' gave opportunities for practitioners to craft their take on how the merger should best be presented within these constraints. This was presented to the markets by acceptable practitioners, namely top management and its financial and legal advisers (who are also part of the institutions of text). These practitioners are well versed in dealing with a range of financial, regulatory and investing institutions, their explicit and implied requirements as well as subtle nuances. Merger practitioner activities were carefully crafted to fit within institutional requirements, such as takeover rules on timing of submissions, the way in which announcements should be made, the mechanism by which new shares are issued etc. In getting the merger approved, there was a very tight binding of the M&A as practice model using just a handful of key practitioners over a short period of time.

Merger integration

Once the merger transaction was completed, new elements emerged in the M&A as practice model. The number and variety of practitioners influencing strategic outcome swelled markedly. In the pre-deal stage, for reasons of secrecy, only a handful of top managers were engaged in the process. Post-deal, the number of employees involved was some 16,000 across many countries and myriad customer and supplier demands made themselves felt.

While the 'text' on financial, economic and legal issues remained intact, additional elements became important. Pre-deal attention focused on two financial markets concerned with the same issues of maximizing share price. The power of the text here was tangible, as it was obligatory to satisfy this hurdle for the companies to merge. Post-merger, the original strategic text remained in place, but other richer texts became apparent. The merger involved integration in several European countries between which there are significant differences in national cultures, work practices and attitudes. In addition the industry situation continued to decline throughout the period.

Tools/text interface

The 'tools' in the case remain linked with the original strategic text. Even though there was a new integration framework, none of the tools took into account the new aspects of text, namely national social and business variations.

There were clashes between 'old' tools and 'new' ones, as shown in Germany where the business was attempting to put in place a regional sales model (which was locally sensitive, providing a rich customer interface, and which was working well) and yet the corporate centre in a different geography and with a different perspective was attempting to strip out such interfaces to reduce costs. This was a fundamental conflict over how to do business in different territories.

The tools also under-recognized the 'integrative' nature of the business. While there was a model to streamline production and sales, other areas of cross-functional integration were ignored, paralyzing many other initiatives aimed at achieving efficiencies – for example, the inability to integrate IT prevented other functions from even starting their own restructurings.

Tools/talk interface

The problem of applying generic and high-level models to plural contexts is difficulty in translation and implementation. In this case, the attempts to merge sales forces in different countries had varied impacts in Sweden, Germany and Italy. The generic model for streamlining manufactured product to customer gave few clues about how this could be operationalized in practice, causing confusion and tensions between myriad manufacturing and marketing links.

Talk/text interface

At the organizational level, a list of strategic imperatives, distinct and conceptual in nature, flowed from the strategic 'text'. However, within the firm at the micro-level, this clarity and distinctness blurred rapidly and could not be translated into local situations. This complexity took the form of interdependencies, with aspects of the organization beyond the control or influence of local managers. The existence of such interdependencies prevented strategic initiatives from being taken. For instance, fragmented IT prevented changes in normal decision patterns because alternative information could not be obtained. The largest single intended synergy was to be achieved through product swapping among manufacturing units for cost efficiencies. However, this couldn't occur because the main sales companies had not been able to achieved unified sales channels. Reasons for this failure were partly political, partly due to local contexts and partly because finance had not been able to put in place invoicing procedures because of fragmented IT – a situation that did not appear likely to be resolved.

To cope with paradoxical demands from the text and their local situations, practitioners on the ground resorted to game playing. Rather than achieve cost savings through business restructuring, they managed to achieve some results through natural wastage of staff and sales offices trading-off manufacturing plants against each other. Initially, in financial terms, the overall effect was that the company was moving towards complying with the strategic 'text'. In practice, though, business restructuring was not taking place and looked unlikely to ever happen.

M&A as practice

Throughout the merger process, the earlier coherence, which was sufficient to allow the merger to take place, slowly fragmented as more practitioners became involved and as textual influences proliferated. It further fragmented as time elapsed. While the process began in a clear, guided way, there was little mechanism in tools to allow a translation of textual imperatives into post-merger strategy on the ground. Nor was there a receptiveness in tools to the variations that began to surface in 'talk'. There were clear elements of resistance throughout the framework. 'Talk' resisted 'tools' and 'text'. 'Tools' resisted changes in 'text' and also feedback from 'talk': innovative actions and activities were being used to avoid the constraints of 'tools' and might have led to the customization or creation of new more appropriate tools. The dominant strategic text was being driven down into the organization with few adjustments or translations for practitioners within the firm to interpret and handle. Through resistance and innovation, the strategy text was re-conceptualized at the micro-level, allowing the company initially to satisfy the 'text' but ultimately causing an irrevocable separation. The deteriorating coherence in the practice of this merger led to textual pressures for the situation to be reconstituted. This did not occur within the firm, which had become mired in complexity. With failing strategic performance, there was an opportunity for another firm to take control to resolve these tensions.

Conclusions

The M&A as practice approach to the case shows the harmful consequences of disconnection between pre-merger intentions and post-merger actions. In this way the M&A as practice framework attempts to cross the divide in the M&A literature between M&A strategy and M&A implementation. It provides some explanation in terms of the increasing complexity throughout the process and the failure of linkages between 'text', 'tools' and 'talk' to accommodate tensions. It also raises important questions. If the majority of intended changes did not make sense on the ground, then why was the merger proposed, and accepted, on this basis? This focuses attention on how firms interface with institutions and the mechanisms of persuasion and argumentation that might be used. The tools employed to implement the merger were clearly too broad for purpose. How might these have been adjusted and customized? Indeed, there is clearly a need for new tools to handle more complex post-merger integrations. There is evidence of practitioner activities that were commercially sensible and innovative in avoiding the simplistic and, in some cases, erroneous prescriptions of 'tools'. Why were some of these activities not anticipated? Why was innovation ignored, with no feedback into post-merger plans and conceptualizations? In what ways can practitioners be involved in the production of text in such a way that alignment may be improved? If reconstitution of the strategic text is more the norm than the exception in mergers, why are there few mechanisms for this to feedback into 'text'?

The M&A as practice perspective, as articulated in this chapter, tries to show through the analysis of a merger how links between what practitioners do and multiple contexts over time can explain strategic outcome. Reflexivity is apparent as a continuous interaction between multiple levels, from macro-environment to micro-contexts. This highlights the translation difficulties and tensions between universal high-level strategy and multifaceted micro-contexts. The advantage of the M&A as practice approach is to extend the insights of the process school from the organizational to the micro-levels as well as to reconnect with outcomes. M&A as practice can also give explanation for financial outcomes observed by the classical school. For this merger and for others, we can perceive how broad strategic intents for certain results can be mutated through the complexity and variance of micro-contexts to achieve different outcomes. The more holistic approach of M&A as practice helps to cross the harmful divide between content and process (Pettigrew, 1992; Rumelt et al., 1994), between M&A formulation and integration, and can provide a richer explanation for merger outcome than is current in the literature. In particular, it draws attention to dynamic interconnections over time across multiple levels of analysis and these may connect, disconnect and reconnect over time to shape strategic outcome.

Chapter 14   M&A as Time

Duncan Angwin, Scott Dacko and Matthew Checkley

Mergers and acquisitions fail in many ways and for many reasons: the deal was transacted at the wrong time; the acquirer failed to achieve quick wins in the first 100 days; after 5 years the merger could only be seen as hugely value destroying; the wave of diversifying acquisitions included some of the worst deals in corporate history. These common pronouncements on M&A performance are all linked to *time* and *timing*. However, this critical perspective of 'time' is rarely made explicit in M&A studies. At best, 'time' is interpreted narrowly and taken for granted as an underlying objective variable. At worst, the effects of time are ignored altogether. Insensitivity to time in M&A studies and by managers has real consequences for understanding M&A. Bringing time to the fore and giving it a more sophisticated treatment may help explain many difficulties that have been observed in M&A as well as offer opportunities for more effective M&A management.

This chapter on 'M&A as Time' will reveal time to be a far richer perspective than is commonly acknowledged. A more sensitive appreciation of temporal challenges may well help to resolve core problems and paradoxes in M&A as well as offer significant opportunities for managers to handle M&A more effectively. How then to get to grips with 'time' – what is time and how does it affect M&A?

Time has its own set of variables and relationships to guide managerial action. A temporal perspective focuses on the pace of activities (Eisenhardt, 1989), their trajectories over time (Lawrence et al., 2001), the cycles they align with (Ancona et al., 2001) and their location along a continuum of time (Blount and Janicik, 2001). It recognizes that different people will have different conceptions of urgency (Perlow, 1999) and focus on time (Zimbardo and Boyd, 1999) and there are variations between cultures in the ways that time affects group behaviour (Bluedorn and Denhardt, 1988). A temporal perspective, therefore, brings out the timing, pace, cycles, rhythms, flows, temporal orientations and cultural meanings of time (Ancona et al., 2001).

This chapter argues that the richness of time presents challenges that must be appreciated by adopting a multi-time perspective on M&A. Furthermore, a

multi-constituent perspective should also be recognized to the extent that different constituents in M&A operate on 'different clocks'. After a brief discussion about
time, this chapter illustrates the importance of a temporal view of time through a
review of earlier chapters contained within this book, a reflection on the time literature in management studies and by way of an experimental case study.[1] These provide insight into how both academicians and managers can understand M&A better
and increase their sensitivity to the richness of a M&A performance frontier.

'Time'

'*Time*' has many definitions. For example, the *Merriam-Webster Dictionary Online*
(www.webster.com) has 98 entries for 'time'. At this point in 'time' (relative to the
reading of this chapter), it is useful to raise awareness of the temporal issue, that
there may be multiple definitions and views of 'time', which may have a broad set
of implications for management research.

  'Time' and timing are key constructs that permeate a wide array of management
and marketing phenomena and research. Until relatively recently, however, much
academic research considered 'time' implicitly rather than explicitly. The series of
conferences on 'time' in Palermo, Sicily, beginning in 2001, however, demonstrates
the growing interest in examining temporal issues in management by making 'time'
and timing explicit. Hoskin (2004, p. 743) considers the Palermo conference as
a sort of kairos in this regard: 'a temporal moment of crystallization that worked
through the coming together of its participants to signal that a new intellectual
path was already, and continues to be, cleared'. On further reflecting on the value
of the concept of timing in obtaining managerial insight, Hoskin (p. 752) argues
that, '. . . even at the simplest levels, we should never forget that timing–spacing
synthesis has been a necessary precondition, or horizon, to signifying and making
sense at all'. In this sense, this last chapter aims to achieve greater managerial insight
into M&A by raising awareness of the importance of 'time' and timing, beginning
with a brief review of the treatment of 'time' in earlier chapters.

A Temporal Perspective on Prior Chapters

A cursory inspection of earlier chapters in this book through a temporal lens is very
revealing. In some instances 'time' and timing is addressed explicitly and in other
cases implicitly. We can also detect different views on the nature of 'time' and timing. For some, 'time' is viewed as a universal standard applicable to all; a clock-based
regularity characterized by an unrelenting inevitability. Others take a more pluralistic view of 'time' as having different qualities and dimensions depending on the

Table 14.1   'Time' as experienced

Chapter	'Time' as . . . Objective/Subjective	'Time' conceptualizations	Managerial approaches
M&A as Success	Objective	'Time' as deadline; single point outcome. Search of speed and value; 'time' is valuable and scarce	Measure and control
M&A as Illusion	Subjective	Hardening perceptions of 'time'; another source of delusion	Understand interplay of subjective 'time' perceptions; understand biases
M&A as Imperialism	Subjective	Conflict between conqueror and conquered; 'time' as another consideration within opportunism	Build, or enforce consensus
M&A as Warfare	Mixed	Dead line to victory/defeat but ongoing wars, cycles, 'time' lessness	'Time' as (mere) context for victory
M&A as Power	Objective	'Time' institutionalized as concrete framing of activities (although this varies by context)	Conform to, or work within, institutional framing of 'time'
M&A as Risk	Objective	'Time' as marking risk events; speed or lethargy as potential sources of risk	Measure and control; anticipate
M&A as Knowledge	Mixed	'Time' as setting project deadline; knowledge as wasting asset; need for speed; conflicting perceptions	Understand interplay of subjective 'time' perceptions and objective requirements
M&A as Stereotypes	Subjective	'Time' as context; zeitgeist; conflicting perceptions	Understand interplay of subjective tie perceptions; build consensus
M&A as Boundaries	Mixed	Interplay of objective clock-'time' and subjective perceptions	Manage convergence of understandings to point of balance or harmony
M&A as Monitoring	Mixed	Interplay of objective frame for outcomes with subjective perceptions and activities	Understand interplay between subjective activities and objective frames of reference

parties involved and context in question. Here the 'rigor' of 'time' may mean different things to different people.

To illustrate the different ways in which 'time' may be explicitly or implicitly handled, a temporal perspective on earlier chapters in the book is set out in Tables 14.1 and 14.2. In several chapters temporality is submerged so inferences have had to be drawn about the treatment of 'time'.

Research suggests that there may be at least six dimensions to 'time' (these are reviewed later) and this complex multidimensionality makes a full temporal treatment very complex. As the aim here is just to reveal how temporal sensitivity gives insights into M&A, just two dimensions of 'time' have been used for analysis. Clearly a fuller appreciation of how these chapters are arranged temporally would require all six dimensions to be employed. The two dimensions chosen for illustrative purposes are: 1) how 'time' is experienced – whether objectively based on an external metric or through human interpretation (see table 14.1); 2) 'time' as a referent anchor – whether the approach is focused on the past, the present or future (see table 14.2). Alongside the approaches to 'time', tables 14.1 and 14.2 also set out what these mean for 'time' conceptualization and what managers actually do – their actions and activities.

The orthogonal nature of these two temporal dimensions allows the creation of a framework to display visually the differences between the chapters in terms of the ways in which they handle 'time' (see figure 14.1). Other frameworks could be created for different temporal dimensions.

- *Group A: Rooted in the past.* Managers need to understand history and path dependencies. M&A strategy is thus seen as critically constrained and managers must 'work in the grain', paying respect to context and past conditions that created it. Clock 'time' is of marginal interest where subjectivity is greater. Cycles or intervals could be critical.
- *Group B: Future oriented.* This group is essentially about information processing and extrapolation. The emphasis is on using frameworks or models to process data to create information. Strategic choice regarding M&A is based on the outcome of analysis. For instance the models might be DCF or CAPM, into which created data, such as cash flow forecasts, are plugged. Clock 'time' and objectivity are critical.
- *Group C: Placed in the present – the deictic flux of being 'here' and 'now'.* Managers need to continuously iterate between the objectivity of plan and subjectivity of activities and interpretations – each informing and altering the other. Where there is greater subjectivity, as in M&A as *illusion*, managers need to understand their fallibility – we are all prone to bias, error and irrationality. These well-established characteristics of our psychology can be the cause of regret in M&A.
- *Group D: Future focused in terms of defining desired states of nature – organizational balance and harmony.* M&A strategy is complex, iterative or incremental and determined by relevant constituents and their perceptions of 'time'.

Table 14.2   'Time' as referent anchor

Chapter	'Time' as . . . Past/Present/ Future	'Time' conceptualizations	Managerial approaches
M&A as Success	Future	Expected gains and costs of the future are anticipated and discounted into today's value	Measure and control: DCF; option theory
M&A as Illusion	Present	Current interaction shapes M&A evolution – in this chapter the past was discounted	Critically reflect on attitudes and the fallibility of our perceptions
M&A as Imperialism	Past	A retrospection on how M&A may be interpreted based on past actions	History creates path dependencies; understand how the imperial legacy forms strategic constraints. Strategize 'in the grain'
M&A as Warfare	Past	Previous dominating warfaring affects outcomes and legitimates further warfaring behaviour and language	History creates path dependencies; understand how the warring legacy forms strategic constraints and opportunities
M&A as Power	Past and Future	Institutions react to the M&A activity of the past and attempt to shape the M&A activity of the future to meet socio-economic expectations	M&A requires navigation within shifting power structures, which can be nationally defined. Strategize 'in the grain'
M&A as Risk	Future	Expected risks are estimated for present action	Measure and control; model prospective financial outcomes and identify points of uncertainty
M&A as Knowledge	Past	Differences in prior histories clash and shape the present	History creates path dependencies; understand how stocks of organizational knowledge form strategic constraints. Strategize 'in the grain'
M&A as Stereotypes	Past and Present	Past differences are employed in the present to shape M&A evolution (but without clear future shape in mind)	History and culture create path dependencies; understand how stereotypes form strategic constraints. Strategize 'in the grain'
M&A as Boundaries	Future	Intended future states guide present interactions and activities.	Manage for shared understanding; strategy as balancing and harmonizing.
M&A as Monitoring	Present	Present plans interact with actual activities in mutual iteration to affect eventual outcome	A continuous measuring, evaluating, adjusting process. Strategy in the making

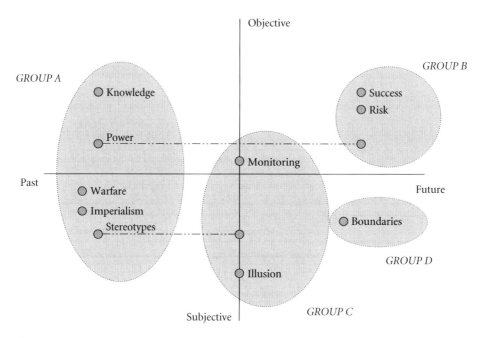

Figure 14.1   Temporal groupings of chapters

Some chapters span parts of these 'time' dimensions, or iterate along a dimension. In this category M&A as *power* is simultaneously balancing past behaviours with desired future states, whereas M&A as *stereotypes* is drawing selectively on interpretations of the past to mould and shape a present.

Reflecting on the chapters in this book from a temporal perspective, some perspectives assume convergence of 'time' perceptions whereas others recognize a persistent underlying dissonance. In some approaches, 'time' is a rigid, rare resource, whereas others view 'time' as abundant and plastic. In just these few chapters on M&A we quickly appreciate a very rich set of temporal treatments, which suggests that a temporal lens provides a new and powerful way to view M&A. In the next section the dimensions of 'time' in management research and their managerial implications in M&A are explored further.

'Time' in Management Research

What precisely is 'time' in the context of management research? The answer is that 'time' is multidimensional and possesses many characteristics. In a useful review of 'time'-based studies in strategy research, Mosakowski and Earley (2000) find that 'time' has five dimensions:

1) *The nature of 'time'*: Is 'time' 'real' in that it is a fundamental category exist-
    ing independently of events, or is 'time' epiphenomenal in that it exists only
    in relation to events? Most management research views 'time' as 'real', but some
    research views 'time' as epiphenomenal, existing only to separate 'procedures'.
    Clearly, one's assumption about the nature of 'time' should have important
    implications in how 'time' can be used and managed.

2) *The experience of 'time'*: Is 'time' experienced objectively in that it is based on
    some external metric, or is 'time' experienced subjectively in that 'time' gains
    significance only through human interpretation? Management research is
    predominantly focused with an objective experience of 'time', suggesting an
    opportunity to explore further the implications of subjective 'time'.

3) *The flow of 'time'*: Is the flow of 'time' novel, cyclical or punctuated? It is novel
    if the view is there is little repetition of events, cyclical if there are repetitive events,
    and punctuated if there are repetitive events punctuated by novel ones. There
    is a diversity of views regarding the flow of 'time' in the management literature.

4) *The structure of 'time'*: Is the structure of 'time' discrete, continuous, or
    epochal? Is 'time' perceived to consist of discrete temporal units of measur-
    able and equal duration, or is it a continuous flow that cannot be broken into
    units but can only be identified with events? Or is it epochal in that 'time' is
    perceived to consist of discrete temporal units, the length of which is perceived
    to vary depending on the subjective experience? There is again a diversity of
    views in the literature regarding the appropriate structure of 'time'.

5) *Time's referent anchor*: Is the most appropriate referent anchor for 'time' the
    past, present, or future? Varying referent anchors are found throughout the
    management literature.

One of the implications of the five dimensions is that dominant assumptions
about 'time' may influence the way mergers and acquisitions and their successes
are evaluated and managed. To illustrate how different 'time' dimensions underlie
treatments of M&A, two of these dimensions were used earlier in the chapter, showing how different researchers treat 'time' explicitly or implicitly and how bringing
'time' and 'timing' to the fore gives rise to new insights. The richness of the M&A
research terrain shows great diversity of treatment of 'time' and although there is
a substantial preponderance of 'time' being treated as 'real', objective, novel, discrete, and with a range of temporal anchors, more recent research has begun to
explore the other sides of these temporal dimensions.

Other notions of 'time' have been proposed in order that a theory of 'time' might
be developed. George and Jones (2000) suggest six dimensions that researchers
should consider – and be constrained by. They include:

1) *The past, future, and present and the subjective experience of 'time'*: 'Time' is
    intimately bound up with human experience so that the past and future are
    reflected in the present. In other words the past preconditions the present while

the future is embedded in the present in terms of expectation, possibilities and strivings (Heidegger, 1962). In this sense the present cannot be artificially separated from the past and future, as is often the tendency in research. To grasp the nature of a phenomenon it is important to understand how its existence at any point in 'time' is a refection of the past and future as they come together. It is subjective, as people's experiences vary depending on the context, task and whether they are 'in flow' or not. The experience of connectedness among past, future and present will vary among both organizations and individuals based on their capabilities and skills.

2) *'Time' aggregations*: People will aggregate, or bracket, their experience of 'time' into episodes (e.g. short; long; 'time' containing only positive events; 'time' containing only negative events) in order to reflect on it and give it meaning (Schutz, 1967). These aggregations will be affected by a person's psychological state, the meaning they attribute to it and its relationship to other phenomena.

3) *Duration of steady states and rates of change*: Duration is how long a phenomenon exists in a steady state or is unchanging. Rate of change is how long it takes to move from one steady state to another. The authors observe that much of the organizational behavior literature ignores or treats poorly the notion of steady state durations, leading to problematic managerial prescriptions and evaluations.

4) *Incremental versus discontinuous change*: Often referred to in the organizational literature as evolutionary or revolutionary change.

5) *Frequency, rhythm and cycles*: This searches for patterns and regularities – for repetitive rhythms. Some organizational phenomena have their own particular rhythms and cycles. Recognizing the extent that frequencies, rhythms and cycles influence various organizational phenomena is therefore an important aspect of promoting shared rhythms within organizations.

6) *Spirals and intensity*: Rather than always oscillating between highs and lows, some phenomena may spiral over 'time', with intensity increasing in an upward or downward direction, nonlinearly and exponentially.

'Time' in M&A

In relation to M&A, the subjective experience of 'time' and its connectedness varying across organizations and individuals is hardly recognized in the literature. While the connectedness of 'time' is captured to some extend in the processual studies of M&A, the multilayered nature of experienced 'time' has not. This suggests that different 'flows' of experienced 'time' may have an affect on the M&A process and its outcome(s). Chapter 8 on 'M&A as Boundaries' provides an example of how different parties engage in different types of boundary creation at different rates of 'time'.

'Time' aggregations are common in the M&A literature in an objectified research sense – for instance, in performance studies reviewed in chapter 2, 'M&A as Success' – but it is rare to find discussion on how 'time' aggregations affect results. Studying different aspects of M&A such as the acquisition decision or the integration process, 'time' aggregation is rarely brought to the fore and yet is likely to be highly significant. For instance a 'time' aggregation consisting of the week before a merger/acquisition is likely to have a very different character to a 'time' aggregation consisting of the $1^1/_2$ years after the merger; the length of 'time' that may be seen as the minimum period for full organizational integration to take effect. An example of different 'time' aggregations on the perceptions of M&A performance can be seen in the many commentaries on the HP–Compaq merger. Just prior to the deal, the preponderance of informed opinion at one point in 'time' was that the merger was seriously flawed – 'two weaklings does not a champion make'. A 1-year retrospective post-completion date described the merger as 'falling apart'. After 2 years, analysts were reported as 'still waiting for the upside'. Now, in 2006, 5 years post-merger, a recent IDC report argues it has been a huge success, with shareholder return up 46%, soaring free cash flow, improved operating margin and dominance of retail shelf space. Clearly the aggregation of 'time' in different ways does matter.

Linked to the previous discussion is when a particular state ends. For instance, when would the post-acquisition integration phase finish? There are also important and largely unanswered questions about the rate and pace of change within an integration phase, with just a handful of studies on early change in the first 100 days (Angwin, 1997; 2004; Ashkenas, 1998). These durations and rates of change are also likely to vary by organization and also within organizations.

Viewing 'time' as incremental or discontinuous will affect judgements about risk and success. Whether post-acquisition change is to be incremental or revolutionary has huge implications for the way in which a process might be planned and how the risks and rewards are perceived. Juxtaposing chapter 4, 'M&A as Warfare', and chapter 9, 'M&A as Knowledge', illustrates how implicitly different views of 'time' as incremental or discontinuous can affect interpretation.

'Time' as frequency, rhythm, and cycles permeates organizations and it is interesting to think about how these may coincide and integrate post-deal. Some cycles will be highly visible and predictable, such as sales cycles or annual budgeting processes whereas others will be difficult to predict and far less visible. In altering some aspects of the organization, internal rhythms and cycles may be disrupted and damage synchronies with other endogenous and exogenous patterns. An example of this interplay is provided in chapter 7, 'M&A as Project', where there is a fascinating interplay of rhythms, cycles and structures, between planning outcomes and operational activities.

'Time' as a spiralling influence, where there can be a rapid escalation in a belief in pursuing a particular course of action, is readily seen in M&A negotiations. In chapter 3, 'M&A as Illusion', there is an example of two senior executives getting caught up in a spiral of 'time', intensifying interaction and distrust, resulting in a suboptimal outcome. In the post-acquisition period, understanding the spiralling dynamic nature of change can be vitally important in helping achieve desired managerial outcomes.

Although George and Jones (2000) present six dimensions of 'time' as distinct, and each does capture a facet of 'time', it is likely that they are interrelated. For instance, rates of change have implications for cycles and spirals. Nevertheless, researchers and managers can benefit greatly by uncovering and then critically examining the temporal assumptions that are implicitly adopted in pursuing particular courses of action based on any general theory or theoretical prescription. Such a temporal evaluation process can lead to greater objectivity in decision making as well as help to increase the likelihood of pursuing strategically optimal options within the organization.

By making temporal assumptions apparent, new 'time'-related concepts may also emerge which would provide alternative ways of looking at management phenomena to obtain fresh insights. For example, the new temporal concept of *timing norms*, described by Ancona et al. (2001) as norms that people experience as shared, expected patterns of paced activity might vary within organizations. In other words, expectations about pace and when actions should begin or end will vary depending on, for example, the level or level(s) involved in the organization and the responsibilities of the individuals involved. There are *timing norms*, for example, that emerge through social interactions, while others result from formally scheduled events. Understanding and explaining what timing norms look like and where they come from, along with their positive and negative effects, could be particularly useful in understanding post-acquisition integration and lead to better managerial decision making.

In summary there are many dimensions to 'time' and incorporating a subjective view requires the examination of individual and social processes. To give a flavour of these dimensions, the following interactive session was crafted for an Improvisational Conference on 'time' at INSEAD, Fontainebleau, France, in July 2004. It involved a simulated merger/acquisition[2] where pre-conference participants experienced events as they unfolded. They were recorded throughout the process and this recording was then relayed to participants at the conference to explore temporal issues in M&A.

A Merger/Acquisition For Temporal Analysis

Pre-session preparation as well as the implementation approach for the session were outlined as follows:

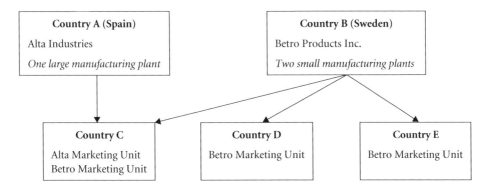

Figure 14.2 Locations of Alta Industries and Betro Products Inc. just prior to amalgamation

Pre-session preparation
1. Four individuals of suitable backgrounds were selected to adopt the roles of different stakeholders involved in a takeover. They were given descriptions of their stakeholder roles (the first four roles in table 14.3). They were also given figure 14.2, showing the locations of the firms.
2. Participants were given a chronology of events for a simulated merger/acquisition that was based on actual M&A experience (table 14.4). Each person read the summary of events up to and including Week −4 (4 weeks before the takeover) but were not allowed to read ahead.
3. Each person was then videotaped in his or her role of a particular stakeholder, and where they expressed their views of the takeover at that particular point in 'time'.
4. The process was repeated for the remaining three 'time' periods (end of Week 0, end of Week 14, and end of Week 130), where, on reading of a summary statement from the M&A chronology, they express their views on videotape.
5. Once all individuals have been interviewed, the videotapes for each stakeholder were then collated to show each of their views, arranged to appear in complete chronological order.
6. The videotape was then ready to present as a simulated merger/acquisition for subsequent temporal analysis by a group of experts at the Improvisational Conference on 'time'.

Session implementation
1. At the Improvisational Conference on 'time', an individual in the audience adopted the role of a fifth stakeholder involved in the takeover, thereby supplementing and complementing the views previously recorded and expressed on videotape. The participating individual was given a description of the stakeholder role (the fifth role in table 14.3).
2. The session moderator adopted the role of 'time'-keeper, i.e. 'clock time'.
3. The 'time'-keeper gave all members of the audience a chronology of events for a simulated merger/acquisition. The 'time'-keeper told the audience member

Table 14.3   Stakeholder descriptions: five perspectives on the 'time' for evaluating the success of the takeover of Betro Products Inc. by Alta Industries

---

Institutional Shareholder in Alta Industries – You are an institutional shareholder in Alta Industries and have been for the past 5 years. Your objectives are to actively support actions that result in the highest possible share price. You are wary of other company stakeholders that may advocate any other view.

Member of the Board of Directors in Betro Products Inc. – You are responsible for major board decisions in the Betro organization during all weeks. In your position, you have made a lot of money in the past. However, after a takeover, you would be the weaker party. There is always a threat that you would be sacked. Regardless of the outcome, head-hunters would probably approach you for possible positions in other companies.

Production Worker in Betro Products Inc. – You have been making gadgets at one of Betro's smaller manufacturing facility for 10 years. You are the primary wage earner for your family. You are often concerned that you have not earned enough to provide for your children's future needs along with your retirement and that of your spouse.

Marketing Manager in Betro Products Inc. – You are responsible for marketing the gadgets of Betro Products Inc. You have been with the company for 2 years and have been more successful than your counterparts at Alta Industries. Your objectives are to actively support actions that are likely to increase the current and future sales of Betro Products' gadgets. You are deeply suspicious of any employee or company stakeholder that advocates actions that may adversely affect Betro Products' gadget marketing and sales efforts.

Production Manager in Alta Industries – You are responsible for the production of high-quality gadgets at world-beating efficiency levels. You have the most modern gadget plant in the world, which has the single biggest gadget capacity of any company in the industry. However, it is currently only operating at 60% capacity. You live near the factory and are married with two children. You enjoy skiing and skating. You've worked in the same company for the past 10 years. Your immediate boss is a main board executive director. Revealed later in the simulation, in week 14: one of the Betro production managers decides to leave the company. Your boss becomes the director of all manufacturing.

---

    to read the summary of events up to and including Week −4 (4 weeks before the takeover) and to not read ahead.

4. The pre-recorded videotape of the interviews with other key stakeholders for the same M&A 'time'-frame (i.e. 4 weeks before the takeover) was then played to the audience.

5. The participating individual who adopted the role of the fifth stakeholder was then 'on stage,' attending a stakeholders' meeting at that particular period in 'time'. In it, the individual expressed his/her personal views, also evaluating the merger. (If needs be, the 'time'-keeper can prompt the individual to be concise in the interest of staying on schedule.)

Table 14.4   Chronology of events for merger/acquisition

Weeks −52 to −5 (1 year before the takeover)
The European context surrounding companies Alta Industries of Spain and Betro Products Inc. of Sweden in the year prior to the acquisition was one of deterioration. The gadget manufacturing industry was very fragmented and competitive and in a slow state of decline. Technology improvements for gadget production were driving overcapacity in gadgets. Customers had grown globally and were using their greater bargaining power to drive down the prices of gadgets. These customers were also preventing a rising end demand for gadgets from feeding through to our businesses. Both Alta Industries and Betro Products Inc. were also seeing rising energy costs from their very large suppliers. The industry mentality of maximizing throughput meant there was no incentive for any competitor in the industry to reduce overcapacity.

Alta Industries was renowned for the superior quality of its manufactured gadgets. In particular, substantial investment in a vast manufacturing plant allowed it to claim the lowest cost of gadget production in the industry in the world. However, where the company had been struggling was selling its gadgets across Europe.

By contrast, Betro Products Inc. had an excellent market presence for gadgets in most of Europe's leading markets. While it had always struggled to keep its costs of gadget production down, it was able to make substantial margins on bespoke gadgets for different markets. Betro Products Inc. attributed its success to a sophisticated gadget marketing and sales team that could communicate customer wishes effectively to its manufacturing plants.

Alta was a public company, well resourced and with a gearing level of 37.3% – close to the industry average. Betro, however, had suffered more through the deterioration in markets, and had seen its gearing rise to 74%.

End of Week −4 (1 month before the takeover)
Alta Industries agreed with Betro Products Inc. that a friendly takeover of Betro would be in both companies' best interests, as the combined group would improve asset utilization, purchasing and market power. Industry consolidation appeared the only way forward. Rumours appear in the newspapers that a takeover is imminent. Staff of both firms are seen at the headquarters of both firms.

Stakeholders are asked: What are your personal views on the likelihood of success of the takeover?

* * *

Week −3 (3 weeks before the takeover)
When Alta Industries announced its agreed cash bid, or Alta equity alternative bid, for Betro Products Inc, it represented a 15% premium on the current share price.

Week −1 (1 week before the takeover)
The arrival of a bid from Cobalt Industries forced Alta to increase its offer to a 30% premium.

Table 14.4   *(cont'd)*

End of Week 0 (the week of the takeover)
Alta Industries acquires the Betro Products Inc. organization. At closing, the majority of Betro Products Inc. shareholders accept either the cash offer or the offer of equity in the enlarged Alta Industries. As a result of the takeover, the value of Alta Industries shares falls by 1%.

As Betro was 25% larger than Alta by capitalization before the takeover, the deal has the effect of the combined group having a gearing higher than Alta's previous level of 37.3%. Many of Betro's banks took the opportunity to redeem their loans when the deal was concluded and the majority of debt was taken on by Alta's bankers.

Alta employees are delighted with the news of the acquisition. Their personalized letters talk about how the deal would solve each firm's problems and reassures them that their jobs are safe. However, Betro Products Inc. employees are concerned about their jobs. Betro manufacturing/production employees in particular are worried that all production would shift to Alta's large plant.

Stakeholders are asked: What are your personal views on the likelihood of success of the takeover?

* * *

End of Week 14 (14 weeks after the takeover)
A little over 3 months into the acquisition, the organization has a new name: New Alta B. Logos of the former companies are changed to New AltaB. A numberof sales offices in the former Alta Industries organization are merged with the loss of 100 jobs. Gadget manufacturing remains untouched as it is unclear which product lines could switch to the central manufacturing facility of former Alta Industries. Efforts are being made for employees in different parts of the business to meet, to improve communications. The European market, however, continues to worsen.

Stakeholders are asked: What are your personal views on the likelihood of success of the takeover?

* * *

Week 52 (One year after the takeover)
A year post merger, a few product lines have been moved to the central manufacturing facility of the former Alta Industries and one small factory of the former Betro Products has been closed with the loss of 300 jobs. However, these cost savings are minimal.

Game playing by sales and manufacturing forces throughout is evident everywhere, with old relationships being maintained and new channels being resisted.

Table 14.4   *(cont'd)*

End of Week 130 (2¹/₂ years after the takeover)

Increasing pressure for cost savings is placed on business units run by the head offices of the former Alta Industries and Betro Products as a result of further deteriorations in the market for gadgets and rising supply costs. Heated debates take place over the rationale for having two head offices. A number of senior directors of the former Betro Products decide to leave the company on the basis that power was shifting to the head office of the former Alta Industries and that the head office of the former Betro Products Inc. would probably be closed. New AltaB imposes travel restrictions on all employees, reducing rich communications.

Stakeholders are asked: What are your personal views on the likelihood of success of the takeover?

---

6. Simultaneously, all individuals in the session are given the task of observing and reflecting on the perspectives and issues raised by the participating individuals, both live and videotaped.

7. The process was repeated for the remaining three 'time' periods (end of Week 0, end of Week 14, and end of Week 130), beginning each period with the reading of a summary statement from the M&A chronology followed by expressions of stakeholder views.

8. Following the above videotaped presentation and live discussions, all individuals in the session were asked to contribute their views, including academic perspectives aimed at 'making sense of what had been said and acted'; that is, offering explanations regarding the views expressed and the dynamics observed. The 'time'-keeper recorded participants' comments. (See table 14.5.)

9. Subsequent to all participants' comments, a summary view was then presented by the researchers regarding their perspectives on the state of knowledge regarding 'time'-scapes in mergers and acquisitions. In the context of the role-

Table 14.5   Session findings: insights from a temporal analysis perspective

---

A summary of the views expressed by the conference participants is presented for each of the stakeholders as well as for the overall merger/acquisition.

Member of the Board of Directors in Betro Products Inc.
*   Temporal contradictions are evident – it's called a takeover and a marriage.
*   All actions are described with future imagery.
*   There is a strategic planning perspective but with a 'set and forget' view.
*   The perspective seems a-temporal – a seamless fantasy of marriage.
*   A 'when we get there, we'll consolidate' view ignores the present.
*   A story-lining, narrative-telling perspective is adopted.
*   The rhythm is bullish and positive.

Table 14.5   (cont'd)

Institutional Shareholder in Alta Industries
- Different positive and negative stories are presented.
- Discussion talks about ups and downs over 'time'.
- 'Time' is viewed as independent.
- The 'time' span is stretched and long.
- In the end, the view is that there is no future possible.
- The tone is direct and all about a business orientation.
- The tone is also monotone with despair, yet rational.
- The shareholder is not excited; he's just doing his job.
- Temporalities discussed are views as *un-calibrated* and out of sync but rational.

Marketing Manager in Betro Products Inc.
- The person is being pushed and under 'time' pressure.
- Present and future actions are imagined but the views are irrational.
- There is a lateness in the person's temporal views.
- In marketing, she sees the future *she* wants.

Manufacturing Production Manager in Alta Industries
- He is consistent in his future view.

Production Worker in Betro Products Inc.
- She is concerned about future job security.

Summary Observations by Case Study Participants
- There is no mechanism to force the company into a communal sensemaking of 'time'.
- All should be aware of different 'time' horizons.
- Some temporal views are 180 degrees apart.
- The M&A is not all about chronological 'time', it's about pace and sequence.
- Anticipation plays a key role in planning and preparation.
- Context matters.
- There is local rationality in that stakeholders have different conceptions of what success is and when it occurs.
- Different conceptions of 'time' interact.
- There are different agendas: 1) personal agenda relative to the institution, 2) business unit agenda, 3) corporate, and 4) M&A agenda – the deal.
- Functional rationality and the agendas combine.
- What is important and priorities vary from stakeholder to stakeholder.
- Interpretations are informed by anticipation and uncertainty.
- There are clearly different types of 'time'.
- 'Time' adds value to the process.
- 'Time' makes a difference.
- There is a shifting temporal profile to the takeover.
- There is no one right answer.
- 'Time' is spatial and geographic/cultural. Example: in one country nothing happens, whereas in another there are clashes.
- There is a functional element to the lens of 'time'.
- Completion 'time' is short for finance and long at the firm level.
- Culture plays a role in the speed of completion.

---

play, for example, comments were given on each perspective in terms of: 1) the 'time'-frame considerations for evaluating the success of the takeover, 2) temporal assumptions involved, 3) implications of the 'time'-frame considered in terms of its pros and cons, and 4) possible interactions among the different temporal perspectives.

Simulation Analysis Summary

Although the case is a substantial simplification of reality, it quickly reveals myriad temporal issues. In essence any M&A involves multiple stages of development and implementation over 'time', multiple organization levels, and multiple stakeholders. In additional, all stakeholders have varying personalities and temporal frames – especially in a global economy – and varying cultural characteristics that, collectively, are likely to strongly influence the temporal expectations and actions of each and interactions among all stakeholders. The case analysis conducted by the audience points to the fragmented nature of temporality; contradictions and interactions; synchronies and misalignments; variance in pace and rhythms; the use of past, present and future referent anchors; different 'time' horizons and shifting temporal profiles; functional, organizational and individual 'time'; spatial 'time'. This temporal richness is rarely explored in the M&A literature but may well have significant influence over our views of M&A and how we think of M&A outcome.

M&A Managers, Performance and Temporality

The preceding discussion of temporal research and the simulation highlights the complexities of social 'time' throughout the M&A process. Managers also have blind spots and biases that affect the M&A process and outcomes simply because decisions and decision outcomes are occurring at sufficiently different points in 'time' as to be influenced by multiple effects of 'time' itself. To explain such temporal bias, Kahneman and Tversky (1979), Mowen and Mowen (1991) and Platt (1973) draw on prospect theory, arguing that when decision makers face situations where gains occur in the present and losses occur in the future, decision-making individuals and organizations may fall into a trap where actions are taken even though the actions lead to severe long-term negative outcomes. In the context of M&A, empirical evidence suggests that many mergers and acquisitions are advocated by managers even though they lead to severe long-term negative outcomes for shareholders.

Similarly, managers and organizations may also be prone to making decisions regarding the timing of M&A activity where such decisions result in companies overpaying to speed-up completion of the deal. Again, empirical findings on M&A

suggest this is indeed the case in many instances. To some extent, this empirical finding is consistent with research by Lowenstein (1988) on speed-up costs involving individuals who are trading off something in the future for the present.

Perhaps an even more critical issue is that of managerial decision making and action involving the selection of appropriate timing for evaluations of M&A performance. Earlier in the chapter, the overall performance of the HP–Compaq merger was shown to vary substantially depending upon the temporal aggregation chosen. Figure 14.3 illustrates a selection of different perspectives on M&A performance throughout the M&A process (Dacko and Angwin, 2005). Within the post-acquisition phase, it is now increasingly familiar to hear top managers, consultants and M&A analysts state that organizational performance during 'the first 100 days' is critical to the success of any new merger or acquisition. Such views are now espoused in the recent literature on mergers and acquisitions as well (see Coopers and Lybrand, 1996; Feldman and Spratt, 1999; Lajoux, 1998).

Yet with all the attention on the supposedly facilitating roles of speed and the elimination of delays in the M&A integration process, scant attention has been given to the temporal assumptions and methodological aspects associated with measuring M&A performance over 'time' or actual evaluations of empirical support. For example, implicit within the focus on early evaluations is the assumption that early actions have bigger effects on outcomes than later actions. This path dependency perspective suggests decreasing latitude for acquirers as 'time' progresses, which constrains their later ability to initiate or even consider other courses of action.

Choosing a 'time' frame for evaluating success is clearly critical and how 'time' is evaluated makes a difference. Table 14.6 lists many approaches to evaluating M&A success and shows their temporal assumptions. It shows that there are trade-offs involved in the use of these methods for assessing M&A performance.

It is also important to consider who is doing the choosing, or framing, of 'time' for performance as each stakeholder has their own ways of aggregating 'time' and temporal anchors. Table 14.7 illustrates this point for a few stakeholders, each of which has unique temporal foci and blind spots.

Top managers should recognize that all stakeholders vary in their views on appropriate strategic performance horizons. Their different ' "time"- spans of discretion' and different 'clocks' suggest different expectations. For these reasons, it is important for top management to be skilled at building and managing multiple 'time'-frames and to overcome the clock 'time' concept (Lee and Liebenau, 1999). They should recognize and not be taken by surprise by the possibility of temporally induced distortions in stakeholder perceptions (including themselves) and they should possess a more sophisticated view of M&A success by using multiple clocks at different points in 'time'.

Discussions in the M&A literature on success tend to be overly framed by single-point evaluations, with few arguments over when that 'point' should be. Such temporal aggregation, however, is an overly crude and arbitrary convenience and not sufficiently subtle to capture real M&A performance. Assessing M&A success

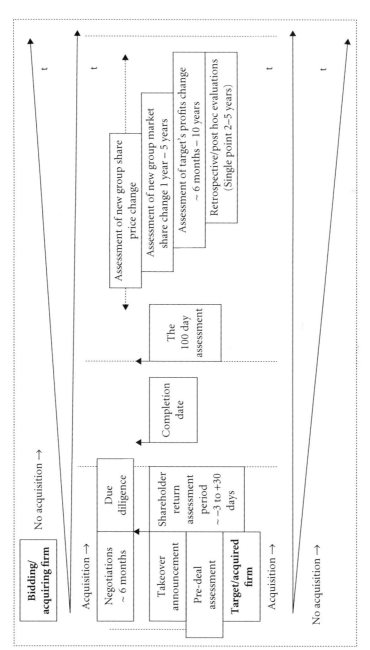

Figure 14.3 Methods for measuring merger or acquisition success

Table 14.6   Methodological choices and M&A performance measurement considerations

Approach, description	How 'time' is considered	'Time' is dependent/ independent variable?	Methodological advantages	Methodological issues/risks
Assess change in price/earnings ratio before merger/ acquisition talks	'Time' is not considered, relying instead on financial engineering	Neither	Easy and convenient	Fails to consider any non-P/E ratio benefits, post-acquisition integration
Assess shareholder returns soon after a takeover announcement	Here, 'time' is not considered, relying instead on perfect market theory	Neither	Fast and convenient	Subject to optimism; risks being unrealistic
Assess share price value years after a completed acquisition	Long 'time' frame over which to measure performance	Independent	Realistic	Difficult to control for influences outside the acquisition itself. Only assess the acquirer
Assess success 100 days after acquisition	Very short 'time'-frame over which to measure performance	Independent	Generally fast and convenient	Subject to premature judgements; risks being unrealistic about subsequent integration
Assessing extent of one aspect of integration planned for completion at a specified future 'time'	A future 'time' is the benchmark for assessing extent of completion of one aspect of integration	Dependent	Establishes early expectations for a success measure	Subject to optimism; risks being unrealistic
Assessing extent of broad integration planned for completion at a specified future 'time'	A future 'time' is the benchmark for assessing extent of completion of broad integration	Dependent	Recognizes process interactions and establishes early expectations for a success measure	Subject to optimism; risks being unrealistic
Cultural influence assessment	Qualitatively examines cultural influences on timing for success expectations and evaluations	Both, reflecting a series of causal influences	Enables adjustments to quantitative methods	Subjective
Personality influence assessment	Qualitatively examines personality influences on timing for success expectations and evaluations	Both, reflecting a series of causal influences	Enables adjustments to quantitative methods	Subjective

Table 14.7 Primary stakeholder foci and blind spots in M&A

	Foci	Blind spots
Equity markets	• Share price • Immediate company announcements • Immediate top management interviews • Preliminary financial announcements and material changes	• Integration process • Detail on integration progress • Intangible issues such as national, regional, industry, corporate and professional cultures
Top management	• Share price • Presenting quick wins to financial markets	• Integration process detail • Long-term integration • Intangible issues such as national, regional, industry, corporate and professional cultures
Divisional management	• Internally set financial targets and budgets • Achieving quick wins through disposals	• Detail on integration process • Cultural alignment
Operational management	• Internally set financial targets • Integration process • Focus on tangible returns • Progress with integration	• Share price • External financial appraisal • Long-term intangible issues
Non-managerial employees	• Meeting operational targets • Coping with uncertainty in a new structure • Job retention • Working with cultural differences	• Share price • External financial appraisal • Group performance

requires the passages of 'time's appropriate for evaluating processes of change throughout multiple levels of organization to capture multilayered learning for instance (Orlikowski, 1996). In research terms, Webb and Pettigrew (1999) argue that such successful evaluation requires rich data collection that is both 'longitudinal and cross-sectional'. But even this holistic organization-level assessment may be in itself too ambitious, or too crude, as there are likely to be significant variances within the firm in terms of pace of performance in different functions, territories, at alternative levels in the organization and by social/organizational groups to name but a few. Perhaps researchers need to be more sensitive to these sorts of variances and should aim at focusing on sub-organizational levels of performance before attempting aggregation.

One suggestion for improving our understanding of M&A performance might be to acknowledge different temporal elements in the organizations affected, so that a multitude of performances are established. Different types of stakeholder are likely to operate on different temporalities, resulting in a cascade of performance horizons so that the notion of whether the merger/acquisition is successful or not at a single point in 'time' can be challenged – what 'time' would be 'right' here?

To provide coherence to such a temporal map, it is suggested here that a 'performance surface' could be created – a surface that connects the frontiers of these different horizons. There may be different performance surfaces for different types of outcome. These performance surfaces could be compared with other temporal surfaces of comparable M&A. Perhaps this approach may allow more sensitive conclusions to be drawn about the shape and profile of such performance surfaces in general and the tensions and coherences that lie within them and allow researchers to move away from over-reliance on single-point assessments. Performance surfaces in M&A may help to overcome the problem of interpreting M&A performance, as illustrated in the HP–Compaq discussion above.

'Time' in M&A Research

This chapter has argued that a temporal lens provides significant insights into understanding M&A. The simulation has illustrated some of the multidimensional aspects of social 'time' and the later discussion on M&A performance shows how the framing and dimensions of 'time' leads to very different outcomes. For researching into M&A it is important to be sensitive to various 'time'-scales. We must recognize that there is 1) an existence interval for organizational phenomena, 2) an observation interval, 3) a recording interval, 4) an aggregation interval, and 5) a validity interval, where each of these intervals is likely to be different (Zaheer et al., 1999). In the context of M&A success evaluation, for example, the existent interval may be the 'time' elapsed since the completion of the deal, but the observation interval may be the first 100 days. The recording interval, where individuals capture data for analysis, may be a set of weekly periods occurring within that 'time'-frame, whereas the aggregation interval may be those weekly periods considered to be representative of the desired outcome for success evaluation. The validity interval is the interval over which the success evaluation is likely to remain applicable, which may, for example, be the weeks following the observational interval. The implication of managers making such 'time'-scales explicit is that it enables a more objective evaluation of the process used to arrive at important conclusions regarding the health and direction of merged or acquired organizations.

Future organizational evaluations should consider whether it is 'clock' 'time' or 'social' 'time' that is dominant in relation to any organizational phenomena as well as whether it is best to treat 'time' as the independent or dependent variable in characterizing the relationship between 'time' and any organizational phenomena (Lee and Liebenau, 1999). Such dimensions lead to the view that there is 1) deciding 'time' (clock 'time' as the independent variable), 2) working 'time' (clock 'time' as the dependent variable), 3) varying 'time' (social 'time' as the independent variable) and 4) changing 'time' (social 'time' as the dependent variable). In the context of M&A, it is *deciding 'time'* that drives or sets the pace for M&A integration, whereas it is *working 'time'* that determines how quickly and how well individuals in the organization work toward integration. Furthermore, it is *varying 'time'* that explains how and why different levels of the organization feel 'time' differently and hence why integration may occur at different speeds at different levels of the organization. It is also *changing 'time'* that ultimately results from the various strategic and tactical actions aimed at influencing expectations about appropriate 'time'-frames for achieving desired performance levels as well as evaluating and framing actual organizational performance.

Conclusions

'Time' and timing rarely takes centre stage as a variable of direct theoretical or empirical importance in M&A. However, throughout this chapter evidence is presented that suggests 'time' is of great importance for a better understanding of M&A, as it has profound implications for what is measured, how it is measured and why, and for prior and post hoc theorizing. Indeed, the more explicit treatment of 'time' and timing may shed light on ongoing debates in M&A research. For this reason, the following are proposed as criteria for critiquing the role of 'time' in extant M&A literature:

'Time' as an independent variable

1. *Omitting 'time' as an important independent variable.* Approaching or suggesting in an M&A research study that a management phenomenon is independent of the effect of either the sequence of 'time' or a location in 'time' when, in fact, it is not. For example, management practices associated with successful business performance may be examined but the effect of when in 'time' such

practices are implemented relative to the age of the firm, tenure of the management etc. may not be examined, where it may be determined that there are also significant temporal influences.

2. *Including 'time' as an important independent variable but using an inappropriate definition or operationalization.* Acknowledging in an M&A research study that a management phenomenon is dependent on either the sequence of 'time' or a location in 'time' but failing to properly characterize, define or operationalize the particular variable. For example, chronological 'time' may be used in a study examining M&A successes and failures, when tempo or speed relative to competitors may be more appropriate in establishing significant effects.

3. *Including one aspect of 'time' as an important and appropriately operationalized independent variable but omitting other independent variables of 'time'.* Properly characterizing, defining and operationalizing one 'time' variable in a study but failing to include others that may influentially interact or provide insights. For example, M&A research examining the influence of a firm's strategic actions on integration speed may consider the rate and duration of capital expenditures but not consider the seasonality of expenditures that is associated with the particular area.

'Time' as a dependent variable

1. *Omitting 'time' as an important dependent variable.* Approaching or suggesting in a research study that a set of management variables is related to a particular outcome or effect but not the temporal sequence or location of the outcome or effect. For example, management practices associated with successful business performance may be examined but not the effect of the practices on business performance over different periods of 'time'.

2. *Including 'time' as an important dependent variable but using an inappropriate definition or operationalization.* Acknowledging in a research study that a temporal variable is influenced by a set of management actions but failing to properly characterize, define or operationalize the 'time' variable. For example, the influence of strategic actions on 'time'-between-purchases of expensive market research data may be examined when 'time'-between-uses of the data may be more appropriate in establishing significant effects.

3. *Including one aspect of 'time' as an important and appropriately operationalized dependent variable but omitting other dependent variables of 'time'.* Properly characterizing, defining and operationalizing one 'time' variable in a study but failing to include other dependent 'time' variables that may provide further insights. For example, management research may examine the influence of a firm's strategic actions on the rate of its chronological integration but fail to examine the influence of the same actions on the firm's integration relative to that of competitors' integration efforts.

Where 'time' is explicit in M&A research, it is almost always an objective view, but there is compelling argument for 'Incorporating a subjective view, which would require that researchers examine individual and/or social processes. A subjective view of "time" allows the researcher to model "time" perceptions as endogenously determined and . . . subject to strategic influence [where] stakeholders' perceptions of a firm's temporal patterns might serve as a valuable resource . . .' The implication is that there are numerous of influences on 'time' that are worth examining – influences from the micro- to the macro-levels, including powerful individuals who shape strategic thinking and decision making. There is a clear need, therefore, for more M&A research at multiple levels of analysis. In addition, 'Awareness of temporal assumptions may highlight inefficiencies associated with resource allocation strategies, shifting the firm to adopt a new causal model'. 'Time' views, therefore, should clearly be matched to firm choices as well as industry conditions and broader contexts.

Researchers should therefore avoid:

1. Failing to account for the potentially significant influence of cultural differences in 'time' perception and/or 'time' use.
2. Failing to account for the potentially significant influence of personality differences in 'time' perception and/or 'time' use.
3. Failing to examine 'time'-frames of appropriate or sufficient duration.
4. Failing to understand or apply methodologies in management research to identify and characterize temporal influences.
5. Failing to recognize opportunities to manage temporal variables to achieve positive effects in management practice.

This chapter has argued for the importance of a temporal perspective on M&A. To date, the role of 'time' has largely been implicit in M&A research. 'Time' has been assumed by researchers and managers alike to be an objective background variable and this continues to have consequences for the way in which M&A activity is viewed and treated. Throughout this chapter, a more sophisticated treatment of 'time' has been proposed in recognition that 'time' and timing varies dramatically across individuals, groups, organizations and contexts. These temporal differences become particularly apparent in an M&A setting, where they come head-to-head in multidimensional 'temporal clashes'. Recognizing the importance and multifaceted nature of 'time' and timing in M&A is therefore vital for researchers and managers alike.

For researchers, temporal sensitivity may well help to deepen understanding of M&A and explain the many paradoxes and problems that litter the field. For senior management, mastering the use of 'time', as a temporal lens, may lead to greater managerial effectiveness – indeed, sensitivity to temporal issues may be viewed as a critical skill. This *temporal leadership* (Ancona and Tushman, 2001) would enable the handling of multiple 'time' frames, the creation of temporal architectures and the creation of a vision that would act as an anchor for the strategic pacing of the M&A.

This final chapter on 'M&A as Time' shows how a temporal perspective under-lies many different schools of thought on M&A. It also reveals a new horizon, which is currently obscured by traditional treatments of M&A. Raising awareness of the richness of a temporal perspective offers many benefits, not least that we may gain a better understanding of the difficulties and challenges in M&A, both as researchers and practitioners. In offering 'time' as another perspective to be explored, conven-tional boundaries of M&A research may be extended and new horizons revealed.

NOTES

1. This experimental case study formed the basis of an interactive session at an improvisa-tional conference on time, INSEAD, Fontainebleau, France, July 2004.
2. Readers of this chapter may also wish to use the M&A case study presented in this chapter as a basis for an exercise and subsequent discussion with peers as a means for making more explicit the temporal assumptions, biases, and judgmental 'time'-frames of the individuals in their organization.

Mergers and Acquisitions: A Primer

Duncan Angwin

What Are Mergers and Acquisitions?

Mergers and Acquisitions (M&A) are dynamic strategies which firms may use to substantially enhance their value to stakeholders – shareholders in particular. For acquiring and merging firms, M&A can be envisaged as a strategic initiative when they are substantial in size, requiring major commitment of resources and are difficult to reverse. These deals achieve rapid growth for the acquirer and may also bring about reinvigoration. Small-scale M&A may also be viewed as strategic if they involve particularly valuable resources or may lead to a reorientation in parent activities. Small-scale M&A may also be part of a larger strategic intent where a series of deals in aggregate allow firms to build substantial strategic positions. Through M&A, firms have a means of responding to, or anticipating, external changes in the environment. M&A may also provide a way for firms to proactively influence their immediate context through affecting industry competitive balance.

Benefits through M&A occur through firm enlargement and by the exchange of resources and capabilities. These should enhance group profitability. Where the acquiring company is publicly listed, share price performance may also improve. However within these generalities are myriad of nuances and complexities that affect the process of M&A and its outcome(s). The following section is intended to provide the reader unfamiliar with M&A with a brief guide to; the terminology 'in-use'; the nature of the phenomena; the main participants; the key part of the process, and a few issues central to conducting M&A research. Against this scene setting, the richness of the chapters in the rest of the book should become apparent.

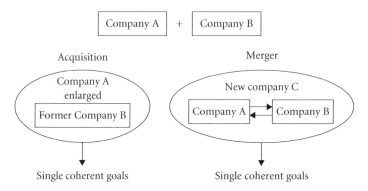

Figure 1   Distinguishing acquisitions and mergers

Defining M&A

First of all what do we mean exactly by mergers and acquisitions? The M&A process is about ownership and control. Through **acquisition**, a firm (A), the 'acquirer', purchases a controlling interest in another firm (B), the 'acquiree'. Acquirers are generally larger companies than their targets, but there are exceptions to this rule.[1] A controlling interest is when the acquirer achieves ownership in excess of 50% of the acquiree's voting shares. In most cases the purchase can be achieved with the use of cash, shares in firm A or a mixture of both. Often it is necessary for the acquirer to pay a price above the existing share price (a premium) to encourage acquiree shareholders to part with their shares. The result is an enlarged firm A (see figure 1).

Where enlarged firm A owns 100% of the target, it has purchased the entirety of the acquired firm (although it should be noted that in negotiations there can be significant variations in what is actually acquired). Within the enlarged A, the management of the acquiring firm is now in a position to do whatever it wishes with the all the resources, capabilities and liabilities of the acquired firm. This loss of ownership and control of firm B is sometimes described as a **takeover**. It may mean for instance that enlarged A decides to do away with firm B's identity, dismember its structure, get rid of its top management and lay off significant numbers of employees. In other situations, enlarged A may decide to retain firm B's name, keep its structure intact, work with the acquired management team and begin a significant investment programme to upgrade assets.

In a **merger**, a new firm (C) is created out of the two original firms (A and B) (see figure 1). Often the firms A and B are of approximately equal size and the deal is achieved through the exchange of shares in firms A and B for new shares in firm C. There is no premium payable. In theory, mergers are about bringing together 'equals' to form a new firm with an emphasis on egalitarianism and trying to keep the best practices of both organizations. It is anticipated that once the merger is completed, management teams will work together to realize synergistic benefits. Often to symbolize this approach, merging companies prefer to keep elements of their identity in the new company name. For example, equality was symbolized in Glaxo's merger with SmithKlineBeecham with a new name being formed from each firm's initials, namely GSK; PriceWaterhouse's merger with Coopers and Lybrand resulted in PWC; Daimler's merger with Chrysler formed DaimlerChrysler. At the time of writing there is a major discussion over the new name for the planned merger between Gaz de France and Suez.

Mergers and acquisitions can also be distinguished in terms of the accounting treatment of **goodwill, share premium** and **pre-acquisition reserves** (depending on national accounting standards). Under acquisition accounting, the pre-acquisition reserves of the acquired company are effectively frozen as permanent capital and hence are not available for distribution. Any excess of the purchase price above the valuation of the assets included in the balance sheet is termed '*goodwill*' and included in the future balance sheet of the acquiring company. This goodwill needs to be amortized over time.

In a merger there is no significant change of ownership and so the consolidated balance sheet is merely a combination of the two existing balance sheets with all assets remaining at their previous book values (subject to adjustments to bring differing accounting policies into line) and *no* goodwill is created (so there is no subsequent amortization required). Shares issued in the share for share exchange required for a merger are recorded at nominal value (not at market value as for shares issued in an acquisition) and hence no non-distributable[2] share premium account is created. A key advantage of merger accounting is that the reserves (pre-combination retained profits) of *both* companies are pooled and any that were distributable before remain available to be distributed as dividends of the new entity. For these reasons merger accounting has proved popular.

In the US, there is a preference for using the term merger to describe both mergers and acquisitions, and there is no doubt that the usage of the terms merger and acquisition have become blurred in practice. However, the term acquisition is used in this book, as the latter are far more common than mergers (which have been estimated to account for less than 2% of all deals). Real mergers are also very rare indeed, as many are viewed by investors as '*zero-premium acquisitions*' – acquisitions in disguise, which allow one party to subsequently dominate the combined organization while avoiding paying a premium to investors. For instance, the Daimler–Chrysler **merger** caused investor Mr Kirk Kerkorian, who had a large stake in Chrysler after his own failed takeover attempt in the mid-1990s, to launch a lawsuit claiming the deal had robbed shareholders of billions of dollars by casting it as a merger when it was really a takeover – the evidence being the brutal way in which Daimler subsequently handled Chrysler management and employees. This was clearly not in the spirit of a merger, which he saw as an **acquisition** in all but name.

Target Ownership

Target firm equity may be held **privately**, perhaps a family owned firm, **closely controlled**, when only a small percentage of shares are available to the general public on a stock market, and **publicly** available on a stock market. For a potential acquirer, if the target company shares are privately owned, the main approach has to be directly to the owners. Where shares are listed on stock markets, acquirers are in a position to purchase these shares from a range of shareholders; from individuals to institutions and in such a way that the target company may not be aware that a predator is building up a stake.

Firms' may also be **state owned**, with their future determined by political rather than purely commercial concerns. In many countries there has a been a great deal of privatization of state owned firms, with companies either completely placed onto the public market, such as a number of major European banks, or with the state retaining a 'golden share', which enables them to influence the firm's governance and its control – this may mean the exercise of a veto in the event of an unsuitable bidder attempting to take control of a sensitive industry like defense for instance, but also might result in firms being put up for sale by the state as a way of reinvigorating these businesses – a technique now in use in China with its State Owned Enterprises (SOEs). To purchase shares in an SOE requires significant negotiation with layers of government. The type of ownership of a target firm is therefore important in affecting the way in which a bid can be mounted, the way in negotiations are conducted, the rules and regulations which apply to acquisition and the conditions of subsequent ownership.

When an acquirer has achieved a controlling share in a public target company they may exhort remaining target shareholders to part with their shares. In some countries this 'minority squeeze-out' process is facilitated by regulations that allow acquirers with high percentage ownership in acquired firms to acquire all remaining outstanding shares. This is for the benefit of outstanding minority shareholders in the target company who would be disadvantaged in holding what would become an illiquid share.

Some acquisitions do not result in the acquirer holding 100% of the shares and control can change hands for as little as 51%.[3] It is possible for the acquirer to make **minority acquisitions** – to purchase a 'minority stake' in a firm (less than 50%), perhaps as a hedge against the target's future performance, or as a way for improving later chances of an acquisition and preventing acquisition by another predator (such as News Corporation's acquisition of shares in BSkyB to prevent NTL from acquiring it). Occasionally, a shareholding of less than 50% is sufficient for the 'acquiring' firm to control the board of directors in the target firm, so that full acquisition may not be necessary. In such circumstances it is evident that level of ownership and control are not entirely coincident. Minority acquisitions tend to be common in countries with restrictive regulations and practices and also in sensitive sectors, such as defence, where there tends to be restriction upon the level of foreign ownership. Throughout this book, the M&A discussed are deals where the acquirer achieves majority ownership.

Paying for an Acquisition

To pay for an acquisition, shares (equity), cash or a mixture of both may be offered to target shareholders in exchange for their shares. If the acquiring company is financing the acquisition largely through debt, this is termed a **leveraged buyout** (LBO). Target shareholder shares in the old company are now cancelled. If the target shareholders received cash as compensation, their association with the enlarged acquirer is now at an end. If however they have received shares in the enlarged acquirer they retain an interest in the future of the enlarged firm.

To persuade target shareholders to give up their shares, the acquirer often has to offer a **premium**. The premium is the difference in price between the market price of shares in the target firm before the bid was announced, and the amount actually paid at completion of the deal. This premium can vary considerably in size depending on the state of the market, but, as a rough guide, friendly takeovers (see below) accept premiums of, on average, around 25% and hostile takeovers require premiums as high as 80%.

No premium is payable in the event of a merger, as there is no significant change in ownership. The shareholders in the 'old' companies have their shares cancelled and new shares in the new merged company are issued pro-rata.

How Common Are M&A?

M&A activity has often been described as occurring in waves. Figure 2 describes the cycles for M&A in the US.

The period of **horizontal consolidation**, or acquisitions between companies in the same industry, can be described as a Darwinian struggle of the survival of the fittest. Drives for efficiency resulted in increased concentration and the creation of industrial giants such as General Electric. The second wave, described as **increasing**

Figure 2   Historical merger waves
Source: DePhamphlis (2001)

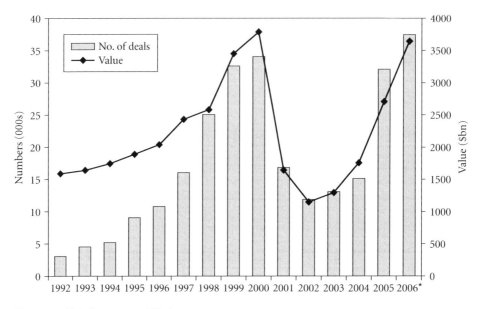

Figure 3   Global announced M&A

concentration, resulted from the US entry into the First World War and the post-war economic boom. Both of these eras ended with stock market crashes. The **conglomerate era** was driven by firms wanting to diversify risk. Large numbers of acquisitions resulted, with parent businesses purchasing in business areas quite different to their core. However, sprawling giants resulted, which became unmanageable. The **dumping decade** followed, when it was widely perceived that conglomerates were value destroying and that their individual parts were worth more than the whole. Hostile takeovers, leveraged buyouts and the use of junk bond finance were significant mechanisms of the time to takeover these bloated companies. The threat of acquisition also spurred firms such as British American Tobacco to begin substantial divestment programmes. The decade dwindled with slowing economies, the bankruptcy of many LBOs and the demise of Drexel Burnham, the market maker for junk bonds. The **era of mega-deals** in the 1990s resulted from deregulation of industries, reductions in trade barriers, the global trend towards privatization and liberalization of economies, and a revolution in information technology. Each year up to 2000 saw record levels of activity by value with $3.43 trillion of deals transacted in that year alone (see figure 3).

The last great wave was characterized by the rise of '*mega-mergers*' (deals in excess of $1bn) and an increase in hostile takeovers on the European continent, encouraged by the drive towards a single market and opportunities for firms to match the advantages in economic scale of US and Far East counterparts. The initial fears of 'Fortress Europe' as well as its size and sophistication made it an attractive hunting ground for non-European multinationals. This not only spurred acquisitions on the continent, but the difficulty in acquiring European firms also necessitated hostile bids. Although commonplace in the US and UK, continental Europe was now in the grip of these acrimonious deals.

In 2001, there was a sharp downturn in global levels of M&A activity, although some mega deals persisted. Since 2003, there has been a resurgence in activity which can partly be ascribed to a sustained rise in world stock markets, historically low costs of borrowing and the rise of economies such as China and India, creating a huge demand for raw materials and energy. Global announced activity for 2006 amounted to $3.6 trillion according to Thomson Financial, exceeding the record set in 2000 at the peak of the dotcom bubble. Interesting features of this recent wave have been the rise in Private Equity deals and the acquisitions of firms with strong cash flows, such as utilities.

Over the same period as figure 3, there has been an important trend in M&A with an acquirer in one nation and a target in another. These **cross-border**[4] deals, see figure 4, kept pace with overall global M&A trends, running at levels of 25%–30% for much of the last wave. However, they have recently begun to assume an increasing importance in relation to overall global levels of M&A, with a record $1,300bn of deals in 2006 – 35.7% of the global total.

The vast majority of cross-border M&A remains between the triad nations. However, a number of non-triad areas are assuming significance. At the end of the 1990s,

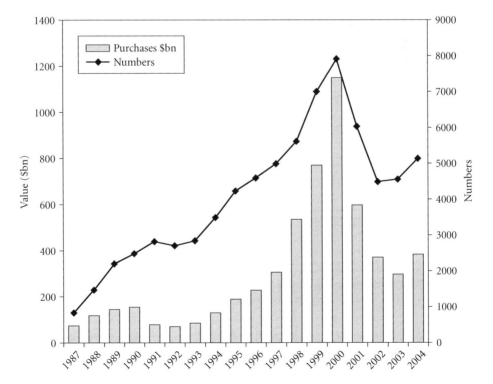

Figure 4   Cross-border M&A deals
Source: UNCTAD (2005)

Latin America saw considerable activity when there was an extensive privatization programme of utility industries. Following the demise of the USSR, Eastern Europe's economies liberalized and many cross-border M&A followed. In Japan, where there had been almost no cross-border activity, a struggling economy brought about a greater appreciation of M&A as a potential force for rejuvenation, and foreign acquirers were received more positively. More recently, China has changed its position from only allowing limited foreign ownership – through joint ventures, for instance – to permitting M&A as a crucial way to invigorate state and semi-state owned firms. Although levels of activity into and out of China are small in relation to global volumes, they are accelerating rapidly (Angwin, Thomas and Li, 2007). This illustrates the role that national authorities can play in using M&A as a policy tool for re-shaping economies.

Explaining the waves of M&A activity has proven to be a significant challenge as each presents different characteristics to previous waves. Nevertheless, there are similarities and a multi-causal view that acknowledges periods of economic recovery, booming stock markets, industrial and technological shocks (such as innovation or supply shocks) and regulatory changes (such as deregulation) (Kastrinaka, 2007) can provide a level of explanation.

M&A Participants

Firms have been described as a nexus of interactions. In their normal business, they are engaged in myriad relationships with many and varied suppliers, multiple customers, competitors and they have a range of links with regulatory authorities. In an M&A deal, all of these relationships are put into question and need to be re-established or dissolved. Firms also have contracts with their employees and these too may need to be renewed or unwound.

To ensure that the process of managing these relationships is handled in a fair and proper way, many rules, regulations and codes exist which acquirers are either obliged or strongly advised to adhere to. In the UK, M&A must conform to the UK Companies Act and parties involved are obliged to follow the City Code, sometimes call 'the Blue Book'. To assist them in this task and to manage the M&A as a whole, firms appoint a range of advisers. This depends on: the size of the deal; the complexity of the transaction (in legal and financial terms); whether it is public or private (as levels of disclosure are more stringent in the former); and the level of in-house skill, resources and experience the acquirer possesses already.

Figure 5 shows the main participants in an acquiring firm's M&A deal (the list is similar for a target firm). **Investment banks** are generally appointed to lead and coordinate the M&A process. They offer strategic and tactical advice, screen candidates for consideration, initiate contact with the seller, conduct and support negotiations, value the transaction, structure deals and coordinate the inputs of other

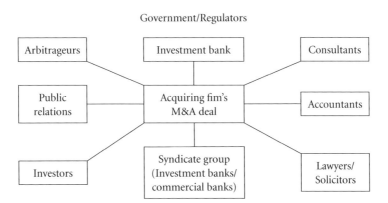

Figure 5 Main participants in M&A for an acquiring firm
Source: Adapted from Angwin (2000)

professional advisers. A critical part of the role of investment banks is to ensure that the directors of its client company fulfil their fiduciary obligations to their shareholders. They need to produce a 'fairness letter' to this effect. Leading investment banks are Goldman Sachs, Citigroup and JP Morgan.

There are myriad **consultants** that can be used in the M&A process. In identifying acquiring firm strategy and potential target companies, strategy consultants may be used, such as McKinsey, Boston Consulting Group and Mercer. Specialist consultants may be used through the M&A process to provide particular types of information. During the investigation phase, consultants may be used to evaluate intellectual property issues, environmental matters and industry-specific concerns. In the post-acquisition period, consultants may be used as general help in integration, or as specialists to integrate particular aspects such as IT systems or managing culture change programmes.

Accountants are used in the M&A process to perform financial due diligence on the target firm (see below) and act as auditors to ensure that the information provided by the target firm is accurate. They also advise on structuring the deal and achieving the best tax structure. The way a deal is structured will affect the type of accounting used and have tax implications for the acquirer. Large firms in this area include KPMG, PwC and Ernst and Young.

Lawyers/solicitors are essential for helping the acquirer deal with the complexities of rules, regulations and codes that surround M&A. There will be many specialists involved, examining corporate, tax, intellectual property, real estate, litigation, antitrust, employee and securities law. The main firms in Europe are Linklaters, Clifford Chance, Slaughter and May.

To raise the funds to finance M&A, a new issue of securities (debt, shares) is offered to a **syndicate group** of investment banks for sale to the investing public. These securities may be offered to the public as an Initial Public Offering (IPO), or privately placed with institutional investors. **Investors** play a key role in M&A. They may be individuals or institutional investors, the latter including insurance companies, investment companies, pension funds. Where the ownership of the target firm is concentrated in the hands of just a few institutional investors, the outcome of the transaction is often decided by their actions. Where the M&A activity is taking place in the public's eye, the image and messages of the acquirer need to be communicated effectively to a wide range of stakeholders.

It is also important for the acquirer management to be seen to be consistent in its approach and communication to avoid its messages losing credibility. Projecting a strong and consistent message is particularly vital in hostile bids where the target firm will be forcefully attacking the position of the acquirer. **Public relations** is therefore a vital component of an acquirer's tactics in launching and fighting a bid.

Arbitrageurs are very active in the lead up to, and during, M&A. They attempt to anticipate the launch of bids, as the moment a bid is launched share prices can move dramatically, allowing them to gain significant profit. If arbitrageurs acquire large quantities of shares, they can place themselves in a position to influence the outcome of the bid.

Surrounding the participants in figure 5 is the influence of **government and regulators**. Their impact may be relatively arm's length through the mechanism of the law, but in large transactions, where there may be concerns over the acquirer achieving monopoly power for instance, there can be direct intervention. Very large transactions with a European Community dimension may fall under European Community regulation. Smaller transactions where there are concerns about competition will be handled by National regulators. In the UK, for instance, all transactions are screened by the Office of Fair Trading (OFT). Where an M&A situation qualifies for investigation, as there are reasons to believe it will result in a substantial lessening of competition (Enterprise Act 2002), it will be referred to the Competition Commission (CC). After an investigation the CC will determine whether the transaction can be: 1) cleared, 2) prevented, 3) allowed to proceed, but with the parties needing to act on a remedies statement from the CC for disposals, adjustments and actions which will remove or mitigate the offending parts of the deal. The criteria for intervention, and government involvement in general, varies substantially from country to country. Different standards between different countries, as well as with supra-national regulators, presents firms with greater risks in cross-border deals that are likely to result in multiple regulator involvement. This is further compounded in recently privatized sectors, such as utility companies, which also have a further body of sector-specific regulators to contend with.

The M&A Process

To illustrate the way in which an M&A deal unfolds, figure 6 shows a simplified linear stage model.[5]

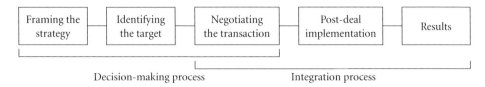

Figure 6   Linear model of M&A
Source: Adapted from Angwin (2000)

Framing the strategy

While it is tempting to leap into making an acquisition, one of the most important things for a potential acquirer to do first is to review its overall strategy and consider all the strategic options. This is to avoid the potential problems of ill-considered opportunistic purchases, which may appear to be bargains in isolation, but may serve to undermine the acquirer's dominant strategy (unless the purpose of the firm is to 'trade' in M&A). Acquirers should also question the need for M&A as the preferred strategy rather than joint ventures, other linking arrangements or organic expansion. Some companies will use management consultants, or investment banks to help them define their M&A strategy.

Motivations

There are a broad range of 'classical' motivations for engaging in M&A. These can be categorized as financial, economic, strategic and behavioural. The financial motives of the acquirer are aimed at improving shareholder wealth through:

- Reducing the cost of capital. This may be through scale effects or through buying a listed company (if a private firm), for instance.
- Reducing tax liabilities.[6] Tax benefits can also be achieved cross-border.
- Adjusting the debt profile of the acquired company.[7]
- Asset stripping (the selling off of acquired assets at a profit).
- Borrowing against the cash balances of the target company.
- Accessing cash in the target company to reduce overall leverage.
- Improve stock market measures such as share price/earnings per share/PE.
- Purchasing a bargain, or 'cheap' deal (Wernerfelt, 1984), where companies may be undervalued.

   Economic motivations are about maximizing long-run profitability of the acquirer through achieving sustained advantage over its rivals. Competitive advantage can be achieved by cost reduction or increasing market power through:

- Economies of scale (i.e. increasing volume of production to reduce unit cost).
- Economies of scope (i.e. spreading advertising costs across more SBUs).

- Increasing bargaining power along the value chain (i.e. increasing market power to capture value from the customer; increasing power over suppliers to reduce transaction costs).

Strategic motivations overlap in part with purely financial and economic motives. However, strategic motivations provide additional ways for generating these benefits:

- Overcapacity reductions: where there is overcapacity in the industry, this has a depressing effect on prices in the market. By purchasing competitors and closing them down, this reduces overcapacity and buoys up prices.
- Collusive synergies (Chatterjee, 1986), where potential entrants to an industry are deterred by the potential competition (Steiner, 1975) of concentric acquisition by a market leader, or mutual forbearance (Porter, 1985) by acquiring in a competitors' main market. These synergies represent wealth transfers from the firms' customers (Trautwein, 1990).
- Greater diversity of business areas may improve stability of earnings and reduce portfolio risk (Haspeslagh and Jemison, 1991).

More recently the strategy school has focused on the unique and valuable characteristics of a firm's resources that are immobile, valuable, rare and difficult to imitate or substitute (Barney, 1991) in a highly imperfect market. This illiquidity makes acquisition one of the few ways in which these idiosyncratic, costly to copy capabilities (Wernerfeldt, 1984; Dierickx and Cool, 1989) may be obtained. Potentially they offer acquirers above-normal economic profits through ownership and the exploitation of valuable, rare and private synergies. The motivations cited here include:

- Acquiring new capabilities – i.e. knowledge acquisition (patents, know-how) and owning innovation (buying entrepreneurial firms).

All of the above are based on the assumption that the deal will make the acquiring firm 'better off' in a demonstrable way using conventional performance indicators (i.e. reported earnings, share price, market share).

All the motivations for M&A mentioned so far assume that managers act purely in the best interest of their shareholders. It is important to note that managers may also be motivated to purchase a firm more for their own self-interest, the so called 'agency problem' (Jensen and Meckling, 1976), and also exhibit 'hubris' (Roll, 1986), an overly self-confident belief in their ability to successfully manage an acquisition. These are common explanations for the high failure rates in M&A. As a counterbalance to these negative views of management, their motivation may also be viewed as acting in the best interests of the firm, which may not always coincide with those of its shareholders (Angwin, Stern and Bradley, 2004). The degree of alignment is affected by national context.

Market relation

	Same	Different
Same	Horizontal M&A	Market extension (Concentric technology) M&A
Production **Long-** *relation* **linked**	Vertical backward M&A*	Vertical forward M&A*
Unrelated	Product extension (Concentric marketing) M&A	Conglomerate M&A

* from the perspective of the acquiring organization

Figure 7 The FTC typology of M&A

Commonly missed from discussions of motivations is the role of context influencing actions, which may not be portrayed to shareholders in these terms (Angwin, 2003). For instance, it should be remembered that institutional pressure may play a very significant role in motivating firms to enter into M&A (e.g. China's pressures on its SOEs; Nigeria's central bank's pressure on Nigerian banks to merge to improve the health of the country's financial system). (For a detailed discussion of motivations in M&A, see Angwin, 2006.)

Growth directions

There are a number of ways of considering how M&A fits with a firm's strategic intent. The classic framework for this purpose was developed by Igor Ansoff and has been used by the Federal Trade Commission (FTC) in the US (see figure 7). It examines how M&A may enable a firm to extend its activities in terms of its products and markets.

The framework classifies M&A in terms of the 'relatedness' between the acquiring and acquired firm: whether their products or markets overlap. For instance, a **horizontal acquisition**, where an acquirer buys a direct competitor, should offer the opportunity for integrating both firms' products and markets. Combining production operations – or, indeed, transferring the output from firm B's facility to firm A's and closing down firm B's facility – would allow a reduction in unit costs through raising throughput in firm A's factory. By reducing the amount of assets held, and improving efficiency through greater throughput, value can be created. There are also benefits to be had from economies of scope, where generic costs such as advertising and R&D can be spread across an enlarged firm. Externally, the combining of the firms should increase bargaining power along the value chain. Greater market power should be one such synergy gain, allowing greater value to be extracted from customers. These acquisitions are sometimes called 'consolidation' acquisitions because they cause an increase in the concentration of the industry, measured by market share, and may arouse the interest of competition regulators, such as the Securities and Exchange Commission in the US or the Competition Commission in the UK, for instance. Techniques exist for the assessment of industry concentration, the most well-known of which is the *Herfindahl-Hirschman index.*

Economies of scope also apply in **related acquisitions**, where the acquirer purchases a firm that is not in the same industry but where there are perceived overlaps with some competencies in the firm's value chain. A **vertical acquisition** is the purchase of a firm upstream or downstream in the value chain. The idea is to reduce the costs of the links in the value chain on the basis that internalizing these links will allow for greater efficiency and so add value or offer advantages in ensuring quality of supply or capturing distribution. For instance, processes carried out by suppliers or customers may be done more efficiently or better when managed by the acquiring company. This may be about maintaining delivery times or quality standards for instance, or ensuring and coordinating supply.

An **unrelated diversification** occurs when an acquirer purchases a firm in a completely unfamiliar market, a new geographic area and with different products and supporting processes. The reasons for such an acquisition may be an attempt by the acquiring firm to 'diversify' out of its current business area, which may be in decline, or perhaps as a way of reducing systematic risk by being in just one industry. The classic example of unrelated acquisitions were in the tobacco industry, which over several decades spent billions acquiring businesses completely unrelated to their own so as to protect themselves against a potential downturn in their core business of tobacco. Another classic form of unrelated acquisition has been practised by conglomerate companies who are in the business of buying and selling businesses that show profit potential in different industries. This is a form of trading, as these firms also dispose of acquired businesses on a regular basis. GE grew to become one of the world's greatest companies using this approach. Unrelated acquisitions might also occur as a form of exploration, as an experiment, and may succeed or fail spectacularly. These acquisitions by definition are highly speculative and tend to occur in fast-moving unpredictable industry sectors, such as high technology.

Although regulators seem to remain with frameworks based in particular on the definition of markets, firms are increasingly using concepts such as '**relatedness**' in terms of internal resource and capability similarities. This can result in quite different conceptions of synergy potential. For instance two firms may have quite different products in different markets, and so appear 'unrelated', but there could be a common underlying process or capability that may benefit through combination and so be a 'related' transaction.

Identifying the target

Assuming that the search for a target firm flows from the acquirer's strategy and value-creating insights, a set of criteria for acquisition targets can be established. It is worth saying that it is often very difficult to find a target firm that actually fits all criteria perfectly and is also likely to be for sale. Acquirers can throw their nets very widely in the initial search stages and may draw on their own industry and trade contacts, a range of advisers (banks, accountants, consultants, lawyers) and, in the case of cross-border deals, embassies (Angwin and Savill, 1997). In addition to the criteria derived from the motivations outlined above, there will also be a set of hygiene factors which can be assessed externally, and which need to be satisfied before any approach may be made. Apart from the issue of whether the target is actually likely to be for sale, these factors will vary depending on the acquirer's ability to address them. For instance, whether the target is financially healthy or not may deter some acquirers if there is likely to be a substantial drain on cash flow. The target may be too small to be bothered with or too large to handle. There may be too much dependence on one customer, or the target might have long-term contractual arrangements with suppliers that would be very expensive to break. Should a target firm appear to satisfy these sorts of concerns, the acquirer will begin to estimate the target's value to itself.

For the acquirer, value is achieved where the combination of acquirer and target firms, less the anticipated costs (the premium and the costs of integration), exceeds the value of both firms standing on their own. This can be expressed as follows:

$$V_{a+b+s} - P - C_{t+i} > V_a + V_b$$

where V = value, a = firm A, b = firm B, s = synergies, P = premium, C = costs, t = transaction costs and i = anticipated integration costs.

Alternatively expressed, the net acquisition value (NAV) is:

$$NAV = V_s - P - C_{t+i}$$

The premium is the additional amount payable, over the market price of the shares, to prize the target company shares from its shareholders. To estimate this figure, financial advisers will take into account market sentiment, the nature of the shareholders, the likely actions of the target firm management and the likelihood of other bidders contesting the bid. As shown in figure 8, the acquirer also has to estimate the costs of integration, which may be very large and require a substantial commitment of funds. For instance, when Ford acquired Jaguar for $2.5bn, J. D. Power (1999)[8] estimated it needed to invest a further $3.5bn to raise Jaguar's initial build quality from second worst in Europe to world class. A large portion of integration costs can be estimated with some certainty but there will always be an unknown

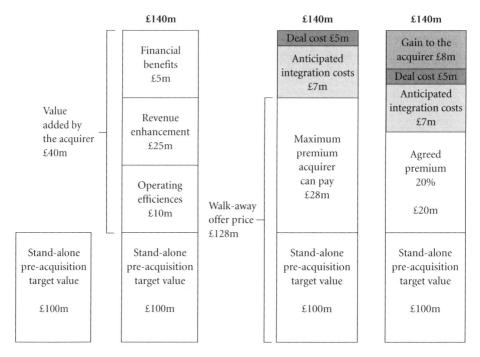

Figure 8   Considerations in thinking about an appropriate offer price

element that must be factored in. Figure 8 shows a way to think of the amount an acquirer can offer for a target.

Figure 8 shows that the target has a stand-alone market value of £100m. However, when combined with an acquirer there are possibilities for creating value – often termed **synergies**. These may come from improving 'operational efficiencies', such as the removal of duplicate activities or improvement in operational processes. For instance, at head-office level there is no need for two company secretaries, or two finance directors; in marketing, one advertising agency may be sufficient; in operations, all production may be channelled through one large efficient plant rather than two or more smaller ones; and there may be duplication of many other assets and activities. Probably the most visible source of duplication in highly integrated mergers is employees, which is why there often follows widespread redundancy (one of the chapters in the book gives an example of 5,000 redundancies). Such redundancies in fully integrated acquisitions are more the rule than the exception. Enhanced bargaining power along the value chain may result in greater value extraction from customers, termed 'revenue enhancements'. By having a larger market presence, the enlarged acquirer may be able to raise prices without significant loss of sales. There may also be 'financial benefits' such as the ability to borrow at more advantageous rates, an improved tax position or stronger cash flow. The actual price paid and how this may work in negotiations is discussed later.

The importance of price in M&A has led to substantial efforts to develop techniques and methods for valuing target companies. Finance and accounting have created a substantial array of techniques and methods for assessing value of a target company and these are critically reviewed in chapter 2 by Mark Whittington and Ken Bates. In practice, practitioners will use several approaches to value a target firm. These will generate a range of values from which a bid range for negotiations and a 'walk-away price' (where in financial terms the deal is not viable for the acquirer) may be established. Although the techniques in themselves promise considerable accuracy, their results should be treated with care due to the large number of variables that cannot be determined with complete confidence at this stage.

Should a target firm appear to fit with strategic motivations, satisfy hygiene factors and be affordable, the acquirer may make a tentative approach to the management of the target company. This can be as casual as a conversation between two chief executives in a hotel lobby, at a conference or on a golf course, or may be through a financial adviser for greater secrecy and to allow the potential acquirer to remain anonymous from the outset.

Negotiating the transaction

For publicly listed acquisitions, there are two main negotiation styles. These are **friendly** and **hostile**. A friendly acquisition is where the management of the target company is approached and they (the target management) recommend the deal to their shareholders with their approval. These direct negotiations can occur in companies with shares **listed** on a stock market, when shares are **closely held** (where company shares are tied up in cross-shareholding agreements with banks, for instance) and when companies' shares are **privately held**. In hostile deals, the acquirer often goes around the target management and appeals directly to target firm shareholders. Going directly to target shareholders is termed a **tender offer**.[9] In these cases, the target management does not recommend the deal. Hostile deals can only be done where shareholders can be directly approached in this way, and this generally only applies to targets that are public companies. In hostile deals, there are many ways in which the target management can resist takeover and there are also many tactics open to the acquiring firm. Defence tactics fall into two areas: 1) pre-bid action and 2) post-bid action.

Pre-bid actions firms can take to discourage predators, through increasing the costs or difficulty of acquisition, include:

- Improve operational efficiency and strategic focus to improve earnings per share and the share price.
- Alter ownership structure (through share buy-back, poison pills, high gearing, dual class shares).

- Change management structure to thwart a predator trying to control the board.
- Introduce management incentives (golden and other parachutes) that would be triggered on acquisition and greatly increase costs to a predator.
- Cultivate unions and workforce.
- Maintain good investor relations to be able to count on their support and to avoid shares being undervalued.
- Monitor share movements to detect the build up of unwanted stakes.

Post-bid, target management will issue a letter to its shareholders attacking the logic of the bid and advising shareholders to reject it. They will then issue defence documents praising their own performance and prospects and will attempt to make the offer look ill-founded and cheap. Other specific actions that might be pursued are:

- Promise higher future dividends: increased returns weakens bidders' promises of superior returns.
- Asset revaluation: properties/intangibles.
- Share support: white knight, ESOP, employee pension fund.
- Regulatory appeal: lobby antitrust authorities.
- Litigation: force disclosure of nominee shareholders.
- Acquisition and divestment: sell 'crown jewels', MBO. Makes target bigger or incompatible.
- Lobby politicians.
- Red herring: attack predator on peripheral issues.
- Advertisement: use media to discredit predator.

Friendly acquisitions can also include those deals where the original approach from the acquiring firm is rebuffed, perhaps as a negotiation ploy, but the offer is ultimately accepted as an agreed deal. Hostile acquisitions are far less common than friendly acquisitions and have been estimated to be less than 2% of all M&A.

If an approach from a potential acquirer is not rebuffed and there appears to be interest from the target firm, a **letter of intent** (sometimes called 'heads of agreement') will be agreed. In essence this sets out some ground rules for conducting further negotiation and enquiries. Although not legally binding in many countries, the letter of intent can have 'teeth' if the acquiring company does not act in good faith. For instance, it has been known for companies to pose as acquirers purely to gain secrets from competitors, without having any intention of purchasing the target. In this sort of circumstance, the target company will have been adversely affected and would have grounds for suing for damages. In countries such as the US, the legal status of the letter of intent is determined by its content.

As negotiations proceed, generally between a small group of top executives from each firm, typically the CEO and finance director, together with professional advisers, considerable effort is applied to a **due-diligence process**. Professional advisers are hired, typically accountants and lawyers, with industry specialists, to verify all the information they have on the target company and to make further enquiries about its condition from the target firm and independent sources. The main task is to establish as well as possible the true state of the target firm and to estimate the health of the business going forwards. There will be a significant emphasis on attempting to gain assurance that there are no '**black holes**', or major liabilities that might destroy the deal or seriously damage the acquirer in the event of a deal being consummated. These problems may be uncovered logically through thinking about the nature of the business process (for instance, a particular industrial activity may be likely to engage in certain types of ongoing relationships which may be damaging to an acquirer). However, some may not be so obvious. In one case in which the author was involved, the industrial process was non-polluting, the firm had only been in its premises for 15 years, the previous occupant had been a service business and the buildings look well maintained. However, the smart acquirer noticed that in the past the previous occupant's major shareholder was an asbestos manufacturer and so guessed that the roof was made of blue asbestos – he was right!

The extent to which the acquirer can carry out due diligence, and its timing, depends on the openness of the target firm and the nature of the deal. Any target firm is likely to want to project the best possible image of itself to achieve the maximum price. It will also minimize its disclosure of negative aspects (to those required by law). Within these extremes is substantial room for manoeuvre depending on the skill of the negotiators, their investigative teams, and the willingness of the target to complete a deal. For a friendly public transaction in the UK, the target company will attempt to satisfy all the acquirer's concerns, but will also be mindful that if an unwanted bidder were to enter into the arena, under law, they would have to supply them with the same level of information. This will constrain their open-ness. Nevertheless, if target management is to remain post-deal, it will want to ensure that there are no unpleasant surprises for the acquirer. In a hostile bid, the target firm will not assist the acquirer in its attempts to uncover information, except that which they are bound to do for their shareholders. To overcome these problems, acquirers may resort to alternative ways of obtaining information, such as the use of investigative consultants.

In all public deals there is also a significant time constraint enshrined in legisla-tion, which varies by country, setting out the maximum amount of time allowed for a bidder to attempt to purchase control of the target firm and appeal to target shareholders. The reason for this constraint is to reduce the uncertainty in the mar-kets around the firms in question. In the UK this is 60 days from the posting date of the offer document. This creates significant pressure on both top management teams and their advisers as they attempt to investigate each other and resolve all issues in a complex situation. It is not at all surprising that M&A deals are often concluded in the early hours of the morning and the protagonists look exhausted.

The information derived from the due diligence is fed into calculations to gener-ate 'accurate' valuations. Where there are concerns, perhaps some of which cannot be adequately investigated in the available time, or access to necessary information is not forthcoming, the acquirer's lawyers will add clauses to the final contract, often termed '**warranties**', to protect the acquirer in the event that, post-deal, further investigation reveals problems or difficulties. This protection may allow the acquirer to not pay all the monies agreed (where there is a deferred payment schedule) or to reclaim monies paid based on subsequent evidence. This may necessitate legal action.

The negotiations offer the acquiring firm the opportunity to understand the target firm management (and visa versa), gain explanation for issues that may have been uncovered during the due-diligence process, agree a price and work out how potential deal blockers may be overcome or avoided. For instance, the acquirer may perceive a particular individual to be critical to post-acquisition success, but this person may want certain working conditions (such as new facilities, guarantees of research spend) or other inducements to stay. The majority of time during negotiations is spent in verifying and apportioning legal obligations, clarifying accounting treatments, negotiating price and discussing how senior management will be treated.

Where the acquirer's intentions are to work with the acquired firm management to achieve post-acquisition synergies, the tenor of the negotiations will be to focus on how the firms and management teams will work together and what issues may cause the process to derail. Only when both sides have some comfort on these issues are attentions likely to turn to price negotiations. Where the acquirer views the target firm as simply a set of assets to be acquired, price discussions will assume a more dominant position.

In considering what price to offer, the acquirer is bounded by 1) the need to pay sufficient premium to win control of the firm and 2) the fear that paying too high a price will wipe out all post-acquisition benefit. Ideally, the acquirer would like to pay as close as possible to the target's stand-alone value (and even get a discount if possible). If this is not possible and the price becomes very high, it will be difficult for the acquirer to generate sufficient value post-acquisition to recover the costs of purchase. The target firm will aim to get its full stand-alone value as well as most if not all of the value that the acquirer may get from extracting post-acquisition synergies. The ability to bargain over this issue will depend on how important the target and its management are to the acquirer, the power and ownership of the target management, how keen they are to sell and also whether there are other potential bidders for the firm. If the price offered is perceived to be low by the target management and other potential bidders, the target management is likely to reject the approach and other bidders may well enter the arena. They may offer their own bids, creating a bidding war, or '**contested offer**'. In this situation, the target firm, if acquired, will generally extract far more value from the eventual acquirer than if there had just been one bidder.

The actual price agreed will depend on the way in which all the data gathered can be used to facilitate negotiations and this depends crucially on the skill of the negotiating teams. The importance of human interaction, the levels of skill and experience in negotiation, and the intentions and expectations held by all parties should not be underestimated in influencing the final price paid.

Post-deal implementation

Once the deal has been completed, the acquirer can now begin to manage the target company. Whether the acquirer acts sensitively and with minimal intervention or aggressively with massive change programmes will be determined by the value-creating insights the parent has. These insights will provide answers to the questions: 1) to what extent do the two firms need to integrate to allow synergy benefits to emerge; 2) to what extent is it important to retain the acquired firm's organizational configuration; 3) how fast should the integration proceed? Based on answers to these questions, four distinct post-acquisition integration styles can be determined, as outlined in figure 9.

Isolation acquisitions can be characterized as being kept at arm's length from the acquirer. They are often in poor financial shape and require substantial change to survive – sometimes referred to as being kept in 'intensive care'. Due to the poor state of the acquired company, post-acquisition actions tend to occur very rapidly with the post-acquisition phase being relatively short-lived. **Maintenance** acquisitions are often good-quality businesses but in areas different to the acquirer's expertise. Acquirers avoid interfering in the running of these acquisitions and instead try to learn from the acquired company's achievements. For this reason it is important that maintenance acquisitions be protected from an overly aggressive parent. The post-acquisition phase tends to see ad hoc changes over a long period of time. It can take years for real benefits to show. In **subjugation** acquisitions, the acquirer does not value the way in which the acquired company is structured and so it is often broken up, its identity lost and top management team removed. Often these acquisitions are in the same industrial sectors, where economies of scale and scope are possible. The integration process is extensive and complex and may bring

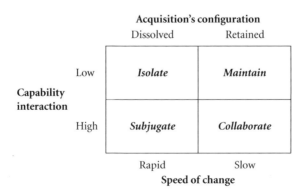

Figure 9   Post-acquisition integration styles

rapid results. **Collaborative** acquisitions are of firms that are of good quality and their configurations are valuable to the acquirer. These acquisitions begin with considerable independence but later there are efforts to work ever more closely together. Over time there is substantial interchange of capabilities but this is a gradual process. Collaborative acquisitions are difficult to manage, there are substantial risks and the benefits are long term. With each of these post-acquisition types there are benefits and risks so that no one type is 'best'. However, consistency of approach appears to be important.

In addition to the approach to integration, there is also the way in which the integration is managed. Although it would be tempting to think that large aggressive change is always bad and few changes are good, the quality of execution of either approach can make the difference between success and failure. For instance, although the realization that the acquirer is to lay-off thousands of jobs is not a pleasant one, an acquirer could simply not tell its new employees until the last moment, which would definitely result in uproar, strikes, malicious action and a destabilization of the remaining staff. Alternatively, the acquiring firm may give employees plenty of warning, incentivize them to remain to help with the integration process, give a bonus at the end of their contracts and actively assist in finding them new jobs. Although the news will still be a blow, employees seem to react more positively to this treatment. In the words of one CEO, '*think dispassionately but act compassionately*'.

The consequences for mismanaging the post-acquisition phase are often described in terms of **culture clash**. This can mean fundamental differences about the core assumptions of employees in each organization. The effect of bringing very different cultures together has been described as a psychological shockwave (Mirvis and Marks, 1992) and can lead to very damaging actions from passive resistance and the loss of good staff to sabotage (Buono and Bowditch, 1989). For this reason, managing expectations and having in place specific well-communicated programmes for post-acquisition integration are a vital part of successful post-acquisition management (for a list of post-acquisition integration actions, see Angwin, 2000).

Results

Although it seems intuitively obvious that an acquirer would want to assess the results of an acquisition, this is surprisingly rare in practice. Explanations may be that: 1) the clock cannot be turned back so it would just be an academic exercise; 2) those involved in achieving the deal were all senior management so finding poor results could be politically difficult; 3) those involved have been overtaken by other large events that obscure the impact of the deal; 4) managers have been overwhelmed by other day-to-day activities.

Academics, however, have pored over M&A data to establish levels of success and the main determinants of results. Different scholars use different performance-related questions, levels and methods of analysis.

Two main schools comprise 1) **financial economists** and 2) **industrial economists**. These schools are distinguished by different measurement approaches, with the former relying on short event windows and the stock market as accurate reflection of company value, and the latter eschewing these indicators and adopting product- and accountancy-based measures as performance indicators. From the myriad studies that have resulted, the overall conclusions are that around 50% of all M&A fail (chapter 2 reviews some of these studies). There is also some evidence to suggest that this figure is rising. This raises an important paradox and a major reason for this book: with such high failure rates in M&A, why do managers continue to do them?

There are many views put forward to explain poor M&A performance, including poor strategy, the lack of good targets forcing acquirers to purchase poor firms, hubris in top management leading to overpayment, overestimation of synergy, inadequate due diligence, lack of planning for post-acquisition integration, poor post-acquisition integration management and culture clash. All of these reasons tend to blame top management. However, we should also look further afield and recognize that the M&A process is embedded in shifting contextual forces. These frame the activities and actions of firms from the outset and continue to constrain and facilitate M&A throughout its process. For example, M&A may result from changes in legislation, governmental intervention or competitor threats. During the negotiation process between two firms, competitors might also launch their own bids and, after the takeover is completed, the same competitors may launch aggressive marketing campaigns while the acquirer is struggling to digest the newly acquired firm. While managers involved in an M&A process will focus on 'doing the deal', it is crucial that they remain aware that the world will not stand still while they negotiate a deal or integrate a firm. As the process evolves, so outcomes may shift.

Some Key Issues in M&A Research

For those interested in researching M&A, it is apposite to raise a few practical issues. The vast majority of empirical papers on M&A rely on large-scale database driven quantitative analysis or in-depth case study research. It is not the intention here to review the pros and cons of these research methods, but to identify some specific issues relevant to conducting this type of research in the M&A field.

Database quality

Researching M&A in countries such as the US and UK is facilitated by databases such as Mergerstat (US), Thomson OneBanker, Datastream, and (UK) Office of National Statistics (ONS). Large databases allow the application of sophisticated statistical techniques to enable strong correlations to be established between aspects of the data. However, a degree of caution needs to be exercised. These databases all have different criteria for the inclusion of deals (size of deal, size of controlling interest) and also have different start dates. They focus on some factors much more than others and, indeed, miss some data that could be regarded as vital for understanding the success of M&A – the intended integration approach, for instance. It is vital for the researcher to be absolutely clear on what definition they are choosing to use to define M&A because to assume that all deals reported in these databases are comparable transactions would be erroneous. In reviewing many of these databases in great detail, it is clear that there is significant variation in including what constitutes an M&A deal, and this net can be widely drawn. For instance, if one is examining transfer patterns within M&A, it makes sense to examine the acquisition of one company by another organization. To include MBOs as M&A in this context would be misleading, as there is no acquiring 'organization' involved, but only a management team. With a different definition of M&A based on change of control, MBOs could be included. Researchers also have to be careful about whether they are examining the acquisition of whole organizations or parts of organizations as the latter can be quite different in nature to an entire organization.

Researchers also should recognize that not only do the databases have very different inclusion standards, but they also misreport M&A on the following bases: 1) M&A transactions being confused with many other types of deal that cannot be viewed as the same or 'similar'; 2) announced deals not actually being completed; 3) deals missed; and 4) a complex deal being reported as several deals rather than one. For these reasons, care should be taken over interpreting papers that are based on large databases where there is no clear definition of what constitutes an M&A deal.

For M&A databases more generally, researchers need to take great care in recognizing that accuracy is affected by whether deals are public or private, as this affects the quality of reported data, and that, for private deals, the quality of data is influenced by size of the deal. It is worth noting that the vast majority of M&A transactions by number are private, and yet studies concentrate on public transactions, presumably because data are of higher quality. For levels of M&A activity, it is wise to look at both numbers of deals as well as value because in some countries the latter figure is not always reported, or significantly understated for tax reasons.

In some countries, such as China, which are of great interest in M&A, databases are in their infancy and extremely unreliable – often with only partial coverage of different markets – and therefore need to be treated with great care.

Case study data

Case study research has the attraction that it is able to reveal a rich picture of what takes place in M&A and find explanations for these observations. There are three general categories: ex-ante, ex-post and real-time case study research.

The problems with case studies are that a great deal of secrecy surrounds M&A deals. This is hardly surprising, as information about an impending deal can significantly affect share prices and, indeed, the future of the transaction. There is also the problem of knowing when a deal is about to happen. Generally, the only case studies seen on ex-ante deals are those where researchers were already in the company looking at something else – for instance, Buono and Bowditch's (1989) classic study on bank mergers. To successfully research a deal before the event can therefore be extremely difficult to achieve.

Most case study research is conducted some time after the event and depends on manager recall of what happened. Access is easier, since market sensitivities are reduced, although this depends on the transaction. However, post-deal, the problems are that:

- Very significant changes can happen immediately, with the loss of key personnel such as the target's top management team. These executives may not be keen to speak of this experience and the acquiring companies generally do not give out forwarding addresses. With access to a major set of actors disrupted, interviews tend be only of 'the winners'.
- The speed of change post-acquisition can be so rapid that the time elapsing between the deal being closed and the arrival of the researcher can lead to significant distortions (Angwin, 2000).
- A single point of time is not sufficient to capture process.
- There is a post hoc problem.

Real-time research is probably the best way to research process in M&A. However, due to the sensitivities mentioned above, it is also the most difficult method to use, as it requires embeddedness in the firm and close association with personnel. This closeness, even if achievable, then runs the risk of introducing bias through the researchers potentially losing objectivity because it is highly unlikely that they would be trusted by both sides in a deal. There is also a real risk that if the deal becomes difficult and sensitive, the researchers may need to leave and if they are allowed to stay they will undoubtedly have to sign legally binding documents that will prevent publication.

Of course, no research method is perfect, and in M&A research – particularly research that seeks to gain a rich understanding of the phenomena – it has been observed that it is almost impossible to analyse the area with conventional techniques. This presents a challenge to researchers that underlies the study of many aspects of management studies. Is it worth trying to deepen our understanding of this difficult area, even though the methodological challenges are considerable, or do we simply continue to focus on those areas where there is readily accessible and convenient data, but data that lead only to very partial understandings of M&A?

Progress in M&A research needs stronger relationships between researchers, practitioners and consultants to better understand the realities of M&A and those who are involved in them. There is also a need for multidisciplinary research with sufficiently robust constructs, models and methodologies to operate across different disciplinary areas to capture the dynamic and complex nature of M&A. This book sets out to demonstrate that it is worth facing up to the difficulties of researching M&A in new ways so as to develop our appreciation of these intricate phenomena. By being open to new perspectives and developing different methods, new horizons in M&A may be revealed.

NOTES

1.   A *reverse takeover* is when a smaller firm or investment vehicle bids for a larger firm.
2.   A reserve is *distributable* if it meets the criteria for being available for shareholders as a dividend; it is *non-distributable* if it is regarded as part of the core capital of the business.
3.   In some instances a minority shareholding can be a way of gaining power in the target boardroom and ultimately gaining leverage over the management of a firm. While technically not an acquisition by direct ownership, it is clear that one firm controls another. This is a relatively rare situation.
4.   Deals between two firms in the same country are termed '*domestic*' M&A.
5.   There are a number of 'stage' models of the M&A process of varying sophistication but readers should be wary of accepting uncritically an inevitable progression between stages. For instance it is common for stages to be reversed and each to iterate with the other.
6.   This may be through judicious application of tax loss carry forwards from the target firm, tax treatment of goodwill, or other special tax treatment, and in leveraged acquisitions the transfer of value through reduction in the cost of capital base on the tax deductibility of interest.
7.   In turnarounds, higher risk debt may be renegotiated down by providing guarantees (Haspeslagh and Jemison, 1991).
8.   J. D. Power (1999) *Jaguar is top make in initial quality*. Special Power Report.
9.   A tender offer is not always associated with a hostile takeover. It may take place with the approval of the target management or be used just to precipitate talks between the two management teams.

Appendix 1 At What Price Should Tesco Buy Greggs?

Specimen Solution and Discussion

Any valuation exercise will start with a review of the past performance of the target company, most likely in comparison with leading players in the sector and/or the prospective acquiring company itself. In practice strategies, key events and trends over several years need to be reviewed in the light of the competitive environment but we only have room here to give a flavour of this by providing a summary analysis of the financial performance of Greggs over the past 2 years.

A detailed description of interpretation of accounts is beyond the scope of this chapter but all good financial accounting textbooks will have a section on interpretation and ratio analysis (for example, see chapter 10 of Black, 2005). Changes in key figures should be highlighted and trends (over several years) identified before using ratio analysis to gain further insights. Ratios are often classified into groups that measure profitability, efficiency, liquidity and solvency, and investment ratios but note that we are mostly interested in profitability and efficiency ratios here. Figure A1.1 shows a DuPont pyramid of ratios, and this approach is discussed below.[1]

A key ratio when looking at performance from a shareholder's point of view is return on equity (ROE), which is profit after tax (PAT) divided by shareholders' funds (equity) and shows the earnings attributable to the ordinary shareholder as a percentage of their stake in the business. Further finance can be raised by the business through fixed interest borrowings and this 'gearing' effectively increases the capital employed available for investment in the business. To take this additional capital employed into account, a key ratio for measuring business performance is return on net assets (RONA), which compares the profit before interest and tax (PBIT) to the total capital employed to earn that profit, as measured by total assets less current liabilities (TA − CL, which is the same as fixed assets plus working capital). Movements in RONA from year to year may be explained by calculating secondary ratios that measure the profitability of sales and the rate of asset utilization. Profitability of sales is measured by net margin (PBIT/sales), and asset utilization is measured by sales/TA − CL. Note the mathematical relationship:

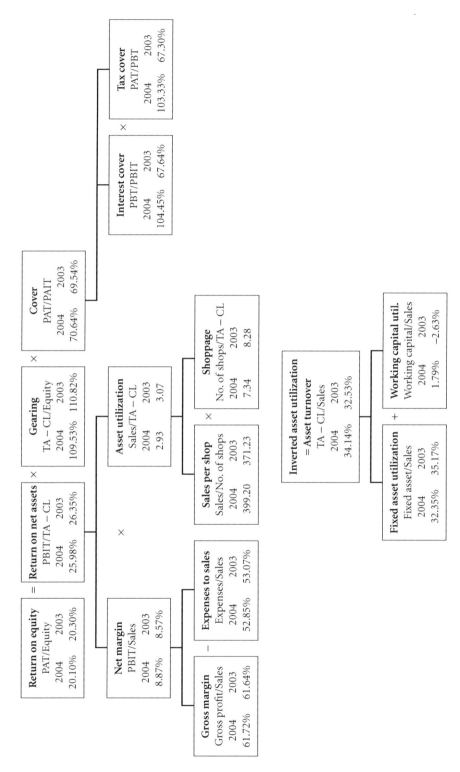

Figure A1.1 DuPont ratio analysis of Greggs plc

RONA = Net margin × Asset utilization

Hence, movements in RONA are fully explained by movements in these two secondary ratios.

Movements in these secondary ratios can be explained by continuing down the pyramid of ratios to explain movements at any level in terms of the ratios at the next level down, for example net margin is explained by gross margin less expenses/sales. This approach to investigating the links and trade-off between ratios is often called DuPont Analysis (after the DuPont Company, which first used it to monitor divisional performance).

Note that the relationship between return to shareholders (ROE) and return on the total investment in the company (including borrowings), as measured by RONA, can be expressed as follows:

ROE = RONA × Cover × Gearing

where cover is PAT/PBIT and gearing is TA − CL/equity.

So, movements in return on equity may be explained by movements in RONA (which can be further investigated through the pyramid of ratios) and movements in cover (i.e. after interest and tax, the proportion of PBIT that gets through to the bottom line) and gearing (e.g. if extra investment can generate a RONA of 20%, it makes sense to borrow money at 7% to finance it).

These ratios have been calculated for Greggs based on 2004 and 2003 results and are shown in figure A1.1 in the pyramid format. They are interpreted in the narrative below.

Review of Greggs's recent financial performance (comparison of 2004 to 2003)

Greggs is clearly growing quite quickly with sales up by over 10% and operating profit and net assets up by 14.2% and 15.8% respectively. RONA has fallen slightly from 26.3% to 26.0%, despite a slight increase in net margin, due to a fall in asset utilization from 3.07 to 2.93 times. Investigating this fall in asset utilization further, we see that the net increase in shops was 32 (2.6%) and there was an impressive 7.5% increase in average sales per shop (so Greggs is both increasing its number of stores and its like-for-like sales at existing stores) – so it is not sales/store that explains falling asset utilization. However, the number of stores per £1m of net assets invested has fallen from 8.28 to 7.34, and we might expect this in a company undergoing rapid expansion and hence now having a bigger proportion of new, costly stores on the balance sheet (compared with older, depreciated stores), but note that the number of stores only increased by 32 in 2004 compared with 29 in 2003 and hence the rate of expansion has not stepped up dramatically.

We can delve further by splitting asset utilization into fixed asset and working capital utilization and we find that fixed asset utilization improves (fixed assets/ sales falls from 35.2% to 32.4%) but working capital utilization gets worse (working capital/sales moves from −2.63% to +1.79%) as Greggs moves from a position of having net current liabilities to one of having net current assets. The question is, why? The reason that the net current liabilities of £12m has turned into £9m net current assets in 2004 is mainly due to an increase in 'cash at bank and in hand' (up 72%) from £36.4m to £62.6m – the latter figure representing 36.4% of the net assets and hence considerably depressing RONA in 2004. Presumably this cash balance is being retained to fuel further rapid expansion, but also note that if cash is excluded from net assets the RONA becomes 40.8% in 2004 compared with 34.9% in 2003, thus highlighting the underlying high returns and increase in profitability.

The small rise in net margin from 8.6% to 8.9% is mainly explained by lower expenses/sales, although gross margin rose very slightly, perhaps due to the additional emphasis on sandwiches and cakes as opposed to (lower margin) bread sales. Distribution and selling expense is the largest item and falls from 45.9% of sales to 45.4% probably due to economies of scale (as sales have grown rapidly while some costs have remained relatively fixed).

Greggs has virtually no long-term debt and hence low gearing (even when treating deferred tax as debt). Although 2004 RONA is a little lower than 2003, cover improves a little to counter a slight fall in gearing and hence ROE falls only from 20.3% to 20.1%. Note that there is net interest receivable due to the large cash balances and hence 104.4% of PBIT gets through to PBT and then 32.4% is lost in tax (in 2003, 103.3% gets through to PBT and 32.7% is lost in tax).

Greggs looks to be a profitable, cash generating business and appears to be able to finance a rapidly growing business from its own retained profits. According to the managing director (p. 14 of accounts), 'investment in shop refurbishment was restrained' in 2004, with 24 comprehensive refurbishments and eight minor refits, but will be accelerated in 2005 with 60 refits planned. Given that much of this can be financed out of the cash balance and cash generated from operations, the refit programme will not push up net assets too much and hence any sales improvement it causes will enhance RONA. A comparison of key ratios (see table A1.1) shows that Greggs considerably outperforms Tesco, especially when the cash balances are eliminated. The effect on key ratios is estimated here by reducing both net assets and shareholders' funds by the amount of the cash balance.

If Tesco were to acquire Greggs it would enable the company to continue expansion in the UK and, even if paying a premium for goodwill, it could probably achieve RONA at least as high as on its UK supermarket business of around 18% and higher than returns overseas of around 10%. RONA on Greggs' business would be higher once the cash balances were no longer part of net assets but would be reduced by any goodwill premium Tesco might pay over book value of Greggs' net assets – this might be more favourable than seeking more expansion overseas at lower RONA and perhaps higher risk. There would be some synergies and savings by bringing

Table A1.1   Key ratios, Greggs vs. Tesco

	Greggs unadjusted	Greggs without cash balance	Tesco
RONA	25.98%	40.82%	14.90%
Net margin	8.87%	8.87%	6.28%
Asset utilization	2.93	4.60	2.37
ROE	20.10%	31.29%	15.20%

Tesco's supply chain expertise to bear on Greggs, and Tesco's expertise would facilitate quicker and cheaper expansion. Key questions would be whether Tesco would retain the Greggs and Baker's Oven brands or convert the shops to the Tesco brand (Tesco's Oven?) and whether Tesco would continue Greggs' expansion into Belgium or close the two overseas stores and concentrate on the UK. Tesco might choose the latter, having ventured into France some years ago and subsequently pulled out in favour of overseas expansion in Eastern Europe and Asia.

We will now use this financial analysis as a platform to estimate levels for the value drivers needed in the valuation model (see tables A1.2 and A1.3).

Value drivers – Greggs remaining in current ownership

Sales growth rate

Over the past 10 years annual sales growth has been between 5.92% and 11.93%. After 11.93% growth in 2002, growth dipped to 8.13% in 2003 and bounced back to 10.33% in 2004, but as this was a 53-week year this should be normalized to 8.25%.

We mentioned above that investment in shop refurbishment was restrained in 2004, but will be accelerated in 2005, with 60 refits planned, so we should expect growth to increase and hence set it at 10% for the next 4 years, tailing off when it becomes harder to find good sites for expansion to 9.0% for years 5 and 6 and to 8% for years 7 and 8. From the terminal year onwards we estimate that growth, without further investment, will be 2.5% per annum, in line with the expected growth of the economy.

EBITDA margin

This has grown gradually from 12.25% in 2001 to 13.1% in 2004 and we set it at 13% for 4 years, falling to 12.5% for the next 3 years as the most favourable sites are exhausted and new sites reduce aggregate margins. A further fall to 12% is predicted for year 8 and from the terminal year onwards the ongoing margin is set at 11% because of competitive pressures.

Table A1.2 Valuation of Greggs in current ownership

Year	Base year	1	2	3	4	5	6	7	8	Terminal year
Sales	504,186	554,605	610,065	671,072	738,179	804,615	877,030	947,193	1,022,968	1,048,542
EBITDA	66,050	72,099	79,308	87,239	95,963	100,577	109,629	118,399	122,756	115,340
Tax		−15,862	−17,448	−19,193	−21,112	−22,127	−24,118	−26,048	−27,006	−25,375
Investment:										
Stock change		−403	−444	−488	−537	−531	−579	−561	−606	−205
Debtors change		−1,361	−1,497	−1,647	−1,812	−1,794	−1,955	−1,894	−2,046	−691
Creditors change		5,042	5,546	6,101	6,711	6,644	7,242	7,016	7,578	2,557
Fixed assets: Enhancing		−22,184	−24,403	−26,843	−26,574	−28,966	−28,065	−30,310	−32,735	0
Fixed assets: Sustaining		−22,184	−24,403	−26,843	−29,527	−32,185	−35,081	−37,888	−40,919	−41,942
Free cash flow		15,146	16,660	18,326	23,112	21,618	27,071	28,714	27,022	49,686
Terminal adjustment										764,393
Discount factor		0.917	0.842	0.772	0.708	0.650	0.596	0.547	0.502	0.502
Discounted flow		13,895	14,023	14,151	16,373	14,050	16,142	15,708	13,561	383,623

Total enterprise value	501,526
Add cash and near cash assets	62,601
Less debt	0
Shareholder value	564,127
No of shares	12,141,892
Estimated share price (£s)	46.46

Working in £000s (except share price).
Coincidentally, share price on 28 February 2006 = £46.46.

Table A1.3   Value drivers: Greggs in current ownership

Year	1	2	3	4	5	6	7	8	Terminal
Sales growth rate	10.0%	10.0%	10.0%	10.0%	9.0%	9.0%	8.0%	8.0%	2.5%
Operating profit margin (before depreciation)	13.0%	13.0%	13.0%	13.0%	12.5%	12.5%	12.5%	12.0%	11.0%
Income tax rate	22.0%	22.0%	22.0%	22.0%	22.0%	22.0%	22.0%	22.0%	22.0%
Stock change (% of sales growth)	0.8%	0.8%	0.8%	0.8%	0.8%	0.8%	0.8%	0.8%	0.8%
Debtors changes (% of sales growth)	2.7%	2.7%	2.7%	2.7%	2.7%	2.7%	2.7%	2.7%	2.7%
Trade creditor changes (−% of sales growth)	10.0%	10.0%	10.0%	10.0%	10.0%	10.0%	10.0%	10.0%	10.0%
Capital equipment investment (enhancing; % of sales growth)	40.0%	40.0%	40.0%	40.0%	40.0%	40.0%	40.0%	40.0%	0.0%
Capital equipment investment (sustaining; % of sales)	4.0%	4.0%	4.0%	4.0%	4.0%	4.0%	4.0%	4.0%	4.0%
Cost of capital	9.0%	9.0%	9.0%	9.0%	9.0%	9.0%	9.0%	9.0%	9.0%

Value growth duration: 8 years (not less than 4).

Tax rate

As a percentage of EBITDA, tax has been consistently between 22.47% and 22.88%. We round down a little and set it at 22% for all years.

Stock change, debtors change and creditors change

These have been set at the same rate for all years at their historical average percentages of sales growth over the past 4 years (after adjusting for anomalies such as a high VAT debtor in 2001). The rates are 0.8%, 2.7% and 10% respectively.

Capital equipment investment – sustaining

Depreciation has been around 4% of sales over the past 4 years and – on the assumption that to simply replace assets as they wear out, capital expenditure needs to be approximately the same as the depreciation charge – this has been set at 4% for all years, including the terminal year.

Capital equipment investment – enhancing

If the capital equipment expenditure sustaining is deemed to be equal to the depreciation charge, the historical capital equipment investment enhancing must be total capital spend less depreciation. As a percentage of sales growth this was 28.12% in 2001, 53.41% in 2002, 36.42% in 2003 and 5.1% in 2004. There may be lag effects and 2004 may be an anomaly due to the 'restrained investment'. We will therefore use the average of the previous three years of 40% times sales growth.

Cost of capital

Using the current UK risk-free rate of 4.5%, expected market risk premium of 8%[2] and Greggs' beta of 0.58[3] the required rate of return (RRR) of ordinary shareholders calculated as follows:

$$RRR = 4.5\% + (8\% \times 0.58) = 9.14\%$$

As Greggs has no borrowings, its weighted cost of capital (WACC) is also 9.14%. We will round down to 9%.

Completing the valuation model

On the value driver sheet, the value driver levels discussed above have to be entered into the model for the planning horizon (we assumed 8 years) and for the terminal year. Note that in the terminal year, capital equipment investment enhancing is set at zero as we are assuming steady state is reached and the only ongoing capital expenditure is that necessary to sustain that level of business.

On the valuation sheet, the base year levels of sales and EBITDA have to be entered – we used the 2004 figures. The total enterprise value will be calculated automatically.

The balance sheet cash balance has to be added and if there were any borrowings (debt) these are deducted to arrive at the valuation of total equity. When the total number of shares is entered the value per share is shown.

As discussed below, sensitivity analysis can be performed by altering any of the value driver levels entered.

Value drivers – Greggs acquired by Tesco

Sales growth rate

The growth rate will remain at 10% for the first year but Tesco will speed up the opening of new shops and increase growth to 11% in year 2 and continue at 11% in year 3 and 4. Tesco will not be immune to the difficulties of obtaining new sites and hence growth will tail off but will be one percentage point higher each year than forecast for Greggs alone. The same 2.5% annual growth rate prediction is used for the terminal year onwards.

EBITDA margin

Tesco's supply chain management expertise and power over suppliers will improve EBITDA margin by half a percentage point (to 13.5%) in year 2 and a full percentage point in year 3. Thereafter the EBITDA margin will be one percentage point higher each year than forecasted for Greggs alone.

Tax rate

As part of Tesco, there should be tax efficiencies and hence the effective tax rate (as a percentage of EBITDA) should fall from 22% to 21%.

Stock change, debtors change and creditors change

Stock change and debtors change have been set at the same rate as for Greggs. Tesco may bring some efficiencies (e.g. better stock control), but it is a relatively immaterial figure anyway. Tesco will be able to command better credit terms and hence creditors change should rise from 10% of sales change to 13%.

Capital equipment investment – sustaining

This was 4% for Greggs but Tesco should be able to make cheaper purchases of replacement capital equipment and hence this will be trimmed to 3.9% of sales.

Capital equipment investment – enhancing

This was 40% times sales growth for Greggs but again Tesco can leverage its buying power and make cheaper purchases to trim this to 36%.

Cost of capital

As Tesco happens to have the same beta as Greggs (0.58), its required rate of return of ordinary shareholders is also 9.14%. But Tesco has geared up the company to take advantage of borrowing at a relatively low interest rate of (say) 6%[4] on average and has a capital structure with approximately 45% debt and 55% equity. Note that interest on debt is an allowable expense for tax purposes and hence if a company pays corporation tax at 30% its after-tax cost of debt is only 70% (1 minus the tax rate) times the actual interest rate paid. We therefore estimate Tesco's after-tax cost of debt as 6% × 70% = 4.2%. Hence Tesco's WACC could be calculated as follows:

Equity	55% × 9.14%	=	5.03%
Debt	45% × 4.2%	=	1.89%
WACC		=	6.92%

We will round up Tesco's WACC to 7%.

Completing the valuation model

Having saved the model for Greggs' value alone, the amended value driver levels discussed above may be entered and the valuation sheet will change to reflect the new assumptions for Greggs under Tesco ownership and management.

Based on these assumptions the value per share of Greggs under Tesco's ownership and management is estimated at £89.89, which is 93.5% above the quoted share price of £46.46, as verified by the Greggs in current ownership valuation section (see tables A1.4 and A1.5).

Sensitivity analysis

Of course, it is quite difficult in practice to predict the value drivers (either for continuation in current ownership or after takeover) even after undertaking a thorough review of past performance, future prospects in the light of expected market conditions and company strategies. What will be useful to improve confidence in the valuations is to perform sensitivity analysis and assess the effect of changes in any of the value drivers. It will be found that changes in some of the value drivers have relatively minimal effect on the overall value and hence these do not need to be laboured over. The overall valuation will be found to be more sensitive to other

Table A1.4 Valuation of Greggs under Tesco's ownership and management

Year	Base year	1	2	3	4	5	6	7	8	Terminal year
Sales	504,186	554,605	615,611	683,328	758,494	834,344	917,778	1,000,378	1,090,412	1,117,673
EBITDA	66,050	72,099	83,107	95,666	106,189	112,636	123,900	135,051	141,754	134,121
Tax		-15,141	-17,453	-20,090	-22,300	-23,654	-26,019	-28,361	-29,768	-28,165
Investment:										
Stock change		-403	-488	-542	-601	-607	-667	-661	-720	-218
Debtors change		-1,361	-1,647	-1,828	-2,029	-2,048	-2,253	-2,230	-2,431	-736
Creditors change		6,554	7,931	8,803	9,772	9,860	10,846	10,738	11,704	3,544
Fixed assets: enhancing		-21,962	-24,378	-27,060	-27,306	-30,036	-29,736	-32,412	-35,329	0
Fixed assets: sustaining		-21,630	-24,009	-26,650	-29,581	-32,539	-35,793	-39,015	-42,526	-43,589
Free cash flow		18,156	23,064	28,300	34,143	33,613	40,278	43,110	42,683	64,956
Terminal adjustment										1,443,464
Discount factor		0.935	0.873	0.816	0.763	0.713	0.666	0.623	0.582	0.582
Discounted flow		16,968	20,145	23,101	26,048	23,965	26,839	26,847	24,842	840,109

Total enterprise value	1,028,863
Add cash and near cash assets	62,601
Less debt	0
Shareholder value	1,091,464
No. of shares	12,141.892
Estimated share price (£s)	89.89

Working in £000s (except share price).

Table A1.5 Value drivers: Greggs under Tesco's ownership and management

Year	1	2	3	4	5	6	7	8	Terminal year
Sales growth rate	10.0%	11.0%	11.0%	11.0%	10.0%	10.0%	9.0%	9.0%	2.5%
Operating profit margin (before depreciation)	13.0%	13.5%	14.0%	14.0%	13.5%	13.5%	13.5%	13.0%	12.0%
Income tax rate	21.0%	21.0%	21.0%	21.0%	21.0%	21.0%	21.0%	21.0%	21.0%
Stock change (% of sales growth)	0.8%	0.8%	0.8%	0.8%	0.8%	0.8%	0.8%	0.8%	0.8%
Debtors changes (% of sales growth)	2.7%	2.7%	2.7%	2.7%	2.7%	2.7%	2.7%	2.7%	2.7%
Trade creditor changes (–% of sales growth)	13.0%	13.0%	13.0%	13.0%	13.0%	13.0%	13.0%	13.0%	13.0%
Capital equipment investment (enhancing: % of sales growth)	36.0%	36.0%	36.0%	36.0%	36.0%	36.0%	36.0%	36.0%	0.0%
Capital equipment investment (sustaining: % of sales)	3.9%	3.9%	3.9%	3.9%	3.9%	3.9%	3.9%	3.9%	3.9%
Cost of capital	7.0%	7.0%	7.0%	7.0%	7.0%	7.0%	7.0%	7.0%	7.0%

Value growth duration: 8 years (not less than 4).

Price per share = £89.89

Table A1.6   Effect of changes in value drivers on value per share, considering each driver change individually

	Value per share (£)	Change
Greggs in current ownership	46.46	–
Changed sales growth rates	47.62	2.50%
Change in EBITDA margin	48.63	4.67%
Change in tax rate	47.63	2.52%
Change in creditors %	47.81	2.91%
Change in capex: enhancing	48.00	3.31%
Change in capex: sustaining	47.47	2.17%
Change to Tesco's WACC	68.65	47.76%

value drivers and hence more research and/or more care and attention should be paid to these.

We can briefly demonstrate this by looking at the percentage increase in per share value of Greggs in Tesco's ownership by making adjustment to each value driver individually, as shown in table A1.6.

As can be seen the changes we have made in EBITDA margins have a larger effect on overall value than changes in sales growth. Changes in capex, enhancing has a larger effect than changes in capex, sustaining – but note that we only changed capex, sustaining by 0.1 of a percentage point (from 4% of sales to 3.9% of sales) and this has still increased value by 2.17%, which is because this driver relates to total sales and not just sales growth. Once the drivers that have the greatest effect on value are identified, appropriate sensitivity analysis can be conducted with attention focused on the most sensitive drivers. At this point it may prove appropriate to test the figures that result from using key value drivers (such as growth rates and EBITDA margin) by undertaking a more complete budgeting exercise. For example a 10% average growth rate may have been estimated but this may be an estimated average of differing growth rates of different segments of the business. For example, the growth rate in the north of England may be lower than in the Midlands and margins may also be lower – have these differences been accurately estimated? What about new stores in Belgium – will growth be slower and at lower margins? Only detailed budgets can prove the accuracy of the estimates.

An alternative, or additional, approach to sensitivity analysis would be to calculate the effect of, say, a 10% decline in each of the value drivers on value per share. This is shown in table A1.7.

We see that value is more sensitive to a 10% change in operating profit than a 10% increase in WACC.

Although Penman (2004) recommends accounting-based valuation methods, he highlights the need to adjust for accounting methods that shift income from current

Table A1.7   Effect of a 10% decline in value drivers on value per share

Value driver	Value per share (£)	Change
Base	89.89	
EBITDA margin	74.52	17.1%
Cost of capital	77.06	14.3%
Sales growth	81.54	9.3%
Fixed assets	82.38	8.4%
Income tax rate	85.81	4.5%
Creditors change	89.06	0.9%
Debtors change	89.72	0.2%
Stock change	89.84	0.1%

earnings to future earnings and states that 'the diligent analyst discerns growth that comes from accounting from growth that comes from real business factors' (p. 203). While the cash flow valuation method avoids the problem of adjusting for accounting methods, its accuracy still depends on the ability of the analyst to understand the real business factors and produce detailed cash flow forecasts to support the value driver rates used.

Note the quite dramatic effect of the change in WACC. The fact that Tesco's WACC is two percentage points lower than Greggs' is increasing value by nearly 48% and this is clearly a key driver of enhanced value. This indicates that we need to check our calculations carefully and we quickly see that because both companies have the same beta they have the same cost of equity and the only reason Tesco has a much lower WACC is simply because of its use of cheaper debt finance. Greggs chooses to have no debt at all. We will return to this point after we have considered structuring the deal.

Structuring the deal

The range for negotiation would appear to be somewhere between £46.46 and £89.89, but of course the directors and current shareholders of Greggs may have an inflated view of the value of the company and directors would be unlikely to recommend acceptance of any offer not appreciably above the current share price. If a premium above the pre-announcement share price of at least 20% is expected, Tesco would have to be prepared to bid at least £55.75 per share. Let us assume that this would be the minimum price for starting negotiations.

Theoretically there can be additional value gained through careful structuring of the deal, but our literature review suggested that both sets of shareholders gained most (or lost least) if the offer was for cash, rather than shares. In this case, unless Tesco directors believe their shares to be overvalued (thus providing an opportunity to utilize that premium to effectively make the bid cheaper) a cash bid would seem appropriate. A motivator for this would be that Greggs' directors might contest the bid and highlight how they could deliver increased value by returning surplus cash to shareholders and this would be more tempting if Tesco were only offering shares. There was conflicting evidence as to whether tender offers provided the same value or more value to target company shareholders but it would seem to be in Tesco's interests to bid high enough to secure agreement from Greggs' directors, but not so high that they give away too much. If the bid is too low initially it will most likely become both hostile and contested, and that increases the likelihood of the winner's curse and loss of value for Tesco shareholders. The ideal bid needs to be high enough to discourage counter-bids and to satisfy Greggs' directors and shareholders but not so high as to give away most of the value of synergies yet to be realized to Greggs' shareholders – a difficult, if not impossible, balance to strike!

Tesco would certainly not want to pay Greggs' shareholders for all the value they bring to the deal (although we have seen from the literature that many acquirers have done just this) and hence the top price should be well below the £89.89 per share valuation. Let us assume that Tesco would go no higher than £74.90, as at that price they would only generate a 20% increase in value if the valuation estimate proved to be accurate. So, the range for negotiation would be £55.75 to £74.90. Ignoring acquisition costs, if the deal was struck at £55.75 the potential increase in value would be split 21% to Greggs' shareholders and 79% to Tesco's shareholders – historical evidence and the discussion above concerning the avoidance of a contested bid would lead us to conclude that this would be too low. If the deal was struck at £74.90 the potential increase in value would be split 65% to Greggs' shareholders and 35% to Tesco's shareholders – perhaps a more likely outcome, and note that the extraction of value by Tesco depends on the accuracy of the valuations together with the ability to actually reap the synergistic savings promised post acquisition.

What WACC?

Let us return to the observation made above that Greggs has no debt and this largely explains its higher cost of capital. Switching to Tesco's lower cost of capital results in a 48% increase in value (or 51% of the total estimated synergies). Some would argue that we should not use Tesco's current WACC to discount cash flows arising from the acquisition of Greggs but should instead use the new WACC of the combined company. This is a fair point but given that Greggs is about 1.75% of the size of Tesco (Greggs has shareholders' funds of £157 million compared with Tesco's shareholder's funds of £9,006 million), it is unlikely that the acquisition will have any material effect on Tesco's WACC.

But, having recognized that a large part of enhanced value is driven by Tesco's lower WACC, which is because of its use of gearing, one has to ask: why does Greggs not make use of gearing? The answer to date would seem to be that Greggs does not need it as the company is generating more cash than it needs to finance the current rate of growth, and in fact has £62.6 million of cash in hand (nearly 40% of equity value). But while that cash is sitting in the bank it is earning very low returns and, presumably in the long term, Greggs' shareholders do not want to take the risk of investing in a company when part of their investment is only earning bank interest rates. If Tesco were to bid for Greggs and offer its shareholders a mixture of cash and Tesco's shares it would be possible for Greggs' directors to offer to give their shareholders some cash by declaring a special dividend or buying back some of its own shares. Greggs could finance future expansion by raising cheaper loan capital and hence at the same time reduce its WACC.

While Greggs would not be able to borrow money as cheaply as Tesco (we estimated Tesco could borrow at 6%), it could probably borrow at 7.5% and would not add much risk to ordinary shareholders if it financed the company 30% debt and 70% equity. Therefore, its after-tax cost of debt would be $7.5\% \times 70\% = 5.25\%$ and its WACC could be calculated as follows:

Equity	70% × 9.14%	=	6.4%
Debt	30% × 4.2%	=	1.575%
WACC			7.975%

If we round up Greggs' revised WACC to 8% and substitute this into our valuation calculation for Greggs in current ownership we increase the per share value to £55.48, a 19.4% increase. The possibility that this can be done (either by Greggs or any other potential acquirer) probably raises the minimum bid price that Tesco must offer to £66.58, a 20% premium, and hence reduces the range within which negotiations may take place.

Alternative approaches

There is one more point before we move on to briefly discuss the post-acquisition step of managing the outcome. Strictly speaking we should have estimated the value of Greggs under Tesco's ownership by calculating the difference in value between Tesco with Greggs and Tesco without Greggs. Given the relatively small size of Greggs, it was felt that such an acquisition could be relatively easily assimilated into Tesco and bringing the two companies together would not create savings at Tesco itself. Hence our simpler approach is likely to be accurate enough, although the costs of the deal and any additional costs at Tesco in relation to the integration of Greggs post acquisition do need to be taken into account. A further possibility is to value only the incremental effects on Greggs of Tesco's ownership (i.e. the extra sales from faster growth and their associated costs and the additional cash flows generated through higher margins, synergistic cost savings, etc.). This may be preferable in simplistic cases but we feel that valuing Greggs in current ownership as compared with Greggs under Tesco's influence is in fact the safest approach.

Post-acquisition integration

There is a considerable difference between the valuation of Greggs under current ownership and the valuation of Greggs if owned and managed by Tesco. Hence there would seem to be an opportunity, in this hypothetical example, to strike a deal that gives a reasonable premium to the target company shareholders and presents the opportunity for the acquirer's shareholders to also gain some value. Some of the extra value under Tesco's ownership is relatively easy to generate as it arises out of Tesco's ability to raise cheap debt finance. More difficult to achieve will be the value created by faster expansion and improved EBITDA margins, as these will depend on quick and effective integration. This requires that Greggs gets the benefit of Tesco's expertise in such areas as supply chain management, and sourcing, acquisition and setting up of new shops. Our advice here is to utilize the information collected during the valuation process and quickly involve Greggs' management in the implementation process. The information needs to be incorporated into budgets at regional and even store level and the targets for potential savings (e.g. from using Tesco's supplier network) need to be debated and agreed, particularly by Greggs' managers. Although these managers inevitably will not have been involved in the valuation exercise, their participation now in revised budgeting and target setting for performance measures would be a sensible first step to achieving the predicted value. Simply imposing new budgets and stretched targets on reticent managers is a recipe for disaster.

It is quite likely that Tesco's performance measurement system for stores is more sophisticated than the one operated by Greggs and much of it will be inappropriate for the somewhat different operation. Undoubtedly some aspects of it will be relevant, as will aspects of the system previously operated by Greggs. Fully involving Greggs' managers in the process of developing a new performance measurement system (e.g. a balanced scorecard) might be a good way to facilitate integration and help develop a new joint culture for Greggs under Tesco ownership. Only by quick and careful attention to detail can the maximum value be extracted from the acquisition.

NOTES

1. For further application of such techniques within the UK food retail industry, see Moon and Bates (1993) and Bates and Whittington (1996).
2. Brealey and Myers (2000, pp. 195–6) say that from past evidence the market risk premium 'appears to be 8 to 9%, although many economists and financial mangers would forecast a lower figure'.
3. London Business School, Risk Management Service, vol. 28, no. 1, January–March 2006.
4. Note 19 of Tesco's accounts states interest rates on borrowings of various rates between 4% and 7.5%.

Glossary of Terms

Abnormal return: The change in value caused by an event (common in event studies as the part of the return that is not predicted).

Acquisition: The purchase of a controlling interest in a firm (generally in excess of 50% of votes).

Adjusted present value (APV): A valuation technique in which operating free cash flows are discounted at the cost of equity and tax shields are discounted at the cost of debt.

Adverse selection: Bad acquisitions will be offered at the same price as good ones when buyers are unable to distinguish between them (sometimes called the 'lemon theory').

Agency problem: Where agents (i.e. managers) have an incentive to act in their own self-interest rather than those of their principals (i.e. the owners or shareholders). The agents may bear less than the total costs of their actions.

Announcement date: The date a deal is formally announced.

Arbitrage: Typically, the purchase of shares for resale at a higher price – to gain a portion of the gains that generally accrue to target shareholders.

Auction: Two or more bidders competing for a single target. This will increase the price paid for the target.

Bear hug: The acquirer notifies, often publicly, the directors of the takeover target of its intention to acquire the firm. This is an attempt to pressurize target directors into a negotiated settlement.

Beta: The systematic risk of an asset in the capital asset pricing model (CAPM). It is the variability of the asset's return in relation to the return of the market.

Bidder: The acquiring firm.

Blockholder: The holder of a significant percentage of voting shares in a firm.

Breach of trust: Changing the terms of a contract.

Capital asset pricing model (CAPM): Calculates the required return on an asset as a function of the risk-free rate plus the market risk premium times the asset's *beta*.

Capital cash flow valuation: A method of valuation in which capital cash flows are discounted at the expected or required rate of return.

Capital cash flows (CCF): Operating free cash flows plus tax shields.

Collaboration acquisition: The aim is to find a way in which both acquired and acquiring firms may work together to create a transformed organization capable of more than the original firms on their own. It is vital to retain top management in the acquired firm and to work on change over a long period.

Completion date: Date when the deal is formally agreed, signed and paid for.

Concentration ratio: Measure of concentration of firms in an industry by sales (see Herfindahl-Hirschman index, HHI).

Concentration merger: When there is a specific combining of functions (i.e. operations, marketing) or a specific complementarity in these strengths rather than a general management overlap (i.e. finance).

Conglomerate: A combination of unrelated firms.

Cost leadership: A strategy based on achieving the lowest costs amongst competitors.

Cross-border acquisition: An acquisition across a national border.

Crown jewels defence: The most valuable part(s) of the target business is locked up through an agreement with a third party to purchase it (often at a low price) if, and only if, the bid succeeds. This removes the *raison d'être* of the takeover.

Culture clash: When the cultures of the acquiring and acquired companies are combined insensitively and/or are sufficiently different to cause significant problems regarding mutual understanding and trust.

Cumulative abnormal return (CAR): The sum of daily abnormal returns over a period relative to the event. This technique is used in event studies.

Discounted cash flow (DCF) valuation: The application of an appropriate cost of capital to a future stream of cash flows.

Dissidents: A group of shareholders who disagree with incumbent management. They may try to make board changes through a proxy contest.

Diversification: Classically this has been defined as an acquisition of a firm that is not in the same market or product area as the acquirer. More recently, diversification has been defined in terms of acquiring different capabilities and competencies.

Divestiture: Sale of part of a company (business unit, assets, product line) for cash or securities.

Dividend growth valuation model: The application of an appropriate discount factor to a future stream of dividends.

DuPont ratio analysis: A system of ratio analysis that disaggregates return on investment into constituent ratios.

Earnings before interest and tax (EBIT): Net operating income before interest and tax. Non-operating earnings and expenses are normally not included.

Earnings before interest, tax, deprecation and amortization (EDITDA): EBIT plus depreciation and amortization.

Earnout: Part of the payment for the target is deferred and based on measures of future performance. The arrangement is often used to incentivize target management to remain with the business.

Economies of scale: Where unit costs fall as the scale of operation increases.

Economies of scope: Where unit costs fall because of the occurrence of common resources such as advertising, distribution, purchasing being applied to the production of more than one product.

Employee stock ownership plan: Defined contribution pension plan designed to invest primarily in the stock of the employer firm. The size of such funds can make them significant players in takeover situations.

Event study: An empirical test of the effect of an event (takeover) on share returns. The event is the reference date from which the analysis of returns is made, regardless of the calendar timing of the occurrences in the sample of firms.

Excess return: See *Abnormal return*.

Free cash flow (FCF): Cash flow in excess of positive net present value investment opportunities available.

Free-rider problem: Shareholders who reason that their decisions have no impact on outcome in a tender offer and so refrain from tendering their shares to free ride on the value increase resulting from the takeover, thus causing the bid to fall.

Game theory: An analysis of the behaviours of participants under specific rules, strategies and information.

Going-concern value: The value of the firm as a whole over and above the sum of the values of each of its parts.

Golden parachute: Provision in top manager contracts for compensation following loss of jobs in the event of the firm changing control.

Goodwill: Excess of the purchase price paid for a firm over the book value received. This is recorded on the acquirer's balance sheet to be amortized over time.

Greenmail: A premium paid by a target firm for its shares to an unwanted acquirer to avoid a takeover. This tactic is illegal in Europe.

Gross cash flows: Net operating profit after taxes plus depreciation.

Growth–share matrix: A strategy technique for determining the competitive position of businesses in terms of market share and market growth rate.

Herfindahl-Hirschman index (HHI): A measure of industry concentration determined by the sum of the squares of the market shares of all the firms competing in the industry. Scores of 1000–1800 suggest a moderately concentrated industry. Where an acquisition increases the HHI by 100 or more points, it may be investigated by merger authorities. Scores above 1800 in the US are likely to be challenged where the acquisition increases HHI by 50 or more points.

Holding company: An organization that holds shares of other companies but has no operating units of its own.

Horizontal acquisition: A combination of firms operating in the same business activity.

Hostile takeover: A tender offer that proceeds even after it has been opposed by the target management team.

Hubris: Characteristic of acquiring firm managers who make mistakes (often over-paying) based on over-optimism caused by excessive pride, past achievements and emotional distortions.

Information asymmetry: This occurs when one party to the transaction has more information than the other.

Initial public offering (IPO): The first offering to the public of common shares.

In-play: Once a bid or rumour of a bid becomes known, the financial community regards the target firm as vulnerable.

Insider trading: Where some parties take actions based on information not available to outside investors.

Internal rate of return (IRR): A method for finding the discount rate that equates the present value of cash inflows and investment expenditures. The IRR must equal or exceed the relevant risk-adjusted cost of capital for the project to be acceptable.

Isolation acquisition: Often poorly run, these acquisitions require the implementation of rigorous controls to turn the business around. There is little integration of operations with the acquiring firm to avoid possible contamination. Change in the acquisition takes place very rapidly.

Joint venture (JV): A combination of subsets of assets contributed by two or more companies for a specific business purpose and for a limited period of time. The contributing firms remain separate and the joint venture is a new business.

Junk bond: A high-yield bond that is below investment grade when issued (below Standard & Poor's BBB rating).

Knock-out bid: An offer price considerably above the prevailing share price, designed to discourage other potential bidders and to persuade target shareholders to sell to the offeror.

Leveraged buyout (LBO): The purchase of a company by a small group of investors financed largely by debt.

Liquidation: The sell-off of all a firm's assets to satisfy creditor claims.

Maintenance acquisition: Often a new business area or platform for the acquiring company in generally good financial condition with strong management. Post-acquisition the aim is to maintain the core competencies of the business and to make very few changes. Some learning benefits for the acquirer may be possible over the longer term.

Management buyout (MBO): The private purchase of a business unit (BU) of a public firm by the BU's management team.

Merger: The bringing together of two or more firms to create a single new firm.

Mezzanine financing: Subordinate debt often issued in connection with LBOs.

Minority squeeze-out: The elimination by controlling shareholders of minority shareholders through forced share purchase.

Monopoly: A totally dominant or sole firm in an industry.

Moral hazard: Opportunistic behaviour where success benefits one party at the expense of another.

Multinational enterprise (MNE): A company with operations in more than one country that are more substantial than just representative offices or just import/export operations.

Net operating income (NOI): Revenues minus all operating costs, including depreciation.

Net operating profit after taxes (NOPAT): *Net operating income* multiplied by one minus the actual cash tax rate applicable to a line of business.

Net present value (NPV): Compares the net present value of cash inflows of a project, discounted at the risk-adjusted cost of capital, with the present value of investment expenditure.

Normal return: The predicted return if no event took place. This is the reference point for the calculation of *abnormal returns* attributable to an event.

Oligopoly: A small number of dominant firms in a market.

Operating free cash flows: Gross cash flows minus investment requirements.

Opportunism: Self-interest seeking with guile, including shirking and cheating.

Poison pill: A takeover defence that creates securities that provide their holders with special rights (i.e. buying target or acquiring firm shares), exercisable only after a triggering event such as a takeover bid. Exercise of these rights would make the acquisition of a target firm more difficult or costly.

Pooling of interests accounting: Assets and liabilities of each firm are combined solely on their previous accounting balances.

Portfolio strategy: The buying and selling of businesses to achieve a 'balance' overall in terms of profitability, cash flow and risk (i.e. to avoid overexposure to one product/market).

Proxy contest: An attempt by a group of dissident shareholders to gain representation on a firm's board of directors.

q-ratio: Sometimes called Tobin's q, this is the ratio of the market value of a firm's securities to the replacement costs of its physical assets.

Raider: A person who attempts to purchase a controlling interest in a firm against its management's interests.

Real options: This is an approach to value flexibility in the context of M&A.

Restructuring: Major changes in the way in which a firm structures its assets, operations, liabilities and equity patterns.

Reverse takeover: The acquisition of a larger firm by a smaller acquirer.

Risk-free rate: The return on an asset with no risk of default. Often the return on short-term government securities is used for this purpose.

Risk premium: The differential of the required return on an asset in excess of the *risk-free rate*.

Scorched earth defence: Actions taken to make a target less attractive to an acquirer. These might include *crown jewels defence*, incurring high levels of indebtedness, substantial raising of dividend payout, major share repurchase. The target firm may be substantially weakened in this process.

Shark repellent: Amendments to a firm's corporate charter or bylaws designed to make a firm less attractive and less vulnerable to acquisition.

Signalling: An action that conveys information to other players.

Silver parachute: A reduced *golden parachute* provision payable to a wider range of managers.

Spin-off: A parent firm distributes its shares in a subsidiary to its own shareholders and creates a new public company.

Staggered board: An anti-*takeover* device that divides a firm's directors into several classes with different election dates. This delays the transfer of control to a new owner.

Stakeholder: An individual or group with an interest in the firm. This includes shareholders, debt holders, management, employees, consumers, local communities etc.

Standard Industrial Classification (SIC): The US Census Bureau's system of categorizing industry groups.

Standstill agreement: A voluntary contract by a large block shareholder not to make further investments in the target company for a specified period of time.

Subjugation acquisition: Often a *horizontal acquisition*, the aim of the acquirer is to incorporate the assets of the acquired firm into the acquirer's structure and so abolish its identity and configuration. The main emphasis will be on reducing duplications between the firms. This generally results in substantial redundancies and large amounts of change in the short term.

Synergy: The combination of two firms to create an output greater than the firms on their own.

Takeover: The acquisition of one firm by another.

Takeover defence: Methods employed by a target firm to prevent takeover by a predator.

Target: The firm subject to a bid from an acquirer.

Tender offer: A public offer to target firm shareholders to buy their shares.

Tin parachute: Payment to a wide range of target firm employees for terminations resulting from takeover.

Tobin's *q*: See q-*ratio*.

Toehold: The initial fraction of a target firm's shares acquired by a bidder.

Undervaluation: A firm's shares selling for less than their intrinsic or potential value.

Underwritten offering: Public share issues sold by a firm to an investment bank at a negotiated price. The investment bank then bears the risk of price fluctuation before the shares are sold to the general public.

Value-based management (VBM): Relating the firm's strategies and operating decisions to measures of economic value created.

Vertical acquisition: The combination of firms that operate along the same value chain of activity.

Wealth transfer: The gain of one type of stakeholder in relation to the losses of another.

Weighted average cost of capital (WACC): The relevant discount rate or investment hurdle rate based on targeted capital structure proportions.

White knight: An acceptable acquirer sought out by a target firm seeking to avoid acquisition by another party.

White squire: A friendly third party who helps a target firm avoid acquisition by an unwanted acquirer, but does not takeover the target itself.

Winner's curse: The tendency in contested bids and auctions for the acquirer to overpay for the luxury of winning the deal. This explains the frequency of negative returns to acquiring firms in contested bid situations.

References and Further Reading

Adams, J. (1999) 'Cars, Cholera and Cows: The Management of Risk and Uncertainty', *Policy Analysis*, no. 335 (March).

Adams, J. S. (1963) 'Toward an Understanding of Inequity', *Journal of Abnormal and Social Psychology*, vol. 67, no. 5, pp. 422–36.

Aiello, R. J. and Watkins, M. (2000) 'The Fine Art of Friendly Acquisitions', *Harvard Business Review*, vol. 78, no. 6, pp. 101–7.

Aldrich, H. and Herker, D. (1977) 'Boundary Spanning Roles and Organization Structure', *Academy of Management Review*, vol. 2, no. 2, pp. 217–30.

Alvesson, M. (2001) 'Knowledge work: Ambiguity, image and identity', *Human Relations: Special Issue on Knowledge Management in Professional Service Firms*, vol. 54, no. 7, pp. 863–86.

Amihud, Y. and Lev, B. (1981) 'Risk Reduction as a Managerial Motive for Conglomerate Mergers (in Short Articles)', *The Bell Journal of Economics*, vol. 12, no. 2 (autumn), pp. 605–17.

Amin, S. (1974) *Accumulation on a World Scale: A Critique of the Theory of Underdevelopment*. New York: Monthly Review Press.

Amit, R. and Livnat, J. (1989) 'Efficient Corporate Diversification: Methods and Implications', *Management Science*, vol. 35, no. 7 (July), pp. 879–97.

Amsden, A. H. (1992) *Asia's Next Giant: South Korea and Late Industrialization*. Oxford: Oxford University Press.

Ancona, G. and Tushman, M. L. (2001) 'Time, technology, and dynamic capabilities: towards temporal leadership', *Academy of Management Review*, vol. 26, no. 4 (October).

Ancona, G., Goodman, P. S., Lawrence, B. S. and Tushman, M. L. (2001) 'Time: A new research lens', *Academy of Management Review*, vol. 26, no. 4 (October), pp. 645–63.

Andersen Consulting (1999) *Global Survey Acquisition and Alliance Integration*. 1999 Report.

Anderson, B. (1983) *Imagined Communities: Reflections on the Origin and Spread of Nationalism*. London: Verso Editions and NLB.

Andrade, G., Mitchell, M. and Stafford, E. (2001) 'New evidence and perspectives on mergers', *Journal of Economic Perspectives*, vol. 15 (spring), pp. 103–20.

Andrews, K. R. (1971) *The Concept of Corporate Strategy*. Homewood, IL: Dow Jones Irwin.

Angwin, D. N. (2000) *Implementing Successful Post-Acquisition Management*. Senior Executive Briefing, Financial Times Management Series/Prentice Hall.

Angwin, D. N. (2001) 'Mergers and acquisitions across European borders: national perspectives on pre-acquisition due diligence and the use of professional advisors', *Journal of World Business*, vol. 36, no. 1, pp. 32–57.

Angwin, D. N. (2003) 'Strategy as exploration and interconnection'. Chapter 8 in S. Cummings and D. W. Wilson (eds) *Images of Strategy*. Oxford: Blackwell, pp. 228–65.

Angwin, D. N. (2004) 'Speed in M&A integration: the first 100 days', *European Management Journal*, vol. 22, no. 4, pp. 418–30.

Angwin, D. N. (2006) 'Motive architypes in mergers and acquisitions (M&A): The implications of a configurational approach to performance', Strategic Management Conference, Vienna.

Angwin, D. N. and Ernst & Young Consultants (1997) *The first 90 days*. Ernst & Young, pp. 1–14.

Angwin, D. N. and Savill, B. (1997) 'Strategic perspectives on European cross-border acquisitions – a view from top European executives', *European Management Journal*, vol. 15, no. 4, pp. 423–35.

Angwin, D. N. and Vaara, E. (2005) ' "Connectivity" in merging organizations: Beyond traditional cultural perspectives', Special Issue, *Organization Studies*, vol. 26, no. 10, pp. 1447–56.

Angwin, D. N., Stern, P. and Bradley, S. (2004) 'Agent or Steward? The target CEO in a hostile takeover: can a condemned agent be redeemed?' *Long Range Planning*, vol. 37, no. 3, pp. 239–57.

Angwin, D. N., Thomas, H. and Li, X. (2007) 'Mergers and Acquisitions into China: A Review and Research Agenda', paper submitted to Academy of International Business Conference, Indianapolis, June.

Ansoff, H. I., Brandenburg, R. G., Portner, F. E. and Radosevich, R. (1971) *Acquisition Behaviour of US Manufacturing Firms, 1946–1965*. Nashville, TN: Vanderbilt University Press.

Arikan, A. M. (2004) 'Does it pay to capture intangible assets through mergers and acquisitions?' In A. L. Pablo and M. Javidan (eds) *Mergers and Acquisitions: Creating Integrative Knowledge*. Oxford: Blackwell Publishing.

Arrow, K. J. (1965) *Aspects of the Theory of Risk Bearing*. Helsinki, Finland: The Academic Book Store.

Ashford, B. E., Kreiner, G. E. and Fulgate, M. (2000) 'All in a Day's Work: Boundaries and Micro Role Transitions', *Academy of Management Review*, vol. 25, no. 3, pp. 472–91.

Ashforth, B. and Mael, F. (1989) 'Social identity theory and the organization', *Academy of Management Review*, vol. 14, no. 1, pp. 20–39.

Ashkenas, R. N., DeMonaco, L. J. and Francis, S. C. (1998) 'Making the deal real: How GE Capital integrates acquisitions', *Harvard Business Review*, vol. 76, no. 1 (January–February), pp. 165–78.

Bacharach, S. B., Bamberger, P. and McKinney, V. (2000) 'Boundary Management Tactics and Logics of Action: The Case of Peer-Support Providers', *Administrative Science Quarterly*, vol. 45, no. 4, pp. 704–36.

Baird, I. S. and Thomas, H. (1990) 'What is risk anyway?' In R. A. Bettis and H. Thomas (eds) *Risk, Strategy and Management*. Greenwich, CT: JAI Press, pp. 21–52.

Barca, F. and Becht, M. (eds) (2001) *The Control of Corporate Europe*. Oxford: Oxford University Press.

Barney, J. (1991) 'Resources and Sustained Competitive Advantage', *Journal of Management*, vol. 17, no. 1 (March), pp. 99–120.

Barney, J. (1999) 'How a firm's capabilities affect boundary decisions', *Sloan Management Review*, vol. 40, no. 3, pp. 137–46.

Bartlett, C. A. and Ghoshal, S. (1987) 'Managing across borders: New organizational responses', *Sloan Management Review*, vol. 29, no. 1, pp. 43–54.

Bartlett, C. A. and Ghoshal, S. (1998) *Managing Across Borders: The Transnational Solution* (2nd edn). Boston: Harvard Business School Publishing.

Bates, K. and Whittington, M. (1996) 'Intense Competition, Revised Strategies and Financial Performance in the UK Food Retailing Sector'. In J. Nilsson and G. van Dijk (eds) *Strategies and Structures in the Agro-food Industries*. Assen, The Netherlands: Van Gorcum.

Bauer, T. N., Morrison, E. W. and Callister, R. P. (1998) 'Organizational socialization: A review and directions for future research'. In G. R. Ferris (ed.) *Research in Personnel and Human Resource Management*, vol. 16. Greenwich, CT: JAI Press, pp. 149–214.

Bebchuk, L. A. and Ferrell, A. (1999) 'Federalism and Corporate Law: The race to protect managers from takeovers', *Columbia Law Review*, vol. 99, p. 1168.

Belcher, T. and Nail, L. (2001) 'Culture clashes and integration problems in cross-border mergers: A clinical examination of the Pharmacia–Upjohn merger'. In L. A. Nail (ed.) *Issues in International Corporate Control and Governance*, vol. 15. Greenwich, CT: JAI Press, pp. 353–70.

Belsky, G. and Gilovich, T. (1999) *Why Smart People Make Big Money Mistakes and How to Correct Them*. New York: Simon & Schuster.

Berglund, J. and Löwstedt, J. (1996) 'The fate of human resource management in a folkish society'. In T. Clark (ed.) *European Human Resource Management*. Oxford: Blackwell.

Billig, M. (1995) *Banal Nationalism*. London: Sage.

Birkinshaw, J. (2000) *Entrepreneurship in the Global Firm*. London: Sage.

Birkinshaw, J. and Hagstrom, P. (eds) (2000) *The Flexible Firm: Capability Management in Network Organisations*. Oxford: Oxford University Press.

Birkinshaw, J., Bresman, H. and Hakanson, L. (2000). 'Managing the post-acquisition integration process: How the human integration and task integration processes interact to foster value creation', *Journal of Management Studies*, vol. 37, no. 3, pp. 395–425.

Björkman, I. and Vaara, E. (2004) *Nordea Markets: Socio-cultural integration challenges*. Published by the case library of the Helsinki School of Economics and the European Case Clearing House.

Black, G. (2005) *Introduction to Accounting and Finance*. Pearson Education.

Bloch, L. and Kremp, E. (2001) 'Ownership and Voting Power in France'. Chapter 4 in F. Barca and M. Becht (eds) *The Control of Corporate Europe*, Oxford: Oxford University Press, p. 106.

Blount, S. and Janicik, G. A. (2001) 'When plans change: Examining how people evaluate timing changes in work organizations', *Academy of Management Review*, vol. 26, no. 4, pp. 566–85.

Bluedorn, A. C. and Denhardt, R. B. (1988) Time and organizations. *Journal of Management*, vol. 14, no. 2, pp. 299–320.

Boons, F. and Strannegard, L. (2000) 'Organizations coping with their environment', *International Studies of Management and Organizations*, vol. 3, no. 3, pp. 7–17.

Bower, J. L. (2001) 'Not all M&As are alike – and that matters', *Harvard Business Review*, vol. 79, no. 3, pp. 93–101.

Bower, J. L. (2004) 'When we study M&A, what are we learning?' Chapter 13 in A. L. Pablo and M. Javidan (eds) *Mergers and Acquisitions: Creating Integrative Knowledge*. Oxford: Strategic Management Society, Blackwell Publishing.

Boyd, J. (2003) 'A quest for Cinergy: The war metaphor and the construction of identity', *Communication Studies*, vol. 54, no. 3, pp. 249–65.

Boyle, R. and Haynes, R. (1996) ' "The Grand Old Game": Football, media and identity in Scotland', *Media, Culture and Society*, vol. 18, pp. 549–64.

Bradley, M., Desai, A. and Kim, E. H. (1983) 'The rationale between interfirm tender offers: information or synergy?' *Journal of Financial Economics*, vol. 11, nos. 1–4, pp. 183–206.

Bradley, M., Desai, A. and Kim, E. H. (1988) 'Synergistic gains from corporate acquisitions and their division between the stockholders of target and acquiring firms'. *Journal of Financial Economics*, vol. 21, no. 1, pp. 3–40.

Breakwell, G. M. and Lyons, E. (1996) *Changing European Identities: Social Psychological Analyses of Social Change*. Oxford: Butterworth-Heinemann.

Brealey, R. A. and Myers, S. C. (1981) *Principles of Corporate Finance*. McGraw-Hill.

Brealey, R. A. and Myers, S. C. (2000) *Principles of Corporate Finance*, 6th edn. New York: McGraw-Hill.

Brealey, R. A., Myers, S. C. and Allen, F. (2006) *Corporate Finance*, 8th edn. New York: McGraw-Hill Irwin.

Bresman, H., Birkinshaw, J. and Nobel, R. (1999) 'Knowledge transfer in international acquisitions', *Journal of International Business*, vol. 30, no. 3, pp. 439–62.

Brookes, R. (1999) 'Newspapers and national identity: The BSE/CJD crisis and the British press', *Media, Culture and Society*, vol. 21, no. 2, pp. 247–63.

Brooks, G. R. (1995) 'Defining market boundaries', *Strategic Management Journal*, vol. 16, no. 7, pp. 535–49.

Broyles, J. (2003) *Financial Management and Real Options*. John Wiley.

Bruner, R. F. (2002) 'Does M&A pay? A survey of evidence for the decision-maker', *Journal of Applied Finance*, vol. 12, no. 1, pp. 48–68.

Bruner, R. F., Eades, K. M., Harris, R. S. and Higgins, R. C. (1998) 'Best practices in estimating the cost of capital: Survey and synthesis', *Financial Practice and Education*, vol. 8, pp. 13–28.

Bruun, S. and Wallén, M. (1999) *Nokian valtatie*. Helsinki: Tammi. [*Nokia's Highway*.]

Buono, A. F. and Bowditch, J. L. (1989) *The Human Side of Mergers and Acquisitions: Managing Collisions Between People and Organizations*. San Francisco: Jossey-Bass.

Buono, A. F., Bowditch, J. L. and Lewis, J. (1985) 'When cultures collide: The anatomy of a merger', *Human Relations*, vol. 38, no. 5, pp. 477–500.

Burt, T. and Harney, A. (1999) 'Le cost-killer makes his move', *Financial Times*, 9 November 1999.

Calas, M. and Smircich, L. (1991) 'Voicing Seduction to Silence Leadership', *Organization Studies*, vol. 12, no. 4, pp. 567–602.

Calori, R. and De Woot, P. (1994) *A European Management Model: Beyond Diversity*. Prentice Hall.

Campbell, A., Yeung, S. and Devine, M. (1993) *A Sense of Mission*. London: FT/Pitman.

Cardoso, F. H. and Faletto, E. (1971) *Dependency and Development in Latin America*. Berkeley: University of California Press.

Carey, D. (2000) 'Lessons From Master Acquirers: A CEO Roundtable on Making Mergers Succeed', *Harvard Business Review*, vol. 78, no. 3 (May–June), pp. 145–54.

Cartwright, S. and Cooper, C. L. (1992) *Mergers and Acquisitions: The Human Factor*. Oxford: Butterworth-Heinemann.

Cartwright, S. and Cooper, C. L. (1995) 'Organizational marriages: "Hard" versus "Soft" issues', *Personnel Review*, vol. 24, no. 3, pp. 32–42.

Cartwright, S. and Cooper, C. L. (1997) *Managing Mergers, Acquisitions and Strategic Alliances: Integrating People and Cultures*. Oxford: Butterworth-Heinemann.

Chamberlain, S. L. and Tennyson, S. (1998) 'Capital shocks and merger activity in the property-liability insurance industry', *The Journal of Risk and Insurance*, vol. 65, no. 4 (December), pp. 563–95.

Chao, G. T. et al. (1994) 'Organizational Socialization: Its Content and Consequences', *Journal of Applied Psychology*, vol. 79, no. 5, pp. 730–43.

Charles, M.-L. and Louhiala-Salminen, L. (2005) 'Kenen kieltä puhutaan, missä kulttuurissa toimitaan: suomalais–ruotsalaiset yritysfuusiot'. In Olli Kangas and Helena Kangasharju (eds) *Ordens makt och maktens ord*. Helsinki: Svenska Litteratursällskapet. [Whose language do we speak? What culture do we operate in? Finnish–Swedish corporate mergers.]

Chatterjee, S. (1986) 'Types of synergy and economic value: the impact of acquisitions on merging and rival firms', *Strategic Management Journal*, vol. 7, no. 2, pp. 119–39.

Chatterjee, S. and Lubatkin, M. (1990) 'Corporate mergers, stockholder diversification and changes in systematic risk', *Strategic Management Journal*, vol. 11, no. 4, pp. 255–68.

Chatterjee, S., Lubatkin, M. and Schoenecker, T. (1992) 'Vertical strategies and market structure: A systematic risk analysis', *Organization Science*, vol. 3, no. 1 (February), pp. 138–56.

Chatterjee, S., Lubatkin, M., Schweiger, D. M. and Weber, Y. (1992) 'Cultural differences and shareholder value in related mergers: Linking equity and human capital', *Strategic Management Journal*, vol. 13, no. 5, pp. 319–34.

Checkland, P. (1993) *Systems Thinking, Systems Practice*. Chichester: Wiley.

Checkland, P. and Scholes, J. (1990) *Soft Systems Methodologies in Action*. Chichester: Wiley.

Chia, R. (1996) 'Metaphors and metaphorization in organizational analysis: Thinking beyond the unthinkable.' In D. Grant and C. Oswick (eds) *Metaphor and Organizations*. Thousand Oaks: CA: Sage, pp. 127–45.

Child, J., Faulkner, D. and Pitkethly, R. (2001) *The Management of International Acquisitions*. Oxford: Oxford University Press.

Chow, I. H. (2002) 'Organizational Socialization and Career Success of Asian Managers', *International Journal of Human Resource Management*, vol. 13, no. 4, pp. 720–37.

Chunlai Chen, Z. and Findlay, C. (2003) 'A review of cross-border mergers and acquisitions in APEC', *Asian-Pacific Economic Literature*, vol. 17, no. 2 (November), pp. 14–39.

Clark, T. (2004) 'Guest Editor's Introduction; Controversies and continuities in management studies: Essays in honour of Karen Legge', *Journal of Management Studies*, vol. 41, no. 3, pp. 367–77.

Clegg, S. (1989) *Frameworks of Power*. London: Sage.

Clegg, S. (1990) *Modern Organisations: Organisation Studies in the Postmodern World.* London: Sage.

Collins, G. (2005) 'The gendered nature of mergers', *Gender, Work and Organization,* vol. 12, no. 3, pp. 270–90.

Collinson, S. C. (2001) 'Knowledge management capabilities in R&D: A UK–Japan company comparison', *R&D Management,* vol. 31, no. 3, pp. 335–47.

Collinson, S. C. and Wilson, D. C. (2006) 'Inertia in Japanese organizations: Knowledge management routines and failure to innovate', *Organization Studies,* vol. 27, no. 9, pp. 1359–87.

Conference Board, The (2000) *Performance Measurement During Merger and Acquisition Integration.* Report 1274-00.

Connery. D. C. (1966) *The Scandinavians.* London: Eyre & Spottiswoode.

Cooke, M. (1993) 'Man retelling the war myth'. In M. Cooke and A. Woollacott (eds) *Gendering War Talk.* Princeton, NJ: Princeton University Press, pp. 177–204.

Coopers and Lybrand (1996) *Speed Makes the Difference: A Survey of Mergers and Acquisitions.* London: Coopers and Lybrand.

Corbett, M. (1994) *Critical Cases in Organisational Behaviour.* London: The MacMillan Press.

Crouch, C. and Streeck, W. (1997) *Political Economy of Modern Capitalism: Mapping Convergence and Diversity.* London: Sage.

Cummings, S. (2004) *Recreating Strategy.* London: Sage Publications.

Cummings, S. and Angwin, D. N. (2004) 'The future shape of strategy: Lemmings and Chimeras', *Academy of Management Executive,* vol. 18, no. 2, pp. 21–36.

Cummings, S. and Davies, J. (1994) 'Mission, Vision, Fusion', *Long Range Planning,* vol. 27, no. 6, pp. 147–50.

Cummings, S. and Wilson, D. W. (eds) (2003) *Images of Strategy.* Oxford: Blackwell.

D'Aveni R. A. and Ilinitch, A. Y. (1992) 'Complex patterns of vertical integration in the forest products industry: systematic and bankruptcy risks', *Academy of Management Journal,* vol. 35, no. 3 (August), pp. 596–625.

Dacko, S. and Angwin, D. N. (2005) '100 Days since the merger or acquisition: time to evaluate success?' *In Search of Time.* Palermo, Sicily, Chapter 5.

Datta, D. K., Narayanan, V. K. and Pinches, G. E. (1992) 'Factors influencing wealth creation from mergers and acquisitions: a meta-analysis', *Strategic Management Journal,* vol. 13, no. 1, pp. 67–84.

Davenport, T. and Prusak, L. (1998) *Working Knowledge: How Organizations Manage What They Know.* Boston: Harvard Business School Press.

Davies, P. L. (2003) 'Institutional investors as corporate monitors in the UK'. In K. J. Hopt and E. Wymeersch, E. (eds) *Capital Markets and Company Law.* Oxford: Oxford University Press.

Davis, G. F. and Stout, S. K. (1992) 'Organization theory and the market for corporate control: a dynamic analysis of the characteristics of large takeover targets, 1980–1990', *Administrative Science Quarterly,* vol. 37, no. 4 (December), pp. 605–33.

Davis, J. H. (1982) 'Social interaction as a combinational process in group decision.' In H. Brandstatter, J. H. Davis, and G. Stocker-Kreichgauer (eds) *Group Decision Making.* London: Academic Press, pp. 27–58.

Davis, P. S., Desai, A. B. and Francis, J. D. (2000) 'Mode of international entry: an isomorphism perspective', *Journal of International Business Studies,* vol. 31, no. 2, pp. 239–58.

Dawes, J. (2002) *The Language of War*. Cambridge, MA: Harvard University Press.

DePamphilis, D. (2001) *Mergers, Acquisitions and other Restructuring Activities: An Integrated Approach to Process, Tools, Cases and Solutions*. San Diego: Academic Press.

Derrida, J. (1978) *Writing and Difference*. London: Routledge.

Dierickx, I. and Cool, K. (1989) 'Asset stock accumulation and sustainability of competitive advantage', *Management Science*, vol. 35, no. 12, pp. 1504–11.

Donaldson, L. (2001) *The Contingency Theory of Organisations*. Sage Publications.

Dranikoff, L., Koller, T. and Schneider, A. (2002) 'Divestiture: Strategy's missing link', *Harvard Business Review*, vol. 80, no. 5 (May–June), pp. 75–83.

Drury, C. (2004) *Management and Cost Accounting*, 6th edn. London: Thompson Learning.

Duhaime, I. M. and Schwenk, C. R. (1985) 'Conjectures on cognitive simplification in acquisition and divestment decision making', *Academy of Management Review*, vol. 10, no. 2, pp. 287–95.

Dunford, R. and Palmer, I. (1996) 'Metaphors in popular management discourse: The case of corporate restructuring'. In D. Grant and C. Oswick (eds) *Metaphor and Organizations*. Thousand Oaks, CA: Sage, pp. 95–109.

Dunning J. H. (1980) 'Towards an eclectic theory of international production: some empirical tests', *Journal of International Business Studies*, vol. 11, no. 1, pp. 9–31.

Dunning J. H. (1993) *Multinational Enterprises and the Global Economy*. Reading: Addison-Wesley.

Eccles R. G., Lanes, K. L. and Wilson, T. C. (1999) 'Are you paying too much for that acquisition?' *Harvard Business Review*, vol. 77, no. 4 (July–August), pp. 136–47.

Economist Intelligence Unit (2002) 'M&A in Japan: Foreign Wind', *Business Asia*, 18 November 2002. London: The Economist Intelligence Unit.

Edwards, J. and Fischer, K. (1994) *Banks, Finance and Investment in Germany*. Cambridge: Cambridge University Press.

Edwards, J. and Nibler, M. (2000) 'Corporate Governance: Banks versus ownership concentration in Germany', *Economic Policy*, vol. 15, no. 31, pp. 239–67.

Eisenhardt, K. (1989) 'Making fast strategic decisions in high velocity environments', *Academy of Management Journal*, vol. 32, no. 3, pp. 543–76.

Ekwall, A. and Karlsson, S. (1999) *Kohtaaminen: kirja kulttuurieroista ja johtajuudesta*. Vaasa: Storkamp media. [*Meeting: A Book on Cultural Differences and Leadership*.]

Emerson, V. (2001) 'An Interview With Carlos Ghosn, President of Nissan Motors, Ltd. and Industry Leader of the Year', *Journal of World Business*, vol. 36, no. 1, pp. 3–10.

Empson, L. (2000) 'Mergers between professional service firms: Exploring an undirected process of integration'. In C. L. Cooper and A. Gregory (eds) *Advances in Mergers and Acquisitions*, vol. 1. Greenwich, CT: JAI Press, pp. 205–37.

Empson, L. (2001) 'Fear of exploitation and fear of contamination: Impediments to knowledge transfer in mergers between professional services firms', *Human Relations: Special Issue on Knowledge Management in Professional Service Firms*, vol. 54, no. 7, pp. 839–62.

Empson, L. (2004) 'Organizational identity change: Managerial regulation and member identification in an accounting firm acquisition', *Accounting, Organizations, and Society*, vol. 29, no. 8, pp. 759–81.

Endlich, L. (2000) *Goldman Sachs: The Culture of Success*. London: Warner Books.

Englich, B. and Mussweiler, T. (2001) 'Sentencing under uncertainty: Anchoring effects in the classroom', *Journal of Applied Social Science*, vol. 31, no. 7, pp. 1535–51.

Evans, P., Pucik, V. and Barsoux, J.-L. (2002) *The Global Challenge: Frameworks for International Human Resource Management.* New York: McGraw-Hill.

Fama, E. F. and French, K. R. (1993) 'Common risk factors in the return on stocks and bonds', *Journal of Financial Economics*, vol. 33, no. 1, pp. 3–56.

Feldman, M. L. and Spratt, M. F. (1999) *Five Frogs on a Log.* Chichester, England: John Wiley & Sons.

Ferrarini G. (2003) 'Shareholder Value and the Modernization of European Corporate Law', Chapter 10 in K. J. Hopt and E. Wymeersch (eds) *Capital Markets and Company Law.* Oxford: Oxford University Press.

Fligstein, N. (2001) *The Architecture of Markets.* Berkeley: University of California Press.

Foucault, M. (1980) *Power/Knowledge.* New York: Pantheon.

Frank, R. and Burton, T. M. (1997) 'Pharmacia & Upjohn faces culture clash; Europeans chafe under U.S. rules', *The Wall Street Journal*, 2 February 1997.

Franks, J. and Mayer, C. (1998) 'Bank control, takeovers and corporate governance in Germany', *Journal of Banking and Finance*, vol. 22, no. 10, pp. 1385–403.

Fursich, E. (2002) 'Nation, capitalism, myth: Covering news of economic globalization', *Journalism and Mass Communication Quarterly*, vol. 79, no. 2, pp. 353–73.

Garsombke, D. (1988) 'Organizational culture dons the mantle of militarism', *Organizational Dynamics*, vol. 17, no. 1, pp. 46–57.

Gates, S. and Very, P. (2003) 'Measuring performance during M&A integration', *Long Range Planning*, vol. 36, no. 2, pp. 167–85.

Gaughan, P. A. (2002) *Mergers, Acquisitions and Corporate Restructurings*, 3rd edn. New York: John Wiley and Sons.

Gellner, E. (1983) *Nations and Nationalism.* Oxford: Basil Blackwell.

George, C. S. (1972) *The History of Management Thought.* Englewood Cliffs, NJ: Prentice Hall.

George, J. M. and Jones, G. R. (2000) 'The role of time in theory and theory building', *Journal of Management*, vol. 26, no. 4, pp. 657–84.

Ghoshal, S. and Bartlett, C. A. (1998) 'Creation, adoption, and diffusion of innovations by subsidiaries of multinational corporations', *Journal of International Business Studies*, vol. 19, no. 3, pp. 365–89.

Gilmore, T. N. (1982) 'Leadership and boundary management', *The Journal of Applied Behavioural Science*, vol. 18, no. 3, pp. 343–56.

Gold, A. R., Hirano, M. and Yokoyama, Y. (2001) 'An outsider takes on Japan', *McKinsey Quarterly*, no. 1, pp. 94–105.

Gordon, N. J. and Roe, M. (eds) (2004) *Convergence and Persistence in Corporate Governance.* Cambridge: Cambridge University Press.

Gospel, H. and Pendleton, A. (eds) (2005) *Corporate Governance and Labour Management: An International Comparison.* Oxford: Oxford University Press.

Granlund, M. (2003) 'Management accounting system integration in corporate mergers: a case study', *Accounting, Auditing and Accountability Journal*, vol. 16, no. 2, pp. 208–43.

Grant, R. M. (2002) 'Corporate strategy: Managing scope and strategy content'. In A. Pettigrew, H. Thomas and R. Whittington (eds) *Handbook of Strategy and Management.* London: Sage.

Grant, R. M. and Spender, J. C. (1996) 'Knowledge and the firm', *Strategic Management Journal*, vol. 17, Winter Special Issue, pp. 5–11.

Greenberg, D. and Guinan, P. J. (2004) 'Mergers and acquisitions in technology-intensive industries: The emergent process of knowledge transfer'. In A. L. Pablo and M. Javidan (eds) *Mergers and Acquisitions: Creating Integrative Knowledge*. Oxford: Blackwell Publishing.

Gundelach, P. (2000) 'Joking relationships and national identity in Scandinavia', *Acta Sociologica*, vol. 43, pp. 113–22.

Haleblian, J. and Finkelstein, S. (1999) 'The influence of organizational acquisition experience on acquisition performance: a behavioral perspective', *Administrative Science Quarterly*, vol. 44, pp. 29–56.

Hall, P. A. and Soskice, D. (2003) 'Varieties of capitalism and institutional change: a response to three critics', *Comparative European Politics, Houndmills*, vol. 1, no. 2, p. 241.

Haltsonen, V. (2001) 'Humour, Jokes and the Finnish–Swedish Relationship: Why Do Finns Tell Jokes About Swedes?' Master's thesis, Helsinki School of Economics.

Hancke, B. (2002) *Large Firms and Institutional Change: Industrial renewal and economic restructuring in France*. Oxford: Oxford University Press.

Handy, C. (1989) *The Age of Unreason*. Boston, MA: Harvard Business School Press.

Hannah, L. (1983) *The Rise of the Corporate Economy*, 2nd edn. London: Methuen.

Harragan, B. (1977) *Games Mother Never Taught You: Corporate gamesmanship for women*. New York: Warner.

Harrington, S. E. (1993) 'The relationship between risk and return: evidence for life insurance stocks', *The Journal of Risk and Insurance*, vol. 50, no. 4 (December), pp. 587–610.

Haspeslagh, P. C. and Jemison, D. B. (1991) *Managing Acquisitions: Creating Value Through Corporate Renewal*. New York: The Free Press.

Haunschild, P. R., Davis-Blake, A. and Fichman, M. (1994) 'Managerial overcommitment in corporate acquisition processes', *Organization Science*, vol. 5, no. 4, pp. 528–40.

Haveman, H. A. and Cohen, L. E. (1994) 'The ecological dynamics of careers: The impact of organizational founding, dissolution, and merger on job mobility', *American Journal of Sociology*, vol. 100, no. 1, pp. 104–52.

Hawley, J. M. (1995) 'Maintaining business while maintaining boundaries: an Amish woman's experience', *Entrepreneurship, Innovation and Change*, vol. 4, no. 4, pp. 315–28.

Hayes, R. H. (1979) 'The human side of acquisitions', *Management Review*, vol. 68, no. 11, pp. 41–6.

Hayes, R. H. and Hoag, G. H. (1974) 'Post-acquisition retention of top management', *Mergers and Acquisitions*, vol. 9, pp. 8–18.

Hayward, M. L. A. and Hambrick, D. C. (1997) 'Explaining the premium paid for large acquisitions: evidence of CEO hubris', *Administrative Science Quarterly*, vol. 42, no. 1, pp. 103–29.

Hedges, C. (2003) *War is a Force that Gives us Meaning*. UK: Anchor.

Hedlund, G. (1986) 'The hypermodern MNC – A heterarchy?' *Human Resource Management*, vol. 25, no. 1 (spring), pp. 9–36.

Heidegger, M. (1962) *Being and Time*. New York: Harper & Row.

Hellgren, B., Löwstedt, J., Puttonen, L., Tienari, J., Vaara, E. and Werr, A. (2002) 'How issues become constructed in the media: "Winners" and "Losers" in the AstraZeneca merger', *British Journal of Management*, vol. 13, no. 2, pp. 123–40.

Hernes, T. (2004) 'Studying Composite Boundaries: A Framework of Analysis', *Human Relations*, vol. 57, no. 1, pp. 9–28.

Hirsch, P. and Andrews, J. (1983) 'Ambushes, shootouts and golden parachutes: The language of corporate takeovers'. In L. R. Pondy, P. J. Frost, G. Morgan and T. C. Dandridge (eds) *Organizational Symbolism*. Greenwich, CT: JAI Press, pp. 145–55.

Hitt, M. A., Harrison, J. S. and Ireland, R. D. (2001) *Mergers and Acquisitions: A Guide to Creating Value for Stakeholders*. Oxford: Oxford University Press.

Hitt, M. A., Hoskisson, R. E. and Ireland, R. D. (1990) 'Mergers and acquisitions and managerial commitment to innovation in M-form firms', *Strategic Management Journal*, vol. 11, no. 5, Special Issue: Corporate Entrepreneurship (summer), pp. 29–47.

Hobday, M. (1995) *Innovation in East Asia: The Challenge to Japan*. Aldershot: Edward Elgar.

Hofstede, G. (1984) *Culture's Consequences: International Differences in Work-related Values*. Beverly Hills, CA: Sage.

Hogg, M. A. and Terry, D. J. (2001) *Social Identity Processes in Organizational Contexts*. Philadelphia, PA: Psychology Press.

Holstein, W. J. (1998) 'All the film in China', *US News Online*, Business and Technology 7/6/98 at: www.usnews.com/usnews/issue/980706/6koda.htm.

Hopt, K. J. and Wymeersch, E. (eds) (2003) *Capital Markets and Company Law*. Oxford: Oxford University Press.

Hoskin, K. (2004) 'Spacing, timing and the invention of management', *Organization*, vol. 11, no. 6, pp. 743–57.

Howell, R. A. (1970) 'Plan to integrate your acquisitions', *Harvard Business Review*, vol. 49, pp. 66–76.

Hunt, J. W. (1990) 'Changing pattern of acquisition behaviour in takeovers and the consequences for acquisition processes', *Strategic Management Journal*, vol. 11, no. 1, pp. 69–77.

Hunt, J., Lees, S., Grumbar, J. J. and Vivian, P. D. (1986) *Acquisitions – The Human Factor*. London Business School/Egon Zehnder International.

Hviid, M. and Prendergast, C. (1993) 'Merger Failure and Merger Profitability', *The Journal of Industrial Economics*, vol. 41, no. 4 (December), pp. 371–86.

Ingham, G. (1984) *Capitalism Divided? The City and Industry in British Social Development*. London: Macmillan.

Ivancevich, J. M., Schweiger, D. M. and Power, F. R. (1987) 'Strategies for managing human resources during mergers and acquisitions', *Human Resource Planning*, vol. 10, no. 1, pp. 19–35.

Janis, I. L. (1982) *Groupthink: Psychological Studies of Policy Decisions and Fiascos*. Boston: Houghton Mifflin.

Javidan, M., Pablo, A., Singh, H., Hitt, M., Jemison, D. (2004) 'Where we've been and where we're going'. Chapter 14 in A. Pablo and M. Javidan (eds) *Mergers and Acquisitions: Creating Integrative Knowledge*. Strategic Management Society, Blackwell Publishing.

Jeffcutt, P. (1994) 'From interpretation to representation in organizational analysis', *Organization Studies*, vol. 15, no. 2, pp. 241–74.

Jemison, D. B. (1984) 'The importance of boundary spanning roles in strategic decision making', *Journal of Management Studies*, vol. 21, no. 2, pp. 131–52.

Jemison, D. B. and Sitkin, S. B. (1987) 'Acquisitions: the process can be a problem', *Harvard Business Review*, vol. 60, no. 6, pp. 107–16.

Jenkinson, T. and Ljungqvist, A. (2001) 'The role of hostile stakes in German corporate governance', *Journal of Corporate Finance*, vol. 7, no. 4, pp. 397–46.

Jensen, M. C. (1986) 'Agency costs of free cash flow, corporate finance, and takeovers', *American Economic Review*, vol. 76, no. 2, May, pp. 323–9.

Jensen, M. and Meckling, W. (1976) 'Theory of the firm: managerial behaviour, agency costs, and ownership structure', *Journal of Financial Economics*, vol. 3, no. 4, pp. 305–60.

Jensen, M. C. and Ruback, R. S. (1983) 'The market for corporate control: the scientific evidence', *Journal of Financial Economics*, vol. 11, nos. 1–4 (April), pp. 5–51.

Johnson, G. (1987) *Strategic Change and the Management Process*. Oxford: Basil Blackwell.

Johnson, G., Melin, L. and Whittington, R. (2003) 'Micro strategy and strategizing: towards an activity-based view', *Journal of Management Studies*, vol. 40, no. 1 (January), pp. 1–22.

Johnson, H. T. and Kaplan, R. S. (1987) *Relevance Lost: The rise and fall of management accounting*. Boston, MA: Harvard Business School Press.

Johnson, J. and Orange, M. (2003) *The Man Who Tried to Buy the World: Jean-Marie Messier and Vivendi Universal*. London: Penguin.

Jones, C. S. (1985) 'An empirical study of the role of management accounting systems following takeover or merger', *Accounting, Organisations and Society*, vol. 10, no. 2, pp. 177–200.

Jönsson, S. (1995) *Goda utsikter – svenskt management i perspektiv*. Stockholm: Nerenius & Santérus Förlag. [*Good Prospects – Swedish Management in Perspective*.]

Jopson, B. (2005) 'IFRS: there is no accounting for taste', *Financial Times*, 4 October.

Kahneman, D. and Tversky, A. (1979) 'Prospect theory: An analysis of decisions under risk', *Econometrica*, vol. 47, no. 2, pp. 262–92.

Kaplan, R. S. and Norton, D. P. (1992) 'The Balanced Scorecard – measures that drive performance', *Harvard Business Review*, vol. 70, no. 1, pp. 71–9.

Kaplan, R. S. and Norton, D. P. (1993) 'Putting the Balanced Scorecard to work', *Harvard Business Review*, vol. 71, no. 5, pp. 134–42.

Kaplan, R. S. and Norton, D. P. (1996) 'Using the Balanced Scorecard as a strategic management system', *Harvard Business Review*, vol. 76, no. 1, pp. 75–85.

Kastrinaka, Z. (2007) 'Macroeconomic and Microeconomic Approaches to Merger waves in the UK'. Unpublished PhD thesis, University of Warwick.

Kelts, R. (2003) 'The Cost Killer Cometh', *J@pan Inc.*, October 2003, Linc Media, www.japaninc.com.

Kesner, I. F., Shapiro, D. L. and Sharma, A. (1994) 'Brokering mergers: an agency theory perspective on the role of representatives', *Academy of Management Journal*, vol. 37, no. 3, pp. 703–21.

Killick, M., Rawoot, I. and Stockport, G. J. (2001) *Cisco System Inc. – Growth Through Acquisitions*, Case Study from the graduate school of Management, University of Western Australia, Perth, Australia.

Kitching, J. (1967) 'Why do mergers miscarry?' *Harvard Business Review*, vol. 45, no. 6 (November–December), pp. 84–101.

Kitching, J. (1973) *Acquisitions in Europe: Causes of Corporate Successes and Failures*. Geneva: Business International.

Klein, N. (2000) *No Logo: Taking Aim at the Brand Bullies*. London: Harper-Collins.

Knight, F. (1921) *Risk, Uncertainty and Profit*. New York: Harper & Row.

Knights, D. and Morgan, G. (1991) 'Corporate strategy, organizations, and subjectivity: A critique', *Organization Studies*, vol. 12, no. 2, pp. 251–73.

Kobrin, S. J. (1982) *Managing Political Risk Assessment*. Berkeley: University of California Press.

Kogan, N. and Wallach, M. (1966) 'Modification of judgmental style through group interaction', *Journal of Personality and Social Psychology*, vol. 4, no. 2, pp. 165–74.

Koke, J. (2004) 'The market for corporate control in a bank-based economy: a governance device?', *Journal of Corporate Finance*, vol. 10, no. 1, pp. 53–80.

Koller, V. (2003) 'Metaphor Clusters in Business Media Discourse: A Social Cognition Approach', PhD Thesis, University of Vienna.

Koller, V. (2005) 'Critical discourse analysis and social cognition: Evidence from business media discourse', *Discourse and Society*, vol. 16, no. 2, pp. 199–24.

Kostova, T. and Roth, K. (2002) 'Adoption of an organizational practice by subsidiaries of multinational corporations: institutional and relational effects', *Academy of Management Journal*, vol. 45, no. 1, pp. 215–33.

Kotter, J. P. (1995) 'Leading change: why transformation attempts fail', *Harvard Business Review*, vol. 85, no. 1 (March–April), pp. 59–67.

Kuhn, T. (1962) *The Structure of Scentific Revolutions*. London: University of Chicago Press.

Kusstatscher, V. and Cooper, C. L. (2005) *Managing Emotions in Mergers and Acquisitions*. Cheltenham: Edward Elgar.

Kynaston, D. (2002) Volume 4: *The City of London: A club no more 1945–2000*. London: Pimlico.

La Ville, V. and Mounoud, E. (2003) 'What do we mean by "Strategy as Practice"?' In B. Czarniawska and P. Gagliardi (eds) *Between Discourse and Narration: How Can Strategy be a Practice?* John Benjamin Publishing.

Laine-Sveiby, K. (1987) *Svenskhet som strategi*. Stockholm: Timbro Förlag. [*Swedishness as Strategy*.]

Laine-Sveiby, K. (1991) *Suomalaisuus strategiana*. Juva: WSOY. [*Finnishness as Strategy*.]

Lajoux, A. R. (1998) *The Art of M&A Integration: A Guide to Merging Resources Processes, and Responsibilities*. London: McGraw-Hill.

Lall, S. (1996) *Learning From The Asian Tigers: Studies in Technology and Industrial Policy*. Basingstoke: Macmillan.

Lampel, J. and Shapira, Z. (2001) 'Judgmental errors, interactive norms, and the difficulty of detecting strategic surprises', *Organization Science*, vol. 12, no. 5, pp. 599–612.

Lane, P. J., Cannella, A. A. and Lubatkin, M. H. (1998) 'Agency problems as antecedents to unrelated mergers and diversification: Amihud and Lev reconsidered', *Strategic Management Journal*, vol. 19, no. 6 (June), pp. 555–78.

Langetieg, T. (1978) 'An application of a three factor performance index to measure stock holder gains from merger', *Journal of Financial Economics*, vol. 6, no. 4, pp. 365–83.

Larsson, R. and Risberg, A. (1998) 'Cultural Awareness and National versus Corporate Barriers to Acculturation'. In M. Cardel Gertsen, A.-M. Søderberg and J. E. Torp (eds) *Cultural Dimensions of International Mergers and Acquisitions*. Berlin: De Gruyter.

Lawrence, T. B., Winn, M. L. and Jennings, P. D. (2001) 'The temporal dynamics of institutionalization', *Academy of Management Review*, vol. 26, no. 4, pp. 624–44.

Le Shan, L. (2002) *The Psychology of War*. New York: Helios.

Lee, H. and Liebenau, J. (1999) 'Time in organizational studies: Towards a new research direction', *Organization Studies*, vol. 20, no. 6, pp. 1035–58.

Leifer, R. P. and Delbecq, A. (1978) 'Organization/environment interchange: a model of boundary spanning activity', *Academy of Management Review*, vol. 3, no. 1, pp. 40–50.

Lenin, V. I. (1916) *Imperialism, the Highest Stage of Capitalism, Selected Works*, Volume 1. Parus Publishers, pp. 667–766.

Lev, B. and Mandelker, G. (1972) 'The microeconomic consequences of corporate mergers', *Journal of Business*, vol. 45, no. 1 (January), pp. 85–104.

Levinson, H. (1970) 'A psychologist diagnoses merger failures', *Harvard Business Review*, vol. 47, pp. 90–102.

Lewellen, W., Loderer, C. and Rosenfeld, A. (1989) 'Mergers, executive risk reduction, and stockholder wealth', *The Journal of Financial and Quantitative Analysis*, vol. 24, no. 4 (December), pp. 459–72.

List, J. (2003) 'Does market experience eliminate market anomalies?', *Quarterly Journal of Economics*, vol. 118, no. 1 (February), pp. 41–71.

Llewellyn, S. (1994) 'Managing the boundary: how accounting is implicated in maintaining the organisation', *Accounting, Auditing and Accountability*, vol. 7, no. 4, pp. 4–24.

Lord, C., Ross, L. and Lepper, M. R. (1979) 'Biased assimilation and attitude polarizations: the effects of prior theories on subsequently considered evidence', *Journal of Personality and Social Psychology*, vol. 37, no. 11, pp. 2098–190.

Love, P. and Gibson, S. (1999) 'Hidden sore points that can thwart a culture match', *Mergers and Acquisitions*, vol. 33, no. 6, pp. 51–6.

Lowenstein, G. F. (1988) 'Frames of mind in intertemporal choice', *Management Science*, vol. 34, no. 2 (February), pp. 200–14.

Lubatkin, M. (1987) 'Merger Strategies and Stockholder Value', *Strategic Management Journal*, vol. 8, no. 1 (January–February), pp. 39–53.

Lubatkin, M. and Chatterjee, S. (1994) 'Extending modern portfolio theory into the domain of corporate diversification: does it apply?', *The Academy of Management Journal*, vol. 37, no. 1. (February), pp. 109–36.

Lubatkin, M. et al. (1998) 'Managing mergers across borders: a two-nation exploration of a nationally bound administrative heritage', *Organization Science*, vol. 9, no. 6, pp. 670–85.

Lukes, S. (1974) *Power: A Radical View*. London: Macmillan. (Second edition, 2004, Palgrave Macmillan.)

Macintosh (1985) *The Social Software of Accounting and Information Systems*. Chichester, UK: John Wiley.

Magnet, M. (1984) 'Help! My company has just been taken over', *Fortune*, July 9, pp. 44–51.

Malkiel, B. G. (1990) *A Random Walk Down Wall Street*, 5th edn. New York: W. W. Norton & Company.

March, J. G. and Shapira, Z. (1987) 'Managerial perspectives on risk and risk taking', *Management Science*, vol. 33, no. 11, pp. 1404–18.

Markowitz, H. M. (1952) 'Portfolio selection', *Journal of Finance*, vol. 7 (March), pp. 77–91.

Marks, M. L. (1991) 'Merger Management HR's Way', *HR Magazine*, vol. 36, no. 5, pp. 60–6.

Marks, M. L. and Mirvis, P. H. (1985) 'Merger syndrome: stress and uncertainty (Part 1)', *Mergers & Acquisitions*, vol. 20, no. 2, pp. 50–6.

Marks, M. L. and Mirvis, P. H. (1986) 'Merger syndrome: management by crisis (Part 2)', *Mergers & Acquisitions*, vol. 20, no. 3, pp. 70–7.

Marks, M. L. and Mirvis, P. H. (1998) *Joining Forces: Making One Plus One Equal Three*. San Francisco: Jossey-Bass.

Marks, M. L. and Mirvis, P. H. (2001) 'Making mergers and acquisitions work: Strategic and psychological preparation', *Academy of Management Executive*, vol. 15, no. 2, pp. 80–94.

Mayo, A. and Hadaway, T. (1994) 'Cultural adaptation – The ICL Nokia-Data merger 1991–92', *Journal of Management Development*, vol. 13, no. 2, pp. 59–71.

McClelland, D. (1961) *The Achieving Society*. Princeton: Princeton University Press.

McKay, C. (1841) *Extraordinary Popular Delusions and the Madness of Crowds*. Three Rivers Press reprint edition (1995).

Meeks, G. (1977) *Disappointing Marriage: A study of the gains from merger*. Cambridge, UK: Cambridge University Press.

Melin, L. (1986) 'The field-of-force metaphor: a study in industrial change', *International Studies of Management and Organization*, vol. 17, no. 1, pp. 24–33.

Melin, L. (1989) 'The field-of-force metaphor', *Advances in International Marketing*, Volume 3. Greenwich: JAI Press, pp. 161–79.

Meyer, J. W. and Rowan, B. (1977) 'Institutional Organizations: Formal Structures as Myth and Ceremony', *American Journal of Sociology*, vol. 83, pp. 340–63.

Meyer, L. (2002) 'Women in war stories: Book Reviews', *Journal of Women's History*, vol. 14, no. 2, pp. 162–71.

Michaelsel, S. and Johnson, D. E. (1997) *Border Theory: the Limits of Cultural Politics*. Minneapolis: University of Minnesota Press.

Millar, F. and Beck, D. (2004) 'Metaphors of crisis'. In D. Millar and R. Heath (eds) *Responding to Crisis: A Rhetorical Approach to Crisis Communication*. Mahwah, NJ: Lawrence Erlbaum, pp. 153–66.

Miller, E. J. and Rice, A. K. (1967) *Systems of Organization: The Control of Sentient Boundaries*. London: Tavistock Publications.

Mintzberg, H. (1973) *The Nature of Managerial Work*. New York: Harper & Row.

Mirvis, P. H. and Marks, M. L. (1992) *Managing The Merger: Making It Work*. Englewood Cliffs, NJ: Prentice Hall.

Moeller, S. B., Schlingemann, F. P. and Stultz, R. M. (2004) 'Firm size and the gains from acquisitions', *Journal of Financial Economics*, vol. 73, no. 2, pp. 201–28.

Moeller, S. B., Schlingemann, F. P. and Stulz, R. M. (2005) 'Wealth destruction on a massive scale? A study of acquiring-firm returns in the recent merger wave', *Journal of Finance*, vol. LX, no. 2, pp. 757–82.

Monin, N. and Monin, D. J. (1997) 'Rhetoric and action: When a literary drama tells the organization's story', *Journal of Organizational Change Management*, vol. 10, no. 1, pp. 47–60.

Moon, P. and Bates, K. (1993) 'CORE analysis in strategic performance appraisal', *Management Accounting Research*, vol. 4, no. 2 (June).

Moore, F. (2000) 'Vorsprung durch sales technique: stereotypes, strategies and identities in a "global" city'. Kingston University School of Business: WPTC-2K-10.

Morosini, P., Shane, S. and Singh, H. (1998) 'National cultural distance and cross-border acquisition performance', *Journal of International Business Studies*, vol. 29, no. 1, pp. 137–58.

Mosakowski, E. and Earley, P. C. (2000) 'A selective review of time: Assumptions in strategy research', *Academy of Management Review*, vol. 25, no. 4 (October), pp. 796–812.

Mowen, J. C. and Mowen, M. M. (1991) 'Time and outcome valuation: Implications for marketing decision making', *Journal of Marketing*, vol. 55, no. 4 (October), pp. 54–62.

Mueller, D. C. (2003) 'The finance literature on mergers. A critical survey'. In M. Waterson (ed.) *Competition, Monopoly and Corporate Governance: Essays in Honour of Keith Cowling*. Cheltenham, UK: Edward Elgar.

Nahavandi, A. and Malekzadeh, A. R. (1988) 'Acculturation in Mergers and Acquisitions', *Academy of Management Review*, vol. 13, no. 1, pp. 79–90.

Narula, R. and Dunning, J. H. (2000) 'Industrial Development, Globalization and Multinational Enterprises: New Realities for Developing Countries', *Oxford Development Studies*, vol. 28, no. 2, pp. 141–68.

Nayyar, P. R. (1992) 'On the measurement of corporate diversification strategy: evidence from large US service firms', *Strategic Management Journal*, vol. 13, no. 3, pp. 219–36.

Nippert-Eng, C. (1996a) 'Calendars and Keys: The Classification of Home and Work,' *Sociological Forum*, vol. 11, pp. 563–82.

Nippert-Eng, C. (1996b) *Home and Work: Negotiating Boundaries Through Everyday Life*. Chicago: University of Chicago Press.

Nohria, N. and Ghoshal, S. (1997) *The Differentiated Network: Organizing Multinational Corporations for Value Creation*. San Francisco: Jossey-Bass.

Nolan, P. (2001) *China and the Global Economy: National Champions, Industrial Policy and the Big Business Revolution*. Houndsmill: Palgrave.

Nolan, P. (2004) *Transforming China: Globalization, Transition and Development*. London: Anthem.

Nonaka, I. and Takeuchi, H. (1995) *The Knowledge Creating Company*. Oxford: Oxford University Press.

Nooteboom, B., Berger, H. and Nooderhaven, N. G. (1997) 'Special research forum on alliances and networks', *The Academy of Management Journal*, vol. 40, no. 2 (April), pp. 308–38.

O'Byrne, D. (2001) 'A boundary model of post acquisition integration', *Proceedings of PhD Colloquium*, UCC Cork.

O'Byrne, D. and Angwin, D. (2003) 'Changing sub-unit boundaries during a merger', *The Irish Journal of Management*, vol. 24, no. 1, pp. 194–215.

O'Sullivan, M. (2000) *Contests for Corporate Control: Corporate Governance and Economic Performance in the United States and Germany*. Oxford: Oxford University Press.

Olie, R. (1994) 'Shades of Culture and Institutions in International Mergers', *Organization Studies*, vol. 15, pp. 381–405.

Orlikowski, W. J. (1996) 'Improving organizational transformation over time: A situated change perspective', *Information Systems Research*, vol. 7, no. 1, pp. 63–92.

Paasi, A. (1999) 'Boundaries as social practice and discourse: the Finnish–Russian border', *Regional Studies*, vol. 33, no. 7, pp. 669–80.

Pablo, A. L. and Javidan, M. (eds) (2004) *Mergers and Acquisitions: Creating Integrative Knowledge*. Oxford: Blackwell.

Paulsen, N. and Hernes, T. (2003) *Managing Boundaries in Organizations: Multiple Perspectives*. Hampshire, UK: Palgrave.

Penman, S. H. (2004) *Financial Statement Analysis and Security Valuation*, 2nd edn. Boston, MA: McGraw-Hill.

Perlow, L. A. (1999) 'The time famine: Towards a sociology of work time', *Administrative Science Quarterly*, vol. 44, no. 1, pp. 57–81.

Petronio, S., Ellmers, N., Giles, H. and Gallois, C. (1998) '(Mis)communication across boundaries', *Communication Research*, vol. 25, no. 6 (December), pp. 571–95.

Pettigrew, A. M. (1985) *The Awakening Giant*. Oxford: Basil Blackwell

Pettigrew, A. M. (1992) 'The character and significance of strategy process research', *Strategic Management Journal*, vol. 13, Special Issue, pp. 5–16.

Pfeffer, J. and Salancik, G. R. (1978) *The External Control of Organizations: A Resource Dependency Perspective*. New York: Harper & Row.

Picconi, M. P. (2004) *The perils of pensions: does pension accounting lead investors and analysts astray?* PhD dissertation, Cornell University. Published by Proquest Information and Learning Company, Ann Arbor, MI.

Pickard, J. (2006) 'The man and the bubble', *FT magazine* (London: Financial Times), 18 February, pp. 14–15.

Platt, J. (1973) 'Social traps', *American Psychologist*, vol. 28, no. 8, pp. 641–51.

Plender, J. (2002) *Going Off the Rails: global capital and the crisis of legitimacy*. London: Wiley.

Porter, M. E. (1985) *Competitive Advantage*. New York: The Free Press.

Prasad, A. (ed.) (2003) *Postcolonial Theory and Organizational Analaysis: A Critical Engagement*. New York: Palgrave Macmillan.

Pritchett, P. (1997) *After the Merger*, 2nd edn. New York: McGraw-Hill.

Procter-Thomson, S. (2005) 'Developing leadership practices: constellations or stars', *Indepth Discussion Paper Series*, Centre For Excellence in Leadership, Lancaster University.

Puddifoot, J. E. (1997) 'Psychological reaction to perceived erasure of community boundaries', *The Journal of Social Psychology*, vol. 137, no. 3, pp. 343–56.

Ramaswamy, K. (1997) 'The performance impact of strategic similarity in horizontal mergers: evidence from the U.S. banking industry', *The Academy of Management Journal*, vol. 40, no. 3 (June), pp. 697–715.

Ranft, A. L. and Lord, M. D. (2002) 'Acquiring new technologies and capabilities: A grounded model of acquisition implementation', *Organization Science*, vol. 13, no. 4, pp. 420–42.

Rappaport, A. (1998) *Creating Shareholder Value*. New York: The Free Press.

Rhodes-Kropf, M. and Viswanathan, S. (2004) 'Market valuation and merger waves', *Journal of Finance*, vol. LIX, no. 6, pp. 2685–718.

Riad, S. (2007) 'Of mergers and cultures: "What happened to shared values and joint assumptions?"' *Journal of Organizational Change Management*, forthcoming.

Rindova, V., Becerra, M. and Contardo, I. (2004) 'Enacting competitive wars: Competitive activity, language games and market consequences', *Academy of Management Review*, vol. 29, no. 4, pp. 670–86.

Risberg, A., Tienari, J. and Vaara, E. (2003) 'Making sense of a transnational merger: media texts and the (re)construction of power relations', *Culture and Organization*, vol. 9, no. 2, pp. 121–37.

Roe, M. (2003) *Political Determinants of Corporate Governance: Political Context, Corporate Impact*. Oxford: Oxford University Press.

Roll, R. (1986) 'The hubris hypothesis of corporate takeovers', *Journal of Business*, vol. 59, no. 2, Part 1 (April), pp. 197–216.

Roll, R. and Ross, S. (1994) 'On the cross-sectional relation between expected returns and betas', *Journal of Finance*, vol. 49, no. 1, pp. 101–21.

Rostow, W. W. (1960) *Stages of Economic Growth: A Non-Communist Manifesto*. Cambridge: Cambridge University Press.

Rouse, M. J. and Daellenback, U. S. (1999) 'Rethinking research methods for the resource-based perspective', *Strategic Management Journal*, vol. 20, no. 5, pp. 487–97.

Rubery, J. and Grimshaw, D. (2003) *The Organisation of Employment: An International Perspective*. London: Palgrave Macmillan.

Rugman, A. M. (1979) *International Diversification and the Multinational Enterprise*. Lexington: D.C. Heath.

Rugman, A. M. and Collinson, S. C. (2004) 'The Regional Nature of the World's Automotive Industry', *European Management Journal*, vol. 22, no. 5, pp. 471–82.

Rumelt, R. (1974) *Strategy, Structure and Economic Performance: Division of Research*. Boston MA: Harvard Business School Press.

Rumelt, R., Schendel, D. and Teece, D. J. (1994) 'Fundamental issues in strategy'. In R. Rumelt, D. Schendel, and D. J. Teece (eds) *Fundamental issues in strategy*. Harvard Business School Press.

Russo, J. E. and Schoemaker, P. J. H. (1989) *Decision Traps: Ten Barriers to Brilliant Decision Making and How to Overcome Them*. New York: Simon & Schuster.

Sahlman, W. A. (1990) 'The structure and governance of venture capital organizations', *Journal of Financial Economics*, vol. 27, no. 2, pp. 473–521.

Saïd, E. (1978) *Orientalism*. New York:Vintage Books.

Sales, A. M. and Mirvis, P. H. (1984) 'When Cultures Collide: Issues in Acquisitions'. In J. R. Kimberly and R. E. Quinn (eds) *Managing Organizational Transitions*. Homewood, IL: Irwin.

Salter, M. S. and Weinhold, W. A. (1979) *Diversification Through Acquisition*. New York: Free Press.

Säntti, R. (2001) *How Cultures Interact in an International Merger*. Acta Universitatis Tamperensis 819. Tampere: University of Tampere.

Schein, E. H. (1978) *Career Dynamics: Matching Individual and Organizational Needs*. Reading, MA: Addison-Wesley.

Schmidt, V. (2002) *The Futures of European Capitalism*. Oxford: Oxford University Press.

Schneider, S. and Dunbar, R. (1992) 'A psychoanalytic reading of hostile takeover events', *Academy of Management Review*, vol. 17, no. 3, pp. 537–67.

Schniederjans, M. J. and Fowler, K. L. (1989) 'Strategic acquisition management: a multi-objective synergistic approach', *The Journal of the Operational Research Society*, vol. 40, no. 4 (April), pp. 333–45.

Schnitzer, M. (1995) ' "Breach of trust" in takeovers and the optimal corporate charter', *The Journal of Industrial Economics*, vol. 43, no. 3 (September), pp. 229–59.

Schoenberg, R. (2001) 'Knowledge transfer and resource sharing as value creation mechanisms in inbound continental European acquisitions', *Journal of Euromarketing*, vol. 10, no. 1, pp. 99–114.

Schuler, R. and Jackson, S. (2001) 'HR issues and activities in mergers and acquisitions', *European Management Journal*, vol. 19, no. 3, pp. 239–53.

Schutz, A. (1967) *The Phenomenology of the Social World*. Evanston, IL: Northwestern University Press.

Schweiger, D. M. (2002) *M&A Integration: A Framework for Executives and Managers*. New York: McGraw-Hill.

Schweiger, D. M. and DeNisi, A. S. (1991) 'Communication with Employees following a Merger: A Longitudinal Field Experiment', *The Academy of Management Journal*, vol. 34, no. 1 (March), pp. 110–35.

Schweiger, D. M. and Goulet, P. (2000) 'Integrating acquisitions: An international research review'. In C. Cooper and A. Gregory (eds) *Advances in Mergers and Acquisitions*, Volume I. Greenwich, CT: JAI/Elsevier Press, pp. 61–91.

Schweiger, D. M. and Goulet, P. K. (2002) *Explaining Acquisition Integration Effectiveness Through Cultural Learning: a Field Experiment*. Academy of Management Proceedings.

Schweiger D. M. and Ivancevich, J. M. (1987) 'The effects of mergers and acquisitions on organizations and employees: a contingency view', Annual Conference of the Strategic Management Society, Boston.

Schweiger, D. M. and Lippert, R. L. (2005) 'Integration: The critical link in M&A value creation'. In G. K. Stahl and M. E. Mendenhall (eds) *Managing Culture and Human Resources in Mergers and Acquisitions*. Palo Alto: Stanford Business Books/Stanford University Press.

Schweiger, D. M. and Very, P. (2003) 'Creating value through merger and acquisition integration'. In C. Cooper and A. Gregory (eds) *Advances in Mergers and Acquisitions*, Volume 2. Oxford: Elsevier Science, pp. 1–26.

Schweiger, D. M. and Walsh, J. P. (1990) 'Mergers and acquisitions: An interdisciplinary view'. In K. M. Rowland and G. R. Ferris (eds) *Research in Personnel and Human Resource Management*, Volume 8. Greenwich, CT: JAI Press, pp. 41–107.

Scott, R. W. (1998) *Institutions and Organizations*. Thousand Oaks, CA: Sage Publications.

Scott, W. R. (1998) *Organizations: Rational, National, and Open Systems* (4th edn). Upper Saddle River, NJ: Prentice Hall.

Searby, F. W. (1969) 'Control post-merger change', *Harvard Business Review*, vol. 5, pp. 139–45.

Selden, L. and Colvin, G. (2003) 'M&A needn't be a loser's game', *Harvard Business Review*, vol. 81, no. 6 (June), pp. 70–9.

Short, J. F. (1984) 'The social fabric at risk: toward the social transformation of risk analysis,' *American Sociological Review*, vol. 49, no. 6 (December), pp. 711–25.

Siehl, C., Ledford, G., Silverman R. and Fay, P. (1988) 'Preventing culture clashes from botching a merger', *Mergers & Acquisitions*, March/April, pp. 52–7.

Sinclair, A. (1998) *Doing Leadership Differently*. Melbourne: Melbourne University Press.

Sirower, M. L. (1997) *The Synergy Trap: How Companies Lose the Acquisition Game*. New York: The Free Press.

Sitkin, S. B. and Pablo, A. M. (1992) 'Reconceptualizing the determinants of risk behavior', *The Academy of Management Review*, vol. 17, no. 1 (January), pp. 9–38.

Smith, B. C. (1996) *On the Origin of Objects*. Cambridge, MA: MIT Press.

Smith, C. (2003) 'Strategy as numbers'. In S. Cummings and D. Wilson (eds) *Images of Strategy*. Oxford: Blackwell.

Smith, P. B., Andersen, J. A., Ekelund, B., Graversen, G. and Arja, R. (2003) 'In Search of Nordic Management Styles', *Scandinavian Journal of Management*, vol. 19, no. 4, pp. 491–507.

Søderberg, A.-M. and Vaara, E. (eds) (2003) *Merging Across Borders: People, Cultures and Politics*. Copenhagen: Copenhagen Business School Press.

Stahl, G. and Mendenhall, M. E. (2005) *Mergers and Acquisitions: Managing Cultures and Human Resources*. Palo Alto: Stanford University Press.

Stahl, G. K. and Voigt, A. (2004) 'Meta-analysis of the performance implications of cultural differences in mergers and acquisitions', *Academy of Management Proceedings*, 2004, pp. 1–5.

Steiner, P. O. (1975) *Mergers: Motives, Effects, Policies.* Ann Arbor: University of Michigan Press.

Stoughton, N. M. (1998) 'The information content of corporate merger and acquisition offers', *The Journal of Financial and Quantitative Analysis*, vol. 23, no. 2 (June), pp. 175–97.

Strearns, L. B. and Allan, K. D. (1996) 'Economic behaviour in institutional environments: the corporate merger wave of the 1980s', *American Sociological Review*, vol. 61, no. 4 (August), pp. 699–718.

Sudarsanam, S. (2003) *Creating Value from Mergers and Acquisitions.* Harlow, UK: FT-Prentice Hall.

Sudarsanam, S. and Mahate, A. A. (2003) 'Glamour acquirers, methods of payment and post-acquisition performance: the UK evidence', *Journal of Business Finance and Accounting*, vol. 30, no. 1 and 2, pp. 299–341.

Sutherland, S. (1992) *Irrationality: The Enemy Within.* London: Constable.

Tajfel, H. (1981) *Human Groups and Social Categories.* Cambridge: Cambridge University Press.

Tajfel, H. and Turner, J. C. (1986) 'The social identity theory of intergroup behaviour'. In S. Worchel and W. G. Austin (eds) *The Psychology of Intergroup Relations.* Chicago: Nelson Hall.

Tallman, B. (2003) 'The organization leader as king, warrior, magician and lover: How Jungian archetypes affect the way men lead organizations', *Organization Development Journal*, vol. 21, no. 3, pp. 19–30.

Terry, D. J. (2001) 'Intergroup relations and organisational mergers.' In M. A. Hogg and D. J. Terry (eds) *Social Identity Processes in Organizational Contexts.* Philadelphia: Psychology Press.

Tetlock, P. E. (2005) *Expert Political Judgement: How Good Is It? How Can We Know?* Princeton, NJ: Princeton University Press.

Thaler, R. (1985) 'Mental accounting and consumer choice', *Marketing Science*, vol. 4, no. 3, pp. 199–214.

Thaler, R. (1992) *The Winner's Curse: Paradoxes and Anomalies in Economic Life.* Princeton, NJ: Princeton University Press.

Thompson, J. D. (1967) *Organizations in Action.* New York: McGraw-Hill.

Thompson, R. S. (1984) 'Diversification strategy and systematic risk: an empirical inquiry', *Managerial and Decision Economics*, vol. 5, no. 2 (June), pp. 98–103.

Thusu, D. and Freedman, D. (2003) 'Introduction'. In D. Thusu and D. Freedman (eds) *War and the Media.* London: Sage, pp. 1–12.

Tienari, J., Holgersson, C., Søderberg, A.-M. and Vaara, E. (2003) 'An uneasy coupling'. In A.-M. Søderberg and E. Vaara (eds) *Merging Across Borders: People, cultures and politics.* Copenhagen: Copenhagen Business School, pp. 228–51.

Tienari, J., Huhtinen, A.-M., Vaara, E. and Syrjänen, M. (2004) 'Björn Wahlroos, suomalainen johtaminen ja sotilasdiskurssi', *Hallinnon tutkimus/Administrative Studies*, vol. 23, no. 2, pp. 41–54.

Tienari, J., Søderberg, A.-M., Holgersson, C. and Vaara, E. (2005) 'Gender and national identity constructions in the cross-border merger context', *Gender, Work and Organization*, vol. 12, no. 3, pp. 217–37.

Tienari, J., Vaara, E. and Björkman, I. (2003) 'Global capitalism meets national spirit: discourses in media texts on a cross-border acquisition', *Journal of Management Inquiry*, vol. 12, no. 4, pp. 377–93.

Trautwein, F. (1990) 'Merger motives and merger prescriptions', *Strategic Management Journal*, vol. 11, no. 4, pp. 283–95.

Turner, J. C. (1985) 'Social categorization and the self-concept. A social cognitive theory of group behaviour'. In E. J. Lawler (ed.) *Advances in Group Processes: Theory and Research*, Volume 2. Greenwich, CT: JAI Press.

Turner, J. R. (1992) *The Handbook of Project-Based Management*, New York: McGraw-Hill.

Tversky, A. and Kahneman, D. (1974) 'Judgement under uncertainty: heuristics and biases', *Science*, vol. 185, pp. 1124–31.

UNCTAD (2000) *The World Investment Report* (WIR). Geneva: The United Nations Commission on Trade and Development.

UNCTAD (2003) *The World Investment Report* (WIR). Geneva: The United Nations Commission on Trade and Development.

Vaara, E. (2002) 'On the discursive construction of success/failure in narratives of post-merger integration', *Organization Studies*, vol. 23 no. 2, pp. 213–50.

Vaara, E. (2003) 'Post-acquisition integration as sensemaking: glimpses of ambiguity, confusion, hypocrisy, and politicization', *Journal of Management Studies*, vol. 40, no. 4 (June).

Vaara, E., Risberg, A., Søderberg, A.-M. and Tienari, J. (2003a) 'Nation talk – the construction of national stereotypes in a merging multinational'. In Anne-Marie Søderberg and Eero Vaara (eds) *Merging Across Borders: People, cultures and politics*. Copenhagen: Copenhagen Business School Press.

Vaara, E., Tienari, J. and Erkama, N. (2003b) 'Ne glider in! Yritysjärjestelyiden metaforisesta rakentumisesta tiedotusvälineissä', *Liiketaloudellinen aikakauskirja/The Finnish Journal of Business Economics*, vol. 2, pp. 288–310. ['On the metaphoric construction of merger and acquisitions in the media'.]

Vaara, E., Tienari, J. and Säntti, R. (2003c) 'The international match: Metaphors as vehicles of social identity-building in cross-border mergers', *Human Relations*, vol. 56, no. 4, pp. 419–51.

Vaara, E., Tienari, J., Piekkari, R. and Säntti, R. (2005) 'Language and the Circuits of Power in a Merging Multinational Corporation', *Journal of Management Studies*, vol. 42, no. 3.

Van den Berg, P. T. and Wilderom, C. P. M. (2004) 'Defining, measuring, and comparing organisational cultures,' *Applied Psychology: An International Review*, vol. 53, no. 4, 570–82.

Van Kippenberg, D. and van Leeuwen, E. (2001) 'Organizational identity after a merger: sense of continuity as the key to postmerger identification.' In M. A. Hogg and D. J. Terry (eds) *Social Identity Processes in Organizational Contexts*. Philadelphia: Psychology Press.

Van Maanen, J. and Schein, E. H. (1979) 'Toward a theory of organizational socialization', *Research in Organizational Behavior*, vol. 1, pp. 209–64.

Van Putten, A. B. and MacMillan, I (2004) 'Making real options really work', *Harvard Business Review*, vol. 82, issue 12, pp. 134–41.

Vanhonacker, W. R. et al. (2000) *Kodak in China (B): A Billion for a Billion*. Case Clearing House (ECCH), www.ecch.cranfield.ac.uk/.

Very, P. (2004) *The Management of Mergers and Acquisitions*. Chichester: Wiley.

Very, P. and Schweiger, D. M. (2001) 'The acquisition process as a learning process: evidence from a study of critical problems and solutions in domestic and cross-border deals', *Journal of World Business*, vol. 36, no. 11, pp. 11–31.

Very, P., Lubatkin, M. and Calori, R. (1996) 'A cross-national assessment of acculturative stress in recent European mergers', *International Studies of Management and Organization*, vol. 26, no. 1, pp. 59–86.

Walsh, J. P. (1988) 'Top management turnover following mergers and acquisition', *Strategic Management Journal*, vol. 9, no. 2, pp. 173–83.

Warner, M. and Campbell, A. (1993) 'Germany/German management'. In D. J. Hickson (ed.) *Management in Western Europe: Society, Culture and Organization in Twelve Nations.* Berlin: Walter de Gruyter, pp. 89–108.

Wasserstein, B. (2000) *Big Deal: Mergers and Acquisitions in the Digital Age.* London: Warner Books.

Webb, D. and Pettigrew, A. (1999) 'The temporal development of strategy: Patterns in the UK insurance industry', *Organization Science*, vol. 10, no. 5 (September–October), pp. 601–21.

Weick, K. (1995) *Sensemaking in Organizations.* Thousand Oaks, CA: Sage.

Wensley, R. (2003) 'Strategy as intention and anticipation'. In S. Cummings and D. W. Wilson (eds) *Images of Strategy.* Oxford: Blackwell.

Wernerfelt, B. (1984) 'A resource based view of the firm', *Strategic Management Journal*, vol. 5, no. 2, pp. 171–80.

Weston, J. F. and Mansinghka, S. K. (1971) 'Tests of the efficiency performance of conglomerate firms', *Journal of Finance*, vol. 26 (September), pp. 919–36.

Weston, J. F., Mitchell, M. L. and Mulerin, J. H. (2004) *Takeovers, Restructuring, and Corporate Governance*, 4th edn. Upper Saddle River, NJ: Pearson Education Inc.

Weston, J. F., Smith, K. V. and Shrieves, R. E. (1972) 'Conglomerate performance using the capital asset pricing model', *Review of Economics and Statistics*, vol. 54 (November), pp. 357–63.

Westwood, R. (2001) 'Appropriating the other in discourses of comparative management'. In S. Linstead and R. Westwood (eds) *The Language of Organization.* London: Sage.

Wheen, F. (2004) *How Mumbo-Jumbo Conquered The World.* London: Harper Perennial.

Whitley, R. (1999) *Divergent Capitalisms.* Oxford: Oxford University Press.

Whittington, M. (2000) 'Problems in comparing financial performance across international boundaries: a case study approach', *International Journal of Accounting*, vol. 35, no. 3, pp. 399–413.

Whittington, M. and Bates, K. (2004) 'Forecasting Financials'. In Crainer, S. (ed.) *FT Handbook of Management*, 3rd edn. London: FT/Prentice Hall.

Whittington, R. (2002) 'Strategy as Practice: Integrating and Developing a Field', Academy of Management, Best Paper Proceedings, Denver, August.

Williamson, O. E. (1994) 'Transactions Cost Economics and Organization Theory'. In N. J. Smelser and R. Swedberg (eds) *The Handbook of Economic Sociology.* Princeton: Princeton University Press and Russell Sage Foundation.

Wilson, B. (1990) *Systems Concepts, Methodologies and Applications*, 2nd edn. Chichester: Wiley.

Wilson, F. (1992) 'Language, technology, gender and power', *Human Relations*, vol. 45, no. 9, pp. 883–915.

Wittgenstein, L. (1958) *Philosophical Investigations.* New York: Macmillan.

Wodak, R., de Cillia, R., Reisigl, M. and Liebhart, K. (1999) *The Discursive Construction of National Identity.* Edinburgh: Edinburgh University Press.

Wright, P., Ferris, S. P., Sarin, A. and Awasthi, V. (1996) 'Impact of corporate insider, blockholder, and institutional equity ownership on firm risk taking', *The Academy of Management Journal*, vol. 39, no. 2 (April), pp. 441–63.

Yamamura, K. and Streeck, W. (eds) (2003) *The End of Diversity? Prospects for German and Japanese Capitalism*. Ithaca: Cornell University Press.

Yan, A. and Louis, M. R. (1999) 'The Migration of Organizational Functions to the Work Unit Level: Buffering, Spanning and Bringing up Boundaries', *Human Relations*, vol. 52, no. 1, pp. 25–47.

Yolles, M. (1999) *Management System: A Viable Approach*. London: FT/Pitman.

Zaheer, S., Albert, S. and Zaheer, A. (1999) 'Time scales and organizational theory', *Academy of Management Review*, vol. 24, no. 4, October, pp. 725–41.

Zander, L. (1999) 'Management in Sweden'. In M. Warner (ed.) *Management in Europe*. Thomson Learning Business Press, pp. 345–53.

Zerubavel, E. (1991) *The Fine Line: Making Distinctions in Everyday Life*. New York: The Free Press.

Zimbardo, P. and Boyd, J. (1999) 'Putting time in perspective: a valid, reliable individual differences metric', *Journal of Personality and Social Psychology*, vol. 77, no. 6, pp. 1271–88.

Index

Page references referring to figures are in *italics* and those referring to tables are in **bold**.
Glossary definitions are indicated by 'g' after the page number.

Blackwell
Publishing

Duncan **Angwin**

Mergers
and Acquisitions

IMAGES SERIES

Mergers and Acquisitions

DUNCAN ANGWIN
University of Warwick

Written by leading experts, this highly topical book provides a multi-disciplinary perspective on the subject of mergers and acquisitions.

- Each chapter introduces key frameworks that relate to a particular perspective and incorporates case studies where these frameworks can be used for interpretive and diagnostic purposes

- Invites readers to apply the frameworks as maps or tools for analysing their own organisational experiences via a series of general discussion questions

- Offers analytical insights into actual experiences of mergers and acquisitions in different global contexts, successful and unsuccessful, presenting new empirically based evidence to support the arguments.

CONTENTS

CONTRIBUTORS INLCUDE

Duncan Angwin *(University of Warwick)*; Ken Bates *(University of Warwick)*; Caroline Brown; Matthew Checkley *(University of Warwick)*; Simon Collinson *(University of Warwick)*; Stephen Cummings *(Victoria University of Wellington)*; Scott Dacko *(University of Warwick)*; Laura Empson *(Said Business School, University of Oxford)*; Stephen Gates *(The Conference Board)*; Erin Mitchell; Glenn Morgan *(University of Warwick)*; Derek O'Bryne *(Waterford Institute)*; Sally Riad *(Victoria University of Wellington)*; David Schweiger *(University of South Carolina)*; Justin Scott; Chris Smith *(University of Adelaide)*; Janne Tienari *(Lappeenranta University of Technology, Finland)*; Eero Vaara *(Helsinki School of Economic & Business Administration)*; Philippe Very *(EDHEC)*; Mark Whittington *(University of Aberdeen)*.

JULY 2007 480 PAGES

HB 978-1-4051-2239-9 £55.00 / PB 978-1-4051-2248-1 £26.99

Order your FREE inspection copy!

Please send me a free paperback examination copy to review for the course I teach:

☐ Mergers and Acquisitions: ANGWIN
978-1-4051-2248-1 pb £26.99

COURSE:

NO. OF STUDENTS: START DATE:

Do you wish to consider this book for course adoption? Paperback examination copies are available to teachers of approved courses with twelve or more students, where English is the primary teaching language. Please note they are sent at the discretion of the publisher.

I am not teaching an appropriate course, but would like to purchase a copy of the book at a 20% discount:

☐ Mergers and Acquisitions: ANGWIN
978-1-4051-2239-9 hb £55.00 £44.00

☐ Mergers and Acquisitions: ANGWIN
978-1-4051-2248-1 pb £26.99 £21.59

* Please include postage: UK: £2.75 for the first book + 50p per book thereafter. Europe: £3.00 per book for the first 5 books + £2.00 per book thereafter. RoW: £5.00 per book for the first 5 books + £4.00 per book thereafter.

☐ I enclose a cheque made payable to Marston Book Services

☐ Please charge my Mastercard / Visa / Amex / Maestro / Delta
(circle as appropriate). Please supply cardholder address if different from delivery address.

TOTAL AMOUNT *(INCLUDING POSTAGE)*:

CARD NUMBER:

ISSUE NUMBER / START DATE: EXPIRY DATE:

SIGNATURE:

NAME OF CARDHOLDER:

ADDRESS OF CARDHOLDER:

DELIVERY DETAILS

NAME:

POSITION:

DEPARTMENT:

INSTITUTION:

ADDRESS:

                                          COUNTY

POSTCODE: COUNTRY:

E-MAIL:

TEL:

PLEASE RETURN THIS FORM TO:
Catherine Fox, Blackwell Publishing, 9600 Garsington Road, Oxford OX4 2DQ UK
Fax: +44 (0)1865 471694   E-mail: Catherine.Fox@oxon.blackwellpublishing.com
Please quote reference: **C6MPD590 / 0 1**

Blackwell Publishing

To be the first to hear about new publications in your field from Blackwell Publishing, please tick here ☐ e-mail ☐ post

NB Your data may be passed to other companies within the Blackwell group. For European customers this would involve the transfer of data outside the EU.

16887735R00267

Printed in Great Britain
by Amazon